Arthur J. Bellinzoni, Jr.

Arthur J. Bellinzoni is Ruth and Albert Koch Professor of Humanities at Wells College in Aurora, New York. He earned the Ph.D. in History and Philosophy of Religion from Harvard University. He is a member of the Studiorum Novi Testamentum Societas, the Society of Biblical Literature, and the American Academy of Religion. This collection is his first book for Mercer University Press.

THE
TWO-SOURCE
HYPOTHESIS

THE TWO-SOURCE HYPOTHESIS

A Critical Appraisal

Edited with an Introduction by
ARTHUR J. BELLINZONI, JR.

with the assistance of
JOSEPH B. TYSON
and
WILLIAM O. WALKER, JR.

MERCER

ISBN 0-86554-096-9

The Two-Source Hypothesis
Copyright ©1985
Mercer University Press
All rights reserved
Printed in the United States of America

All books published by Mercer University Press are produced
on acid-free paper that exceeds the minimum standards set by the
National Historical Publications and Records Commission.

Library of Congress Cataloging in Publication Data

Main entry under title:
The two-source hypothesis

Bibliography: p. 453.
Includes indexes.
1. Two source hypothesis (Synoptics criticism)—
Addresses, essays, lectures. I. Bellinzoni, Arthur J.
II. Tyson, Joseph B. III. Walker, William O.
BS2555.2.T86   1985   226'.066   84-29447
ISBN 0-86554-096-9 (alk. paper)

Contents

PREFACE.. ix

INTRODUCTION 1

THE CASE FOR THE PRIORITY OF MARK 21

The Priority of Mark
   B. H. Streeter..23

The Priority of Mark
   J. A. Fitzmyer...37

In Support of Markan Priority
   W. G. Kümmel...53

The Priority of Mark
   G. M. Styler...63

The Priority of Mark
   H. G. Wood..77

The Synoptic Problem
   F. Neirynck..85

THE CASE AGAINST THE PRIORITY OF MARK 95

The Synoptic Problem
   B. C. Butler 97

Lachmann's Argument
   N. H. Palmer 119

The Lachmann Fallacy
   B. C. Butler 133

Critique of the Main Arguments for Mark's Priority
      as Formulated by B. H. Streeter
   D. L. Dungan.. 143

A New Introduction to the Problem
   W. R. Farmer.. 163

Suggested Exceptions to the Priority of Mark
   E. P. Sanders 199

The Second Gospel Is Secondary
   P. Parker 205

THE CASE FOR THE Q HYPOTHESIS 219

The Document Q
   B. H. Streeter.. 221

In Support of Q
   W. G. Kümmel.. 227

Luke's Use of Q
   J. A. Fitzmyer.. 245

Q: A Reexamination
   C. K. Barrett... 259

Towards the Rehabilitation of Q
   F. G. Downing 269

In Defense of Q
 E. L. Bradby 287

The Original Order of Q
 V. Taylor 295

THE CASE AGAINST THE Q HYPOTHESIS 319

On Dispensing with Q
 A. M. Farrer 321

The Words of Jesus and the Future of the "Q" Hypothesis
 T. R. Rosché 357

Evidence for the View that St. Luke Used St. Matthew's Gospel
 A. W. Argyle 371

The Major Agreements of Matthew and Luke Against Mark
 R. T. Simpson 381

A Fresh Approach to Q
 W. R. Farmer 397

The Argument from Order
 and the Relationship Between Matthew and Luke
 E. P. Sanders 409

Critique of the Q Hypothesis
 D. L. Dungan 427

CONCLUSION 435

The Two-Source Hypothesis: A Critical Appraisal
 Joseph B. Tyson 437

BIBLIOGRAPHY 453

INDEXES 471

 Biblical Citations 471

 Names 483

Preface

This volume of essays has grown out of my participation over a period of several years in the Consultation on the Relationships among the Gospels of the Society of Biblical Literature. Professor William R. Farmer of the Perkins School of Theology of Southern Methodist University invited me to participate in the Consultation in the hope that, through my earlier research on the development of the gospel sayings tradition in the writings of Justin Martyr, I might bring some new insights from second-century literature to the question of gospel relationships in the first century. Instead, I became interested in the various solutions to the synoptic problem.

Early in my discussions with Professor Farmer, I commented that too little of the literature on the principal issues of gospel interrelationships is easily available or sufficiently well-known to many scholars and students and that a collection of essays on critical questions might serve to advance interest in the various solutions to the synoptic problem. I suddenly found myself in charge of a major project. Even before the scope of this volume of essays was clearly defined, Watson E. Mills, publisher of Mercer University Press, had expressed an interest in publishing the material.

Professor Joseph B. Tyson of Southern Methodist University and Professor William O. Walker, Jr., of Trinity University agreed to serve with me as an advisory board to define the focus of the project and to assist in identifying the essays that would be most valuable for inclusion in the collection. Their advice and wisdom has been invaluable throughout these many years, as has the warm and continued support of Professor Farmer, whose own work has been in many ways a major inspiration in the creation of this volume.

After the advisory board defined the project and selected the essays, the task of editing each of the essays for this volume fell to me, as did the task of writing a general introduction to the collection and a brief synopsis of each essay. Professor Tyson kindly agreed to write the concluding essay.

I should like to acknowledge the generosity of the many publishers who gave permission to reprint the material that forms the heart of this volume. Original publication is documented and acknowledged at the beginning of each essay in this volume. I am grateful for the generosity of Wells College and Southern Methodist University for the award of grants to assist in the research and publication costs of this volume. I wish also to acknowledge the contribution of Mercer University Press in seeing the project through its various stages.

I was aided in the reading of proofs and in the preparation of the indices by Lech Gora, who gave unselfishly of his time in what can only be considered a labor of love.

This volume is dedicated to the memory of my mother and father.

Wells College   A. J. B.
Aurora, New York
1 December 1984

INTRODUCTION

INTRODUCTION

Arthur J. Bellinzoni, Jr.

Simply stated, the synoptic problem is the question of the relationship among the gospels of Matthew, Mark, and Luke,—the so-called "synoptic gospels." It has long been acknowledged that these three gospels share much of the same material, that the arrangement or organization of that material is similiar, and that the similarities often extend to exact or nearly exact verbal agreement in the presentation of the material. Yet at the same time there are among the gospels of Matthew, Mark, and Luke striking dissimilarities that also seek explanation. Indeed, the peculiar similiarity and dissimilarity, agreement and disagreement, consistency and inconsistency, congruity and incongruity, conformity and disparity constitute the synoptic problem.

Historical criticism has tended to deal with this evidence in one of two ways: either the authors of the synoptic gospels made use of a common written source or sources or of a common oral tradition, or else they made use of one another.[1] Research of the nineteenth century largely rejected the

---

[1]Johann Gottfried Eichhorn, "Über die drei ersten Evangelisten," *Allgemeine Bibliothek der biblischen Literatur* (1794) 5:766. See also Hans-Herbert Stoldt, *History and Criticism of the Marcan Hypothesis* (Macon GA: Mercer University Press, 1980) 3.

former alternative, and attention in recent synoptic criticism has tended to focus instead on the question of the literary relationship among the three gospels, what Stoldt calls "the inner synoptic" rather than the "the pre-synoptic" solution.[2] Twentieth-century studies of the synoptic problem have tended to focus on literary solutions; much less attention has been paid to whether a larger role must be attributed to the place of oral tradition, not only prior to the writing of the gospels, but also continuing and influencing the texts of the various gospels for a rather long period of time after they were written.

Among the many literary solutions to the synoptic problem, the examples of Augustine, Griesbach, Farrer, and Lindsey can serve to illustrate the wide range of models that have over the centuries been proposed. The synoptic problem was certainly not a preoccupation of the patristic age; however, it is worth noting that St. Augustine (354-430) believed that Matthew was the earliest gospel, that Mark depended on Matthew, and that Luke depended on both Matthew and Mark. Augustine in one passage calls Mark a "foot-follower and abbreviator" of Matthew.[3]

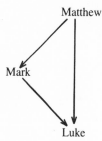

                                        AUGUSTINIAN MODEL

Like Augustine, J. J. Griesbach (1745-1812) maintained that Matthew was the earliest gospel. He further argued that the very extensive agreement between Matthew and Luke was best explained by Luke's use of Matthew. Mark was the last of the synoptic gospels and was dependent on both Matthew and Luke. Griesbach observed that Mark almost never diverged from Matthew in order and seldom diverged from Matthew in content unless he was following the order and content of Luke.[4]

---

[2]Stoldt, *Marcan Hypothesis*, 3.

[3]Augustine, *De consensu evangelistarum* 1. 2. 4 (*Patrologia Latina* 34:1044).

[4]Johann Griesbach, "A Demonstration that Mark was Written after Matthew and Luke," *Johann Jakob Griesbach Bicentenary Colloquium 1776-1976: J. J. Griesbach, Synoptic and Text Critical Studies 1776-1976* (1978).

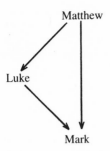

GRIESBACH MODEL

Contrary to Augustine and Griesbach, Austin Farrer holds to the priority of Mark. He regards Matthew as an amplified version of Mark and maintains that Luke presupposes both Matthew and Mark. In the triple tradition Luke follows Mark as his basic source but is also acquainted with and shows the influence of Matthew; and, according to Farrer, the double tradition in Luke is borrowed from Matthew.[5]

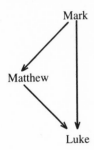

FARRER MODEL

Robert L. Lindsey, by contrast, argued that Luke was the earliest gospel. He maintained that Luke made use of two principal (hypothetical) sources, the so-called Proto-Narrative (PN) and the sayings source (Q). Mark also used two principal sources, PN and Luke (the dotted line to Q in the diagram suggests, according to Lindsey, the possibility that Mark may have remembered an occasional Q passage). Matthew, the last of the gospels, used Mark, PN, and Q.[6]

---

[5]Austin M. Farrer, ''On Dispensing with Q,'' *Studies in the Gospels: Essays in Memory of R. H. Lightfoot* (1955) 55-88.

[6]R. L. Lindsey, *A Hebrew Translation of the Gospel of Mark* (n.d.), see especially pp. 44-45. See also R. L. Lindsey, ''A Modified Two-Document Theory of Synoptic Dependence and Interdependence,'' *NT* 6 (1963):239-63.

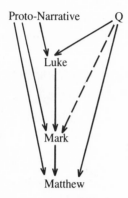

LINDSEY MODEL

It is not our intention here to give the impression that the solutions to the synoptic problem are limited to a handful of hypotheses, all of which are simple, literary solutions. Yet, whether justifiably or not, one of the most widely accepted conclusions of twentieth-century New Testament scholarship has been a simple literary solution—namely the hypothesis that Mark was the earliest written gospel, that the authors of Matthew and Luke in writing their gospels used Mark and a second source, commonly designated "Q," and perhaps one or more additional sources.[7]

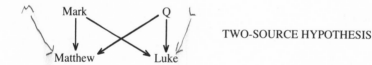

TWO-SOURCE HYPOTHESIS

More than a century of scholarly research amassed such overwhelming evidence in support of the priority of Mark and the use by Matthew and Luke of Mark and Q that alternative solutions had virtually been aban-

---

[7]It is not my purpose to rehearse here the history of the synoptic problem. That has already been done in a more complete fashion than this volume can hope to do. See especially, H. J. Holtzmann, *Die Synoptische Evangelien* (1863); L. Vaganay, *Le problème synoptique* (1954); E. Fascher, *Die formgeschichtliche Methode* (1924); K. Grobel, *Formgeschichtliche und synoptische Quellenanalyse* (1937); W. R. Farmer, *The Synoptic Problem: A Critical Analysis* (1976); Stoldt, *History and Criticism*. See also O. E. Evans, "Synoptic Criticism Since Streeter," *ET* 72 (1961): 295-99; W. G. Kümmel, *Introduction to the New Testament* (1975) 44-52.

doned, not only by most Protestant scholars, but also by the great majority of Roman Catholic scholars, who earlier might have been regarded as having had a vested interest in the priority of Matthew.[8] Indeed, Willi Marxsen in his *Introduction to the New Testament: An Approach to its Problems* goes so far as to state:

> This Two-Source theory has been so widely accepted by scholars that one feels inclined to abandon the term 'theory' (in the sense of 'hypothesis'). We can, in fact, regard it as an assured finding—but we must bear in mind that there are inevitable uncertainties as far as the extent and form of Q and the special material are concerned.[9]

This position, shared in perhaps a less dogmatic form by the overwhelming majority of scholars, helps us to define the focus of this volume of essays. In citing Marxsen, we do not endorse his view; we merely acknowledge it as a representative, if somewhat extreme, statement of what may still be regarded as the *status quo* in synoptic studies.

In 1951 B.C. Butler challenged the priority of Mark and reopened the case for Matthean priority.[10] Butler maintained that if conjectural sources are not excluded from consideration, then it is possible that Matthew and Mark, on the one hand, and Matthew and Luke, on the other hand, are connected by the common use of a lost gospel, which Butler characterized as a Proto-Matthew, a gospel of which our Matthew is a fairly faithful "second edition." But if conjectural sources are excluded from consideration, then the evidence suggests that Matthew was written first, that Mark made use of Matthew, and that Luke made use of both Matthew (for his "Q" material) and Mark. Butler's model is basically that of Augustine.

---

[8]On 19 June 1911 the Biblical Commission enacted a decree affirming the traditional authorship, date of composition, and historical character of the Gospel of Matthew. "In deciding the priority of St. Matthew's Gospel in its original language and substance, the Biblical Commission has solemnly disapproved of any form of these theories which maintains that St. Matthew's original work was not a complete Gospel or the first in the order of time." Francis E. Gigot, "Synoptics," *The Catholic Encylcopedia* (1912) 14:394.

[9]Willi Marxsen, *Introduction to the New Testament: An Approach to its Problems* (1968) 118.

[10]B. C. Butler, *The Originality of St. Matthew: A Critique of the Two-Document Hypothesis* (1951); see also "The Synoptic Problem," *A New Catholic Commentary on Holy Scripture* (1969) 815-21.

BUTLER MODEL

Two years later Pierson Parker also questioned Markan priority.[11] Parker argued that both Matthew and Mark depended on a common *Grundschrift*, which he called K (for *koinos*), a sort of Proto-Matthew or perhaps a Proto- or Ur-Markus. Parker also argued that Luke made use of Mark and that Matthew and Luke drew upon Q, and he argued strongly for a Proto-Luke. Parker also argued that Mark shortened and altered K to suit the needs of his Gentile audience and that Matthew merged K with other materials. In his 1981 essay Parker, noting that " 'Q' was those portions of Proto-Luke (or of Luke?) that appealed to the final redactor of Matthew," presented the following diagram of his modified view:[12]

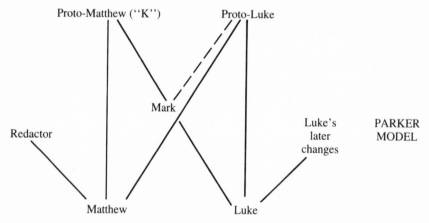

PARKER MODEL

---

[11]Pierson Parker, *The Gospel Before Mark* (1953); Parker's views have recently been updated in an essay "A Second Look at *The Gospel Before Mark*," *JBL* 100 (1981): 389-413. The above discussion of Parker's views reflects the modifications contained in this article.

[12]"A Second Look," 410.

Then in 1964 William R. Farmer reopened the synoptic problem by rejecting the priority of the Gospel of Mark and the whole idea of the use of the hypothetical source ''Q'' by the authors of Matthew and Luke and called for a return to the hypothesis of Johann Griesbach that Matthew is the first of the synoptic gospels, that Luke copied his Markan and non-Markan parallels from Matthew, and that Mark put together his gospel as a conflation of Matthew and Luke.[13]

The importance of these studies of Farrer, Lindsey, Butler, Parker, and Farmer is clear.[14] The synoptic problem lies at the heart of so many issues of New Testament scholarship that a change in our model of synoptic relationships affects meaningfully such other areas of New Testament research as form criticism, textual criticism, the quest of the historical Jesus, etc. The history of Christian theology, of early Christian sacraments, and of church institutions and government is affected significantly by our answer to the question of the order of composition of the synoptic gospels and the matter of their literary interrelationship. Since Markan priority is an assumption of so much of the research of the last century, many of the conclusions of that research would have to be redrawn and much of the literature rewritten if the consensus of scholarship were suddenly to shift. The priority of Mark has been so much the basis of most gospels research in the twentieth century that any meaningful erosion from that position would affect many conclusions that have found consensus. Not only would the substitution of Matthean for Markan priority have such an effect, but were scholars to move to a position that no consensus can be reached about the synoptic problem or that the synoptic problem is fundamentally unsolvable, we would then have to draw more tentatively the conclusions that have sometimes been drawn on the basis of what were earlier regarded as the assured results of synoptic studies.

---

[13]Farmer, *The Synoptic Problem*. See also Griesbach, ''A Demonstration,'' and the Griesbach model diagram above.

[14]As an indication of the persistence of the challenge to the two-source hypothesis it is appropriate to note, for example, some of conferences dealing with the subject in recent years: The Pittsburgh Festival on the Gospels (April 6-10, 1970), see *Jesus and Man's Hope*, 2 volumes (1970); The Johann Jakob Griesbach Bicentenary Colloquium (July 26-31, 1976), see *J. J. Griesbach: Synoptic and Text-Critical Studies 1776-1976* (1978); The Trinity University Colloquy on the Relationships among the Gospels (May 26-29, 1977), see *The Relationships Among the Gospels: An Interdisciplinary Dialogue*, ed. W. O. Walker, Jr. (1978); the Society of Biblical Literature Consultation on the Relationships of the Gospels; and the forthcoming (1984) Jesusalem Conference.

It is probably too early to predict whether new hypotheses or modifications of old hypotheses will establish themselves when the evidence has been re-examined; but it is appropriate to test the regnant hypothesis and to consider seriously the suggestions that have disturbed, if not shaken, the critical consensus that has developed in synoptic research over the last century or more.

No single collection of essays on the synoptic problem can hope to address all of the issues that have been raised in connection with that problem over the last century or even over the last two or three decades. Therefore, in defining the focus of this volume, it is necessary to exclude points of view that may be critical to a good understanding of certain issues. The focus of this volume is principally the case for and the case against the two-source hypothesis, in large measure because that particular hypothesis has so dominated twentieth-century scholarship. Yet defining the focus of this volume around the two-source hypothesis already begs a number of very important questions about the synoptic problem and presupposes a number of very important matters that simply cannot be ignored. These include:

1. Whether the synoptic problem is, in fact, solvable at all. A number of scholars argue that it is not, that the evidence is just not sufficient to suggest a single compelling solution;[15]

2. Whether, if the synoptic problem is solvable, the correct solution is strictly, or even primarily, a "literary" one, or whether a larger role must be attributed to the influence of the oral tradition;[16]

3. Whether, if the correct solution to the synoptic problem is a "literary" one, it is necessarily a simple linear one (two-source, Griesbach-Farmer, Augustine, Farrer-Enslin, Lindsey) rather than a more complex

---

[15]See the discussion in Joseph A. Fitzmyer's essay, "The Priority of Mark and the 'Q' Source in Luke," *Jesus and Man's Hope* (1970) 1:132-33.

[16]See, for example, Birger Gerhardsson, *Memory and Manuscript: Oral Tradition and Written Transmission in Rabbinic Judaism and Early Christianity* (1961).

one (Vaganay,[17] Léon-Dufour,[18] Boismard,[19] Gaboury[20]).

Although the two-source hypothesis is still quite clearly the regnant theory of synoptic relationships, there has been serious erosion in the past few years from the dogmatic position that prevailed, largely unchallenged, throughout most of this century. Yet in spite of that partial erosion, most contemporary New Testament scholarship continues to assume the theory and to build upon its foundation without serious regard to the possibility that we are building on a foundation of sand rather than on a foundation of rock.

Since the publication of William Wrede's *Das Messiasgeheimnis in den Evangelien* in 1901,[21] there has been in critical circles a reluctance to assume the historical value of even the broad outline of the Markan Gospel. Yet the Gospel of Mark has still stood as the focus of attention, whether attention was being directed to the historical Jesus or to the beliefs of the earliest church.[22] Were we suddenly to shift to a theory of Matthean priority, we would have to reopen the question of *kerygma* and history in the earliest tradition of the church. Rather than assigning the Birth Narratives and the Resurrection Appearances to a later stage in the development of the church's tradition, we would instead be faced with the earlier appearance of these traditions and the question of why they have been omitted by Mark rather than why they were added later by Matthew and Luke. Altering the order of the gospels requires altering virtually all of our arguments about the origin and growth of each unit of the synoptic tradition.

This volume of essays assumes that it is appropriate to examine the question of inter-synoptic relationships. It does not seek to address itself to the matter of pre-synoptic tradition, except in the form of hypothetical

---

[17]L. Vaganay, *Le problème synoptique: Une hypothèse de travail.* Bibliotheque de théologie, 3/1 (1954).

[18]X. Léon-Dufour, "Les Évangiles synoptiques," *Introduction à la Bible,* II (1959); "Interpretation des Évangiles et problème synoptique," *De Jésus aux Évangiles: Tradition et rédaction dans les Évangiles synoptiques,* Volume II (1976); "The Synoptic Problem," *Introduction to the New Testament* (1965).

[19]M.-E. Boismard, *Synopse des quatre évangiles en français* II: *Commentaire* (1972).

[20]A. Gaboury, *La structure des évangiles synoptiques. La structure-type à l'origine des Synoptiques* (1970).

[21]Trans., *The Messianic Secret,* by J. C. G. Grieg (1971).

[22]See the important study by James M. Robinson, *The Problem of History in Mark* (1957).

sources (such as "Q"). The growth of oral tradition is not dealt with, and the oral theories of Gerhardsson and others are not considered. We do not mean thereby to raise questions about the legitimacy of the scholarship that deals with these issues. We mean only to draw perimeters around this particular project, to state that the question of the literary relationship among the synoptic gospels can and should be examined, at least in part, as an inner-synoptic problem.

Farmer, who excludes from consideration hypothetical sources and who effectively seeks to limit the discussion to the direct literary dependence of the three synoptic gospels on one another, maintains that "there are eighteen and only eighteen fundamental ways in which three documents, among which there exists some kind of direct literary dependence, may be related to one another.[23] Quite clearly introducing the possibity of hypothetical sources into the discussion increases the mathematical possibilities significantly, but it is not our purpose here to give a hearing to every theory of synoptic relationships that has ever surfaced. Our purpose, as we have said, is rather quite simply to present the arguments for and the arguments against the two-source hypothesis, the prevailing theory of synoptic interrelationships. It is entirely appropriate that this theory be given the preeminence that it occupies in this volume, because it is the basis for most study of the gospels in this century.

Basically, the purpose of this collection of essays is to afford to the reader easy access to the literature that is most critical to an understanding of the question of synoptic relationship, or more particularly to an understanding of the two-source hypothesis. Specifically, the volume is divided into two main sections: the first dealing with the question of the priority of the Gospel of Mark, and the second dealing with the question of the hypothetical source "Q." In each principal section we have tried to assemble those essays which argue most strongly, most forcefully, most convincingly the case for and the case against Markan Priority and Q. Some of the arguments are repeated in more than one essay, but each essay makes a special contribution to the question of synoptic relationships.

Effectively, the volume should be read as a whole, although it may serve some readers simply as a convenient source for the individual essays being consulted. Each main section is viewed as a unit; together the several essays within the section argue the case for or the case against Markan

---

[23]Farmer, *The Synoptic Problem*, 208.

Priority or the use of Q. The effect of the case made by each section must be weighed as the reader tries to judge whether the two-source hypothesis deserves to continue to serve as the basic model for contemporary gospel research.

The purpose of this volume, however, is not simply to afford easier access to material that has already been published elsewhere, but in addition to encourage further research on the synoptic problem. Most New Testament scholars seem to consider the synoptic problem solved, or essentially solved, and hardly worth devoting further research to untangling. But there are too many voices now crying for a reexamination of the two-source hypothesis for the problem to continue to go unheeded. The neater theories are seen to pose problems that need to be addressed with an open mind and with the critical eye of unbiased research. In the past difficulties have often been swept under the rug or treated as minor issues in a problem that has essentially been regarded as solved. The problems that stand in the way of one model or another are often treated as minor issues to be explained away rather than treated as serious obstacles to the continued acceptance of a preferred model.

Many scholars have not felt it necessary to study closely and critically the basic literature, because they have tended to accept the consensus that developed around the two-source hypothesis and because they have considered it more appropriate to devote their time and research to the new frontiers of New Testament scholarship rather than to an issue that was judged to lie behind us, that had been ''solved.'' But the synoptic problem is not behind us. It is very much with us, and it is clear that we are embarking upon a new state in the study of synoptic interrelationships.

Any anthology must include some materials and exclude others. The limitation of space places restrictions on a volume even beyond the limitations determined by the editor in defining the scope of the project. Beyond our intention of trying to identify those statements that argue each case most convincingly, some other principles have emerged that have affected (but not limited) the choice of materials:

1. The volume includes for the most part essays that are independent works or portions of essays that can easily be read as a unit. In large part we have avoided including chapters of books that are dependent upon other material in the same volume.

2. When critical decisions had to be made, preference was sometimes given to less easily accessible essays. However, classical or critical material is included, whatever its source.

3. Within each section we have tried to avoid including more than one essay by any single author. This has been particularly difficult, because certain authors have written extensively on critical issues, and certain positions are closely associated with particular scholars. But we have tried in these instances to find a single essay to represent that author's case and include arguments on the subject from as many other scholars as possible. It is essential not to draw the conclusion that a position is narrowly held by a single scholar or a handful of scholars when this is very definitely not the case.

4. It has often been desirable, even essential, to give preference to shorter articles over longer ones, or not to reproduce the whole of a longer essay.

This volume does not represent a single point of view. It has no particular model that it seeks to promote. It has no axe to grind other than to offer the strongest arguments possible on both sides of the issues, to give a hearing to alternative solutions to the synoptic problem, and to encourage further research in the area. This volume has no pretense of being exhaustive, but these essays and their bibliographical references are important resources for any scholar interested in synoptic studies.

As stated earlier, the two-source hypothesis has dominated synoptic studies for the past century. The case for the two-source hypothesis has remained much the same since its classic statement by B. H. Streeter in 1924. Likewise the case against the two-source hypothesis has focused for the most part around certain identifiable issues. What we have tried to do here is to present representative literature in which the case for and against the two-source hypothesis can be carefully reviewed and analyzed by student and scholar alike with an aim toward furthering research on the question of gospel relationships. To this end, it seems appropriate in this introduction to identify the principal issues that are examined in detail in the essays that follow.

THE CASE FOR THE PRIORITY OF MARK

The case for the priority of Mark has focused, for the most part, on five arguments that are laid out in detail in the six essays under this rubric.

1. *The Argument from Shared Content*. Matthew shares 90 percent and Luke 55 percent of the subject matter of Mark in language very largely identical with that of Mark. This argument is developed in much the same way in the essays of Streeter, Fitzmyer, Kümmel, and Styler.

2. *The Argument from Wording*. In the passages contained in all three synoptic gospels, either Matthew or Luke or both are in close verbal agreement with Mark, including even the collection of words and the structure of sentences. Matthew and Luke almost never agree against Mark. The essays of Streeter and Fitzmyer develop this argument.

3. *The Argument from Order or Sequence of Incidents*. The order or sequence of episodes in Mark is clearly the more original and is, in general, supported by both Matthew and Luke. Where either one departs from the Markan order, the other is usually found supporting Mark. This argument is developed in the essays of Streeter, Fitzmyer, Kümmel, Wood, and Neirynck.

4. *The Argument from Mark's More Original or More Primitive Character*. Matthew and Luke improve upon and refine Mark's language, style, and grammar. Streeter, Fitzmyer, Kümmel, Wood, and Neirynck advance this argument. Styler speaks of Mark's more original character in several critical passages. Even Butler, an opponent of Markan priority, concedes that this argument deserves serious attention.

5. *The Argument from Distribution of Markan and Non-Markan Material throughout Matthew and Luke*. The way in which Markan and non-Markan material is distributed throughout Matthew and Luke suggests that each was working independently with Mark and with material from other sources. Streeter advances this argument, but Fitzmyer frankly calls this the weakest of Streeter's arguments for the priority of Mark.

With regard to the question of Markan priority a critical question has been whether the Mark used by Matthew and Luke is the same as our Gospel of Mark or an earlier edition of that Gospel, a so-called "Ur-Markus." Streeter maintains that Matthew and Luke used a source *practically identical* with Mark; Fitzmyer maintains that it is quite possible that Ur-Markus is the form of Mark that underlies Matthew and Luke. Kümmel states clearly that Mark, in the form handed down to us, has been used by both Matthew and Luke and that none of the arguments for an Ur-Markus is convincing. The matter of Mark vs. Ur-Markus is critical, because part of the case against Markan priority rests on issues that the Ur-Markus theory is designed to answer.

THE CASE AGAINST THE PRIORITY OF MARK

The case against the priority of Mark is not as easy to pinpoint as the case for Markan priority. Although several arguments are repeated from one essay to another, clearer focus of the objections to Markan priority is needed if study on the subject is to be advanced. Butler proposes a three-part critique of the priority of Mark as opposed to his own position of Matthean priority: (1) there is apparent overlap between Mark and Q; (2) there are several passages in which Matthew and Luke cannot have been drawing from Mark, an argument advanced as well by Sanders and Parker in their essays (Sanders collects 34 instances in which Matthew or Luke is thought to have a more original form of certain passage than does Mark, and Parker finds some 163 passages that, in his view, suggest the secondary character of Mark.); and (3) there are several passages where Matthew shows us the sort of thing which Mark's source would have contained.

In his other essay in this section, Butler discussed the so-called "Lachmann Fallacy." Specifically, the argument from order has been used to prove Markan priority. Lachmann took it for granted that all three synoptic evangelists derived their material from a common source, a pre-evangelical source, whether written or oral (see Palmer's essay). This conclusion was the basis of the theory of Ur-Markus as a first edition of Mark and as a source for Matthew and Luke. Later identification of Ur-Markus with Mark meant that Lachmann's inference no longer held good. Although Lachmann himself is not guilty of this so-called Lachmann Fallacy, others are (for example, Stanton, Abbott, Wellhausen, Burkitt, Hawkins, Streeter, Rawlinson, Narborough, and Redlich). Butler observes that once the theory of Ur-Markus is rejected, all that can be argued is that Mark is necessarily the connecting link between Matthew and Luke in the Triple Tradition, but not necessarily the source of more than one of them.

Dungan reviews critically the issues regarding each of the five traditional arguments in favor of Markan priority and finds them inconclusive. Butler and Farmer both argue that in seeking a soluton to the Synoptic Problem it is a good working hypothesis that simpler solutions are to be preferred, other things being equal, to more complicated ones and that conjectural or nonextant sources are not to be supposed unless the data of the problem require them. This point of view leads Farmer to present his argument for the Griesbach Hypothesis, namely the view that Mark wrote

after Matthew and Luke and is dependent on both. Clearly a point of view that strikes at the use of hypothetical sources in the working model strikes at the heart of the two-source hypothesis. Farmer also observes that the phenomena of agreement and disagreement in the respective order and content of the material and the so-called minor agreements of Matthew and Luke against Mark are more readily explicable on a hypothesis where Mark wrote after and used both Matthew and Luke. Indeed, as Neirynck maintains, it is generally agreed that the minor agreements of Matthew and Luke against Mark are the most serious stumbling block to Markan priority.

THE CASE FOR THE Q HYPOTHESIS

It is clear from the outset that the case for Q rests on the assumption of the priority of Mark, and so any evidence that argues against Markan priority argues as well against the Q hypothesis. It is also clear that the case for Q is not built, as is the case for Mark, on several independent arguments. Rather the case for Q is basically a single argument with several parts or, perhaps, several steps:

1. There are about 200 verses of mostly sayings material common to Matthew and Luke not found in Mark (Streeter, Kümmel, and Fitzmyer).

2. This material occurs in Matthew and Luke in quite different contexts, but the order of the parallel material is regarded by some (but not others) as so strikingly similar as to prove a common source (Streeter, Kümmel, and Taylor).

3. The degree of verbal agreement between the non-Markan parallel passages in Matthew and Luke is so thoroughgoing as to force the assumption of a common source (Streeter, Kümmel, Fitzmyer, and Barrett).

4. Subsequent to the Temptation story, there is not a single case in which Matthew and Luke agree in inserting the same saying at the same point in the Markan outline (Streeter).

5. Sometimes it is Matthew, sometimes it is Luke, who gives a saying in what is clearly the more original form (Streeter).

6. The evidence of doublets and double traditions in Matthew and Luke, once in a setting that is paralleled in Mark, proves that Matthew and Luke must have used a second source in addition to Mark (see especially Kümmel and Fitzmyer).

Although developed differently in the essays in this section, these features are, in the view of supporters of the Q hypothesis, best explained if both Matthew and Luke, in addition to their use of Mark, are independently drawing from a common document and making slight modifications of their own in their use of that document. Actually not all scholars would identify Q as a written document. Of those whose essays are included here, however, Streeter does consider Q a written source; Kümmel clearly sees it as a common written source; and Fitzmyer speaks of the postulated Q source, clearly implying it was written. Barrett, on the other hand, argues that the material we have called Q was probably not from *one* written document but rather from a number of non-Markan sources which were used by Matthew and Luke, and Downing refers to Q as "this source" or "these sources." Taylor considers the argument from the order reflected in the so-called Q sayings the most objective and decisive argument in support of Q. He concludes that Q is a written collection of sayings and parables which actually existed when Matthew and Luke wrote. Many scholars, however, regard Q as a body of common oral tradition.

It is generally agreed that the Q hypothesis depends on the improbability that Luke used Matthew (so Kümmel, Farrer, Bradby, and Downing); and at the outset of his defense of Q, Fitzmyer even sets forth the five principal reasons for denying Luke's dependence on Matthew.

THE CASE AGAINST THE Q HYPOTHESIS

Farrer maintains that the hypothesis of Luke's use of Matthew must be exploded before we can consider that Matthew and Luke have both drawn from a common source (or sources), Q. He believes that the case for Q would be strengthened (1) if the passages common to Matthew and Luke had a strong, distinctive flavor; or (2) if the passages common to Matthew and Luke cried out to be strung together in one order rather than in any other, and being so strung together made up a satisfyingly complete little book; or (3) if the lost source proposed were a sort of book known to be plentiful at the time.[24] But Farrer finds the evidence for Q weak and opts rather for Luke's use of Matthew. Likewise, Argyle, in noting the so-called minor agreements of Matthew and Luke against Mark, concludes

---

[24]James M. Robinson has attempted to address this point by reference to the Gospel of Thomas; see his "Logoi Sophon: On the Gattung of Q," *Trajectories Through Early Christianity* (1971), 71-113.

that Luke's use of Matthew is not only possible but very probable; and Simpson argues that although the synoptic problem may well turn out to be insoluble, a study of the major agreements of Matthew and Luke against Mark undermines the Q hypothesis and greatly strengthens the probability that Matthew was one of the sources used by Luke. Farmer, as well, believes that there is great uncertainty about Q and that the evidence points to Luke's use of Matthew; and Sanders likewise argues for contact between Matthew and Luke rather than their independent employment of the same two sources, Mark and Q. Rosché correctly indicates that Q is meaningful only for those who have accepted the priority of Mark, and he maintains that the future demands the adherents of the "Q" theory to appraise realistically the ways in which Matthew and Luke used Markan sayings and those who reject the document "Q" to define more carefully what is common in Matthew and Luke and how this common element is to be explained.

Let us now turn to the essays themselves, to the case for and against the two-source hypothesis. Only then will the reader be able to judge whether the two-source hypothesis deserves to continue to serve as the regnant theory of synoptic interrelationships.

THE
CASE FOR THE
PRIORITY OF
MARK

THE
PRIORITY
OF MARK

B. H. Streeter*

Streeter argues that the main facts and considerations that establish the priority of Mark and the dependence of Matthew and Luke upon Mark are:

(1) Matthew reproduces 90 percent and Luke more than half of the subject matter of Mark in language very largely identical with that of Mark (the argument from content).

(2) In the passages contained in all three gospels, either Matthew or Luke or both are in close verbal agreement with Mark. They almost never agree against Mark (the argument from wording).

(3) The order of incidents in Mark is clearly the more original and is, in general, supported by both Matthew and Luke. Where either one departs from the Markan order, the other is usually found supporting Mark (the argument from arrangement).

(4) Matthew and Luke improve upon and refine Mark's language, style, and grammar.

(5) The way in which Markan and non-Markan material is distributed throughout Matthew and Luke suggests that each was working independently with Mark and with material from other sources.

Matthew and Luke made use of a source that in content, in order, and in actual wording must have been *practically identical* with Mark.

---

*Burnett Hillman Streeter, ''The Priority of Mark,'' *The Four Gospels: A Study of Origins* (London: Macmillan and Co., 1924) 157-69, 195-97.

Such being the almost universal method of ancient historians, whether Jewish or Greek, it is natural to ask whether the remarkable resemblance between the first three Gospels, which has caused the name Synoptic to be applied to them, would not be most easily explained on the hypothesis that they incorporate earlier documents. A century of disussion has resulted in a consensus of scholars that this is the case, and that the authors of the First and Third Gospels made use either of our Mark, or of a document all but identical with Mark. The former and the simpler of these alternatives, namely, that they used our Mark, is the one which I hope . . . to establish beyond reasonable doubt.

The attempt has recently been made to revive the solution, first put forward by Augustine, who styles Mark a kind of abridger and lackey of Matthew, *"Tanquam breviator et pedesequus ejus."* But Augustine did not possess a Synopsis of the Greek text conveniently printed in parallel columns. Otherwise a person of his intelligence could not have failed to perceive that, where the two Gospels are parallel, it is usually Matthew, and not Mark, who does the abbreviation. For example, the number of words employed by Mark to tell the stories of the Gadarene Demoniac, Jarius's Daughter, and the Feeding of the Five Thousand are respectively 325, 374, and 235; Matthew contrives to tell them in 136, 135, and 157 words.[1] Now there is nothing antecedently improbable in the idea that for certain purposes an abbreviated version of the Gospel might be desired; but only a lunatic would leave out Matthew's account of the Infancy, the Sermon on the Mount, and practically all the parables, in order to get room for purely verbal expansion of what was retained. On the other hand, if we suppose Mark to be the older document, the verbal compression and omission of minor detail seen in the parallels in Matthew has an obvious purpose, in that it gives more room for the introduction of a mass of highly important teaching material not found in Mark.

Further advance, however, towards a satisfactory solution of the Synoptic Problem has been, in my opinion, retarded by the tacit assumption of scholars that, if Matthew and Luke both used Mark, they must have used it in the same way. To Professor Burkitt, I believe, belongs the credit of first protesting against this assumption: "Matthew is a *fresh edition* of Mark, revised, rearranged, and enriched with new material; . . . Luke is a

---

[1]Cf. J. C. Hawkins, *Horae Synopticae*[2] (1909) 159.

new historical work made by combining parts of Mark with parts of other documents."[2] The distinction thus stated by Burkitt I shall endeavour to justify and to elaborate in a new direction.[3] . . . I conceive it to be one of fundamental importance in any attempt to estimate the value of the Third Gospel as an historical authority for the life of Christ.

Partly in order to clear the way for a more thorough investigation of this point, partly because this book is written for others besides students of theology, I will now present a summary statement of the main facts and considerations which show the dependence of Matthew and Luke upon Mark. Familiar as these are to scholars, they are frequently conceived of in a way which tends to obscure some of the remoter issues dependent on them. They can most conveniently be presented under five main heads.

I. The authentic text of Mark contains 661 verses. Matthew reproduced the substance of over 600 of these. Mark's style is diffuse, Matthew's succinct; so that in adapting Mark's language Matthew compresses so much that the 600 odd verses taken from Mark supply rather less than half the material contained in the 1068 verses of the longer Gospel. Yet, in spite of this abbreviation, it is found that Matthew employs 51 percent of the actual words used by Mark.[4]

The relation between Luke and Mark cannot be stated in this precise statistical way—for two reasons. First, in his account of the Last Supper and Passion, Luke appears to be ''conflating''—to use the convenient technical term for the mixing of two sources—the Markan story with a parallel version derived from another source, and he does this in a way which often makes it very hard to decide in regard to certain verses whether Luke's version is a paraphrase of Mark or is derived from his other source. Indeed there are only some 24 verses in this part of Luke's Gospel which can be identified with practical certainty as derived from Mark, though it would be hazardous to limit Luke's debt to Mark to these 24.[5] Secondly, there are also, outside the Passion story, a number of cases where Luke appears deliberately to substitute a non-Markan for the Markan version of a story or piece of teaching. Thus the Rejection at Nazareth, the Call of Peter, the parable of the Mustard Seed, the Beelzebub controversy, the

---

[2]F. C. Burkitt, *The Earliest Sources for the Life of Jesus* (1922).

[3]B. H. Streeter, *The Four Gospels* (1924) 199-222.

[4]*Oxford Studies in the Synoptic Problem*, ed. W. Sanday (1911) 85ff.

[5]Cf. Streeter, 216-17.

Great Commandment, the Anointing, and several less important items are given by Luke in a version substantially different from that in Mark, and always, it is important to notice, in a context quite other from that in which they appear in Mark.

Another striking feature in Luke's relation to Mark is his "Great Omission," so called, of a continuous section of 74 verses, Mk. 6:45-8:26. Besides this he omits several shorter sections, which added together amount to 56 verses. If we leave out of account all passages where there is reason to suspect that Luke has used a non-Markan source, it appears on an approximate estimate that about 350 verses (*i.e.* just over one half of Mark) have been reproduced by Luke. When following Mark, Luke alters the wording of his original a trifle more than Matthew does; on the other hand he retains many details which Matthew omits, and he does not compress the language quite so much. The result is that on an average Luke retains 53 percent of the actual words of Mark, that is, a very slightly higher proportion than does Matthew.

From these various figures it appears that, while Matthew omits less than 10 percent of the subject matter of Mark, Luke omits more than 45 percent but for much of this he substitutes similar matter from another source. Each of them omits numerous points of detail and several complete sections of Mark which the other reproduces; but sometimes they both concur in making the same omission. The student who desires to get a clear grasp of the phenomena would do well to prepare for himself, by the aid of the lists in the Additional Note at the end of this chapter, a marked copy of the second Gospel, indicating by brackets of four different shapes or colours—(a) passages peculiar to Mark; (b) those reproduced by Luke, but not by Matthew; (c) those reproduced by Matthew, but not by Luke; (d) those which Luke omits, but for which *in another context* he substitutes a parallel version.[6]

II. Let the student take a few typical incidents which occur in all three Synoptists—I would suggest Mk. 2:13-17 and 11:27-33 to begin with—and having procured a Synopsis of the Gospels, underline in red words found in all three, in blue words found in Mark and Matthew, in yellow words found in Mark and Luke. If this is done throughout the Gospels it

---

[6]Such a comparison is facilitated by the use of William R. Farmer's *Synopticon: The Verbal Agreement between the Greek Texts of Matthew, Mark and Luke Contextually Exhibited* (1969). [editor's note]

will appear that a proportion varying from 30 percent to over 60 percent of the words in Mark are underlined in red, while a large number of the remainder are marked *either* in blue *or* yellow.[7] What is still more significant, if the collocation of words and the structure of sentences in Matthew and Luke be examined, it will be found that, while one or both of them are constantly in close agreement with Mark, they never support one another against Mark.[8] This is clear evidence of the greater originality of the Markan version, and is exactly what we should expect to find if Matthew and Luke were *independently* reproducing Mark, adapting his language to their own individual style.

III. The order of incidents in Mark is clearly the more original; for wherever Matthew departs from Mark's order Luke supports Mark, and whenever Luke departs from Mark, Matthew agrees with Mark. The section Mk. 3:31-35 alone occurs in a different context in each gospel; and there is no case where Matthew and Luke agree together against Mark in a point of arrangement.

A curious fact[9] . . . is that, while in the latter half of his Gospel (chap. 14 to the end) Matthew adheres strictly to the order of Mark (Mk. 6:14 to the end), he makes considerable rearrangements in the first half.[10] Luke, however, though he omits far more of Mark than does Matthew, hardly ever departs from Mark's order, and only in trifling ways.[11] On the other hand, wherever Luke substitutes for an item in Mark a parallel version from another source, he always gives it *in a different context* from the item in Mark which it replaces. This, as we shall see later, is a fact of very great significance for the determination of the source of Luke's non-Markan material.

---

[7]The happy possessor of W. G. Rushbrooke's magnificent *Synopticon* will find the work done for him by the use of different types and colors. Of Greek Synopses on a smaller scale, the most conveniently arranged are A. Huck's *Synopsis* and Burton and Goodspeed's *Harmony of the Synoptic Gospels*. For those who have little or no knowledge of Greek an admirably arranged Synopsis based on the English of the Revised Version is *The Synoptic Gospels* by J. M. Thompson.

[8]Except as stated in Streeter, 179ff.

[9]The matter is explained by Streeter, 274.

[10]A convenient chart showing Matthew's rearrangement of Mark's order is given in the *Commentary on Matthew* by W. C. Allen (1907), xiv. The discussion of the relation of Matthew and Mark in this work, i-xl, is the most valuable known to me: I cannot, however, accept the theory of Matthew's second main source, xliff.

[11]These are enumerated and discussed in *Oxford Studies*, 88ff.

We note, then, that in regard to (a) items of subject matter, (b) actual words used, (c) relative order of sections, Mark is in general supported by *both* Matthew and Luke, and in most cases where they do not both support him they do so alternately, and they practically never agree together against Mark. This is only explicable if they followed an authority which in content, in wording, and in arrangement was all but identical with Mark.

IV. A close study of the actual language of parallel passages in the Gospels shows that there is a constant tendency in Matthew and Luke—showing itself in minute alterations, sometimes by one, sometimes by the other, and often by both—to improve upon and refine Mark's version. This confirms the conclusion, to which the facts already mentioned point, that the Markan form is the more primitive. Of these small alterations many have a reverential motive. Thus in Mark, Jesus is only once addressed as "Lord" κύριε, and that by one not a Jew (the Syrophoenician). He is regularly saluted as Rabbi, or by its Greek equivalent διδάσκαλε (Teacher). In Matthew κύριε occurs 19 times; in Luke κύριε occurs 16, ἐπιστάτα (Master) 6 times. In the same spirit certain phrases which might cause offense or suggest difficulties are toned down or excised. Thus Mark's "he *could* do there *no* mighty work" (6:5) becomes in Matthew (13:58) "he *did not many* mighty works"; while Luke omits the limitation altogether. "*Why callest thou me good?*" (Mk. 10:18) reads in Matthew (19:17) "Why askest thou me concerning the good?" Much more frequently, however, the changes merely result in stylistic or grammatical improvements, without altering the sense.

But the difference between the style of Mark and of the other two is not merely that they both write better Greek. It is the difference which always exists between the spoken and the written language. Mark reads like a shorthand account of a story by an impromptu speaker—with all the repetitions, redundancies, and digressions which are characteristic of living speech. And it seems to me most probable that his gospel, like Paul's Epistles, was taken down from rapid dictation by word of mouth. The Mark to whom tradition ascribes the composition of the Gospel was a Jerusalem Jew, of the middle class;[12] he could speak Greek fluently, but writing in an acquired language is another matter. Matthew and Luke use the more

---

[12]His mother had a house large enough to be a meeting-place for the church, and kept at least one slave girl (Acts 12:12-13), and his cousin Barnabas had some property.

succinct and carefully chosen language of one who writes and then revises an article for publication. This partly explains the tendency to abbreviate already spoken of, which is especially noticeable in Matthew. Sometimes this leads to the omission by one or both of the later writers of interesting and picturesque details, such as "in the stern . . . on a cushion" (Mk. 4:38), or "they had not in the boat with them more than one loaf" (Mk. 8:14). Usually, however, it is only the repetitions and redundancies so characteristic of Mark's style that are jettisoned. Sir John Hawkins[13] collects over 100 instances of "enlargements of the narrative, which add nothing to the information conveyed by it, because they are expressed again, or are directly involved in the context," which he calls "context-supplements." The majority of these are omitted by Matthew, a large number by Luke also; though Luke sometimes omits where Matthew retains, as well as *vice versa*. Again, Mark is very fond of "duplicate expressions" such as "Evening coming on, when the sun set" (1:32).[14] In these cases one or other of the later Evangelists usually abbreviates by leaving out one member of the pair; and not infrequently it happens that Matthew retains one and Luke the other. Thus in the above example Matthew writes "evening coming on," Luke "the sun having set."

Matthew and Luke regularly emend awkward or ungrammatical sentences; sometimes they substitute the usual Greek word for a Latinism; and there are two cases where they give the literary equivalent of Greek words, which Phrynichus the grammarian expressly tells us belonged to vulgar speech. Lastly, there are eight instances in which Mark preserves the original Aramaic words used by our Lord. Of these Luke has none, while Matthew retains only one, the name Golgotha (27:33); though he substitutes for the Markan wording of the cry from the cross, "Eloi, Eloi . . . " the Hebrew equivalent "Eli, Eli . . . " as it reads in the Psalm (Mk. 15:34 = Mt. 27:46 = Ps. 22:1).

The examples adduced above are merely a sample given to illustrate the general character of the argument. But it is an argument essentially cumulative in character. Its full force can only be realized through the immense mass of details which Sir John Hawkins has collected, analyzed and tabulated on pages 114-153 of his classic *Horae Synopticae*. How any one who has worked through those pages with a Synopsis of the Greek text can

---

[13]Hawkins, 125.

[14]Cf. Hawkins, 139ff, where 39 instances are given.

retain the slightest doubt of the original and primitive character of Mark I am unable to comprehend. But since there are, from time to time ingenious persons who rush into print with theories to the contrary, I can only suppose, either that they have not been at the pains to do this, or else that—like some of the highly cultivated people who think Bacon wrote Shakespeare, or that the British are the Lost Ten Tribes—they have eccentric views of what constitutes evidence.

V. An examination of the way in which the Markan and non-Markan material is distributed throughout the Gospels of Matthew and Luke respectively is illuminating. The facts seem only explicable on the theory that each author had before him the Markan material already embodied in one single document; and that, faced with the problem how to combine this with material from other sources, each solved it in his own way—the plan adopted by each of them being simple and straightforward, but quite different from that chosen by the other.

Certain elements in the non-Markan matter clearly owe their position in the Gospels to the nature of their contents. For example, the two first chapters of Luke, with their account of the Birth and Infancy of Christ, differ so much in style and character from the rest of the Gospel that they are almost certainly to be referred to a separate source, whether written or oral we need not now discuss; and the same remark applies to the first two chapters of Matthew. Obviously, however, these stories, whencesoever derived, could only stand at the beginning of a Gospel. Similarly the additional details, which Matthew and Luke give in their accounts of the Temptation and the Passion, could only have been inserted at the beginning and at the end of their Gospels. But the greater part of the non-Markan matter consists of parables or sayings which do not obviously date themselves as belonging to any particular time in the public ministry. It would appear that the Evangelists had very little to guide them as to the exact historical occasion to which any particular item should be assigned. That, at any rate, seems to be the only explanation of the curious fact (to which my attention was drawn by Sir John Hawkins) that, subsequent to the Temptation story, there is not a single case in which Matthew and Luke agree in inserting a piece of Q material into the same context of Mark. The way, then, in which materials derived from the Markan and from non-Markan sources are combined must have been determined mainly by literary considerations, and very little, if at all, by extrinsic historical information.

The student who wishes to get a thorough grasp of the facts is advised to mark off in blue brackets—in a New Testament, *not* in a Synopsis of the Gospels—all passages of Matthew and Luke which appear to be derived from Mark. For this purpose the list of parallels in Additional Note B will be of assistance. He will then see clearly the difference in the methods adopted by Matthew and by Luke.

Matthew's method is to make Mark the framework into which non-Markan matter is to be fitted, on the principle of joining like to like. That is to say, whenever he finds in a non-Markan source teaching which would elaborate or illustrate a saying or incident in Mark, he inserts that particular piece of non-Markan matter into that particular context in the Markan story. Sometimes he will insert a single non-Markan verse so as most appropriately to illustrate a context of Mark, for example, the saying about faith (Mt. 17:20), or about the Apostles sitting on twelve thrones (Mt. 19:28). Sometimes he expands a piece of teaching in Mark by the addition of a few verses from another source on the same subject; for example, the non-Markan saying on divorce, Mt. 19:1-12, is appropriately fitted on to Markan discussions of the same theme. So the Markan saying, repeated in Mt. 19:30, "The first shall be last and the last first," suggests to him the addition in that particular context of the parable of the Laborers in the Vineyard which points the same moral. Similarly the moral of the Markan parable of the Wicked Husbandmen, Mt. 21:33ff. (which is directed against the Jewish authorities), is reinforced by the addition immediately before and after it of the anti-Pharisaic parables of the Two Sons and the Marriage Feast.

Examples of this kind of adaptation of non-Markan matter to a Markan context could be indefinitely multiplied. But it is worthwhile to call special attention to the bearing of this process on the longer discourses in Matthew. All of them are clear cases of "agglomeration," that is, of the building up of sayings originally dispersed so as to form great blocks. Four times, starting with a short discourse in Mark as a nucleus, Matthew expands it by means of non-Markan additions into a long sermon. Thus the seven verses of Mark's sending out of the Twelve (Mk. 6:7ff.) became the 42 verses of Mt. 10. The three parables of Mk. 4 are made the basis of the seven parable chapter, Mt. 13—one only being different. The 12 verses, Mk. 9:33-37, 42-48, are elaborated into a discourse of 35 verses in Mt. 18. The "Little Apocalypse" (Mk. 13) is expanded, not only by the addition of a number of apocalyptic sayings (apparently from Q), but also by hav-

ing appended to it three parables of Judgment, Mt. 25. To some extent
analogous is the way in which the Sermon on the Mount, far the longest
and most important block of non-Markan matter, is connected with the
Markan framework. It is inserted in such a way as to lead up, and thus give
point, to the Markan saying, ''And they were astonished at his teaching:
for he taught them as one having authority, and not as the scribes'' (cf.
Mk. 1:22; Mt. 7:29). That the Sermon on the Mount is itself an agglomeration of materials originally separate [I have demonstrated elsewhere].[15]

Luke's method is quite different and much simpler. There are half-a-
dozen or so odd verses scattered up and down the Gospel in regard to
which it is disputable, whether or not they are derived from Mark. Apart
from these, we find that, until we reach the Last Supper (Lk. 22:14),
Markan and non-Markan material alternates in great blocks. The sections,
Lk. 1:1-4:30 (in the main); 6:20-8:3; 9:51-18:14; and 19:1-27 are non-
Markan. The intervening sections, 4:31-6:19; 8:4-9:50; 18:15-43; 19:28-
22:13; are from Mark, with three short interpolations from a non-Markan
source. From 22:14 onwards the sources, as is inevitable if two parallel
accounts of the Passion were to be combined, are more closely inter-
woven. This alternation suggests the inference that the non-Markan materials, though probably ultimately derived from more than one source,
had already been combined into a single written document before they
were used by the author of the Third Gospel.[16] . . . The net result of the facts
and considerations briefly summarized under the foregoing five heads is to
set it beyond dispute that Matthew and Luke made use of a source which
in content, in order, and in actual wording must have been *practically
identical* with Mark. Can we go a step farther and say simply that their
source *was* Mark?

To the view that their common source was *exactly* identical with our
Mark there are two objections.

(1) If the common source used by Matthew and Luke was identical
with our Mark, why did they omit some whole sections of their source?

(2) How are we to account for certain minute agreements of Matthew
and Luke against Mark in passages which, but for these, we should certainly suppose were derived from Mark?

---

[15]See Streeter, 249ff.

[16]The further inference that *this combined non-Markan document* was regarded by Luke
as his main source and supplied *the framework into which he fitted extracts of Mark* is
worked out elsewhere. See Streeter, 199-222.

It has been suggested (a) that the omissions of material found in Mark would be explicable on the theory that the document used by Matthew and Luke did not contain the omitted items—that it was an earlier form of Mark, or "Ur-Markus," of which our present Gospel is an expanded version; (b) that if the text of Ur-Markus differed slightly from that of Mark, the same theory would account for the minute agreements of Matthew and Luke.

Clearly a decision as to the merits of an Ur-Markus hypothesis can only be made after a study of the actual passages omitted by Matthew and Luke respectively, and a careful scrutiny of the so-called "Minor Agreements." But there is one preliminary consideration which ought not to be overlooked.

In estimating the probability of Matthew or Luke purposely omitting any whole section of their source, we should remember that they did not regard themselves merely as scribes (professedly reproducing exactly the manuscript in front of them), but as independent authors making use, like all historians, of earlier authorities, and selecting from these what seemed to them to be most important. Moreover, for practical reasons they probably did not wish their work to exceed the compass of a single papyrus roll. If so, space would be an object. As it is, both Matthew and Luke would have needed rolls of fully thirty feet long; and about twenty-five feet seems to have been regarded as the convenient length.[17] And, when compression of some kind is necessary, slight reasons may decide in favour of rejection. Very often we can surmise reasons of an apologetic nature why the Evangelists may have thought some things less worthwhile reporting. But, even when we can detect no particular motive, we cannot assume that there was none; for we cannot possibly know, either all the circumstances of churches, or all the personal idiosyncrasies of writers so far removed from our own time.

ADDITIONAL NOTES

(A) Omissions from Mark

(N.B.—These lists do not include odd verses which add nothing material to the sense.)

---

[17] Cf. *Oxford Studies*, 25ff.

(a) The passages of Mark which are absent from both Matthew and Luke are:—1:1; 2:27; 3:20-21; 4:26-29; 7:3-4; 7:32-37; 8:22-26; 9:29; 9:39b; 9:48-49; 11:11a; 13:33-37;* 14:51-52; total, 32 verses.

(b) The passages of Mark which are absent from Matthew but present in Luke are:—1:23-28; 1:35-38; 4:21-24;** 6:30; 9:38-40; 12:40-44; total, 23 verses.

(c) The passages of Mark which, though present in Matthew, have no equivalent in Luke are:—1:5-6; 4:33-34; 6:17-29; 9:10-13; 9:28; 9:41; 9:43-47; 10:1-10; 10:35-41; 11:12-14, 20-22; 11:24; 13:10, 18, 27, 32; 14:26-28;*** 15:3-5; total, 62 verses. To which must be added the long continuous passage of 74 verses, 6:45-8:26, commonly spoken of as Luke's "great omission." As, however, the two miracles of gradual healing (7:32-37 and 8:22-26) which Matthew also omits occur in this section of Mark, we must beware of counting these 11 verses twice over in estimating the total omissions by Luke from Mark. Thus the total of Luke's *complete* omissions will then amount to 155 verses.

(d) The passages of Mark—*excluding* the Passion story (i.e. Mk. 14:17ff. = Lk. 22:14ff.)—which do not appear in Luke in the same context as in Mark, but for which there is substituted a different version in another context, are:—Mk. 1:16-20, cf. Lk. 5:1-11; 3:22-27, cf. Lk. 11:14-23; 3:28-30, cf. Lk. 12:10; 4:30-32, cf. Lk. 13:18-19; 6:1-6, cf. Lk. 4:16-30; 8:15, cf. Lk. 12:1; 9:42, cf. Lk. 17:2; 9:50, cf. Lk. 14:34; 10:11-12, cf. Lk. 16:18; 10:31, cf. Lk. 13:30; 10:42-45, cf. Lk. 22:25-27; 11:23, cf. Lk. 17:6; 11:25, cf. Lk. 11:4; 12:28-34, cf. Lk. 10:25-28; 13:15-16, cf. Lk. 17:31; 13:21-23, cf. Lk. 17:23; 14:3-9, cf. Lk. 7:36-50; 15:16-20, cf. Lk. 23:11; total, 58 verses. The Passion story in Mk. 14:17-16:8 contains 100 verses; *at least* 20 (perhaps over 30) of these appear in Luke.**** In the main Luke follows a non-Markan source, but in many passages it is not possible to differentiate the two.

(B) The Non-Markan Parallels in Matthew and Luke

(N.B.—Where Mark and Q overlap the reference to Mark is given within round brackets. Where the version in Matthew is probably in the main not derived from Q the reference is within square brackets.)

LUKE		MATTHEW
3:7-9, 16-17	=	3:7-10, 11-12 (cf. Mk. 1:7-8)
4:1-13	=	4:1-11 (cf. Mk. 1:12-13)
6:20-23	=	5:[3-4, 6], 11-12
6:27-33, 35-36	=	[5:44, 39-40, 42; 7:12; 5:46-47, 45, 48]
6:37-38, 39-40, 41-42	=	7:1-2; [15:14; 10:24-25]; 7:3-5
6:43-45	=	7:16-18, 20; 12:33-35

*But Matthew has similar matter, Mt. 24:42; 25:13-15; cf. also 12:38-40; 19:12.

**But Matthew has matter similar to Mk. 4:21, 22, 24 elsewhere, i.e. Mt. 5:15; 10:26; 7:2; and has already (Mt. 13:9) given Mk. 4:23, but in the form in which it occurs in Mk. 4:9. Mk. 4:25 is placed by Matthew a little earlier, Mt. 13:12.

***But for 14:30 Luke in another context has an equivalent, Lk. 22:34.

****See Streeter, 222.

6:46	=	[7:21]
6:47-49	=	7:24-27
7:1-10	=	8:5-10, 13
7:18-20, 22-28, 31-35	=	11:2-11, 16-19
9:57-60	=	8:19-22
10:2	=	9:37-38
10:3-12	=	10:16, 9, 10*a*, 11-13, 10*b*, 7-8, 14-15
		(cf. Mk. 6:6-11)
10:13-15	=	11:21-24
10:21-22	=	11:25-27
10:23-24	=	13:16-17
11:2-4	=	[6:9-13]
11:9-13	=	7:7-11
11:14-23	=	12:22-27 (cf. Mk. 3:22-27)
11:24-26	=	12:43-45
11:29-32	=	12:38-42 (cf. Mk. 8:12)
11:33	=	5:15 (cf. Mk. 4:21)
11:34-35	=	6:22-23
11:39-44, 46-48	=	23:[25-26], 23, 6-7*a*, [27], 4, 29-31
		(cf. Mk. 12:38-40)
11:49-52	=	23:34-36, 13
12:2-9	=	10:26-33 (cf. Mk. 4:22, *hidden*,
		and Mk. 8:38, *ashamed*)
12:10	=	12:32 (nearer than Mk. 3:28-29)
12:22-32	=	6:25-33
12:33-34	=	6:19-21
12:39-46	=	24:43-51
12:51-53	=	10:34-36
12:54-56	=	16:2-3 (om. B‭א‬ 13 etc. Orig.)
12:58-59	=	[5:25-26]
13:18-19	=	13:31-32 (cf. Mk. 4:30-32) ✓
13:20-21	=	13:33
13:23-24	=	[7:13-14]
13:26-27	=	7:22-23
13:28-29	=	8:11-12
13:34-35	=	23:37-39
14:11 = Lk. 18:14*b*	=	23:12
14:26-27	=	10:37-38 (cf. Mk. 8:34)
14:34-35	=	5:13 (cf. Mk. 9:50)
15:4-7	=	[18:12-14]
16:13	=	6:24
16:16	=	11:12-13
16:17	=	5:18
16:18	=	5:32 (cf. Mk. 10:11-12)
17:1-2	=	18:6-7 (cf. Mk. 9:42)
17:3-4	=	[18:15, 21-22]
17:6	=	17:20 (cf. Mk. 11:22-23)
17:23-24	=	24:26-27 (cf. Mk. 13:21)
17:26-27	=	24:37-39

17:34-35	=	24:40-41
17:37	=	24:28
22:30*b*	=	[19:28*b*]

To this list may be added the parables:

19:11-27 (Pounds)	=	[25:14-30] (cf. Mk. 13:34) (Talents)

And still more diverse:

14:15-24 (Great Supper)	=	[22:1-10] (Marriage Feast)

THE
PRIORITY
OF MARK

J. A. Fitzmyer*

Fitzmyer enumerates and discusses critically the arguments most often presented to establish the priority of Mark over Luke (and Matthew), developing the discussion basically around the arguments of Streeter:

(1) The bulk of Mark is found in Luke (55 percent of it) and in Matthew (90 percent of it).

(2) The order or sequence of episodes in Luke is very similar to that of Mark, even when other material is interspersed in Luke. This sequence is, moreover, even more strikingly compared to Mark's, when Matthew's order is taken into account, for Matthew and Luke agree in sequence only to the extent that they agree with Mark.

(3) The priority of Mark has been espoused because within the Triple Tradition the actual wording of the passages is frequently the same, including even the collation of words and the structure of sentences.

(4) The priority of Mark has been found in the more primitive character of the narrative of Mark, or what has been called its "freshness and circumstantial character" (namely, Mark's phrases that are likely to cause offense, his roughness of style and grammar, and his preservation of Aramaic words).

*Joseph A. Fitzmyer, "The Priority of Mark," from "The Priority of Mark and the 'Q' Source in Luke," *Jesus and Man's Hope* (Pittsburgh Theological Seminary, 1970) 1:134-47, 164-66.

(5) Streeter's fifth point is the weakest of his arguments for the priority of Mark (namely, the distribution of Markan and non-Markan material throughout Matthew and Luke).

Fitzmyer considers it quite possible that Ur-Markus is the form of Mark that underlies Matthew and Luke.

This survey of the study of the relationship of the Lukan Gospel to the Synoptic Problem may be begun with the priority of Mark. I propose to set forth briefly the main arguments that have normally been proposed for it and comment on them from the standpoint of some recent reactions.

First of all, the priority of Mark over Luke (and Matthew) has been espoused in recent times because the bulk of Mark is found in Luke (55 percent of it, according to Streeter) and in Matthew (90 percent of it).[1] This common agreement in subject-matter is often referred to as the Triple Tradition. In itself, the mere common possession of the same matter does not argue for the priority of Mark. The situation could be due to Mark's dependence on Luke (and/or Matthew), as Augustine once held with reference to Matthew (*De consensu evangelistarum*, 1,2,4), and as J. J. Griesbach,[2] and more recently W. R. Farmer,[3] have held with reference to both Matthew and Luke. In other words, "Mark is necessarily the connecting-link between Matthew and Luke in these passages, but not necessarily the source of more than one of them."[4] Thus stated theoretically and abstractly as a propositional argument (often with the aid of diagrams and arrows), the intermediary position of Mark is certain, but the priority of Mark over the other two is still to be shown.

When the argument is thus left on the theoretic level, as it often is, the priority of Mark appears to be more of an assumption than a conclusion. But the retort is made that the priority of Mark over Matthew and Luke

---

[1]B. H. Streeter, *The Four Gospels: A Study of Origins* (1930) 151, 159-60. See also G. Bornkamm, "Evangelien, synoptische," *RGG*, 3d ed., (1958) 2:753-66.

[2]See J. J. Griesbach, *Synopsis Evangeliorum Matthaei Marci et Lucae una cum iis Joannis pericopis quae omnino cum caeterorum Evangelistarum narrationibus conferendae sunt* (Halle: 2d ed., 1797; 3d ed., 1809; 4th ed., 1822); translated into English by B. Orchard, "A Demonstration that Mark was written after Matthew and Luke," *J. J. Griesbach: Synoptic and Text-critical Studies* (1977). Cf. X. Léon-Dufour, "The Synoptic Problem," *Introduction to the New Testament*, ed. A. Robert and A. Feuillet; trans. P. W. Skehan, et al. (1965) 266.

[3]W. R. Farmer, *The Synoptic Problem: A Critical Analysis* (1964) 199-232. See the reprint of this chapter in this volume.

[4]B. C. Butler, *The Originality of St. Matthew: A Critique of the Two-Document Hypothesis* (1951) 65.

depends as well on the concrete comparison of individual texts and on the complex of subsidiary questions related to it that must be answered. For instance, in the case of the latter one may ask a series of questions: (1) Why would anyone want to abbreviate or conflate Matthew and Luke to produce from them a Gospel such as Mark actually is? (2) Why is so much of Matthew and Luke omitted in the end-product? Why is so much important Gospel material that would be of interest to the growing and developing church(es) eliminated by Mark? Why, for example, has he omitted the Sermon on the Mount and often encumbered narratives in the retelling with trivial and unessential detail (for example, the cushion in the boat, Mark 4:38; the "four men" in Mark 2:3 and so on). In other words, given Mark, it is easy to see why Matthew and Luke were written; but given Matthew and Luke, it is hard to see why Mark was needed in the early Church. (3) How could Mark have so consistently eliminated all trace of Lukanisms? If he were a modern practitioner of *Redaktionsgeschichte*, the elimination might be conceivable. But was he so inclined? (4) What would have motivated Mark to omit even those elements in the infancy narratives of Matthew and Luke that are common? His alleged interest in narratives, rather than teaching, would have led him instead to present a conflated and harmonized infancy narrative. (5) Mark's resurrection narrative, even if it be limited to 16:1-8, is puzzling. Can it really be regarded as an abbreviation or conflation of the Matthean and/or Lukan accounts? (6) What sort of early theologian does Mark turn out to be if his account is based on Matthew and Luke? Having behind him the certainly more developed Christologies and ecclesiologies of Matthew and Luke, what would be his purpose in constructing such a composition? There is an unmistakable Markan theology, with which one has to cope, as is now evident from the study of the *Redaktionsgeschichte* of the second Gospel. But that this was produced by an abbreviation or conflation of Matthean and/or Lukan theologies is incomprehensible to most students of the Synoptics.

These considerations are admittedly subsidiary; but they do affect the argument that is based on the bulk of the material that is common to the Triple Tradition. It might even be admitted that no one of these reasons is in itself cogent or sufficient to prove the priority of Mark.

This does not mean that there have been no attempts to answer such questions from other points of view.[5] But does the conviction that these other attempts have carried outweigh the more common interpretation?

---

[5] See, for instance, W. R. Farmer, *Synoptic Problem*, 278-283, 230-232, 253, 227-228, *et passim*; X. Léon-Dufour, "The Synoptic Problem," 269-274.

A second reason usually given for asserting that Luke depends on Mark is the order or sequence of episodes in the Third Gospel that is so similar to that of Mark, even when other material is interspersed in Luke. This sequence is, moreover, even more strikingly compared to Mark's, when Matthew and Luke agree in sequence only to the extent that they agree with Mark. When one departs from the Markan sequence, and pursues an independent course, the other still agrees with the Markan order. Or, to put it another way, within the Triple Tradition, Matthew and Luke never agree with one another against Mark in regard to the order of episodes. As far as the common sequence of material in Luke and Mark is concerned, one sees it best in the six blocks of material set forth below.

(1) Mk. 1:1-15	= Lk. 3:1–4:15 (five episodes)[6]
(2) Mk. 1:21-39	= Lk. 4:31-44 (four episodes)
(3) Mk. 1:40–3:19	= Lk. 5:12–6:19 (seven episodes)
	(Luke's "small interpolation" follows: 6:20–8:3)
(4) Mk. 4:1–9:41	= Lk. 8:4–9:50 (nineteen episodes)
	(After Lk. 9:17, Luke's "big omission" [= Mk. 6:45–8:26])
	(Luke's "big interpolation," 9:51–18:41)
(5) Mk. 10:13–13:32	= Lk. 18:15–21:33 (twenty-one episodes)
(6) Mk. 14:1–16:8	= Lk. 22:1–23:11 (eighteen episodes)

Within these major blocks of material common in sequence to Mark and Luke, there are occasional insertions from the Double Tradition or from Luke's special source that fill out an episode. Yet they do not affect the common order, for despite them the blocks of material in Mark are still seen as units in Luke. Such insertions can be found at Luke 3:7-14 (John's preaching); 3:23-38 (the genealogy of Jesus); 4:2b-13 (the temptation); 19:1-27 (Zacchaeus and the parable of the pounds); 19:41-44 (lament over Jerusalem); 22:27-32, 35-38 (the discourse at the Last Supper); 23:27-32 (the road to Calvary); 23:39b-43 (two criminals on crosses); 23:47b-49 (Calvary).

Moreover, within these large blocks smaller units are confirmed by the same order or sequence in Matthean episodes:

Mt. 9:1-8, 9-13, 14-17	Mk. 2:1-12, 13-17, 18-22	Lk. 5:17-26, 27-32, 33-39
Mt. 12:1-8, 9-14, 15-21	Mk. 2:23-28; 3:1-6, 7-12	Lk. 6:1-5, 6-11, 17-19
Mt. 13:1-9, 10-17, 18-23	Mk. 4:1-9, 10-12, 13-20	Lk. 8:4-8, 9-10, 11-15
Mt. 16:13-23, 24-28; 17:1-9	Mk. 8:27-33; 8:34–9:1; 9:2-10	Lk. 9:18-22, 23-27, 28-36

---

[6]The numbering of the episodes differs with the way various scholars divide up the blocks of material. The exact numbering is immaterial. It is intended merely to give a general indication of incidents involved.

Mt. 22:15-22, 23-33, 34-40, 41-46	Mk. 12:13-17, 18-27, 28-34, 35-37	Lk. 20:20-26, 27-40, 41-44

Once again the query is in order, whether the sequence of sections and incidents in Matthew and Luke over against Mark argues for anything more than the intermediary position of Mark, or for anything more than Mark as a connecting-link between Matthew and Luke.[7] To assert that it actually proves the priority of Mark would be to fall into the so-called "Lachmann Fallacy."[8] Yet again, one has to make a distinction between the theoretic and abstract presentation of this argument, and the concrete application of it in the Triple Tradition. For many students the telling factor is not simply the comparison of Luke with Mark, but also with Matthew, and the more plausible reasons that can be assigned for the Lukan omission and addition of material within the Markan order.

It is undoubtedly this argument more than any other that has been assailed as "inconclusive or fallacious." The "fallacious" character of it has been stressed by E. W. Lummis, H. G. Jameson, B. C. Butler, and W. R. Farmer, to cite only the main names.[9] It was especially Butler who insisted on the intermediary position of Mark, and maintained that Mark

---

[7]One could also argue that all three evangelists copied an earlier source independently and thus account for the common order. This argument for a sort of *Urevangelium* has been used. But it is of little concern today, and we need not pursue this possibility further.

[8]This title for the error in logic involved was first coined by B. C. Butler, *Originality*, 62-71, even though he was careful not to ascribe directly to Lachmann what he calls a "Schoolboyish error of elementary reasoning." This has been made clear in the article of N. H. Palmer, "Lachmann's Argument," *NTS* 13 (1966-67), which provides an abridged English translation of Lachmann's article. [This article is reprinted in this volume; editor's note]. Farmer (*Synoptic Problem*, 66) traces the fallacy itself to F. H. Woods, "The Origin and Mutual Relation of the Synoptic Gospels," *Studia biblica et ecclesiastica: Essays Chiefly in Biblical and Patristic Criticism* (1890) 2:59-104. More recently he has pointed out that the first person in the English-speaking world to attribute the error to Lachmann was F. C. Burkitt in his Jowett Lectures for 1906 ("The Lachmann Fallacy," *NTS* 14 [1967-68]: 441-443).

[9]See E. W. Lummis, *How Was Luke Written: Considerations Affecting the Two-Document Theory with Special Reference to the Phenomenon of Order in the Non-Marcan Matter Common to Matthew and Luke* (1915); H. G. Jameson, *The Origin of the Synoptic Gospels: A Revision of the Synoptic Problem* (1922); B. C. Butler, *Originality*, 62-71. W. R. Farmer is content to remark "Since Streeter's first three reasons for accepting the priority of Mark were exposed as fallacious by Jameson in 1922 and again by Butler in 1951, there is no need to give them further consideration" (*Synoptic Problem*, 169). O. E. Evans, however, still considers the argument from order to be of "decisive importance." See *ET* 72 (1960-61): 296. And in this he is not alone.

"was not necessarily the source of more than one of them." But H. G. Wood has put his finger on a difficulty in Butler's own solution, which argues from this intermediary position, namely, "that Mark is a source only for Luke, and the knowledge of Matthew's order comes to Luke through Mark. This is very strange because Dom Butler claims to have proved that Luke is also dependent on Matthew. Why, having Matthew in his hands, Luke should follow Matthew's order only when it reappears in Mark is difficult to understand and explain. If Dom Butler's thesis were true, there should be numerous agreements in order between Matthew and Luke against Mark, and admittedly there are none or next to none."[10] Wood also criticizes Butler for not having examined the question of order "in detail;" he devotes a large part of his short article precisely to the refutation of Butler in the matter [of] sequence or order. Unfortunately, it cannot be reproduced here, but many of his points are quite telling; his article should not be overlooked.

One last remark in this matter of order pertains to the so-called Lukan transpositions. In at least five places Mark and Luke do not have the same order of episodes, where they might have: (1) The imprisonment of John the Baptist (Mk. 6:17-18) is found in Luke 3:19-20. (2) Jesus' visit to Nazareth (Mk. 6:1-6) is found at the beginning of the Galilean ministry in Luke 4:16-30. (3) The call of the four disciples (Mk. 1:16-20) appears later in Luke 5:1-11. (4) The choosing of the Twelve (Mk. 3:13-19) and the report of the crowds that followed Jesus (Mk. 3:7-12) are presented in an inverted sequence in Luke 6:12-16, 17-19. (5) The episode about Jesus' real relatives (Mk. 3:31-35) is found after the parables in Luke 8:19-20. Of less significance are two other episodes that appear in a different order: the parable of the mustard seed (Mk. 4:30-32), which is found in Luke 13:18-19 (in this instance an independent Lukan source may be involved); and the betrayal of Jesus (Mk. 14:20-21 and Lk. 23:21-23, an episode of the passion narrative). In any case, a more plausible reason can be assigned for the transposition of the five episodes by Luke than for their transposition by Mark.[11] This would again argue for the priority of Mark over Luke.

---

[10]H. G. Wood, "The Priority of Mark," *ET* 65 (1953-1954): 17-19 [reprinted in this volume]; cf. O. E. Evans, 296.

[11]In each case Matthew has preserved the Markan order of these five "transpositions," except for a partial transposition of his own in Matthew 10:1-4. Luke moves up the report

Thirdly, the priority of Mark has been espoused because of the actual wording of the passages within the Triple Tradition, which is frequently the same. This affects even the collocation of words and the structure of sentences. Yet from this observation, baldly stated, one might wonder how one can conclude the priority of Mark. What makes the difference, however, for many scholars is the concrete comparison. Streeter suggested using different colors to distinguish the words that agree in all three, and those that agree in Matthew and Mark, or in Luke and Mark. Such a comparison is facilitated by the use of W. G. Rushbrooke's *Synopticon* or by the more recent book of W. R. Farmer with the same title.[12] Rushbrooke's work openly espoused the Two-Source Theory and presented the matter in colored columns accordingly; Farmer's *Synopticon* presents the text of each of the first three Gospels in its entirety, and not in parallel columns, and "hi-lites" the agreements between the various compositions in different colors. It is thus better designed to assist the student to determine the nature and extent of the verbatim agreements without reference to any particular source-theory. Yet even the use of Farmer's book pushes one in the direction of the Two-Source Theory. I cannot help but still be impressed by that part of the argument that singles out the agreement of Matthew or Luke with Mark, when the other disagrees. This aspect must be taken into account in conjunction with the agreement of all three. When it is so considered, I find it hard to see Mark as a mere connecting-link. And

---

of the Baptist's imprisonment in an effort to finish off the story of the Baptist before the baptism and ministry of Jesus is begun, either because John does not belong to the period of Jesus (Conzelmann) or he represents a separate preparatory period within the time of fulfillment (W. Wink). The visit to Nazareth is transferred to the beginning of the ministry for a programmatic purpose, to present in capsule form the theme of fulfillment and to symbolize the rejection that marks the ministry of Jesus as a whole. The call of the four disciples is given a more plausible, psychological position by Luke in its later appearance, when it is narrated after a certain portion of Jesus' ministry; it makes the response to the call more intelligible than in Mark. The version of the choosing of the Twelve and the report of the crowds again produces a more logical setting for the Sermon on the Plain (6:20-49). And the shifting of the episode about Jesus' real relatives provides an audience for Jesus' sermon (8:19-20).

[12]See W. G. Rushbrooke, *Synopticon: An Exposition of the Common Matter of the Synoptic Gospels* (1880); W. R. Farmer, *Synopticon: The Verbal Agreement between the Greek Texts of Matthew, Mark and Luke Contextually Exhibited* (1969).

even less can I find a plausible reason for saying that Mark borrowed from Matthew or Luke.

A fourth reason for espousing the priority of Mark over Luke (and Matthew) has been found in the more primitive character of the narrative of the second Gospel, or what has been called its "freshness and circumstantial character." This refers to the greater quantity in Mark of vivid, concrete details, phrases likely to cause offense, roughness of style and grammar, and the preservation of Aramaic words. These traits abound in Mark and are present in Matthew and Luke to a less degree. One cannot regard them as evidence for Mark's "greater historical candor,"[13] since they do not really support such a judgment. Again, they are not found solely in the so-called Petrine passages in Mark, but in others as well.[14]

Streeter's analysis of the details of this Synoptic is well known; he regards the differences in Matthew and Luke as improvements and refinements of Mark's version. For instance, he maintains that "the difference between the style of Mark and of the other two is not merely that they both write better Greek. It is the difference which always exists between the spoken and written language. Mark reads like a shorthand account of a story by an impromptu speaker—with all the repetitions, redundancies and digressions which are characteristic of living speech."[15] He cites as further evidence the "context-supplements" of J. C. Hawkins, those enlargements of the narrative which add nothing to the information conveyed by it,[16] the majority of which are omitted by Matthew, and a large number of which are omitted by Luke as well.

Butler also treated this material, and he admitted that this point was the only one of Streeter's five arguments that tended "to support the theory of Markan priority to the exclusion of all other solutions . . . , an argument deserving serious attention."[17] Faced, however, with a mass of data on this point, Butler sought a solution in Mark's dependence on Matthew, by insisting that the references in Mark to Peter's remembering (11:21) reveal him to have been a preacher who "was using Matthew as his *aide-mém-*

---

[13]See D. Guthrie, *New Testament Introduction: The Gospels and Acts* (1965) 127.

[14]See V. Taylor, *The Gospel according to St. Mark* (1953), 44-66, 102.

[15]*The Four Gospels* 162-64. Cf. B. C. Butler, *Originality*, 147-56.

[16]J. C. Hawkins, *Horae synopticae: Contributions to the Study of the Synoptic Problem*, 2d ed. (1909) 114-53 esp. 125-26.

[17]*Originality*, 68.

oire.''[18] "Peter made use of Matthew as the source-book for his own 'instructions', he selected passages which his own memory could confirm and enlarge upon, he omitted incidents that occurred before he met our Lord, and most of Matthew's discourse-material, as not suitable for his purpose and not such as he could reinforce with a personal and independent recollection. He altered his Palestinian-Jewish source in various ways to make it more palatable to his Gentile audience.''[19] Thus Butler returned to a form of Augustine's solution, but apparently he has had little following in such an opinion. It is noteworthy that Butler had to interpose between Matthew and Mark a *preacher*, in effect, an oral source. As such, this becomes another stage in his solution of the Synoptic Problem, which he does not formally acknowledge. It is a hypothetical element that is really devoid of any control, and this is its deficiency.

A more frontal attack on this argument, however, was made by Farmer, who pointed out several defects in the argument as it was used by Streeter. Indeed, he turns the usual argument around and maintains that precisely those things that point to the "primitivity" of Mark's language are indications of the Gospel's lateness. It is understandable that Farmer is critical of Streeter's facile distinction between characteristics of spoken and written languages, of his idea that Mark has resulted from dictation, and of his assigning of the second Gospel to John Mark of Acts.[20] But Farmer's attribution of the "interesting and picturesque" details to the "well-attested tendency in the church to make the tradition more specific by the addition of just such details" goes undocumented.

What is really needed in this argument is a set of independent criteria. The recent book of E. P. Sanders, *The Tendencies of the Synoptic Tradition*,[21] has addressed itself to this question in some detail. But whereas the Synoptic and pre-canonical tradition of what Jesus did and taught was formerly studied in comparison with the tendencies of folk tradition, or of rabbinical tradition, or of the early church as revealed in the Epistles, Sanders seeks criteria from the post-canonical tradition. Under three main headings (increasing length, increasing detail, and diminishing Semitism, as pos-

---

[18]Ibid., 168.

[19]Ibid., 168-69.

[20]*Synoptic Problem*, 170-71.

[21]E. P. Sanders, *The Tendencies of the Synoptic Tradition*, SNTS Monograph Series 9 (1969).

sible tendencies of the tradition) he compares the post-canonical tradition and the Synoptic Gospels. From the standpoint of increasing length, Sanders finds that the evidence "weighs against the two-document hypothesis, and especially against Mark's priority, unless it can be offset by the *redaktionsgeschichtlich* consideration that Matthew and Luke were abbreviators."[22] Under the second heading Sanders concludes that "the simple priority of any one Gospel to the others cannot be demonstrated by the evidence of this chapter [that is, increasing details]. It is clear, rather, that the questions which finally emerge from this section concern redactional method and the relation of Mark to the eyewitness period. The categories which argue for Matthew's priority to Mark are just those which some would explain as containing material which Mark owes to the eyewitness source." "In summary, we must conclude that the principal lesson to be learned from the study of details is that of caution; . . . the criterion of detail must not be used too quickly to establish the relative antiquity of one document or another."[23] Finally, Sanders concludes that "Semitic syntax and grammar do not necessarily prove a tradition to be either relatively or absolutely early," and that Mark is richer in parataxis, asyndeton, and the use of the historic present. "It certainly suited Mark's redactional style to write vernacular Greek more than it did the style of Matthew or Luke, but we cannot thereby prove Mark to be the earliest of the Gospels."[24] The study of Sanders deserves greater attention than this one paragraph I have devoted it, since it bears on a vital aspect of what has been called "an argument deserving serious attention."[25] But the book significantly ends in a *non liquet*: "while certain of the useful criteria support Mark's priority, some do not. Both Matthean priorists and Lukan priorists can find some support in this study."[26] Sanders's study is important, but it is really limited in scope; it has to be considered alongside of the other comparative studies of the Synoptic and similiar tendencies. It remains to be seen whether this detailed study really undermines the so-called primitive character of the Markan Gospel.

---

[22]Ibid., 87.

[23]Ibid., 188.

[24]Ibid., 255.

[25]This book came into my hands unfortunately only at a date when the sketch was practically finished.

[26]Sanders, *Tendencies*, 276.

Undoubtedly the weakest point in the usual line-up of reasons set forth for the Two-Source Theory is Streeter's fifth point. When it is scrutinized today from the vantage-point of hindsight, his presentation is seen to be not so much an argument as a preliminary statement and a preoccupation to answer two objections: (1) Why did Matthew and Luke omit certain sections of Mark (namely, Mk. 1:1; 2:27; 3:20-21; 4:26-29; 7:2-4, 32-37; 8:22-26; 9:29, 48-49; 13:33-37; 14:51-52)? These represent a total of some thirty verses. (2) How can we explain certain minor verbal agreements (omissions or alterations) of Matthew and Luke against Mark in the Triple Tradition?[27]

To explain the omitted sections of Mark, Streeter appealed to a variety of reasons which were not always cogent. To explain the minor verbal agreements of Matthew and Luke against Mark, Streeter classified the passages and offered reasons for the independent changes. In the main, his classification used these headings:[28] (a) *Irrelevant agreements*: since unnecessary or unimportant Markan words were often omitted by Matthew or Luke in their compression of details, "coincidence in omission" in these parallel passages proves nothing. Similarly, the common shift in some parallel passages from the historic present to imperfects or aorists, the common substitution of δέ for καί, the common insertion of noun-subjects in sentences where Mark merely has "he" or "they", and the common introduction of ἰδού in five parallel passages (whereas Mark never uses it in narrating). In all of these details Streeter's point was that changes were otherwise widespread in Matthew or Luke and inevitably led to coincidental, and hence irrelevant, cases of agreement, constituting "considerably more than half the total number of the Minor Agreements."[29] (b) *Deceptive agreements*: "When Mark uses a word which is linguistically inadmissible, the right word is so obvious that, if half-a-dozen independent correctors were at work, they would all be likely to light upon it. For instance Mark uses φέρειν of animals or persons as objects, and every time Matthew and Luke concur in altering it to ἄγειν (or

---

[27]See the lists in E. A. Abbott, *The Corrections of Mark Adopted by Matthew and Luke*, Diatesserica II (1901), 307-324; or J. C. Hawkins, *Horae Synopticae*, 143-153, 208-212; B. de Solages, *A Greek Synopsis of the Gospels: A New Way of Solving the Synoptic Problem* (1959) 1052-66.

[28]*The Four Gospels*, 179-81, 293-331.

[29]Ibid., 298.

some compound of it).[30] Similarly, common corrections are made for κράββατον, θυγάτριον, κεντυρίων, βασιλεύς (used of Herod), and so on. Streeter applied the same judgment to "coincidences" that extended beyond single word agreements (for example, the five-word sequence in Mt. 9:7; Lk. 5:25 over against Mk. 2:12—showing that four of the five words are derived from the immediate Markan context); cf. Mk. 16:8; Mt. 28:28; Lk. 24:9—Mk. 3:1; Mt. 12:9-10; Lk. 6:6—Mk. 4:10; Mt. 13:10; Lk. 8:9—Mk. 4:36; Mt. 8:23; Lk. 8:22; and so on. (c) *The Influence of Q*: Certain phrases were commonly introduced into passages derived from Mark by Matthew and Luke because of the overlaping of Q and Mark (that is, because Q also contained versions of John's preaching, the baptism of Jesus, the temptation, the Beelzebub controversy, and so on). Yet Streeter used this influence to explain the agreements in Matthew and Luke in their parallels to only three Markan passages:

Mk. 4:21 = Mt. 5:15 = Lk. 8:16 = Lk.11:33
Mk. 4:22 = Mt. 10:26 = Lk. 8:17 = Lk. 12:2
Mk. 8:12 = Mt. 12:38 = Mt. 16:4 = Lk. 11:29

(d) *Textual corruption*: " . . . in nearly every case where a minute agreement of Matthew and Luke against Mark is found in B‭א‬ it is absent in one or more of the other early local texts." From this Streeter concluded, "A careful study of the MS. evidence distinctly favors the view that all those minute agreements of Matthew and Luke against Mark, which cannot be attributed to coincidence, were absent from the original text of the Gospels, but have crept in later as a result of 'assimilation' between the texts of the different Gospels." (e) *Some Residual Cases*: Here Streeter treated chiefly Mark 14:65, Matthew 26:67-68 and Luke 22:64: the plural participle λέγοντες and the phrase τίς ἐστιν ὁ παίσας σε, "the most remarkable of the minor agreements." To handle it, Streeter appealed to the addition of the phrase in the Markan text of mss. W, Θ, 13, etc., 579, 700, and after a rather lengthy discussion concluded that the phrase is really "an interpolation into Matthew from Luke."[31]

The fifth point in Streeter's presentation has often been criticized, and this loophole in the Two-Source Theory has been exploited by its oppo-

---

[30]This point is discussed in greater detail in my article, "The Use of *Agein* and *Pherein* in the Synoptics," in the *Festschrift* for F. W. Gingrich.

[31]*The Four Gospels*, 325-329. Cf. W. R. Farmer, *Synoptic Problem*, 284-86 (and 148-51).

nents.[32] For instance, in seeking to dispense with Q, A. M. Farrer drew an argument precisely from Luke's "small alterations in the wording of his Markan original" which were made in common with Matthew.[33] Though Farrer admits that Luke worked directly "upon the more ancient narrative of St. Mark," yet his alterations of Mark were due to "Matthean echoes," because Luke was after all acquainted with Matthew. Farrer's premise is that the Two-Source Theory was erected "on the incredibility of St. Luke's having read St. Matthew's book,"—a presupposition that has undergone a change in recent times and that enables Farrer simply to *assert* to the contrary. Farrer criticizes Streeter for classifying the minor agreements and for finding a distinct hypothesis for each class of them (such as scribal error assimilating Luke to Matthew or Matthew to Luke, or scribal errors subsequently effacing the text of Mark, or stylistic and doctrinal changes, or dependence on a Q parallel). "Thus the forces of evidence are divided by the advocate, and defeated in detail."[34] Farrer's criticism of Streeter on this point was, however, analyzed by R. McL. Wilson, who retorted with the observation that his criticism was written "with the balance tilted against it from the beginning"—an admirable "example of the demolition of one's opponent by means of the gentle art of ridicule."[35]

The one more or less valid point of criticism that Farrer levelled against Streeter—that of classifying the minor agreements and then finding a distinct hypothesis for each—was subsequently developed by W. R. Farmer, who labelled Streeter's procedure as "the atomization of the phenomena."[36] By this he means the separate classification and discussion of the phenomena in one group at a time, which obscured the total concatenation of agreements in a given Synoptic passage. So treated, the reader would scarcely become aware of the "web of minor but closely related agree-

---

[32]See A. W. Argyle, "Agreements between Matthew and Luke," *ET* 73 (1961-1962): 19-22; N. Turner, "The Minor Verbal Agreements of Mt. and Lk. against Mk.," SE 1 TU 73 (1959): 223-234; X. Léon-Dufour, "The Synoptic Problem," 271-274. Cf. L. Vaganay, *Le problème synoptique: Une hypothèse de travail* (1954) 69-74, 405-425; J. Schmid, *Matthäus und Lukas: Eine Untersuchung des Verhältnisses ihrer Evangelien* (1930).

[33]Austin Farrer, "On Dispensing with Q," *Studies in the Gospels: Essays in Memory of R. H. Lightfoot* (1957) 55-88, esp. 61 [reprinted in this volume].

[34]Ibid., 62.

[35]"Farrer and Streeter on the Minor Agreements of Mt and Lk against Mk," *SE* 1 TU 73 (1959): 254-257.

[36]Farmer, *Synoptic Problem*, 118.

ments'' of Matthew and Luke against Mark in any given passage.[37] Farmer analyzes in great detail the arguments of Streeter under four main headings; many of his analyses have detected historical defects in Streeter's presentation and some of them unveil a rather cavalier procedure.

Yet not all of Farmer's remarks are as telling as they might seem to be. For instance, his claim that the readers of Matthew and Luke ''were used to a Greek upon which the influence of Latin had long been felt. At least this is a presumption that would follow naturally from the historic and cultural realities of the times.''[38] One would have expected a little documentation here instead of a presumption. Or again, Farmer's comment on the common Lukan and Matthean shift from the Markan λέγει (an historic present) to εἶπειν in 20 passages: ''Possibly all twenty instances of this particular agreement are irrelevant. In each case, however, it is necessary to see this particular agreement in the context of all related phenomena in the concrete passage in which the agreement occurred.''[39] In this regard Farmer seems to be uncovering a defect in the process of atomization; indeed, in the abstract it appears to be a point well made. However, if one fishes out the 20 passages (which are undocumented) and compares them, even using Farmer's new colored *Synopticon*, it is difficult to see what the telling ''web of minor but closely related agreements'' is in most of the passages. True, one will find in these passages other words than εἶπειν ''hi-lited'' in red, that is, common to Matthew and Luke. Sometimes a few significant words are common, but at times a common καί or δέ or ιδού (for example, Mt. 8:1-4; 9:3-4; 12:48) might be the words. In such cases, it is hard to discern what the ''web'' really is. Consequently, until Farmer spells out what is meant by this ''web of *closely related* agreements,'' one may have to live with the atomizing explanation. In some instances, to be sure, Streeter's explanations still command stronger assent.

Concerning these common minor agreements of Matthew and Luke against Mark in the Triple Tradition, one should recall that they represent only a small fraction of the data to be considered in the Synoptic Problem. They constitute a real problem, which cannot be denied; they are one of the loopholes in the Two-Source Theory. Whatever explanation (or explanations) may account for this phenomenon, it scarcely weighs as evidence

[37]Ibid., 125.

[38]Ibid., 124.

[39]Ibid.

that completely counterbalances the other data pointing to a dependence of Luke (and of Matthew) on Mark. Furthermore, the distinction made long ago between significant and insignificant agreements of Matthew and Luke against Mark may still be valid. The longest list of significant agreements, constructed from four earlier attempts at collecting them, numbers only 46. And when these are further examined, they can be reduced to six; Mt. 26:68, 75; 17:3, 17; 9:7, 20 (and parallels).[40] The last word on this issue has not been said, and unfortunately what has at times been written about it has been laced with more emotion than reason.

These are the main reasons that have been proposed for the priority of Mark over Luke (and Matthew). They are not without their difficulties, and some of them are less cogent than others. But, as I see the situation, the day has not yet come "when the absolute priority of Mark [is] regarded as an a priori position in an obsolete stage of criticism."[41]

Before leaving the topic of the priority of Mark, a word should be said about the form of Mark that is thought to underlie Matthew and Luke. If the majority consensus seems to favor the priority of Mark over Luke (and Matthew), it can be said to be largely against the idea of *Ur-Markus*, that is, against a form of Mark that Matthew and Luke would have used which was earlier than and slightly different from canonical Mark. V. Taylor, in his commentary, *The Gospel according to St. Mark*, surveyed the various forms in which this hypothesis had been proposed up to that time and felt "compelled to reject all known forms of the Ur-Markus hypothesis"; yet he admitted that "there is something unseemly in an investigation which ends with *Requiescat Ur-Marcus.*"[42] Unfortunately, the hypothesis has not quite died. Some of the earlier forms in which it had been proposed have, indeed, proved inadequate; but some recent studies have been supporting one or other aspect of it. Aside from the problems of the commonly omitted Markan passages in Matthew and Luke and the minor verbal

---

[40]See S. McLoughlin, "Les accords mineurs Mt-Lc contre Mc et le problème synoptique: Vers la théorie des Deux Sources," *De Jésus aux Évangiles: Tradition et rédaction dans les évangiles synoptiques* (1967) 17-40. This article must be used, however, with great caution. It is cited here only because it indicates some of the lines along which one may have to proceed in evaluating the thrust of these minor agreements in the Two-Source Theory.

[41]X. Léon-Dufour, "The Synoptic Problem," 277.

[42]Vincent Taylor, *The Gospel according to St. Mark* (London: Macmillan, 1953) 68-77.

agreements, there is also the problematic ending of Mark, the textual evidence for a "Western" (or perhaps "Caesarean") form of Mark, and the textual evidence for a second century revision of Mark.[43] These are, in the main, the reasons invoked for the Ur-Markus hypothesis. None of this evidence, however, is as cogent as the other factors favoring the Two-Source Theory, and this is basically the reason for the reluctance of many to accept it. Then, too, there is the more recent emphasis on *Redaktionsgeschichte*, which may allow for some of the differences that the hypothesis itself was seeking to handle. To my way of thinking, the possibility of Ur-Markus is still admissible.[44]

---

[43]See T. F. Glasson, "Did Matthew and Luke Use a 'Western' Text of Mark?" *ET* 55 (1943-1944): 180-184 (and the debate that ensued with C. S. C. Williams, *ET* 56 [1944-1945]: 41-45; 57 [1945-1946]: 53-4; 58 [1946-1947]: 251; 77 [1965-66]: 120-21); J. P. Brown, "An Early Revision of the Gospel of Mark," *JBL* 78 (1959): 215-27 (and the note by T. F. Glasson with the same title, *JBL* 85 [1966]: 231-33); O. Linton, "Evidences of a Second-Century Revised Edition of St. Mark's Gospel," *NTS* 14 (1967-68): 321-355; A. F. J. Klijn, "A Survey of the Researches into the Western Text of the Gospels and Acts," *NT* 3 (1959): 162.

[44]R. Bultmann, (*Form Criticism: A New Method of New Testament Research* [1934] 13-14) has made use of this hypothesis; see also G. Bornkamm, *RGG* 2:756. The arguments commonly brought against it can be found in Feine-Behm-Kümmel, *Introduction to the New Testament* (1966) 49-50.

IN
SUPPORT
OF MARKAN
PRIORITY

W. G. Kümmel*

Kümmel presents the following evidence in support of the priority of Mark:

(1) A comparison of the synoptic gospels shows strikingly extensive agreement with regard to the extent of material between Matthew and Mark and between Luke and Mark.

(2) Decisive is the comparison of the sequence of the accounts in the synoptic gospels: within the material that they have in common with Mark, Matthew and Luke agree in sequence only insofar as they agree with Mark; when Matthew and Luke diverge from Mark, each goes his own way.

(3) Decisive is the comparison of language and content. Matthew and Luke have changed the colloquial or Semitic texts of Mark into better Greek.

It can be concluded from a comparison of all three synoptics that Mark, in the form handed down to us, has been used by both Matthew and Luke as a common source. None of the arguments for an Ur-Markus is convincing.

---

*Werner Georg Kümmel, "Attempt at a Solution of the Synoptic Problem," *Introduction to the New Testament* (Nashville: Abingdon Press, 1973) 56-63.

A comparison of all three Gospels with each other shows strikingly extensive agreement as regards extent of material between Matthew and Mark and between Luke and Mark. Only three short accounts (Mk. 4:26-29, the seed growing of itself; 7:31-37, the healing of the deaf-mute; 8:22-26, the blind man of Bethsaida) and three quite short texts from Mark (3:20, Jesus' relatives consider him to be mad; 9:49, salt with fire; 14:51, the fleeing young man) are found neither in Matthew nor in Luke (that is, about 30 verses out of 609). This attests that the Markan material is to be found almost totally in both Matthew and Luke, or indeed in either Matthew or Luke. This set of facts based on the pericopes as a whole is also confirmed by word count. In sections common to Matthew and/or Luke there are 10,650 words of Mark, 8,189 of which are in both other gospels (7,040 in Luke and 7,678 in Matthew).[1] In the material that is common to all three, Matthew and Luke have extensive congruence with Mark. On the basis of the resulting presupposition indicated by this evidence—that Mark could be the common source for Matthew and Luke— the omission of small bits of Markan special material by Matthew and Luke is thoroughly comprehensible; the two healings (by means of magical manipulations) and the position adopted by the relatives of Jesus are offensive; Mk. 9:49 is incomprehensible; the note in 14:51 is no longer of any interest; only the omission of the seed parable is inexplicable, although Mt. 13:24ff. does have at this place in the Markan structure the parable of the tares among the wheat. That Matthew and Luke must have used a very similar source is implied in any case by a comparison of the extent of the material. For the dependence of Mark on Matthew and/or Luke, or of Matthew on Luke, or of Luke on Matthew is inconceivable, since the omissions which would have to be assumed are incapable of explanation.[2]

Decisive is the comparison of the sequence of the accounts in the Gospels: within the material that they have in common with Mark, Matthew and Luke agree in sequence only insofar as they agree with Mark; where

---

[1]B. de Solages, *Greek Synopsis of the Gospels* (1959)1049, 1052. By a somewhat different count, R. Morgenthaler, *Statistische Synopse* (1971) asserts that Matthew has 8,555 of Mark's 11,078 words, while Luke has 6,737.

[2]D. L. Dungan's reference to Marcion's abbreviation of the gospel text also does not prove that Mark could have mishandled the tradition in the same way (''Mark—The Abridgement of Matthew and Luke,'' *Jesus and Man's Hope* [1970] 1:51 ff.). See the reprint of this article in this volume [editor's note].

they diverge from Mark, each goes his own way.[3]

For example, in the section Mark 2-3 par. all three Gospels proceed together at first: Mk. 2:1-22; Mt. 9:1-17; Lk. 5:17-39. In 9:18, however, Matthew goes off on his own, and presents several healings, the mission discourse (9:35-10:42), and pericopes about Jesus and the Baptist, about woes, thanksgiving, and salvation (11:2-30), all of which are units that Luke has too, though in different places. Mk. 2:23-3:6 once again agrees in essence with Mt. 12:1-14 and Lk. 6:1-11, but now Luke, with his sermon on the plain (6:20-49) and the material from 7:1-8:3, diverges from the sequence common to Mk. 3:7-35 and Mt. 12:15-50 (except that Mk. 3:13-19 = Mt. 10:1-14, and Mt. 12:33-45 is lacking in Mark). Only in 8:4 does Luke return to the sequence of pericopes followed by Mark and Matthew.

This fact—that Mark's sequence of material represents the common term between Matthew and Luke—was first recognized by Lachmann,[4] who concluded from this that Mark had best preserved the primitive gospel. Though later scholars have drawn from this correct observation of Lachmann's the conclusion that the common term was Mark itself, that is by no means a "Lachmann fallacy,"[5] if indeed the divergence of Matthew

---

[3]E. P. Sanders, "The Argument from Order and the Relationship Between Matthew and Luke," *NTS* 15 (1968-1969): 255, names four exceptions to this rule, of which three concern only single verses, however, and one is an OT citation. That Matthew and Luke united together in divergence from Mark quite sporadically proves nothing (contrary to Sanders, 256). The statistical investigation of A. M. Honoré, "A Statistical Study of the Synoptic Problem," NT 10 (1968): 95 ff., also comes to the same result: that no common divergences of Matthew and Luke from Mark are present. However, on the expert information of Frau Prof. A. Hampe that the method employed in this work is unclear, I leave to one side the essay in the following discussion. On the other hand, Morgenthaler (283-84) is instructive.

[4]See W. G. Kümmel, *Introduction to the New Testament* (1973) 48.

[5]By dispensing with the *Urmarkus* hypothesis, B. C. Butler, *The Originality of St. Matthew* (1951); W. R. Farmer, "The Lachmann Fallacy," *NTS* 14 (1967-1968): 441 ff; N. H. Palmer, "Lachmann's Argument," *NTS* 13 (1966-1967): 368ff.; Sanders; and Dungan have characterized the argument based on word order as a "fallacy," since it only proves that—in this view—Mark is still the middle point between Matthew and Luke. Even though Lachmann rejected the conclusion that Matthew and Luke were directly dependent on Mark, he at times comes close to implying it; see W. G. Kümmel, *The New Testament: The History of the Investigation of its Problems* (1972) n. 212. And this conclusion obtrudes itself since it makes readily comprehensible the deviations of Matthew and Luke

and Luke from Mark can be rendered comprehensible, but not the divergence of Mark from Matthew and Luke.

And that is indeed the case. Since from Mk. 6:7 on, Matthew and Luke practically never deviate from Mark's sequence, even though at completely different points they offer substantial supplements to Mark (an exception is Lk. 22:21-23, 56-66), the only section of Mark for which the sequence needs to be checked in relation to the parallels in Matthew and Luke is 1:1-6:6.[6]

It is really apparent that Luke presents only four deviations from the Markan order:

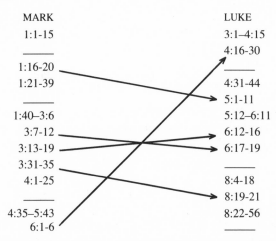

MARK	LUKE
1:1-15	3:1–4:15
————	4:16-30
1:16-20	————
1:21-39	4:31-44
————	5:1-11
1:40–3:6	5:12–6:11
3:7-12	6:12-16
3:13-19	6:17-19
3:31-35	————
4:1-25	8:4-18
————	8:19-21
4:35–5:43	8:22-56
6:1-6	————

(a) The rejection of Jesus in Nazareth (Mk. 6:1-6) is made into a programmatic scene for the inception of Jesus' activity; (b) the call of the disciples (Mk. 6:16-20) is placed after the first of Jesus' works because in this way the response of those called is more plausible; (c) the call of the twelve (Mk. 3:13-19) is placed before the crowding of the people around Jesus (Mk. 3:7-12), because in this way Luke has hearers on hand for the sermon on the plain which he inserts at 6:20ff.; (d) the transposition of the rejection of Jesus' family (Mk. 3:31-35) before the parable speech provides

---

from Mark in some instances. Farmer has not shown that Mark, when he agrees with one of the other two Gospels in word order, also agrees in exact wording; See Farmer, *Synoptic Problem*, 218; see also Morgenthaler, 292.

[6]In this case A. Barr's *A Diagram of Synoptic Relationships* (1938) is very helpful; further Morgenthaler, 227ff.

the crowds necessary for the scene. Thus in all four cases Luke's alteration of the Markan sequence is readily explicable, and furthermore detailed features show that Luke had the Markan sequence before him: Lk 4:23 speaks of miracles that took place in Carpernaum which Luke does not report until 4:31ff., even though he has placed Mk. 6:1ff. before Mk. 1:21ff. (par. Lk. 4:31ff.) and in this connection has mentioned the miracles that took place in Capernaum. In Lk. 4:38 Simon is mentioned, although his call is first narrated in 5:1ff. (transposed from Mk. 1:16ff.).

Basically Matthew diverges from the Markan order only in a twofold way.

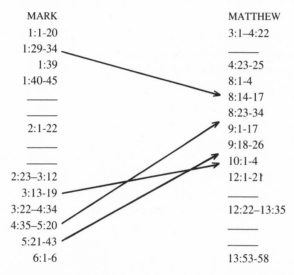

MARK	MATTHEW
1:1-20	3:1–4:22
1:29-34	———
1:39	4:23-25
1:40-45	8:1-4
———	8:14-17
———	8:23-34
2:1-22	9:1-17
———	9:18-26
———	10:1-4
2:23–3:12	12:1-21
3:13-19	———
3:22–4:34	12:22–13:35
4:35–5:20	———
5:21-43	———
6:1-6	13:53-58

(a) In connection with the first great discourse of Jesus (Mt. 5-7), there follows a string of ten miracle stories by way of illustrating 4:23; thus Matthew brings together in chs. 8 and 9 miracles that are scattered throughout the first half of Mark (1:29ff.; 4:35ff.; 5:21ff.). (b) Matthew attaches to these miracle chapters a mission address (10:5ff.), as an introduction to which he has moved forward the call of the twelve (Mk. 3:13ff.). Here also can be observed in detail Matthew's alteration of Mark's sequence; the two controversy sayings in Mt. 9:9-17 are out of place in a cycle of miracles and can be accounted for only on the ground that this is where they occur in Mark. Very significant likewise is the comparison of the parable chapter, Mk. 4:1-34, with Mt. 13:1-52: because Mt. 13:36-52 has been added even though the Markan sequence has been maintained, the

explanation of the parable of the weeds has been separated from the parable itself by the parables of Mt. 13:31-33 and by a concluding statement in Mt. 13:34-35; further, a second concluding statement follows in Mt. 13:51.

The opposite position—that Mark has altered the sequence of Matthew or Luke—offers no clarification in any of the cases mentioned (Wood offers other examples), so that the hypothesis of Griesbach, according to which Mark has excerpted the other two synoptists, is disproved, as well as the theory that Mark has used and abbreviated either Matthew or Luke.[7]

Decisive, however, for the recognition of the priority of Mark over Matthew and Luke is the comparison of language and content.[8] The strict agreement between the synoptists in the text that they share with Mark[9] proves in the first instance only that a literary relationship exists. But when the word usage of Matthew and Luke is compared with Mark, it is apparent either that Matthew and Luke have in large measure changed the colloquial or Semitic text of Mark into better Greek, and have done so in the same or similar ways, or that only Matthew or Luke has affected any such alteration: cf. the replacement of κράβατος (Mk. 2:4) by κλίνη (Matthew) or κλινίδιον (Luke), or the change of the difficult construction τί οὗτος οὕτως λαλεῖ; βλασφημεῖ (Mk. 2:7) in different ways by Matthew and Luke.[10] That in every case Mark is primary cannot be doubted, so that the thesis of Vaganay is untenable that on the basis of the oral tradition of Peter's preaching Mark has expanded the Aramaic Matthew which lies be-

---

[7]The attempt to show that Matthew has improved on the logical sequence of Mark and, therefore, is dependent on Mark, as in E. M. Dalmau, *A Study on the Synoptic Gospels* (1964), is based on a false allegorical interpretation of the parable of the sower and is, therefore, not demonstrable. On the redactional reworking of Mark 1:29-6:11 by Matthew, see F. Neirynck, "Rédaction et structure de Matthieu," *Festschrift Coppens*, 65ff.

[8]See on this recently G. Styler, "The Priority of Mark," in C. F. D. Moule, *The Birth of the New Testament* (1962) 223-32; reprinted in this volume; and D. Guthrie, *NT Introduction* (1965) I:126ff.

[9]See Kümmel, 43.

[10]Lists of such changes in P. Wernle, *Die synoptische Frage* (1899), 11ff., 18ff., 131ff., 146ff.; J. C. Hawkins, *Horae Synopticae*[2] (1909), 131ff. The eight Aramaic words in Mark (Hawkins, 130) are entirely lacking in Luke and Matthew has only two (27:33, 40). E. P. Sanders, *The Tendencies of the Synoptic Tradition* (1969) 10, 190ff., contests that these linguistic differences could prove the priority of Mark, but he investigates only features which could be characterized as semitisms, and even then he can explain the dominance of parataxis and the historical present in Mark, which is supposedly secondary as contrasted with Luke and Matthew, solely on the ground of Mark's personal preference!

hind Mark and Matthew, but which is preserved in a better text by Matthew.

More decisive than the purely linguistic alterations of the Markan text are the indications of substantive changes. In Mt. 3:16. εὐθύς before ἀνέβη ἀπὸ τοῦ ὕδατος is incomprehensible, but is readily explained on the basis of Mk. 1:10 εὐθὺς ἀναβαίνων . . . εἶδεν. In Mt. 9:2 the reason for the remark "Jesus saw their faith" cannot be discerned; Mk. 2:4, however, reports the most unusual undertaking of bringing the sick man to Jesus by digging a hole in the roof, a detail which Matthew has obviously omitted. In Mt. 14:1 the correct title for Antipas is used, τετράρχης instead of the popular βασιλεύς in Mk. 6:14, but in 14:9, Matthew has βασιλεύς (= Mk. 6:26), which can only be understood as a careless taking over of the Markan text. Still more striking is the replacement of Mk. 10:18 τί με λέγεις ἀγαθόν by the inoffensive τί με ἐρωτᾷς περί τοῦ ἀγαθοῦ in Mt. 19:17, and the strengthening of ἐθεράπευσεν πολλούς (Mk. 1:34) to πάντας (Mt. 8:16) and ἑνὶ ἑκάστῳ (Lk. 4:40). Here, as in other places, Luke appears to be secondary: instead of the ambiguity of the subject in Mk. 2:15, "As he sat at table in his house," Lk. 5:29 has the clarification "Levi arranged a great feast in his house." In Lk. 23:18 it is incomprehensible why the crowd suddenly asks for Barabbas to be freed, especially since he is not even identified until the following verse, but Luke has omitted the information given in Mk. 15:6 about Pilate's custom of releasing a prisoner.[11]

On the basis of all these facts it may be inferred from a comparison of the material common to all three Synoptics that Mark has been used by Matthew and Luke as a common source.

But is it really Mark and not a pre-Markan source that Matthew and Luke—as well as Mark—have used? Earlier Lachmann and H. J. Holtzmann took the position that Matthew and Mark were dependent on a earlier version of Mark, and the hypothesis of an *Urmarkus* which in different forms was used by Matthew and Luke has often been defended,[12] espe-

---

[11]Further examples of this kind in Styler, 228-29.

[12]Older advocates in V. Taylor, *The Gospel According to St. Mark* (1952) 67ff. More recently, F. Hauck, *Theologische Hand-Kommentar zum NT* (1931); P. Feine and J. Behm, *Einleitung in das Neue Testament* (1963); G. Bornkamm, *Handbuch zum NT* (1949ff.); E. Barnikol, *Das Leben Jesu der Heilsgeschichte* (1958) 264ff.; C. Masson, *L'Évangile de Marc et l'Église de Rome* (1968) 525-26, 117-18. A. Fuchs, "Sprachliche Untersuchungen zu Mt und Lk. Ein Beitrag zur Quellenkritik," *AB* 49 (1971) tries to show that Matthew and Luke have used an edited Deutero-Mark rather than our Mark.

cially the view that Mark as well as Matthew and Luke is dependent on an Aramaic Matthew.[13] In support of the theory, it is asserted that (a) the fact that Mk. 6:45-8:26 is lacking in Luke (the so-called "greater omission") can be explained only if Luke did not have this section in his copy of Mark; (b) the negative and positive agreements of Matthew and Luke against Mark in texts otherwise common to them and Mark force the conclusion that they used a common version different from Mark; (c) cases in which Matthew represents an older form of material shared in common with Mark lead to the same conclusion.

None of these arguments is persuasive, however.[14] (a) Numerous individual pericopes of Mark are missing in Luke, and in many cases the omission of a Markan text or the replacement of a Markan text by a parallel text can be explained objectively.[15] That Mk. 6:45-8:26 is lacking is admittedly "enigmatic," but at the same time Luke gives evidence that he has read this section (Schürmann).[16] The view that Luke had access to a truncated version of Mark is as unsatisfactory an explanation for the evidence as any hypothesis of an *Urmarkus*. (b) The agreements of Matthew and Luke over against Mark in the Markan material are of very different sorts. (i) Some of these agreements are only the consequence of textual

---

[13]See Kümmel, 47-50.

[14]Opposed to the *Urmarkus* or primitive document hypothesis are R. H. Fuller, *A Critical Introduction to the New Testament* (1966); A. F. J. Klijn, *An Introduction to the New Testament* (1967); W. Michaelis, *Einleitung in das NT. Eine Einführung in ihre Problem* (1963); A. Vögtle, *Das NT und die neuere katholische Exegese, I. Grundlegende Fragen zur Entstehung und Eigenart des NT* (1966); S. E. Johnson, *A Commentary on the Gospel according to St. Mark* (1960); V. Taylor; J. Heuschen, *Recherches Bibliques* 2 (1957); 11ff.; B. H. Streeter, *The Four Gospels: Study of Origins* (1924); F. C. Grant, *The Gospels: Their Origin and Their Growth* (1957); H. Schürmann, "Sprachliche Reminiszenzen an abgeänderte oder ausgelassene Bestandteile der Spruchsammlung im Lk und Mt," *NTS* 6 (1959-1960): 196; R. Schnackenburg, *Synoptische Studien für A. Wikenhauser* (1953) 205; T. Schramm, *Der Markus-Stoff bei Lukas* (1971) 5, n.2; see especially J. Schmid, *Mt und Lk*, 70ff.; *Synoptische Studien für A. Wikenhauser* (1953), 159ff.; *Lexikon für Theologie und Kirche*, 2d ed., 9:1242.

[15]See H. Schürmann, "Die Dublettenvermeidungen im Lk" (The Avoidance of Doublets in Lk), *Zeitschrift für Kirchengeschichte* 76 (1954): 83ff = H. Schürmann, *Traditionsgeschichtliche Untersuchungen zu den synoptischen Evangelien* (1968), 279ff.

[16]According to Morgenthaler, 248, Luke recognized the close relationship of some texts with the texts taken over from Mark and wanted to leave room for his own special material.

corruptions and disappear when the text is corrected.[17] But as a consequence of the uncertainty of the wording in the Synoptics the explanation is also uncertain in many cases. (ii) By far the majority of the agreements concern grammatical or stylistic improvements over against Mark (see the list in de Solages, 1055ff.), by which a convergence is either unavoidable or easily explicable. Furthermore, at least as often variations such as these are found only in Matthew or in Luke or were carried out for different purposes.[18] These agreements cannot therefore be used as the basis for a *Vorlage* differing from Mark that was used by Matthew and Luke. (iii) Finally there are a small number of agreements which can scarcely be depicted as accidental:[19] for example, Mt. 13:11 par Lk. 8:10 ὑμῖν δέδοται γνῶναι τὰ μυστήρια against ὑμῖν τὸ μυστήριον δέδοται in Mk. 4:11; Mt. 26:68 par. Lk. 22:64 τίς ἐστιν ὁ παίσας σε which is lacking in Mk. 14:65. These few instances may be explained through the influence of the oral tradition and are not extensive enough to justify the hypothesis of an *Urmarkus* or the theory that Matthew and Luke have used a version of Mark that preserved the "Caesarean" text (so Brown).[20] (c) There remain only those cases in which Matthew is supposed to present an older form of the tradition than Mark. Especially pointed to in this connection are Mk. 7:1ff., 24ff.; 10:1ff. and par. because here Matthew evidences a more

---

[17]Thus κύριε is surely to be read in Mk. 1:40 (= Mt. 8:2 = Lk. 5:12); another view though not persuasive, in T. Schramm (see note 14), 92 n3; and τοῦ κρασπέδου in Lk. 8:44 (= Mt. 9:20 against Mk. 5:27; cf. Streeter, 306ff.); and possibly in Mk. 9:19 διεστραμμένη belongs in the Markan text (= Mt. 17:17 = Lk. 9:41); cf. S. McLoughlin, "Le Problème synoptique. Vers la théorie des deux sources. Les accords mineurs," *Festschrift Coppens*, 30.

[18]Lists are in Hawkins, 129-30, 135-34, 139ff., and Schmid, *Mt und Lk* 38-39, 41-42, 66-67. Cf. Morgenthaler, 301ff., who erroneously traces the agreements to a subsequent dependence of Luke on Matthew.

[19]Lists are in Hawkins, 210-11. McLoughlin in his outstanding study tests forty-six instances of "remarkable agreements"and concludes that the only convergence which cannot be accounted for as an unambiguously text-critical or independent alteration is Mt. 26:68 = Lk. 22:64 (against Mk. 14:65) τίς ἐστιν ὁ παίσας σε; even here McLoughlin, on the basis of a conjecture, wants to eliminate these words as secondary, but if that seems too problematical it is still the case that the number of agreements between Matthew and Luke against Mark that lack explanations is very small.

[20]T. F. Glasson, "An Early Revision of the Gospel of Mark," *JBL* 85 (1966): 231ff., wants to consider that there was a version of Mark into which the "Western" readings intruded.

Jewish version; but Schmid[21] has shown convincingly that in all these texts Matthew has reworked—in the direction of judaizing—texts which in Mark are radically critical of the Law.

Since none of the arguments for an *Urmarkus* or for a document used also by Mark is convincing, by far the most probable conclusion is that in the form handed down to us Mark served as a source for Matthew and Luke.

---

[21]Schmid, 171ff.; cf. also R. Hummel, *Die Auseinandersetzung zwischen Kirche und Judentum in Mt* (1966) 46ff. When the texts which are supposed to be secondary in Mark are assembled, at the most one (Mk. 1:29) can be shown to be secondary in Mark as compared with Matthew and Luke.

THE
PRIORITY
OF
MARK

*G. M. Styler**

With regard to B. C. Butler's *The Originality of St Matthew,* Styler examines Butler's severe criticism of the Q hypothesis and of the priority of Mark. Styler discusses critically Butler's principal agreements on which, Styler maintains, the decision must turn. Styler attempts to demonstrate that in spite of Butler's criticisms the priority of Mark is securely grounded.

(1) As far as the material common to all three synoptics is concerned, Mark is the *middle term* or *link* between Matthew and Luke. Although the priority of Mark will satisfactorily *explain* these phenomena, so too, Butler argues, will other hypotheses. Styler concedes that although the advocates of the priority of Mark have been wrong in claiming to establish Markan priority though statistics, there are cogent arguments that retain their force. Styler maintains that Butler has not succeeded in destroying these arguments for Markan priority.

(2) Butler's attack on Q is an important preliminary to his attack on the priority of Mark. It is generally agreed, Styler says, that Matthew has not borrowed from Luke. The two possible explanations of the fact that Matthew and Luke have some closely similar passages, are, then, either (a) that Luke borrowed from Matthew or (b) that both of them depend upon a

*G. M. Styler, "The Priority of Mark," in C. F. D. Moule, *The Birth of the New Testament* (Harper and Row, 1962) 223-32.

common source (or sources), that is, the Q hypothesis. Any argument against (a) is, therefore, *ipso facto* an argument in favor of Q. Styler identifies three principal arguments against Luke's use of Matthew, which, therefore, serve as arguments in support of Q.

(3) Styler examines some of Butler's examples of passages in which Matthew's version is judged to be more original than Mark's and finds the more natural conclusion to be that Mark is indeed prior to Matthew.

After a century or more of discussion, it has come to be accepted by scholars almost as axiomatic that Mark is the oldest of the three synoptic gospels, and that it was used by Matthew and Luke as a source. This has come to be regarded as "the one absolutely assured result" of the study of the synoptic problem.

It has also been usually agreed that, besides Mark, Matthew and Luke shared another source of material, denoted by the symbol "Q." Many have explored and accepted the hypothesis that it was a single clearly defined document, which can to a great extent be reconstructed. Others, however, have postulated a number of documents or traditions, known to both Matthew and Luke, sometimes in language closely similar, at other times less so. It may therefore be better to employ the symbol Q to denote the material common to Matthew and Luke (but absent from Mark) rather than to denote a document, and thus prejudge the question of its unity. For the purpose of reexamining the priority of Mark, the unity of the Q document or Q material is irrelevant. But the validity of the Q hypothesis in some form or other is not wholly irrelevant, as will be seen.

The priority of Mark and the hypothesis of Q have been widely accepted in the present century, and are conveniently denoted by the name "The Two-document Hypothesis," although it should be noted that the documents may well have been many more than two. The classical statement and defense was made by B. H. Streeter,[1] who attempted to reconstruct Q as a unitary document, but restricted it more narrowly than previous scholars. He gave the labels "M" and "L" to the material peculiar to Matthew and Luke, or (to be more precise) to the sources from which he took most of their peculiar material to be derived. Here again it may be noted that some scholars have been cautious in accepting the unity of the M or L material, and that since this material appears in only one gos-

---

[1]Streeter, *The Four Gospels* (1924).

pel any reconstruction of its alleged source is even more speculative than the reconstruction of Q.

It was not necessary to maintain that Mark's version must at every point be older than Matthew's parallel version, since it was possible to say that anything in Matthew which in fact seemed more original than Mark could have been derived from Q. Further, there had been lingering doubts about the existence of Q. But it came as a shock when in 1951 Dom B. C. Butler published his book *The Originality of St Matthew,* attacking the Q hypothesis and the priority of Mark at the same time. In a minutely detailed study he subjected both hypotheses to a severe criticism, and argued strongly for the priority of Matthew. Mark, he argued, was dependent on Matthew; Luke was dependent on Mark for the material which the two had in common, and on Matthew for the Q material. Once the Q hypothesis is abandoned, the priority of Matthew, he claimed, quickly follows[2] from the existence of those passages in which Matthew's text seems clearly more original than Mark's or in some other way superior to it.

In spite of much close and careful reasoning, and the existence of at any rate *some* passages which tell in favor of Butler's conclusion, scholars have not abandoned the usual belief in the priority of Mark. In this Excursus it will not be possible to examine all Butler's arguments and instances one by one.[3] But an attempt will be made to show that the belief in the priority of Mark is in fact securely grounded, and to make clear the principal arguments on either side, on which the decision must turn.

First of all, we must admit that Butler has exposed a serious logical error in many expositions of the priority of Mark. Many of its advocates have begun by stating certain formal relationships that hold between the three Synoptic Gospels, namely:

(i) The bulk of Mark is contained in Matthew, and much of it in Luke; there is very little that is not contained also in one or the other.

(ii) The Markan material usually occurs in the same order in all three gospels; where Matthew's order diverges from Mark's, Luke supports Mark's order, and where (but this is very rare) Luke's order differs from Mark's, Mark's order is supported by Matthew. In other words, Matthew

---

[2]Butler agreed with the general assumption that there is no case for maintaining the priority of Luke; see his *The Originality of St. Matthew: A Critique of the Two-Document Hypothesis* (1951).

[3]Nor to consider the various articles that have appeared subsequently.

and Luke never agree with one another against Mark in respect of the order in which material common to all three Gospels is arranged.

(iii) The same relationship holds good for the most part in respect of wording. Matthew and Luke are often closely similar in wording in Q passages (that is, where Mark has no close parallel), but in Markan passages it is exceptional[4] for Matthew and Luke to have significant words in common unless Mark has them also; frequently Mark and Matthew will share the same phrasing, while Luke diverges, or Mark and Luke will do so, while Matthew diverges.

From these facts it is clear that, as far as material common to all three is concerned, Mark is the *middle term* or *link* between Matthew and Luke; Matthew and Luke are not directly related here, but only through Mark.

Now it is obvious that the priority of Mark will satisfactorily *explain* these phenomena. But its advocates have made a serious mistake in arguing (or assuming) that no *other* hypothesis will explain them.[5] Butler is correct in claiming that they are guilty of a fallacy in reasoning. If Matthew were the original, followed by Mark with variations, and if in turn Luke followed Mark, again with variations, these phenomena could well be the result. Alternatively, (as far as the phenomena go) Luke might be the earliest of the three, Mark the second, and Matthew the last; Butler agrees that on other grounds that suggestion may be set aside. But he rightly insists that the phenomena are satisfied equally well by the standard view, that Mark is the common source of Matthew and Luke, or by the view which he supports, namely, that Matthew is the oldest Gospel, that Mark used Matthew, and that Luke in turn used Mark.

Butler is correct, therefore, in saying that the formal relationships do not by themselves compel one solution to the synoptic problem. The texts of the Gospels must be carefully studied side by side before we can decide on the question of priority. With this we agree. But we part company when

---

[4]There are a number of exceptions. Some of these may be coincidental; others are probably due to corruptions and assimilations in the course of the transmission of the text; see Streeter, 179ff. Perhaps there are still more than can easily be accounted for. But they remain few compared with the large number of passages when the generalization given in the text holds true. Butler agrees, and does not attempt to use them to establish Luke's knowledge of Matthew.

[5]A variant theory is that the common source of Matthew and Luke was not the Mark we possess but an "Ur-Markus," an earlier edition of Mark, similar but not identical. The only objection to this theory is that it seems to be unnecessary.

he goes on to claim that this comparison points to the priority of Matthew. Although the advocates of the priority of Mark have been wrong in claiming to establish it through the statistics, yet there are cogent arguments which retain their force. In the present writer's judgment Butler has not succeed in destroying them, and they outweigh the arguments that Butler has adduced on his side.

Before turning to them, however, let us examine the place of the Q hypothesis in the enquiry. It is relevant to the priority of Mark to this extent: there are passages, especially in sections of teaching, where Matthew's version may well be judged more original than Mark's parallel. If the existence of a non-Markan source is denied, it will be difficult to maintain that in such passages Mark is prior to Matthew; rather, they support the priority of Matthew to Mark. But if Matthew had access to a non-Markan source, then there is no problem for advocates of Markan priority. Q is therefore relevant, since it is just what is required—namely, a non-Markan source. The evidence of Luke therefore will be relevant to the enquiry if it supports the existence of Q. If, however the Q hypothesis is rejected, the position of "Markan priorists" is weakened; they must still postulate a non-Markan source for Matthew to have used, but they can no longer point to Q as constituting that source.

Butler's attack on Q, therefore, is an important preliminary to his attack on the priority of Mark. If the former succeeds it increases his chance of succeeding in the latter also. But only slightly. Markan priorists will be driven on to more uncertain ground; they must now postulate an unknown source, instead of being able to point to one which is partially known. But in this there is no intrinsic improbability.[6] In other words, it is perfectly possible to believe that Luke obtained his so-called Q material directly from Matthew, and at the same time that Matthew obtained it from an earlier source, possibly known to Mark.[7]

It is agreed that Matthew has not borrowed from Luke. The two possible explanations of the fact that they have some closely similar passages

---

[6]Butler rightly asserts the principle that sources should not be multiplied needlessly. But there is no objection to postulating such a source; and it may be necessitated by other reasons, namely the arguments for the priority of Mark, if they prove to be sound.

[7]A. M. Farrer holds (like Butler) that Luke knew and used Matthew (as well as Mark), but continues to accept the standard view that Matthew used Mark. Cf. his essay "On Dispensing with Q" in *Studies in the Gospels* (1955) 55-88 [reprinted in this volume]; and *St Matthew and St Mark* (1954).

are (a) that Luke borrowed from Matthew, and (b) that both depend on a common source (or sources), that is, the Q hypothesis. Any argument against (a) is therefore *ipso facto* an argument in favor of Q. There are three principal ones: first, that in at least some of the parallel passages Luke's version seems more original than Matthew's;[8] secondly, that it is hard to see why, if Luke has borrowed material from Matthew he has so violently and frequently disturbed Matthew's order; and thirdly, it seems inexplicable why he has consistently ignored[9] Matthew in any passage where he follows Mark, and has no parallel account—for example, of the Nativity stories and Resurrection appearances.

Butler faces these arguments, and dismisses them. He denies that there are any cogent examples of Q passages in which Luke's version is more original than Matthew's; and he claims that Luke makes no attempt to put material derived from Matthew into the Markan context in which Matthew had it. He claims that it would be a tricky task to find out what that context was, since already there are large variations in order in the first half of Matthew and Mark.[10]

But in spite of Butler's arguments, which deserve careful study, the present writer continues to find it hard to believe that Luke used Matthew.

After disposing of Q, Butler turns to the question of the relative priority of Matthew and Mark, and rightly asks that it should be discussed on the basis of a direct comparision of the parallel passages without prejudice. This is a fair challenge, which the "Markan priorist" need not evade. Butler himself examines a large number of passages, and claims that here on a straight comparison of Matthew and Mark the preference will nearly always go to Matthew's version as the more original. The most convincing of his examples are cases[11] where Matthew's version is a coherent whole, and Mark's seems to be an excerpt, in which knowledge is betrayed of

---

[8]Cf., for example, Lk. 6:20 ("Blessed are you poor") with Mt. 5:3 ("Blessed are the poor in spirit"). Although it is true that Luke's version fits his own special interests, it still seems to the present writer that it is nearer to the probable original than Matthew's "poor in spirit." Cf. also Lk. 3:8 with Mt. 3:9; Luke's μὴ ἄρξησθε may well be nearer to the original than Matthew's μὴ δόξητε.

[9]Or "almost entirely ignored"; cf. above, n 4.

[10]A. M. Farrer, "On Dispensing with Q," 67ff. [reprinted in this volume] argues that Luke's order is typological, and was never intended to reflect the order of Matthew. But although his argument is persuasively written, the present writer finds his thesis incredible.

[11]Cf., for example, the preaching of John the Baptist.

some phrase or fact which Mark does not reproduce. Unless we are allowed to appeal to Q, and say that it is some knowledge of Q[12] (not Matthew) which Mark betrays, Butler's conclusion does indeed seem to be forced on us. Rather less convincing are passages where Mark refers to Jesus' teaching, or to parables (in the plural), and goes on to produce only one example. Certainly Mark here betrays knowledge of more than he reproduces, and certainly Matthew shows more knowledge than Mark; but it is gratuitous to suppose that it must be from Matthew that Mark's knowledge comes.

Less convincing still are passages where Matthew's version is more smooth than Mark's; rather, they tell the other way. In all his arguments of this type, Butler defeats himself: the better his defense of Matthew, the harder it becomes to see why Mark should have altered something smooth into something less smooth. In fact, the relative roughness of Mark is one of the strong arguments on the other side. In textual criticism it is an accepted canon that, other things being equal, the harder reading is to be preferred, since it is more probable that the harder should have been altered to the easier than *vice versa*. Numerous examples can be produced in which, in one way or another, Matthew's version looks easier than Mark's. They may be grouped under several heads.

(a) Grammatical variants, where Mark is wrong and Matthew correct; for example, Mk. 10:20 ἐφυλαξάμην (wrong), = Mt. 19:20 ἐφύλαξα (right).

(b) Stylistic variants, where Mark is sprawling, and Matthew, tidy; for example, Mk. 10:27 = Mt. 19:26. Butler argues regularly for the superiority and greater originality of Matthew in such cases, on the ground that his version is closer to an authentic Semitic parallelism and even an original poetic strain in the teaching of Jesus. To the present writer it seems far more probable that Mark represents the earlier version, and that Matthew by careful rewriting has achieved a greater polish.

(c) There are the well-known examples[13] where Mark's version appears lacking in respect for the apostles or even in its estimate of the person

---

[12]That is, of Matthew's source for this passage.

[13]For example, Mk. 4:38 (= Mt. 8:25); Mk. 6:5-6 (= Mt. 13:58); Mk. 10:17-18 (= Mt. 19:16-17), where Matthew's question τί με ἐρωτᾷς περὶ τοῦ ἀγαθοῦ, and the appended comment εἷς ἐστιν ὁ ἀγαθός are intelligible as a rewriting of Mark, but most odd otherwise.

of Christ, and where Matthew's version avoids all such implications. Without attempting to establish any rigid law of development, we must surely say that all such passages tell strongly in favor of the priority of Mark, and that Butler's attempts to evade this inference are unconvincing.

(d) In some passages Mark is suggestive but obscure, and Matthew's parallel looks like an attempt to leave the reader with an edifying message; but we are left with the suspicion that Matthew has not penetrated to the real sense. Compare, for example, Mk. 8:14-21 with Mt. 16:5-12 where Matthew interprets the "leaven" against which Jesus warns his disciples as "the teaching of the Pharisees and Sadducees."

But the best instance is the difficult passage about the purpose (or effect) of parables.[14] Butler's treatment[15] of this leaves me quite unconvinced. Matthew seems here to be trying hard to extract a tolerable sense from the intolerable statement that Mark appears to be making, namely that Jesus taught in parables to prevent the outsiders from having a chance of understanding and being converted. He assumes that Mark's "all things are (done) in parables" means "I speak in parables." But recent commentators have suggested a line of interpretation of Mark's text which the present writer finds wholly satisfying; namely that the same teaching is put before all by Jesus, but whereas some by God's grace penetrate to its inner meaning, for others it remains external, a parable and nothing more;[16] and herein the dark purpose of God, as predicted in Isaiah, is fulfilled. Mark may have partly misunderstood what he recorded; but it seems certain to the present writer that his words are closer to the original, and that Matthew's version is an unsuccessful attempt to simplify what he found intolerable.

Another example of misunderstanding by Matthew may be claimed at Mk. 2:18 (= Mt. 9:14). Mark's first sentence ("the disciples of John and the Pharisees were fasting") sets the scene; then "they" ask Jesus why his disciples, unlike those of John and of the Pharisees, do not fast. The persons who ask are surely *not* the ones who were the subject of the previous sentence; they are persons unspecified.[17] Matthew's sentence is much

---

[14]Mk. 4:10-12 = Mt. 13:10-15.

[15]Butler, 90-92.

[16]Or even "a riddle"; the same word in Hebrew or Aramaic can mean "parable" or "riddle." Cf. J. Jeremias, *The Parables of Jesus* (ET 1954; 2d ed. 1963) 12-14.

[17]For another clear example of Mark's "impersonal" plural cf. 5:35; 3:21, 32 are other probable examples.

shorter and neater. But he obviously assumes that "they" are the disciples of John and the Pharisees.

We have passed on to an argument which to the present writer puts the priority of Mark beyond serious doubt, namely, that there are passages where Matthew goes astray through misunderstanding, yet betrays a knowledge of the authentic version—the version which is given by Mark. The two accounts of the death of the Baptist (Mk. 6:17-29; Mt. 14:3-12) contain clear examples of this. Mark states fully the attitude of Herod to John; he respected him, but was perplexed; and it was Herodias who was keen to kill him. And the story that follows explains how in spite of the king's reluctance she obtained her desire. Matthew, whose version is much briefer, states that Herod wanted to kill John. But this must be an error; the story, which perfectly fits Mark's setting, does not fit Matthew's introduction; and at 14:9 Matthew betrays the fact that he really knows the full version by slipping in the statement that "the king"[18] was sorry. It is surely clear that Matthew, in a desire to abbreviate, has oversimplified his introduction.

Further, both Mark and Matthew relate this story as a "retrospect" or "flashback," to explain Herod's remark that Jesus was John risen from the dead. Mark quite properly finished the story, and then resumes his main narrative with a jump; Matthew, failing to remember that it was a "retrospect," makes a smooth transition to the narrative which follows: John's disciples inform Jesus; and "when Jesus heard . . . " (Mt. 14:12-13).

Butler rightly asks that the comparison should be made without prejudice. But, in the course of it, impressions are necessarily received. One impression which is received of Matthew is that he regularly aims at giving a smooth version, without any kind of roughness; and also that he is somewhat pedantic.[19] It is at least in line with this impression if, as the Markan priorists maintain, Matthew regularly conflates Mark and his other source.

---

[18]Mark calls Herod "king"; Matthew correctly calls him "tetrarch" in 14:1, but lapses into calling him "king" at 14:9. Butler attempts to base an argument for the priority of Matthew on his superior knowledge at this point; and also on the knowledge he displays from time to time of Jewish and Palestinian customs. Such arguments are tenuous, and are more than counterbalanced by Mark's superior knowledge of the story he is relating.

[19]Cf. 21:2ff., where he apparently takes Zech. 9:9 to mean two animals. Cf. also 14:21, where he speaks of 5,000 men "apart from women and children"; surely this is a pedantic gloss on Mark's plain ἄνδρες.

Butler pours scorn on the suggestion, regarding it as cumbrous and point-less; but if Matthew really was pedantic he may not have thought it so.

Of all the arguments for the priority of Mark, the strongest is that based on the freshness and circumstantial character of his narrative.[20] Tradition connects his Gospel with St. Peter and this trait has strengthened the belief that the tradition may be sound. But it should be noticed that the same character is to be found even in narratives of events at which St. Peter was not present. Butler concedes this quality to Mark and explains it by a dar-ing suggestion: he accepts the tradition that St. Peter is often Mark's source—hence a vividness and wealth of detail greater than in Matthew—and saves the priority of Matthew by suggesting that St. Peter himself[21] had access to a copy of Matthew while speaking.

In effect, this suggestion amounts to the view that Mark had direct ac-cess to what was in fact Matthew's ultimate source; to the authentic ver-sion of the story which Matthew has often abbreviated or modified. Clearly it makes dependence on Matthew unnecessary. These are the cases on which the priority of Mark strongly rests, and they counterbalance the rival group of passages, mostly teaching and not narrative, on which But-ler relies for his hypothesis. In those, it will be remembered, Markan prior-ists are sometimes on the defensive, and appeal to Q.[22]

For those passages,

our diagram will be   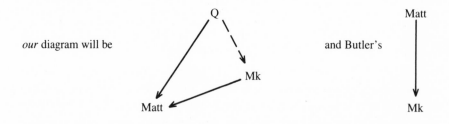   and Butler's

---

[20]Including touches that might well come almost directly from an eyewitness, for ex-ample, the cushion in the boat (Mk. 4:38) and the Aramaic words and phrases, of which Mark preserves more than Matthew.

[21]Or, presumably, it might have been that Mark, while using Matthew as his written source, called to mind the fuller account he had heard from St. Peter. In any case, Matthew is acquainted with the same account as Mark.

[22]Cf. *supra*; "Q" need not here mean a source common to Matthew and Luke; all that is needed is a source used by Matthew which Mark knew, and occasionally used.

In the narrative passages, the situation is exactly reversed; here the simple view is that Matthew depends on Mark; and it is now Butler who requires a three-term diagram, namely,

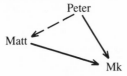

But whereas it seems perfectly credible to the present writer that (i) a non-Markan source existed, known to both Mark and Matthew, and (ii) Matthew conflated it with Mark, Butler's suggestion on the other hand seems to be pure fantasy. Our explanation of *his* favorable cases may be cumbersome; but his explanation of *our* favorable cases is incredible.

In the next place, Mark, if he is using Matthew, has used only about 50 percent of his subject-matter, but has expanded it in the telling.[23] But it is hard to see why he should have omitted so much of value *if* he was using Matthew: not only the Sermon on the Mount and much teaching besides, but also the narratives of the Infancy of Jesus. Mark *does* include teaching; and so it cannot be replied that he was only interested in narrative.[24]

The point may be put like this: given Mark, it is easy to see why Matthew was written; given Matthew, it is hard to see why Mark was needed.[25]

If Matthew was using Mark, and incorporating other material, it is easy to understand why he should regularly have abbreviated Mark whenever he could safely do so.[26] In spite of the postulate of the form critics,[27]

---

[23]But has expanded it in a natural way; the extra sentences seldom look like extraneous insertions.

[24]True, he has in any case made his selection from the material available to him. Butler urges this point, and claims that if there is a difficulty here it is almost as great for us as for him. But surely not. It is harder to see why Mark should have omitted these if they were already incorporated in a full-scale document accessible to him.

[25]That is, by the early Christians. Mark is of course valued most highly by the modern scholar.

[26]The story of Jarius's daughter is a good example (Mk. 5:21-43 = Mt. 9:18-26). Matthew omits one whole episode in the story. His version is more compact, but as a result it is historically far less credible; according to him, the father tells Jesus that his daughter has just *died*, and begs him to come and restore her to life. In Mark, the girl is *near* to death, and the father appeals to Jesus for help.

[27]The form critics postulate that conformity to a regular pattern is an indication that a passage goes back to an earlier date than one which does not conform to the pattern.

it is likely that Mark's sprawling and circumstantial stories are more original than Matthew's shorter and more formal ones.

Lastly, an examination of Matthew's additions tells heavily against his
priority. Under this head there are two classes of passage. (i) First, pieces
of teaching included by Matthew but absent from the parallel section of
Mark. Butler claims that Matthew's whole context hangs together; and
that if he has really inserted them into a framework provided by Mark he
has done so with a felicity that is beyond belief. But, with some exceptions,[28] this judgment will be challenged. Thus, in spite of Butler's claim
that the famous *Tu es Petrus* passage has parallels or antitheses with both
the preceding and the following verses, few will find him convincing. On
the contrary, the passage will still seem to many to be an insertion into
Mark's account of Peter's confession of faith[29]—although not, of course,
necessarily an invention.

(ii) There are also some narrative additions in Matthew which seem to
stem from later apologetic, or even from the stock of legendary accretions
which are evident in the apocryphal Gospels. Butler argues strongly that
any such judgment is premature and unwarranted; that if the detailed comparison of Matthew and Mark proves Matthew to be older, then that verdict must be accepted, and any suspicion that Matthew's special narratives
are "late" must be mistaken. But since we hold that the detailed comparison of Matthew and Mark tells in the other direction, in favor of Mark's
priority, then the judgment that Matthew's narratives are late, and sometimes close to the legendary, must be given full weight.

In conclusion it should be said that, although Butler naturally gives
most space to the passages which seem to tell in his favor, he does not attempt to conceal the fact that there are strong arguments on the other side.
To some extent, however, he weakens their force by admitting them
quickly, and attempting to explain them all away in a few words by his

---

[28]Namely, the passages where an overlap of Mark and Q is postulated by Markan priorists.

[29]Mk. 8:27-33 = Mt. 16:13-23. Cf. also Matthew's parable of the Labourers in the
Vineyard (20:1-16), which is placed after πολλοὶ δὲ ἔσονται πρῶτοι ἔσχατοι καὶ
ἔσχατοι πρῶτοι, and rounded off with a variant of the same logion. But the real point
of the parable is different; in inserting it after this logion, Matthew has accentuated a secondary feature.

suggestion that St. Peter had access to a copy of Matthew. Until some less incredible explanation is forthcoming, the natural conclusion that Mark is prior to Matthew will continue to hold the field.[30]

---

[30]For a review of the way in which the priority of Mark came to be accepted, and the dubious arguments often used in its defense, cf. W. R. Farmer, "A 'Skeleton in the Closet' of Gospel Research," *BR* 6 (1961): 3ff., which the present writer had not seen at the time of writing. But it seems that, however insecure the arguments used in the past, the reasons for accepting the priority of Mark are in fact strong.

THE
PRIORITY
OF
MARK

H. G. Wood*

Wood addresses B. C. Butler's plea for the originality of Matthew, stating that Butler's critique of the two-document hypothesis cannot be dismissed or lightly set aside.

Wood argues that if Butler's thesis is correct, namely that Mark and Luke both depend on Matthew, then there should be numerous agreements in order between Matthew and Luke against Mark, but there are none or next to none. Wood maintains that had Butler examined the question of order in detail, he would almost certainly have been forced to recognize that again and again Mark's order is original and Matthew's secondary and derivative.

After examining in detail the question of order in several passages, Wood concludes that the argument based on a comparison of the order and arrangement of incidents in Mark and Matthew is still valid. Wood also calls attention to the fact that Butler himself concedes that one argument in favor of the priority of Mark which deserves serious attention is the ꞌpresence in Mark of phrases likely to cause offense, which are then omitted or toned down in Matthew and Luke.

It remains conclusive that Mark is the first of the synoptic gospels.

*H. G. Wood, "The Priority of Mark," *The Expository Times* 65 (1953-1954): 17-19.

We are so accustomed to regarding the priority of Mark as the most assured result of the critical study of the Synoptic problem, that we have almost forgotten the evidence that established the conclusion. It is just as well that this confident assumption should be challenged if only to arouse us from what John Stuart Mill called "the deep slumber of a decided opinion." Such a challenge has now been issued by Dom B. C. Butler in his plea for the recognition of the originality of St. Matthew.[1] His critique of the two-document hypothesis cannot be lightly set on one side. He presents his case with great ingenuity and marshals his evidence with commendable care and critical insight. If he fails to convince, we shall still gain from a reconsideration of the relations of Mark and Matthew.

Dom Butler starts from the examination of some five passages in Matthew usually assigned to the hypothetical Logia-document Q, to which parallels may be found both in Mark and Luke. These are the Parable of the Mustard Seed, the saying on giving scandal, the Beelzebub controversy, the mission charge to the Twelve, and the dual precept of charity.[2] In these passages it will be seen that Mark has phrases in common with Matthew, and Luke has phrases in common with Matthew, but Mark and Luke do not agree against Matthew. This recalls the kind of consideration first adduced by Lachmann to support the priority of Mark, namely, the fact that in the order and arrangement of the material common to the first three Gospels, Matthew and Luke each agree with Mark to a considerable extent, but Matthew and Luke seldom agree together against Mark. Where Matthew has a different order from Mark, Luke usually follows Mark; where Luke has a different order from Mark, Matthew usually follows Mark. The conclusion is that the order of the narrative as it stands in Mark is presupposed in Luke and Matthew.

Most scholars would say that the evidence produced by Dom Butler suggests, not that Mark and Luke depend on Matthew for their records of the teaching, but that Matthew represents the lost document Q more fully and more accurately than Luke and Mark. Matthew stands nearer to the common source. But, asks Dom Butler, is this hypothetical document Q really necessary? For a long time scholars talked of Ur-Markus as the source of the triple tradition, and at last realized that this was superfluous.

---

[1]B. C. Butler, *The Originality of St. Matthew: A Critique of the Two-Document Hypothesis* (1951).

[2]Mt. 13:31-33; 18:6-7; 12:25-32; 10:3-15; 22:35-40.

Mark was accepted, not just as the Gospel nearest to the source of the triple tradition, but as actually the source from which Matthew and Luke drew the framework and much of the content of their narratives. Why should we not dismiss Q, like Ur-Markus, and see in Matthew the source of the material in Luke and Mark which is usually assigned to Q? This, however, lands the critic in a serious and obvious difficulty. The same type of reasoning leads most scholars to regard Matthew as dependent on Mark, and Dom Butler to regard Mark as dependent on Matthew. The two-document hypothesis avoids this difficulty by making Mark depend not on Matthew but on Matthew's source. As this does not satisfy Dom Butler's thesis, he has to show that the same type of reasoning is valid as he uses it but fallacious as ordinarily presented. The evidence in either case is susceptible of more than one interpretation. In the case of the triple tradition, Mark holds a mediating position. There are three possible solutions, which may be indicated diagrammatically.

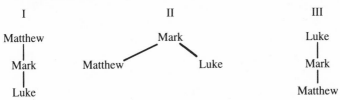

All are agreed that solution No. III is ruled out, but it is a fallacy to suppose that No. II is necessary. According to Dom Butler, solutions I and II have an equal chance of being correct. ''There is one chance in two that Matthew copied Mark; and there is one chance in two that Mark copied Matthew.''

In the case of the common traditions regarding the teaching of Jesus, we have three similar solutions. Matthew now holds the mediating position, but Dom Butler claims to have demonstrated that the second solution is here the most probable, if not the only possible one. If, then, Mark and Luke are both dependent on Matthew for Q material, we must accept the first solution for the triple tradition, and recognize the originality of Matthew.

The first solution implies that ''Mark is necessarily the connecting link between Matthew and Luke, but not necessarily the source of more than one of them.'' So Dom Butler contends that Mark is a source only for Luke, and the knowledge of Matthew's order comes to Luke through

Mark. This is very strange because Dom Butler claims to have proved that Luke is also dependent on Matthew. Why, having Matthew in his hands, Luke should follow Matthew's order only when it re-appears in Mark is difficult to understand and explain. If Dom Butler's thesis were true, there should be numerous agreements in order between Matthew and Luke against Mark, and admittedly there are none or next to none. The observation of Lachmann and the deduction from it cannot be dismissed as a fallacy. It is the most likely of the three solutions, and the choice between No. I and No. II is by no means a choice between solutions which have an equal chance of being correct.

Unfortunately, Dom Butler does not examine the question of order in detail. If he had done so, he would almost certainly have been forced to recognize that again and again Mark's order is original and Matthew's secondary and derivative. Indeed, one clear instance would suffice. In Mk. 1, the call of the first four disciples is followed by the entry of Jesus into Capernaum where He takes up His residence in Simon's house. On the Sabbath He teaches in the synagogue and heals a demoniac. Returning to Simon's house, He cures Simon's mother-in-law of a fever. Then at even, when the sun was set, crowds come to be healed. These incidents are naturally interconnected. The call of Simon is naturally followed by the journey into Capernaum. The scene in the synagogue on the Sabbath is linked with the healings at sunset. Because it was the Sabbath, the people waited till the Sabbath was over before bringing their sick to be healed. The series of events reads like Simon's recollection of his first Sabbath with the Master. Of this interconnected series, Matthew has only the call of the four disciples and the healing of Simon's mother-in-law, followed by healings at sunset. The call of the four disciples is related in ch. 4, and the other two incidents are related in ch. 8 after the healing of the centurion's servant. By linking the healing of Simon's mother-in-law with the healing of the centurion's servant Matthew gets the place right. He brings Jesus into Capernaum and so into the house of Peter, but he misses the note of time. He does not hint that these two cures took place on the Sabbath, as he has omitted the scene in the synagogue. Consequently, there is no point in his saying that the cures on a large scale took place "at even." Only if the healing in Simon's house took place on the Sabbath would the people have waited till sunset before bringing their sick to be healed.

Dom Butler rather rashly is prepared to test his case by the use of this particular phrase, ὀψίας γενομένης, "at even" or "when it was eve-

ning.'' He says, ''This is characteristically Matthaean: there are six other occurrences of this phrase in Matthew (besides 16:2); five in Mark, all probably borrowed from Matthew (at Mk. 4:35 the phrase probably comes from Mt. 8:16);[3] no other example in the New Testament.'' Later on Dom Butler adds, ''If we were right in regarding ὀψίας γενομένης as a typical Matthæan phrase, then we have to explain St. Mark's use of the phrase, every time probably in parallel with Matthew (for at Mk. 4:35 it is probably derived from Mt. 8:16); if he owes the phrase to Matthew, then that by itself settles the case.'' Unfortunately for his argument Dom Butler has overlooked the fact that Mt. 8:16 is parallel to and almost certainly derived from Mk. 1:32. As we have seen, in Mk. 1:32 it is natural and full of significance, since it is part of the story of a Sabbath in Capernaum. In Mt. 8:16 it is pointless, and *the writer only retained it because he found it in his source.* In Mk. 4:35 the phrase is again perfectly appropriate, and Mark did not need to borrow it from Matthew or any one else. Matthew 8:16 is undeniably borrowed from Mk. 1:32, and, as Dom Butler says, that settles the case.

If this single instance suffices to establish the priority of Mark, it is of course no isolated case. It has long been recognized that Mk. 2:1-3:6 presents a series of incidents, not necessarily connected in time or place, but linked together by the theme of the growth of Pharisaic opposition. In the healing of the paralytic Jesus challenges the unspoken censure of His critics. After the call of Levi, the Pharisees question the disciples about the conduct of their Master in eating with publicans and sinners: then they question Jesus about the conduct of His disciples who neglect fasting. This is followed by the censure of the disciples for Sabbath-breaking, and the climax is reached when Jesus Himself is condemned by the Pharisees for healing on the Sabbath.

The progress from doubt and suspicion to definite hostility is clearly brought out. Either Mark found these stories so arranged in his source, or he imposed this order on stories which probably came to him as separate fragments of tradition. If he derived this set of stories in this order from his source, that source was not Matthew, for though Matthew has the stories in the same order, he puts the first three in ch. 9 and the second two

---

[3]''On that day, when it was even, he said to his disciples, 'Let us go over to the other side' '' (Mk. 4:35). ''And when even was come, they brought unto him many possessed with devils'' (Mt. 8:16).

in ch. 12. Again, the probable conclusion is that the order is original in Mark and that Matthew took it over from Mark but failed to perceive the connexion in theme between the first three and the last two incidents.

Admittedly, in this case it is barely possible Mark found the two sets in Matthew and by a stroke of genius saw that they could effectively be linked together. But this is highly improbable. The chances of Matthew borrowing from Mark and of Mark borrowing from Matthew are certainly not equal. The odds are in favour of the first hypothesis. And the hypothesis is confirmed when we examine instances where the order of certain incidents is clearly due to Mark's methods as an evangelist and where Matthew accepts the order in whole or in part without understanding it. In two instances Mark presents incidents in a form resembling the Greek device chiasmus, or, more simply, in the order a b b a. The two parts of a single incident or two closely associated incidents are separated by the whole of another single incident or by two incidents closely associated with each other. Apparently Mark adopts this procedure to suggest the interval between the beginning and the end of his first chosen incident. Thus in ch. 3 we are told in verses 20, 21 that the relatives of Jesus set out to arrest Him because people were saying that He was out of His mind. This is the beginning of incident a. But instead of completing it at once, Mark inserts the judgment of the Scribes from Jerusalem, 'He hath Beelzebub.' This is incident b. Mark proceeds to complete incident b by giving the reply of Jesus to this criticism. Then he records the arrival of the relatives and the answer of Jesus to them, thus completing incident a. The pattern, a b b a, is obvious. Similarly in ch. 6, Mark first records the mission of the Twelve (a 1), then inserts Herod's speculation about Jesus (b 1), adds the story of the death of John the Baptist (b 2), and follows this with the return of the Twelve (a 2), the retirement into the desert and the feeding of the multitudes. Again the pattern, a b b a, is clearly present. The use of this framework may be attributed to the Evangelist himself. In so ordering these blocks of material, Mark is almost certainly original. But if this is doubted, and if the arrangement came to him from his source, then that source cannot have been Matthew. For though Matthew's narrative is affected by the marshaling of the events in this order, these two blocks as arranged in Mark are not to be found in Matthew. In the first instance, Matthew's narrative has b b a. He appends the repudiation of his relatives by Jesus to the criticism of the Pharisees, and Jesus' answer to them. But the first part of Mark's a b b a is missing. In consequence, the reason for Jesus' refusal to

speak to His relatives is left unexplained, and His apparent discourtesy becomes unintelligible. Nor is there any ground in Matthew for associating this incident with what immediately precedes. The connexion of the intervention of the relatives with the verdict of the scribes, which is patent in Mark, is lost in Matthew. The conclusion seems inevitable. The order is original in Mark; it is secondary and derivative in Matthew.

The second instance is even more striking.

Matthew records the mission of the Twelve in ch. 10. He nowhere troubles to mention their return. Much later in ch. 14 he records the judgment of Herod that Jesus is John the Baptist risen from the dead, and relates the story of the death of John the Baptist. He follows this with the withdrawal of Jesus to the desert and the feeding of the multitude. Here, again, Matthew seems to have had Mark's pattern a 1, b, b, a 2 before him, but having separated a 1 from the rest of the block, he has no real grounds for following b b by a 2, and he proceeds to make a quite impossible connection between b and a 2. Misunderstanding his source and the situation, he assumes that the death of John the Baptist took place just before the feeding of the multitude and is the occasion for the withdrawal of Jesus to the wilderness. He tells us that the disciples of John buried John's body and went and told Jesus who, on hearing this, withdrew to a desert place apart. But manifestly the death of John the Baptist had taken place some time before the Twelve set out on their mission and before Herod could say of Jesus, this is John the Baptist risen from the dead. The juxtaposition of the story of the death of John the Baptist with the story of the feeding of the multitude is original in Mark. Mark is not correcting a blunder in his source, presumed to be Matthew. Matthew is misunderstanding a succession of incidents which he found in his source, which appears to be Mark.

Dom Butler thinks that the only arguments in favor of the priority of Mark which are deserving of serious attention are the presence in Mark of phrases likely to cause offense; which are omitted or toned down in the other Gospels, and the fact that ''Mark reads like a transcript of the words of an impromptu speaker, while Matthew and Luke use the most succinct and carefully chosen language of one who writes and then revises an article for publication.'' These characteristics of Mark's narrative, which Dom Butler frankly recognizes and which remain presumptive evidence for Mark's priority in spite of the ingenuity of his attempt to weaken their force, do not consitute the only arguments deserving of serious attention.

The argument based on a comparison of the order and arrangement of incidents in Mark and Matthew still holds good and, as I think I have shown, it remains conclusive.

THE
SYNOPTIC
PROBLEM

F. Neirynck*

Recent discussion of the two-document hypothesis has concentrated principally upon three points: the minor agreements of Matthew and Luke against Mark, the argument from order, and the style of Mark.

1. THE MINOR AGREEMENTS. The minor agreements of Matthew and Luke against Mark are the most serious stumbling block to the hypothesis of Markan priority. Without abandoning the priority of Mark, several solutions to the problem of the minor agreements have been proposed: (a) a Proto-Mark or Deutero-Mark; (b) Luke's subsidiary dependence on Matthew; (c) a common source for Matthew and Luke besides Mark (and Q).

2. THE ARGUMENT FROM ORDER. Neirynck examines critically the contention that the relative order of sections in Mark is in general supported by both Matthew and Luke. He discusses criticisms of the logic of the argument from order, disagreements in order between Matthew and Mark, and the matter of Luke's tendency to follow very closely the order of Mark.

3. THE STYLE OF MARK. The roughness of Mark's style is a well-known argument for the gospel's priority. The evidence of stylistic im-

---
**F. Neirynck, "Synoptic Problem," *The Interpreter's Dictionary of the Bible* (Nashville: Abingdon, 1976) Supp: 845-48.

provement and of Christological corrections in Matthew and Luke is impressive, although Neirynck briefly examines the alternatives.

The two-document hypothesis is undoubtedly the most widely accepted source-critical hypothesis in NT introductions, gospel commentaries, and monographs. It is presupposed in a considerable number of redaction-critical investigations, and in particular, the recent study of the Matthean as well as the Lukan redaction and theology has shown the practicability of the theory.[1] Nevertheless, the existence of the hypothetical ''Q'' source is still contested,[2] and objections raised against the priority of Mark have tended to call the two-document hypothesis into question and, in some quarters, have led to other theories (oral tradition, gospel fragments, primitive gospel, priority of Matthew).

The recent discussion has concentrated upon three problems: the minor agreements, the argument from order, and the style of Mark.

1. *The minor agreements.* On the hypothesis of the independent editing of Mark by Matthew and Luke the minor agreements of these gospels against Mark (in the triple tradition) are the most serious stumbling block. Occasionally, textual corruption and harmonization can be the cause of the agreement, but only on a more limited scale than was proposed by Streeter. Because of the great number of these coincidences in content, vocabulary, style, and grammar, the concatenation of agreements in certain sections, and the combinations of positive and negative agreements, many authors do not accept accidental coincidence as a satisfactory explanation for the whole of the phenomenon. Without abandoning the priority of Mark, several solutions have been proposed.

(a) *Proto-Mark or Deutero-Mark.* Matthew and Luke used a Markan text which is slightly different from our Mark, either a Proto-Mark[3] or a Deutero-Mark, due to textual corruption,[4] revision,[5] or edition (West: Primitive Luke;[6] Fuchs: Mark already combined with Q[7]).

---

[1]R. T. Fortna, "Redaction Criticism, NT," *IDB* (1976) Supp: 733-35.

[2]F. Neirynck, "Q," *IDB* (1976) Supp: 715-16.

[3]M.-E. Boismard, *Synopse des quatre évangiles en français* 2: *Commentaire* (1972).

[4] F. Glasson, "Did Matthew Use a 'Western' Text of Mark?," *ET* 55 (1943-1944): cols. 180-84; and "An Early Revision of the Gospel of Mark," *JBL* 85 (1966): 231-33.

[5]J. P. Brown, "An Early Revision of the Gospel of Mark," *JBL* 78 (1959): 215-27.

[6]H. P. West, "A Primitive Version of Luke in the Composition of Matthew," *NTS* 14 (1967) :75-95.

[7]A. Fuchs, "Sprachliche Untersuchungen zu Matthäus und Lukas," *AB* 49 (1971).

(b) *Luke's subsidiary dependence on Matthew*. Luke, who follows Mark as his basic source in the triple tradition, is also acquainted with and influenced by Matthew. According to some authors the double tradition, too, is borrowed from Matthew,[8] but others suggest that the minor agreements (in the triple tradition) and the double tradition or Q sections are to be explained differently.[9]

(c) *Common source*. Both Matthew and Luke depend on another source besides Mark: a primitive gospel, Proto-Matthew,[10] gospel fragments,[11] or oral tradition.[12]

In the two-document hypothesis it is a common assumption that some of the agreements should be assigned to Q (especially the *major* agreements in the sections parallel to Mk. 1:7-8, 12-13; 3:22-30; 4:30-32; 6:7-11, and, less convincingly, 12:28-34). The great bulk of minor agreements, however, can be explained by coincident correction and the common tendencies of the independent editors, Matthew and Luke, and are therefore highly significant for the redactional study of the gospels.[13] Only a small number of residual cases are attributed to the influence of oral tradition,[14] or to textual corruption.[15]

---

[8]A. Farrer, "On Dispensing with Q," *Studies in the Gospels* (1955) 55-88.

[9]R. Morgenthaler, *Statistische Synopse* (1971) 301-305.

[10]L. Vaganay, *Le Problème synoptique* (1954) 69-74, 319, 423-25; cf. Boismard.

[11]X. Léon-Dufour, "Les Évangiles synoptiques," *Introduction à la Bible* (1959) 2:291-95.

[12]N. A. Dahl, "Die Passiongeschichte bei Matthäus," *NTS* 2 (1956): 17-32; T. Schramm, *Der Markus-Stoff bei Lukas* (1971) 72-7.

[13]F. Neirynck, "Urmarcus redivivus? Examen critique de l'hypothèse des insertions matthéennes dans Marc," in *L'évangile selon Marc* (1974) 103-45; "The Argument from Order and St. Luke's Transpositions," *The Minor Agreements*, 291-322; "The Gospel of Matthew and Literary Criticism: A Critical Analysis of A. Gaboury's Hypothesis," *L'é- vangile selon Matthieu* (1972) 37-69; *Duality in Mark. Contributions to the Study of the Markan Redaction* (1972). F. Neirynck in collaboration with T. Hansen and F. Van Segbroeck, *The Minor Agreements of Matthew and Luke Against Mark with a Cumulative List* (1974).

[14]W. G. Kümmel, *Introduction to the NT* (rev. ed., 1975).

[15]J. Schmid, *Einleitung in das NT* (1973), revision of A. Wikenhauser's *Introduction*; cf. B. de Solages, *A Greek Synopsis of the Gospels* (1959) and *La Composition des évangiles. De Luc et de Matthieu et leurs sources* (1973); S. McLoughlin, "Le problème synoptique," in *De Jésus aux évangiles: Tradition et rédaction dans les évangiles synoptiques* (1967) 17-40.

On the Griesbach Hypothesis, with the assumption of some direct literary relationship between Matthew and Luke, the minor agreements are explained by Mark's "own peculiar stylistic preferences" as he conflated the two earlier gospels.[16]

2. *The argument from order.* The relative order of sections in Mark is in general supported by both Matthew and Luke: where Matthew diverges from Mark, Mark's order is supported by Luke, and where Luke differs from Mark, Mark's order is supported by Matthew. From this statement of the absence of agreement in order between Matthew and Luke against Mark (in the triple tradition), proponents of the two-document hypothesis draw the conclusion that Mark is the common source, independently edited by Matthew and Luke.

a. The validity of the argument. B. C. Butler[17] has contended that there is a logical error in the traditional argument from order. A number of scholars, among them some who continue to espouse the two-document hypothesis on other grounds,[18] have in fact dismissed the argument as useless. It is allowed that the argument has probative force on the assumption of a common gospel source.

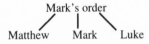

But, it is claimed, once this solution is abandoned the phenomena of order are satisfactorily explained not only on the hypothesis of Markan priority, but also on any other hypothesis which proposes Mark as the middle term.

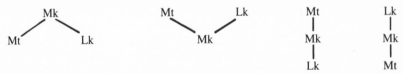

However, some other observations need to be made.

1. If the relative order of the gospel *episodes* is studied as a specific literary phenomenon, it becomes clear that there are virtually no places

[16]W. R. Farmer, *The Synoptic Problem* (1964).

[17]B. C. Butler, *The Originality of St. Matthew* (1951).

[18]G. M. Styler, "The Priority of Mark," in C. F. D. Moule, *The Birth of the New Testament* (1962) 223-32 [reprinted in this volume]; R. H. Fuller, E. P. Sanders, and T. R. W. Longstaff, "The Synoptic Problem: After Ten Years," *PSTJ* 28 (1975): 63-74.

where Matthew and Luke agree against Mark. (Sanders,[19] however, also considers individual sentences or phrases where there is agreement in order and regards this as indicative of Luke's dependence on Matthew).

2. The description of the evidence as "alternating support" (i.e., when Matthew diverges from Mark, Mark's order is supported by Luke, and when Luke diverges from Mark, Mark's order is supported by Matthew) should be corrected by a more concrete approach. In fact, the basic phenomenon to be reckoned with is the common order between Mark and Matthew and between Mark and Luke. The changes of order are exceptional: in Luke the alterations of the Markan order are limited in number, and in Matthew the transpositions are confined to 4:23-11:1. (In the Griesbach hypothesis, too, the argument from order is based on the so-called "alternating support," explicable only by the deliberate intention of a writer, on this hypothesis, by Mark's decision to remain close to at least one of his sources, Matthew and Luke).

3. The evidence of the relative order excludes the oral tradition hypothesis and the fragments theory.

4. The appellation "Lachmann fallacy"[20] is misleading, not because Lachmann's observations (1835) were made within the primitive gospel hypothesis, but also because he did not use the formulation of "Mark's order supported either by one or the other," which originated in the Griesbach hypothesis and was first employed in the Markan hypothesis by Weisse (1838).[21]

5. Lachmann's concern was to determine the reasons which could have influenced the evangelists in altering the sequence of the gospel sections in some *Urgospel*. His argument for the priority of Mark's order is still a valuable one insofar as an acceptable explanation can be given for Matthew's and Luke's transpositions, and no good reason has been found why Mark would change the order of Matthew or Luke.

b. Matthew and Mark. The disagreements in order are found in the first part of Matthew. From 14:1 on, Matthew follows faithfully the Markan sequence (Mk. 6:14-16:8): there are only a few omissions (Mk. 8:22-26;

---

[19]E. P. Sanders, "The Argument from Order and the Relationship between Matthew and Luke," *NTS* 15 (1969): 249-61.

[20]B. C. Butler, *Originality*.

[21]C. H. Weisse, *Die evangelische Geschichte kritisch und philosophisch bearbeitet* ("A Critical and Philosophical Study of the Gospel Story") 2 vols. (1938).

12:41-44; 14:51-52), and the alterations of order in Mt. 15:3-6; 19:4-6; and 21:12-13 are merely inversions within the same context; the discourse fragment of Mt. 10:17-22 (cf. Mk. 13:9-13), which is sometimes quoted as the only transposition in the gospel, is a redactional duplication (cf. 24:9, 13-14; Mk. 13:9-10, 12c-13). The presence of transpositions in the first part of Matthew does not necessarily point to a different tradition (Gaboury: multiple sources in a less advanced state). Matthean editorial concentration is a much more plausible explanation. In the discourses of Mt. 5-7 and 9:37 ff. Matthew combined the double tradition parallels with other Q sections. If we can admit, as most authors do, that the original order of Q is better preserved in Luke, then Matthew not only anticipated these sections but also reversed the order of the Baptist and the mission sections.

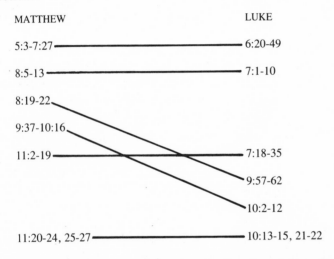

MATTHEW   LUKE

5:3-7:27 ——————————————— 6:20-49

8:5-13 ————————————————— 7:1-10

8:19-22

9:37-10:16

11:2-19 ——————————————— 7:18-35

                              9:57-62

                              10:2-12

11:20-24, 25-27 ——————————— 10:13-15, 21-22

A similar observation is to be made regarding the triple tradition: the transpositions are found in the great complex of 4:23-11:1, from the Sermon on the Mount to Jesus' answer to John the Baptist. The section opens with a solemn introduction in which Matthew combined several motifs from Mark's "Day at Capernaum" (Mk. 1:21-39), and also from other summaries in Mark.

MATTHEW   MARK

4:23a   1:39a; 6:6b

4:23b	1:14-15
4:23c	1:39b
4:24a	1:28
4:24b	1:32, 34
4:25	3:7-8
5:1a	3:13
5:2	1:21

The Sermon on the Mount is the only one of the five great discourses in Matthew (5-7; 10; 13; 18; 24-25) for which the occasion is not provided by a rudimentary discourse in Mark (cf. Mk. 6:7-11; 4:31-34; 9:33-50; 13). Perhaps the first mention of Jesus' *teaching* in Mk. 1:21 explains why Matthew placed the first sermon here and used Mk. 1:22 in his description of the reactions of the multitude: Mt. 8:1-17 combines the miracle story which followed the sermon in Q (Lk. 7:1-10) with miracle stories from Mk. 1. The first place is given to the cleansing of the leper (8:2-4, with the *inclusio* in 9:30b-31; cf. Mk. 1:43-45). The inversion of the order has to do with Matthew's interest in the composition of 8:1-9:34. At the same time Mk. 10:40-45 is introduced within the "First Day" of Jesus' ministry, Matthew's replacement of the "Day at Capernaum" in Mark (5:1-8:17).

In the second section of miracles (8:19-9:34) Matthew anticipated Mk. 4:35-5:43 and duplicated other miracle stories in 9:27-34. However, the insertion of the Q passage in 8:19-22 clearly shows that the editorial interest is not merely in the miracles of Jesus. The summary of Jesus' ministry is echoed in 10:1, 7-8 and unites the activity of Jesus and the mission of the disciples. Thus, Matthew's editing can be seen in a double anticipation: that of the miracles from Mk. 4:35-5:43, and that of the disciples sections from Mk. 6:6b-11 (combined with 3:13-19), and from Q (cf. Luke 9:57-10:12). Mt. 8:18-9:34 is the evangelist's own composition around the Markan sequence of 2:1-22. In 12:1 he comes back to Mk. 2:23 and from there on follows the order of Mark, with the exception only of the anticipated pericopes.

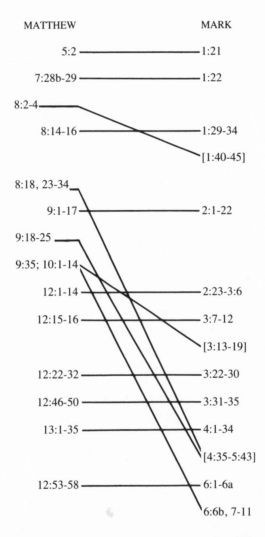

c. *Luke and Mark*. The situation in Luke is quite different. There is no such rearrangement as we have in Mt. 4:23-11:1. Luke normally follows the order of Mark. It has been argued that Luke, where he borrowed from Mark, *always* follows the Markan order and that the few instances of divergence in the ministry, and the more frequent alterations of order in the Passion Narrative, are explainable only by the influence of non-Markan sources (Proto-Luke). However, for each transposition a valuable redac-

tional explanation can be adduced, although many exegetes admit a non-Markan tradition behind pericopes such as:

Luke		from Mark
4:16-30		6:1-6a
5:1-11		1:16-20
6:12-16, 17-19		3:13-19, 7-12
7:36-50		14:3-9
8:19-21		3:31-35
(after 8:4-18)		(before 4:1-34)
10:25-28		12:28-34
(cf. 20:39-40)		
22:21-23		14:19-21
22:24-27		10:42-45
22:31-34		14:29-30

3. The style of Mark. The roughness of Mark's style is a well-known argument for the gospel's early dating. The evidence of stylistic improvements and Christological corrections in Matthew and Luke is impressive, although those who question Mark's priority dismiss it as unconvincing and argue, to the contrary, that there are passages in Mark which suggest that Mark is secondary to Matthew and Luke.[22]

The new defense of the Griesbach hypothesis holds that duplicate expressions, of which one element has a parallel in Matthew and the other in Luke, are the result of conflation. According to Boismard and some other exegetes, the sources combined by Mark are not the gospels of Matthew and Luke but Proto-Mark and Proto-Matthew, or other gospel sources. However, a re-examination of the evidence shows that duplicate expressions and other forms of duality form a characteristic feature of Mark's style. The two-step expressions, in which the second statement adds precision to the first, is typical. It points to the originality of Mark rather than to conflation and combination of sources.

---

[22]For example, W. R. Farmer, *The Synoptic Problem.*

THE
CASE AGAINST
THE PRIORITY
OF MARK

THE
SYNOPTIC
PROBLEM

*B. C. Butler**

After reviewing Streeter's arguments for the priority of Mark, Butler concludes that the extent and similarity of the synoptic gospels is so great as to require some theory of connection, direct or indirect. He argues that in seeking a solution to a literary problem of this type, it is a good working hypothesis that simpler solutions are to be preferred, other things being equal, to more complicated ones; and that conjectural or nonextant sources are not to be supposed unless the data of the problem require them.

After reviewing the question of whether oral or written sources are the best solution to the synoptic problem, Butler concludes that we have to search for a *written* source (or written sources) as the solution to our problem, but we should allow for the possibility of augmentation from the oral tradition.

Butler singles out for mention several solutions to the synoptic problem: (1) The Two-Document Hypothesis: original form (Weisse and Holtzmann: i.e., a first edition of Mark [or Proto-Mark] and a conjectural Discourse Source [later named Q]); (2) The Two-Document Hypothesis: modern form (McLoughlin: i.e., Mark and Q); (3) The Four Document Hypothesis (Streeter: i.e., Mark, Q, M. [the source of Matthew's peculiar material], and L [the source of Luke's peculiar material]); (4) Lagrange's

*B. C. Butler, "The Synoptic Problem," *A New Catholic Commentary on Holy Scripture,* ed. R. C. Fuller, L. Johnston, and C. Kearns (Nelson, 1969) 815-21.

Modified Two-Document Hypothesis (that is, an effort by Roman Catholic scholars to reconcile the priority of Matthew with the Two-Document Hypothesis); (5) The Priority of Matthew (Chapman); (6) Pierson Parker (Matthew and Mark depend on a common source, named by Parker K, a sort of Proto-Matthew); (7) A Post-Lagrange Hypothesis (Vaganay); (8) Mark a conflation (Farmer).

Butler proceeds to a detailed examination of certain aspects of the Two-Document Hypothesis: (1) a seven-part critique of the so-called Q passages, and (2) a three-part critique of the priority of Mark as opposed to the priority of Matthew. He concludes that the evidence requires that Mark depends on Matthew, and that Luke depends on both Matthew (for his so-called Q material) and on Mark. If conjectural sources are not excluded from consideration, then Butler believes that it is possible that Matthew and Mark on the one hand, and Matthew and Luke on the other hand, are connected by the common use of a lost Gospel, which can best be described as a Proto-Matthew, a document of which our canonical Matthew is a fairly faithful "second edition."

The synoptic problem is posed by the similarities and differences between the first three (or "Synoptic") Gospels. These are the data which lead us to ask whether there are any direct dependencies between two or more of these Gospels, and whether two or more of them share one or more common sources (literary or oral). The data may be summarized as follows:

A. Through a total of about 200 verses, mainly comprising discourse material and scattered about in various parts of the Gospels (often in different contexts), there runs a strong similarity, or even virtual identity, between Matthew and Luke in content, presentation and language; but there are no parallels for most of these verses in Mark. They constitute what we shall here call the "Q" material or the "Q" passages (*Quelle*, "source" in German). The detailed temptations of Christ after his baptism are a good example of Q material. The temptations are not specified in Mark, but are given in almost identical detail in Matthew and Luke; yet the order of the temptations is different, and there are a few differences in wording.

B. (1) Mark contains 673 verses. The substance of over 600 of these is found also in Matthew; and of about 350 out of the 673 the substance is found in Luke.

(2) Where a section of Mark has parallels in both Matthew and Luke, the majority of Mark's actual Greek words is usually found in both Matthew and Luke; or at least in one of them. When a section of Mark has a

parallel in only one of the other two, there is again a marked similarity between Mark and the other passage. This parallelism of content and wording is combined with a similarity of approach to the incidents recorded that emerges very clearly if contrasted with the highly individual approach of John in the few passages (few, that is, till the Passion narrative is reached) where he relates an incident also recorded in one or more of the Synoptics.

(3) The order of Mark's sections or incidents is generally found also in Matthew or Luke or in both; and Matthew and Luke hardly ever agree in their order of incidents *against* the order of Mark.

(4) Where all three are parallel, the frequent agreements in detail of all three, and the frequent agreements of Mark with one of the others against the third, stand in marked contrast with the relative paucity of agreements of Matthew with Luke *against* Mark.

(For the above summary I am indebted to B. H. Streeter[1]).

The full force of these data is only appreciated when the Greek text of the three Gospels is carefully studied and compared. This is best done with the help of a Greek Synopsis. The extent of similarity is too great to be explained by similarity of purpose coupled with coincidence. Some theory of connection is required. Such connection may be direct or indirect. (Thus, if documents X and Y are connected, the reason may be that (a) the author of X used Y as his source; or *vice versa*; or (b) that the two authors used some third document (or oral tradition) as their common source; or (c) that some third author or oral teacher used X or Y as his source, and in turn became a source for Y or X—this third author or teacher would then have provided a "missing link" between X and Y. The Synoptic Problem is a specimen of a type of literary problem that frequently occurs when some historical event or tradition is recorded in two different authorities).

In seeking a solution of a problem of this type, it is a good working hypothesis that simpler solutions are to be preferred, other things being equal, to more complicated ones; and that conjectural, or nonextant, sources are not to be supposed unless the data of the problem require them.

Oral Sources or written? A theory which sought to explain the data of our problem purely by the common use of the same oral traditions would hardly, in the judgment of most scholars, do justice to the extent and character of the parallels and similarities. And it would have to suppose a *Greek* oral tradition more rigidly fixed than we have the right to assume.

---

[1]B. H. Streeter, *The Four Gospels: A Study of Origins* (1930).

Moreover, it is equivalent, critically speaking, to the hypothesis that all three Gospels are derived, in their 'Markan' sections, from a Proto-Evangelium, a conjectural (nonextant) original Gospel. This was Lachmann's presupposition, and he showed conclusively, on the basis of the existing agreements, *coupled with the relative absence of agreements* (in these sections) of Matthew and Luke against Mark, that the Proto-Evangelium must have been something very similar to Mark: in fact, we may say a (lost) *first* edition of Mark, a Proto-Mark. If this solution was to be accepted, it became desirable to determine the extent of the differences between Mark and Proto-Mark, and this must be done by examining the agreements of Matthew and Luke against Mark in the relevant passages. Their total determinable extent was however found to be exiguous, and at length, in the early years of the present century, the followers of this trail gave up the theory that Mark itself was used as a source by the authors of Matthew and Luke. They failed to notice that, by taking this step, and thereby admitting that there is *direct* dependence (between Matthew and Mark on the one hand, and Mark and Luke on the other), they had not only thrown overboard the presupposition of Lachmann's arguments, but had in consequence destroyed the basis of his logic. *If* the explanation of the similarities and differences between Matthew, Mark, and Luke in their "Markan" sections is not due to direct utilization of one Gospel by another but to common use of a source other than any or them, then the source must have been remarkably like Mark. But *if* the possibility of direct utilization is entertained, then we have three alternative solutions, all equally probable on the evidence so far discussed: (a) Matthew may have been the source of Mark, and Mark the source of Luke; or (b) Mark may have been the source of Matthew on the one hand and Luke on the other; or (c) Luke may have been the source of Mark, and Mark the source of Matthew (W. R. Farmer[2] suggests that the evidence can be met by supposing that Matthew was the source of Luke, while the author of Mark "conflated" Matthew and Luke. It seems to be correct procedure to suppose, at least provisionally, that we have to search for a *written* source (or written sources) as the solution to our problem. But in view of what we know, or can reasonably assume, about the primitive Church, we should allow for the possibility of considerable interference from oral tradition.

---

[2]W. R. Farmer, *The Synoptic Problem* (1964).

Alternative solutions. In patristic times the existence of this problem was hardly noticed. It is, however, worthy of remark that Augustine held that the author of Mark was a ''foot-follower and abbreviator'' of Matthew (*De Consensu evang.*, 1, 2, 4. Among the numerous solutions put forward in more recent times the following may be singled out for mention here:

(1) *The Two-Document Hypothesis, original form.* As propounded by C. H. Weisse;[3] his arguments were perfected by H. J. Holtzmann.[4] On this hypothesis, the data listed under B above were to be explained by a conjectural *first edition* of Mark (or Proto-Mark), which would have been utilized as a source by the authors of Matthew, Mark and Luke. The data described under A above were similarly explained by a conjectural Discourse Source (later named, for convenience, ''Q''), utilized as a source by Matthew and Luke.

(2) *The Two-Document Hypothesis, modern form.* This solution eliminates Proto-Mark, and makes Mark itself a source used by Matthew and Luke. It retains Q, though it is prepared to understand by that symbol not a single document but a number of small written collections of the sayings of Jesus. This solution has recently been reargued by S. McLoughlin.[5]

(3) *The Four-Document Hypothesis.* An elaboration of (2) by Streeter, which takes account of the fact that, besides their Q material and the material which they share with Mark, Matthew and Luke have each also material which is peculiar (that is, without parallel in another Gospel). (a) The ''four documents'' are thus Mark, Q, M (the source of Matthew's peculiar material), and L (the source of Luke's peculiar material). Streeter held that Matthew's infancy Narrative probably came from oral sources, and Luke's from a document which may have been composed in Hebrew. (b) Streeter also suggested that Luke's Q material and L may have been combined, before Luke was composed, to form what we call a Proto-Luke; this the author of Luke will have combined with his borrowings from Mark to produce Luke.

(4) *Lagrange's Modified Two-Document Hypothesis.* In 1911 and 1912 the Pontifical Biblical Commission published a series of Replies concerning the Gospels of Matthew, Mark and Luke and their mutual rela-

---

[3]C. H. Weisse, *Die Evangelische Geschichte* (1838).

[4]H. J. Holtzmann, *Die Synoptische Evangelien* (1863).

[5]S. McLoughlin, *The Synoptic Theory of Xavier Léon-Dufour* (unpublished, 1965).

tions.[6] The effect of these, so far as concerns our problem, was to discountenance the Two-Document Hypothesis as put forward at that time, and to give weight to the argument that tradition points to the priority of Matthew. In the years that followed, solutions based on varying degrees of literary dependence and oral tradition found favor with many Catholic scholars anxious to reconcile the priority of Matthew with the Two-Document Hypothesis. The one worked out by Lagrange in his commentaries on Mark, Luke and Matthew was widely accepted in Catholic manuals, introductions and commentaries between 1911 and 1950, and even today is only slowly yielding ground to other views, notably that of Vaganay and Benoit. Lagrange's detailed survey and analysis of the basic data of the problem remain a classic of Catholic scholarship, eminently worthy of the attention of a serious student. A simple outline of his position in nontechnical language will be found in his *Gospel of Jesus Christ.*[7] He held that Mark (through Peter's preaching) and Aramaic Matthew depended on the oral apostolic catechesis; that Greek Matthew reproduced and freely edited, with additions, the substance of Aramaic Matthew, depending also on Mark; that Luke depended on Mark and (partially, especially as regards Discourses) on Matthew; further, that the authors of Matthew and Luke each used some smaller proper sources for material peculiar to them individually.

(5) *The Priority of Matthew.* H. J. Chapman[8] revolted against the Two-Document Hypothesis. He argued that Matthew is the first of our extant Gospels and was a source for Mark (he thought that Matthew could have been used by some early Christian teacher—Peter?—as a basis for oral teaching, and that Mark is a written record of such oral teaching; thus Matthew is not the immediate, but the ultimate, source of Mark). He agreed however that the author of Luke used Mark as a source. As regards Luke's "Q" material, he held that this derives directly from Matthew; Q itself is thus eliminated.

(6) *Pierson Parker*[9] agreed with Chapman that Mark shows abundant evidence of dependence on a source, and that Matthew shows us the sort of source that this will have been. But he held that Matthew is not itself

---

[6]Denzinger-Bannwart, *Enchiridion Symbolorum,* 3561-78.

[7]M.-J. Lagrange, *Gospel of Jesus Christ,* (1938) 1:2-6.

[8]H. J. Chapman, *Matthew, Mark and Luke* (1937).

[9]P. Parker, *The Gospel Before Mark* (1953).

Mark's source, but that both Matthew and Mark depend on a source, named by him K, which was a sort of Proto-Matthew. He also accepted the dependence of Luke on Mark. He disagreed with Chapman on the subject of Q, arguing on grounds of vocabulary that Matthew's "Q" material stands out from the rest of Matthew as derived from a special source. He therefore held that Matthew and Luke depend on Q.

(7) *A Post-Lagrange Hypothesis: Vaganay,*[10] *Benoit.*[11] Vaganay's *Le Problème Synoptique* attempts to push beyond Lagrange's hypothesis and to find concrete and specific answers to points which it had left in shadow. Is Mark really independent of all written sources? Through what stages, in Aramaic and in Greek, did Aramaic Matthew pass before its substance was incorporated in Matthew? As for Luke: what specifically is meant by saying that it shows "partial" dependence on Matthew, that is, for the Discourses? And what is the literary origin of the "great interpolation" Lk. 9:51-18:14, much of the contents of which is found dispersed in Matthew, especially in Matthew's Discourses? In face of such questions, Vaganay and, in substantial agreement with him, Benoit have evolved a somewhat complex hypothesis, postulating not a few conjectural and nonextant documents. As this hypothesis is gaining ground just now and is favored by the commentators on Matthew and Luke in the present volume, we here expound it in less summary fashion than the others, making free use of the account given of it by A. Jones[12] and using also Vaganay and Benoit.

Like Lagrange, these authors identify the source Q with the Apostle Matthew's alleged original Aramaic gospel. This represented the Jerusalem apostolic catechesis (Baptism to Resurrection) which Peter preached. Of Aramaic Matthew many Greek translations were very soon made (Papias). "These translations were used by our three evangelists each of whom adjusted his source to his purpose. Thus Mark, for example, omitted many sayings of our Lord, notably the opening discourse, and arranged the narrative-matter in his own way. In this Luke has followed him fairly closely but filled in many of his omissions of discourse. The Greek Matthew completely re-organizes the narrative-sequence and, to some extent, the discourses—though apparently his arrangement of the five great discourses is due to his source, the Aramaic Matthew." Mark therefore does

---

[10]L. Vaganay, *Le Problème Synoptique* (1954).

[11]P. Benoit, *L'Évangile selon S. Matthieu* (1961).

[12]A. Jones in *Catholic Commentary on Holy Scripture* (1953) 853-54.

not depend exclusively on an oral source (Peter), but probably also on a Greek form of Aramaic Matthew.

Besides Aramaic Matthew and supplementary to it, it is conjectured that there soon grew up, also in Aramaic, an autonomous Sayings Collection, R(= Recueil), a kind of miniature or supplementary Q, considerably smaller than Aramaic Matthew. Of this, too, many Greek translations were made. Our canonical Matthew is based on Mark, on a Greek form of Aramaic Matthew and on R. The author of Matthew in fact undertook to present the content of the oral catechesis (and so of Aramaic Matthew) "more fully than Mark, his predecessor, of whose work however he made considerable use . . . From the original gospel of Matthew he took over the discourses in their entirety, even adding to them with the help of other traditions," in particular the sayings of R, which he "quarries for the structure of his great discourses."

Luke is based on Mark, on one of the Greek translations of Aramaic Matthew, and on R which he incorporates into 9:51-18:14. Thus Luke and Greek Matthew are independent of each other; there is no direct dependence of Mark on Matthew; but there is direct dependence of Luke on Mark and of Matthew on Mark. (As in other hypotheses, Matthew and Luke have each their own sources for what is proper to them respectively, such as their Infancy Narratives).

The present writer, while admiring the industry that has gone into the construction of the Vaganay-Benoit solution, and welcoming the considerable inroads that it has made on the supposed "priority of Mark," may be allowed to offer two comments. (1) The complexity of the hypothesis makes its truth doubtful. Methodologically, and other things being equal, a theory is to be recommended for its simplicity; and a theory involving five nonextant sources and ten lines of dependence, even if true, could hardly be *shown* to be true. (2) As usual, the hypothesis needs to be tested in comparative analysis of actual passages in the Gospels. Vaganay has offered specimens of such work in illustration of his hypothesis.[13]

(8) *Mark a conflation.* As indicated above, Farmer has recently declared his adherence to a solution of the problem which is substantially that

---

[13]Reference may be made to B. C. Butler, "The Synoptic Problem Again," *DR* 73 (1954-1955); and "M. Vaganay and the 'Community Discourse,' " *NTS* 1 (1955), where one such specimen is subjected to detailed examination and doubts are cast on the validity of Vaganay's analysis.

offered by Griesbach in 1783: Matthew, he suggests, is a source for Luke; Mark is the latest of the three Gospels, and results from a conflation of Matthew and Luke. The reaction of the critical world to this *revenant* among solutions remains to be seen. Here it may be said that, while it deals with most of the data, it supposes an extraordinary and perservering virtuosity on the part of the author of Mark which some will find hard to believe.

Critique of The Two-Document Hypothesis. In its modern form this has held such a central place in NT studies, that a critique of it may serve to open up the whole subject in a useful way. This is now offered, in brief compass.

THE SO-CALLED "Q" PASSAGES

(1) "Q" is a conjectural, non-extant, document. The onus of proof lies on anyone who appeals to a conjectural document. The interpretation of Papias's reference to a work which he calls the "dominical Logia" is too uncertain to afford a firm basis for "Q".

(2) If Q existed, its extent, and to some degree its nature, are uncertain. (a) It need not have included *all* the material shared by Matthew and Luke but missing from Mark. Where a saying is preserved in Matthew and Luke in widely divergent forms, it may have been transmitted to them along different channels. It almost certainly must have been so transmitted if, in any instance, Matthew and Luke appear to give divergent translations of a single Aramaic saying (it is here assumed that Christ usually spoke in Aramaic); for Q, if it existed, must have been a Greek document by the time at which it was utilized by the authors of Matthew and Luke; and the closeness of their actual Greek wording in very many Q passages shows that they were using the *same* Greek translation of the Aramaic sayings.

(b) Q could have included a great deal that is *not shared* by Matthew and Luke; there is no guarantee that either author included in his Gospel the *whole* of any of his sources—and we know that (if they both used Mark) neither of them included the whole of Mark. This consideration may be of great importance. If, for instance, it can be shown that the Q material regularly coheres organically with its contexts in Matthew, while it is only loosely and artificially inserted into its contexts in Luke, there will be a strong argument for reckoning to the supposed Q document a good deal of the Matthaean contexts of the Q material; Q will thus tend to

swell to something like the proportions, and to approximate to the character, of Matthew. Taken by itself, however, the so-called ''Q'' adds up to a rather shapeless mass of unconnected sayings, with one or two possible indications of narrative settings.

(3) There are five passages in which all three Synoptic Gospels are connected, but in which the agreements between Matthew and Luke are too numerous to be coincidences: (a) Mt. 13:31-32; cf. Mk. 4:30-32 and Lk. 13:18-19; (b) Mt. 18:6, 7; cf. Mk. 9:42 and Lk. 17:1b, 2; (c) Mt. 12:25-32, cf. Mk. 3:23-30 and Lk. 11:17-23, 12:10; (d) Mt. 10:9-14; cf. Mk. 6:8-11 and Lk. 10:4-11; (e) Mt. 22:34-40; cf. Mk. 12:28-34 and Lk. 10:25-28.

In these passages we have agreements among all three Gospels; agreements between Matthew and Luke against Mark; agreements between Matthew and Mark against Luke; relative *absence* of agreements between Mark and Luke against Matthew; and the fact that the Luke passages are not in the same contexts as their parallels in Mark—but where Mark and Luke are *directly* connected they nearly always follow the same order of narration (that is, they agree as regards contexts). The natural interpretation of these data is that, in these passages *Matthew is the connecting link* between Mark and Luke; or in other words (since Luke can hardly be the direct source of Matthew and an indirect source of Mark) that in these passages Luke is dependent on Matthew (unless we suppose the dependence of both Luke and Matthew on a conjectural Proto-Matthew). If, however, Luke is dependent on Matthew (or a Proto-Matthew) in these five passages, it becomes probable that the same explanation is applicable on a far wider scale. Thus the data which have given rise to the Q Hypothesis (which is a constituent part of the Two-Document Hypothesis) would be explained by Luke's direct dependence on Matthew (or Proto-Matthew).

These five passages are an embarrassment to the supporters of the Two-Document Hypothesis. Streeter suggested that they indicate ''overlapping'' between Mark and Q, that is, these incidents or sayings were recorded independently by the authors of Mark and Q. He then argued that, in these passages, Luke used Q (and did not use Mark), whereas Matthew ''conflated'' Q and Mark, that is, he built up his own version by combining elements from his two sources. This explanation does not arise naturally from the data, but is dictated by the exigencies of the Two-Document Hypothesis. Perhaps no solution of the problem can avoid supposing a certain amount of conflation of sources, but Matthew's alleged behavior in

(a) and (d) above seems very irrational. On (a), Streeter himself comments: the differences between the Q and Mark versions of the parable "are entirely unimportant . . . no one antecedently would have expected that Matthew would take the trouble to combine the two versions." And in reference to (d) he points out "the almost meticulous care with which Matthew conflates Mark and Q—the only real additions he has to make are the words 'gold' and 'Gomorrah'."

It will be observed that we have left the door open for the possibility that the link between Matthew and Luke in these passages (and therefore, presumably, in other Q passages) was a conjectural Proto-Matthew. It is important to bear in mind that, if this solution is accepted, it rules out the dependence of Matthew on Mark in these passages; Mark must, in this hypothesis, depend either on Matthew or on Proto-Matthew.

(4) If Q existed, it presumably contained a sermon, the source of Matthew's Sermon on the Mount and Luke's Sermon on the Plain. Luke's sermon is far shorter than Matthew's; and, apart from the "Woes" and about three longish verses, it contains hardly anything not found in Matthew's sermon. There are parts of Matthew's sermon which are found not in Luke's sermon but elsewhere in Luke. Luke's sermon is almost destitute of special Jewish coloring and relevance; it is practically a colorless discourse on love of neighbor. Admitting that Matthew's sermon may have been enlarged by insertion into it of material not originally belonging to this context, we must still ask: Was the supposed Q sermon unrelated to the Palestinian situation of our Lord's preaching; and has it been "Judaized" by the author of Matthew? Is it not more probable that the original sermon was strongly Palestinian in coloring and relevance, and that Luke has "edited this coloring out" in order to make the sermon suitable for Gentile readers? And why should not Luke have exercised this editing process on Matthew itself? Why suppose Q?

At the end of the Sermon on the Plain, Luke has "After he had ended all his sayings in the hearing of the people . . . " (7:1). This corresponds to the transitional clause at the end of Matthew's Sermon on the Mount: "Afterwards, when Jesus had finished these sayings . . . " (7:28). But this clause in Matthew is a typical "Matthaean formula," repeated in substance at 11:1; 13:53; 19:1; and 26:1. In each case, as in 7:28, it occurs at the end of one of Matthew's five great blocks of discourse, and is thus part of this Gospel's structural plan. If Luke is not dependent on Matthew, his reproduction (in his own language) of the formula at Lk. 7:1 suggests that

Q must have contained the five great discourses and the narrative matter to which the formula is, in each case, the transition and introduction.

(5) Another Matthaean formula ("there men will weep and gnash their teeth;" six occurrences in Matthew) is found in Luke 13:28-29, which is parallel to Mt. 8:11-12, the first occurrence of the formula in Matthew. Again, Luke 9:57-10:24 seems to show Luke's editing of material borrowed from Mt. 8:19-22; 11:21-23, 25-27; 13:16-17.

(6) Luke's verbal divergences from Matthew in his Q passages are nearly always towards typically Lukan *style,* or in some other way give the impression that they are less primitive than the Matthew versions. The criterion of poetical form led C. F. Burney[14] to conclude that in most Q cases ("though not all") Matthew preserves the original form of our Lord's sayings.

(7) Frequently, a Q passage which fits organically into its context in Matthew seems to have only an artifical *editorial* link with its context in Luke. This suggests that Luke is borrowing from a source which, if not Matthew itself, is utilized more extensively by Matthew. Q begins to expand in Matthew into the contextual field of the certain Q passages in that Gospel; it begins to approximate to a Proto-Matthew, if not to Matthew itself.

An argument urged against Luke's dependence on Matthew is that Q passages in Luke hardly ever have the same contexts as the corresponding passages in Matthew; why should an author regularly put his borrowed material into new contexts? (It should be noticed that, if Matthew and Luke are both borrowing from Q, at least one of them has, on nearly every occasion, altered the Q context of his loan—unless Q was simply a hotchpotch of *disjecta membra.*) The answer is probably to be sought in Luke's editorial problems. (a) For whatever reason, Luke hardly ever interferes with what he borrows from Mark, except to alter its style; he will not insert new material inside a Markan paragraph (he did in fact try to conflate Mark with another source—Q, Matthew, or Proto-Matthew—at 3:1ff., where synoptic parallelism first begins in his Gospel; he soon gave it up, perhaps because it proved too difficult—conflation undoubtedly is a very difficult literary procedure). But the Q material in Matthew is often embedded in Markan contexts, from which, therefore, Luke had to extract it if he was to be faithful to his rule: do not interfere with Markan material. (b) On a

---

[14]C. F. Burney, *The Poetry of Our Lord* (1925) 7.

generous estimate, the Q material constitutes less than a quarter of the whole of Luke. He had also, among his sources, Mark and his special sources (for example, for the Infancy Narrative). If it was at a rather late stage of composition that he decided to utilize Matthew, the easiest way would have been to *mark,* in his copy of Matthew, the passages which he intended to use, and then fit them in wherever he could.[15]

The important result of the arguments listed above is, that there seems little reason to believe in a Q consisting of a mere haphazard collection of sayings. The Q material, when it came into Luke's hands, was probably part of a larger whole, in fact of a kind of Gospel—whether Matthew or Proto-Matthew (should good reason be found for conjecturing a Proto-Matthew). Note that Luke's source for the main body of his Q passages must have been in Greek.

MARK'S PRIORITY, OR MATTHEW'S?

The relative paucity of agreements between Matthew and Luke against Mark in passages (except in the five listed above) where all three Gospels have parallels is commonly taken to mean that Mark is, in these passages, the "connecting link" or "middle term" between Matthew and Luke. (Farmer, however, regards the agreements of Matthew and Luke against Mark in these passages as extensive enough to constitute a stubborn surd on the hypothesis of the Two Documents. His own theory—that Luke used Matthew and that Mark conflated Matthew and Luke—resolves this surd.) There are three ways in which Mark could have been such a connecting link: either (a) Matthew was written first, and was used as a source by Mark, which in turn became a source for Luke; or (b) Mark has the priority and was used as a source by the authors of Matthew on the one hand and Luke on the other; or (c) Luke has the priority and was used as a source for Mark, which in turn became a source for Matthew.

These alternatives are exhaustive (if we exclude Farmer's theory of an all-pervading conflation), unless we take into consideration the possibility of a Proto-Evangelium as a source for two, or all three, of our Gospels. If such a Proto-Evangelium was the source of all three Gospels, then, as Lachmann rightly argued, it must be envisaged as a Proto-Mark. If it was the source only of Matthew and one of the other two Gospels, then it could have been either a Proto-Mark or a Proto-Matthew or Proto-Luke, and

---

[15]H. G. Jameson, *The Origin of the Synoptic Gospels* (1922).

Mark itself must have been the remaining Gospel's source for the common material. Proto-Mark is under a cloud (and in the opinion of the present writer is to be rejected); and no one, so far as he knows, wishes to make Luke or a Proto-Luke the source of the common material in both Mark and (indirectly, via Mark) Matthew. It therefore seems reasonable to ask whether any of the three other hypotheses will meet the facts: priority of Mark, priority of Matthew, or priority of a Proto-Matthew as the source of both Matthew and Mark. In each case, we should be forced to infer the dependence of Luke on Matthew (and this is in fact commonly conceded).

As, however, Proto-Matthew, if it ever existed, is not extant, it will be convenient to compare Mark directly with Matthew, while bearing in mind that evidence which appears to point to Mark's dependence on Matthew may, at least in some cases, be equally well explained by the dependence of both Matthew and Mark on Proto-Matthew. We shall only accept the Proto-Matthew hypothesis if driven to do so, since it supposes a nonextant document, and two lines of dependence (Proto-Matthew source of Matthew; Proto-Matthew source of Mark) instead of one (Matthew source of Mark).

(1) A. E. J. Rawlinson,[16] a convinced adherent of the Two-Document Hypothesis, suggested that at various points Mark "perhaps" or "probably" or "no doubt" depends on (a Roman edition of) Q. Cf. his remarks on Mk. 1:2; 1:12-13; 3:22-30; 4:21-25; 6:7-13; 8:15; 8:34-9:1; 9:33-37 (a "catena of Sayings" probably derived from Q); 10:30; 10:35-40. Mk. 10:38 (the reference to baptism, omitted by Matthew in the parallel passage, may be an editorial edition); 12:38-40 (Mark appears to be summarizing from memory the anti-Pharisaic discourse which apparently stood in Q, and which Matthew reproduces "at fuller length"); 13:9-13 (probably stood in Q). We may add that Rawlinson thought that in ch. 4 Mark was probably drawing upon some existing collection of parables; this could have been Q, though Rawlinson does not suggest it.

Thus Rawlinson finds signs of dependence on a previous source (usually Q) in passages scattered through nine of the first 13 chapters of Mark, although Q is supposed to be mainly discourse, and Mark has little discourse. V. Taylor[17] prefers dependence not on Q but on "the Lesson Book of the Roman community"—a document at least as conjectural as Q. We

---

[16]A. E. J. Rawlinson, *The Gospel according to St. Mark* (1947).
[17]V. Taylor, *The Gospel according to St. Mark* (1952).

have already suggested doubts about the reality of Q, and in each of the above-mentioned cases it is Matthew which guides us to the probable version contained in Mark's source (except for the "collection of parables," not further determined). Here then is evidence, provided by an ardent believer in the Two-Document Hypothesis, that Mark utilized a source or sources; and it is clear that this source could have been Matthew or Proto-Matthew. But if Mark is prior to Matthew and was Matthew's usual source, we have the awkward result that, time and time again, Matthew must have turned from a passage in Mark which we now recognize to show traces of editing, and restored the more original form of Mark's source. No impartial critic could fail to recognize the gravity of these facts for the supporters of the Two-Document Hypothesis. Note that, in his contribution to *Oxford Studies in the Synoptic Problem* (1911),[18] Streeter himself had held that it was "beyond reasonable doubt" that Mark was familiar with Q; in *The Four Gospels: A Study of Origins*, he withdrew from this position, in the year before the publication of Rawlinson's commentary on Mark.

(2) C. F. Burney, who accepted the Q hypothesis, examined the poetic forms of the sayings of Christ in *The Poetry of Our Lord*. He says that there are passages in Mark's versions of sayings where "a characteristically clearcut form of antithesis" preserved in the other Gospels "has been to some extent lost in Mark. . . . The inference is that the other Synoptists cannot, in these passages, have been drawing from Mark, but that both they and Mark were dependent upon a common source (Q)." But if we reject the notion of Q, we can explain Burney's data by Mark's dependence on Matthew or by the dependence of both Matthew and Mark on Proto-Matthew.

(3) There is thus good reason to pursue a paragraph-by-paragraph comparison of Matthew and Mark, in order to determine (a) when Mark would seem to be the source which explains what we find in Matthew; (b) when Mark itself seems to be based on a source; (c) when Matthew shows us the sort of thing which Mark's source would have contained—whether because Matthew was actually Mark's source, or because Matthew and Mark are both dependent on Proto-Matthew. Such a complete examination cannot, of course, find place here,[19] but a few examples can be given.

---

[18]*Oxford Studies in the Synoptic Problem*, ed. W. Sanday (1911).
[19]Cf. Chapman and Butler.

(a) Mk. 13:33-37; cf. Mt. 24:37-25:46. Mk. 13 contains the longest discourse given by Mark. Up to verse 32 inclusive it is closely paralleled in Matthew, though Mt. 24:9-14, which is contextually parallel to Mk. 13:9-13, seems to come from a different source (Matthew's real parallel to Mk. 13:9-13 is Mt. 10:17-22). But the relations between Matthew and Mk. 13:33-37 are odd. These verses bring Mark's discourse (already long, compared with others in Mark) to a conclusion. In place of them, we find in Matthew 61 verses of continuing discourse. These 61 verses of Matthew include practically everything contained in Mark's five verses, but these contents are *scattered* among Matthew's 61 verses, always in appropriate contexts (note that the *faithful servant* of Mt. 24:45 would, for the evangelist, suggest Peter, the *key-bearer* of the Kingdom, for whom compare the *door-keeper* [also provided with keys] of Mk. 13:34b). The Matthaean parallels to these items in Mk. 13:33-37 cannot be accidental; this must be excluded by reason of the identity of general context. But it is hardly possible that the author of Matthew could have broken Mk. 13:33-37 into small pieces and fitted these pieces, one by one, into a number of new contexts derived from some other source, and could have done it so well that each item seems to belong organically to the context in which it occurs in Matthew. The only reasonable view is that these verses of Mark are a "telescoping" of what we find in Matthew's 61 verses (or of such paragraphs among them as contain the items found also in these verses of Mark).

This view is raised almost to a certainty, when we remark that Mark's *absent master*, who may (very unreasonably) come back "suddenly" and at night, and will yet expect to find his servants on the watch for him (though presumably they had also been hard at work during the daylight), is really a combination or "conflation" of the *master* of the Talents parable (Mt. 25:14-30), who keeps normal and expected hours, with the *thief in the night* (Mt. 24:43-44; verse 42 should be appended to Matthew's previous paragraph). By "telescoping" these two figures Mark has produced an incongruity.

This example, then, suggests that Mark was not the source of Matthew, but that either Matthew was the source of Mark, or both of them depended on Proto-Matthew.

(b) As mentioned above, Mk. 13:9-13 has the same *context* as Mt. 24:9-14; but its real *parallel* is Mt. 10:17-22. Burney states that this passage of Mark is distinguished from the rest of the discourse in which it is placed in Mark by its rhythm. He further points out that the discourse as a

whole is "eschatological" in content, but this is not true of these verses (Mk. 13:9-13). But Mt. 24:9-14, like its context in Matthew, *is* remarkedly eschatological; whereas Mt. 10:17-22 (= Mk. 13:9-13, though in different context) is, as it should be, in a non-eschatological context in Matthew.

Burney therefore, accepting the Two-Document Hypothesis, suggests that these verses were borrowed by Mark from Q, whence also the author of Matthew would have borrowed them at Mt. 10:17-22. We should then have to assume that Matthew, copying Mark up to this point, recognized that he had already utilized the Q extract (Mk. 13:9-13) in his own ch. 10; he therefore omitted it here (though he does not normally mind having doublets), and substituted for it Mt. 24:9-14. But whence did he obtain these substituted, and contextually far superior, verses? Did he "make them up"? Is it not far more probable that Mt. 24:9-14 belonged originally to their present context, and that it is Mark who has departed from his source (whether Matthew or Proto-Matthew) by substituting for these verses those which Mt. 10:17-22 gives in their proper context? (The author of Mark may have thought that the references to Christian degeneration in Mt. 24:9-14 were too strong meat for his readers). It will be observed that if Mark is here the source of Matthew, we have to suppose a dislocation of source material by *both* authors: first, Mark deserts his current context and inserts a piece of Q; then Matthew deserts his Markan source and inserts a passage of unknown provenance. But if Matthew (or Proto-Matthew) is the source of Mark, only one dislocation has occurred, namely that in Mark.

Once again, a subsidiary point serves to confirm the verdict against Mark's priority. Burney not only separated Mk. 13:9-13 from its context on rhythmical grounds; he further pin-pointed Mk. 13:10 (within this little group of verses) as a rhythmical intruder. He subsequently noticed that the Matthaean parallel (Mt. 10:17-22) *lacked this intrusive gloss.* However, the "gloss" does occur in Matthew—at 24:14, rounding off Matthew's alleged *substituted* passage. There is no critical evidence that Mk. 13:10 is unauthentic (unless its omission by Luke be taken as such). If it is authentic, then it is a nail in the coffin of Mark's priority. We cannot believe that Matthew not only excised the major rhythmical intrusion from Mark and was able to fill the gap by invisible mending with a fragment of tradition whose origin is quite unknown, but also (a) purified the verses thus taken from Mark of the "sub-intrusion" (and used them, thus purified, in his ch.

10), and (b) used this sub-intrusion to complete the "invisible" patch which he inserted in his ch. 24 to replace the major excision from Mark. We conclude that, unless Mark depends on Matthew, both depend on a common source which contained, in different places, both Mt. 10:17-22 and Mt. 24:9-14. If this source is to be called "Q," then Q swells beyond any proportions which Luke justifies us in assigning to it. The source would more truly be a Proto-Matthew.

(c) It will be observed that the results of our examination in (a) and (b) are convergent. The conclusions separately reached are immensely strengthened thereby. Similarly, the total case against the priority of Mark is largely built up by an accumulation of such convergent evidence. This evidence is scattered *passim* in the first 13 chapters of Mark, compared with parallel passages in Matthew (as for Mk. 1:2, the data here are so awkward for the Two-Document Hypothesis that supporters of it have suggested, without any basis in the manuscript tradition, that this verse in Mark is inauthentic).

We are driven to the conclusion that either Mark used Matthew as a source, or both Matthew and Mark used Proto-Matthew as their source. In either case, unless we accept Dr. Farmer's revival of the Griesbach solution and regard Mark as a conflation of Matthew and Luke, Mark will have been used as a source by Luke.

The Proto-Matthew hypothesis appeals to a nonextant conjectural document, and the burden of proof therefore rests on those who support it. One argument often proposed is that Matthew's version of the common material is more polished, reverent, and refined than Mark's; this might suggest that while Mark has copied Proto-Matthew rather closely, Matthew has "improved" his source. Matthew, it is said, is a literary composition, while Mark reads "like a shorthand account of a story by an impromptu speaker." Matthew lacks picturesque details which are found in Mark, and often lacks Mark's redundancies. Again, on six occasions when Mark puts *Aramaic* words on Christ's lips, Matthew lacks them.[20] The argument is a strong one, though it might possibly be turned by appeal to "oral interference"; if an oral teacher had used Matthew as a basis for his teaching, and if Mark were the written record of such oral teaching, then Mark's informality and crudity would have a natural explanation. (As

---

[20]Cf. Streeter, 162-64.

regards Mark's Aramaic words, F. P. Badham[21] says: "It is a thing to be felt, not argued about, that it was a later generation that required . . . the actual wonder-words." Evidence is abundant in Mark that this Gospel caters for the interests of "a later generation," and does not cater for the Jewish-Palestinian interests of the readers of Matthew. Defenders of the Two-Document Hypothesis who appeal to Mark's Aramaicisms should note that the linguistic substratum of Matthew is profoundly Semitic, and that this substratum is considerably blurred or diminished in Mark.)

Vaganay holds that there are traces in Mark of a special *Petrine* oral teaching, and he further argues that such Petrine elements in Mark have left their print, here and there, on Matthew. If that is so, we are practically bound to concede that Matthew had access to Mark and therefore that Mark's source could not have been Matthew; the case for Proto-Matthew would thus be established. We may be permitted to think that the case is still *sub judice*.

Meanwhile, we can perhaps make some progress towards determining more closely the contents and structure of Mark's source, leaving the option between Matthew and Proto-Matthew momentarily open. Matthew, as all admit, is a carefully edited composition—see, for example, the five great discourses. One of Matthew's editorial devices is his use of the recurrent formula, as in the phrase "And it came to pass, when he had finished . . . " which succeeds each of the great discourses. Another is a system of "referring back" from one context to another by a procedure which produces what have come to be called "doublets." Now whereas a formula coheres with its context on each occasion of its use, one member of a doublet will cohere with its context, the other member may be only loosely attached to its context; in such a case, the function of the loosely attached member is to "refer" to the other member and its context. Thus, Mt. 5:32 and 19:9 constitute a doublet. The former member of this pair, 5:32, is required by its context, with which it inseparably coheres. But the latter member, 19:9, is necessary to its context; indeed, it has been appended to a paragraph already completed in 19:8. In other words Matthew (or his source) has added the saying in ch. 19 in order to remind his readers of what was said on the subject of divorce in ch. 5. (In a modern book a footnote reference could serve the same purpose.)

---

[21]F. B. Badham, *St. Mark's Indebtedness to St. Matthew* (1897) 48-49.

One would suppose that such an editorial device as this would come at a late stage of Gospel-building. When, therefore, we find that, in this and other instances, Mark has the doublet saying or verse in the context in which, in Matthew, it constitutes a "reference back," it may be felt that we have an argument in favor of Mark's dependence on Matthew itself, not on some earlier Proto-Matthew.

Similarly, of the 25 examples of Matthaean formulas listed by Hawkins, 12 are found to have one or two occurrences in Mark. Such use of formulas by Matthew again suggests a relatively late stage in the crystallization of our Gospels, and Mark's dependence on them again militates against the view that his link with Matthew is by way of their common use of Proto-Matthew. In any case, we seem justified in thinking that, if Proto-Matthew had a real existence and was Mark's source, Matthew must be a not very greatly altered "second edition" of it. It should however be noted that Proto-Matthew could have lacked Matthew's opening genealogy of Christ and his Infancy Narrative (though I think Luke's "Matthaean" source probably had both of these).

External Evidence. (a) When passages elsewhere in the NT raise the suspicion that they may have a connection with the material contained in the Synoptic Gospels, they nearly always seem to reflect the influence of the Matthaean form of this material. Thus 1 and 2 Thessalonians present an eschatological teaching which (with the exception of 1 Thess. 5:3 which suggests Lk. 21:34-36, but here it is probably Luke that is dependent on 1 Thessalonians, not vice versa) is totally explicable—where not distinctively Pauline—only by reference to the eschatological material in Matthew.[22] Again, Gal. 2:7-8 seems to show a knowledge of what is found in Matthew's version of Peter's confesson at Caesarea (Mt. 16). C. H. Dodd[23] pointed out various elements in Paul which he shares with Matthew and not with the other Synoptic Gospels. James has numerous links, especially with the Sermon on the Mount, though occasionally the similarity seems to be to Luke rather than to Matthew.[24]

(b) In the sub-Apostolic age allusions to the Synoptic tradition nearly always approximate to Matthew more than to Luke or Mark. The witness

---

[22]Cf. B. Orchard, "Thessalonians and the Synoptic Gospels," *Biblica* 19 (1938).

[23]C. H. Dodd, "Matthew and Paul," *ET* 58 (1947): 293ff.

[24]J. Chaine, *L'Épître de S. Jacques*, lxivff., as referred to in B. C. Butler, "St. Paul's Knowledge and Use of St. Matthew," *DR* 64 (1948): 367ff.

of these allusions is sometimes minimized by the suggestion that often they may relay oral tradition rather than any of our written Gospels. Even so, it would be significant that the common oral tradition of the churches, judging by this evidence, agreed rather with Matthew than with Mark or Luke. Reference may be made particularly to the Didache, which depends, for most of its evangelical allusions, on Matthew or on a Matthaean form of the tradition.[25] This would be extremely important if we could accept Audet's dating of the Didache (A.D. 50-70, more or less); but this dating is doubtful.[26]

Early patristic statements throw little clear and direct light on our problem. The meaning of Papias's statement that Matthew "composed the dominical Logia in the Hebrew language" is disputed.[27] His other statement, on the authority of "the Elder," that Mark wrote down the oral teaching of Peter, probably refers to Mark; it cannot however be pressed so far as to exclude all use of documentary sources by the author of Mark, and in any case would be consistent with Peter's dependence on Matthew or Proto-Matthew.

Conclusion. The Synoptic Gospels are probably interrelated by literary, not merely oral, links. If all conjectural sources are to be excluded, the evidence requires that Mark depends on Matthew; and that Luke depends on Matthew (for his Q material) and on Mark (unless, as Farmer holds, Mark is a conflation of Matthew and Luke). If conjectural sources are not excluded, it is possible that Matthew and Mark on the one hand, and Matthew and Luke on the other, are connected by the common use of a lost Gospel which could best be described as a Proto-Matthew, a document of which our Matthew is a fairly faithful "second edition"—but it would still remain possible that both Mark and Luke depend on Matthew.[28] If Proto-Matthew is admitted, then it would be possible to argue that Matthew itself is lightly indebted to Mark.

---

[25]B. C. Butler, "The Literary Relations of the Didache, ch. 16," *JTS* 11 (1960): 265-83; "The 'Two Ways' in the Didache," *JTS* 12 (1961): 27-38. Note, however, that Didache ch. 16 shows clear dependence on Luke or "Proto-Luke."

[26]J. P. Audet, *La didaché* (1958).

[27]Cf. M. Jouvyon, "Papias," *Dictionnaire de la Bible*, Supplement (1960) 6:1104-09.

[28]Pierson Parker sought to establish the reality of Q by statistics of style; the present writer (Butler) has criticized his findings in "The Synoptic Problem Again," *DR* 73 (1954-1955): 26ff.

Further progress may be expected along the lines of Form Criticism; an example is to hand in Dupont.[29] Such study may enable us to say with confidence whether or not a conjectural Proto-Matthew is required. Unless it is required, it should be excluded: *entia non sunt multiplicanda praeter necessitatem.* For the sake of clarity, it must be emphasized that the Proto-Matthew which may prove to be required must have been in the Greek language (that is, our problem would not be solved in an "Aramaic Matthew"). It is indeed possible that some of Luke's so-called Q material is derived, independently of Matthew, from Aramaic sources. But much of Luke's Q material, like Mark in general, is too similiar in its Greek to the Greek of the corresponding passages in Matthew to be explained as resulting from independent translations of Aramaic originals.

---

[29]J. Dupont, *Les Béatitudes* (1954).

LACHMANN'S
ARGUMENT

N. H. Palmer*

In the Triple Tradition Matthew and Luke never agree against Mark in their arrangement of passages—that is, in the order of pericopes. This absence of agreement in order against Mark is often used to prove that these passages were taken by Matthew and Luke, independently, from Mark— that is, as an argument for Markan priority. This inference is commonly attributed to K. Lachmann. B. C. Butler has pointed out an error in this inference.

Palmer notes that it is disturbing that Gospel critics have for so long relied on an argument now seen to be invalid and that it is, therefore, of some interest to discover just how this so-called "Lachmann fallacy," as Butler termed it, came to be committed. In fact, Palmer points out, even Butler concedes that Lachmann did not so much commit a fallacy as make an unwarranted assumption; namely, Lachmann took it for granted that all three synoptic evangelists derived their material from a common source, a pre-evangelical source, whether written or oral.

Lachmann made the narrative sequence in the synoptic gospels (that is, what came to be regarded as the argument from order) the sole subject of his investigation in his critical essay. Inasmuch as Lachmann's argument is not easily accessible to scholars, Palmer sets out in the main body

*N. H. Palmer, "Lachmann's Argument," *New Testament Studies* 13 (1966-1967): 368-78.

of his article to give an English version of the relevant sections of Lachmann's original Latin article of 1835: "De ordine narrationum in evangeliis synopticis" (On the order of stories in the synoptic gospels).

Palmer concludes that Lachmann's article contains no trace of an argument from the absence of agreement in order against Mark or what, according to Palmer, Butler overhastily dubbed "the Lachmann fallacy." Others may be guilty of the so-called "Lachmann fallacy," but Lachmann himself apparently is not.

The gospels of Matthew and Luke rarely agree against Mark in details of the passages which are common to all three: and they never do so in their arrangement of those passages. Of all the other four possible types of agreement-and-disagreement, there are abundant instances. Let us call this composite fact "the absence of agreement against Mark." (Writing M for Matthew, K for Mark, L for Luke, and a dot for disagreement, we have just five types of combination: MKL; MK.L; KL.M; LM.K; M.K.L.)

The absence of agreement against Mark is often used to prove that these passages were taken by Matthew and Luke, independently, from Mark. (To save space, this "pedigree" may be written K—M, L.) This inference, which is commonly attributed to Lachmann, proceeds as follows:

> Although each variation in the detail or ordering of these passages may be taken to represent a decision of the borrowing evangelist to depart at that point from the gospel he was following, a considerable asymmetry between the resulting combinations (agreements-and-disagreements) should be taken as a property of their actual relationship, and can therefore be used to show which evangelist borrowed from which. Thus in any pedigree in which Mark could differ from, say, Matthew without thereby affecting the reading of Luke, he should quite frequently stand alone against their joint witness. As he so rarely does so, we must assume that the relationship of the documents made it difficult or impossible: that is, that in the actual pedigree Mark could not differ from Matthew (or Luke) without thereby affecting the reading of Luke (or Matthew). Now the pedigree possessing this property is K—M, L. We should therefore hold, on grounds of ordering, that Matthew and Luke derived the common material independently from Mark, and should explain away their "minor agreements" of detail against him as due to coincidence or to later assimilation of the texts.

B. C. Butler has pointed out an error in this inference:[1] K—M, L is not the only pedigree to possess the required property. In any pedigree in

---

[1] B. C. Butler, *The Originality of S. Matthew* (1951) chapter V, "The Lachmann Fallacy," 62-71. [Reprinted in this volume]

which Mark stands "between" the other two, his differing from one of them will affect the other, thus eliminating variations of the type ML.K. Divergent pedigrees of no less than five different patterns put Mark in this "medial position":

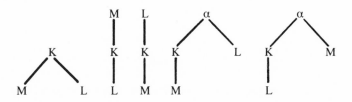

Mark also stands middle in such convergent pedigrees as

Until the relationship among these gospels is uniquely determined, very little progress can be made with questions of date or editorial policy; thus there is little point in discussing why Luke made certain changes when borrowing from Mark, as long as the possibility remains open that it was Mark who borrowed from Luke. As the absence of agreement against Mark does not determine the pedigree uniquely, appeal will have to be made to other and less objective arguments. Thus Butler finds some details of Matthew's text more "original"; while G. M. Styler is equally convinced, on similar grounds, of the priority of Mark.[2] The "one assured result" of Synoptic criticism (on which even form critics have been accustomed to rest some of their arguments) is once more in dispute.

It is disturbing that Gospel critics should for so long have relied on an argument now seen to be invalid: and it is therefore of some interest to discover just how this "Lachmann fallacy" came to be committed. Butler points out that Lachmann himself did not so much commit a fallacy as make an unwarranted assumption. He took it for granted that all three evangelists derived their material from a common source, whether written

---

[2]G. M. Styler, "The Priority of Mark," in C. F. D. Moule, *The Birth of the New Testament* (1962) 223-32. [Reprinted in this volume]

down or recited orally. On this assumption, the absence of agreement against Mark does show that Mark stood "nearest" to the source.

Assuming that this common source was in writing (*Grundschrift*), later scholars came to regard it as an earlier version of Mark ("Urmarcus"); then when a second document (Q) was postulated to account for the non-Markan parallels between Matthew and Luke, no reason remained for distinguishing Urmarcus from our Mark. Thus the familiar two-source theory was evolved, no one noticing that on these conditions the absence of agreement against Mark would no longer prove the priority of Mark.

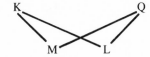

This account of the development of Synoptic argument has recently been set out in considerable detail by W. R. Farmer.[3] The general conclusion must be that Synoptic criticism took a large step backwards in this century, as critics from Streeter onwards went on using the argument from order as proof of Markan priority, after abandoning the assumption on which its validity depends.

Lachmann's argument was set out in a Latin article, "De ordine narrationum in evangeliis synopticis," in *Theologische Studien und Kritiken* for 1835. It was reprinted in the preface to the second volume of his *Novum Testamentum Graece et Latine* (1850). These volumes are not easy to come by, and it may be that few scholars know his reasoning at first hand. I therefore give an English version of the relevant sections.[4] They contain several remarks of quite contemporary interest to Synoptic students. They do not, as far as I can see, contain the fallacious "Lachmann argument." The account just given of the (perverse) development of Synoptic criticism will therefore need correction at some points.

---

[3]W. R. Farmer, *The Synoptic Problem* (1964).

[4]The translation has been made from *Theologische Studien und Kritiken* (1835): 570-90. The relevant material appears on 573-84.

On the order of the stories in the synoptic gospels
by Karl Lachmann, professor at Berlin

[Introduction, replying to critics of his edition of the New Testament and dedicating this work to the memory of F. Schleiermacher.]

Many have inquired how it came about that three of the gospels accepted by the judgment of the Church should be so similar in form throughout, and yet should in various places both agree and differ together in order, in additions and omissions, and in the actual events and words.

Some are sure they will solve his problem one day by comparing and harmonizing not these passages alone, but all that remains of the gospel tradition, even including apocrypha. These scholars work very hard, but not very intelligently. Some others thought the whole explanation lay in the origins of these books, which they could discover. I would not say they were entirely wrong, but they could not provide all they had promised. Their wide claims should therefore be reduced; their acute observations need supplementing by further discoveries, if one is to climb to the summit rather than to fly up there. Now I should like to take a proper middle course; and it seems clear that in approaching the matter one must make a start either from one of those three gospels, or from one of the respects in which they both differ and agree. I have therefore decided to consider for the present only their ordering. This is much the simplest element, and no one, to my knowledge, has considered it before. So let us see how much progress can be made from this starting point.

The ordering of the gospel stories does not vary as much as most people think. The variation appears greatest if all three writers are compared together, or if Luke is compared with Matthew; it is less if Mark is compared with the others one by one. That shows what I should do: first compare Mark with Matthew, and afterwards consider the order of Luke and Mark.

The points in which Mark differs from Matthew all come together in one section (Mk. 1:21-6:13; Mt. 4:24-13:58). It is therefore an easy matter to set out their differences in a table, as follows:

According to Mark	*According to Matthew*
Simon, Andrew, James, and John are called.	Simon, Andrew, James, and John are called. [*Great crowds follow*. Sermon on the mount.]
They were astonished at his doctrine.	They were surprised at his doctrine.
I (II Mt.)	I (II Mk.)
Peter's mother-in-law. [Let us go to the nearby villages and towns.]	Leper: you can cleanse me, if you will.
II (I Mt.)	II (I Mk.)

Leper: you can cleanse me, if you will.   [Centurion] Peter's mother-in-law.

III (V Mk.)

He gives orders to cross the sea. [The Son of Man has nowhere to lay his head. Let the dead bury their dead.] He commands the wind and the sea. The Gerasenes.

III (IV Mt.)   IV (III Mk.)

Paralytic. Levi. Why does he eat and drink   Paralytic. Matthew. Why does he eat with
with publicans and sinners?   publicans and sinners?
Why don't your disciples fast?   Why don't your disciples fast?

V (VI Mk.)

The ruler's daughter, and the woman suffering from an issue of blood. [Two blind men. The dumb man.]

VI (VIII Mk.)

[The harvest indeed is great.]
The apostles are called together.
[*Their names.*] They are sent out.
[Further address to them. The messengers sent by John. Discourse about John.]

IV (VII Mt.)   VII (IV Mk.)

They pluck ears of corn on the sabbath.   They pluck ears of corn on the sabbath.
Withered hand healed. [*Great crowds fol-*   Withered hand healed.
low. The apostles' names.] He has Beel-   [The blind dumb man.] He casts out de-
zebub and casts out demons in the name   mons in the name of Beelzebub.
of the prince of demons.
Discourse. His mother and brethren.   [continued.] His mother and brethren.
Parable of the sower. [Lantern under a   Parable of the sower.
bushel. With what measure ye mete. If a   [Tares.]
man casts a seed on the ground.]
Grain of mustard. Without a parable he did   Grain of mustard. [Leaven.] Without para-
not speak.   bles he did not speak.
                                                  [Interpretation of the parable of the tares.
                                                  Other parables.]

V (III Mt.)

Let us cross over. He threatens the wind and
 says "Silence!" to the sea.
The Gerasene.

VI (V Mt.)

Jairus' daughter, and the woman who had a
 flow of blood.

VII (VIII Mt.)

Is not this the carpenter?

VIII (VII Mk.)

Is not this the carpenter's son?

VIII (VI Mt.)

The twelve are called together and sent out.

IX

And King Herod heard.

IX

Herod the tetrarch heard the report of Jesus.

No further difference can be found between these two gospels. If I can make out the reasons for the differences here set out, I shall bring them into agreement again. It is clear that they have not all been jumbled together indiscriminately. The entire difference concerns eight sections, two of which have been simply interchanged, so that what each put first stands second in the other. The remaining sections can be divided into two parts in such a way that in neither did the writers differ in their ordering: for the sections standing third, fourth and seventh in Mark stand fourth, seventh and eighth in Matthew; while Mark's fifth, sixth and eighth equal Matthew's third, fifth and sixth. This shows that each followed the same source,[5] not departing from the order held by the other, unless compelled by some necessity. Which of them departed, then? And by what necessity? It used to be said that Matthew must have put back into correct temporal order the events at which he was present. No scholars, I suppose, would now hold this view; for recent learned controversy can hardly have left anyone supposing the gospel attributed to Matthew to be either more accurate than the others chronologically, or to have been written by an apostle. Even more plausible (since it makes less sense of the necessity which I mentioned) is the view of Mark as a bungling dilettante, unsure of his way, borne hither and thither between Matthew's and Luke's gospels by boredom, desire, carelessness, folly or design. Adherents of this view must have been taken in by a certain discussion of Griesbach's which, though it looks clever and subtle, is really not ingenious at all, but an absolute frost. Anyway, I hold that no good reason can be found by which we could suppose that Mark was led to alter Matthew's order here, especially as Luke agrees with Mark on almost all these points: but I think I can show why the order of Mark and Luke could not be used in the gospel of Matthew; so it was here, not there, that the order had to be broken by certain devices. Now

---

[5] *Ut adpareat idem utrumque secutum esse.*

the gospel of Matthew I regard as originally composed of discourses of the Lord Jesus Christ, collected and woven together, with other stories stuck in afterwards (this view of Schleiermacher's needed expounding only, not arguing, since it is obviously true; so it should be accepted even if you differ from him in interpreting Papias). In this gospel the sermon on the mount in Galilee precedes the group of sections under discussion; the sixth section (on the numbering given just above) contains a discourse on the duties of apostles (Mt. 9:37, 38; 10:5-42), and another about John the Baptist (11:7-19 or 30): the seventh section gives a discourse about Satan, with various other things added in, which may or may not derive from Matthew the apostle (12:25-45); the same section also contains a large number of parables (13:3-52). Mark, on the other hand, has part of the discourse on Satan in his fourth section, plus some parables, and in his eighth section gives a bit of the discourse to the apostles. Anyone who thinks about this will agree that he can see why Mark's final section was put after his second, in Matthew's gospel, and Mark's eighth before his fourth. It is quite clear that Matthew the apostle put the sermon which is said to have been given on the mount right at the beginning of his book. It would therefore have seemed more appropriate that the leper should be said to have run and met Jesus when he came down from the mount and before he entered the town of Capernaum, in which he healed the centurion's servant according to the Gospel of Matthew, and Peter's mother-in-law according to both evangelists. Again it is quite likely, and not unreasonable, that Matthew the apostle put the discourse on duties of apostles and the one about John before the discourse on Satan and before the parables: in which case it is not surprising that those who composed the gospel according to Matthew, being afraid to change this order, preferred to change the arrangement in which the stories had been handed down to them. There were, then, compelling reasons for the arrangement in Matthew's gospel of most of Mark's sections (the order was this, sections two, one, three, eight, four, seven of Mark: for the third, fourth and seventh kept their positions, and I have just discussed the first second and eighth); it remained only to assign convenient positions to sections five and six. In discussing this we must of course beware of the penalties attached to excessive curiosity; I will, however, venture to say that they put Mark's sixth section, containing the raising of the ruler's daughter, in front of his eighth section (= Matthew's sixth), and added two blind men and the dumb one, so that the message there sent to John, that "the blind receive their sight and the deaf hear and the dead are raised up" (Mt. 11:5),[6] should not seem pointless, that is, without examples. It is less obvious why they preferred not to put Mark's fifth section before his sixth, but put it over in front of his third instead; but as Jesus had twice already been said to have brought help to demoniacs also (Mt. 4:24; 8:16), they may have thought it more suitable for the Gerasenes, as a fine example of this type, to come immediately after the curing of the fever of Peter's mother-in-law, and for the paralytic to be put aside for a moment, as the centurion's servant, who suffered from just the same disease, had come only a little earlier, in Matthew's second section (8:6). But everyone can form his own opinion about this instance: it will suffice if compelling reasons for changing the order are found in some of these sections, since it is likely that the evangelist's own preferences also played a part at times. Both factors can be observed in the section I come to now. Mark, before the first discourse, in his fourth section (3:7-19), says that many followed Jesus "from Gal-

---

[6]Passages within quotation marks are given by Lachmann in the Greek.

ilee and from Judaea and from Jerusalem and from Idumaea, and beyond Jordan, and about Tyre and Sidon,'' but he then goes on to list the apostles' names; Luke also has both these sections in the same position (6:14-19). But in the gospel according to Matthew the apostles' names had to be put in the sixth section (10:2-4), which corresponds to Mark's eighth and contains instructions to them as they were setting out. Now that other bit could have been put in the same place, but was moved elsewhere: for before the first discourse, that is, the one on the mount, it says, ''and there followed him great multitudes from Galilee and Decapolis and Jerusalem and Judaea and beyond Jordan'' (4:24, 25); but a similar opening is given to the discourse in both Luke and Matthew, ''blessed are the poor, for yours is the kingdom of God.''

I have now explained where and why Matthew departs from the order given in Mark. Fair and straightforward readers will, I think, agree with me. If others read this in the conviction that whatever I say will be wrong, I shall not exert myself to deceive them with a long discourse in a fine style, to drag them over unwillingly to my side. But not even obstinacy and scepticism, I suppose, could drive them to deny that Luke hardly ever departs from Mark, once they have examined a little more closely those places where there is some difference. These fall into two classes: in some the order changes while the words in both are very much the same; other sections are set in different positions and also differ in the matter and the words. There are two instances of the former class, and three of the latter. I shall discuss each class separately.

First comes the instance I mentioned just now in Matthew. Mark (3:7-19, 20-30) after the curing of the withered hand stated that a great crowd followed from Galilee and Judaea and from the other parts, and then at once put down the names of the apostles, and the discourse on the division of Satan's kingdom. Luke, however, changes the order a little at this point (6:12-19), that is, after the withered hand, first listing those who were chosen as apostles, then saying from whence the great multitude of the people had been gathered together: but he put the discourse about Satan elsewhere in the gospel (11:14-26), in a section peculiar to him and not shared with the others. The other instance is very similar to this, in every respect. In the very next passage (3:31-4:25, 4:30-32) Mark places first that saying of Jesus, ''Behold my mother and my brethren,'' next the parable of the sower, and about the lantern under a bushel, and ''To him that hath shall be given,'' and lastly the saying about a grain of mustard; Luke, however, (8:4-18, 19-21) starts with the sower and the lantern covered by a vessel, and adds at this point ''To him that hath shall be given,'' but puts the parable about the grain of mustard away in another place (13:18, 19). It may seem rather bold of me to say, he puts them away from here: but when I see such clear and almost continuous agreement, from which Luke departs only once or twice, I am bound to consider that in the parable of the grain of mustard and in the discourse on Satan he departed deliberately from the order of the others, which was known to him, to avoid writing the same things twice or taking anything away from that account of Jesus' journey to Jerusalem, which he thought more reliable. The fact that he placed the apostles' names and ''Behold my mother'' in slightly different positions from the others makes so little difference to my case that I need not now inquire why he did so.

There remains the other class of instances in which displacement is accompanied by a remarkable difference in the facts and the words. This has so impressed some writers that they thought Luke was telling different stories, rather than the

same stories in a different dress. Luke himself, however, must certainly be supposed to have held a different view; if it now seems credible that he was acquainted with the gospel stories in the order in which Mark used them, it is surely inconceivable that he should have omitted those unless he was sure he could present them as received from other authorities in a different and indeed more reliable manner. Consequently where Mark describes the calling of Simon and Andrew and the sons of Zebedee (1:16-20), and again where he records that Jesus in reply to those in his home town who jeered "Is not this the carpenter, the son of Mary?" said that a prophet is not without honor except in his own country (6:1-6), and lastly where Mark writes that the woman of Bethany anointed Jesus' head in the house of Simon the leper (14:3-9), in all these places Luke has nothing of that sort. Other writers have, I think, sufficiently explained why Luke transferred to the first part of his gospel (4:16-30) the saying to the Nazarenes, that no prophet is acceptable in his own country. Moreover on Luke's reading of the tradition about Simon and the sons of Zebedee, they did not merely leave their nets and their father, as the others wrote (Mk. 1:18, 20; Mt. 4:20, 22), but left *all* that they had (Lk. 5:11) and followed Jesus; Luke may therefore have thought it inappropriate to mention Simon's *house* (Lk. 4:38) after this, like the others, in reporting that his mother-in-law was suffering from fever there. Luke therefore preferred to put the call of Simon and his friends (5:1-11) after the healing of Simon's mother-in-law, rather than (supposing the story of the demon who knew Christ were transposed or dropped[7] along with the words "he rose up from the synagogue" [4:31-38]), leave a problem, though not a difficult one, to the prudence of the reader: this, however, is what he did in another and rather similar case (5:28, 29), where he writes that Levi, who had just then left all his things and was following Jesus, made a great feast at his house. Finally, there is the woman who anointed Jesus' feet in the house of Simon the Pharisee: here Luke had received certain things which would have seemed inappropriate if said a few days before Jesus' death (for example, 7:49, "who is this that even forgiveth sins?", which could hardly have been placed after the snub to those who asked, 20:2, "tell us by what authority you do these things"): he therefore decided—if I may hazard a guess—that he might conveniently recount this matter at the point (7:38-50) where, following some authority of his own, he had to list the women who were ministering to Jesus (8:1-3).

How stands the matter now? If my suggestions are correct and there is such precise and comprehensive agreement between both Matthew and Luke and the order of the gospel according to Mark that what little variations there are can be supposed made by them each for his own purposes, and if it is clear, in spite of this complete agreement, that they did not have before them a copy of Mark to imitate, the only remaining possibility is to say that the more or less prescribed order which all three follow was settled and established by some authority and tradition of the gospel, before they themselves wrote. Whether that order was shown to the evangelists in writing, or acquired by them through an already fixed custom of teaching and hearing, I prefer not to decide for the moment, so as not to spoil my case by taking on another. I shall be satisfied if it is understood that in determining the precise chronology of the history of Jesus, and deciding which events should be thought to have happened before or after others, no greater weight can be placed on the witness of three evangelists than if a single and indeed unknown author had testified. It may

---

[7]*vel traiecta vel recisa.*

also be helpful to point out to those who compose harmonies (or synopses as they are called nowadays), and who are usually put to great trouble by the difference of order and sequence, that in carrying out their task they should not be too contemptuous of Mark's authority. Finally, I think I can properly advise students of the sources of each gospel always to distinguish very carefully between material derived from the first writers and effects due to assembling the stories in a predetermined order; here even Schleiermacher may, I fear, have been oversubtle in ascribing to Luke's authorities some cases of linking different stories which a more correct view would see as coming together only by chance, being forced by the predetermined order to reach the same position in the story.

I have explained briefly with what caution gospel questions would have to be treated if anyone is minded not to neglect this small contribution of mine but to find a proper application for it in other fields. As learned readers do not need to be supplied with instances, I would have nothing more to add, were I not stimulated and roused to further discussion by what I said just now: that, even before our gospels were written, that order by which they were to be arranged was already settled. The first point that seems to me to be worth further inquiry is not who the first author of it was, but how and by what means that order was composed and the stories arranged.

Let me begin at this point. No one, I suppose, will believe that this whole body of gospel history, which has come down to us in three versions, came out full and complete in every part as though at one birth, at the same time as the separate stories were framed in a more or less fixed verbal form: and there is evidence by which certain smaller collections of stories can be easily made out, the elements of which though very posssibly handed down by different authors are fitted and linked together by a sort of common bond and can even be marked off from the passages on either side of them by certain fixed and definite signs and formulae. Now I think I can show with sufficient precision how many such "molecules" of gospel history there were for our writers to use, and what were the limits of each one. As I said, it makes no difference to my case whether you regard them as written tracts or suppose that those who told stories were accustomed when speaking and teaching to link those parts together, though if we have to admit that those learned in the gospel history would bring out several stories all together, what was there to prevent those stories, linked in that way and put in those same words, from being written down, before bolder spirits turned their minds to the composition of complete gospels? [Outline division of the common tradition by reference to subject-matter and closing formulae.]

Although in this article clarity is sometimes sacrificed to brevity, the general line of argument is clear and needs no commentary. Like modern critics, Lachmann regards these gospels as assemblages of paragraphs. Like the harmonists, he tries to reconcile or explain the variant arrangements of these paragraphs. Unlike them, he treats this as a literary problem: we are not to decide which order is most likely to be historically correct but which arrangement was earlier and which resulted from alterations to it at a later date.

Lachmann had some experience in juggling paragraphs, for in his second edition of Propertius (1829) he reassembled some poems cut in half by a dislocation in the manuscript. The transpositions in the gospels were not to be explained by chance and mechanical means, but by finding reasons which could have influenced one or another evangelist in altering the order that he found. This recalls the familiar method of choosing between readings in manuscripts: is it easier to conceive reasons or processes by which the reading of A could be turned into the reading of B, or is the reverse change, from B to A, more easily conceivable? (For example, if copyists tended to interpolate, then *brevior lectio potior.* . . .) The reasons which Lachmann found may still deserve attention; it may also be that we could find "reasons" telling the opposite way in each single case. His argument, then, does not rest on facts about different gospels or evangelists so much as on a comparison of plausibility in various conjectures of ours about the evangelists. Lachmann also takes for granted a theory about the double composition of Matthew without which his conjectures would appear even less plausible. The main point, however, is the complete absence of the argument we were led to expect, that triple comparison among types of variation, whose overhasty conclusion Butler dubbed (overhastily) "the Lachmann fallacy." Lachmann's article contains no trace of an argument from the absence of agreement against Mark.

We may therefore take a more cheerful view of the progress, gradual but not completely interrupted, of Synoptic criticism. Lachmann first tried arguing from the phenomena of order. His successors in Germany worked out several forms of *Grundschrift* and Urmarcus theory. The first clear case of the argument from absence of agreement is cited from Abbott: "In the case of the three narratives A, B, and C, if A contains much that is common to A and B alone, and much that is common to A and C alone, and *all that is common to B and C*, it follows generally that A contains the whole of some narrative from which B and C have borrowed parts."[8]

It was natural that the new principle should first be recognized in a concrete case; and that general statements of it should not at first make the limitations and qualifications very precise. Abbott may not have realized that, if A copied B, adding new material, and C then copied most of A, giving a linear pedigree B—A—C, text A would indeed "contain the whole of

---

[8]E. A. Abbott and W. G. Rushbrooke, *The Common Tradition of the Synoptic Gospels* (1884) vii; cf. Farmer, 77.

some narrative from which B and C "*present* some parts, without proving that documents B and C both borrowed their text from that of document A.

A formal and nearly correct treatment of the argument from absence of agreement against one of three texts was first given by Quentin, in discussion of the Vulgate text.[9] The precise application of this technique of triple comparison to the Synoptic problem is probably due to Butler, himself, although he does not mention Quentin, and writes as though the principle of the argument were well known to all, and the fallacy committed by Stanton, Abbott, Wellhausen, Burkitt, Streeter, Rawlinson, Narborough, Redlich and perhaps Hawkins[10] were an elementary error to which not even a schoolboy would fall prey. But arguments are tricky things to handle and even more difficult to conceive in the abstract or to describe. We shall all of us commit logical sins in the future: it is some comfort to learn that we are in good company.

---

[9]H. Quentin, *Essais de critique textuelle* (1926) ch. III.
[10]See Butler, *Originality,* 63.

THE
LACHMANN
FALLACY

B. C. Butler*

According to Butler, the priority of Mark rests, in part, on an inference that is obviously false. Lachmann himself drew a correct inference on the assumption that the Synoptic Gospels are only indirectly connected by dependence of them all on a lost document or oral tradition; namely, that the phenomena of order show that the lost document is most faithfully preserved in Mark. This conclusion was the basis of the theory of Ur-Markus as a sort of first edition of Mark and as a source for Matthew and Luke. In the course of time it was seen that Ur-Markus must have been so similar to Mark as to have been practically identical with it, and the proper step was taken of abandoning this conjectural document. But it was not noticed that by identifying Ur-Markus with Mark the terms of Lachmann's problem were essentially altered and his inference no longer held good. In the theory of Markan priority Ur-Markus's ghost presides over his own sepulchre.

Butler quotes Streeter, interposing his own comments: ''We note, then, that in regard to (a) items of subject matter, (b) actual words used, (c) relative order of incidents, Mark is in general supported by *both* Matthew and Luke, and in most cases where they do not both support him they do so alternately [that is, one or the other supports him], and they practi-

*B. C. Butler, ''The Lachmann Fallacy,'' *The Originality of St. Matthew: A Critique of The Two-Document Hypothesis* (Cambridge: University Press, 1951) 62-71.

cally never agree together against Mark. This is only explicable [here is the vicious inference] if they followed an authority which in content, in wording, and in arrangement was all but identical with Mark.''

This mistake, although not actually made by Lachmann, was apparently fathered upon him and has been repeated in modern times by Stanton, Abbott, Wellhausen, Burkitt, Hawkins, Streeter, Rawlinson, Narborough, Redlich, and others. In fact, Butler maintains, once the theory of Ur-Markus is rejected, all that can be argued is that Mark is necessarily the connecting-link between Matthew and Luke in the Triple Tradition, but not necessarily the source of more than one of them. The data simply do not support a more precise determination of the relationship among the synoptic gospels.

Butler does concede that Mark's use of phrases likely to cause offense and his roughness of style and grammar and use of Aramaic words is an argument for Markan priority deserving serious attention.

''A century of discussion,'' says Streeter,[1] ''has resulted in a consensus of scholars . . . that the authors of the First and Third Gospels made use either of our Mark, or of a document all but identical with Mark. The former and the simpler of these hypotheses, viz. that they used our Mark, is the one which I hope . . . to establish beyond reasonable doubt.'' In the following pages I assume it is agreed that ''a document all but identical with Mark''[2] need not be introduced to complicate the argument; we need only consider the three extant Gospels.

Streeter proceeds to set out, under five heads, ''the main facts and considerations which show the dependence of Matthew and Luke upon Mark.'' The first three ''heads'' comprise the familiar facts that about nine-tenths of Mark's subject-matter is found in Matthew, and rather more than half in Luke, in language ''very largely identical with that of Mark,'' the majority of Mark's actual words, in any average section of the common matter, being found in one or both of the other Gospels; that Mark's order of sections and incidents is generally found also in Matthew and Luke, and when one of these has an order different from that of Mark, the other usually follows Mark's order; and that Matthew and Luke, in genuinely ''Markan'' passages, never agree together *against Mark* in point of order and very rarely in words, collocation of words, or structure of sentences.

On the basis of this accurate statement of highly important data, Streeter, following in the wake of a distinguished line of critics, and him-

---

[1]B. H. Streeter, *The Four Gospels* (1924) 157.

[2]Whether Ur-Markus or a ''second edition'' of Mark.

self not the last in the ranks, rests an inference which is obviously false. As the matter is so vital it may be well to quote his actual words: "We note, then, that in regard to (a) items of subject-matter, (b) actual words used, (c) relative order of incidents, Mark is in general supported by *both* Matthew and Luke, and in most cases where they do not both support him they do so alternately [that is, one or the other of them supports him], and they practically never agree together against Mark. This is only explicable [here is the vicious inference] if they followed an authority which in content, in wording, and in arrangement was all but identical with Mark."

The mistake, though not actually made by Lachmann (1835),[3] is apparently fathered upon him, and it has been repeated over and over again in modern times—for instance by V. H. Stanton (apparently) in 1899,[4] by E. A. Abbott (1901),[5] by Wellhausen (1905),[6] by Burkitt (1906),[7] perhaps by Sir J. Hawkins (1911),[8] by Streeter, as we have just seen (1924), by Bishop Rawlinson (1925),[9] by Bishop Narborough (1928),[10] and by Canon Redlich (1936).[11] Since the argument conceals a schoolboyish[12] error of

---

[3]*De Ordine Narrationum in Evangeliis Synopticis*, in *Theologische Studien und Kritiken* (1835): 570ff. I quote from the preface to the second volume of Lachmann's edition of the New Testament (Berlin, 1850). Lachmann took it for granted that neither Matthew nor Luke is dependent on Mark and held that all three Synoptic Gospels depend on a common written or oral source. On this assumption his argument (that the Markan order of events is a faithful reproduction of the source's order) holds good. It is Lachmann's followers who had inadvertently committed themselves to a fallacy. Lachmann prefaces his inference with the vital proviso (discarded by his modern followers): *Si eos* [St. Matthew and St. Luke] *exemplar Marci propositum quod imitarentur non habuisse manifestum est.*

[4]"Gospels," *Hastings Dictionary of the Bible* (1889) 239.

[5]"Gospels," *Encyclopaedia Biblica* (1901) col. 1765, referring only to contents.

[6]*Einleitung in die drei ersten Evangelien* (1911) 43-44.

[7]*The Gospel History and its Transmission* (1906) 36-37.

[8]*Oxford Studies in the Synoptic Problem*, ed. W. Sanday (1911) 29.

[9]*The Gospel according to St. Mark* (1947) xxxv: "It is obvious that these facts are most simply explained by the hypothesis" that Mark was a source of Matthew and Luke.

[10]"The Synoptic Problem," in *A New Commentary on Holy Scripture* (1928): "It seems to follow," from the data, that either Mark or a document resembling it "has largely shaped the other two Synoptic Gospels."

[11]*Student's Introduction to the Synoptic Gospels* (1926) 31: "Each of the three arguments by itself [that is, common contents, common diction, common arrangement] would not have proved our thesis, but the three arguments together furnish decisive evidence that Mark is the primary Gospel." That the error should be so persistently propagated may be pleaded as a justification for exposing it once and for all, as the text attempts to do.

[12]Or schoolmasterish; see n16.

elementary reasoning at the very base of the Two-Document hypothesis as commonly proposed for our acceptance, we may be forgiven for devoting to its refutation more space than it intrinsically deserves.

Burkitt wrote as follows:

> Lachmann started from the central fact that the common order of the three Synoptic Gospels is Mark's order. "There is not so much diversity," he says, "in the order of the Gospel tales as most people imagine. It is indeed very great if you compare the Synoptic Gospels indiscriminately together, or compare Luke with Matthew; but if you compare Mark with both the others separately the diversity is inconsiderable." And he goes on to draw the conclusion that the order of the narrative, as we have it in Mark, is presupposed by and underlies the narratives in Luke and Matthew.[13]

Since Lachmann's time the investigation has been extended, as we have seen, to cover the very wording of Mark. The theory of a common oral tradition has been (rightly) excluded, though Lachmann did not apparently himself finally close the door upon it. And the gap between ''a

---

[13]Burkitt, *Gospel History*, 37. Lachmann's statement runs as follows: *Narrationum evangelicarum ordinis non tanta est quam plerisque videtur diversitas; maxima sane si aut hos scriptores eadem complexione omnes aut Lucam cum Matthaeo composueris, exigua si Marcum cum utroque seorsim* (*Novum Testamentum Graece et Latine*, 2:xiv). For his inference, see *ibid.*, xx, where, having premised that the authors of Matthew and Luke did not have Mark before them, he proceeds: *Quid superest nisi ut illum quem omnes velut sibi praescriptum sequuntur ordinem, prius quam ipsi scriberent, auctoritate ac traditione quadam evangelica et confirmatum fuisse dicamus?* The clause *prius quam ipsi scriberent* shows that Lachmann was not recommending the theory of his modern followers, that Mark itself was the source of the other two. So also C. H. Weisse (according to Stanton in the article referred to above) took the view that Mark "more simply and fully embodied a document used by the other two," that is, Ur-Markus (*Die Evangelische Geschichte*, 1838). He also held that "Matthew's 'Logia' " was also used both in our first and our third Gospel. Here for the first time was the "two-document hypothesis" (Stanton, 236). It is not without interest that the two-document hypothesis started off with Ur-Markus, which has since been discarded, and apparently with an appeal to Papias (the Logia) which is no longer regarded as essential. Is it ncessary to point out that Streeter in 1911 and Burney held Mark to be dependent on Q? Substitute Ur-Markus for Mark, in order to restore to Lachmann's argument its original cogency, and admit that Ur-Markus may have not been merely dependent on Q but *comprised in the same document with it*, and Ur-Markus then becomes indistinguishable from Matthew, on which Mark (our present Mark) will then depend; and Luke must depend on our present Mark (for the Markan sections) and on Matthew (for the Q passages). The two-document hypothesis can thus be resolved into the hypothesis which is worked out in the course of our present study [that is, in the whole of Butler's book].

tradition embodied in Mark,'' or Ur-Markus, and Mark itself as we now possess it has been successfully narrowed and in fact almost closed. Thus was reached the firm position held by Streeter, that our present Mark was a written source for Matthew and Luke.

The argument in its modern form was stated by Burkitt in the following way:

> In the parts common to Mark, Matthew, and Luke, there is a good deal in which all three verbally agree; there is also much in common to Mark and Matthew, and much common to Mark and Luke, but hardly anything common to Matthew and Luke which Mark does not share also. There is very little of Mark which is not more or less adequately represented either in Matthew or in Luke. Moreover, the common order is Mark's order; Matthew and Luke never agree against Mark in transposing a narrative. Luke sometimes deserts the order of Mark, and Matthew often does so; but in these cases Mark is always supported by the remaining Gospel. Now what is the deduction to be drawn from these facts? There is only one answer. We are bound to conclude that Mark contains the whole of a document which Matthew and Luke have independently used, and, further, that Mark contains very little else besides.

And after further examination Burkitt decides that there is no necessity to suppose that the document thus used by Matthew and Luke was in fact any other than Mark itself—Ur-Markus resigns its place to Mark.[14]

But once Ur-Markus is rejected, *the terms of the problem are altered.* ''The deduction to be drawn from these facts'' is no longer that ''Mark contains the whole of a document which Matthew and Luke have independently used,'' but that (a) there is a relation of dependence, *one way or the other*, between Matthew and Mark, and again between Mark and Luke; (b) the similarities between Matthew and Luke in the ''triple tradition'' are not, as a rule,[15] due to immediate dependence of Matthew on Luke or *vice versa*, but to the fact that either Matthew or Luke depends on Mark, while the other either depends on Mark *or is Mark's source*. In other words, *Mark is necessarily the connecting link between Matthew and Luke in these passages, but not necessarily the source of more than one of them.*

The data adduced by Streeter in the ''heads of evidence'' referred to at the beginning of this chapter and by Burkitt in the above quotation are quite incapable of giving any indication leading towards a more precise de-

---

[14]Burkitt, *Gospel History*, 58.

[15]The qualifying clause is intended to allow for possible occasional agreements between Matthew and Luke against Mark, in case these cannot be explained away.

termination of the relations obtaining between the three documents than that stated in the last sentence of the paragraph just written. We are left with three possible "solutions" of the problem of the "triple tradition," and none of them is more probable than the other, on the evidence so far presented.

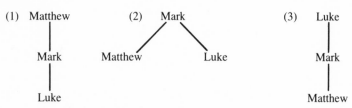

In mathematical terms, the solution which Lachmann's followers consider to be dictated by the facts turns out to have one chance in three of being correct; there is a probability of two to one against it.[16]

We can at once concede that the third solution, supposing as it does that Luke was the original Gospel, is absurd—though for reasons not included in Streeter's first "three heads" of evidence. Rejecting it, we are left with a choice between solutions (1) and (2), and their claims on our acceptance, up to date, are exactly equal. There is one chance in two that Matthew copied Mark; and there is one chance in two that Mark copied Matthew. To decide between these precisely equal alternatives we must turn to an entirely different set of considerations, and the arguments so far adduced will not give any "accumulative" force to such further arguments as we may discover.

---

[16]There is unconscious humor in the following passage from E. A. Abbott (*The Fourfold Gospel*, I:11-12): "Matthew and Luke are in the position of two schoolboys, Primus and Tertius, seated on the same form, between whom sits another, Secundus (Mark). All three are writing (we will suppose) a narrative of the same event. . . . Primus and Tertius copy largely from Secundus. [It may be noted that Abbott begs his question only a little more blatantly than some other Markan priorists.] Occasionally the two copy the same words; then we have agreement of three writers. At other times Primus (Matthew) copies what Tertius (Luke) does not. . . . At others, Tertius (Luke) copies what Primus (Matthew) does not. . . . But Primus and Tertius cannot look over one another's shoulders," and hence agreement of them "against" Secundus is only possible by accident. As the same results (exactly) will follow if Secundus copied from Primus (or Tertius) and was himself copied by Tertius (or Primus), we must hope that Abbott, who was headmaster of a famous school, is not illustrating from real life. Otherwise, it would be interesting to hear what Primus (or Tertius) thought of the acumen and justice of his headmaster.

Is it too much to hope that the "Lachmann fallacy" will no longer be displayed—with every appearance of superior logic—before the imagination of an unsuspecting public, prone to submit to the claim to reason, and slow to examine its validity? The catena of authors listed above as propagating this fallacy[17] should at least suggest a doubt whether the present dominance of the theory of Markan priority is really due, as is commonly supposed, to a triumph of honest criticism over traditionalism and fantasy. The truth is probably that Lachmann drew a correct inference on the assumption that the Synoptic Gospels are only indirectly connected by dependence of them all on a lost document or oral tradition; namely that, in that case, the phenomena of order show that the lost document is most faithfully preserved in Mark. This conclusion was the basis of the theory of Ur-Markus as a sort of first "edition" of Mark and as source for Matthew and Luke. In course of time it was seen that Ur-Markus must have been so similar to Mark as to have been practically identical with it, and the proper step was taken of abandoning this conjectural document. But it was not noticed that by identifying Ur-Markus with Mark the terms of Lachmann's problem were essentially altered and his inference no longer held good. In the theory of Markan priority Ur-Markus's ghost presides over his own sepulchre.

The data summarized above, though inadequate for the purpose to which Streeter sought to apply them, have nevertheless carried us a long way on the road towards a solution of the Synoptic Problem. They have reduced the nine possible solutions (apart from appeals to oral tradition and conjectural documents) to three, and they enable us, for practical purposes, to exclude the oral theory in its pure form, since the oral tradition (an unwritten Ur-Markus) appealed to would have to be indistinguishable from Mark in order to satisfy the data. Burkitt's critique of Ur-Markus[18] is sound, and tells equally against the oral hypothesis.

It will be remembered that of Streeter's five "heads of evidence" we have so far considered only the first three. The fifth turns out to contain no evidence in proof of Streeter's theory, but a series of deductions from it, with a rather closer examination than that hitherto attempted in *The Four Gospels* of the placing of the "Markan tradition" in Matthew and Luke.

---

[17]We can add Armitage Robinson to the list; see *The Study of the Gospels* (1902) 15 ("The most natural explanation").

[18]Burkitt, *Gospel History*, 40-41.

Thus, only the fourth head of evidence contains any argument tending to support the theory of Markan priority to the exclusion of all other solutions. Not five converging sets of evidence, but one only.

This set is summarized by Streeter as follows: "The primitive character of Mark is . . . shown by (a) the use of phrases likely to cause offense, which are omitted or toned down in the other Gospels; (b) roughness of style and grammar, and the preservation of Aramaic words," and he points out in particular that the difference between the style of Mark and of the other two "is the difference which always exists between the spoken and the written word (p. 163); Mark in fact reads like the transcript of the words of 'an impromptu speaker,' while Matthew and Luke use the more succinct and carefully chosen language of one who writes and then revises an article for publication."[19]

Here at last we have an argument deserving serious attention, and it is discussed [elsewhere].[20] For the moment, it may be enough to say:

1. The stylistic evidence to which Streeter here appeals is susceptible of a different explanation from that which, in his view, it dictates. It is often taken to indicate, as indeed Streeter's words suggest, that Mark is, practically speaking, not a work of literature but a deposit of oral teaching from the lips of one teacher, and the assumption is often made, not without powerful arguments in its favor, that this oral teaching sprang direct from the recollections of the eyewitness who gave it. Evidence is adduced to suggest that this oral teacher was St. Peter, and it is easy to understand the fascination that this idea exerts on many minds and the prejudice it engenders against any theory of a written source behind Mark.

However, as will be pointed out below, Burney (like Streeter in 1911, though on different grounds from his) held that Mark was dependent on Q, and his argument is cogent for those who believe in that "'lost document'"; for others it tends directly to suggest Mark's dependence on Matthew. Bishop Rawlinson,[21] again, holds that St. Mark's materials came to him from tradition, the arrangement of them being largely his own—this as against those who hold that Mark is a direct report of St. Peter's oral teaching. In this view he was probably influenced by Wellhausen, who in some respects prepared the way for the Form Critics of the last thirty years. Pro-

---

[19]Streeter, *Four Gospels*, 157.
[20]See Butler, *The Originality of St. Matthew* (1951) 162, 164ff.
[21]A. E. J. Rawlinson, *St. Mark* (1952) 110.

fessor Lightfoot[22] summarizes the Form Critics' attitude to Mark as follows: "We are now bidden to see 'in that Gospel' a compilation of materials of different date, origin, character and purpose, many of which may have had a considerable history—whether oral or literary or both—before they were finally inserted in this Gospel." Thus a powerful current of thought in modern critical circles tends to see in Mark *an editor of preexisting materials*. It is probable that the Form Critics do less than justice to the intrinsic and external arguments for Mark's close connection with St. Peter's oral teaching, but they have prepared the ground for a theory which would accept that connection *and at the same time look, for an explanation of the signs of editorial work in Mark, not to a purely conjectural evolution of oral or at least subliterary "tradition," but to a document lying under our hand and controlling our hypotheses.*[23] We have shown that Streeter's "stylistic" argument must carry virtually the whole weight of the hypothesis of Markan priority (I exclude, for the moment, "higher critical" theories of evolving doctrine and "legendary accretions");[24] and the Form Critics (along with Burney and Bishop Rawlinson) have undermined its validity in so far as there is force in their contention that Mark is in the last resort dependent on a source or sources (written or oral) other than the oral teaching of an eyewitness, or indeed of any one teacher.

2. I therefore suggest that it is desirable, before further examining the stylistic argument, to undertake an investigation (never, so far as I am aware, attempted in modern publications of the Two-Document school) of the actual point-to-point relations revealed by a comparative study of the texts of either Matthew and Mark, or Mark and Luke, or of both these pairs. I propose that we must study the Matthew-Mark pair; I agree, in fact, with the adherents of Markan priority that Luke is dependent on

---

[22]R. H. Lightfoot, *History and Interpretation in the Gospels* (1935) 25.

[23]Mark might, for instance, derive from an oral paraphrase or "Targum" of Matthew.

[24]A quotation from Burkitt, *Gospel History*, 38-39, may be not out of place: "Far be it from me to disparage the high studies of history and philosophy in favour of literary [or should we say, documentary] criticism: but as the wise man said, 'To everything there is a season,' and in the particular study before us the season of literary criticism comes logically first. As long as those who studied the Synoptic Problem attacked it by considering mainly the actual contents of the Gospels, they seemed to be unable to shake off a certain confusion between the earliest Synoptic Gospel and the primitive preaching of Christianity."

Mark, and if it emerges from our study of the Matthew-Mark pair that Mark is dependent on Matthew, Luke's dependence on Mark follows automatically.[25]

As I have said, such a study seems never to be offered to the public by the modern Markan priorists. The reason is, no doubt, that through a combination of false inference (from the first three heads of evidence) with the conclusion to which they have jumped from the fourth "head," they have supposed that their case is proved, so that this minute documentary comparison is unnecessary. Nevertheless such comparison is of the essence of the kind of criticism involved in a problem such as ours. It can give results practically immune, in their cumulative force, from variable subjective judgments; and if the Markan priorists believe in their own theory they should welcome the test to which it will be put by such an investigation: if their theory is true, then either our investigation will provide no results, or the results obtained will confirm their theory

It may not be amiss to draw attention to the fact that our investigation, if it is to have probative value, must be approached with an "open mind." Otherwise it will in fact become a study exactly similar to Harnack's study of the Q passages in *The Sayings of Jesus*—a study whose results . . . can only be used in support of the Q hypothesis after a most searching process of weeding out those among them which depend on a prior acceptance of the hypothesis. This "open mind," in the matter of the "triple tradition," is something which the adherents of Markan priority find it peculiarly difficult to achieve,[26] for the dominant theory is in possession, and it tends to blind the eyes to evidence which, for the unprejudiced, is overwhelmingly cogent. I suggest, then, that we frankly recognize that the first three "heads of evidence" have not afforded any support to Markan as against Matthaean priority; and that we put away from our minds, for the time being, the conclusion suggested but not necessitated by the fourth "head of evidence." We turn to the first two Gospels and examine them side by side in a purely objective and scientific spirit. Let the argument lead us where it will, and at the end of it we shall be able to decide whether its bearing corroborates, or tends to undermine, the conclusion derived by Markan priorists from stylistic comparison.

---

[25]If, however, Matthew depends on Mark, it does not automatically follow that Mark does not depend on Luke.

[26]I write with feeling, having been myself at one time an adherent of the school.

CRITIQUE
OF THE MAIN ARGUMENTS
FOR MARK'S PRIORITY
AS FORMULATED
BY B. H. STREETER

D. L. Dungan*

Dungan reviews the recent critical comment that has gradually accumulated around each of the traditional arguments in favor of Mark's priority to Matthew and Luke.

A. The Argument from Shared Matter. This is in no way an argument for Markan priority. Streeter's argument proves only that Mark is in some sort of literary relation with Matthew and Luke.

B. The Argument from the Lack of Significant Verbal Agreements Between Matthew and Luke Against Mark. Against Streeter two points should be raised: (1) Streeter's reason for ignoring the evidence of the *joint omissions* of Markan material by Matthew and Luke is not sound, and (2) Streeter's *method* for handling the positive agreements against Mark *distorts the evidence.*

C. The Argument from the Order of Incidents and Sections. Although stated in an inexcusably prejudicial manner, Streeter has got the facts largely right; but the inference that the argument from order demonstrates the priority of Mark is obviously false.

*D. L. Dungan, "Mark—The Abridgement of Matthew and Luke," *Jesus and Man's Hope* (Pittsburgh Theological Seminary, 1970) 1:54-74.

D. The Argument from Mark's Primitive Language and Theology.
Dungan maintains that the argument from Mark's primitive language does
not conclusively demonstrate Mark's priority. In fact, the argument has in
the past been used to show precisely the opposite. Streeter's argument for
the priority of Mark using style, grammar, and vocabulary collapses, since
the evidence is quite inconclusive.

*E. The Argument from the Distribution of Markan and Non-Markan
Material in Matthew and Luke.* Dungan notes that since Streeter believes
that Luke was inserting chunks of Mark into another Gospel (Proto-Luke),
his argument is really a fallacy. In fact, says Dungan, the priority of Mark
is clearly closely tied to the assumption of a hypothetical sayings-collection (Q). The two are inextricably intertwined.

Since the formulations of B. H. Streeter have become very widely
used, indeed, classics in the discussion, they will be used here.[1]
"Five reasons for accepting the priority of Mark" (Streeter's heading
for the arguments that follow):
A. The argument from shared matter. "Matthew reproduces 90 percent of the subject matter of Mark in language very largely identical with
that of Mark; Luke does the same for rather more than half of Mark."[2] Al-

---

[1]We shall be quoting the statements given in the synopsis at the beginning of Chapter
VII, which is entitled "The Fundamental Solution," *The Four Gospels* (1924) 151-52.
Clear signs of his influence are evident in both German as well as English-speaking scholarship; for example, P. Feine, J. Behm, *Introduction to the New Testament*, 13th German
ed. rev. by W. G. Kümmel (1964; ET 1966) 45-50; J. L. Price, *Interpreting the New Testament* (1961) 162; A. H. McNeile, *An Introduction to the New Testament*, 2d ed. (1953)
60-61. For the older period, see the simliar formulations by C. H. Weisse, one of the first
to combine the Q hypothesis with the idea of Mark's priority (W. R. Farmer, *The Synoptic
Problem* [1964] 24), in A. Schweitzer, *The Quest of the Historical Jesus* (ET 1961) 123-
24. Some might think Rudolf Bultmann does not belong to this group since he always kept
to the Ur-Markus theory; thus: "it is . . . probable that the text of Mark which the two other
evangelists used lay before them in an older form than that in which we have it today. This
Urmarcus (as it is usually called) was altered and enlarged at certain points; *but it cannot
be distinguished from the present text of Mark in any important way"* (*Form Criticism*, ed.
F. C. Grant [1962] 13-14). See further E. P. Sanders, *The Tendencies of the Synoptic Tradition* (1969) 6, n2. The italics were added to Bultmann's remarks to prove that he fell prey
to precisely the same methodological error that all of the later advocates of the Two-Document hypothesis made from H. J. Holtzmann and William Sanday on down; see Farmer,
23, 49-50, 65, *et passim.* Bultmann regarded the work of Streeter with some favor; see,
for example, *History of the Synoptic Tradition*, 2d ed. (1968, ET of 2d German ed., 1931)
3, n4.
[2]Streeter, for example, 151; see more fully, 159-60.

though the statement of the literary evidence is prejudicially slanted in favor of his conclusion, it is correct enough in itself. How Streeter was able to maintain his inference from it, however, is incomprehensible. This is in no way an argument [for] Mark's *priority*. As H. G. Jameson pointed out before Streeter wrote his book, "the facts here stated . . . do not give even a hint why one of these alternatives [namely, whether Matthew or Mark was the source for the other] should be true rather than the other. The argument, that is, does not bear either for or against the priority of Mark."[3] All Streeter's statement proves is that Mark is in some sort of literary relation with Matthew and Luke.[4] This is the true significance of this statement: it asserts that the Synoptic Problem is primarily a question of literary interrelationships.[5]

B. The argument from the lack of significant verbal agreements between Matthew and Luke against Mark. "In any average section, which occurs in the three Gospels, the majority of the actual words used by Mark are reproduced by Matthew and Luke, either alternately or both together."[6] What Streeter means here is that there are no significant agreements between Matthew and Luke against Mark such as would seriously undercut the priority of Mark. Against this two points should be raised: 1) Streeter's reason for ignoring the evidence of the *joint omissions* of Markan material by Mathew and Luke is not sound, and 2) Streeter's *method* for handling the positive agreements against Mark *distorts the evidence.*

1. The joint omissions of Mark by Matthew and Luke. Streeter considered Matthew's and Luke's omissions of Markan material of no special importance.

> If the agreement consists in an omission, it is almost invariably of the unnecessary or unimportant words which are characteristic of Mark's somewhat verbose style. Matthew and Luke both compress Mark: *it would be hard to find three consecutive verses in the whole of his Gospel of which either Matthew or Luke have not*

---

[3]H. G. Jameson, *The Origin of the Synoptic Gospels* (1922) 10.

[4]Farmer discusses the argument in connection with F. H. Woods's statement of it, *Synoptic Problem,* 63-64, and again when he examines the arguments of E. A. Abbott (77ff.). His rebuttal is based mainly on Jameson's argument quoted above which he reprints (288-89, see further 113-14, 152-53). For Farmer's treatment of this phenomenon on Griesbachian terms, see 202-203.

[5]Ibid., 203; Streeter, *Four Gospels,* 155ff.

[6]Streeter, *Four Gospels,* 151; see more fully 160-61.

omitted some words, apparently with this object. Since, then, both Matthew and Luke independently compress Mark by the omission of unnecessary words or sentences, and since in any sentence only certain words can be spared, they could not avoid *frequently concurring in the selection of words to be dispensed with. Under such circumstances, coincidence in omission calls for no explanation.*[7]

This justification is logically distressing and factually impossible since Streeter obviously presupposes Mark's priority in his explanation of the phenomenon of Matthew's and Luke's joint omissions of Markan passages. Thus he begs the question. In addition, he apparently never noticed that the agreements in omission, that is, those passages where Matthew and Luke depart from the text of Mark together and return together (a so-called "negative agreement"), frequently fit into a surrounding network of positive agreements (joint alterations or additions) between Matthew and Luke against Mark. Because of this, they must be taken into consideration, and *Streeter never discussed them.* For those who still think there is no new evidence to consider and, therefore, disregard Farmer's plea for a reconsideration of the Synoptic Problem, here, on Streeter's own description of the literary facts, is some new evidence: *in nearly every verse.*[8]

2. Atomization of the evidence. In the second place, Streeter—following J. C. Hawkins's lead—relied upon a basic methodological approach which systematically prevented him from ever having to account for the significance of the totality of agreements between Matthew and Luke against Mark in any given passage. This enabled him to ignore the chief sort of agreement against Mark: *the network itself.*

---

[7]Ibid., 180, cf. 295-96; italics in the last sentence are Streeter's.

[8]See Farmer's observations on V. H. Stanton, *Synoptic Problem*, 101-102, cf. 110, 120. A. W. Argyle's comment is precisely to the point, "Agreement [between Matthew and Luke] on which passages to omit is just as significant as agreement in alterations and additions," "Evidence for the View that St. Luke used St. Matthew's Gospel," JBL 83 (1964): 394 [reprinted in this volume]. Léon Vaganay has one of the rare discussions of this phenomenon of joint omissions *as it relates* to other types of agreement against Mark; see *Le Problème synoptique*, 69-74. They are most striking in such accounts as, for example, the Gerasene Demoniac (Mt. 8:28-34 par), Jairus' Daughter (Mt. 9:18-26 par), feeding of the 5000 (Mt. 14:3-12 par), and the Healing of the Epileptic Boy (Mt. 17:14-21 par). H. J. Held's discussion, "Matthew as Interpreter of the Miracle Stories," in G. Bornkamm, et al., *Tradition and Interpretation in Matthew* (1963), pays no attention whatever to this phenomenon. On Held's discussion, see now E. P. Sanders, *The Tendencies of the Synoptic Tradition* (1969) 24, 83-87.

In the chapter of *The Four Gospels* dedicated to this problem, Streeter approaches the data *already split up into four groups or kinds*: "irrelevant agreements," "deceptive agreements," "influence of Q," and "textual corruption."[9] Farmer objects:

> This procedure tends to atomize the phenomena. If one restricts the discussion of these phenomena to one group at a time, as Streeter did, . . . *the total concatenation of agreements in a given Synoptic passage will never be impressed upon the mind of the reader of such a discussion.* For example, if a particular passage exhibits a web of minor but closely related agreements of Matthew and Luke against Mark, there is the prospect that these different agreements will be divided into two or more of Streeter's different categories, thus dissipating the full impact which these same agreements would make on the mind of the reader if he were to have them all brought to his attention at the same time, and discussed together in the concrete wholeness of the particular context which they have in the passage concerned.[10]

As noted above, dismemberment of the context was Hawkins's way of investigating the phenomena,[11] and before him, that of E. A. Abbott as well.[12] On the other hand, none of them ever made a list or found a category to deal with the manifold variety of evidence possible in the agreements of omission.

Once again, for those who are oppressed by the prospect of reopening the Synoptic Problem, who see it as nothing more than "going back over plowed ground," as it was recently put at a meeting of the Society of Biblical Literature, here is plenty of *fresh evidence* virtually untouched by plow, virgin soil in nearly every section of the Gospels.[13]

---

[9]Streeter, *Four Gospels*, 293.

[10]Farmer, *Synoptic Problem*, 119.

[11]See Farmer on Hawkins, Ibid., 104ff.

[12]E. A. Abbott, *The Corrections of Mark Adopted by Matthew and Luke* (1901) 307-324.

[13]See Farmer, *Synoptic Problem,* 104, 138. Cf. A. Farrer's similar objection to Streeter's many sources: "What does Dr. Streeter do? He divides the evidence into several groups and finds a distinct hypothesis for each. . . . Thus the forces of evidence are divided by the advocate, and defeated in detail. His argument finds its strength in the fewness of the instances for which any one hypothesis needs to be invoked; but the opposing counsel will unkindly point out that the diminution of the instances for each hypothesis is in exact proportion to the multiplication of the hypotheses themselves." See "On Dispensing with Q," *Studies in the Gospels: Essays in Memory of R. H. Lightfoot,* ed. D. E. Nineham (1955) 62 [reprinted in this volume]. For an interesting example of the proper method of handling the several types of agreement against Mark, see A. W. Argyle, "Evidence," 390-396 [reprinted in this volume].

Furthermore, as the article of Argyle [see n8] indicates, a clear grasp of this pervasive concatenation and harmony of agreements dooms the Q hypothesis, for one soon notices that the network of agreement runs from Q sections straight through Markan sections of Matthew and Luke and on into other Q sections. N. Turner rightly warns Two-Document theorists that great care must be exercised in the way the agreements of Matthew and Luke against Mark in the Markan contexts are explained, or Q will become very large indeed, "for these verbal agreements are widespread throughout the Markan sections."[14]

---

[14]See N. Turner, "The Minor Verbal Agreements of Matthew and Luke against Mark," *SE* 1, TU (1957): 223-43, quotation from 223. In fact, Q begins to take on the appearance of a Gospel itself, complete with passion narrative; see Farmer, *Synoptic Problem*, 150-51, n20. The problem is even more acute than Turner realizes, for, as R. T. Simpson points out, "there is in a few cases [of the Q-Mark overlap] a very close connection between the Q material [which Matthew and Luke are allegedly using] and that taken from Mark, so that *the Q material is quite unable to stand alone*. It is rather strange that this latter point was very convincingly made by Streeter himself in his *earlier* essay in *Oxford Studies*"; see Simpson, "The Major Agreements of Matthew and Luke Against Mark," *NTS* 12 (1966): 273-84, quotation from 274 [reprinted in this volume]. Simpson refers to Streeter's essay, "St. Mark's Knowledge and Use of Q," in *Studies in the Synoptic Problem*, ed. William Sanday (1911) 166-83. On this occasion Streeter's investigation brought him to the extraordinary result that *"Mark may well be a mutilation of Q"* (165, italics Streeter's). The passages he discussed were John's preaching, the temptation, the Beelzebub controversy, the parable of the mustard seed, the mission instructions, and some others. He later disavowed this article and its conclusions, but he could not eliminate an unresolved question, for he apparently did not fully realize just where his logic required him to go: if Mark is frequently being passed over in section after section where Matthew and Luke seem to correspond to Mark, then the basis for holding to Mark's priority dissolves at just the places where it should be strongest—namely, in the Markan passage (Triple Tradition). On the other hand, Q begins to puff up to enormous proportions as it threatens to designate the whole chain of similarities up and down the entire length of Matthew and Luke *including many Markan sections* since Mark's parallel (in the Triple Tradition sections) on several occasions seems "a mutilated excerpt from Q," to use Streeter's words. But it is then no hard step to decide, as E. W. Lummis, J. Chapman, B. C. Butler, and many others have done, that the relationship between Luke and Matthew may well be more scientifically explained, not by invoking some imaginary source as the link between the two, but by trying to discover whether Luke is directly dependent upon Matthew.

. . . the crucial weakness both of the priority of Mark and of the Q hypothesis is the extensive concatenation of agreements between Matthew and Luke *where all three Gospels are together and where Matthew and Luke are allegedly relying upon both Q and Mark*. In another article, Argyle asserts that Streeter ignored many of these sections in *The Four Gospels*; see A. W. Argyle, "Agreement between Matthew and Luke," *ET* 73 (1961-

C. The argument from the order of incidents and sections. We now turn to one of the most well-known and, for many, most obvious arguments in behalf of Mark's priority. (The other widely used argument rests upon Mark's primitive Greek and vivid narrative detail. We will consider it in the next section, D.) Let us hear once more Streeter's formulation of this argument: "The relative order of incidents and sections in Mark is in general supported by both Matthew and Luke; where either of them deserts Mark, the other is usually found supporting him."[15]

Once again, although stated in an inexcusably prejudicial manner, Streeter has got the facts largely right. *The inference that it demonstrates the priority of Mark is obviously false.* This evidence concerning the order of incidents and sections simply is not a "reason for the priority of Mark." That such a mistaken idea could take root and become an axiom of international biblical science, capturing the minds and hearts of even the most sharpeyed men of renown, is a brilliant spot of comedy in an otherwise rather sober profession. It seems that it is not only in politics and love that men do foolish things.[16]

1962): 19-22. Farmer seems to have reached the same conclusion; see "Streeter's Fatal Omission," *The Synoptic Problem*, 90ff. It is true that F. C. Burkitt actually did absent-mindedly ignore his own promise to discuss this kind of evidence against the priority of Mark, see Farmer, 90-91. F. C. Burkitt, *The Gospel History and Its Transmission* (1906) 42 and 58ff. But Streeter is not so forgetful; in *The Four Gospels*, he does discuss the same passages he covered in his earlier article, but one might not realize this, for they are to be found here and there under the different rubrics of his many specifically constructed source hypotheses: see, for example, under "Mark-M overlaps" (259ff.), "Mark-Q overlaps" (186ff.), passages where Q is attested in one Gospel only (185), Mark-proto-Luke overlaps (280ff.), and, in case he might have overlooked some overlaps (or places where overlaps overlapped), overlaps in general (242ff.). It is immediately clear that every one of these categories has one function: to explain why a parallel in Mark can have manifest signs of lateness in such a way that Mark's general priority can still be maintained. The only trouble is, there are so many it is precisely Mark's general priority that is seriously threatened when they are considered in the aggregate. To be sure, many different hypotheses can explain these phenomena; for a Griesbachian suggestion, see Farmer 209-210.

[15]Streeter, *Four Gospels*, 151; see more fully 161-62.

[16]Farmer seems to have had his eyes opened by the initial observations on this fundamental error in B. C. Butler, *The Originality of St. Matthew: A Critique of the Two-Document Hypothesis* (1951) 62-71 [reprinted in this volume]. Going back and following step-by-step the rise of the Two-Document hypothesis, Farmer saw each new move in the direction of this fundamental mistake as it occurred. His general conclusion confirmed that of Butler, that the argument concerning the order of sections was originally a part of an

As we might expect, a lone cry of protest was heard, complaining that the argument made no sense at all, and again, as we might expect, it was promptly squelched. Indeed, H. J. Jameson, in his book, *The Origin of the Synoptic Gospels. A Revision of the Synoptic Problem* (1922), seems to have been the first to notice out loud that—as currently stated—the evidence Streeter here points to was quite *inconclusive* . . . and was open to at least four simple interpretations (we shall leave it to our learned Catholic friends to decide how many complicated interpretations): the Two-Document hypothesis, the Augustinian hypothesis (Jameson's view), the Griesbach hypothesis, and any Urgospel hypothesis. Streeter rebuked Jameson's obduracy (who else could he have meant?), chiding him for displaying a quite unprofessional unacquaintance with the work of England's *guru* in Synoptic criticism, Sir John Hawkins.

> Since there are from time to time ingenious persons who rush into print with theories to the contrary [of Mark's priority], I can only suppose, either that they have not been at pains [to study carefully J. C. Hawkins' *Horae Synopticae*], or else that—like some of the highly cultivated people who think Bacon wrote Shakespeare or that the British are the Lost Ten Tribes—they have eccentric views of what constitutes evidence.[17]

Urgospel hypothesis, first formulated by K. Lachmann, according to whom Mark was singled out as reproducing most faithfully the order of incidents and sections of a lost original Urgospel *lying behind all of the Synoptics*. But then this Urgospel shrank more and more down to Mark's size, mostly because the non-Markan parts of it were being siphoned off into another hypothesis, the so-called "Logia-source" (a precursor of Q). Finally, this Ur-Markus (as it was now being called) was simply identified with canonical Mark itself (the later Holtzmann, Burkitt, Streeter). And precisely in that moment the original argument from order lost its logical footing entirely. It had gradually changed from the claim that Mark's order best preserved an order belonging to a prior Urgospel (because by comparison Matthew and Luke have many derivations Mark does not) to a very different claim that since Mark's order is a common denominator in some sense between Matthew's and Luke's order of sections and incidents it is prior to them (which is a *non sequitur*); see Farmer, *Synoptic Problem*, 16-17, 23, 49-50, 64-67, 89-90; for a Griesbachian interpretation of the phenomenon of order, see 211-12. Further, Butler, "The Lachmann Fallacy," *Originality*, 62-71 [reprinted in this volume]; Butler opted for the Augustinian solution. N. H. Palmer has translated the essay in which Lachmann originally discussed the phenomenon of order; "Lachmann's Argument," *NTS* (1967): 368-78 [reprinted in his volume]. Certain comments at the conclusion of this article seem a bit confused and drew from Farmer a clarification the following year; W. R. Farmer, "'The Lachmann Fallacy,' " *NTS* 14 (1968): 441-43.

[17]Streeter, *Four Gospels*, 164.

Prior to this Streeter had already scoffed at Jameson's alternative solution, namely, that Mark was an abridgement of Matthew (Augustine's view).[18]

> There is nothing antecedently improbable in the idea that for certain purposes an abbreviated version of the Gospel might be desired; *but only a lunatic* would leave out Matthew's account of the Infancy, the Sermon on the Mount, and practically all the parables in order to get room for purely verbal expansion of what was retained.

Quite apart from the fact that proponents of the Augustinian hypothesis are perfectly capable of giving plausible explanations for what seemed sheer lunacy to Streeter,[20] Streeter seems to imagine that the literary abbreviation he describes would have been quite unlikely for the early church. As we shall show [elsewhere],[21] this reaction of Streeter is surprisingly inconsistent with well-known facts about the early church.

Needless to say, Jameson's objections were ignored. He did raise one question from within the Two-Document hypothesis's own terms of discussion, however, which is quite penetrating. To put it into Farmer's reformulation: if Streeter is right about the way Matthew and Luke independently or jointly seem constantly to support Mark's order, then "*why* does Matthew usually support Mark when Mark is deserted by Luke? And, as if to compound the difficulty, *why should* Luke, in a singular way support Mark when Mark is deserted by Matthew?"[22] How did it happen that *the whole* of Mark, almost, is covered precisely by one or the other or both Matthew and Luke, acting as if in divinely foreordained harmony and invisible guidance (for, as we all know, neither was aware of what the other was doing)? Just when Luke goes off into a special passage, there appears at Mark's side faithful Matthew, as if by magic, and just when Matthew suddenly departs on an errand of his own, in the nick of time back comes Luke, as if in response to a providential *bath qol*. How is it possible?

On the other hand, consider what Arrian, the compiler of Epictetus's discourses, said about the way he wrote a biography of Alexander the

---

[18]But see Dungan, 81-88.

[19]Streeter, *Four Gospels*, 158; italics added.

[20]See, for example, John Chapman, *Matthew, Mark, and Luke. A Study in the Order and Interrelation of the Synoptic Gospels* (1937).

[21]Dungan discusses this point in his essay, 93-97.

[22]Farmer, *Synoptic Problem*, 213; italics added.

Great: "Wherever Ptolemy son of Lagus and Aristobulus son of Aristobulus give an identical account in their works on Alexander, son of Philip, I follow this with absolute confidence in its accuracy. Where they disagree, I choose the version which, in my judgment, is the more credible and at the same time the more interesting of the two."[23]
    Why couldn't the author of Mark have done the same with his two sources? Does it sound so impossible? Later on we shall come back to this question of how Mark may have conflated the two other Gospels.[24] At this point, let it be emphasized that Farmer's objection seems quite well taken.

> Streeter's statement, that "the relative order of incidents and sections in Mark is in general supported by both Matthew and Luke; where either of them deserts Mark, the other is usually found supporting him," is a *tour de force* by which a serious problem for the Markan hypothesis is converted into an argument in behalf of the priority of Mark.[25]

One might understand, using Arrian's description of his method as an example, how this phenomenon would have come about if Mark were last, but it is precisely what we cannot explain if Mark is first.[26]

---

[23]*Anabasis*, I, 1, quoted from A. J. Toynbee, *Greek Historical Thought from Homer to the Age of Heraclitus* (1952) 70; further R. M. Grant, *The Earliest Lives of Jesus* (1961) 48-49.

[24]See Dungan, 90-93.

[25]Farmer, *Synoptic Problem*, 213.

[26]Ibid., 50, 289ff., where Jameson's argument is quoted *in extenso*. It was not until B. C. Butler's *The Originality of St. Matthew* (1951) appeared that a distinct shock registered throughout the tower of biblical research. Butler raised the same objection Jameson had, that Streeter and others who made use of the argument from order of incidents as if it supported exclusively the hypothesis of Mark's priority were committing "a schoolboyish error of elementary reasoning" (63). Butler went beyond Jameson to show how this error had come about as a result of the unconscious alteration of the initial assumptions of the discussion. It now appears that this objection is finally beginning to change some minds. Two recent signs: the excursus by G. M. Styler, "The Priority of Mark," in C. F. D. Moule, *The Birth of the New Testament* (1962) 223-32 [reprinted in this volume], in which he concedes that Butler proved conclusively that the argument from order will not support any particular hypothesis. Nevertheless, Styler still held to Mark's priority, mostly on the usual grounds of its primitive style and theology—Streeter's fourth argument which we shall discuss in the next section. The other straw in the wind is an article by H. Meynell, "The Synoptic Problem: Some Unorthodox Solutions," *Theology* 70 (1967): 386-97. Meynell also cites Butler as having been decisive for showing up the inconclusiveness of the argument from order, and thus opening the situation for a fresh consideration of alternative hypotheses—in this case, Pierson Parker's *The Gospel Before Mark* (1953) and the work

Before we continue, it should be noted that Streeter separates off these three "reasons for the priority of Mark" from the following two with this statement: "this conjunction and alternation of Matthew and Luke in their agreement with Mark as regards (a) content, (b) wording, (c) order, is only explicable if they are incorporating a source identical, or all but identical, with Mark."[27] We have demonstrated, instead, that Streeter has not successfully proved his case up to this point. On the contrary, Styler is completely correct when he asserts, "from these facts [namely, (a), (b), and (c) above], it is clear that, as far as material common to all three is concerned, Mark is the *middle term or link* between Matthew and Luke. . . . Now it is obvious that the priority of Mark will satisfactorily *explain* these phenomena. But its advocates have made a serious mistake in arguing (or assuming) that no *other* hypothesis will explain them."[28] Thus, before we proceed any further, it should be made clear that Streeter's case for the priority of Mark will have to depend entirely on the strength of the next two arguments alone.

D. The argument from Mark's primitive language and theology. Streeter's formulation of this very influential argument is as follows: "The primitive character of Mark is further shown by (a) the use of phrases likely to cause offense, which are omitted or toned down in the other Gospels, (b) roughness of style and grammar, and the preservation of Aramaic words."[29] Since this statement does not fully and clearly set forth all the kinds of judgments Streeter actually brings to bear, let us elaborate his view more carefully.

First, he finds a general tendency "in Matthew and Luke . . . to improve upon and refine Mark's version."[30] For example, many such improvements "have a reverential motive." How Streeter was able to decide when something was more reverential than a close parallel, and thereby later, is still something of an enigma. He apparently had in his possession

---

of W. R. Farmer. As the Pittsburgh Festival on the Gospels itself shows, however, there is much more discussion going on behind the scenes than an outsider might surmise judging from the number of articles that have appeared. [The two volumes of essays, *Jesus and Man's Hope*, in which Dungan's essay first appeared, is the collection of papers presented in connection with the Pittsburgh Festival on the Gospels—editor's note.]

[27]Streeter, *Four Gospels*, 151; cf. 162.
[28]Styler, "Priority of Mark," 225.
[29]Streeter, *Four Gospels*, 151-52, 162ff.
[30]Ibid., 162.

some sort of calibrated scale of reverentialness as it obtained in the early days of the church along which he was able confidently to range the various Gospel texts in terms of earlier or later reverentialness. Where he chanced to discover such a handy implement is a mystery to everyone, for many of us have searched for years in hopes of finding our own, but all in vain. Until we each have one and can thus check our results against those of Canon Streeter, perhaps we should set these impressions of his aside until we have carefully considered the literary evidence.

Streeter also proposed numerous literary axioms, such as (a) "better Greek" (Matthew and Luke) is later Greek; (b) repetitious, redundant style (Mark) is earlier than shorter, "succinct and carefully chosen language" (Matthew and Luke); (c) "interesting and picturesque details . . . which add nothing to the information conveyed" (Mark) is earlier; (d) "duplicate expressions" (Mark) is earlier than, as it were, single expressions: "not infrequently it happens that Matthew retains one [member of such duplicate expressions] and Luke the other;"[31] Latinized (or Aramaized) Greek (Mark) is earlier than better Greek (Matthew and Luke); (e) the presence of "the original Aramaic words used by our Lord" (Mark has eight) is earlier than not having any at all in the same stories (Luke), or only rarely (Matthew has one case—the crucifixion—but there it is Hebrew). This list is obviously redundant. What it boils down to are four contentions: (a) a roughter Greek style does not tend to stand in literary dependence upon a better, smoother Greek style; (b) a full, picturesque, conversational narrative does not tend to stem from a sparse, shorter narrative; (c) pleonastic phrases do not stand in literary dependence upon simpler phrases (this is really a part of (a) but it is so frequently singled out, it is worthy of special consideration); (d) Aramaic words are not added in the midst of narratives that originally did not have them. Add these all together and they point to an earlier, more primitive Gospel (Mark) which has been smoothed out and touched up in two later ones (Matthew and Luke).

The fact is, however, not a single one of these arguments, nor all of them together, conclusively demonstrates Mark's priority. Every single one of them has been turned, in fact, to show precisely the opposite. Mark's rougher Greek, with its Latin loanwords and heavy use of the his-

---

[31]Ibid., 164.

toric present used to be considered good evidence for a mid-second century date, according to the Tübingen School. On the other hand, the presence of the Aramaic words in Mark is not what is so interesting. It is the fact that these are so often accompanied by *translations*. Furthermore, in two healing pericopes, they are Jesus' ''healing word'' along with other magical gestures mentioned by Mark. Thus, they could easily be later additions, that is, to provide the church with the magical, healing formulas used by Jesus—naturally in his own tongue.

The sense one has in reading Mark of full, vivid, *inconsequential* detail is precisely characteristic of the second-century apocryphal acts. And as for Mark's well-known pleonastic style, could this not be the natural result of an author combining two sources?—especially because, as Streeter himself declares,[32] it seems most remarkable to view it the other way, where, as if guided by the left hand and right hand of the Holy Spirit, Matthew independently selects precisely one-half of a Markan pleonasm, and Luke the other, time after time.

Incidentally, a literary test Streeter does not seem to have discussed is one concerning the relative distribution of certain favorite phrases or formulistic expressions. It is rather interesting as Farmer describes it in Griesbachian terms. The formulas in question are of a very particular type: those that occur in one Gospel, which also occur in another Gospel at a parallel point *and also occur independently in the first Gospel elsewhere.*[33] Farmer finds that the examination of this type of literary evidence produced the following results: '' 'Favorite or habitual expressions' of Matthew are found frequently both in Mark and Luke in parallel passages where there is evidence of copying. Such formulas of Luke also occur fairly frequently in Mark. *There seem to be no such expressions characteristic of Mark, however, which show up either in Matthew or Luke.* This fact is particularly difficult to understand on Streeter's theory concerning Markan priority. For if Matthew and Luke copied Mark, presumably they would inadvertently copy at least a few of Mark's characteristic expressions into the texts of their Gospels. This would seem to be especially true in the case of Matthew, where the amount of verbatim agreement between Matthew and Mark is so great that if Matthew copied Mark it would seem to be

---

[32]Ibid.

[33]See for a list of such cases, J. C. Hawkins, *Horae Synopticae*, 2d ed. (1909) 168-69.

highly unlikely that he would have averted all characteristic expressions of Mark.''[34]

But we may argue back and forth about aspects of Streeter's literary criteria, what they mean, and so forth, "till the cows come home," and fail to come to a much more fundamental problem at the root of this entire tree of arguments. When has a single one of these four arguments ever been itself scientifically tested to see whether and to what extent it is a reliable criterion for deciding between early or late traditions? When has anyone scrutinized these axioms themselves to see how valid they are?

One would think that this had been done many times, judging from the bland confidence with which so many use them as picks and shovels to quarry out of Matthew and Luke the many hypothetical sources which so fill the literature. But unbelievable as it must seem, with the possible exception of E. DeWitt Burton's study on *Principles of Literary Criticism and the Synoptic Problem* (1904), I do not know of a single careful, scientific test of the limitations and validity of such arguments in the older literature. One would think that *somewhere* in the works of such source-theorists as Pierson Parker or Léon Vaganay or Wilhelm Bussmann one would find a careful, extensive critique of their chief literary instruments, establishing the correct way to use them, and specifying the precise weight and character the results obtained by their use should have. But such is not the case. Indeed, one cannot help drawing the conclusion that it is no doubt precisely because so many have no clear idea of the correct way to use such

---

[34]Farmer, *Synoptic Problem*, 157. For the older literary axioms of Streeter, Farmer shows how Mark's poor Greek was widely recognized in the nineteenth century as evidence of Mark's having spoiled the Greek of his sources in precisely the same fashion that the *Acts of Pilate* or the Gospel of Peter do, both of which rely on the canonical Gospels; see 120-28, 159-69. See further, L. Vaganay, *L'évangile de Pierre* (1930). 52-53, 141-46. On the Latinisms in Mark, see especially the intriguing article by P.-L. Couchoud, ''Was the Gospel of Mark Written in Latin?'' *CQ* 5 (1928): 35-79. This translation by M. S. Enslin of an earlier French article (*RHR* [1926]: 161-92) provided Couchoud with the opportunity thoroughly to revise and supplement his argument. In general, see B. W. Bacon, *Is Mark a Roman Gospel?* (1919) for documentation of Mark's ignorance of Palestinian geography, political customs, and general anti-Jewish bias. On the question of the difference between true Semitisms and the use of actual Aramaic or Hebrew words *with translations*, see Farmer, 124, 172ff.; further B. C. Butler, *Originality*, 68ff. Indeed, Mark's transliterations are curiously inconsistent with known forms of the alleged Aramaic or Hebrew words he translates and transliterates; see I. Robinowitz, '' 'Be opened' = 'Εφφαθά (Mark 7:34): Did Jesus Speak Hebrew?'' *ZNW* 53 (1962): 229-38.

criteria that the literature on the Synoptic Problem is so filled with references to hypothetical sources and their constant, uncontrollable "overlapping."

At least the Augustinians (for example, Lummis, Jameson, Chapman, Butler, Argyle) have this advantage: their view gives one a much easier conscience. With them one is not so likely to lie awake nights wondering how to figure out how much Q overlapped M.[35] To join up with them, all one needs is to postulate the altogether charming scene of the aged St. Peter, preaching at last in Imperial Rome, holding a copy of Matthew in his hand as an aid to his fading memory. At his feet sits St. Mark, faithfully copying down his every word. Thus St. Peter, his memory gloriously jogged, reminiscences on the times when the Lord walked among men, expanding slightly the sparse, concentrated accounts of Matthew from his own memory of the things that happened and Mark records those vivid narratives in the Gospel called by his name.[36] Perhaps I haven't described this view as persuasively as it could be, but the general idea should be clear enough: Mark's brevity in over-all scope and contents, as well as its frequently considerably expanded sections where it does contain Matthean material, can be explained without recourse to any hypothetical sources, and, at the same time, one is able to take into account and comply with the traditions handed down by the early church fathers concerning the origins of these two Gospels, something the Two-Document hypothesis must disregard.

However this may be, a careful, exhaustive *testing of these common literary arguments* has finally appeared. *The Tendencies of the Synoptic Tradition*, by E. P. Sanders, is devoted precisely to this question, namely, the reliability of such arguments as the presence of Semitisms, good or poor grammatical constructions, longer or shorter versions of the same pericopes, and the like. The testing ground selected could not have been more scientifically conceived, for Sanders carried out his research, not only within the canonical Gospels, and compared the results of that with conclusions arrived at from a comparison between the canonical Gospels and the aprocryphal Gospels, he also checked out comparisons between these writings and citations in the early Fathers. Then, equally significant, Sanders worked through the important manuscript traditions, the Caesa-

---

[35]See Streeter, *Four Gospels*, 243-44, 249-54, 181-85.
[36]See, for example, J. Chapman, *Matthew, Mark, and Luke* (1937) 83-93.

rean, the Western, the Alexandrian, and others, to see how they supported
or conflicted with these literary axioms. He arrived at an astonishing conclusion: *"there are no hard and fast laws of the development of the Synoptic tradition. On all counts the tradition developed in opposite
directions.* It became both longer and shorter, both more and less detailed,
and both more and less Semitic. . . . For this reason, dogmatic statements
that a certain characteristic proves a certain passage to be earlier than another are *never justified."*[37]

Sanders's exhaustive study indicates that it *might* be true that the explanation of Mark's rough Greek, vivid detail and small size, as compared
to Matthew and Luke, is because it is older, that is, more primitive, than
they are. But it *might* be just as true that all of these characteristics are signs
of its lateness, putting it in the group of early second century writings em-
anating from Rome which have many of the same features it does. In short,
Streeter's argument for the priority of Mark using style, grammar, and vocabulary collapses, since the evidence is quite inconclusive.

---

[37]E. P. Sanders, *The Tendencies of the Synoptic Tradition,* SNTS Monograph Series 9
(1969) 272; italics added. This extraordinarily thorough treatment fills a large gap in the
literature. Long overdue is Sanders's introductory discussion in which he points to case
after case in which these arguments have been used in utterly contradictory ways by various
men, leaving the entire discussion in a state of grave disarray (1-29). Unfortunately, Sanders did not discuss the only other full-length test of typical literary-critical axioms which
has appeared: M. P. Brown's masterfully conceived and executed analysis of arguments
frequently employed to decide the authenticity or inauthenticity of certain Pauline letters
such as Colossians or Ephesians; see *The Authentic Writings of Ignatius. A Study of Linguistic Criteria* (1963). Using the two sets of Ignatian letters, whose authenticity and inauthenticity respectively have been conclusively verified through manuscript evidence,
Brown ran tests on such commonly used criteria as length of sentences, use of certain prepositions, favorite grammatical constructions, the appearance of key concepts or terms, and
so on. In his conclusion he ranked in degree of reliability each of the criteria, giving the
necessary warnings and suggestions on the proper way to employ them. More studies like
these are badly needed, for example, in the whole area of how copying was carried out in
antiquity; just how copying, conflating material, abridging, expanding, and so on was carried out. We need more scientifically verified guidelines to help us understand what is
probable and what is not in this whole area. T. R. Rosché's penetrating critique, "The
Words of Jesus and the Future of the 'Q' Hypothesis," *JBL* 79 (1960): 210-220 [reprinted
in this volume], is actually a petition for just this sort of information. An excellent step in
this direction is the study of A. Pelletier, *Flavius Josèph, Adaptateur de la Letter d'Aristée.
Une réaction atticisante contre la Koiné* (1962). The best general discussion is still that of
H. J. Cadbury, *The Making of Luke-Acts,* 2d ed. (1958).

In my opinion, although Streeter never said it in so many words, his insulting crack about Jameson's proposal to adopt the Augustinian view reveals another argument which was quite decisive for him. It was not a literary argument exactly, but rather a historical one. It seems to have been impossible for Streeter to imagine why anyone in the early church who had Matthew (much less Matthew *and Luke* as the Griesbach hypothesis must contend) would even want to create out of them such a truncated, sayingsless abridgment as Mark represents. What purpose would such a mutilation serve that could not be surpassingly better served by either Matthew or Luke (much less both together) in a far more glorious way? This crucial question must be answered before Mark's lateness can ever seem very plausible, no matter how neat and simple the Griesbach solution may be on purely literary grounds.[38]

E. The argument from the distribution of Markan and non-Markan material in Matthew and Luke. Streeter gives a very roundabout statement of this argument in the Synopsis at the head of his chapter,[39] so we shall pass straight to the most crucial part of it which he brings up later in the text: "subsequent to the Temptation story, there is not a single case in which Matthew and Luke agree in inserting a piece of Q material . . . into the same context of Mark."[40] Connoisseurs of Two-Document *arcana* seem especially fond of this argument. To be adept enough to bandy it about in public is immediate proof of a very advanced degree of initiation into the mysteries. The real mystery is why anyone (including myself) ever took it seriously. For one thing, Streeter has no business offering as an argument for the priority of Mark something which, as B. C. Butler rightly complained, contained "no new *evidence* in proof of [the Two-Document] theory, but a series of deductions from it."[41]

But not only is this not a "reason for the priority of Mark," Streeter repeatedly contradicted the statement itself in other contexts. It would be fitting to reiterate what Jameson originally said about this.

> Now [Streeter's statement] looks very convincing, until we remember the well-known fact, which Canon Streeter himself draws attention to in more than one place, that, except in the chapters dealing with John the Baptist and the Temptation

---

[38]Dungan deals with this matter later in his article, 93-97.

[39]Streeter, *Four Gospels*, 152.

[40]Ibid., 165.

[41]Butler, *Originality*, 67; italics added.

(where the contexts agree), *Luke does not attempt to insert his "Q" matter into the Markan context at all, but collects it all into some three or four large sections, which are interposed between* similar large sections of Markan matter.[42]

As a matter of fact, Streeter did not think Luke was inserting anything into the Markan outline, but precisely the reverse. According to him, what Luke really did was insert chunks of Mark into *another Gospel*: "this combined non-Markan document [namely Q + L, which he called "proto-Luke," and which was a Gospel; see 199 ff.] was regarded by Luke as his *main source* and supplied the framework into which he fitted extracts of Mark."[43] Or again, "the *non-Markan* sections [of Luke] represent a single document, and to Luke this was the framework into which he inserted at convenient places, extracts from Mark."[44]

Now although his argument is not really an argument at all but a fallacy (even if it were not, one could hardly decide what Streeter means to assert since he seems to be claiming contradictory things), nevertheless, this "fifth reason" is important and has one great virtue. It shows how closely tied together the priority of Mark is with the assumption of a hypothetical sayings-collection. The two are inextricably intertwined. This state of affairs may be explained historically by remembering that originally it was not Mark which was understood to be joined with Q, but *Urmarcus*. Originally, there were *two* hypothetical sources understood to lie within the three Synoptic Gospels. As Farmer comments:

> The Markan hypothesis was first regarded as "scientifically established" only in connection with an Ur-gospel, on the one hand, and Papias' *Logia* on the other. Without these two ideological presuppositions, pure products of the creative imagination of Lessing and Schleiermacher, the Markan hypothesis, in the nineteenth century, would . . . probably never have been accepted by New Testament scholars acquainted with the realities of the Synoptic Problem.[45]

If this is the case, we should be very mistaken to think that we have successfully destroyed the grounds for believing in the priority of Mark just because not a single argument Streeter advanced in behalf of it has been left standing. Never mind that the very definition of Q requires the priority of Mark to be soundly established. Even though this must strike the logi-

---

[42]Jameson, *Origin*, 15-16; cf. A. M. Farrer, "On Dispensing with Q," 66 [reprinted in this volume].

[43]Streeter, *Four Gospels*, 167-168; italics added.

[44]Ibid., 208.

[45]Farmer, *Synoptic Problem*, 24-25.

cally-minded as a bit strange, the fact is the priority of Mark has been traditionally defended directly, and, as it were, indirectly—that is, from arguments for Q. Streeter is a classic example of this procedure. Thus even though one head of the "Pushmi-pullyu" has been lopped off, the beast is still very much alive and the other head still intact! So now we must go round and scrutinize the other end of this hypothesis, for it seems that the existence of Q has always been essential to the argument for Mark's priority—precisely as the loophole to invoke anytime one finds a pericope that is more primitive in Matthew and/or Luke when they were supposedly using Mark: the blessed overlap! We are grateful to Mr. Styler for putting this with exquisite aplomb when he casually let on how scholars really went about using the Q hypothesis in their work: "it was not necessary to maintain that Mark's version must at every point be older than Matthew's parallel version, since it was possible to say that *anything in Matthew* which in fact seemed more original than Mark could have been derived from Q."[46] With that kind of system, how could you lose? It recalls Bert Taylor's humorous ditty about the Brontosaur:

Behold the mighty brontosaur,
Famous in prehistoric lore,
Not only for his power and strength
But also for his intellectual length.
You will observe by these remains,
The creature had two sets of brains!
One in his head (the usual place),
The other at his spinal base.
Thus he could reason a priori
As well as a posteriori.
No problem bothered him a bit;
He made both head and tail of it.
If one brain found the pressure strong,
It passed a few ideas along.
If something slipped his forward mind,
'Twas rescued by the one behind.
And if in error he was caught,
He had a saving afterthought.
Thus he could think, without congestion,
Upon both sides of every question.
Oh, gaze upon this model beast—
Defunct ten million years, at least!

---

[46]Styler, "The Priority of Mark," 223, italics added [reprinted in this volume].

A NEW
INTRODUCTION
TO THE PROBLEM

W. R. Farmer*

Matthew appears to be the earliest Gospel, and Luke seems next in order. Matthew was evidently used extensively by the author of Luke, who undoubtedly had access to other written materials besides Matthew. But Luke seems to be dependent on Matthew for the general order and form of his Gospel. Mark throughout the whole extent of his Gospel seems to be working closely with texts of Matthew and Luke before him. Arguments against this view are unconvincing, whereas it is possible to raise serious objections to alternative views that have been proposed. In sixteen steps, Farmer presents an argument intended to support the view that Mark wrote after Matthew and Luke and is dependent on both, and also that Luke was dependent on Matthew.

1. The similiarity between Matthew, Mark, and Luke is such as to justify the assertion that they stand in some kind of literary relationship to one another.

2. There are eighteen and only eighteen fundamental ways in which three documents, among which there exists some kind of direct literary dependence, may be related to one another.

*W. R. Farmer, "A New Introduction to the Problem," *The Synoptic Problem: A Critical Appraisal,* 2d ed. (Macon GA: Mercer University Press, 1976) 199-232.

3. While it is possible to conceive of an infinite number of variations of these eighteen basic relationships by positing additional hypothetical documents, these eighteen should be given first consideration.

4. Only six of the eighteen basic hypothetical arrangements are viable.

5. There are isolable and objectively identifiable categories of literary phenomena that have played a prominent role in the history of the Synoptic Problem that when properly understood are more readily explicable when Mark is placed third than when either Matthew or Luke is placed third.

6. The phenomena of agreement and disagreement in the respective order and content of material in each of the Synoptic Gospels constitute a category of literary phenomena that is more readily explicable on the hypothesis that places Mark third with Matthew and Luke before him than on any alternative hypothesis.

7. The minor agreements of Matthew and Luke against Mark constitute a second category of literary phenomena that is more readily explicable on a hypothesis where Mark is regarded as third with Matthew and Luke before him than on any alternative hypothesis.

8. A positive correlation exists between agreement in order and agreement in wording among the Synoptic Gospels that is more readily explicable on the hypothesis that Mark was written after Matthew and Luke and is the result of a redactional procedure in which Mark made use of both Matthew and Luke.

9. It is possible to understand the redactional process through which Mark went, on the hypothesis that he composed his Gospel based primarily on Matthew and Luke.

10. The most probable explanation for the extensive agreement between Matthew and Luke is that the author of one made use of the work of the other.

11. The hypothesis that Luke made use of Matthew is in accord with Luke's declaration in the prologue to his Gospel concerning his purpose in writing.

12. Assuming that there is direct literary dependence between Matthew and Luke, internal evidence indicates that the direction of dependence is that of Luke upon Matthew.

13. The weight of external evidence is against the hypothesis that Matthew was written after Luke.

14. The weight of external evidence is against the hypothesis that Matthew was written after Mark.

15. That Mark was written after both Matthew and Luke is in accord with the earliest and best external evidence on the question.

16. A historical-critical analysis of the Synoptic tradition, utilizing both literary-historical and form-critical canons of criticism, supports a hypothesis that recognizes that Matthew is in many respects secondary to the life situation of Jesus, and the primitive Palestinian Christian com-

munity, but that his Gospel was nonetheless copied by Luke, and that Mark was secondary to both Matthew and Luke, and frequently combined their respective texts.

The Synoptic Problem is difficult but not necessarily insoluble. Matthew, Mark, and Luke were almost certainly written in some particular chronological order. Reduced to its simplest terms the Synoptic Problem sets the task of discovering that order. However important the part oral tradition and other written sources may have played in the composition of the synoptic Gospels, the problem of determining which was written first, which second, and which third still persists. One of the three was written before the other two. One was written after the first, and before the third. And one was written after the other two.[1]

If a critic, on the basis of his own research, thinks that he knows the order in which Matthew, Mark, and Luke were written, and is asked to write about this question, there are two possible courses of action for him

---

[1] A critic's conviction of the proper order in which the Synoptic Gospels were written, however, does not necessarily enable him to prove his beliefs. Even if his understanding is right, it is not likely that he will be able to settle the question with finality in the mind of another critic. This is partly because it is not practical for him to set forth all the arguments and evidence that conceivably could lead impartial investigators to the conclusion that the question had been settled once and for all. Certainly, to retrace the history of his own thinking on the Synoptic Problem, however interesting that might be, and even instructive, would have dubious probative value.

But if it is impractical for a critic to set forth all the arguments and evidence that might conceivably lead impartial investigators to the solution of the Synoptic Problem he believes to be correct, what can he do? If the solution he thinks is the correct one is a solution that has already been proved, he is first obligated to review the history of the Synoptic Problem to show why his solution was first proposed favorably, and why critical opinion in favor of this solution did not develop into a lasting consensus. But once this has been done, how could he proceed to formulate his argument? He could next attempt to clarify for his readers the nature of the problem, and then suggest a way to approach the problem which will lead the interested investigator more readily to more fruitful results than any other known way.

It follows from all this that the difficulty of the Synoptic Problem does not justify an attitude of resignation. Attention has been drawn to the complexity of the problem in order to discourage the reader from thinking that the work of another investigator would ever produce in his mind that degree of reasonable certainty and conviction that more justly comes from his own work of verification and further discovery. Whether a given reader will ever come to the point that he recognizes that there is no longer any reason for him to doubt that a particular solution is the true solution will and should depend upon his own further investigations. There is no substitute for firsthand study of the Gospels themselves.

to take. (1) He can attempt to write as if in fact he did not know the truth, and strive to approach the problem with an objectivity that would reflect no particular point of view. In that case, if he set forth the solution he thought to be correct, he would be obligated to treat other possible solutions equally fully. The resulting study would be very extensive, and therefore no such book has ever been written. One reason it has never been written is that the number of solutions which have been propounded is so very great that the human heart and hand falters before a task of such magnitude. (2) Another course he can follow is to write about the problem from his own point of view. In this case he is obligated to disclose to his readers the solution to the Synoptic Problem he accepts, and indicate something of the degree of probability he attaches to his views on the matter.

The latter course is followed in this book.[2] And the time has now come for the reader to know the point of view from which this book has been written.

Matthew appears to be the earliest Gospel, and Luke seems next in order. Matthew was evidently used extensively by the author of Luke, who also may have been the author of Acts. Luke undoubtedly had access to other written materials besides Matthew, and some of this material was probably parallel to material which Luke also found in Matthew. But Luke seems to be dependent on Matthew for the general order and form of his Gospel, and in many passages he clearly copied his text from Matthew.

There seems to be no sound literary or historical ground on which to base a denial of the premise that Mark is throughout the whole extent of his Gospel working closely with texts of Matthew and Luke before him.

It is probable that there were other written sources and some kind of oral tradition also available to each of the Evangelists. Matthew and Luke possibly had access to one or more common written sources, but the use of hypothetical written sources (and/or oral tradition) by the Evangelists is not the best way to account for the major phenomena of similarity, and the extensive verbal agreement among Matthew, Mark, and Luke.

On the whole, this view of the matter is not new. Many investigators have held essentially the same view as the best solution to the problem of the Synoptic relationship. The works of critics who have held this view are

---

[2]The reference is to Farmer's *The Synoptic Problem*, in which the section reproduced here is chapter VI (editor's note).

more cogent than what has been written by those who adhere to alternate views. That is, the arguments of these critics can be verified by an appeal to the phenomena of the Gospels themselves in a way that is not true of other hypotheses.

Arguments against the view that Matthew is the earliest Gospel, Luke second, and Mark third, are unconvincing. On the other hand, it is possible to raise serious objections to alternate views that have been proposed.

Thus it has been possible in Chapters I through V[3] to review the history of the Synoptic Problem in such a way as to help the reader understand that this view was abandoned in favor of another that was less satisfactory, for reasons which scholars would not justify.

Within this particular historical context, the reader finds himself confronted with a view which calls into question a long-established consensus concerning one of the Gospels, namely, Mark. This view proposes for that Gospel a relationship to Matthew and Luke, that is virtually the opposite to the relationship which it has on the usual view. It may be helpful, therefore, if an effort is made to cut through the whole history of the problem and attempt to follow an argument intended to support the view that Mark wrote after Matthew and Luke and is dependent upon both, and also that Luke was dependent on Matthew.

Although the particular argument which follows draws upon much that has been done previously, both in form and content, it is to a large extent new. It is intended to encourage a serious reconsideration of a solution which was first formulated in the eighteenth century, flourished in the first half of the nineteenth century, but which for the past one hundred years has been eclipsed by the two-document hypothesis.

The argument is presented in steps. At first it is important to take one step at a time and always in order. But as one advances through the initial steps, it matters little in which order he takes the later steps, some of which indeed may be skipped without serious loss. That is, the cogency of the argument does not presuppose that the separable theses presented at each step in the argument are like the ''links of a chain,'' which, as a chain, can be no stronger than the weakest link. On the contrary, the cogency of his argument depends upon a web of evidence structured by innumerable arguments, some of which touch only the most minute points, but which, nevertheless, taken together with all the rest, constitute a supportive basis

---

[3]See again Farmer, *Synoptic Problem*.

that will bear the full weight of the conclusion: "It is historically probable that Mark was written after Matthew and Luke and was dependent upon both." The destruction of one or more of the strands of evidence which have been woven into this web would not destroy the web. Nor can it be doubted that others in favor of the same conclusion may see ways in which the web of evidence may be strengthened by adding an argument here and by reconstructing another one there.

It may be possible to damage the web so that it can no longer hold up the conclusion it has been spun to support. But that will not happen unless one is able to cut one or more of the main strands set forth in the initial steps, or unless one is able to destroy several closely related theses supporting some decisive section in the web of argumentation.

Step One

Thesis: *The similarity between Matthew, Mark, and Luke is such as to justify the assertion that they stand in some kind of literary relationship to one another.*

The nature of this similarity is such as to warrant the judgment that the literary relationship between these Gospels could be one involving direct copying. That is, the degree of verbatim agreement in Greek between any two of these three Gospels is as high or higher than that which generally exists between documents where it is known that the author of one copied the text of the other. The same degree of verbatim agreement could be accounted for on the hypothesis that each Evangelist independently copied one or more common or genetically related sources. But this alternative way of explaining the phenomena of agreement between any two Gospels should not be utilized until after an attempt has been made to explain it on the simplest terms, namely on the hypothesis that one Evangelist copied the work of the other. The reason for this procedure is not that the simplest explanation is necessarily the correct one, but that it is wrong to multiply hypothetical possibilities unnecessarily. There is nothing wrong in hypothecating the existence of an otherwise unknown source or sources, if there exists evidence that is best explained thereby. But for the sake of economy this is not to be done without good reason. This is not an infallible rule, but it is accepted procedure in literary criticism as well as in other disciplines, and one which commends itself by the results achieved

when it is followed, compared to those which are achieved when it is ignored.

The following specimens of texts of Matthew, Mark, and Luke are presented as illustrations of the kind of verbal similarity which exists among these Gospels, and which suggests the possibility of direct copying.

Every word underlined is found in the parallel text(s) of the other Gospel(s) printed on the same page. If the underlining is unbroken, the agreement is exact with reference to case, declension, number and gender of nouns, articles, pronouns, adjectives, and participles: and exact with reference to mood, voice, tense, number and person of verbs, etc. Broken underlining indicates agreement as to the word concerned, but where the agreement is not exact in one or more points of grammar. Differences in the endings of words merely occasioned by the circumstance of their position in the sentence, like the movable ν, or by the circumstance of the quality of the initial letter of the word following as with the ending of the negative οὐ, are disregarded.

A continuation of underlining between words indicates that the same words not only occur in the other gospel(s) printed on the same page, but that they also occur in exactly the same order. Agreement in word order between the last word in a line and the first word in the next line is indicated by an extension of the underlining into the left-hand margin at the beginning of the second line.

THE FEEDING OF THE FOUR THOUSAND
(Not in Luke)

Matthew 15: 32-39

Ὁ δὲ Ἰησοῦς προσκαλεσάμενος τοὺς μαθητὰς αὐτοῦ εἶπεν· σπλαγχνίζομαι ἐπὶ τὸν ὄχλον ὅτι ἤδη ἡμέραι τρεῖς προσμένουσίν μοι καὶ οὐκ ἔχουσιν τί φάγωσιν· καὶ ἀπολῦσαι αὐτοὺς νήστεις οὐ θέλω, μήποτε ἐκλυθῶσιν ἐν τῇ ὁδῷ· καὶ λέγουσιν αὐτῷ οἱ μαθηταί· πόθεν ἡμῖν ἐν ἐρημίᾳ ἄρτοι τοσοῦτοι ὥστε χορτάσαι ὄχλον τοσοῦτον; καὶ λέγει αὐτοῖς ὁ Ἰησοῦς· πόσους ἄρτους ἔχετε; οἱ δὲ εἶπαν· ἑπτά, καὶ ὀλίγα ἰχθύδια. καὶ παραγγείλας τῷ ὄχλῳ ἀναπεσεῖν ἐπὶ τὴν γῆν, ἔλαβεν τοὺς ἑπτὰ ἄρτους καὶ τοὺς ἰχθύας καὶ εὐχαριστήσας ἔκλασεν καὶ ἐδίδου τοῖς μαθηταῖς, οἱ δὲ μαθηταὶ τοῖς ὄχλοις· καὶ ἔφαγον πάντες καὶ ἐχορτάσθησαν, καὶ τὸ περισσεῦον τῶν κλασμάτων

ἦραν ἑπτὰ σπυρίδας πλήρεις. οἱ δὲ ἐσθίοντες ἦσαν τετρακ-
ισχίλιοι ἄνδρες χωρὶς γυναικῶν καὶ παιδίων. καὶ ἀπολύσας
τοὺς ὄχλους ἐνέβη εἰς τὸ πλοῖον καὶ ἦλθεν εἰς τὰ ὅρια Μα-
γαδάν.

Mark 8:1-10

Ἐν ἐκείναις ταῖς ἡμέραις πάλιν πολλοῦ ὄχλου ὄντος καὶ μὴ
ἐχόντων τί φάγωσιν, προσκαλεσάμενος τοὺς μαθητὰς λέγει αὐ-
τοῖς· σπλαγχνίζομαι ἐπὶ τὸν ὄχλον, ὅτι ἤδη ἡμέραι τρεῖς
προσμένουσίν μοι καὶ οὐκ ἔχουσιν τί φάγωσιν· καὶ ἐὰν ἀπολύσω
αὐτους νήστεις εἰς οἶκον αὐτῶν, ἐκλυθήσονται ἐν τῇ ὁδῷ· καί
τινες αὐτῶν ἀπὸ μακρόθεν ἥκασιν. καὶ ἀπεκρίθησαν αὐτῷ οἱ
μαθηταὶ αὐτοῦ ὅτι πόθεν τούτους δυνήσεταί τις ὧδε χορτάσαι
ἄρτων ἐπ' ἐρημίας; καὶ ἠρώτα αὐτούς· πόσους ἔχετε ἄρτους; οἱ
δὲ εἶπαν· ἑπτά. καὶ παραγγέλλει τῷ ὄχλῳ ἀναπεσεῖν ἐπὶ τῆς
γῆς· καὶ λαβὼν τοὺς ἑπτὰ ἄρτους εὐχαριστήσας ἔκλασεν καὶ
ἐδίδου τοῖς μαθηταῖς αὐτοῦ ἵνα παρατιθῶσιν, καὶ παρέθηκαν τῷ
ὄχλῳ. καὶ εἶχον ἰχθύδια ὀλίγα· καὶ εὐλογήσας αὐτὰ εἶπεν καὶ
ταῦτα παρατιθέναι. καὶ ἔφαγον καὶ ἐχορτάσθησαν, καὶ ἦραν περ-
ισσεύματα κλασμάτων ἑπτὰ σπυρίδας. ἦσαν δὲ ὡς τετρακισχί-
λιοι. καὶ ἀπέλυσεν αὐτούς. καὶ εὐθὺς ἐμβὰς εἰς τὸ πλοῖον μετὰ
τῶν μαθητῶν αὐτοῦ ἦλθεν εἰς τὰ μέρη Δαλμανουθά.

Often the agreement between Matthew and Mark is more extensive than
in this passage, though many times it is less so. This passage, however, is not
atypical. Compare Matthew 26:20-29 ‖ Mark 14:17-25 and Matthew 26:36-
46 ‖ Mark 14:32-42 as examples where the verbatim agreement between Matthew and Mark is greater than in the specimens cited.

JESUS IN THE SYNAGOGUE AT CAPERNAUM
(Not in Matthew)

Mark 1:21-28

Καὶ εἰσπορεύονται εἰς Καφαρναούμ. καὶ εὐθὺς τοῖς σάββασιν
εἰσελθὼν εἰς τὴν συναγωγὴν ἐδίδασκεν. καὶ ἐξεπλήσσοντο ἐπὶ τῇ
διδαχῇ αὐτοῦ· ἦν γὰρ διδάσκων αὐτοὺς ὡς ἐξουσίαν ἔχων, καὶ
οὐχ ὡς οἱ γραμματεῖς. καὶ εὐθὺς ἦν ἐν τῇ συναγωγῇ αὐτῶν ἄνθρωπος ἐν πνεύματι ἀκαθάρτῳ, καὶ ἀνέκραξεν λέγων· τί ἡμῖν καὶ

σοί, Ἰησοῦ Ναζαρηνέ; ἦλθες ἀπολέσαι ἡμᾶς. οἶδά σε τίς εἶ, ὁ ἅγιος τοῦ θεοῦ. καὶ ἐπετίμησεν αὐτῷ ὁ Ἰησοῦς λέγων· φιμώθητι καὶ ἔξελθε ἐξ αὐτοῦ. καὶ σπαράξαν αὐτὸν τὸ πνεῦμα τὸ ἀκάθαρτον καὶ φωνῆσαν φωνῇ μεγάλῃ ἐξῆλθεν ἐξ αὐτοῦ. καὶ ἐθαμβήθησαν ἅπαντες, ὥστε συζητεῖν αὐτοὺς λέγοντας· τί ἐστιν τοῦτο; διδαχὴ καινὴ κατ' ἐξουσίαν· καὶ τοῖς πνεύμασι τοῖς ἀκαθάρτοις ἐπιτάσσει, καὶ ὑπακούουσιν αὐτῷ. καὶ ἐξῆλθεν ἡ ἀκοὴ αὐτοῦ εὐθὺς πανταχοῦ εἰς ὅλην τὴν περίχωρον τῆς Γαλιλαίας.

Luke 4:31-37
Καὶ κατῆλθεν εἰς Καφαρναοὺμ πόλιν τῆς Γαλιλαίας. καὶ ἦν διδάσκων αὐτοὺς ἐν τοῖς σάββασιν. καὶ ἐξεπλήσσοντο ἐπὶ τῇ διδαχῇ αὐτοῦ, ὅτι ἐν ἐξουσίᾳ ἦν ὁ λόγος αὐτοῦ. καὶ ἐν τῇ συναγωγῇ ἦν ἄνθρωπος ἔχων πνεῦμα δαιμονίου ἀκαθάρτου, καὶ ἀνέκραξεν φωνῇ μεγάλῃ· ἔα, τί ἡμῖν καὶ σοί, Ἰησοῦ Ναζαρηνέ; ἦλθες ἀπολέσαι ἡμᾶς; οἶδά σε τίς εἶ, ὁ ἅγιος τοῦ θεοῦ. καὶ ἐπετετίμησεν αὐτῷ ὁ Ἰησοῦς λέγων· φιμώθητι καὶ ἔξελθε ἀπ' αὐτοῦ. καὶ ῥῖψαν αὐτὸν τὸ δαιμόνιον εἰς τὸ μέσον ἐξῆλθεν ἀπ' αὐτοῦ μηδὲν βλάψαν αὐτόν. καὶ ἐγένετο θάμβος ἐπὶ πάντας, καὶ συνελάλουν πρὸς ἀλλήλους λέγοντες· τίς ὁ λόγος οὗτος, ὅτι ἐν ἐξουσίᾳ καὶ δυνάμει ἐπιτάσσει τοῖς ἀκαθάρτοις πνεύμασιν καὶ ἐξέρχονται; καὶ ἐξεπορεύετο ἦχος περὶ αὐτοῦ εἰς πάντα τόπον τῆς περιχώρου.

The verbatim agreement between Mark and Luke is not as extensive as between Mark and Matthew. But the reader can readily see from this specimen and a comparison of the following examples that the verbal similarity between Mark and Luke is quite extensive: Mark 5:1-20 ‖ Luke 8:26-39; Mark 9:37-40 ‖ Luke 9:48-50; Mark 10:17-31 ‖ Luke 18:18-30; Mark 12:38b-44 ‖ Luke 20:46-21:4.

THE CENTURION'S SERVANT
(Not in Mark)

Matthew 8:7-10
λέγει αὐτῷ· ἐγὼ ἐλθὼν θεραπεύσω αὐτόν. ἀποκριθεὶς δὲ ὁ ἑκατόνταρχος ἔφη· κύριε, οὐκ εἰμὶ ἱκανὸς ἵνα μου ὑπὸ τὴν στέγην εἰσέλθῃς· ἀλλὰ μόνον εἰπὲ λόγῳ, καὶ ἰαθήσεται ὁ παῖς μου. καὶ γὰρ ἐγὼ ἄνθρωπός εἰμι ὑπὸ ἐξουσίαν, ἔχων ὑπ' ἐμαυτὸν στρα-

τιώτας, καὶ λέγω τούτῳ· πορεύθητι, καὶ πορεύεται καὶ ἄλλῳ· ἔρχου, καὶ ἔρχεται, καὶ τῷ δούλῳ μου· ποίησον τοῦτο, καὶ ποιεῖ. ἀκούσας δὲ ὁ Ἰησοῦς ἐθαύμασεν καὶ εἶπεν τοῖς ἀκολουθοῦσιν· ἀμὴν λέγω ὑμῖν, παρ' οὐδενὶ τοσαύτην πίστιν ἐν τῷ Ἰσραὴλ εὗρον.

Luke 7:6-9

Ὁ δὲ Ἰησοῦς ἐπορεύετο σὺν αὐτοῖς. ἤδη δὲ αὐτοῦ οὐ μακρὰν ἀπέχοντος ἀπὸ τῆς οἰκίας, ἔπεμψεν φίλους ὁ ἑκατοντάρχης λέγων αὐτῷ· κύριε, μὴ σκύλλου· οὐ γὰρ ἱκανός εἰμι ἵνα ὑπὸ τὴν στέγην μου εἰσέλῃς· διὸ οὐδὲ ἐμαυτὸν ἠξίωσα πρὸς σὲ ἐλθεῖν· ἀλλὰ εἰπὲ λόγῳ, καὶ ἰαθήτω ὁ παῖς μου. καὶ γὰρ ἐγὼ ἄνθρωπός εἰμι ὑπὸ ἐξουσίαν τασσόμενος ἔχων ὑπ' ἐμαυτὸν στρατιώτας, καὶ λέγω τούτῳ· πορεύθητι, καὶ πορεύεται, καὶ ἄλλῳ· ἔρχου, καὶ ἔρχεται, καὶ τῷ δούλῳ μου· ποίησον τοῦτο, καὶ ποιεῖ. ἀκούσας δὲ ταῦτα ὁ Ἰησοῦς ἐθαύμασεν αὐτόν, καὶ στραφεὶς. τῷ ἀκολουθοῦντι αὐτῷ ὄχλῳ εἶπεν· λέγω ὑμῖν, οὐδὲ ἐν τῷ Ἰσραὴλ τοσαύτην πίστιν εὗρον.

The verbatim agreement between Luke and Matthew in this passage is equaled or exceeded at many points. Compare for example: Luke 3:7-9 ‖ Matthew 3:7-10; Luke 4:1-13 ‖ Matthew 4:1-11; Luke 6:41-42 ‖ Matthew 7:3-5; Luke 7:18-35 ‖ Matthew 11:2-19; Luke 11:29-32 ‖ Matthew 12:38-42; Luke 13:34-35 ‖ Matthew 23:37-39.

Not only is there extensive agreement between any two of the Synoptic Gospels, but there are many passages which are characterized by extensive agreement among all three. For example: Matthew 8:2-4 ‖ Mark 1:40-45 ‖ Luke 5:12-16.

THE HEALING OF A LEPER

Matthew 8:2-4
καὶ ἰδοὺ λεπρὸς προσελθὼν προσεκύνει αὐτῷ λέγων· Κύριε, ἐὰν θέλῃς, δύνασαί με καθαρίσαι. καὶ ἐκτείνας τὴν χεῖρα ἥψατο αὐτοῦ λέγων· θέλω, καθαρίσθητι. καὶ εὐθέως ἐκαθαρίσθη αὐτοῦ ἡ λέπρα. καὶ λέγει αὐτῷ ὁ Ἰησοῦς· ὅρα μηδενὶ εἴπῃς, ἀλλὰ ὕπαγε σεαυτὸν δεῖξον τῷ ἱερεῖ καὶ προσένεγκον τὸ δῶρον ὃ προσέταξεν Μωϋσῆς, εἰς μαρτύριον αὐτοῖς.

Mark 1:40-45
Καὶ ἔρχεται πρὸς αὐτὸν λεπρὸς παρακαλῶν αὐτὸν καὶ γονυπετῶν

λέγων αὐτῷ ὅτι ἐὰν θέλῃς δύνασαί με καθαρίσαι. καὶ σπλαγχνι-
σθεὶς ἐκτείνας τὴν χεῖρα αὐτοῦ ἥψατο καὶ λέγει αὐτῷ· θέλω,
καθαρίσθητι. καὶ εὐθὺς ἀπῆλθεν ἀπ' αὐτοῦ ἡ λέπρα, καὶ ἐκαθαρίσθη. καὶ ἐμβριμησάμενος αὐτῷ εὐθὺς ἐξέβαλεν αὐτόν. καὶ λέγει αὐτῷ· ὅρα μηδενὶ μηδὲν εἴπῃς, ἀλλὰ ὕπαγε σεαυτὸν δεῖξον
τῷ ἱερεῖ καὶ προσένεγκε περὶ τοῦ καθαρισμοῦ σου ἃ προσέταξεν
Μωϋσῆς, εἰς μαρτύριον αὐτοῖς. ὁ δὲ ἐξελθὼν ἤρξατο κηρύσσειν
πολλὰ καὶ διαφημίζειν τὸν λόγον, ὥστε μηκέτι αὐτὸν δύνασθαι
φανερῶς εἰς πόλιν εἰσελθεῖν, ἀλλ' ἔξω ἐπ' ἐρήμοις τόποις ἦν·
καὶ ἤρχοντο πρὸς αὐτὸν πάντοθεν.

Luke 5:12-16
Καὶ ἐγένετο ἐν τῷ εἶναι αὐτὸν ἐν μιᾷ τῶν πόλεων καὶ ἰδοὺ ἀνὴρ
πλήρης λέπρας· ἰδὼν δὲ τὸν Ἰησοῦν, πεσὼν ἐπὶ πρόσωπον ἐδεήθη
αὐτοῦ λέγων· κύριε, ἐὰν θέλῃς, δύνασαί με καθαρίσαι. καὶ ἐκτείνας τὴν χεῖρα ἥψατο αὐτοῦ λέγων· θέλω, καθαρίσθητι· καὶ
εὐθέως ἡ λέπρα ἀπῆλθεν ἀπ' αὐτοῦ. καὶ αὐτὸς παρήγγειλεν αὐτῷ
μηδενὶ εἰπεῖν, ἀλλὰ ἀπελθὼν δεῖξον σεαυτὸν τῷ ἱερεῖ, καὶ προσένεγκε περὶ τοῦ καθαρισμοῦ σου καθὼς προσέταξεν Μωϋσῆς, εἰς
μαρτύριον αὐτοῖς. διήρχετο δὲ μᾶλλον ὁ λόγος περὶ αὐτοῦ, καὶ
συνήρχοντο ὄχλοι πολλοὶ ἀκούειν καὶ θεραπεύεσθαι ἀπὸ τῶν
ἀσθενειῶν αὐτῶν· αὐτὸς δὲ ἦν ὑποχωρῶν ἐν ταῖς ἐρήμοις καὶ
προσευχόμενος.

Among the other passages which exhibit extensive agreement among all
three Synoptics the following may be considered as more or less representative: Matthew 9:1-8 ‖ Mark 2:1-12 ‖ Luke 5:17-26; Matthew 16:24-28 ‖ Mark
8:34-9:1 ‖ Luke 9:23-27; Matthew 19:13-15 ‖ Mark 10:13-16 ‖ Luke 18:15-
17; Matthew 21:23-27 ‖ Mark 11:27-33 ‖ Luke 20:1-8; Matthew 21:33-46 ‖
Mark 12:1-12 ‖ Luke 20:9-19; Matthew 22:23-33 ‖ Mark 12:18-27 ‖ Luke
20:27-40; Matthew 24:4-8 ‖ Mark 13:5-8 ‖ Luke 21:8-11.

Step Two

Thesis: *There are eighteen and only eighteen fundamental ways in
which three documents, among which there exists some kind of direct literary dependence, may be related to one another.*

If the second copied the first, and the third copied the second but not
the first, they may be related to one another thus in six different ways.

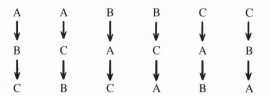

If the first and second were independent of one another, and the third copied both his predecessors, they may be related to one another thus in three different ways.

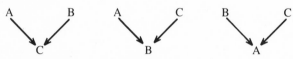

If the second and third independently copied the first, they may be related to one another thus in three different ways.

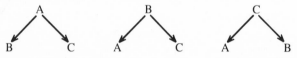

If the second copied the first, and the third copied both his predecessors, they may be related to one another thus in six different ways.

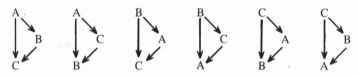

Step Three

Thesis: *While it is possible to conceive of an infinite number of variations of these eighteen basic relationships by positing additional hypothetical documents, these eighteen should be given first consideration.*

The reasons for this have been indicated in the discussion of Step One. This does not mean that the investigator should assume that there were no additional hypothetical documents. On the contrary, he should be open to the possibility that such actually existed. There are instances in literary-historical studies where circumstantial evidence requires the investigator to posit the existence of a document for which he has no direct evidence. But a critic should not posit the existence of hypothetical documents until

he has made an attempt to solve the problem without appeal to hypothetical documents. Only after the investigator has been unable to understand the relationship among Matthew, Mark, and Luke without appealing to unknown sources is he justified in hypothecating the existence of such sources, in order to explain phenomena otherwise inexplicable.

Step Four

Thesis: *Only six out of eighteen basic hypothetical arrangements are viable.*

This follows from the circumstances that there are agreements between any two of the Synoptic Gospels against the third.

This is a verifiable point, recognized by all careful investigators, and it provides an important clue to the solution of the problem once it is properly understood. For if one does not begin by appealing to hypothetical documents, but rather concentrates his attention on the eighteen basic arrangements set forth in Step Two, it follows that where any two Gospels agree, and the third does not (either because the third has something different or is silent), that the Gospel which was written earlier was copied by the author of the later Gospel. The agreement could not be explained otherwise.

But if there are agreements between Matthew and Mark against Luke, and Matthew and Luke against Mark, and Luke and Mark against Matthew, then none of these eighteen basic hypotheses is valid that does not allow for direct literary dependence among all three.

Thus all six instances where the second Evangelist copied the work of the first, and the third copied the second but not the first, can be eliminated from further consideration. For under such circumstances it would be impossible for the first and third to agree with one another against the second.

The three instances where the first and second are independent of one another and the third copied both may also be eliminated from further consideration. For under such circumstances it would be impossible for the first and the second to agree with one another against the third.

Similarly, the three cases where the second and third independently copy the first may be eliminated from consideration. For this suggestion would fail to explain how the second and third could agree against the first.

But those six cases where the second writer copied the first, and the third had direct access to both the first and the second, cannot be rejected

at this point. For they do afford the opportunity for any two of the Synoptic Gospels to agree against the third. Thus, for example, agreements between the first and the second against the third would result from circumstances where the second copied something from the first which the third did not copy exactly or at all, either from the first or the second. And agreements between the second and the third against the first would result from circumstances where the third copied something from the second which was not in the first. And finally, agreements between the first and the third against the second would result from circumstances where the third copied something from the first which the second had copied less exactly or not at all.

It follows from the above that whichever Evangelist was third faced the problem of working with two Gospels between which there already existed a relation of direct literary dependence, in that the second had copied the first. There are certain definite redactional limitations and possibilities within which a writer under such circumstances is able to function, and this ought to provide a clue for discerning which of the three Evangelists was in the position of being third. A writer in the position of being third can (1) follow the text to which both earlier Gospels bear concurrent testimony; (2) deviate from one, but follow the other, when his sources disagree; (3) attempt to combine them where they disagree; (4) deviate by omission or alteration from both when they disagree; (5) deviate by omission or alteration from both even when they agree.

Isolable and objectively definable categories of literary phenomena are necessary which are more readily explicable when one of the Evangelists is placed third than when either of the other two is placed third.

Step Five

Thesis: *There are isolable and objectively definable categories of literary phenomena which have played a prominent role in the history of the Synoptic Problem which when properly understood are more readily explicable when Mark is placed third than when either Matthew or Luke is placed third.*

These are two in number: (1) The phenomena of order and content; (2) The so-called minor agreements of Matthew and Luke against Mark. (See esp. *Synoptic Problem*, 94-152.)

There is a third literary phenomenon which has seldom been noted, but which is also more readily explicable when Mark is third than in any other position. This is the strange positive correlation of order and degree of similarity between Matthew and Mark on the one hand and Luke and Mark on the other. That is, Mark tends to agree more closely with Matthew when they follow an order different from Luke, but more closely with Luke when they follow an order different from Matthew.

Step Six

Thesis: *The phenomena of agreement and disagreement in the respective order and content of material in each of the Synoptic Gospels constitute a category of literary phenomena which is more readily explicable on a hypothesis which places Mark third with Matthew and Luke before him than on any alternative hypothesis.*

With very few exceptions, which are more difficult for one hypothesis than for any other, the order of material in Mark never departs from the order of material common to Matthew and Luke. Therefore, Matthew and Luke almost never agree in order against Mark. If Mark were third, this fact would be readily explained by the reasonable assumption that the Evangelist writing third had no chronological information apart from that which he found in Matthew and Luke, or that if he did, he preferred not to interrupt the order of events to which these two Gospels bore concurrent testimony.

The most striking agreement in order between Matthew and Luke against Mark is the placing of the Cleansing of the Temple on the same day as the Triumphal Entry, whereas Mark places it on the day following. This is not readily explicable on any hypothesis, though on the Griesbach hypothesis it simply entails the recognition that Mark did not slavishly adhere to the order common to Matthew and Luke.

When the order of Matthew and Luke is not the same, the order of Mark tends to be the same as either the one or the other. If Mark was third, this fact would be readily explained by the same assumption stated above, and the recognition that when Mark was confronted by a situation where his sources departed from one another in order, so that there was no longer a common order to follow, he tended to follow the order of one or the other of his sources, rather than depart from both. This cannot be imagined as an unnatural procedure for Mark to have followed under such circum-

stances. A similar statement can be made concerning the content of Mark. Mark seldom has a story or a saying that is not found either in Matthew or Luke or both. The major exceptions to this statement are two healing stories (Mk. 7:32-35; 8:22-26) and one parable (Mk. 4:26-29).

On the Griesbach hypothesis this is readily explained either by the circumstances that Mark was in fact limited very largely to Matthew and Luke for almost all the stories and sayings found in his Gospel, or that he chose to limit himself to these sources.

While the Markan hypothesis is not one of the viable six, set forth in Step Four, the phenomenon of order and content has played such a prominent role in the history of that hypothesis that a discussion of this matter on both the Ur-Marcus and the Streeterian form of that hypothesis is in order.

On the Markan hypothesis, within Streeter's terms, it is possible to explain how Matthew and Luke would sometimes independently reproduce the same order and content for their material through their use of Mark. But this hypothesis would afford no explanation for Luke's following the order and content of Mark whenever Matthew deviated from Mark, and Matthew's following the order and content of Mark whenever Luke deviated from Mark. Since on this hypothesis Matthew has no knowledge of what Luke has done, he could not so consistently have supported Mark's order if he had wanted to, and the same holds true for Luke. The fact that both Luke and Matthew frequently deviate from Mark, either in order or by omission of Markan material, raises the question of their failure to deviate from Mark's order to omit his material more often at the same place than they do.

The problem of Markan order can be posed this way: It is as if Matthew and Luke each knew what the other was doing, and that each had agreed to support Mark whenever the other departed from Mark. Such concerted action is excluded by the adherents of Markan priority in their insistence that Matthew and Luke were completely independent of one another. Streeter's statement, ''The relative order of incidents and sections in Mark is in general supported by both Matthew and Luke; where either of them deserts Mark, the other is usually found supporting him,''[4] was a tour de

---

[4]B. H. Streeter, *The Four Gospels: A Study of Origins* (1924) 151.

force, by which a serious problem for the Markan hypothesis was converted into an argument in behalf of the priority of Mark.

Since it cannot be imagined that Matthew and Luke each consciously decided to support Mark, even when the other deserted him, Streeter's statement on the matter only sharpens the issue. Why *does* Matthew usually support Mark when Mark is deserted by Luke? And, as if to compound the difficulty, why should Luke in a similar way support Mark when Mark is deserted by Matthew? Since both frequently desert Mark, either by departing from his order or by omitting his material, and since neither knows what the other is doing, why do not their desertions of Mark coincide more frequently?

The Markan hypothesis on Lachmann's terms, where it is thought that each Evangelist independently copied an Ur-gospel, affords a ready explanation for some but not all the phenomena of order. Thus agreement among all three and between any two against the third would be readily explained by assuming that such agreement derived from the common order given in the Ur-gospel. If an Ur-gospel could be firmly established, then the fact that Matthew and Luke almost never agree with one another against Mark in order could be taken as a sign that Mark had deviated from the order of the Ur-gospel less than either Matthew of Luke.

But one fact still remains unexplained;[5] namely that whenever Matthew deviated from the order of the Ur-gospel, Luke tended to follow that order, and that whenever Luke deviated from the order of the Ur-gospel, Matthew tended to follow that order. Since both Matthew and Luke deviated from the order of the Ur-gospel, and since neither had knowledge of the action of the other, why do not their deviations from the order of the Ur-gospel coincide more often? Why are there not more instances where neither Matthew nor Luke supports the order found in Mark? There should be some adequate reason to account for this strange alternation where the order in Mark, when unsupported by both Matthew and Luke, is almost always supported either by one or the other. This fact of alternating support suggests some kind of conscious intention for which the Markan hypothesis offers no ready explanation on either the terms of Lachmann or Streeter.

---

[5]A. Jülicher, *Introduction to the New Testament*, 348ff., felt that there was another decisive objection to the Ur-Marcus hypothesis; see Farmer, *Synoptic Problem*, 64-65, n33.

Nor does the Augustinian hypothesis afford a ready explanation for this fact. If Mark was second and sometimes followed the order of Matthew and Luke was third and had access to both, then Luke, by following the order to which Matthew and Mark bore concurrent testimony, would reproduce an order where all three agree. But then it would be necessary to imagine that he not only chose to deviate from the order common to Matthew and Mark on certain occasions, which might not be so difficult to explain, but that whenever the order of Matthew and Mark was not the same, he rather consistently followed the order of Mark. This cannot be explained as due to his preference for Mark's Gospel, since Luke frequently deviated from Mark either in the order that he gave to his materials or in his omission of Markan material. The problem is this: Why would Luke frequently deviate from Mark either by changing the order of Mark's material or by omitting Mark's stories at times when Mark's order and content were supported by Matthew, but then rather consistently adhere to the order of Mark's material and the substance of his content when Mark's order and content were not supported by Matthew?

This appears to be a rather erratic redactional procedure for a writer, and unless it can be explained by the adherents of the Augustinian hypothesis, it must be counted as an unresolved difficulty for that hypothesis.

A similar argument could be made against a hypothesis which placed Matthew third, for here again there would be no ready explanation for the fact that Matthew's order would then deviate frequently from that of Mark when Mark's order was supported by Luke, but rather consistently follow the order of Mark whenever Mark's order was not supported by Luke.

Thus confining the possibilities to the six viable hypothesis set forth in Step Four, it is possible to say that only the two hypotheses which place Mark third afford a ready explanation for the phenomenon of agreement in order and content among Matthew, Mark, and Luke. Thus:

The choice between these two hypotheses cannot be made on the basis of order and content but must be settled on other grounds.

Step Seven

Thesis: *The Minor Agreements of Matthew and Luke against Mark constitute a second category of literary phenomena which is more readily explicable on a hypothesis where Mark is regarded as third with Matthew and Luke before him than on any alternative hypothesis.*

In a typical passage where all three Gospels have parallel material there tend to be seven distinguishable categories of literary phenomena: (1) agreement among all three; (2) agreements between Matthew and Mark against Luke; (3) agreements between Mark and Luke against Matthew; (4) agreements between Matthew and Luke against Mark; (5) words unique to Matthew; (6) words unique to Mark; and (7) words unique to Luke.

Categories (2), (3), and (4) are manifestly distinguishable from (1), (5), (6), and (7). When categories (2), (3), and (4) are compared, it is found that (4) is distinguishable from (2) and (3), in that the agreements in (2) and (3) tend to be more extensive and substantial than those in (4). That is, in passages where all three Gospels are parallel, the agreement between Matthew and Luke against Mark tend to be minor in extent, inconsequential in substance, and sporadic in occurrence, as compared to the corresponding phenomena in categories (2) and (3). This is not true without exception. But it is true in the great majority of cases, and it requires some explanation.[6]

There is no ready explanation for this phenomenon, except on the hypothesis that Mark was third and had access to the texts of both Matthew and Luke. The Augustinian hypothesis offers no ready explanation. For if Luke were third and conflated Matthew and Mark, it would be necessary to think that whenever he copied Mark he frequently compared the parallel passage in Matthew and then allowed the text of Matthew to influence his wording only slightly while he followed closely the text of Mark, frequently copying Mark when Mark deviated from Matthew, but almost

---

[6]It is a merit of B. de Solages's work, *A Greek Synopsis of the Gospels* (1952), that he has isolated this phenomenon, and has recognized it as "the fundamental problem." It is very clear from his arrangement of the Synoptic material into separate frames that the material he puts in frame #3, namely the agreements between Matthew and Luke against Mark, is significantly less than the material in the frames containing agreements between Mark and Luke against Matthew.

never copying Matthew when Matthew deviated from Mark, though departing frequently from both Matthew and Mark in places where they bore concurrent testimony to the same text. Such a redactional procedure would appear to be unnecessarily erratic. On this arrangement, Luke would not show any consistent preference for Mark's text, since he departs readily from the text of Mark when Mark's text is supported by that of Matthew. Furthermore, there are a number of passages, especially in the section of Luke 9:51-18:14, where on the Augustinian hypothesis it would be necessary to say that Luke showed a preference for Matthew, since his text in that section is closer to Matthew's than to Mark's in passages where all three agree.[7]

Similar difficulties would be faced by any hypothesis in which Matthew was placed third. No such objections can be raised, however, against the view that Mark may have been third, providing it be granted with Burton that it is conceivable that a writer in his situation could have been guided by the literary purpose not to deviate from the text to which his predecessors bore concurrent testimony.[8] It would be inhuman to expect a writer so motivated never to deviate in the slightest degree from the common text in his two sources. It is enough to expect him to depart only when so to do would not affect the sense or the intention of the text to which his sources bore concurrent testimony. This is a fair description of the great bulk of the agreements of Matthew and Luke against Mark. Generally speaking, these agreements do not seriously affect the literary purpose or theological intention of the passages concerned.

On this hypothesis there would also be a ready explanation for the extensive agreements of Mark with Matthew against Luke, and of Mark with Luke against Matthew. These agreements would be created whenever Mark, having reached a point in the texts of Matthew and Luke where they deviated from one another, sometimes followed the one and sometimes the other. In such cases, by departing from both, which would have been quite natural at times, there would have been no agreement at all among the three. Thus, on this hypothesis there is a ready explanation for all seven categories of literary phenomena listed above. The only question which remains unanswered is that of the relationship between Matthew and Luke.

---

[7]Cf. J. C. Hawkins, "Three Limitations to St. Luke's Use of St. Mark's Gospel: The Disuse of the Marcan Source in St. Luke ix. 51-xviii. 14," *Oxford Studies in the Synoptic Problem*, ed. W. Sanday (1911) 29-59.

[8]See Farmer, *Synoptic Problem*, 78.

Step Eight

Thesis: *There exists a positive correlation between agreement in order and agreement in wording among the Synoptic Gospels which is more readily explicable on the hypothesis that Mark was written after Matthew and Luke and is the result of a redactional procedure in which Mark made use of both Matthew and Luke.*

When Matthew, Mark and Luke do not all three agree in order, as has been pointed out, either Matthew and Mark will agree, or Luke and Mark will agree. The point is that when Matthew and Mark are following the same order, but Luke exhibits a different order, the texts of Matthew and Mark tend to be very close to one another. And when Luke and Mark are following the same order, but Matthew exhibits a different order, the texts of Luke and Mark tend to be very close to one another. This is quite noticeable in the first half of Mark, and requires an explanation.

This phenomenon is especially difficult to explain on any hypothesis which presupposed that Matthew and Luke independently copied Mark or Ur-Marcus. For, since Matthew had no knowledge of Luke's redactional use of Mark, there is no way he could have known to begin copying the text of Mark more closely where Luke's order was different from that of Mark. Conversely, thère is no way in which Luke could have known to begin copying the text of Mark more closely at the point where Mark's order and that of Matthew departed from one another.

The Augustinian hypothesis affords a ready explanation for a part of this phenomenon, but not for the whole of it. For on that hypothesis, although Luke might naturally have followed the text of Mark more closely when he chose Mark's order in preference to that of Matthew, there is no obvious reason why Mark would have copied Matthew more closely when drawing a passage from Matthew while following Matthew's order than when not following Matthew's order.[9]

---

[9] It is true that when Mark would have departed from Matthew's order and turned to another place in the text of Matthew and copied out a passage, he would have had to create some kind of ligature of his own to tie in the passage with what he had been copying from Matthew at the previous place, and that this would have sometimes made it difficult for him to copy such a passage closely in its opening verse. This would be a partial explanation for the correlation of order and proximity of text between Matthew and Mark. But the phenomenon of correlation tends to extend to the whole of such passages, and not just the transitional verses. For this there seems to be no ready explanation on the Augustinian hypothesis.

Therefore, on the Augustinian hypothesis, there is a ready explanation for the positive correlation between agreement in order and closeness of text between Mark and Luke, but not for the similar correlation between Mark and Matthew.

On the Griesbach hypothesis, however, there is a ready explanation for the whole of this phenomenon. For it would not have been unnatural for Mark to have given some preference to the text of Matthew when he had deliberately chosen to follow Matthew's order instead of that of Luke, and conversely, it would not have been unnatural for him to have given some preference to the text of Luke when he had deliberately chosen to follow Luke's order in preference to that of Matthew. One would not expect Mark to follow such a procedure inflexibly. Indeed the phenomenon is ambiguous enough to indicate that if in fact Mark was third, he did not follow this pattern with absolute consistency. Nevertheless a positive correlation does exist, which was recognized by the advocates of the Griesbach hypothesis. "When the same facts, which are recorded by the evangelist whom he (Mark) is following at any time, are narrated also by the other, he makes use of the later also, to guide him in his manner of description, and even of expression, but he keeps mainly to the former."[10] Assuming Mark to be third and working with Matthew and Luke, this is a statement which does justice to a particular literary phenomenon of the Gospels themselves. The point is that it does not seem possible on any other hypothesis to make a similar statement which will take into account the same phenomenon equally as well.[11]

Step Nine

Thesis: *It is possible to understand the redactional process through which Mark went, on the hypothesis that he composed his Gospel based primarily on Matthew and Luke.*

---

[10]F. Bleek, *An Introduction to the New Testament* (1883) 267.

[11]The reader is referred to Chapter VII of *The Synoptic Problem* for the specific confirmation of this thesis. It is very important not to think that this correlation can be easily verified. There are places where no correlation seems apparent. But there is generally an understandable reason for the fact that in some places the matter is ambiguous, that is readily forthcoming on the Griesbach hypothesis.

A demonstration of this thesis is given in Chapter VIII of *The Synoptic Problem*. The reader is further referred to the works of De Wette and Bleek.[12]

It is possible to arrange a presentation of the results of an analysis of Mark on the Griesbach hypothesis in various ways. Therefore, the differences between the ways in which various advocates of the Griesbach hypothesis divide up the Gospel of Mark are not especially important. The point is that it is possible to proceed through the Gospel of Mark on the hypothesis that he based his gospel on Matthew and Luke, and not encounter redactional problems which create serious and peculiar difficulties for that hypothesis. The demonstration of this thesis . . . is mainly distinguished from the results of previous analyses of Mark on the Griesbach hypothesis by the influence of advances in Synoptic studies which have been made during the past one hundred years in the areas of environmental research and form criticism.

Step Ten

Thesis: *The most probable explanation for the extensive agreement between Matthew and Luke is that the author of one made use of the work of the other.*

Such a direct literary dependence between Matthew and Luke is not incompatible with their mutual use of common sources. Where each has material that is similar, but where there is insufficient evidence to warrant the judgment that there was direct copying by one Evangelist of the work of the other, the explanation that a common source has been copied is al-

---

[12]See especially W. M. L. De Wette, "Erklärung des Verhältnisses zwischen Marcus und den beiden andern Evangelisten durch die Annahme, dass er sie benutzt hat," *Lehrbuch der historisch-kritischen Einleitung in die kanonischen Bücher des Neuen Testaments*, 5th ed. (1848) 167-79; and "Evangelium des Marcus," *Kurze Erklärung der Evangelien des Lukas und Markas*, in *Kurzgefasstes exegetisches Handbuch zum Neuen Testament*, Ersten Bandes zweiter Theil, 127-200. See also Friedrich Bleek, *Einleitung in das Neue Testament*, 2d ed. (1866), paragraphs 93-97. In the English translation of Bleek's *Introduction to the New Testament*, in Clark's *Foreign Theological Library*, this section is set forth under the heading: "Dependence of Mark upon Matthew and Luke," 258-275. See also Samuel Davidson's "The Gospel of Mark—'Analysis of Contents,' and 'Relation of Mark to Matthew and Luke,' " *An Introduction to the Study of the New Testament, Critical, Exegetical, and Theological*, 2d ed. (1868) I:542-63.

together plausible. But where the evidence for direct literary dependence is strong, the most probable explanation would be that one of the Evangelists had copied the work of his predecessor.

The hypothesis that either Matthew or Luke had the work of the other before him not only affords a ready explanation for the extensive agreement in content between the works of these two Evangelists, but also their remarkable similarities in literary form.

Both Matthew and Luke begin with birth narratives, contain genealogies, begin Jesus' ministry with his baptism by John, record the teaching of John, picture Jesus tempted by Satan in the wilderness, describe Jesus' ministry in Galilee, introduce into their narrative framework large collections of Jewish gnomic and parabolic materials—including primitive sayings reflecting the historical solidarity between Jesus and John, narrate Jesus' journey to Jerusalem with his disciples, his triumphal entry, his cleansing of the Temple, the Last Supper with his disciples, the arrest in Gethsemane, the trial before the High Priest, and before Pilate, and finally the crucifixion, death, burial, and resurrection of Jesus.

The fact that in some parts of this outline Luke introduced different content only indicates that he had ample reason to write a new Gospel, and in no way explains why he follows a literary scheme so similar to that found in Matthew. When compared to other Gospel literature in particular, and to contemporary Hellenistic and Jewish literature in general, Matthew and Luke bear a striking resemblance to one another both in form and content.

The form of Matthew and Luke is unique in literature. It is unlikely that two writers would independently have created such unique and similar literary works. It is altogether probable that one was the original literary creation, and that the author of the other took this original work as his literary exemplar, making such improvements and modifications as may have been dictated by his literary and theological purposes.

It is not possible to explain the similarity in content and form between Matthew and Luke by positing their mutual dependence upon either John or Mark, without making appeal to one or more hypothetical sources to explain material held in common by Matthew and Luke not found in either John or Mark. Therefore, as long as one seeks to solve the Synoptic Problem without having recourse to such conjectural sources, he is led to posit direct literary dependence between Luke and Matthew.

Step Eleven

Thesis: *The hypothesis that Luke made use of Matthew is in accord with Luke's declaration in the prologue to his Gospel concerning his purpose in writing.*

The usual interpretation of Luke 1:1, to mean that at the time Luke wrote there were many Gospels in existence, is linguistically possible though not necessary. Lessing interpreted Luke as meaning that "Many have undertaken to rearrange a narrative," and concluded that this referred to an original narrative, composed by the apostles, which Lessing identified with the Gospel of the Nazarenes.[13] The important point linguistically is that the word διήγησις is singular. Therefore, it would be possible to understand Luke to have referred to a single narrative, which he did not think of as the work of a single individual, but of πολλοί. For it is not necessary to translate ἀνατάξασθαι by "rearrange." The Greek can be rendered "many have undertaken to *compile* a narrative."

This was a possible way for Luke to have viewed the Gospel of Matthew. For while it is not impossible that a single individual played an important part in the final stage in the redaction of all the tradition which was included in Matthew, the total work of compilation, arrangement and development of the tradition in that Gospel can with justice be viewed as the work of more than one person, perhaps even a school.

When Luke defined the intention of the διήγησις which was compiled by πολλοί as being concerned to set forth "the things which have been fulfilled among us," his words describe one of the characteristic features of the Gospel of Matthew. For in Matthew the motif of the fulfillment of prophecy is prominent.

When Luke referred to the tradition which had been compiled by πολλοί into διήγησις, as having been "delivered to us by those who were from the beginning eyewitnesses," he clearly associated himself with the "many" compilers, in distinction from those who were from the beginning "eyewitnesses."

The Gospel of Matthew seems to have been composed after the eyewitness period, and reflects the results of the very process of composition Luke describes. That is, Matthew can be justly referred to as διήγησις,

---

[13]See Farmer, *Synoptic Problem*, 4, n5.

made up of tradition which had been handed down from an earlier "eye-witness" period.

It is preferable, therefore, on Lessing's terms, where διήγησις is taken to refer to a single narrative, to identify this narrative with the known Gospel of Matthew, rather than an eye-witness "apostolic" Gospel of the Nazarenes, which after all is highly conjectural.

There is no doubt that from the point of view of readers who were sensitive to the prevailing standards of Hellenisitic historiography, the Gospel of Matthew was defective διήγησις. It was not set within an adequate chronological framework, so that readers acquainted with world history could view it within the context of that history. It contained duplicate accounts of certain events, and reported these as if they were completely separated in time and circumstance, when it was clear that they were but different accounts of the same matter. There were defects in the order in which certain material appeared in Matthew. Thus no sufficient reason is given for Jesus to have left Nazareth for Capernaum at the beginning of his ministry in Galilee, though a story of his being rejected by the people of his native place is included later in the narrative. And the call of the disciples after his great Sermon on the Mount is subject to the criticism of being anachronistic, in view of the indications that the sermon was for the disciples.

At all such points Luke's Gospel seems to reflect the results of a prolonged and careful study of Matthew, with a view to the creation of a new διήγησις which would be free of such defects.

In addition, of course, Luke obviously had access to other material which had been compiled and handed down from the earlier period. And Schleiermacher was no doubt correct in perceiving that it was largely out of such earlier compilations of material that both Matthew and Luke were composed.[14] To what extent these briefer compilations could also have been in Luke's mind when he referred to διήγησις having been compiled by πολλοί, remains uncertain. What is certain, however, is that Luke's Gospel is the result of careful study of the work of earlier redactors engaged in the task of producing διήγησις. And it is quite possible that the Gospel of Matthew was in his mind, and in the minds of those for whom he had prepared his work, when he composed the words of his prologue.

---

[14]See Ibid., 18, n26.

Step Twelve

Thesis: *Assuming that there is direct literary dependence between Matthew and Luke, internal evidence indicates that the direction of dependence is that of Luke upon Matthew.*

In support of this thesis is the fact that passages found in Matthew which express a point of view antithetical to the mission to the Gentiles, such as Matthew 10:5, "go nowhere among the Gentiles," or the continuing importance of Jewish practice, such as Matthew 24:20, "pray that your flight may not be in winter *or on a sabbath*," are not found in Luke. Words and customs which would have become increasingly less intelligible, as the frontiers of the Christian movement expanded farther and farther from its place of origin, such as *Raca* for fool, in Matthew 5:22, and the wearing of *phylacteries*, in Matthew 23:5, are not found in Luke.

The Semitic parallelism of passages in Matthew, like that in Matthew 7:24-27, is frequently broken in the parallel passage in Luke (*compare* Lk. 6:47-49). The assumption is that during the oral period certain tradition was cast in the form of Semitic parallelism, for purposes of oral communication. When this was included in a written Gospel, the possibility existed for the writer to be conservative in editing his material, and thus to preserve the form of Semitic parallelism. However, to do so was not necessary for purposes of written communication, and in fact to reproduce certain cases of parallelism in all their formal fullness was, in some circles, to make the author's writing subject to the criticism of redundancy. It may be assumed, therefore, that the fact that in Luke Semitic parallelism is frequently broken, whereas in the parallel passages in Matthew it is frequently preserved, indicates that Luke has altered Matthew and not vice versa.[15]

---

[15]See C. F. Burney, *The Poetry of our Lord* (1925), for a decisive study of the bearing of the phenomena of Semitic parallelism on the question of the original form of sayings attributed to Jesus in the Gospels. Burney went beyond the evidence in suggesting that all material cast in the form of Semitic parallelism had come from Jesus. All his work actually proves is that it is possible to recover in many cases the more original form of sayings in the Gospels, by studying them in the light of available knowledge of the formal characteristics of Hebrew poetry. For the purpose of settling the question of whether Luke is more likely to have altered Matthew or vice versa, however, Burney's work provides reliable criteria for a general determination of the probabilities of the matter.

Step Thirteen

Thesis: *The weight of external evidence is against the hypothesis that Matthew was written after Luke.*

It is not possible to settle with finality the question of the extent to which one should rely upon the unanimous testimony of the Church Fathers that Matthew was written before the other canonical Gospels. But whatever weight is to be given to this external evidence goes against the view that Matthew was written after Luke, and in favor of the view that Luke was written after Matthew.

Although the earliest statements by the Fathers on this matter are quite late, from the third and fourth centuries, they cannot be dismissed as totally irrelevant. These Fathers all came out of the great central, mainline Church which formulated the canon in which Matthew and Luke were included. That Church and its canon were a result of the mission to the gentiles in the apostolic period. As between Matthew and Luke, the latter was more suited for use in the gentile Churches. By comparison with Luke, Matthew still retained features which were peculiarly Jewish, and reflected the interests of the earlier Jewish-Christian mission (see Step Twelve). Therefore, it is unlikely that a unanimous tradition would have developed in the gentile Church which reversed the true relationship between Matthew and Luke. That is, if Luke had been written before Matthew and had been copied by Matthew, so that Matthew then would have been a later Judaized version of Luke, it would be unlikely for a unanimous tradition to have developed among the gentile Churches which gave pride of place to Matthew. It is historically more probable that attributing pride of place to the more Jewish Gospel reflects a reliable historical memory in the gentile Churches as to the true chronological relationship between these two Gospels.

Step Fourteen

Thesis: *The weight of external evidence is against the hypothesis that Matthew was written after Mark.*

The same considerations set forth in support of the thesis advanced in Step Thirteen argue in favor of this thesis. Where the reader finds "Luke" in the discussion of Step Thirteen, he need only substitute "Mark," and

the same conclusions that apply to the relationship of Luke to Matthew apply also to the relationship of Mark to Matthew.

Step Fifteen

Thesis: *That Mark was written after both Matthew and Luke is in accord with the earliest and best external evidence on the question.*

Papias's testimony throws no light on the question of order in which the Gospels were written. The earliest statement on the question of order in which the Gospels were written is given by Clement of Alexandria, who stated that he had it from the elders that the Gospels with genealogies were written before the Gospels without them. This statement reflects no critical interest in the technical question of literary dependence, and is likely to have been first formulated in response to some question about the validity or theological significance of the genealogies in Matthew and Luke, or in response to some question about the reliability of Gospels which had conflicting genealogies, as compared with those which had none. In any case, the statement of Clement clearly implies that Mark, which has no genealogy, was written after Matthew and Luke, which do have genealogies.

The value of Clement's statement is uncertain. But it probably takes the investigator back to the middle of the second century, and represents an Alexandrian understanding of the chronological relationship between Mark on the one hand and Matthew and Luke on the other.

In view of the tradition that Mark founded the Church in Egypt, it seems unlikely that Egypt would have been the place for a tradition to develop placing the Gospel of Mark after Matthew and Luke unless there were some foundation for this tradition. The most probable basis for this tradition would seem to have been the historical memory among the Churches of Egypt that the Gospel of Mark had been written after those of Matthew and Luke.

The earliest extant citation of the Gospel of Mark is found in Justin Martyr's *Dialogue with Trypho* (106). There is some question as to whether Justin actually had reference to Mark, though it seems likely that he did. Even assuming that Justin's reference constitutes a bona fide citation of Mark, however, there is no clear external evidence for the existence of Mark before the middle of the second century. Or if it be argued that Justin's citation of Mark implies his acceptance of Mark as an apostolic Gospel, it would be possible to say that Mark was probably known in

the Churches of Syria as early as the middle of the first half of the second century, and possibly earlier, that is, between A.D. 100 and A.D. 125. But it would not be possible on the basis of external evidence to place it any earlier than that. This does not mean that it could not have been written earlier. It only means that there is no external evidence that it was.

By way of contrast, there are clear citations of Gospel texts which are distinctive of Matthew and Luke, not only in Justin, but in writings earlier than Justin. In balance these citations seem to constitute reliable external evidence for the existence of the Gospels of Matthew and Luke before A.D. 125, and possibly before A.D. 100 (compare *The Letters of Ignatius* and *The Didache*).

All of this earliest evidence is in complete accord with a view that Mark may have been written after Matthew and Luke. Furthermore, if Mark were written as late as A.D. 100 or A.D. 125, Clement's statement would be based upon tradition he had received from elders who in turn had direct access to the living memory of teachers who had lived in the period when Mark was composed.[16]

Step Sixteen

Thesis: *A historico-critical analysis of the Synoptic tradition, utilizing both literary-historical and form-critical canons of criticism, supports a hypothesis which recognizes that Matthew is in many respects secondary to the life situation of Jesus and the primitive Palestinian Christian community, but that this Gospel was nonetheless copied by Luke, and that Mark was secondary to both Matthew and Luke, and frequently combined their respective texts.*

A full demonstration of this thesis goes beyond the scope of this book, and rightly belongs to a detailed history of the Synoptic tradition. However, the reader can find a variety of examples of the way in which this thesis may be supported in the criticisms of arguments for Markan priority given in Chapters III and IV (see esp. 159-69); and the notes on the Synoptic tradition in Mark, given in Chapter VII. (See esp. *Synoptic Problem*, 265-78.)

The canons of criticism utilized in the analysis of the Synoptic tradition referred to in this thesis are as follows:

---

[16]For a further discussion of this matter see Farmer, *Synoptic Problem*, 282-83.

(1) Assuming that the original events in the history of the Christian movement took place in Palestine, within predominantly Jewish circles, and that by the time the Gospels were written, Christianity had expanded outside of Palestine and outside of circles which were predominantly Jewish in orientation: *That form of a particular tradition found in the Gospels, which reflects an extra-Palestinian or non-Jewish provenance is to be adjudged secondary to a form of the same tradition which reflects a Palestinian or Jewish provenance.*

(2) (In the first edition of this book[17] it was assumed that there was a tendency for the Gospel tradition to become more specific. But E. P. Sanders in *The Tendencies of the Synoptic Tradition*, Cambridge 1969, has shown that the opposite happens often enough to vitiate any canon based upon "specificity." For this reason, I have withdrawn the canon that formerly stood in this place. W. R. F.)

(3) Assuming the redactional tendency to add explanatory glosses, and otherwise to expand tradition to make it applicable to new situations in the churches: *That form of a tradition which exhibits explanatory redactional glosses, and expansions aimed to make the tradition more applicable to the needs of the Church, is to be adjudged secondary to a form of the tradition which is free of such redactional glosses and expansions.*

(4) Assuming the tendency of all writers to use some words and phrases more often than is generally true for other writers when dealing with the same subject: *That form of a tradition which exhibits words or phrases characteristic of a redactor whose hand is clearly traceable elsewhere in the same Gospel is to be adjudged secondary to a form of the same tradition which is free of such words and phrases.* And, as a corollary to this: *That form of a tradition which exhibits words or phrases characteristic of a redactor whose hand is only traceable in another Gospel is to be adjudged secondary to the form of the parallel tradition in the Gospel where the redactor's hand can be clearly traced, provided the characteristic word or phrase occurs in the former Gospel only in passages closely paralleled in the latter, where the verbatim agreement indicates direct literary dependence.*

No one of these canons of criticism is decisive in any given instance. Only when they combine to reinforce one another in indicating that one particular form of a tradition is clearly secondary to another form of the

---

[17]W. R. Farmer, *The Synoptic Problem* (1964).

same tradition can the critic with confidence render a judgment between primary and secondary material.

These canons do not exhaust all the literary and form-critical guides available to the student of the Gospels. The first canon, however, is especially inclusive and is intended to cover all such valid considerations as pertain to the presence or absence of Semitic parallelism in the formal structure of Gospel material, and the presence or absence of such literary forms as may be distinctive of the Hellenistic world.

These four canons[18] supplement six set forth by Ernest De Witt Burton in his monograph, *Some Principles of Literary Criticism and Their Application to the Synoptic Problem* (198). Burton stated that in questions of literary dependence between two documents, that document is to be adjudged dependent which contains features of a secondary character. The following he regarded as evidences of a secondary character: ''(1) manifest misunderstanding of what stands in one document on the part of the writer of the other; (2) insertion by one writer of material not in the other, and clearly interrupting the course of thought or symmetry of plan in the other; (3) clear omission from one document of matter which was in the other, the omission of which destroys the connection; (4) insertion of matter the motive for which can be clearly seen in the light of the author's general aim, while no motive can be discovered for its omission by the author if he had had it in his source; (5) vice versa omission of matter traceable to the motive natural to the writer when the insertion (of the same matter in the other Gospel) could not thus be accounted for; (6) alterations of other kinds which conform the matter to the general method or tendency of the author.''

The six evidences of the secondary character of a document, outlined by Burton, together with the preceding [three] canons for the analysis of Synoptic tradition, provide the most important guides necessary for a study of the history of the redaction of the Synoptic tradition at the hands of the canonical Evangelists.[19]

---

[18]There are only three canons, according to the revision of canon 2 mentioned by Farmer above.

[19]There are additional canons of criticism which must be observed when the critic attempts to trace the history back to its beginning, and to make a judgment about its probable authenticity considered as a saying of Jesus, or its reliability considered as tradition about him. These, however, do not play a decisive part in the study of the Synoptic Problem, and therefore are not set forth here.

Considerations which sometimes have influenced students of the Gospels in their statements about the Synoptic Problem, but which are either irrelevant or inconclusive, and therefore have little or no probative value in settling a question of literary dependence, may be listed as follows:

1. *The relative length of a given passage.* Since writers sometimes enlarge, and sometimes condense, their sources, the relative length of a given passage, by itself, offers no criteria by which it may be adjudged primary or secondary to another.

2. *The grammar and style of a writer.* Since some writers improve the grammar and style of their sources, while others spoil it, such considerations provide no objective basis by which one document may be adjudged primary or secondary to another. There is no provable correlation between style and chronology in matters involving the question of literary dependence between documents of the same general period and class of literature.

3. *The Christology of a given passage.* Since the letters of Paul disclose the fact that Christology was already both complex and highly developed in some circles in the period before the Gospels were written, and since our knowledge of Christological developments in the Churches in the post-Pauline period depends upon a correct solution to the problem of the chronological and literary relationship between the Gospels, and not vice versa, the Christology of a given passage in the Gospels affords the critic no reliable criteria by which to adjudge it primary or secondary to its parallel in another Gospel.

This is not to deny the fact that the life situation of Jesus can be distinguished from that of the later Church. The tendency of the later Church was to modify the tradition from Jesus in the light of the post-Easter faith in him as the risen Lord. The nonchristological statements of Jesus can therefore be distinguished from the Christological traditions of the early Church.

But there is no reliable way in which to adjudge the Christology of Mark as earlier or later than that of Matthew or Luke. All three Gospels came from the post-Pauline period of the early Church, about which very little is known apart from inferences derived from the Gospels themselves. Apart from the Gospels there is no objective basis upon which to reconstruct a scheme of Christological development in this period against which to measure the relative date of a specific Christological reference in the Gospels. For this reason, the Christology of a given passage offers no se-

cure criteria by which it can be judged primary or secondary to a related Christology in a parallel passage. Neither can the omission, nor the insertion, of such a detail offer proof of the relative primary or secondary character of a given passage, unless it be connected in some way with one of the objective canons of criticism listed above or some other valid canon of criticism.

One classic example of the inconclusiveness of the Christological, or "theological," argument will suffice to illustrate the lack of probative value in such considerations. It is sometimes argued that Mark is earlier than Matthew or Luke because the latter two with their birth narratives have clearly been written after the time when the idea of a virgin birth of Jesus had been accepted, whereas Mark, with no such birth narrative, is more likely to have been written before this idea had been accepted in the Church. In response to this view of the matter Samuel Davidson wrote:

> The absence of that history which records the conception, birth and childhood of Christ, should not be adduced as a proof of the gospel's early origin, as it is done by some, for the writer presupposes it as the (other) synoptics, and develops it even to its negative consequences. Instead of Matthew's "Is this not the carpenter's son? Is not his mother called Mary?" Mark has "Is not this the carpenter, the son of Mary?" which agrees better with birth from a virgin than the genealogical registers, where Joseph intervenes in order to deduce the Davidic descent of Jesus.[20]

The implication of Davidson's reply to those who would appeal to the absence of the Virgin Birth stories in Mark as a sign of its primitivity is that if the acceptance of the Virgin Birth of Jesus be made a canon by which a Gospel can be dated, Mark would be dated after Matthew, since Mark's Gospel represents Jesus as the son of Mary but not of Joseph, whereas Matthew, even with the Virgin Birth story, elsewhere in his Gospel represents Jesus as the son of Joseph.

In truth, however, the matter is inconclusive, so long as the outcome of the debate hinges on some preconceived idea of development of dogma in the early Church. For there is no way in which it can be known in which Churches, and at what times, any particular idea about Jesus came to be regarded as an article of faith.

This is not to be taken to mean that Christology is of no importance in a study of the Synoptic Problem. For example, in the case above, once it is recognized that it was not the custom of Jews to identify a man by re-

---

[20]Davidson, *Introduction*, 564-65.

ferring to him as the son of his mother, it can be seen that, as between Matthew and Mark, the text of Mark is the least Jewish, and therefore the most likely to have been influenced by a secondary factor, in this case possibly a developing doctrine concerning the birth of Jesus to a virgin. In balance, then, this consideration would weigh in favor of dating Mark at a time, and locating its place of origin in a region, where the Virgin Birth stories were known and understood in such a way as to preclude the idea of a human father for Jesus.

If it could be proved that in the different churches where Matthew and Mark were written, the dogma that Jesus could not have had a human father was accepted at about the same time, then it would be possible to interpret this consideration by itself as weighing in favor of a date for Mark after this development, and a date for Matthew before this development. But precisely the information upon which any such proof would rest is not available to the critic, and for that reason he will find very little, if any, probative value in such considerations.

SUGGESTED
EXCEPTIONS
TO THE
PRIORITY OF MARK

E. P. Sanders*

Sanders has collected from the work of a few representative scholars, all of whom accept the two-document hypothesis in one form or another, thirty-four instances in which either Matthew or Luke is thought by one or more of these scholars to have a more original form of a certain passage than does Mark. In a few of the passages, the relative primitiveness of the passage in Matthew and Luke may be thought to be the result of the influence of Q.

In addition, Sanders lists from Stanton twelve passages in our Mark which Stanton thinks must have stood otherwise in the Mark used by Matthew and Luke, since one or the other seems to have an earlier form.

From a survey of the work of a few representative scholars—all of whom accept the two-document hypothesis in one form or another—has been culled the following list of instances in which either Matthew or Luke is thought by one or more of these scholars to have a more original form of a certain passage than does Mark.[1] In some instances it is only said that Matthew and/or Luke has a form independent of Mark's. A few passages

*E. P. Sanders, "Appendix II: Suggested Exceptions to the Priority of Mark," *The Tendencies of the Synoptic Tradition* (Cambridge: University Press, 1969) 290-93.

[1]E. P. Sanders, *The Tendencies of the Synoptic Tradition* (1969) 7, 279, 289.

are also listed in which the relative primitiveness of the passage in Matthew or Luke may be thought to be the result of the influence of Q. Such passages—whether the scholar in question has explicitly mentioned Q or not—are marked with an asterisk (*). A brief explanation is given for each passage, but for fuller details the reader will have to consult the work of the scholar cited.

*1. Mk. 1:11, cf. Lk. 3:22 (D). D has the original reading in Luke and Lk. 3:22 depends on Q. Mark here also depends on Q, but gives it in a weakened form. J. Weiss, *Das älteste Evangelium*, 133.

2. Mk. 1:29, cf. Mt. 8:14 and Lk. 4:38. Mark's "Andrew with James and John" is secondary. J. Weiss, *Evangelium*, 148n; R. Bultmann, *Die Geschichte der synoptischen Tradition* (ET, 212).

3. Mk. 1:33, cf. Mt. and Lk. The verse is missing in Matthew and Luke, and was added by a redactor to Mark. J. Weiss, *Evangelium*, 148. Vincent Taylor states that the verse is in Mark's style, and so must have been known to Matthew and Luke. He does not explain why they agree together in omitting it; *The Gospel according to St. Mark*, 181.

4. Mk. 1:35, cf. Lk. 4:42. Mark's "and there he prayed" may have been added by a redactor. J. Weiss, *Evangelium*, 148.

5. Mk. 2:3, cf. Mt. 9:2 and Lk. 5:18. Mark's "borne by four" is the addition of a redactor. J. Weiss, *Evangelium*, 155.

6. Mk. 4:31-32, cf. Mt. 13:31-32. Matthew retains the original antithetic parallelism. M. Black, *An Aramaic Approach to the Gospels and Acts*, 123 (3d ed, 165).

7. Mk. 4:41, cf. Mt. 8:27. Bultmann first raised the possibility that Matthew preserved the earlier text (*Die Geschichte*, 230, ET, 216) but later retracted (see the *Ergänzungsheft* ["Supplementary Notes"] for the pages cited).

8. Mk. 6:8-9, cf. Mt. 10:9-10 and Lk. 9:3-4. Mark softens the mission requirements. Karl Kundsin, "Primitive Christianity in the Light of Gospel Research," *Form Criticism*, 108.

9. Mk. 7:24-31, cf. Mt. 15:21-28. Bultmann thought that Mt. 15:24 is an old and independent logion, and that part of Mk. 7:27 is a secondary addition to the text of Mark. Streeter thought that Matthew here had access also to M. See Bultmann, *Die Geschichte*, 38 (ET, 38); B. H. Streeter, *The Four Gospels*, 260. Note also Bultmann, *Die Geschichte*, 277, n1 (ET, 258, n2): in Mt. 15:21-28, Matthew has "corrected the text of Mark on the basis of a like tradition."

10. Mk. 8:27-33, cf. Mt. 16:13-23 and Lk. 9:18-22. Mt. 16:17-19 is the original ending of the pericope, while Mk. 8:32-33 (missing in Luke) is a later addition. Bultmann, *Die Geschichte,* 277n (ET, 258n).

11. Mk. 8:32-33, cf. Mt. 16:22. Matthew's "far be it from you, Lord," etc., partially supported in Mark by *a b sy*[s], represents the "original Markan text." V. Taylor, *St. Mark,* 379.

12. Mk. 9:14, cf. Mt. 17:14 and Lk. 9:37. The scribes mentioned in Mark are "a belated addition." Bultmann, *Die Geschichte,* 55 (ET, 51).

13. Mk. 9:37, cf. Mt. 10:40. Matthew's form is independent of Mark's and more authentic. Taylor, *St. Mark,* 406.

14. Mk. 9:43-47; cf. Mt. 5:29 (see also Mt. 18:8-9). Mark's reference to the foot is secondary; Bultmann, *Die Geschichte,* 90 (ET, 86). (Mt. 5:29 is sometimes included in Q, even though there is no Lukan parallel, so perhaps this passage should be marked with an asterisk. We should note what Bultmann failed to mention, however: that Mt. 18:8-9 also makes no mention of the foot.)

*15. Mk. 10:11, cf. Lk. 16:18 and Mt. 5:32. Mark's forbidding the wife to marry again is secondary. Bultmann, *Die Geschichte,* 140 (ET, 132).

16. Mk. 10:37, cf. Mt. 20:21. Matthew's "in your kingdom" may be earlier than Mark's "in your glory." Taylor, *St. Mark,* 440.

17. Mk. 10:43 ff., cf. Lk. 22:24 ff. Luke's version is independent of Mark. Black, *Aramaic Approach,* 267 (3d ed., 222).

18. Mk. 10:45, cf. Lk. 22:27. Mark depends upon "the redemption theories of Hellenistic Christianity." Luke is more original. Bultmann, *Die Geschichte,* 154 (ET, 144).

19. Mk. 11:25, cf. Mt. 5:23-24. Matthew's form is earlier and "presupposes the existence of the sacrificial system in Jerusalem." Bultmann, *Die Geschichte,* 140 (ET, 132).

20. Mk. 12:25, cf. Lk. 20:34-36. Luke's version is independent of Mark's. Taylor, *St. Mark,* 483.

21. Mk. 12:28-34, cf. Lk. 10:25-26. In Luke, "another version of the text is being used than Mark's edition." Bultmann, *Die Geschichte,* 21 (ET, 23).

22. Mk. 12:28, cf. Mt. 22:36. Matthew's "great" may be a more literal translation from the Semitic than Mark's "first of all." Taylor, *St. Mark,* 486.

23. Mk. 12:36, cf. Mt. 22:43. Matthew's "in the Spirit" is earlier than Mark's "in the Holy Spirit." Procksch in Kittel, *TWNT* (ET, *TDNT*) 1:103, n53.

24. Mk. 13:1-2, cf. Lk. 21:6. Luke may be from a different source. Taylor, *St. Mark*, 501.

25. Mk. 13:9, cf. Lk. 21:12-13. Luke is independent of Mark. Taylor, *St. Mark*, 507.

26. Mk. 13:13*b*, cf. Lk. 21:19. Luke is independent of Mark and more original. Taylor, *St. Mark*, 510.

27. Mk. 13, cf. Lk. 21:20-36. Luke is independent of Mark 13 and earlier. Taylor, *St. Mark*, 512.

28. Mk. 13:11, cf. Mt. 10:20. Matthew's "the Spirit of your Father" is earlier than Mark's "The Holy Spirit." Procksch, *TDNT* 1:103, n53; also Taylor, *St. Mark*, 509.

29. Mk. 14:17-21, cf. Lk. 22:21-23. Bultmann originally thought Luke to be earlier (*Die Geschichte,* 284; ET, 264), but later changed his mind (see the *Ergängzungsheft* for the verses cited).

30. Mk. 14:22-25, cf. Lk. 22:14-18. Luke has here the older tradition. Lk. 22:19-20 (which parallels Mk. 14:22-25) is in its entirety an interpolation in the text of Luke. Bultmann, *Die Geschichte*, 286 n1 (ET, 265-66, n1).

31. Mk. 14:58, cf. Mt. 26:61. Although Bultmann apparently thinks Matthew used Mark in this passage, he thinks Mark's "made with hands" and "not made with hands" to be secondary in comparison with Matthew. See *Die Geschichte*, 126 (ET, 120).

32. Mk. 14:62, cf. Mt. 26:64 and Lk. 22:70. Taylor (*St. Mark*, 568) thinks Mark must originally have written "you say that I am" (a similar phrase is in Matthew and Luke). J. A. T. Robinson (*Jesus and His Coming,* 49) comes to a similar conclusion.

33. Mk. 15:5, cf. Mt. 27:14. Black writes "either (a) Matthew here preserves the true Marcan reading, or (b) (which seems more likely) Matthew has access to a Semitic tradition in addition to his Marcan source." *An Aramaic Approach*, 252; see also 86.

34. Mk. 14:44-45, cf. Mt. and Lk. These verses are not in Matthew and Luke. Bultmann regards them as legendary and thinks Matthew and Luke did not have them in their Mark. *Die Geschichte*, 296 (ET, 274).

In addition, we may note that Stanton (*The Gospels as Historical Documents*, 142-5) gives a list of passages in our Mark which he thinks must

have stood otherwise in the Mark used by Matthew and Luke, since one or the other seems to have an earlier form.

1. Those instances in which Mark uses "the gospel" absolutely (1:1; 1:14, 15; 8:35; 10:29).

2. "The Carpenter," Mk. 6:3, is due to a revising hand. When it is compared with the expression in Matthew and Luke, it is seen that their expressions might easily have been misunderstood.

3. "The anointing of the sick with oil" may have come from the practice of the church (6:13).

4. "The saying 'the Sabbath was made for man,' etc. at Mk. 2:27 has the appearance of being an insertion."

5. Mk. 9:35-37 "seems to have been rearranged." The phrase "and the servant of all" is probably a later insertion.

6. In Mk. 11:17 the phrase πᾶσιν τοῖς ἔθνεσιν has been inserted later.

7. The phrases in Mk. 4:35, 36 "on that day when even was come" and "they take him with them as he was in the boat" are probably later insertions.

8. The linking statements in Mk. 9:30-31 seem to be secondary to Matthew's blunt statement in the parallel.

9. Mark's dating of the cleansing of the Temple may be due to revision, the original being maintained in Matthew and Luke.

10. The word δίς in Mk. 14:30, 72 seems later.

11. The same is true of the statement that Jesus was crucified at the third hour (15:25).

12. Possibly later are the statement in Mk. 2:26 "while Abiathar was the high priest" and the mention of the scribes in Mk. 9:14.

THE
SECOND
GOSPEL
IS SECONDARY

*P. Parker**

Parker, impressed with the secondary character of the Gospel of Mark, argues that the Second Evangelist was a latecomer and a Gentile. In a detailed study of individual passages in Mark, Parker notes that there are 163 places where Mark favors Gentiles, proclaims a marked universalism, ignores matters that would interest Jews, plays down the Torah, runs down the Jerusalem Church leaders, reinterprets the Christian message on Gentile lines, or displays vast ignorance of Judaism, Palestinian geography, history, and the Hebrew scriptures. The author of the Gospel of Mark cannot have been a disciple of Peter (that is, John Mark) or *any* first century Jew or Jewish Christian. The author must have been a Gentile convert to Christianity.

More than ever, I am impressed with the *secondary character* of our Second Gospel. Negatively, it cannot be Petrine, and cannot be the work of John Mark of Jerusalem. These two points were argued at the 1977 annual meeting of the SBL, in a presentation that need not be repeated here,[1]

*P. Parker, "The Second Gospel is Secondary," from "A Second Look at *The Gospel Before Mark*," *Journal of Biblical Literature* 100 (1981): 395-405; published also in *Society of Biblical Literature 1979 Seminar Papers* (Scholars Press, 1979) 1:151-61.

[1]See P. Parker, "The Authorship of the Second Gospel," *Perspectives in Religious Studies* 5 (1978): 4-9.

though, inevitably, some points must be recalled. Let me now argue, more positively, that the Second Evangelist was himself a *latecomer* and a *Gentile*.

Some of the following items are discussed in the 1953 book,[2] so are but briefly summarized here. Many, however, have not hitherto been put in print, or not by me.

1. *The Second Gospel is late.* Whatever its calendar date, its viewpoint is often strangely subsequent to those of Matthew, Luke and even John. For instance, the Second is the only Gospel which, like the Apostles' and Nicene Creeds, never alludes even remotely to Mary's husband. And, for whatever reason, it is the only NT book that calls Jesus "Son of Mary" (6:3). Again, only at Mark 1:8 does the Baptist say "I baptized," past tense; that looks like an inadvertent throwback from a later standpoint.

In numerous other places the Second Gospel looks definitely less original than the First. Mt. 15:4, "*God* said, Honor thy father . . . ," adheres to earliest Jewish and Jewish-Christian concepts of scriptural inspiration; at Mk. 7:10 it becomes "*Moses* said . . . ," which would be clearer to Gentiles and accord better with their attitudes toward the Torah. At Mk. 11:25, the saying on forgiveness is put so completely out of context as to make little sense; its proper context is in Mt. 6:14-15, beside which, Mark's "stand praying" seems to echo Mt. 6:5. The 1953 book gives other examples of this sort of thing.

2. *Errors in the Second Gospel.* The mistakes in Mark are *so various* and *so numerous* that it seems futile to try to explain them away (though many have tried). This Evangelist just cannot have been familiar with Palestine, its people or its religion.

(a) *Mistakes about Judaism.* Mk. 5:22, "one (*heis*) of the rulers of the synagogue." Diaspora synagogues may sometimes have had more than one ruler, as at Pisidian Antioch (Acts 13:15), but Palestinian synagogues normally had only one.[3]

2P. Parker, *The Gospel Before Mark* (1953).

3A reader opines that Mark customarily used *heis* in the sense of *tis*, and has done so here; cf. Vincent Taylor, *The Gospel According to Mark* (1953), 287, 572. But (a) *heis* for *tis*, a Semitic usage, is typical of *Matthew*, not of Mark. The only clear occurrence in Mark is at Mk. 10:17 = Mt. 19:16; cf. John C. Hawkins, *Horae Synopticae: Contributions to the Study of the Synoptic Problem*, 2d ed. (1909) 3-15. (b) *Heis* for *tis* properly takes a singular noun, or else no noun at all; Mk. 5:22 has a plural. In fact, (c) the expression "one

Mk. 14:12, "On the *first* day of unleavened bread *when they sacrificed the Passover*," confuses Nisan 15 with Nisan 14. Some will say that this is another conflation.

Mt. 26:17:	the *first* day of unleavened bread
Lk. 22:7:	the day of unleavened bread *on which the Passover must be sacrificed*

In any case, only the Second Evangelist seems not to have known the difference.

Mk. 14:13 (also Lk. 22:10) says the disciples were to be met by a man carrying a pitcher of water. Since adult male Jews did not do that, it would have aroused jeers, and excited the very attention that Jesus sought to avoid. (Perhaps the guide had a priestly seal ring with the picture of a water jar; but neither Mark nor Luke says that).[4]

Only Mark supposes that, for Jesus' hearing, "the entire Sanhedrin" met *twice* (14:55, 15:1). That is most improbable. Some will again be disposed to find conflation here, of Mt. 26:58 with Lk. 22:66.

Mk. 15:42, "When *evening was already come*, because it was Friday (Paraskeyē) that is, the day before the Sabbath. . . ." If this be taken literally, either *that* Friday began with *that* sunset, and Jesus had died on Thursday; or else the Evangelist forgot that the Jewish day began at evening.

Mk. 15:46 says that presently, that same evening, Joseph of Arimathea "*bought* a linen cloth." Again, either it was now Friday, and Jesus had died on Thursday; or else somebody has quietly got around the Jewish Sabbath laws.

No Jew, nor any one familiar with Judaism, would have produced the caricature at Mk. 7:3, 4. The caricature is made worse by the gratuitous remark at verse 13, "and many such like things you do."

---

of the ——s," plural, is a typical Markanism, and always means that there were more than one: "one of the Prophets" (Mk. 6:15; 8:28), "one from the crowd" (9:17), "one of the scribes" (12:28) "one of his disciples" (13:1), "one of the Twelve" (14:10, 20, 43), "one of you" (14:18), "one of the high priest's maids" (14:66; Mt. 26:67, 71 has two maids). Mk. 5:22 fits the same usage exactly.

[4]In a panel discussion, George Wesley Buchanan suggested that the man was an Essene monk who had to carry his own jug. But that too would have attracted attention, especially since, by this time, few Essenes remained in Jerusalem.

(b) *Mistakes about Scripture* are less significant, for the ancients had no easy way to look up texts, and had to depend on memory. Those in Mark are interesting chiefly as part of a broader pattern. Mk. 1:2 ascribes Mal. 3:1 to Isaiah. Mk. 1:11 misquotes Isa. 42:1. So does Lk. 3:22, but not Mt. 3:17. Mk. 2:26, "Abiathar" should be "Ahimelech." Mk. 10:19 misquotes the Decalogue, and inserts one, in some manuscripts two, extra commandments, "Do not defraud" (*mē apostereses*), "Do not practice prostitution" (*mē porneyses*). Lk. 18:20 is like Mark, but without these additions. Mt. 19:18-19 quotes correctly and then, like many rabbis, adds Lev. 19:18.

Had Jesus quoted Ps. 22:1 in Aramaic (*Eloi*) as Mk. 15:34 asserts, by-standers could hardly have supposed he was calling for Elijah. Jesus must have used Hebrew *Eli*, as at Mt. 27:46. (Did the Aramaic *Grundschrift* first give *Eli*, then *Eloi* as its translation, and did this confuse the Second Evangelist? or confuse a prior Greek translator? One can only guess. All one *knows* is that the Matthean account makes better sense than the Markan.

(c) *Mistakes about geography*. Except at Mk. 2:4, which describes a Palestinian roof-top better than Lk. 5:19 does, the Second Evangelist appears woefully uninformed about Jesus' land.

"In the wilderness," declares Mk. 1:13, Jesus "was with the wild beasts." The only *beasts* thereabouts were a few goats! (If Jesus had left there and gone into the mountains, he might have heard, at night, a long way off, a jackal or a hyena; but even these would not have been "with" him.)

Only Mk. 6:21 says that Antipas's birthday party was for "the chief men *of Galilee*." Yet (6:27) Antipas had the Baptist beheaded and his head brought in to the party. So the festivities were still in progress. Therefore they must have been at Marchaerus in *Perea*[5]—*a good 100 miles from Antipas's Galilean* seat. Did "the chief men of Galilee" walk or ride their beasts all that way to a birthday party? Or did the Second Evangelist simply have no idea how far it was from Tiberias to John's prison?

---

[5]Josephus, *Antiquities* 18. 5. 2 sets John's imprisonment there. Machaerus was near where John had done most of his preaching; cf. C. C. McCown, "The Scene of John's Ministry and Its Relation to the Purpose and Outcome of His Mission," *JBL* 59 (1940): 113-31.

At Mk. 6:45, Jesus and his disciples cross to Bethsaida after the feeding of the five thousand. Yet (6:55) that crossing brings them to Gennesaret! Lk. 9:11 puts the feeding itself near Bethsaida, and the same is implied at Jn. 6:1, 5, 16 and (probably) Mt. 14:13, 34.

Mk. 7:31 says that Jesus and his companions jouneyed "out from the borders of Tyre . . . through Sidon, to the Sea of Galilee, through the midst of the borders of Decapolis." Let the reader try to make sense out of that!

There apparently was no such place as Dalmanutha (Mk. 8:10). "Magadan" at Mt. 15:39 is likewise a problem; but it, at least, could be a variant form of "Magdala." It is sometimes suggested that the Second Evangelist here just misread his source; but that itself would not speak well for his knowledge.

Mk. 8:27 speaks, without qualification, of "the *towns* of Caesarea Philippi," as though Caesarea Philippi were not itself a town.

Those are just too many geographical absurdities. Our author cannot have been told much about Palestine, still less ever have seen the country.

(d) *Mistakes about current history*. Mk. 6:14-27 repeatedly calls Herod Antipas a "king." Except in the confused text of Mt. 14:9, no other NT writer commits that error. The correct title "tetrarch" appears at Mt. 14:1; Lk. 3:19; 9:7; Acts 13:1; but *never* in the Second Gospel.

Mk. 6:17 says that Antipas took his brother *Philip's* wife. Actually she was the wife of a different brother.[6] The name "Philip" is absent from Lk. 3:19 and is textually doubtful at Mt. 14:3.

It is most unlikely that the Jerusalem populace and their chief priests acclaimed Jesus as the King of the Jews. Only Mk. 15:11-12 imagines that they did.

(e) *Other mistakes?* In virtually all the foregoing, the Second Gospel stands alone. The errors are so eccentric that one is bound to wonder about other Markan statements, when these find no support elsewhere. Whence came the following bits of information?

—that Andrew dwelt at Capernaum, nay, in the very same house as his brother's mother-in-law (Mk. 1:29).
—that Levi was the son (or brother?) of Alpheus (2:14). And does that make Levi a son, or brother, or nephew, or uncle of James (3:18)?
—that Antipas feared John the Baptist (6:14). Perhaps he did, but both Mt. 14:5 and Josephus[7] say he really feared the reaction of the populace.

---

[6]Josephus, *Antiquities* 15. 5. 4.
[7]Ibid., 18. 5. 2.

—that Jesus and the "apostles" (*sic*) took a vacation (6:31). Of course, such a rest period is not inconceivable.

—that a maid *of the high priest* first accused Peter (14:66)

—that Peter's first two denials were both addressed to that same maid (14:68-70).

3. *Doubtful Statements About Jesus.* In the light of what has been said, some Markan statements about Jesus himself fall open to question. In all of the following, the Second Gospel stands alone. In a number of them, there are additional reasons for doubt.

(a) *Geography of Jesus' activities.* Only Mark (1:9) places Jesus in Nazareth immediately before his baptism. It achieves this simply by omitting the article *ho.* With the article (as at Mt. 21:11; Jn. 1:45; Acts 10:38), *Iēsous ho apo Nazaret* would have been merely a title, with no indication as to where, in Galilee, Jesus had just been. (Mt. 3:13 is the only other to mention Galilee at all, in this connection.)

Only Mark (2:1-12) sets the healing of the paralytic in Capernaum. Mt. 9:1 seems to put it in Jesus' "own city," whatever that means. Luke is vaguer still, and could be thinking of a desert area (Lk. 5:16) or Gennesaret (5:1) or some city (5:12) somewhere in Galilee or Judea (5:17).

Only in Mark, Jesus occupies at least six different houses: in Capernaum (Mk. 2:1; 9:33), on a mountain (3:13 + 19), somewhere in Galilee (7:17), at the foot of the mount of transfiguration (9:28), in Perea (10:10) and, yes (7:24), in "the borders" of Tyre and Sidon! Moreover, each of these dwellings has room for Jesus' entire entourage plus other people. How did Jesus come by all this real estate? Did he own it? rent it? borrow it? We are not told.

(b) *Jesus' chronology.* Only Mark (3:6) has Pharisees and Herodians conspiring together in Galilee and right after Jesus got there. Elsewhere the conspiracy is set much later, and in the southland (Mt. 22:15-16 = Mk. 12:13); Acts 4:27; cf. Lk. 13:31). Only Mark has scribes come from Jerusalem as early as 3:22; and only here (3:23) is Jesus' discourse directed to that group. Only Mark has no Judean ministry before Mk. 10:46. Mt. 23:37, a "Q" passage, speaks of such a ministry, while Luke, Acts and John mention it constantly. Perhaps the Second Evangelist's silence here is due to bias in the source he used, and which he did not know enough to correct. Only Mark (11:15-19) puts the temple cleansing on the *second* day of the final visit to Jerusalem. Mt. 21:12-17 and Lk. 19:45-46 put it on the *first* day. Jn. 2:13-22 has it much earlier still. Only Mark (11:11, 15) has

two visits to the temple on those first two days. Only Mark (11:20-26) puts the aftermath of the fig tree incident on the *third* day. Only Mark (14:17) explicitly identifies the Last Supper as the Passover meal the disciples had prepared. Lk. 22:14 *may* equate them, but is unclear. Mt. 26:20 does not say that it was that meal. Jn. 13:1-2 says flatly that the Supper was *before* Passover. This looks like a culminating item in Mark's highly individual calendar of the Passion Story.

(c) *Jesus' own stance.* Only Mark (3:14-15) suggests what Jesus' motives were in calling the Twelve, namely, that they should be with him, and go forth to preach, and exorcise demons. Any Christian writer could surmise such motives, without any actual knowledge at all.

Only Mark says that Jesus was himself a "carpenter" (*tektōn*, 6:3). Is that history? Or does it reflect the Evangelist's unwillingness to notice Joseph?

At the temple cleansing, only Mark (11:16) says that Jesus "would not let any one carry a vessel through the temple." Is Jesus here denigrating temple worship? Or, contrariwise, does he so revere the temple that he will not let it be made a thoroughfare? In any case, *where were the temple police?*

(d) *Jesus' desire for secrecy.* Granted that Jesus was unwilling to channel his ministry along lines either of a mere healer or of a political leader, even so, his demands in Mark seem excessive. At Mk. 7:24, Jesus wants his Tyre and Sidon whereabouts kept secret. No other Gospel recalls a desire for secrecy that early.

Still more astonishing, at Mk. 5:43 he wants it *kept secret* that Jairus's little girl has been raised from death! At 7:36, an erstwhile deaf-mute now hears and speaks, and Jesus demands that he *not let anybody know about it!*

We seem to be dealing, here, not with sober reportage, but with a literary idiosyncrasy of the Second Evangelist. Perhaps it stemmed from his idea of a *Messianitätsgeheimnis.*[8] Whatever its origin, it can hardly be called history.

(e) *Jesus' teaching.* In the parable of the Wicked Husbandman, Mk. 12:8 has the villains first kill the son, then throw him out of the vineyard. At Mt. 21:39 and Lk. 20:15, they first throw him out, then kill him. As a

---

[8]Cf. W. Wrede, *Das Messiasgeheimnis in den Evangelien* (1901; 2d ed. 1913; 3d ed. 1963); also English translation by J. C. G. Grieg, *The Messianic Secret* (1971).

real-life crime, the Markan order appears more probable: kill the unwelcome visitor, then get rid of his body. Matthew-Luke would then have the *lectio difficilior*, so would appear more primitive. They are *a fortiori* original if, as I think, the "son" here originally meant not Jesus but John the Baptist: John *was* first removed from the scene, and afterward killed.

Jn. 2:19 reports that Jesus said, "Destroy this temple and in three days I will raise it up." The saying is echoed at Acts 6:14, and is not denied at Mt. 26:21. Only Mark (14:57-58) brands the report as false.

4. *The Second Evangelist Was a Gentile.* Of his pro-Gentile *sympathies* numerous examples are given in my 1953 book. For the most part those passages will be recalled, here, by a mere "See" or "See also." But there are other items, and they lead beyond the findings of a quarter-century ago.

(a) *Jesus' mission to Gentiles.* At Mk. 3:8, Jesus has followers from Idumea. No other Gospel says that. At Mk. 5:18-20, a Gentile, an erstwhile demoniac, goes at Jesus' bidding on an extended mission to the Decapolis. The mission is more restricted at Lk. 8:37b-39, and is not mentioned in Matthew. At Mk. 7:31 + 8:1, Jesus himself conducts a mission to the Decapolis. (See also 8:3.) Mt. 15:29 does not say this; at most, Mt. 15:39 may mean that the feeding of the four thousand had occurred *somewhere* on the eastern shore. Far more than in Matthew, Luke or John, Jesus in Mark expresses intense concern for a world-wide mission. Mk. 8:19-21 lays heavy emphasis, in the two feedings, on 12 baskets on Jewish territory and 7 on Gentile. The treatment is not nearly so explicit at Mt. 16:9, and is lacking in Luke and John. At Mk. 13:27, the elect are to be gathered "from the uttermost part of the earth," a phrase absent from the others. At Mk. 14:9, "*the* gospel shall be preached *throughout* the whole world." Mt. 26:13 is more limited: "*this* gospel [of the woman's deed?] shall be preached *in* the whole world." Jn. 12:7-8 and Lk. 7:44-47 are still more remote from Mark. See also Mk. 11:17 vs. Mt. 21:13 and Lk. 19:46; also, still more striking, the remarkable differences between First and Second Gospel accounts of the woman near Tyre and Sidon (Mt. 15:21-28; Mk. 7:24-30).

(b) *The larger group.* Even among Jews, Jesus' mission in Mark constantly reaches a wider circle than in the other Gospels. In the north, only Mark says "his name had become known" (6:19). In the south, only Mark said, "*Ho polys ochlos* heard him gladly" (12:37). At Mt. 19:23, Jesus "said to his disciples . . . ," but at Mk. 10:23, he "*looked round about*

and said to his disciples. . . . '' Compare also Mk. 3:34 with Mt. 12:36; Mk. 4:10 with Mt. 13:10; Mk. 8:34 with Mt. 16:24; Mk. 9:35 with Mt. 23:11; Mk. 10:44 with Mt. 20:27; Mk. 11:23 with Mt. 17:30 and 21:21. This difference between the two Gospels is much too widespread to be accidental.

(c) *Absence of Jewish details.* In its parallels to Matthew, the Second Gospel constantly ignores items where the primary thrust is Jewish. Mk. 1:14-15 lacks (I should have preferred to say, omits) an elaborately Jewish description of Capernaum (Mt. 4:13). So does Lk. 4:31, which explains instead that Capernaum was ''a city of Galilee.'' Mk. 7:37 lacks the clause, ''They glorified the God of Israel'' (Mt. 15:31). Mark does not have the healing of two blind men (Mt. 9:27-31), possibly because this resembles Mt. 20:29-34 = Mk. 10:46-52. The command to secrecy (Mt. 9:30) gets transferred to Mk. 5:43 where, as we saw, it makes no sense. Mk. 5:43-44 lacks two other Matthean stories, namely, the healing of a dumb man (Mt. 9:32-34) which stresses the Pharisees' reactions and *the faith of Israel;* and the blind and dumb man (Mt. 12:22-23) where *the son of David* is emphasized. One of these, probably the first, would be ''Q'' (cf. Lk. 11:14), but not both of them.

In the Apocalyptic Discourse, Mk. 13:13 is not like Mt. 24:9-13, and *is* like the mission charge of Mt. 10:22. And Mark lacks entirely these Jewish-Christian elements of the Matthean discourse.

Mt. 24: 9:	''you will be hated by all Gentiles for my name's sake''
Mt. 24:10:	''many will be caused to stumble (*skandalisthēsontai*)''
Mt. 24:11:	''false prophets will arise and lead many astray''
Mt. 24:12:	''because of violation of the Law (*anomia*), the love of many will grow cold''
Mt. 24:20:	''pray that your flight be not on a sabbath''

For propagandizing fellow Jews, Jewish Christians made heavy use of *testimonia.* Such apologetic would carry far less weight with Gentiles. (That is doubtless why the first half of Acts contains 14 appeals to *testimonia*, the second half only three, of which two are addressed to Jews.) The Second Gospel lacks nearly every *testimonium* of Matthew (Mt. 4:15-16; 8:17; 12:18-21; 13:14-15, 35; 17:5; 21:4, 5, 15, 16) and it has none to take their place. In fact, Mark's only *testimonia* are four that *Matthew shares with Luke:* two about John the Batpist (Mk. 1:2 = Mt. 11:10 = Lk. 7:27; Mk. 1:3 = Mt. 3:3 = Lk. 3:4); two spoken by Jesus himself

(Mk. 12:10 = Mt. 21:42 = Lk. 20:17; Mk. 12:36 = Mt. 22:44 = Lk. 20:42-43). See also Mk. 6:7-13, which lacks Mt. 10:5; and Mk. 9:33-37, which lacks Mt. 17:24-27. Both Matthean passages would have been unclear and, probably, offensive to early Gentile Christians.

(d) *Mosaic Law abrogated.* Mt. 12:5-7 appeals to the Torah, and also to Hosea. Mk. 2:27 makes no such appeal, but simply sets aside or, at least, modifies the Sabbath requirement. Mk. 7:19b, a comment *by the Evangelist* asserts that Jesus declared all foods clean. (Recall that at Acts 10:11-14 and 11:5-8, Peter has never heard of this![9]) Mk. 9:4 names Elijah before Moses. A good Jew would have named Moses first, as at Mt. 17:3; Lk. 9:30. See also Mk. 12:31, 33-34, where the Torah is subordinated first to love and then to the Kingdom. Contrast Mt. 22:40. It is interesting that Luke lacks every Markan passage where a Mosaic ordinance is abrogated or toned down.

(e) *Jewish features explained.* The Second Evangelist does not explain matters of Gentile knowledge, such as who Pilate was. He does explain Jewish customs and traditions, as though these were unfamiliar to his readers. Sometimes his explanations are not quite accurate. After quoting Jesus' simile, Mk. 2:19 explains that "as long as they have the bridegroom with them, they cannot fast." Mk. 2:25 explains that David took the showbread "when he had need." Not only is Mk. 7:2-13 a caricature. No Jew would have needed any explanation here, however accurate. Mt. 22:31 reads, "spoken to *you* by God." Mk. 12:32 has "*in the book of Moses, in the account of the bush,* how God spoke to *him.*" However, Lk. 20:37 reads, "*Moses showed, in the account of the bush,* when *he called on the Lord . . . ,*" so that, to some, Mark here will again look like a conflation. Only Mark (12:42) explains that a *lepton,* a coin used in Palestine, was worth half a *quadrans.*

(f) *Adapts message to Gentile interests.* Sometimes, instead of explaining, the Second Evangelist just uses phrasing that was more readily understood by non-Jews. Where Matthew's "Heaven" means God, Mark always reads "God," as does Luke. Where Mt. 12:50 has "my father in heaven," again Mk. 3:35 (and Lk. 8:20) reads simply "God." Mt. 24:15 reads, "standing *in the Holy Place*"; Gentiles would find Mk. 13:14 clearer, "standing *where he ought not.*"

---

[9] This is but one among scores of items where Acts and Mark disagree; cf. Pierson Parker, "A Second Look at the Gospel Before Mark," *JBL* 100 (1981): 392, n7.

This may be why Mk. 15:25 sets the crucifixion at "the third hour." By Jewish ways of counting time, that would mean 9 a.m., which is much too early. But by Roman it meant noon, and that agrees with Jn. 19:14 and, apparently, with Mt. 27:45; Lk. 23:44. Besides the whole of Mk. 15:25 forms an awkward interruption.

Other Markan adaptions involve not just types of expression, but a whole range of Gentile ideas. The concept *automatos* (Mk. 4:28) is most un-Jewish, whereas it appears repeatedly in Greek literature. (Its only NT occurrence is at Acts 12:10.)[10]

At Mt. 8:30, the herd of swine is "a long way off" from Jesus and the group. But Mk. 5:11 (also Lk. 8:32) says the pigs were right *there*. Only Mark adds that there were about two thousand of them.

Only in Mark (10:38-39) does Jesus ask the sons of Zebedee, "Are you able to be baptized with the baptism I am baptized with?" *Baptizesthai* was a common Greek metaphor for overwhelming calamity. It was not Semitic (cf. Lk. 12:50).

Only in Mark (10:12) does Jesus forbid women to divorce their husbands and remarry. But Jewish women could not do that! The teaching would have seemed outlandish to a Jew of Palestine.[11] It was, however, an appropriate expansion for people of pagan background.

(g) *Aramaic* is, to the Second Evangelist, a foreign and exotic tongue. He includes it at 7:34 (*Ephphatha*) and 5:41 (*Talitha cumi*) as if these were incantations for healing, which he then explains. At 3:17 and 10:46 he similarly explains the meanings of Aramaic surnames. We have seen how, in Jesus' cry from the cross (15:34), the Evangelist appears confused about both Aramaic and Hebrew.

(h) *Derogatory of apostles*. The Second Evangelist displays almost unremitting impatience with the Jerusalem apostles—which is understandable if they opposed admission of the uncircumcised into the Church. As I pointed out in 1953, this Gospel pictures the Twelve as uncomprehending (6:52; 9:32; Lk. 9:45 accepts the latter, but explains that a divine decree kept them in the dark). They were extremely discourteous to Jesus (Mk. 4:38; 5:31; 6:37; 9:34). Jesus himself upbraided them severely (4:13; 8:17-18; 9:19).

---

[10]Cf. O. Weinreich, *Tübinger Beiträge zur Altertumswissenschaft* (1929) 330ff.

[11]Unless, what Mark does not say, the words were directed against Herodias; cf. the words of John the Baptist, Mt. 14:4; Mk. 6:18.

Further, says Mark, the three chief disciples had no idea what "rising from the dead" meant (9:10). Yet their forebears had been discussing that topic for centuries.

At Mk. 10:24, the disciples are amazed at Jesus' words about riches and Jesus enlarges on the subject. Neither Matthew nor, surprisingly, Luke has this. At Mk. 10:32 the disciples are again "amazed," "afraid."

At Mk. 10:35-45, the disciples James and John try to undercut their fellows, whereas at Mt. 20:20-28 it is their mother who tries it. We have already seen reason for thinking Mark secondary here. Further, Matthew would hardly have let a woman play so leading a role unless she really did so. Also, in *both* Gospels, the other ten get angry not "at" the two brothers (*pros* or *epi*), but "about" them (*peri*); *that fits the Matthean context*, but is out of place in Mark.[12]

Mk. 14:20 emphasizes the fact that *one of the Twelve* betrayed Jesus. The sentence itself comes in awkwardly (unless there were others at the table). At Mk. 14:40, the disciples "did not know how to answer him." Mk. 9:14-29 fails to mention Jesus' word, "Nothing shall be impossible to you" disciples (Mt. 17:20).

Also peculiar to this Gospel is the derogation of Jesus' "friends" (3:21) and "his own kin" (6:4), but it is hard to say whether these belong with the foregoing.

(i) *Attitude toward Peter.* The Second Gospel names Peter less often than the others do, though perhaps not in disproportion to its length. Further, however: It never acknowledges Peter's authority. Contrast Mt. 16:17-20; Lk. 22:28-32; Jn. 21:15-27. It never calls him "Simon Peter." Contrast Mt. 16:16; Lk. 5:8; and 16 times in John. It says nothing about his walking on water. Contrast Mt. 14:28-31. At Mt. 15:15, Peter asks Jesus to explain a parable; but at Mk. 7:17, it is merely "his disciples" who ask.

As to Peter's perfidy, both Matthew and Mark say he had promised to be loyal, but only Mark (14:31) says that Peter declared his faithfulness "exceeding vehemently." At the Sanhedrin hearing, only Mark (14:54) has the bitter note about Peter "sitting and warming himself" at the officer's fire. (Jn. 18:18, 25 is much milder.) Note, further, that only *Matthew*

---

[12]Incidentally, Mt. 20:20 + 29 places the mother in Jericho. Does that say anything about Zebedee's habitat?

puts Peter's denials in proper Jewish form, (a) simple denial, (b) denial with an oath, (c) denial with a curse (Mt. 26:70-74).

Recall, finally, that the Second Gospel contains very little that reads like personal reminiscence, and *nothing at all that need have come from Peter*. Peter ignored, Peter denigrated—are those the ways that John Mark would write of his friend?

Now, as B. S. Easton remarked decades ago, "In work of this sort, only bulk counts."[13] Some individual items, in the foregoing study, might be explained away in one fashion or another. But dismiss one or two or ten or a dozen as we may, the *bulk* of them remains. Noted above are at least 150 (I make it 163) places where the Second Evangelist favors Gentiles, proclaims a marked universalism, ignores matters that would interest Jews, plays down their Torah, runs down the Jerusalem Church leaders, reinterprets the Christian message on Gentile lines, or displays vast ignorance of Judaism, and Palestinian geography, and history, and the Hebrew Scriptures. Often this Gospel seems misinformed about Jesus' companions, and about Jesus himself. Not only can these things not have come from Peter or John Mark. They cannot have come from *any* first-century Jew or Jewish Christian. The author *must* have been a Gentile convert. If his name was Marcus, it was some other Marcus.

On the positive side, this Gentile Evangelist has left us some of the subtlest and deepest theology in the NT. Its very subtlety and depth, however, make "Markan" thought a huge and separate field of study.[14] In the present essay I have ventured to touch on only a few of the most striking theological considerations.

---

[13]B. S. Easton, *The Gospel According to St. Luke: A Critical and Exegetical Commentary* (1926) xxv.

[14]On Markan theology I am particularly indebted to some recent, richly rewarding studies by Paul J. Achtemeier, most of which have yet to be published.

THE CASE
FOR THE
Q HYPOTHESIS

THE
DOCUMENT
Q

B. H. Streeter*

Of the material in Matthew and Luke that is not derived from Mark, about 200 verses appear in *both* Matthew and Luke—mostly sayings material. Streeter makes two observations about this common material: (1) it occurs in quite different contexts and is arranged in a different order in Matthew and Luke; and (2) the degree of resemblance between these non-Markan parallel passages in Matthew and Luke varies considerably.

The obvious suggestion that Luke copied this material from Matthew (or *vice versa*) breaks down for two reasons: (1) subsequent to the Temptation story, there is not a single case in which Matthew and Luke agree in inserting the same saying at the same point in the Markan outline; and (2) sometimes it is Matthew, sometimes it is Luke, who gives a saying in what is clearly the more original form.

These features are best explained if both Matthew and Luke are independently drawing from a common document and making slight modifications of their own in their use of that document—a hypothetical source by general consent referred to as "Q." Streeter maintains that we are justified in assuming the existence of Q, so long as we remember that the assumption is one which, though highly probable, falls just short of certainty. While the phenomena make the hypothesis of the existence of a

---

*B. H. Streeter, "The Document Q," *The Four Gospels: A Study of Origins* (London: Macmillan, 1924) 182-86.

written source Q practically certain, Streeter notes that its exact delimitation is a matter of a far more speculative character.

Although Matthew embodies about eleven-twelfths of Mark he compresses so much that the Markan material amounts to about half of the total
contents of his Gospel. It is remarkable that the additional matter consists
preponderantly of parable and discourse.[1] Of Luke rather less than one-
third appears to be derived from Mark, though owing to the greater length
of his Gospel—1149 verses as compared with 661—and to some compression of Mark's style, this one-third of Luke includes the substance of
slightly more than half of Mark. Luke's additional matter includes both
more narrative and more parables than Matthew's, but not quite as much
discourse. The discourse occurs in shorter sections, and is not to the same
extent as in Matthew collected into large blocks.

We notice that, of this large mass of material which must have been
derived from elsewhere than Mark, a certain amount, approximately 200
verses, appears in *both* Matthew and Luke. This matter, which they have
in common, includes most of John the Baptist's Preaching, the details of
the Temptation, the Sermon on the Mount, the Healing of the Centurion's
Servant, John's Message, "Art thou he that should come," "Be not anxious for the morrow," and many more of the most notable sayings in the
Gospels. But there are two facts of a puzzling nature. (1) The common material occurs in quite different contexts and is arranged in a different order
in the two Gospels.[2] (2) The degree of resemblance between the parallel
passages varies considerably. For example, the two versions of John the
Baptist's denunciation, "Generation of vipers . . ." (Mt. 3:7-10 = Lk.
3:7-9), agree in 97 percent of the words used; but the two versions of the
Beatitudes present contrasts as striking as their resemblances.

How are we to account for the common matter? The obvious suggestion that Luke knew Matthew's Gospel (or *vice versa*) and derived from it
some of his materials breaks down for two reasons.

---

[1]Narratives peculiar to Matthew, apart from generalized statements of healing like
15:30 and 21:14, are as follows: the Infancy, 1-2; Peter walking on the water, 14:28ff.; the
coin in the fish's mouth, 17:24ff.; various small additions to Mark's story of the Passion
(that is, 26:52-54; 27:3-10, 19, 24-25, 51b-53, 62-66); the Resurrection Appearances. The
two miracles, 9:27-34, are possibly intended to be the same two recorded by Mark, which
otherwise Matthew has omitted. Cf. B. H. Streeter, *The Four Gospels* (1924) 170.

[2]Cf. Ibid., 273ff.

1. Sir John Hawkins once showed me a Greek Testament in which he had indicated on the left-hand margin of Mark the exact point in the Markan outline at which Matthew has inserted each of the sayings in question, with, of course, the reference to chapter and verse, to identify it; on the right-hand margin he had similarly indicated the point where Luke inserts matter also found in Matthew. It then appeared that, subsequent to the Temptation story, there is not a single case in which Matthew and Luke agree in inserting the same saying at the same point in the Markan outline. If then Luke derived this material from Matthew, he must have gone through both Matthew and Mark so as to discriminate with meticulous precision between Markan and non-Markan material: he must then have proceeded with the utmost care to tear every little piece of non-Markan material he desired to use from the context of Mark in which it appeared in Matthew—in spite of the fact that contexts in Matthew are always exceedingly appropriate—in order to reinsert it into a different context of Mark having no special appropriateness. A theory which would make an author capable of such a proceeding would only be tenable if, on other grounds, we had reason to believe he was a crank.

2. Sometimes it is Matthew, sometimes it is Luke, who gives a saying in what is clearly the more original form. This is explicable if both are drawing from the same source, each making slight modifications of his own; it is not so if either is dependent on the other.

A second explanation of the phenomena that has been suggested is that Matthew and Luke had access (in addition to the written Gospel of Mark) to different cycles of oral tradition, or to documents embodying such, and that these cycles, though in the main independent, overlapped to some extent. For those cases where the degree of verbal resemblance between the parallel passages is small I myself believe that some such explanation is a true one. For the more numerous examples where the verbal resemblances are close and striking it is far from convincing.

Accordingly a third hypothesis, that Matthew and Luke made use of a single common document that has since disappeared, has secured, if not quite universal, at any rate an all but universal, assent from New Testament scholars. This hypothetical source is now by general consent referred to as ''Q,'' though in older books it is spoken of as ''the Logia'' or ''the Double Tradition.'' Seeing that Q, if such a document ever existed, has disappeared, the hypothesis that it was used by Matthew and Luke cannot be checked and verified as can the hypothesis that they used Mark. But it

explains facts for which some explanation is necessary, and it has commended itself to most of those who have studied the subject minutely in all
its bearings, as explaining them in a simpler and more satisfactory way
than any alternative suggestion which has so far been put forward. We are
justified, then, in assuming the existence of Q, so long as we remember
that the assumption is one which, though highly probable, falls just short
of certainty.

But it does not follow, because we accept the view that Q existed, that
we can discover exactly which passages in Matthew and Luke were, and
were not, derived from it. Nearly all writers on the Synoptic Problem have
attempted to do this. I have done so myself.[3] But, for reasons which [are]
developed in Chap. IX,[4] I now feel that most of these attempts to reconstruct Q have set out from false premises. (1) Critics have underestimated
the probability that in many cases slightly differing versions of the same
sayings or parables would be in circulation. They have therefore been un-
duly anxious to extend the boundaries of Q by including passages, like the
Lord's Prayer and the parable of the Lost Sheep, where the parallelism between Matthew and Luke is not exact enough to make derivation from a
common written source its most likely explanation. Even if items like
these stood in Q, it is probable that one or other of the Evangelists also had
before him another version as well. Further study of the facts convinces
me that a substantial proportion of the 200 verses in question were probably derived from some other source than Q. (2) On the other hand, since
Matthew and Luke would presumably have treated Q much in the same
way they treated Mark, it is fairly certain that some passages which are
preserved by Matthew only or by Luke only are from Q; but I feel less confidence than heretofore in the validity of some of the principles by which
it has been sought to identify them. (3) Not enough allowance has been
made for the extent to which sayings of a proverbial form circulate in any
community. One such, ''It is more blessed to give than to receive,'' which
does not appear in any of the Gospels, is quoted by Paul (Acts 20:35). At
the present day, at the Bar, in the Medical Profession, in every College in

---

[3]*Oxford Studies,* ed. W. Sanday (1911) Essay VI. On the hazards of reconstructing
Q there are some valuable warnings in Burkitt's review of Harnack's attempt, *Journal of
Theological Studies* (April 1907): 454ff. I cannot, however, accept his own suggestion that
Q contained an account of the Passion.

[4]Streeter, *Four Gospels,* 223-70.

Oxford or Cambridge, professional maxims, or anecdotes and epigrams connected with names well known in the particular society, are handed down by word of mouth. The same thing must have happened in the early Church; and it does not at all follow that a saying of this character, even if it occurs in almost identically the same form in two Gospels, was derived from a written source. Where, however, a number of consecutive sayings occur in two Gospels with approximately the same wording, or where a detached saying is not of a quasi-proverbial character, a documentary source is more probable. Hence, while the phenomena make the hypothesis of a written source Q practically certain, its exact delimitation is a matter of a far more speculative character.[5]

---

[5]Streeter himself attempted a tentative reconstruction of Q in *Four Gospels*, 271-92 [editor's note].

IN SUPPORT OF Q

W. G. Kümmel*

That Matthew and Luke, in addition to their use of Mark, used a second common source, customarily called Q, builds on the observation that Matthew and Luke have in common extensive non-Markan material that Luke could not have drawn from Matthew nor Matthew from Luke.

Kümmel observes that no one any longer defends Matthew's dependence on Luke, and Luke's dependence on Matthew is inconceivable. Why, for example, would Luke shatter Matthew's Sermon on the Mount? And why following the story of the Temptation does Luke not once place material that he has in common with Matthew at the same point in the Markan framework?

Although Kümmel argues that it must be accepted that there was a common source for this non-Markan material found in both Matthew and Luke, he observes that many scholars consider it more likely that Q was not a written source but a common oral tradition. Kümmel, however, believes certain facts are decisive in establishing that Q was a common written source.

(a) The word-for-word agreement between Matthew and Luke is so thoroughgoing as to force the assumption of a common text archetype;

---

*W. G. Kümmel, "Attempt at a Solution to the Synoptic Problem," *Introduction to the New Testament* (Nashville: Abingdon Press, 1973) 63-67.

(b) although Matthew and Luke insert this common material into their Markan framework in different ways, the order of the parallel material is so strikingly similar as to prove a common written source;

(c) the evidence of doublets and double traditions in Matthew and Luke, once in a setting that is paralleled in Mark, incontrovertibly proves that Matthew and Luke must have used a second written source in addition to Mark.

Although the exact compass and order of Q are beyond our reach, Kümmel believes some conjectures about its literary character may be advanced. Although principally sayings material, Q must have included some narrative material as well. Apparently the need arose early for a fixed form of the words of Jesus, and the arrangement of the sayings into sayings groups in Q indicates that this arrangement was made on the basis of content. Q probably arose in Palestine not later than *ca.* 50 to 70 and probably had no literary link with Mark. Q displays a didactic or catechetical character and was probably intended for the instruction of Christians on the religious, moral, and communal life. It is likely that the *Sitz im Leben* of the sayings source is the oldest Christian community, who believed in the resurrection of the One crucified, and who sought and found in the words of Jesus instructions for their missionary preaching and for their life as disciples. Q owed its existence to the need of a Christian community that separated itself from Judaism, to strengthen its faith in the Advent and the awaited fulfillment of the Kingdom of God by appeal to the traditional words of the risen Jesus, and to provide guidelines for its preaching.

Eichhorn was the first to postulate a common source for Matthew and Luke, while Schleiermacher inferred the existence of a sayings source from the Papias reference. Weisse linked these proposals with the thesis of the priority of Mark.[1] The two-source hypothesis—that Matthew and Luke used Mark as a source as well as a second common source, customarily called Q[2]—builds on the observation that Matthew and Luke have extensive common material but that Luke could not have drawn directly from Matthew nor Matthew from Luke. The dependence of Matthew on Luke is no longer defended today and can drop from consideration. On the other hand, that Luke took his common material over directly from Matthew is

---

[1]See W. G. Kümmel, *Introduction to the New Testament* (1973) 45-50.

[2]The usual view that the abbreviation "Q" is from the German word for source, *Quelle*, has been characterized by C. F. D. Moule as improbable (*The Birth of the New Testament* [1962], 84, n1); but this meaning for the abbreviation is indeed rendered probable by the first attestation of its use, in J. Weiss, *Die Predigt Jesu vom Reiche Gottes* (1892) 8, where "Mark and Q" and "LQ" (= Luke's special material, *Lukasquelle*) are mentioned together. Contrary to D. Lührmann, *Die Redaktion der Logienquelle* (1969) 1, n1, P. Wernle, *Die synoptische Frage* (1899) is not the first witness for this term.

championed again and again.[3] This position is completely inconceivable, however.[4] What could possibly have motivated Luke for example, to shatter Matthew's sermon on the mount, placing part of it in his sermon on the plain, dividing up other parts among various chapters of his Gospel, and letting the rest drop out of sight? How could anyone explain the fact that not once does Luke place material that he has in common with Matthew at the same point in the Markan framework,[5] apart from the baptism texts and the temptation stories in Lk. 3:7-9, 17, if he took that material from Matthew and was therefore dependent on the Markan order that is likewise encountered in Matthew?[6] Is it conceivable that Luke would have taken over none of Matthew's additions to the text of Mark?[7] On this question Schmid

---

[3]K. H. Rengstorf, *Das Evangelium nach Lukas* (1962); A. Schlatter, *Der Evangelist Matthäus* (1929); J. H. Ropes, *The Synoptic Gospels* (1934); B. C. Butler, *The Originality of St. Matthew: A Critique of the Two-Document Hypothesis* (1951); A. M. Farrer, "On Dispensing with Q," *Studies in the Gospels: Essays in Memory of R. H. Lightfoot* (1955) 55-88 [reprinted in this volume]; Cassian, "The Interrelation of the Gospels: Matthew—Luke—John," *SE* 1, TU, 73 (1958) 129ff.; N. Turner, "The Minor Verbal Agreements of Mt. and Lk. against Mk.," *SE* 1, TU, 73 (1959) 223-24; W. R. Farmer, *The Synoptic Gospels: A Critical Analysis* (1964); A. W. Argyle, "Evidence for the View that St. Luke used St. Matthew's Gospel," *JBL* 83 (1964): 390-96 [reprinted in his volume]; R. T. Simpson, "The Major Agreements of Matthew and Luke Against Mark," *NTS* 12 (1966): 273-84 [reprinted in this volume]; W. Wilkens, "Zur Frage der literarischen Beziehung zwischen Matthäus und Lukas," *NT* 8 (1966):48-57; E. P. Sanders, "The Argument from Order and the Relationship Between Matthew and Luke," *NTS* 15 (1968-1969): 249-61 [reprinted in this volume] and *The Tendencies of the Synoptic Tradition* (1969).

[4]The attempt by Argyle and Wilkens to make Luke's method of composition understandable by means of Luke's alleged use of Matthew proves on the contrary that this assumption is untenable. See the arguments against Luke's use of Matthew in J. Fitzmyer, "The Priority of Mark and the 'Q' Source in Luke," *Jesus and Man's Hope* (1970) 1:148ff. [reprinted in this volume].

[5]E. P. Sanders, "Argument from Order," 257-58 [reprinted in this volume] mentions several exceptions to this rule, but none of his examples is capable of proof.

[6]The state of affairs is clearly discernible in the colored tables of J. Weiss, *Synoptische Tafeln zu den drei älteren Evangelien* 3d. ed. (1929), revised by R. Schutz; and in B. de Solages, *A Greek Synopsis of the Gospels: A New Way of Solving the Synoptic Problem* (1959) 1089ff.

[7]Cf. J.Schmid, *Matthäus und Lukas: Eine Untersuchung des Verhältnisses ihrer Evangelien* (1930) 25ff.; E. L. Bradby, "In Defence of Q," *ET* 68 (1956-1957): 315-18 [reprinted in this volume]. F. G. Downing, "Toward the Rehabilitation of Q," *NTS* 11 (1964-1965): 169-81 [reprinted in this volume] has shown convincingly that Luke knows the material he has in common with Matthew only in a form that lacks the addition Matthew has made to the material that he—in common with Luke—has taken over from Mark.

and Vaganay[8] have shown that Matthew and Luke alternate in offering the original form of the material they have in common: so that with respect to all these arguments the assumption of a direct dependence of Luke on Matthew must be described as untenable.

Though it must therefore be accepted that there was a common source for the material common to Matthew and Luke, the hypothesis of a written Q source is disputed from various points of view and it is accordingly assumed to be much more likely that a common oral tradition is involved.[9] This position is based on the claim that the supposed source has been imagined on the basis of personal preference and cannot be reconstructed accurately, that the verbal agreements are fewer in the sayings of Jesus than in the text taken over from Mark, that a sayings source without a passion story would be inconceivable, and that the verbal associations point to an oral tradition. But the indications of the use of a common written source are so clear that the majority of scholars consider this position to be inescapable.[10] Decisive are the following facts:

[8]Schmid, *Matthäus*, 183ff.; L. Vaganay, *Le problème synoptique: Une hypothèse de travail* (1954) 293ff.

[9]E. E. Ellis, *The Gospel of Luke* (1966); R. M. Grant, *A Historical Introduction to the New Testament* (1964); D. Guthrie, *New Testament Introduction: The Gospels and Acts* (1965); H. Höpfl-B. Gut, *Introduction in sacros utriusque Testamenti libros compendium*, III: *Introductio specialis in Novum Testamentum* (4th ed., 1938; 6th ed., 1962), curavit A. Metzinger; J. Jeremias, "Zur Hypothese einer schriftlichen Logienquelle Q," *ZNT* 29 (1930): 147ff.; W. L. Knox, *The Sources of the Synoptic Gospels,* I: *St. Mark;* II: *St. Luke and St. Matthew* (1957); S. Petrie, " 'Q' Is Only What You Make It," *NT* 3 (1959): 28-33; T. R. Rosché, "The Words of Jesus and the Future of the 'Q' Hypothesis," *JBL* 79 (1960): 210-20 [reprinted in this volume]; R. North, "Chenoboskion and Q," *CBQ* 24 (1962): 154ff.; F. Rehkopf, "Synoptiker," *Biblisch-historisches Handwörterbuch* (1966) 3:1910ff.; O. Betz, *What Do We Know About Jesus?* (1968) 22; H.-T. Wrege, *Die Überlieferungsgeschichte der Bergpredigt* (1968) 1ff., 57, 108-109, 131, 172.

[10]Recently, in addition to the supporters of the two-source hypothesis (see Kümmel, *Introduction*, 48, n8), R. A. C. Cole, *The Gospel According to Mark* (1961); S. M. Gilmour, "Exegesis of the Gospel According to Saint Luke," *The Interpreter's Bible* (1952); W. Grundmann *Das Evangelium nach Markus*, 5th ed. (1971) and *Das Evangelium nach Lukas*, 2d ed. (1961); A. R. C. Leaney, *A Commentary on the Gospel According to St. Luke* (1958); D. W. Riddle and H. H. Hutson, *New Testament Life and Literature* (1946); H. F. D. Sparks, *The Formation of the New Testament* (1952); A. Wikenhauser, *Einleitung in das Neue Testament* (1953; 4th ed. 1961, slightly revised by A. Vögtle; translated into English by J. Cunningham, 1958, from the 2d ed.); O. E. Evans, "Synoptic Criticism Since Streeter," *ET* 72 (1960-1961); V. Taylor, *Behind the Third Gospel* (1926); cf. also "The Original Order of Q," *New Testament Essays* (1970) 95-118 [reprinted in this vol-

a. The word-for-word agreements between Matthew and Luke in their common text are in part so thoroughgoing (for example, Mt. 3:7-10; 7:7-11; 11:4-6; 12:43-45; 24:45-51 par.) as to force the assumption of a common text archetype, but in part also rather slight (for example, Mt. 10:26-33; 25:14-30 par). Furthermore, the common vocabulary in all the sections which come under consideration is over 50 percent,[11] which can hardly be accounted for by simple oral tradition.

b. Matthew and Luke have inserted into the Markan framework the sayings material that goes beyond Mark, and have done so in quite different ways. Matthew presents large sayings sections: 5-7; 10; 11; 18:10ff.; 23; 24:37ff.; 25; when this material is set aside, what remains is on the whole the Markan material. Luke presents the material that goes beyond Mark for the most part in 6:20-8:3 and 9:51-18:14, the so-called lesser and greater insertions. In view of the very different arrangement of this common material by Matthew and Luke one would expect no community of sequence of these texts in Matthew and Luke. The opposite is the case, however. If the sections in Luke for which Matthew has a more or less equivalent parallel are numbered in their Lukan order and placed beside the Matthean parallels with the numbers of Matthew's sequence (omitting individaul sayings) the following picture results:[12]

---

ume]; E. Hirsch, *Frühgeschichte des Evangeliums* I: *Das Werden des Markus* (1940, 1951) II: *Die Vorlagen des Lukas und das Sondergut des Matthäus* (1941); B. H. Throckmorton, "Did Mark Know Q?," *JBL* 67 (1948): 319-29; H. Helmbold, *Vorsynoptische Evangelien* (1953); F. Bussby, "Is Q an Aramaic Document?," *ET* 65 (1953-1954): 272-75; H. E. Tödt, *Der Menschensohn in der synoptischen Überlieferung* (1959) 215ff.; J. P. Brown, "An Early Revision of the Gospel of Mark," *JBL* 78 (1959): 215-27; "Mark as Witness to an Edited Form of Q," *JBL* 80 (1961): 29-44; H. Schürmann, "Sprachliche Reminiszenzen an abgeänderte oder Bestandteile der Spruchsammlung im Lukas- und Matthäusevangelium," *NTS* 6 (1959-1960): 193-210; P. Hoffmann, "Die Anfänge der Theologie in der Logienquelle," *Gestalt und Anspruch des Neuen Testaments* (1969); D. Lührmann, *Die Redaktion;* F. Neirynck, "Rédaction et structure de Matthieu," *De Jésus aux Évangiles: Tradition et rédaction dans les Évangiles synoptique* (1967) 65; E. Schweizer, *Jesus Christus im vielfältigen Zeugnis des NT* (1968) 124-25.

[11]Thus B. de Solages, *Greek Synopsis*, 1047; similarly R. Morgenthaler, *Statistische Synopse* (1971) 165. C. E. Carlston and D. Norlin, "Once More—Statistics and Q," *HTR* 64 (1971): 71, 77, estimate a verbal agreement in the material common to Matthew and Luke at 71 percent—27 percent higher than in the Markan material they have in common.

[12]See the table in H. Appel, *Einleitung in das Neue Testament* (1922); V. Taylor, "The Order of Q," *JTS* New Series 4 (1953): 29-30 (= *New Testament Essays* [1970] 92-3); Morgenthaler, *Statistische*, 250ff.

	LUKE		MATTHEW	
1	3:7-9, 16-17	Baptist's Preaching	3:7-12	1
2	4:2-13	Temptation of Jesus	4:2-11	2
3	6:20-23, 27-30, 32-36	Sermon on the Plain I	5:3-6, 11-12, 39-42, 45-48	3
4	6:37-38, 41-49	Sermon on the Plain II	7:1-5, 16-21, 24-27	7
5	7:1-10	Centurion from Capernaum	8:5-13	9
6	7:18-35	John the Baptist's Sayings	11:2-19	13
7	9:57-60	Sayings on Discipleship	8:19-22	10
8	10:1-12	Mission Discourse	9:37-10:15	11
9	10:13-15, 21-22	Woes and Joys	11:21-23, 25-26	14
10	11:1-4	Lord's Prayer	6:9-13	5
11	11:9-13	On Prayer	7:7-11	8
12	11:14-23	Beelzebub Controversy	12:22-30	15
13	11:24-26	Saying on Backsliding	12:43-45	17
14	11:29-32	Against Request for Miracles	12:38-42	16
15	11:33-35	Sayings on Light	5:15; 6:22-23	4
16	11:39-52	Against the Pharisees	23:4, 23-25, 29-36	19
17	12:2-10	Summons to Confession	10:26-33	12
18	12:22-34	Cares and Treasures	6:25-33, 19-21	6
19	12:39-46	Watchfulness	24:43-51	22
20	13:18-21	Mustard Seed and Leaven	13:31-33	18
21	13:34-35	Predictions Concerning Jerusalem	23:37-39	20
22	17:22-37	Discourse on the Parousia	24:26-28, 37-41	21
23	19:11-28	Parable of the Talents	25:14-30	23

In spite of the different methods of composition, the texts underlined appear in the same order in Matthew and Luke. Taylor has shown that the same holds true for numerous details as well, if one compares the individual sayings of Matthew with the Lukan order, rather than working from the entire sequence of Matthew.[13] Such agreement can be no accident and proves a common, written source.

c. The decisive evidence for a common, written source for Matthew and Luke is offered by the doublets, or double traditions (double traditions are texts presented by both evangelists, but in different forms; doublets are texts which one evangelist presents twice). It is noteworthy that Luke reports the sending of disciples twice: Lk. 9 and Lk. 10, the first time in parallel with Mk. 6:7-13 and the second in parallel with Mt. 10. Of course,

---

[13]See also A. Barr, *A Diagram of Synoptic Relationships* (1938).

in Lk. 10:1 there are seventy disciples, but as Lk. 22:35 shows, the saying in Lk. 10:4 was originally addressed to the twelve. Mt. 10:1-16 makes contact alternately with Mk. 6:7-13 and Lk. 10:1-12. Similarly there are doublets in Matthew, some of which parallel Mark while others parallel Luke's sayings material, for example, Mt. 18:8-9, and 5:29-30; 19:9 and 5:32.

Furthermore, there is a string of sayings of Jesus appearing twice in Matthew and Luke, once in a setting which Mark also has, a second time in a sayings setting which is found only in Matthew and Luke. The most important examples of this are:

> *a*) "He who has, to him will be given" (Mt. 13:12; Mk. 4:25; Lk. 8:18; cf. Mt. 25:29; Lk. 19:26).

> *b*) "If any man will follow me, he must deny himself" (Mt. 16:24-25; Mk. 8:34-35; Lk. 9:23-24; cf. Mt. 10:38-39; Lk. 14:27; 17:33).

> *c*) The eschatological retribution for the rejection of Jesus (Mt. 16:27; Mk. 8:38; Lk. 9:23-24; cf. Mt. 10:32; Lk. 12:8-9).

> *d*) Persecution of the disciples on account of Jesus (Mt. 24:9, 13; Mk. 13:9, 13, Lk. 21:12, 17; cf. Mt. 10:19-20, 22; Lk. 12:11-12).

> *e*) Mk. 3:23-30 is lacking in Luke; but Lk. 11:17-23 offers a different version of the defense of Jesus against the charge of complicity with the demons. Mt. 12:25-31, however, recalls alternately Mk. 3 and Lk. 11.[14]

When this evidence of doublets and double traditions in Matthew and Luke is placed beside the fact that Mark presents a single doublet (Mk. 9:35; 10:43),[15] it is incontrovertibly proved that Matthew and Luke must have used a second source in addition to Mark. That this source was available to Matthew and Luke in written form cannot be doubted in view of the extensive common sequence and the doublets, including Matthew's mingling of sources. The linguistic agreements demonstrate that this source was in Greek. Though among the sayings of Jesus transmitted in Q there are indubitable Aramaisms or translation variants, it cannot be inferred from that that the Greek Q source as a whole was translated from Ara-

---

[14]See the complete list of doublets in J. C. Hawkins, *Horae synopticae: Contributions to the Study of the Synoptic Problem*, 2d ed. (1909); B. de Solages, *Greek Synopsis*, 928ff.; and especially Morgenthaler, *Statistische*, 128ff.

[15]See de Solages, *Greek Synopsis*, 1069; Morgenthaler, *Statistische*, 140.

maic,[16] since the transition from Aramaic to Greek may very well have taken place at the oral stage of the tradition.

Attempts have been made to reconstruct Q,[17] but without any certain, agreed-upon results. That merely goes with the fact that we have as little certain knowledge of the exact extent of Q as we have of the wording of Q in detail. For if we can infer the existence of Q from the points of contact between Matthew and Luke in material lacking in Mark, what belongs to Q can be indicated only where there is extensive agreement in wording. But does that mean that texts such as the beatitudes (Mt. 5:3ff.; and Lk. 6:20ff.), that are transmitted in the same context, or the parable of the talents (or pounds), which in both Matthew and Luke comes at the end of the Q material, cannot stem from Q, since here, in spite of similar structure, the wording is only occasionally identical? And if we know on the basis of Matthew's and Luke's working over of the Markan material that each of them has omitted a string of Markan texts, could not Mark and Luke have preserved Q texts in their special sources, especially in those sections (such as Mt. 11:28-30 or Lk. 9:61-62) where on the whole the texts are reproduced in both Gospels? Because no unambiguous answer can be given to these questions, possible proof has been sought, and Schürmann, for example, thinks he can show by means of words used rarely or not at all in Luke or Matthew, that Matthew or Luke has read a certain text in Q but has omitted it. But that is entirely too hypothetical to lead to a sure conclusion about the extent of Q. Even if by stylistic, linguistic, or conceptual arguments we can infer an original text lying behind Matthew and Luke corresponding to a saying of Jesus that we find in Matthew or Luke,[18] it remains uncertain whether that version of the text stood in Q or is assumed as lying behind Q. Although the exact compass and order of Q is beyond our reach, some conjectures about its literary character may be advanced.

---

[16]Thus Bussby, "Aramaic Document"; in opposition, N. Turner, "Q in Recent Thought," *ET* 80 (1968-1969): 324-28; Lührmann, *Die Redaktion*, 85ff.; H.-W. Kühn, "Der irdische Jesus bei Paulus als traditionsgeschichtliches und theologisches Problem," *ZTK* 67 (1970): 309-10.

[17]Cf., for example, A. von Harnack, *Sprüche und Reden Jesu; Beiträge zur Einleitung in das Neue Testament* II (1907); B. H. Streeter, *The Four Gospels: A Study of Origins* (1924); W. Bussmann, *Synoptische Studien* I (1925); II (1929); III (1931); Taylor, "The Original Order"; E. Hirsch, *Frühgeschichte.* Lührmann, *Die Redaktion*, seeks to reconstruct the wording of Q for many individual pericopes.

[18]Thus, for example, Mt. 13:16-17 = Lk. 10:23-24. Cf. W. G. Kümmel, *Verhesissung und Erfüllung*, 3d ed. (1956) 105, n21 (= *Promise and Fulfillment* [1957] 112, n21).

Examination of the material which must be seriously considered as Q shows that mostly sayings material is involved, but that Q must have included some narrative material (cf. Lk. 4:2-13; 7:1-10; 7:18-23; 11:14-23; 11:29-32). But the claim that Q was a complete gospel[19] is an undemonstrable postulate. It is probable that from the beginning the arrangement of the material in Q was based on content, since this "gospel" seems to have been created for the practical needs of the church. We know from the letters of Paul that the sayings of the Lord in the apostolic age were assigned authority (cf. I Thess. 4:15; I Cor. 7:10, 12, 25; 9:14; 11:23ff.). But then one must reckon with the fact that the need arose very early for a fixed form of the words of Jesus. The beginnings of the process of fixation certainly reach back into the primitive Palestinian community, probably into its early period. As the arrangement of the sayings into sayings groups in Q indicates, this arrangement was done on the basis of content, probably because such an organization corresponded most closely to the purpose which this "gospel document" was to serve. But, for the arrangement of the writing as a whole, no conceptual principle may be inferred other than the fact that in Q as in Mark an account of the Baptist comes at the beginning and the parousia/judgment comes at the end.[20] By observing the differing ways in which Matthew and Luke have introduced the Q material into the Markan framework, we find that Matthew has strung the Q material throughout the whole of his Gospel, while Luke has it largely in two great blocks (6:20-7:35; 9:57-13:34), so that Luke preserves the sequence of Q better than Matthew. And Taylor's investigation of the sequence of Q material in the speeches in Matthew confirms the conjecture that Luke has followed the Q order on the whole, while Matthew has many times departed from the Q order, in keeping with the systematic recasting of his sources.

Even if this theory about the sequence of Q material as a whole is propounded, nothing generally valid can be said for the wording itself, because at times in Matthew (for example, 4:22ff.), at other times in Luke (6:20ff.), the more original tradition can be recognized. This circum-

---

[19]Hirsch, *Frühgeschichte*; Helmbold, *Vorsynoptische*.

[20]E. Bammel, "Das Ende von Q," *Verborum Veritas: Festschrift for G. Stählin* (1970) 39ff., would like to see Lk. 22:29, 30b (the transfer of power to the disciples before Jesus' death) as the ending of Q and infers from this the influence of the "testament" literature on the formation of Q. But the evidence that Lk. 22:29, 30b in its Lukan form stems from Q and stood at the end of it is hardly convincing.

stance, together with the presence of translation variants in Matthew and Luke[21] and the sharp difference between common texts (Mt. 25:14ff. par. Lk. 19:11ff.), often leads to the conjecture that Matthew and Luke had Q before them in somewhat different forms. If this conjecture were made more precise, that is, that Q consists only of a stratum of tradition in the process of growth,[22] that would clearly not be adequate to explain the state of affairs mentioned above [under headings a-c]. But if it is supposed that the written source Q developed in different directions,[23] so that perhaps on occasion the Greek form of one text or another was replaced by a divergent form from the oral tradition, this assumption best corresponds to the observation about a common text for Matthew and Luke.

If the attempt is made to classify the Q source historically and form-critically, no stress need be placed on the fact that the author is completely unknown to us. The oft-repeated hypothesis that the author was the apostle Matthew[24] is based entirely on Schleiermacher's problematical interpretation of the Papias witness about Matthew.[25] Q probably arose in Palestine, because it obviously consists of a collection influenced by the oral tradition of the sayings of Jesus even after the first written record was made.[26] In attempting to fix a time when Q was written, the question has

---

[21]Cf. M. Black, *An Aramaic Approach to the Gospels and Acts*, 3d ed. (1967) especially 186ff.

[22]R. H. Fuller, *A Critical Introduction to the New Testament* (1960); A. F. J. Klijn, *An Introduction to the New Testament* (1967); A. Schaefer, *Einleitung in das Neue Testament* (4th ed., rev. by M. Meinertz, 1933; 5th ed., 1950); G. Bornkamm, "Evangelien, synoptische," *RGG*, 3d ed. (1958) 2:754-70; M. Dibelius, *From Tradition to Gospel* (1935) 235; X. Léon-Dufour, "Interpretation des Évangiles et problème synoptique," *De Jésus aux Évangiles: Tradition et rédaction dans les Évangiles synoptiques* (1967) 16; E. Fascher, *Textgeschichte als hermeneutisches Problem* (1953) 76.

[23]Lührmann, *Die Redaktion*, 111ff., where it is made clear that Matthew used a form of Q expanded along Jewish-Christian lines.

[24]For example, Cole, *Mark;* M.-J. Lagrange, *L'Évangile selon Matthieu, Études bibliques,* 4th ed. (1927); M. Albertz, *Die Botschaft des Neuen Testaments* I, 1 (1947) I, 2 (1952); W. Michaelis, *Einleitung in das Neue Testament, Eine Einführung in ihre Probleme* (1963); A. H. McNeile, *An Introduction to the Study of the New Testament* (1927; 2d ed., 1953, ed. C. S. C. Williams).

[25]See Kümmel, *Introduction*, 45-46.

[26]Lührmann, *Die Redaktion*, 85ff., suggests a Syrian provenance because Mt. 11:27 par. stems from a Greek-speaking Hellenistic church and Q presupposes the Gentile mission; but both presuppositions are appropriate in the same way for the Palestinian church "in the mid 50s and 60s" (Lührmann).

been asked whether Q is older or more recent than Mark and whether a literary link between the two gospel documents exists. Since a detailed comparison of those texts where Mark and Q converge[27] shows that often Mark offers older tradition (for example, 3:28-29; 6:7ff.), but occasionally Q is older (for example, Lk. 3:16; Mt. 7:2 par.), it cannot be proved in a general way whether Mark or Q is the older text. That there is some sort of traditional connection between Mark and Q cannot be denied, but that does not lead to the assumption that this connection—which concerns only an extremely small part of the material in Q and Mark—is to be explained on the basis of a literary link between the two.[28] The assumption of literary dependence, which in view of the strong linguistic differences between Mark and Q in the double tradition (cf. for example, Mk. 4:30-32 with Lk. 13:18-19) is an extremely remote possibility, and is a consequence of the mistaken presupposition that the contacts among the traditional material can be explained solely on the basis of literary dependence. We have to perceive the relationship of the gospel writings to each other and to the oral tradition in an essentially looser way.[29]

Since any literary link between Mark and Q is improbable, the time of writing of Q cannot be determined in this way. Especially since Wellhausen, the attempt has been made to fix a *terminus a quo* by means of Lk. 11:50-51 (par. Mt. 23:35), where we read that "of this generation [will be

---

[27]See a list of double traditions in F. C. Grant, *The Gospels: Their Origin and Their Growth* (1957).

[28]According to A. Jülicher, *Einleitung in das Neue Testament* (1894; 7th ed. 1931, rev. in collaboration with E. Fascher) and J. Wellhausen, *Einleitung in die drei ersten Evangelien*, 2d ed. (1911), Q is dependent on Mark; similarly W. Schmithals, "Kein Streit um des Kaisers Bart," *Evangelische Kommentare* (1970) 3:80. According to M. Goguel, *Introduction au Nouveau Testament* I-IV, 1/2 (1922-1926, incomplete); J. P. Brown, "Mark as Witness;" J. Lambrecht, "Die Logien-Quelle von Markus 13," *Biblica* 47 (1966): 321-60; S. Schulz, *Die Stunde der Botschaft. Einführung in die Theologie der vier Evangelisten* (1967), Mark is dependent on Q. Any literary relationship is rejected by Albertz, *Die Botschaft*; P. Feine and J. Behm, *Einleitung in das Neue Testament* (1963); E. J. Goodspeed, *An Introduction to the New Testament* (1937) and *New Chapters in New Testament Study* (1937); W. Michaelis, *Einleitung*; G. Strecker, "Zur Geheimnistheorie im Mk," *SE* III, TU, 88 (1964) 87ff.; Bussmann, *Synoptische Studien*; Throckmorton, "Did Mark Know Q?"; E. Güttgemanns, *Offene Fragen zur Formgeschichte des Evangeliums. Eine methodische Skizze der Grundlagenproblematik der Form- und Redaktionsgeschichte* (1970); R. H. Stein, "What is Redaktionsgeschichte?," *JBL* 88 (1969): 45-56 and "The 'Redaktionsgeschichtliche' Investigation of a Markan Seam (Mk. 1:21f.)," *ZNW* 61 (1970): 70-94.

[29]See Kümmel, *Introduction*, 76-80.

required] the blood of all the prophets that has been poured out since the creation of the world, from the blood of Abel [Matthew adds, the righteous] to the blood of Zachariah [Matthew adds, the son of Berechaiah] who fell [Matthew: was murdered] between the altar and the house [Matthew: between the temple and the altar].'' In this threatening statement, which is essentially preserved in an older form in Luke,[30] Matthew's version mentions ''Zachariah, the son of Berechaiah,'' who has been identified with a certain Ζαχαρίας υἱὸς Βάρεις whose murder in the temple in A.D. 68 is reported by Josephus.[31] If it is considered probable that this man is intended,[32] it is hardly likely that mention of the father's name would have been omitted by Luke; rather, it must have been inserted by Matthew. The Zechariah named in the Q version of the saying, without indication of the father, can then only be the prophet Zechariah, son of Jehoida, whose stoning in the forecourt of the temple under King Joaz is recounted in 2 Chron. 24:20-21.[33] Even though questions still remain concerning this, it may be said with a high degree of probability that in the textual form in which it stood in Q this warning saying does not refer to the event of the year 68, so that from this passage no *terminus a quo* can be inferred for the editing of the sayings source.

Even though any possibility of a more exact dating of Q is impossible, it is unlikely that this document was completed later than *ca.* 50 to 70.

In what historical connection are we to understand the origin of this source? Since the material in Q is largely sayings material arranged topically, and since allusion to the passion story is completely lacking in what may be recognized as Q material, it has already been maintained in connection with a purely literary-critical consideration of the Gospels that the Q source displays a didactic or catechetical character, so that it was probably intended for the instruction of Christians on the religious, moral, and

---

[30]Cf. the outstanding analysis of O. H. Steck, *Israel und das gewaltsame Geschick der Propheten* [Israel and the violent fate of the prophets] (1967) 29ff., 33ff., where all the older literature is given.

[31]Josephus, *Jewish Wars* IV, 335-43. The name of the father, Βάρεις, is not transmitted consistently in the tradition, so its Hebrew equivalent is uncertain; see *De bello judaico*, edited by O. Michel and O. Bauerfeind, II, 1 (1963) 54, n137, and 219, n86.

[32]So Steck, *Geschick der Propheten*, 37ff.

[33]So once again Steck, ibid., 33ff.

communal life and pursued no evangelistic aims.[34] The form-critical approach too has contented itself with establishing that this collection of the sayings of Jesus was arranged in the interests of paraenesis. But since the fundamental importance of the Easter faith has been recognized, this collection of the sayings of Jesus could only be thought to have arisen and to have been made to serve paraenetic aims as a consequence of a progressive development of the primitive Christian community.[35] With some justification the opponents of a hypothesis of a Q source have objected that a source of this type is nowhere attested and one cannot conceive that in early Christianity there would be a collection of words of Jesus that left the passion story out of account. Accordingly Bornkamm and Tödt represent another historical understanding: a not inconsiderable part of the Q material cannot be shown to be paraenetic, but serves outspokenly Christological aims (cf. only Lk. 10:21-22) even though it does not presuppose a passion kerygma.[36] The words of Jesus were collected rather with the aim of extending the proclamation of the message of Jesus about the coming of God's kingdom and of the Son of man. Robinson[37] went a step farther and attempted to show by drawing together numerous parallels that sayings collections of this type were designated by the title of λόγοι, and that in Q Jesus was "considered as the Agent of Wisdom," so that the taking over of Q into the frame of Mark by Matthew and Luke implied criticism of this genre (*Gattung*). And according to Köster,[38] Q domesticated the *logoi*, in that the collector has carried out an equation of Jesus with the com-

---

[34]Goguel, *Introduction*; Jülicher, *Einleitung*; Wernle, *Synoptische Frage*. While T. W. Manson, *The Sayings of Jesus* (1949) 15-16, has noted the almost complete absence of polemic in Q, Lührmann would like to demonstrate that Q directs its polemic against all who close their minds to the preaching of the disciples. But the attempt at proof of a redaction of Q has hardly achieved its goal. On "more recent research on the sayings source," see Tödt, *Son of Man*, 235ff.

[35]M. Dibelius, *From Tradition to Gospel.*

[36]Among those in agreement, Fuller, *Introduction,* 73-74. Cf. also H. C. Kee, *Jesus in History: An Approach to the Study of the Gospels* (1970) 62-63, esp. 101-102, 105.

[37]J. M. Robinson, *Trajectories through Early Christianity* (1972) 71ff., esp. 86-87. Similarly H.-W. Kühn, "Der irdische Jesus," 310-11; M. J. Suggs, *Wisdom, Christology, and Law in Matthew's Gospel* (1970) 7-8.

[38]H. Koester, "Gnomai Diaphoroi," *Trajectories Through Early Christianity,* 114ff., and "One Jesus and Four Primitive Gospels," *Trajectories,* 158ff.

ing Son of man, while in the original λόγοι collection used by the Gospel of Thomas, sayings which speak of Jesus Christologically and apocalyptic pronouncements are lacking. But it must be said first of all against Robinson and Köster that neither through Jewish parallels nor through linguistic usage in the Synoptic Gospels is it demonstrable that the sayings source was designated as λόγοι and Jesus was represented as wisdom teacher, even though some of the Jesus words in Q can be characterized as "wisdom words." Köster can support his assumption of a more original λόγοι collection earlier than Q, and not yet containing the apocalyptic expectation of the Son of man, only by asserting that only the message of the coming kingdom of God corresponds to the preaching of Jesus and to the oldest gospel tradition.[39] But this thoroughly dubious reduction of the message of Jesus[40] can in no way prove the existence of this original collection, nor can it show that faith is here understood to be faith in the word of Jesus. Bornkamm, Tödt, and Hoffmann have far more justification for their thesis that the words of Jesus were collected with the aim of continuing proclamation and through faith in their enduring validity, so that Q's taking over of the self-utterances of Jesus (for example, Mt. 12:32; 13:16-17 par.) serves the same kerygmatic goals in Mark. It is questionable, however, whether the lack of any reference to the suffering of Jesus or to any passion story of whatever kind may be made to mean that Q presupposes no passion kerygma. Even if the *argumentum e silentio* is given weight—in reality, of course, we know nothing certain about the original extent of Q!—we must consider that in the Palestinian community in which Q must have originated[41] the passion kerygma repeated by Paul (1 Cor. 15:3ff.) was formulated at a very early date and that it attests the redemptive significance of the death of Jesus. In that case the collecting of the words of Jesus could not have taken place in conscious disregard of this basic confession (see also 1 Cor. 11:25). It is much more likely that Käsemann,[42] is right and that the *Sitz im Leben* of the sayings source is in the

---

[39]So Koester, ibid., 171ff., where he invokes P. Vielhauer, *Aufzätze zum Neuen Testament* (1955) 55ff., 92ff.; and N. Perrin, *Rediscovering the Teaching of Jesus* (1967) 164ff.

[40]See my objections against Perrin in *Journal of Religion* 49 (1969): 59ff., (esp. 64-65) and W. G. Kümmel, *The Theology of the New Testament According to Its Major Witnesses* (1973) 76ff.

[41]Cf. Hoffmann, "Die Anfänge."

[42]E. Käsemann, "On the Subject of Primitive Christian Apocalyptic," *New Testament Questions for Today* (1969) 108ff.

oldest Christian community, who believed in the resurrection of the One crucified, and who sought and found in the words of Jesus instructions for their missionary preaching and for their life as disciples. Others have rightly drawn attention[43] to the fact that the words of Jesus were collected under the presupposition that the risen Lord is giving his community instructions in full exercise of his authority, so that coping theologically with the death and resurrection of Jesus is the presupposition for the formation of the sayings source. The sayings source also presupposes the interpretation of the death of Jesus as a victorious conflict (cf. Lk. 12:20 par.; 13:34-35 par.; 14:27 par.) The question why the community which stands behind the Q collection ''did not make the passion and resurrection part of its proclamation'' (Tödt) takes the absence of statements about the passion and resurrection from what can be surely identified as Q material as sure evidence of the original compass of Q, and is itself accordingly problematical. As a hypothesis one can still refer to the theory that apparently Q was organized for the need of the community itself, for whose existence the primitive Christian kerygma was a presupposition.[44] Beyond this we have no knowledge as to whether or not the oldest literary form of ''gospel'' as it is accessible to us in Mark emerged in the same community and at the same time. In any case, the source Q owes its existence to the need of a Christian community that separated itself from Judaism, to strengthen its faith in the Advent and the awaited fulfillment of the kingdom of God by appeal to the traditional words of the risen Jesus and to provide guidelines for its preaching.

---

[43]H. R. Balz, *Methodische Probleme der neutestamentliche Christologie* (1967) 167ff.; W. Thüsing, ''Erhöhungsvorstellung und Parusieewartung in der ältesten nachösterlichen Christologie,'' *BZ* Neue Folge 12 (1968): 60ff. (= W. Thüsing, ''Erhöhungsvorstellung . . .'' *Stuttgarter Bibelstudien* 42 [1969]: 55ff.); T. Boman, *Die Jesusüberlieferung im Lichte der neueren Volkskunde* (1967) 103ff.; K. Lehmann, ''Aufweckt am dritten Tag nach der Schrift,'' *Questiones disputatae* 38 (1968): 123-24.

[44]In view of the already mentioned interpretation of the death of Jesus as a victorious conflict and the presence of such Christological expressions as Mt. 13:16-17 par.; Lk. 12:8-9 par.; Mt. 11:27 par., the assumption is false that for Q ''the continuity between Jesus and the church is provided in eschatology, not in the kerygma,'' and that not Jesus but the coming judgment was the content of the preaching (Lührmann, *Die Redaktion*, 96-97). The assertion that ''the passion Kerygma . . . must lie behind Q'' is by no means ''an impermissible harmonization'' (against H.-W. Kühn, ''Der irdische Jesus,'' 309) and the absence of a passion narrative cannot be accounted for on the basis of a postulated genre, ''words of a wise man'' (against M. J. Suggs, *Christology and Law*, 9).

Even if the formation of a collection of sayings of Jesus and stories about him without passion narrative is conceivable in this way, the attempt has been made to dismiss the further objection that a collection of this sort with no narrative framework has no parallel, by pointing to the Coptic Gospel of Thomas, which belongs to the Gnostic papyrus discovery from Nag Hammadi.[45] The text, which is designated at the conclusion as "The Gospel according to Thomas," consists of 114 sayings of Jesus, placed after each other disconnectedly; in a majority of cases they are introduced with the words "Jesus said," but occasionally a disciple's question is answered or even a completely detached saying is linked with an indication of the circumstances. In addition to catchwords, the organizing principle of the sequence of sayings can be recognized almost solely at the beginning. A portion of the sayings are purely Gnostic, but a larger part more or less agree with the synoptic words of Jesus, or at least strongly resemble the type of sayings of Jesus in the Synoptics. It has often been asserted that the possibility of the existence of a sayings source has been demonstrated by this discovery.[46] And many scholars have sought to demonstrate that the Gospel of Thomas is dependent, not on the Synoptics, but on a tradition of the words of Jesus which is independent of the Synoptics, perhaps even of the transmission process which underlies them.[47] The case for bas-

---

[45]English translations by A. Guillaumont et al., *Gospel of Thomas*, with Coptic text (1959); by B. M. Metzger, in K. Aland, *Synopsis*, 517ff.; in Hennecke-Schneemelcher, *New Testament Apocrypha*, ed. R. McL. Wilson (1963) 1:286ff. Survey of bibliography by E. Haenchen, *TR* Neue Folge 27 (1961): 147ff., 306ff.; by H. Quecke in *La Venue du Messie*, Recherches Bibliques 6 (1962) 217ff.; by K. Rudolph, "Gnosis und Gnostizismus, ein Forschungsbericht," *Theologische Rundschau* Neue Folge 34 (1969): 181ff.

[46]Thus, for example, C.-H. Hunzinger, "Aussersynoptisches Traditionsgut im Thomas-Evangelium" *TL* 85 (1960): 843-46; O. Cullmann, "Das Thomas-Evangelium und die Frage nach dem Alter der in ihm enthaltenen Tradition" [The Gospel of Thomas and the question of the age of the tradition it contains] *TL* 85 (1960): 330-31; H. K. McArthur, "The Gospel according to Thomas," *New Testament Sidelights: Essays in Honor of A. C. Purdy* (1960) 44; F. V. Filson, "New Testament Greek and Coptic Gospel Manuscripts," *BA* 24 (1961): 17; F. G. Downing, "Towards the Rehabilitation of Q," *NTS* 11 (1964-65): 181.

[47]Thus, for example, Hunzinger, "Aussersynoptisches Traditionsgut"; Cullmann, "Das Thomas-Evangelium"; G. Quispel, "Some Remarks on the Gospel of Thomas," *NTS* 5 (1958-1959): 277; R. McL. Wilson, " 'Thomas' and the Growth of the Gospels," *HTR* 53 (1960): 231-50; R. Haardt, "Das koptische Thomasevangelium und die ausserbiblischen Herrenworte," in *Der historische Jesus und der Christus unseres Glaubens*, ed.

ing the Gospel of Thomas on a tradition independent of the Synoptics is by no means convincing. It is much more likely that the Gospel of Thomas cites the canonical Gospels according to the oral tradition and freely alters them, and that in this way non-Gnostic sayings of Jesus have been taken up throughout from the free tradition.[48] But from this it follows that the Gospel of Thomas is undoubtedly not a later form of the same literary genre as Q, but is a later, wholly different stage in the development of the tradition of the words of Jesus.[49] That conclusion results not only from the lack of any narrative or of any conceptual order, but above all from the lack of any Christology and so of any sort of relationship with the development of the gospel that is for the first time evident in Mark. The Gospel of Thomas presupposes the transformation of Jesus into the role of a Gnostic revealer, and shows in this way that it is a literary form of a later period.

Although the Gospel of Thomas can teach us nothing about the origin and the literary character of Q, by juxtaposition and blending of altered synoptic texts with texts taken from the tradition, it nevertheless shows us a phenomenon which is of great importance for the understanding of the Synoptic Gospels.

---

by K. Schubert (1962) 277; H. Montefiore in H. Montefiore and B. W. Turner, *Thomas and the Evangelists* (1962) 78; H. Quecke, 237; J. B. Bauer, "The Synoptic Tradition in the Gospel of Thomas," *SE* III, TU, 88 (1964) 314; T. Schramm, *Der Markus-Stoff bei Lukas* (1971) 9ff.; J. M. Robinson, *Kerygma und historischer Jesus*, 2d ed. (1967) 130 (with reservation); H. Koester, *Trajectories* (1971) 129, 163ff. According to Koester, no one has weakened Bultmann's contention that Saying 31 in the Gospel of Thomas is more original than Mk. 6:1-6; but H. Schürmann, "Das Thomasevangelium und das luk. Sondergut," *BZ* Neue Folge 7 (1963): 237-38, has shown that this saying is dependent on Lk. 4:22ff. See also A. J. B. Higgins, "The Gospel of Thomas," *The Tradition About Jesus* (1969) 30ff.

[48]Cf. H. K. McArthur, "The Gospel according to Thomas," 61, 65; E. Haenchen, *TR* Neue Folge 27 (1961): 314; H. E. W. Turner, *Thomas and the Evangelists;* Schürmann, "Das Thomasevangelium," 253; W. Schrage, *Das Verhältnis des Thomas-Evangeliums zur synoptischen Tradition und zu den koptischen Evangelienübersetzungen* [The Relation of Thomas to the synoptic Gospels and to the translations of the Gospels into Coptic]; *Beiheft, ZNW* 29 (1964); K. Rudolph, "Gnosis und Gnostizismus," 189-90; E. P. Sanders, *Tendencies,* 42.

[49]Thus rightly R. McL. Wilson, *Studies in the Gospel of Thomas* (1960) 143; J. B. Bauer in R. M. Grant and D. N. Freedman, *The Secret Sayings of Jeus* (1960) 106ff.; E. Haenchen, *Theologische Rundschau,* Neue Folge 27 (1961): 316; B. Gärtner, *The Theology of the Gospel of Thomas* (1961) 30; K. Rudolph, "Gnosis und Gnostizismus," 186; Lührmann, *Die Redaktion,* 91.

LUKE'S USE OF Q

J. A. Fitzmyer*

The non-Markan material common to Matthew and Luke could be due to Matthew's borrowing from Luke, or Luke's borrowing from Matthew, or their common use of an earlier source, commonly called "Q." Fitzmyer summarizes the five principal reasons for denying Luke's dependence on Matthew.

1. The apparent reluctance of Luke to reproduce typically Matthean "additions" within the Triple Tradition;

2. it is difficult to explain adequately why Luke would want to break up Matthew's sermons, especially the Sermon on the Mount;

3. with two exceptions, Luke has never inserted the material of the Double Tradition into the same Markan context as has Matthew;

4. analysis of the Double Tradition material in Matthew and Luke shows that sometimes Matthew, sometimes Luke has preserved the more original setting of a given episode;

5. if Luke depends on Matthew, why has he almost constantly omitted Matthean material in episodes where there is no Markan parallel (for example, the infancy and resurrection narratives)?

*J. A. Fitzmyer, "Luke's Use of Q," from "The Priority of Mark and the 'Q' Source," *Jesus and Man's Hope* (Pittsburgh Theological Seminary, 1970) 1:147-56.

These five reasons for denying Luke's dependence on Matthew form the background for Fitzmyer's more specific discussion of the reasons for the postulated Greek written source "Q."

1. The number of crucial texts in which Matthew and Luke agree with almost identical wording is such that common dependence on a source is called for;

2. the material of the Double Tradition inserted into Matthew and Luke in different contexts manifests a common general and underlying sequence or order;

3. doublets (that is, the same event or saying occurring twice) in either Matthew or Luke seem to be part of the Triple Tradition (that is, derived from Mark), on the one hand, and of the Double Tradition (that is, derived from Q), on the other.

Fitzmyer believes that the postulated Q source may have been part of the *didache* of some early communities, representing mainly a collection of sayings of Jesus gathered from various oral traditions and formulated anew in view of the various *Sitze im Leben* (preaching, controversy, casuistry, catechetics, liturgy). Despite the obvious problem that Q is a hypothetical entity, the Q source will continue to command attention until a more useful hypothesis is convincingly proposed.

Once again it is almost impossible to discuss the hypothesis of Luke's use of Q without bringing in the question of Matthew's use of it too, since by definition Q is the postulated Greek written source underlying some 225 verses common to Matthew and Luke and not found in Mark. This non-Markan material in Matthew and Luke is usually referred to as the Double Tradition. Such common non-Markan material could be due to Matthew borrowing from Luke, or to Luke borrowing from Matthew, or to their common use of an earlier source. Today, very few would consider it likely that Matthew has derived such material from Luke.[1] A number of Gospel commentators, however, do maintain that Luke has used Matthew, but the majority rather espouse their common use of a postulated source, called Q.[2] To establish the independent existence of this source is more difficult than to establish the priority of Mark. Moreover, it is to be noted

---

[1]See the discussion in L. Vaganay, *Le Problème synoptique* (1954) 294-95. A nuanced position is found in the article of H. P. West, Jr., "A Primitive Version of Luke in the Composition of Matthew," *NTS* 14 (1967-1968): 75-96.

[2]For attempts to trace the origin of this siglum, see W. F. Howard, "The Origin of the Symbol 'Q'," *ET* 50 (1938-1939): 379-80.

that some commentators who admit the priority of Mark over Luke[3] deny the existence of the postulated second source (maintaining either the priority of Matthew over both Mark and Luke, or at least that Luke depends on both Mark and Matthew.

Before the survey of the reasons for the postulated Q is begun, the more general question of Luke's dependence on Matthew has to be posed.[4] For Luke's dependence on Matthew is an issue that is not restricted only to the Double Tradition. We have already noted Farrer's contention that the Two-Source Theory was erected on "the incredibility" of Luke having used Matthew. Some of the main reasons for denying such use must now be reviewed, before we proceed to the more specific question of Q. They can be summed up under the following five headings.

First, the apparent reluctance of Luke to reproduce typically Matthean "additions" within the Triple Tradition. In thus phrasing the matter, I may seem to be prejudging the issue. But I am only trying to refer to the fuller Matthean formulation of parallels in Mark, such as the exceptive clause on divorce (Mt. 19:9; cf. Mk. 10:11);[5] Jesus' promise to Peter (Mt. 16:16b-

---

[3]For example, B. C. Butler, *The Originality of St. Matthew: A Critique of the Two-Document Hypothesis* (1951); A. M. Farrer, "On Dispensing with Q," *Studies in the Gospels: Essays in Memory of R. H. Lightfoot* (1955).

[4]It has been espoused by J. H. Ropes, *The Synoptic Gospels*, 2d ed. (1960); H. G. Jameson, *The Origin of the Synoptic Gospels: A Revision of the Synoptic Problem* (1922) 6; B. C. Butler, *Originality*, 22, and "St. Luke's Debt to St. Matthew," *HTR* 32 (1939): 237-308; W. R. Farmer, *The Synoptic Problem: A Critical Appraisal* (1964) 221-25; R. T. Simpson, "The Major Agreements of Matthew and Luke against Mark," *NTS* 12 (1965-1966): 273-84 [reprinted in this volume]; W. Wilkens, "Zur Frage der literarischen Beziehung zwischen Matthäus und Lukas," *NT* 8 (1966): 48-57; A. W. Argyle, "The Methods of the Evangelists and the Q Hypothesis," *Theology* 67 (1964): 156-57; K. H. Rengstorff, *Das Evangelium nach Lukas* (1962) 8-9; A. Schlatter, *Das Evangelium des Lukas: Aus seinen Quellen erklärt,* 2d ed. (1960) 472-561.

[5]W. R. Farmer treats this passage in *Synoptic Problem*, 255-57, using it as a prime example for the Griesbach solution. He regards the Lukan text (16:18) as "a conflation" of Mt. 19:9 and 5:32 and is mainly concerned with the genuine problems of the assumed remarriage of the divorced woman and of the Roman practice that is reflected in the Markan version. But he devotes little time to what seems to be a crucial problem: What would have led Luke to excise the exceptive clause in Matthew? An appeal to Paul's absolute formulation of the prohibition of divorce in 1 Cor. 7:10 scarcely solves the problem, because it only raises the larger one whether Luke was acquainted with Paul's letters at all. Again, to picture Mark twice confronted with the exceptive clause in Mt. 5:32 and 19:9 and twice excising it because he was more influenced by Luke's version from which it is absent is not a convincing argument. For another view of this passage, see A. Isaksson, *Marriage and Ministry in the New Temple* (1965) 96-104.

19; cf. Mk. 8:29);[6] Peter's walking on the waters (Mt. 14:28-31; cf. Mk. 6:50);[7] and the peculiar Matthean episodes in the passion narrative. When Matthew and Mark are considered alone, it may be difficult to decide the dependence or priority in such cases. To my way of thinking, they are more readily intelligible as Matthean "additions" than as Markan excisions. But the real issue is to explain Luke's failure to adopt the extra Matthean materials in his parallels, or at least some of them, if he has written in dependence on Matthew—or used Mark as his main source and quarried Matthew only for such material as would suit his own edifice.[8] The few examples cited above, having to do with pericopes, do not give a full picture of this phenomenon; it is necessary to compare a whole list of smaller Matthean additions to Mark, which are absent in Luke.[9] For instance,

---

[6] See W. R. Farmer's treatment of this passage in "The Two-Document Hypothesis as a Methodological Criterion in Synoptic Research," *ATR* 48 (1966) 380-96. B. C. Butler, *Originality*, 168, sought to defend the Matthean priority of Mt. 16:16ff. But his explanation that Peter, in "telling the Caesarea Philippi incident" and using Matthew as his *aide-memoire*, tore out "the story of the high praise of himself and the promise of his peculiar status vis-à-vis the Church, while leaving the stinging rebuke," because he had learned "the lesson of Christian humility" is too rhetorical to be convincing. I personally see no difficulty in understanding this passage as a Matthean addition, along with the stories about the coin in the mouth of the fish that Peter is to catch and his walking on the waters. They are three episodes in the First Gospel that were added to the so-called ecclesiastical section to enhance Peter's role.

[7] In the hypothesis of Luke's dependence on Matthew, the problem of his apparent reluctance to reproduce Matthean material can also be illustrated in the Double Tradition (for example, the fuller form of the Beatitudes [Mt. 5:3, cf. Lk. 6:20; Mt. 5:6, cf. Lk. 6:21]; the fuller form of the Lord's Prayer [Mt. 6:6-13, cf. Lk. 11:2-4]). See J. Dupont, *Les béatitudes*, new ed. (1958), 43-128. What seems to be an issue here is a Matthean pattern of additions made to dominical sayings, a pattern that accounts readily for his differences from Mark and Luke in the Triple Tradition and from Luke in the Triple Tradition and from Luke in the Double Tradition.

[8] To paraphrase the words of A. M. Farrer, "On Dispensing with Q," 65.

[9] See F. G. Downing, "Toward the Rehabilitation of Q," *NTS* 11 (1964-1965): 168-81 (arguing against Farrer) [reprinted in this volume]; E. L. Bradby, "In Defence of Q," *ET* 68 (1956-1957): 315-18 (despite its title, this article really deals with this issue) [reproduced in this volume]. *Pace* N. Turner, "The Minor Verbal Agreements of Mt. and Lk. against Mk.," *SE* 1 TU, 73 (1959): 223-34, this evidence is not all the result of a subjective approach, or the use of the English text alone, nor does it really involve the minor agreements of Matthew and Luke against Mark. Several arguments are confused by him; cf. J. Schmid, *Matthäus and Lukas*, 25ff.

Lk. 3:22	Mt. 3:17	(the public proclamation)	Cf. Mk. 1:11
Lk. 5:3	Mt. 4:18	("who is called Peter")	Cf. Mk. 1:16
Lk. 5:27	Mt. 9:9	("Matthew")	Cf. Mk. 2:14
Lk. 6:4-5	Mt. 12:5-7	(plucking grain on the Sabbath)	Cf. Mk. 2:26-27
Lk. 8:18b	Mt. 13:12a	(being given in excess)	Cf. Mk. 4:25
Lk. 8:10-11	Mt. 13:14	(quotations of Is. 6:9-10)	Cf. Mk. 4:12
Lk. 9:1-5	Mt. 10:7	(nearness of the kingdom)	Cf. Mk. 6:7-11
Lk. 9:20b	Mt. 16:16b	(Peter's confession)	Cf. Mk. 8:29b

Similar instances could still be added. The question is how to account for the Lukan omission of such Matthean material, in the hypothesis that Luke used Matthew. It is not convincing merely to state that he preferred the simpler Markan form.[10]

Secondly, it is difficult to explain adequately why Luke would want to break up Matthew's sermons, especially the Sermon on the Mount, in order to incorporate a part of it in his Sermon on the Plain and scatter the rest around in an unconnected and disjointed fashion in the loose context of the travel account. Even though one must admit that this central portion of Luke is redactionally very important in the composition of the Third Gospel and that it constitutes a "mosaic" in its own right, yet the tension between its matter and its form (that is, between its loosely connected or almost unconnected episodes or sayings and its unifying preoccupation

---

[10]Perhaps one should also consider the converse phenomenon in Luke; for example, his apparent failure to follow Matthew in omitting Markan passages (for example, Lk. 4:33-37 = Mk. 1:23-28 [Jesus in the synagogue of Capernaum]; Lk. 9:49-50 = Mk. 12:41-44 [the widow's mite]). Farrer has sought to offset this and other arguments which bear on Luke's omission of Matthean material by implying that they are based on an antiquated view of Luke as a collector of Jesus' sayings and a failure to realize that he is really "building an edifice" ("On Dispensing with Q," 63). In one form or another Farrer continually comes back to this line of argumentation: Luke using a Markan skeleton, clothed with material cut from Matthew; or Luke as the gardener, expressing his preference for his own new arrangement over that which his predecessor has left him (65). To describe Luke's edifice, Farrer indulges in ingenious typological eisegesis. The major part of his article is given over to establishing a pattern between Luke (and Matthew) and the Hexateuch. With the advance of *Redaktionsgeschichte* it is certainly wrong to say that Luke is regarded simply as a collector of Jesus' sayings; most of the modern commentators who espouse the Two-Source Theory would reject this and insist on the theological "edifice" in the Third Gospel as much as Farrer does. That this edifice was constructed, however, as Farrer sketches it is another matter. In the matter of typological interpretation one must always ask the question: Who is seeing the connections and patterns, Farrer or the Evangelist? In this regard one would do well to consult the estimate of Farrer's work on Mark by no less a literary critic than Helen L. Gardner, *The Business of Criticism* (1959) 108-22.

with Jesus' movement toward Jerusalem that appears from time to time [Lk. 9:51, 53; 13:22; 17:11; 19:28]) has always been a problem.[11] Whatever explanation is to be given for it and for Luke's redactional purpose in constructing this central section, the explanation that he has quarried the material from Matthew's sermons is the least convincing.

Thirdly, aside from 3:7-9, 17 and 4:2-13 Luke has never inserted the material of the Double Tradition into the same Markan context as Matthew. If he derives such material from Matthew—and otherwise manifests such respect for a source that he is following, as his dependence on Mark would suggest[12]—it is surprising that at least some of the remaining Double Tradition material does not occur in contexts that parallel Matthew, which are often quite appropriate to this material. The frequent disagreement with the Matthean order in this regard is crucial to any judgment about Luke's dependence on Matthew; in fact it suggests that he does not depend.

Fourthly, analysis of the Double Tradition material in Matthew and Luke shows that sometimes Matthew, sometimes Luke has preserved what can only be described as the more original setting of a given episode.[13] This would seem to be scarcely the case if Luke were always dependent on Matthew within this tradition. It is, however, readily intelligible in the hypothesis that both of them have been following and editing a common source.

Fifthly, if Luke depends on Matthew, why has he almost constantly omitted Matthean material in episodes where there are Matthean, but no Markan parallels, for example, in the infancy and resurrection narratives?

These are the five main reasons for denying Luke's dependence on Matthew. They have to be coped with in a real way whenever the contrary thesis is maintained. They form, moreover, the background for the more specific discussion of the Lukan and Matthean use of Q.

That Matthew and Luke both used a common source is a partial hypothesis of the Two-Source Theory. Farrer has maintained that this ''is its

---

[11]See. W. C. Robinson, Jr., ''The Theological Context for Interpreting Luke's Travel Narrative (9:51ff.),'' *JBL* 79 (1960): 20-31; L. Vaganay, *Le problème synoptique*, 106-108.

[12]For some keen observations on this problem, see T. R. Rosché, ''The Words of Jesus and the Future of the 'Q' Hypothesis,'' *JBL* 79 (1960): 210-20 [reprinted in this volume].

[13]See L. Vaganay, *Le problème synoptique*, 295-99; B. H. Streeter, *The Four Gospels: A Study of Origins* (1924) 183.

weakness," and that the Lukan use of Matthew is not "a contrary hypothesis."[14] This view of the situation was exposed by F. G. Downing, who maintained "that Luke used Matthew must in the nature of the case remain as much an hypothesis as the one-time existence of Q."[15] It is but another reason for my own preliminary remark about "the truth of the matter" and the hypothesis with which one must deal in this matter. Q is admittedly a hypothetical entity, but it remains to be seen whether it is "an unnecessary and vicious hypothesis," as Butler has labeled it, or "a nebulosity, a capriciousness, an intractability," as S. Petrie has called it.[16]

The following are the main reasons for the postulated Greek written source Q.[17] First, the number of crucial texts in which Matthew and Luke agree almost with identical wording, at times even word-for-word, is such that common dependence on a source is called for.[18] Thus in passages such as these:

Mt. 3:7b-10	Lk 3:7b-9	The speech of John the Baptist; 61 of 63 words are identical and the two differences are clearly Lukan stylistic improvements (ἄρξησθε for δόξητε; an added adverbial καί).
Mt. 6:24	Lk 16:13	The saying about serving two masters; 27 out of 28 words are identical.
Mt. 7:3-5	Lk. 6:41-42	On judging; 50 out of 64 words are identical.
Mt. 7:7-11	Lk. 11:9-13	The efficacy of prayer; 59 out of 74 words are identical.
Mt. 11:4-6, 7b-11	Lk. 7:22-23, 24b-28	Jesus' answer and testimony about John the Baptist; 100 out of 121 words are identical.

---

[14]Farrer, "On Dispensing with Q," 66 [reprinted in this volume].

[15]Downing, "Towards the Rehabilitation of Q," 180, n5 [reprinted in this volume]. See also W. H. Blyth Martin, "The Indispensability of Q," *Theology* 59 (1956): 182-88; esp. 182.

[16]B. C. Butler, *Originality*, 170; S. Petrie, " 'Q' Is Only What You Make It," *NT* 3 (1959): 28-33.

[17]For an attempt to make Q out to be a "written Aramaic source," see F. Bussby, "Is Q an Aramaic Document?" *ET* 65 (1953-1954): 272-75.

[18]Strictly speaking one might object that such data argue only for the dependence of Luke on Matthew, or more generically, of one on the other. This would have to be admitted if this argument stood alone. It must, however, be considered against the background of the general issues already discussed above, which rule out the dependence of Luke on Matthew.

Mt. 11:21-23	Lk. 10:13-15	Woes against the towns of Galilee; 43 out of 49 words are identical.
Mt. 11:25-27	Lk. 10:21-22	Jesus' praise of the Father; 50 out of 69 words are identical.
Mt. 12:43-45	Lk. 11:24-25	Return of the evil spirit; 53 out of 61 words are identical.
Mt. 23:37-38	Lk. 13:34-35	Lament over Jerusalem; 46 out of 55 words are identical.
Mt. 24:45-51	Lk. 12:42-46	Sayings about vigilance; 87 out of 104 words are identical.

The differences in the above list may seem at times a little high; but one would have to look at the concrete cases, which often enough involve stylistic variants (for example, Luke eliminates a paratactic καί that Matthew has preserved).

Secondly, it is scarcely coincidental that the material of the Double Tradition inserted into the First and Third Gospels in different contexts manifests a common general underlying sequence or order. This can hardly be due to oral tradition and seems rather to argue for a written source. Most of this material is inserted in Matthew into Markan contexts and sermon blocks, whereas in Luke it scarcely ever appears in Markan contexts but is generally grouped in separate, interpolated blocks—or, as Streeter once put it, "Matthew conflates his sources, Luke alternates them."[19] Given this situation, one would scarcely expect a common sequence of any sort in the Double Tradition. And yet, there is a trace of such a sequence.

One way of detecting this common sequence is found in the two-column line-up of parallels of the Double Tradition frequently presented in Introductions to the New Testament (for example, in that of Feine-Behm-Kümmel[20]). This list begins with the order of the Lukan material and compares the Matthean with it; the common order is more apparent at the beginning and the end of the list than in the middle. A better way, however, has been discovered by V. Taylor,[21] who at first set forth the Double Tradition in seven columns: the first of which presented the Lukan order, the

---

[19]Streeter, *Four Gospels*, 187.

[20]P. Feine, J. Behm, W. Kümmel, *Introduction to the New Testament*, 14th ed., trans. A. J. Mattill, Jr. (1966) 52.

[21]V. Taylor, "The Order of Q," *JTS* 4 (1953): 27-31; "The Original Order of Q," *New Testament Essays: Studies in Memory of T. W. Manson 1893-1958* (1959) 246-69 [reprinted in this volume].

next five columns the common material as it appears in each of the five great Matthean sermons, and the seventh as it appears in Matthew outside of the sermons. Taylor's method respects the Matthean scattering of the material, mainly in the sermons, and beyond them. In his first discussion of this matter Taylor had eliminated certain questionable material; but he returned to the issue later and did a more comprehensive study, comparing the Lukan order in detail with each of the sermons in Matthew and the extra-sermon passages. What is striking in this detailed comparison is the amount of agreement in sequence that is revealed, not in the overall order, but in the individual Matthean sections when they are compared with Luke. When there is lack of agreement, it frequently occurs because Matthew inserts Double Tradition material into blocks of his own special material (M), and strives for a topical arrangement. At times this argument from the order of the Double Tradition material has been impugned, but I have so far uncovered no real attempt to cope with or refute the Taylor presentation of it.[22]

A third reason for postulating Q is found in the doublets in Luke (and in Matthew). By a "doublet" is meant here an account of the same event or saying occurring twice in either Luke or Matthew and related in such wise that they seem to be part of the Triple Tradition on the one hand and of the Double Tradition on the other—or to put it another way, that one belongs to a tradition parallel to Mark and one to a tradition not parallel to Mark. The conclusion drawn from this phenomenon is that Matthew and Luke have retained in their gospels the double accounts of the same event or saying as they inherited them independently from Mark and from Q. Thus in Luke we note the following doublets.

From the Markan Source		*From the Q Source*	
8:16	(= Mk. 4:21)	11:33	(= Mt. 5:15)
8:17	(= Mk. 4:22)	12:2	(= Mt. 10:26)
8:18	(= Mk. 4:25; Mt. 13:12)	19:26	(= Mt. 25:29)

---

[22]Cf. C. K. Barrett, "Q: A Re-examination," *ET* 54 (1942-1943): 320-23, for an earlier denial of the validity of this argument [reprinted in this volume]. Taylor quotes some of the results of the investigation of P. Parker, *The Gospel Before Mark*, 30, to support his contention: "since Q has not been assimilated to Matthean types of expression" and "the style of Q does not pervade M, therefore Q and M have different origins" and "Q is really from an autonomous source"; see Taylor, "The Original Order," 269. O. E. Evans, "Synoptic Criticism Since Streeter," *ET* 72 (1960-1961): 298 is also favorably impressed by Streeter's argument.

9:3-5	(= Mk. 6:8-11)	10:4, 5-7,	
		10-11	(= Mt. 10:1, 10-12, 14)
9:23-24	(= Mk. 8:34-35;	14:27	(= Mt. 10:38-39)
	Mt. 16:24-25)		
9:26	(= Mk. 8:38; Mt. 16:27)	12:9	(= Mt. 10:33)[23]

These are the three main reasons for postulating Q. Admittedly, no one has ever seen this source isolated; attempts to ferret it out have certainly not been able to claim success or to command universal agreement.[24] It may never have been the literary unit that Mark is (or that Ur-Markus was). Part of the problem encountered here is the lack of agreement as to how much really belongs to Q; this is the loophole in this part of the theory. There is also the difficulty of passages that, considered globally, would seem to belong to the Q source and yet display such a disagreement in word order and vocabulary that one hesitates to label them clearly as derived solely from Q. V. Taylor lists seven such passages:

Lk. 10:25-28	Mt. 22:34-39	(Saying about the Great Commandment)
Lk. 12:54-56	Mt. 16:2-3	(Saying about signs of the times)
Lk. 13:23-24	Mt. 17:13-14	(Saying about the narrow gate)
Lk. 13:25-27	Mt. 7:22-23; 25:10-12	(Saying about the shut door)
Lk. 14:15-24	Mt. 22:1-10	(Parable of the great supper)
Lk. 15:4-7	Mt. 18:12-14	(Parable of the lost sheep)
Lk. 19:12-27	Mt. 25:14-30	(Parable of the pounds)[25]

---

[23] See further J. C. Hawkins, *Horae Synopticae: Contributions to the Study of the Synoptic Problem,* 2d ed. (1909) 99-106. Matthew has about 20 doublets (Hawkins, 82-99). The "doublet" is not a Gospel feature derived solely from Mark, since this Gospel has only one of them, or possibly two (see 9:35-37 and 10:43-44; and possibly 6:31-44 and 8:1-10). The occurrence of this feature in Mark raises a different issue, which is not related to that of the Matthean and Lukan "doublets."

[24] See the attempts of B. H. Streeter, *Four Gospels,* 197ff.; A. von Harnack, *The Sayings of Jesus: The Second Source of St. Matthew and St. Luke,* translated by J. R. Wilkinson (1908); cf. J. Moffatt, *An Introduction to the Literature of the New Testament,* 3d ed. (1918), 194-204, for a survey of 16 attempts to reconstruct Q. Many of these attempts, however, go back to the pioneer days of the investigation; the astronomical figures sometimes found in them for Q verses have in large measure been reduced in recent studies. Even though one cannot cite a consensus, recent writers tend to count the common verses of the Double Tradition in the neighborhood of 225. *Redaktionsgeschichte* in the study of Matthew and Luke has affected this question too; there is a tendency to allow more for the compositorial work of the Evangelists in this area.

[25] Taylor, "The Order of Q," 28.

How can one account for the verbal disagreement in such passages? Is it due to the simultaneous dependence of such passages on another source which had a parallel to Q (for example, M)? Is it due simply to the redactional work of Matthew or Luke? Is it due to the fact that Q existed in different forms? Was Q possibly a composite document? Taylor believes that there is a "wide consent" that Matthew is dependent on a second source other than Q, and would apparently ascribe such verbal disagreement to the conflation of M and Q.[26] A common understanding of Q maintains that Luke presents substantially the original order of Q, while the more original wording is found in Matthew, since Luke has undoubtedly modified Q stylistically as he has done Mark. Sometimes the verbal disagreement can be ascribed to a known Lukan or Matthean characteristic; yet this does not account for all of it. It is precisely this difficulty of the verbal disagreement in certain Lukan and Matthean passages that one would otherwise be inclined to label as Q that hampers scholars from agreeing on the extent of Q.

It is sometimes argued that Q existed in different forms that were used independently by Matthew and Luke. Thus C. K. Barrett would distinguish two written forms of it.[27] This suggestion, however, might be acceptable, if it meant that a passage in the written source was from time to time replaced by a better form of the same story or saying which was derived from oral tradition. So revised, the Q source might have been used at different times by Matthew and Luke. Plausible though this suggestion is, it is admittedly quite speculative.

---

[26] *Ibid.*, cf. his older article, "Some Outstanding New Testament Problems: I. The Elusive Q," *ET* 46 (1934-1935): 68-74. J. P. Brown, "The Form of 'Q' Known to Matthew," *NTS* 8 (1961-1962): 27-42, has suggested a combination of Q and M Sayings (without the parables) as the form of Q which Matthew used along with Mark, that is, a "larger sayings-document-Q^{mt}." If Taylor's suggestion has any merit then perhaps Brown's suggestion may prove to be an interesting refinement of it. X. Léon-Dufour criticizes this blending of Q and M into Q^{mt}; admitting that "all this solves the difficulty, but at the cost of raising up two logical entities that transform the Two-Source Theory into a Four-Source Theory." So what? Such a transformation may be needed as a refinement of the Two-Source Theory. Moreover, if M or L were regarded merely as an oral source, then the modification of Q by such material would allow for the influence of later oral tradition on the Gospel formation, such as Léon-Dufour himself argues for.

[27] Barrett, *ET* 54 (1942-1943): 320-23; cf. W. Bussmann, *Synoptische Studien* (1931) 2:110-56. Also R. S. Cherry, "Agreements between Matthew and Luke," *ET* 74 (1962-1963): 63.

Some writers have suggested that Q represents only layers of tradition that existed largely in an oral, catechetical, or liturgical form.[28] To admit such a multitude form of Q, however, fails to account for the almost word-for-word identical phrasing that is met at times, and that we mentioned above. It would mean, in effect, a return to a form of the *Traditionshypothese* with all its consequent difficulties.

An objection to Q has often been derived from its content, that it consists almost entirely of sayings of Jesus, contains very few narratives (for example, the temptation, the cure of the centurion's servant, the disciples of John the Baptist), and lacks a passion narrative. This last defect is claimed to be crucial, for how could the early church have composed an evangelical text that lacked the kerygmatic proclamation of the saving event itself? This objection, however, stems from a modern, preconceived idea of what *euaggelion* was in the early church. No one will deny that *euaggelion* was related to *kerygma*, but the two are not necessarily coextensive terms. Moreover, regardless of the position one takes about the origin of the sayings ascribed to Jesus in the Coptic *Gospel according to Thomas*—whether they are to be regarded as derived from canonical sources, from Gnostic composition, or from an independent ancient oral tradition—the significant thing is that this collection of 114 sayings was frankly labeled "Gospel" in antiquity. Save for a few small sections (No. 13, No. 22, No. 100, which contain the tiniest bit of narrative, the *logoi* ascribed to Jesus in this text are devoid of contextual settings, and there is no passion narrative. and yet it was entitled *peuaggelion pkata Thōman.*[29] This apocryphal Gospel, then, shows us at least that the argument against Q drawn from its content is not necessarily valid. To argue thus, however, does not mean that one ascribes a link between Q and the Coptic apocryphal Gospel; if there be a relation, it must be established on other grounds. Finally, to my way of thinking, the postulated Q source may not represent a kerygmatic document of the early church at all. It may rather have been part of the *didachē* of some early communities, representing mainly a col-

---

[28]See J. Jeremias, "Zur Hypothese einer schriftlichen Logienquelle Q," *ZNW* 29 (1930): 147-49; M. Dibelius, *From Tradition to Gospel* (1935) 76.

[29]See H. Koester, "*Gnomai diaphoroi:* The Origin and Nature of Diversification in the History of Early Christianity," *HTR* 58 (1965): 279-318, esp. 293-99. Cf. J. M. Robinson, "*Logoi sophon:* Zur Gattung des Spruchquelle Q," *Zeit und Geschichte: Dankesgabe an R. Bultmann* (Tübingen: Mohr, 1964) 77-96, esp. 79-84. [Both articles appear in English in *Trajectories Through Early Christianity* (1971) 114-57, 71-113.]

lection of sayings of Jesus gathered from various oral traditions and formulated anew in view of various *Sitze im Leben* (for example, preaching, controversy, casuistry, catechetics, liturgy).

Anyone who has made use of the Two-Source Theory in Synoptic Gospel study is aware of the difficulties and the inadequacies of the Q hypothesis. Part of the problem is, as Farrer has rightly recognized, that it is a hypothetical entity. That it is unnecessary is another matter; and this is still to be established. In my opinion, the Q source will continue to command the attention of students, despite its difficulties, until a more useful hypothesis is convincingly proposed—one that is freer of serious objections to it than is Q.

A subsidiary question involving Q must finally be mentioned, before this section is brought to a close. It is the so-called overlapping of Q and Mark in the Gospels of Matthew and Luke. This refers to the suggestion that some episodes or sayings were found in both Mark and Q and have been combined in passages basically related to the Triple Tradition. For instance, the preaching of John the Baptist (Lk. 3:1-18), the baptism of Jesus (Lk. 3:21-22), the temptation of Jesus (Lk. 4:1-13), the parables of the mustard seed (Lk. 13:18-19) and of the leaven (Lk. 13:20-21). In these cases there is evidence of a conflationary composition. Streeter's view was that Mark and Q represent independent traditions in these passages; this seems to be commonly accepted, and only a few would maintain that Mark depends on Q or has incorporated part of Q.[30]

---

[30] See T. E. Floyd Honey, "Did Mark Use Q?" *JBL* 62 (1943): 319-31; B. H. Throckmorton, Jr., "Did Mark Know Q?" *JBL* 67 (1948): 319-29; J. P. Brown, "Mark as Witness to an Edited Form of Q," *JBL* 80 (1961): 29-44.

Q: A REEXAMINATION

C. K. Barrett*

Barrett questions the theory that the material we have called Q was all derived from one written document; rather it was derived from a number of
non-Markan sources that were used by Matthew and Luke. Barrett's investigation is directed toward two issues.

(1) The degree of agreement not only in words but also in traditional
background (*Sitz im Leben*) between Matthew and Luke when they are reporting sayings of the same purport. Barrett finds, in this regard, that in
some of the Q passages the agreement is so close that there is no reason to
doubt they were drawn from a common source or sources, but in other passages the agreement is much less close. He concludes that the part of the
Q material where agreement is closest may be satisfactorily explained as
derived from a single common Greek source, but that the remainder cannot be explained without recourse to some parallel version. Barrett maintains that it is simpler to suppose that Matthew and Luke in collecting their
material used traditions that were similar but not identical than that they
each had identical copies of one source, which in the case of one of them
was contaminated with a parallel version.

(2) If Matthew and Luke are both using the same continuous source,
we should expect them to show in their use of it the same agreements in

*C. K. Barrett, "Q: A Re-examination," *The Expository Times* 54 (1942-1943): 320-
23.

order that, in general, they show when both are following Mark. Barrett finds, in this regard, that the argument that the order of the Q sections in Matthew and Luke indicates that they were drawn from a common document, breaks down. The common order of much of the Q material in Matthew and Luke is afforded rather by the outline of Mark.

In conclusion, Barrett argues that behind Q we should probably see a wider editorial research and a greater number of sources than have commonly been allowed for.

It is unfortunate that the widely used symbol Q is employed in different senses by different writers. Most scholars denote by it a document, now vanished but supposed once to have existed, which was known to both Matthew and Luke, and which supplied them with the material which they have in common in those passages which have no parallel in Mark. Others[1] restrict their use of the term to the common non-Markan material itself, regarded as a stratum of the Gospel tradition but not necessarily as derived from any one source. The latter definition of Q is the more scientific since it makes no assumptions which, however probable, in the nature of the case cannot be proved; and it is that which we shall adopt. It is, of course, possible that behind Q thus defined lies a common written source (Bacon's S), but it seems better, with Bacon, to denote this hypothetical source by another letter.

It is, however, the purpose of this article to call in question the theory that the material which we have called Q was all derived from one written document, and to suggest that the explanation of this common matter is not quite so simple. For it is not to be assumed that the best solution of the Synoptic Problem is the simplest. Such at least is the tendency of the most recent criticism. For example, most critics, even those who do not accept all Streeter's views, would prefer to speak, with him, of a "Four Document Hypothesis" rather than of a "Two Document Hypothesis."[2] Bussmann's[3] even more complicated analysis of the Gospel material carries the process a step further. In particular we may observe Streeter's recognition of the overlapping of his "Q" and "M," and Bussmann's

---

[1] Few in number: B. W. Bacon in several works, for example, *Studies in Matthew* (1930) viii; C. H. Dodd, *Parables of the Kingdom* (1935) 39.

[2] B. H. Streeter, *The Four Gospels: A Study of Origins* (1924) 223-70.

[3] W. Bussmann, *Synoptische Studien*, 3 vols. (1925, 1929, 1931). In vol. 2 Bussmann argues at length that Q was drawn from two sources, one in Aramaic, one in Greek.

division of the Sayings source (*Redenquelle*) into two distinct documents. It is these two points which we wish to develop in the suggestion that the Q material, as we have defined it, is derived not from one common source, but from a number of non-Markan sources which were used by Matthew and Luke, Matthew's "Sayings collection" overlapping with Luke's.[4] Just as our Mark (as is now recognized) is the product of the combination of a multiplicity of sources, so, perhaps, the Q material has been drawn from more than one source.

Towards establishing this position we can in this article take only the first negative step, of arguing that the usual view of Q (that is, that which regards it as all drawn from a single source) does not meet all the facts of the situation. As in all synoptic questions, two chief considerations arise— verbal agreement and coincidence of order. As to the general facts of the matter we cannot do better than quote Stanton:[5] "Portions of the non-Markan matter common to the first and third Gospels are so closely alike in them that the two evangelists must have possessed these portions at least in the same written form. The arrangement, however, even of these closely similar portions is very different, not only relatively to the Synoptic outline (which is accounted for by the independent use of a second document), but also considered by themselves. The same pieces are differently united to other pieces; the same Sayings occur in wholly different contexts. Furthermore the degree of verbal similarity varies greatly in different parts. It is necessary to ask whether these differences are to be traced solely to the diverse revision and adaptation of the same document by the two evangelists." Our investigation will therefore be directed as follows:

(1) We must consider the degree of agreement not only in words but also in traditional background (*Sitz im Leben*) between Matthew and Luke when they are reporting sayings of the same purport.

(2) If Matthew and Luke are both using the same continuous source we should expect them to show in their use of it the same agreement in order which (in general) they show when both are following Mark. We must examine whether this is in fact the case.

---

[4]In an important review of Bussmann's second volume, in *Theologisches Literaturblatt* (Feb. 1931), J. Jeremias asks why the division of R (= *Redenquelle*) should stop at R_1 and R_2; why not R_3, R_4, . . . ?

[5]V. H. Stanton, *The Gospels as Historical Documents* (1909) 2:46-47.

I

When both Matthew and Luke are following Mark their agreement is greatest, and is consistently great, when they repeat the words of Jesus. Since a very great part of Q consists of sayings we should expect that the Matthean and Lukan forms of these sayings, if they were derived from a common source, would reveal the same verbal similarity. In some of the Q passages this is indeed the case, and in them the agreement is so close that there is no reason to doubt that they were drawn from a common written source or sources. There are, however, other passages where the agreement is much less close, and we must inquire whether it can plausibly be maintained that they too were derived by both Matthew and Luke from a common document.

By way of example we may notice first some short sayings which appear in different forms in Matthew and Luke but which must go back to the same root in the tradition.[6]

> Lk. 6:29   Coat-stealing
>   11:44   Pharisees and tombs
>   12:6   The price of sparrows
>   16:16   The Kingdom of God and violence

It can hardly be doubted that in each of these cases Matthew and Luke both give what is substantially the same tradition; but they give it in different forms, and the differences cannot be accounted for by editorial activity. Why should Matthew have turned Luke's highway robbery into a law-suit, or vice-versa? Was either evangelist really concerned about the difference between two a penny and five for twopence? These differences are just such as we should expect to find between sayings which had been independently transmitted. The other two instances which we have mentioned are even more interesting. In Lk. 11:44 and Mt. 23:27 the same charge is brought against the same persons by means of the same simile; but the simile is used so differently as to make the sayings entirely different. Lk. 16:16 (= Mt. 11:12-13) is a saying of well-known difficulty and we shall not attempt to elucidate it; but it is clear that, whatever the original form

---

[6]Perhaps to the same sayings of Jesus; but we are not here concerned with the question of authenticity.

of the logion may have been, it reached Matthew and Luke by different channels.

It is true that in the first two of these four cases Streeter explains the discrepant versions by the theory that the Matthean form has been conflated with M. This concession, however, in effect allows the point that we are making: two parallel versions of the saying existed in the tradition, and it is at least as simple to suppose that one was given by Luke, another by Matthew, as to think that Matthew has conflated the two.

We may consider also two longer Q sections. Lk. 6:20-26 (the Beatitudes and Woes) is ascribed by Streeter to Q; he himself says, however, of the divergence between Luke and Matthew at this point that it "is not plausibly explained as the result of editorial modification of a written source;" his own explanation is based upon the hypothesis that a second set of Beatitudes occurred in the source M. There is probably truth in this view; as we have shown, it confirms our opinion that pieces of the Gospel tradition were collected in different forms by Matthew and Luke. But the question is, whether Matthew knew the Lukan form at all; and this turns upon the Woes, which appear in Luke only. It is clear from the symmetry of expression that the Lukan Woes and Beatitudes belong together. If therefore Matthew knew the Beatitudes he knew the Woes too; and it seems improbable that the Evangelist who expanded a few woes against the Pharisees (Lk. 11) into a whole chapter (Mt. 23) would show no trace in any part of his Gospel of this set of Woes. Probably then we should conclude that in the Beatitudes Matthew and Luke were using allied but different sources. Lk. 13:22-30 is a very instructive passage. The first verse is apparently editorial. Then follows a saying about the narrow door, introduced by a question. In the Matthean parallel (7:13-14—in the Sermon) there is no question, and the linguistic agreement is at a minimum. The only common words are εἰσελθ (εῖν) διὰ τῆς στενῆς, ὅτι, πολλοί, εἰσ(ελθεῖν): without which the saying could hardly exist at all. That the two versions represent the same saying seems hardly open to doubt; but it is almost equally certain that the two streams of tradition must have diverged long before the time of Matthew and Luke. Luke proceeds (verses 25-30) with a passage whose only link with the foregoing is the word θύρα—a mnemonic relationship which itself is probably an indication of oral tradition. It has (not very close) parallels in several parts of Matthew—in 25:10-12; 7:22-23; 8:11-12; 20:16. The first of these passages is an inseparable part of a parable, apparently unknown to Luke. We may

therefore feel confident that these two verses at least reached Matthew and Luke by different channels. The claims made by the expelled "many" in the two Gospels are entirely different; in Matthew they themselves are Christian prophets and exorcists, while in Luke they are men who have heard Jesus teach and had table fellowship with him (that is, Luke's form of the saying is much more probably original). It is quite conceivable that Matthew himself detached the saying about those who came from the East and the West from its Lukan context and placed it in the very appropriate context which it has in his Gospel. The last verse (Lk. 13:30) occurs in Mark as well as Q—an important reminder that we know certainly that there were parallel versions of the same saying.

It will be interesting to observe the case of Luke 12:54-56. There is a Matthean parallel (16:2-3) but it is omitted (without doubt rightly) by ℵ B, other Greek manuscripts, the old Syriac, Coptic, and Armenian versions. The parallel is in any case not close verbally to Luke. The course of events is clear. The original text of Matthew contained no parallel to Lk. 12:54ff. An early editor, noting the deficiency, supplemented the text. But he did not derive his supplement from Luke, but from a similar tradition of the same saying, which must still have been in oral or written circulation. If such an independent tradition was available then, we cannot but suppose that many more were available when, say, fifty years earlier, Matthew was writing his Gospel.

We may briefly refer to one point more in this section. There are cases where differences between Matthew and Luke may be explained as translation variants. It is true that a certain amount of doubt must always attach to reconstructions of Aramaic documents, and that the Semitic experts do not always agree in their explanations. But it does seem that a sufficient number of instances[7] can be made out with sufficient probability to justify us in supposing that Matthew and Luke had, in addition to their common Greek source or sources, at least one Aramaic source.

At this point we may pause and tentatively summarize our conclusions. Neglecting the question of order, which remains to be considered,

---

[7]For example, Lk. 6:22 (= Mt. 5:11); 6:23 (= Mt. 5:12); 10:5 (= Mt. 10:12); 11:39 (= Mt. 23:23); 11:41 (= Mt. 23:26); 11:48 (= Mt. 23:31). See J. H. Moulton, *A Grammar of New Testament Greek*, II: *Accidence and Word Formation*, ed. by W. F. Howard (1929, 1956) 471-72; J. Wellhausen, *Einleitung in die drei ersten Evangelien*, 1st ed. (1905) 36-37; C. C. Torrey, *The Four Gospels* (1933) and *Our Translated Gospels* (1936) passim.

we may say that the part of the Q material where agreement is closest may be satisfactorily explained as derived from a single common Greek source; but that the remainder cannot be explained without recourse to some parallel version, and that it is simpler to suppose that Matthew and Luke in collecting their material used traditions which were similar but not identical than that they each had identical copies of one source (a supposition sufficiently improbable on geographical and historical grounds), which in the case of one of them was contaminated with a parallel version.

II

The only scientific method of investigating the question of order is to read through Q in Matthew, noting where the parallel to each verse or part of a verse occurs in Luke, and vice versa. To describe this process in detail would take far too much space and we must therefore be content merely to illustrate it, and to summarize the results.

In this case also it will be best to discriminate between the larger and smaller blocks of Q; for it is generally agreed that Matthew has treated Q with a free editorial hand, and subordinated his material to his scheme of presenting the teaching of Jesus in great discourses. We must therefore observe whether he has retained groups of small sayings in the same order which we find in Luke, and also whether any common order can be observed in the larger blocks.

First we may take as our example Matthew's longest discourse, the Sermon on the Mount, which contains 107 verses. Of these 59 (making a liberal count) appear in Luke, that is, they may be designated Q; and of the Q verses only 25 occur in Luke's Sermon on the Plain. When we pass to the other Q verses we find the Lukan parallels scattered throughout the central section of the Third Gospel. The saying about salt (Mt. 5:13) occurs in Lk. 14:31-32, where it fits admirably into a discourse on discipleship (and cf. Mk. 9:50). With this saying Matthew associates that about lamps and measures (5:15), which Luke gives in 11:33, in connexion with the discourse on signs, and another saying (11:34-36) which Matthew gives in a different part of the sermon (6:22-23). The saying about agreement with the adversary (Mt. 5:25-26) appears in Luke's apocalyptic chapter (12:57-59). The saying on divorce (Mt. 5:32) has an isolated parallel in Lk. 16:18, which in the Lukan context is associated with the saying about the Kingdom of God and John, the Matthean form of which is in Mt.

11:12-13 (cf. also 5:18). The Lord's Prayer (Mt. 6:9-15) Luke gives (with other teaching which appears in Mt. 7) in his chapter 11. So the list might be continued for the whole sermon; but it will perhaps be sufficient merely to write out the Lukan parallels, and let them speak for themselves. They are: Lk. 14:34-35; 11:33; 12:57-59; 11:2-4; 12:33-34; 11:34-36; 16:13; 12:22-31; 11:9-13; 13:23-24; 13:26-27.

It is quite clear that no common order can be traced here. If it be urged that Matthew's editorial methods provide an adequate explanation of the phenomena, it must be answered that the explanation itself is a confession that the evidence *as it stands* affords no grounds for belief in a single common source as the origin of the Q material. Besides, the editing which we are asked to accept is, sometimes at least, of a surprising nature. Why should an editor, desiring to take over Lk. 11:33-34, place the two verses in different contexts (Mt. 5:15; 6:22-23), and give them, by their new contexts, new meanings?

It will be well to examine next a Lukan section; we shall take one which is given by Streeter[8] as an example of agreement in order. The "five items" he cites occur in Lk. 10:13-11:32. The passage opens with woes on the Galilean cities, and there follows immediately (with a small intermission in Luke) the great Thanksgiving. It seems very probable that these two complementary sayings were connected with one another in a source common to Matthew and Luke. Next, however, comes Lk. 10:23-24, which Matthew has placed in his parable chapter (13:16-17). Luke adds a Q version of the question about the great commandment, of which Matthew gives a conflated version in the Markan position. Next come (in Luke) the Parable of the Good Samaritan and the story of Martha and Mary (both L); 11:1-4, the Lord's Prayer (parallel, Mt. 6:9-15); the Friend at Midnight (L); and the Answer to Prayer (parallel, Mt. 7:7-11). Up to this point we have observed nothing that could seriously be used as evidence for the existence of a document. The next three sections in Luke (the Beelzebul controversy, the return of the evil spirit, the sign of Jonah)[9] occur together, as Streeter points out, in Matthew, though with the second and third reversed. But we should do well to notice this rearrangement, and also the fact, to which Streeter does not draw attention, that in the corresponding Matthean passage (12:25-45) there appear also one Markan verse

---

[8] Streeter, *Four Gospels*, 274.
[9] Omitting the L saying (11:27-28) about the mother of Jesus.

(31), three M verses (34, 36-37), and three Q verses (32, 33, 35; parallels in Lk. 12:10, 6:43-45). Streeter's argument, therefore, in the passage referred to, appears much less convincing when attention is given to detail.

Finally we must examine Q in broader outline. If we neglect small blocks and attend only to larger aggregations the material may be summarily presented as follows:

	LUKE	MATTHEW
A. Matter relating to John, Baptism, and the baptism of Jesus	3:2-22	3:7-17
B. Temptations	4:1-13	4:1-11
C. The Sermon	6:20-49	5:1–7:27
D. The Centurion	7:1-10	8:5-13
E. John's Question; Discourse on John	7:18-35	11:2-19
F. On Discipleship	9:57–10:24	8:19-22 9:37–10:14
G. On signs; Beelzebul and Jonah	11:14-32	12:22-45
H. Against the Pharisees	11:39-52	23
I. For disciples in persecution	12:2-12 12:22-34	10:26-33 6:19-33
J. Preparedness	12:35-59 13:22-30	24:43-44, et al.
K. Lament over Jerusalem	13:34-35	23:37-39
L. Church discipline	17:1-6	18:6-7, 13, 21-22; 17:20
M. The Q Apocalypse	17:22-37	24

It is clear that the latter part of the list furnishes no argument in favor of a single common source of Matthew and Luke on the grounds of common order. There is no such common order. But the case is different at the beginning of the list; for here the sections A B C D F G follow one another in the same order in both Matthew and Luke. The hypothesis is admittedly tenable (as far as evidence derived from order alone is concerned) that the reason why Matthew and Luke present these sections in the same order is that they derived them from the same written source. There is however another hypothesis which satisfies the requirements of the data without postulating any unknown quantity; and an explanation which explains without making further assumptions is to be preferred to one which in solving one problem creates another. It will be observed that the order of the sections A B C F G is not only the same in both Matthew and Luke; it also corre-

sponds with the outline of Mark. Mark too begins his Gospel with an account of John and his work (A). Next follows the brief Markan temptation
narrative (B).[10] Both Matthew and Luke insert their different forms of the
Q sermon (C) at points where a body of teaching is implied by the Markan
narrative (Mt. 1:38-39; 3:7-12). There is no warrant in Mark for the connection of C and D; accordingly we should suppose that this connection
was a piece of tradition (perhaps written tradition) common to Matthew
and Luke. F is given its place in Matthew and Luke by the Markan report
of the appointment and sending out of the Twelve; after which follows, in
Mark as in Q, an account of the Beezlebub controversy (G). It is noteworthy that as soon as Matthew and Luke step off firm Markan ground, in
section H, they at once begin to diverge from one another.

The argument, then, that the order of the Q sections in Matthew and
Luke indicates that they were drawn from a common document, breaks
down.

The results of this investigation are admittedly negative. It has appeared probable that behind Q we should see a wider editorial research and
a greater number of sources than have commonly been allowed for; but we
have taken no steps to analyze Q and consider its constituent elements.
These are, however, tasks which lie ahead of Synoptic critics, and they
promise a field of singular interest because it is one in which the two rewarding disciplines of form criticism and source criticism may be pursued
side by side.

---

[10]The argument admits of simple adaptation if it be held that Lk. 3:1-4:30 is "Proto-
Luke" and does not depend on Mark at all.

TOWARDS
THE REHABILITATION
OF Q

*F. G. Downing**

Downing tests Farrer's challenge to dispense with Q by calling for an examination of Luke's supposed use of passages where Matthew has apparently conflated a Markan record of teaching with similar but distinct material of his own from some other source: the Baptism narrative, the Beelzebul controversy, the Sending out of the Twelve and the Sending of the Seventy, and the Synoptic Apocalypses.

Downing tests Farrer's hypothesis in a detailed analysis of the parallel Greek texts of the Beelzebul controversy (Mt. 12:22-45; Mk. 3:20-29; Lk. 11:14-26). Downing concludes that it seems much more sensible to assume that Luke did not know Matthew's use of Mark (as Farrer's hypothesis maintains); rather it appears that Luke here reproduced his own version of the Q material with no reference either to Matthew or to Mark.

Downing includes a somewhat less detailed analysis of the Baptism narrative, the Sending out of the Twelve, and the Apocalypses. He maintains after reviewing the evidence that it is more reasonable to suppose that Luke's avoidance of every clear use by Matthew of Mark (as Farrer's hypothesis demands) is due rather to Luke's ignorance of Matthew's use of Mark. Downing maintains that Luke knew Matthew's source (or sources)

*F. G. Downing, "Towards the Rehabilitation of Q," *New Testament Studies* 11 (1964-1965): 169-81.

before it had its parallels with Mark conflated with Mark, and this source (or "these sources") is what has come to be known in part as Q.

Downing observes that Farrer himself admitted that the Q hypothesis depends on the incredibility of Luke's having used Matthew. Downing believes that he has shown a greater degree of incredibility in this regard than has generally been realized.

The question of Q is of more than academic importance. Matthew and Luke together reproduce material which does not appear (or not in the same form) in Mark. If it can be shown to have been taken from a source common to them both, then we have four "witnesses" to the synoptic tradition: Mark, the common source (Q), the material peculiar to Matthew, and that peculiar to Luke. And should all four preserve independently some aspect of Jesus' teaching (for example, parables of crisis), then we may fairly be confident of its authenticity. On the other hand, should, for instance, Q omit all reference to Jesus as Messiah, and all (at least explicit) reference to the suffering of "the Son of Man," then we are given serious cause to doubt whether Jesus spoke of himself this way.

However, it seems at present uncertain what should be done about Q. Dr. A. M. Farrer suggested some years ago that the hypothesis be dropped.[1] A recent contributor to the *Journal of Theological Studies* relegated it to a footnote, and argued quite happily without it.[2] Dr. J. Jeremias, in a lecture, thought it hardly fruitful for discussion, and fails to mention it in his published lecture on the "Sermon on the Mount," though there accepting the independence of Luke from Matthew.[3] By way of contrast, both R. Bultmann[4] and G. Bornkamm[5] appear to accept Q without question; and F. W. Beare, in *The Earliest Records of Jesus*, writes, "The present writer must say that he has been more and more impressed, as he went on with the making of this book, with the strength of the evidence that Luke and Matthew have indeed used a second source in common, and that the phenomena of the non-Markan parallels are far more plausibly explained on this theory than by any other hypothesis that has been put for-

---

[1]A. M. Farrer, "On Dispensing with Q," in *Studies in the Gospels*, ed. by D. E. Nineham (1955) [reprinted in this volume].

[2]M. D. Goulder, "The Composition of the Lord's Prayer," *JTS* New Series 14:35 n1.

[3]J. Jeremias, in a lecture in Lincoln, 1961, and in *The Sermon on the Mount* (1961) 17ff.

[4]R. Bultmann, *The History of the Synoptic Tradition* (1963) 2.

[5]G. Bornkamm, *Jesus of Nazareth* (1960) 215.

ward.''[6] But this was not the work in which to discuss these impresssions in detail.

Dr. Farrer rightly explained that "the hypothesis wholly depends on the incredibility of St. Luke's having read St. Matthew's book. . . . If there is no difficulty in supposing St. Luke to have read St. Matthew, then the question (of a 'lost document' lying behind them both) never arises at all.''[7] Dr. Farrer suggested instead that Luke used Mark as a framework into which to fit material he had quarried from Matthew's additions to Mark (as well as other material he already had), to produce a new, patterned, reasoned theological structure: Luke had a definite enough purpose to provide him with a credible motive for "destroying" Matthew's work. And Dr. Farrer pointed out that this supposed use by Luke of Matthew would explain all the awkward little resemblances in their use of Mark that B. H. Streeter[8] had to exercise such ingenuity to argue away: of course there are resemblances in their use of Mark, for Luke used Matthew.

I

Of particular importance in testing Dr. Farrer's hypothesis[9] are Luke's supposed use of passages where Matthew has apparently conflated a Markan record of teaching with similar but distinct material of his own from some other source. The most important of these passages are the Baptism narrative (Mt. 3:1-4:11; Mk. 1:1-13; Lk. 3:1-22; 4:1-13—that is, including the Temptation); the Beelzebul controversy (Mt. 12:22-45; Mk. 3:20-29; Lk. 11:14-26, with 12:10 and 6:43-45); the Sending out of the Twelve (Mt. 9:35-10:16; Mk. 6:13-19 with 6:6, 7, 8-11, 34; Lk. 9:1-5, with 6:13-16, and—the Sending of the Seventy—Luke 10:1-12); and The Synoptic Apocalypse (Mt. 24:4-26; Mk. 13:5-37; Lk: 21:8-36, etc.)[10] In most places (on the hypothesis we are testing) it will have been fairly easy

---

[6]F. W. Beare, *The Earliest Records of Jesus* (1962) 14.

[7]Farrer, "On Dispensing with Q," parenthesis added.

[8]B. H. Streeter, *The Four Gospels* (1924).

[9]Dr. Farrer claimed that his was no hypothesis, and that Q was merely hypothesis, "On Dispensing with Q," 66; but that Luke used Matthew must in the nature of the case remain as much a hypothesis as the one-time existence of Q.

[10]In what follows these will be compared as they stand in A. Huck and H. Lietzmann, *Synopsis of the First Three Gospels*, English ed. by F. L. Cross (1951); cf. especially B. H. Throckmorton, *Gospel Parallels* (1949), for a version of this synopsis using the RSV text.

for Luke to lift Matthean material quite cleanly from its place in the Markan narrative, whether the latter is preserved largely intact or reshaped by Matthew. But in the places we have listed, Luke will have been faced with a much more complex task. It will be interesting to see how he must be supposed to have gone about it.

We shall examine first the Beelzebul controversy.[11] It is necessary first to note how Matthew appears when compared with Mark (see Table 1). There is very little of Mark that he reproduces verbatim: only at verse 29 (Mk. 3:27) does he present largely the same words, syntax, and order; though verse 31a is fairly close to Mk. 3:28, differing only in an inversion. This will be referred to as A material (Matthew $\backsimeq$ Mark). Of 41 words in Matthew, 33 are in Mark.

There are then further sentences where Matthew has perhaps an important word, perhaps a phrase in common with Mark (and is of course dealing quite definitely with the same sort of topic). In verse 24b he has eight words in common, though only three in the same sequence. In the next he has seven, though the verbs are used differently (μερισθεῖσα twice and σταθήσεται), and again the order is not the same. In verse 26a there are two phrases, of four words each, practically identical; but the syntax of the apodosis is quite different, and only σταθήσεται parallels Mark (στῆναι). Lastly verse 32b has ὃς δ' ἂν . . . τοῦ πνεύματος τοῦ ἁγίου οὐκ ἀφεθήσεται (Mark οὐκ ἔχει ἄφεσιν . . . αἰῶνι, which again is fairly like the Markan sequence. Here, of 82 words in Matthew, only 32 appear in Mark, and then with often different sequence and syntax. This we shall call B material (Matthew ‖ Mark). It presents a problem; one that is sadly insoluble. What is Matthew doing in these verses? Is he arbitrarily changing Mark? Or is he conflating Mark with another source that deals in quite similar terms with the same topics? Or is he even reproducing largely this other source, which just happens to use from time to time the same words and phrases as Mark? After all, it might well be expected to, if the subject were the same. The questions must remain rhetorical, though we would suggest the second or the third are nearer the mark. When Matthew has obviously nothing to add to *verba domini* in Mark (for instance, in the parables, Mt. 13; Mk. 4) he consistently allows Mark to provide much more than 40 percent of his words.

---

[11]Its significance is noted without further explanation by F. W. Beare, *The Earliest Records*, 102; cf. *Studies in the Synoptic Problem*, ed. W. Sanday (1911) 53, 171.

And in this section, as of course we have noted, Matthew has a great deal of material on the same sort of subject as Mark presents, which has however no real verbal parallel in Mark at all. Verses 22, 23, 24a, 25a, 26b, 27, 28, 30, 31b, 32a, 33-45 are completely ''new.'' This is C material (Matthew alone). On its own it presents a coherent narrative. Jesus heals a man possessed (verses 22-23), is accused (verse 24a), denies (what must have been in the accusation) that he works through Beelzebul (verse 27), asserts that the exorcism is by the spirit of God, and proof of the in-break of the Kingdom (verse 28), and announces that blasphemy against this power is unforgivable (verses 31b-32a). (He continues with some sayings about ''fruit,'' rejects a request for signs, and returns to the topic with the story of the returning evil spirit—verses 33-43). And the B material would so easily fit with these C verses that at least some weight is added to our suggestion above that B may be largely or even entirely part of Matthew's non-Markan material. B and C were already joined in Matthew's source, so that the parallels there between Matthew and Mark may well be incidental. Still, this suggestion must rest for the moment. We have now analyzed the sort of material which Dr. Farrer believed faced Luke as he set about his reconstruction, and can try to find how he must have gone about it.

Luke includes *none of the A material* (Matthew $\triangleq$ Mark). He reproduces most of the B material (Matthew ‖ Mark), in slightly different forms. These latter ''emendations'' do not however make his text look more like Mark, but diverge even further from Mark than does Matthew. There is nothing corresponding to Mt. 12:25c, with its slight parallels in Mark; in the next verse, Luke has διεμερίσθη for Matthew's and Mark's ἐμερίσθη. Lk. 12:10b (in which Luke reverts to this subject in another setting) lacks the ὃς δ' ἄν and τῷ αἰῶνι which echo Mk. 3:29 in Matthew. He does, however, have εἰς (τὸ ἅγιον πνεῦμα) and uses βλασφημέω of the offence (and ἐφ' ἑαυτήν for καθ' ἑαυτῆς, verse 17b). Whereas Luke reproduces 38 of Matthew's words in these sections, he has only 31 of Mark's. Of the C material (Matthew, not in Mark), he reproduces, here or elsewhere, *almost everything*. There are only fairly slight resemblances in Lk. 11:14 to Mt. 12:22-23, but Luke normally recognizes editorial padding and feels free to produce his own. Verse 17a (and b) of Luke is very similar to its Matthean equivalent; verses (18a), 18b-20, 23 and 12:10a, repeat Matthew almost verbatim. Luke uses elsewhere the substance of Mt. 12:33-35, but not verse 36; none of this fits the context of dispute

about "spirits." He goes straight on to the Return of the Evil Spirit (Mt. 12:43-45; Lk. 11:24-26, where there is hardly a word that is not also in Matthew), adds a pericope of his own on the Blessedness of Christ's Mother (11:27-28), and then has a discourse Against Seeking for Signs (Lk. 11:29-32; Mt. 12:28-42), where again almost every sentence is precisely as in Matthew.

TABLE 1
A SYNOPSIS OF MT. 12:22ff., LK. 11:14ff., MK. 3.20ff.

The text is marked to make three points:

(a) Words (or parts of words) in Matthew that appear also in Mark are underlined (··············). This is to justify the division of the Matthean text into three columns, A, very like Mark; B, fairly similar; C, quite different.

(b) Words that appear in Luke and in Matthew are underlined (————) in both; if they appear also in Mark, they have a double marking (·············). This is to illustrate the relation between Luke and Matthew, and in particular Luke's failure to include any of column A of Matthew (that closely reproducing Mark).

(c) Finally, words in Luke that occur in Mark but not Matthew are underlined twice (·············) to illustrate (largely by absence) the point made (for this passage alone) that Luke has here practically none of the Markan material that Matthew omits.

LUKE'S SUPPOSED USE OF MATERIAL WHICH MATTHEW HAS CONFLATED WITH MARK		
Mark 3:20ff.	Matt. 12:22ff.	Luke 11:14ff.
	A-material (MT ≏ MK) B-material (MT ‖ MK) C-material (MT, not MK)	
20 Καὶ ἔρχεται εἰς οἶκον· καὶ συνέρχεται πάλιν ὁ ὄχλος, ὥστε μὴ δύνασθαι αὐτοὺς μηδὲ ἄρτον φαγεῖν. 21 καὶ ἀκούσαντες οἱ παρ᾽ αὐτοῦ ἐξῆλθον κρατῆσαι αὐτόν· ἔλεγον γὰρ ὅτι ἐξέστη.	C 22 Τότε προσηνέχθη αὐτῷ δαι-	14 Καὶ ἦν ἐκβάλλων δαιμόν-

22 καὶ οἱ γραμματεῖς οἱ
ἀπὸ Ἱεροσολύμων κατα-
βάντες ἔλεγον
ὅτι Βεελζεβοὺλ
ἔχει, καὶ ὅτι ἐν τῷ ἄρχ-
οντι τῶν δαιμονίων ἐκβάλ-
λει τὰ δαιμόνια.

23 Καὶ προσκαλεσάμενος
αὐτοὺς ἐν παραβολαῖς
ἔλεγεν αὐτοῖς· πῶς δύνα-
ται σατανᾶς σατανᾶν
ἐκβάλλειν;
24 καὶ ἐὰν βασιλεία ἐφ᾽
ἑαυτὴν μερισθῇ, οὐ δύνα-
ται σταθῆναι ἡ βασιλεία
ἐκείνη·
25 καὶ ἐὰν οἰκία ἐφ᾽
ἑαυτὴν μερισθῇ, οὐ δυ-
νήσεται ἡ οἰκία ἐκείνη
σταθῆναι.
26 καὶ εἰ ὁ σατανᾶς
ἀνέστη ἐφ᾽ ἑαυτὸν καὶ
ἐμερίσθη, οὐ δύναται
στῆναι ἀλλὰ τέλος ἔχει.

μονιζόμενος τυφλὸς καὶ κωφός·
καὶ ἐθεράπευσεν αὐτόν, ὥστε
τὸν κωφὸν λαλεῖν καὶ βλέπειν.
23 καὶ ἐξίσταντο πάντες οἱ ὄχλοι καὶ ἔλεγον· μήτι οὗτός ἐστιν ὁ υἱὸς Δαυίδ;
24 οἱ δὲ Φαρισαῖοι
ἀκούσαντες εἶπον·

B
οὗτος οὐκ ἐκβάλλει τὰ δαιμόνια εἰ
μὴ ἐν τῷ Βεελζεβοὺλ ἄρχοντι τῶν
δαιμονίων.

C
25 Εἰδὼς δὲ τὰς ἐνθυμήσεις
αὐτῶν εἶπεν αὐτοῖς·

B
πᾶσα βασιλεία μερισθεῖσα καθ᾽
ἑαυτῆς ἐρημοῦται,

καὶ πᾶσα πόλις ἢ οἰκία μερισθεῖσα καθ᾽ ἑαυτῆς οὐ σταθήσεται.

26 καὶ εἰ ὁ σατανᾶς τὸν σατανᾶν
ἐκβάλλει, ἐφ᾽ ἑαυτὸν ἐμερίσθη·

C
πῶς οὖν σταθήσεται ἡ βασιλεία
αὐτοῦ;

C
27 καὶ εἰ ἐγὼ ἐν Βεελζεβοὺλ ἐκβάλλω τὰ δαιμόνια, οἱ υἱοὶ
ὑμῶν ἐν τίνι ἐκβάλλουσιν; διὰ
τοῦτο αὐτοὶ κριταὶ ἔσονται
ὑμῶν.

ιον, καὶ αὐτὸ ἦν κωφόν·
ἐγένετο δὲ τοῦ δαιμονίου
ἐξελθόντος ἐλάλησεν ὁ
κωφός· καὶ ἐθαύμασαν οἱ
ὄχλοι·
15 τινὲς δὲ ἐξ αὐτῶν
εἶπον·

ἐν Βεελζεβοὺλ τῷ ἄρχ-
οντι τῶν δαιμονίων ἐκβάλ-
λει τὰ δαιμόνια·
16 ἕτεροι δὲ πειράζοντες
σημεῖον ἐξ οὐρανοῦ
ἐζήτουν παρ᾽ αὐτοῦ.
17 Αὐτὸς δὲ εἰδὼς αὐτῶν
τὰ διανοήματα εἶπεν
αὐτοῖς·

πᾶσα βασιλεία ἐφ᾽ ἑαυτὴν
διαμερισθεῖσα
ἐρημοῦται,

καὶ οἶκος ἐπὶ οἶκον
πίπτει.

18 εἰ δὲ καὶ ὁ σατανᾶς
ἐφ᾽ ἑαυτὸν διεμερίσθη,

πῶς σταθήσεται ἡ βασι-
λεία αὐτοῦ; ὅτι λέγετε
ἐν Βεελζεβοὺλ ἐκβάλλειν
με τὰ δαιμόνια.
19 εἰ δὲ ἐγὼ ἐν Βεελζε-
βοὺλ ἐκβάλλω τὰ δαιμόνια,
οἱ υἱοὶ ὑμῶν ἐν τίνι ἐκ-
βάλλουσιν; διὰ τοῦτο αὐ-
τοὶ ὑμῶν κριταὶ ἔσονται.

	28 εἰ δὲ ἐν πνεύματι θεοῦ ἐγὼ ἐκβάλλω τὰ δαιμόνια, ἄρα ἔφθασεν ἐφ' ὑμᾶς ἡ βασιλεία τοῦ θεοῦ.	20 εἰ δὲ ἐν δακτύλῳ θεοῦ ἐγὼ ἐκβάλλω τὰ δαιμόνια, ἄρα ἔφθασεν ἐφ' ὑμᾶς ἡ βασιλεία τοῦ θεοῦ.
	A	
27 ἀλλ' οὐ δύναται οὐδεὶς εἰς τὴν οἰκίαν τοῦ ἰσχυροῦ εἰσελθὼν τὰ σκεύη αὐτοῦ διαρπάσαι, ἐὰν μὴ πρῶτον τὸν ἰσχυρὸν δήσῃ, καὶ τότε τὴν οἰκίαν αὐτοῦ διαρπάσει.	29 ἢ πῶς δύναταί τις εἰσελθεῖν εἰς τὴν οἰκίαν τοῦ ἰσχυροῦ καὶ τὰ σκεύη αὐτοῦ ἁρπάσαι, ἐὰν μὴ πρῶτον δήσῃ τὸν ἰσχυρόν; καὶ τότε τὴν οἰκίαν αὐτοῦ διαρπάσει.	
		21 ὅταν ὁ ἰσχυρὸς καθωπλισμένος φυλάσσῃ τὴν ἑαυτοῦ αὐλήν, ἐν εἰρήνῃ ἐστὶν τὰ ὑπάρχοντα αὐτοῦ· 22 ἐπὰν δὲ ἰσχυρότερος αὐτοῦ ἐπελθὼν νικήσῃ αὐτόν, τὴν πανοπλίαν αὐτοῦ αἴρει, ἐφ' ᾗ ἐπεποίθει, καὶ τὰ σκῦλα αὐτοῦ διαδίδωσιν.
	C	
	30 ὁ μὴ ὢν μετ' ἐμοῦ κατ' ἐμοῦ ἐστιν, καὶ ὁ μὴ συνάγων μετ' ἐμοῦ σκορπίζει.	23 ὁ μὴ ὢν μετ' ἐμοῦ κατ' ἐμοῦ ἐστιν, καὶ ὁ μὴ συνάγων μετ' ἐμοῦ σκορπίζει.
	A	
28 ἀμὴν λέγω ὑμῖν ὅτι πάντα ἀφεθήσεται τοῖς υἱοῖς τῶν ἀνθρώπων τὰ ἁμαρτήματα καὶ αἱ βλασφημίαι, ὅσα ἐὰν βλασφημήσωσιν·	31 διὰ τοῦτο λέγω ὑμῖν, πᾶσα ἁμαρτία καὶ βλασφημία ἀφεθήσεται τοῖς ἀνθρώποις, ἡ δὲ τοῦ	
	C	12:10
	πνεύματος βλασφημία οὐκ ἀφεθήσεται. 32 καὶ ὃς ἐὰν εἴπῃ λόγον κατὰ τοῦ υἱοῦ τοῦ ἀνθρώπου, ἀφεθήσεται αὐτῷ·	καὶ πᾶς ὃς ἐρεῖ λόγον εἰς τὸν υἱὸν τοῦ ἀνθρώπου, ἀφεθήσεται αὐτῷ· τῷ δὲ εἰς τὸ ἅγιον πνεῦμα βλασφημήσαντι οὐκ ἀφεθήσεται.
	B	
29 ὃς δ' ἂν βλασφημήσῃ εἰς τὸ πνεῦμα τὸ ἅγιον,	ὃς δ' ἂν εἴπῃ κατὰ τοῦ πνεύματος τοῦ ἁγίου, οὐκ ἀφεθήσεται αὐτῷ	

οὐκ ἔχει ἄφεσιν εἰς τὸν αἰῶνα, ἀλλὰ ἔνοχός ἐστιν αἰωνίου ἁμαρτήματος. 30 ὅτι ἔλεγον· πνεῦμα ἀκάθαρτον ἔχει.	οὔτε ἐν τούτῳ τῷ αἰῶνι οὔτε ἐν τῷ μέλλοντι.	
	For verses 33-42 C, *see* Huck, *Synopsis.*	For 6:43-45; 11:29-32, *see* Huck, *Synopsis.*
	C 43 ὅταν δὲ τὸ ἀκάθαρτον πνεῦμα ἐξέλθῃ ἀπὸ τοῦ ἀνθρώπου, διέρχεται δι᾽ ἀνύδρων τόπων ζητοῦν ἀνάπαυσιν, καὶ οὐχ εὑρίσκει. . . .	11:24 ὅταν τὸ ἀκάθαρτον πνεῦμα ἐξέλθῃ ἀπὸ τοῦ ἀνθρώπου, διέρχεται δι᾽ ἀνύδρων τόπων ζητοῦν ἀνάπαυσιν, καὶ μὴ εὑρίσ- κον. . . .

If Luke has Matthew and Mark before him, fairly obviously he is using only Matthew. He reproduces Matthew's C material (Matthew, not in Mark) almost entire; and where Matthew has parallels with Mark is much closer to Matthew's than to Mark's version. Matthew has retained more or less the Markan context (he has only displaced the Call of the Twelve which immediately preceded the Beelzebul controversy in Mark); Luke has not even preserved that. He has no significant independent parallels with Mark.

If Luke has Mark and Matthew before him, fairly obviously he is using only Matthew. But is he using Matthew? We have noticed that Luke uses none of the A material, none of the material in which Matthew is at all obviously or precisely reproducing Mark. He uses most of the C material (Matthew only), and a lot of the B material, which may well, we suggested, have in large part originally been integral with the C material in Matthew's source. Luke in fact seems to be using Matthew's extra material without Matthew's obviously Markan additions. *But Matthew's extra material without the Markan additions is not Matthew's Gospel;* it is Matthew's other source(s). For convenience, we shall call it Q + M.

This seems to be the only intelligible solution of the problem of "the Lukan omissions of pure Mark from his rendering of material similar to that which Matthew has conflated with Mark."

Of course, the problem hinges on the question of the B verses (Matthew ‖ Mark): do these really belong with the C ones (Matthew, not in Mark), to make up Q; or are they Matthew's artibrary adaptation of Mark to fit his C material, so that Luke's rendering of them in the same relation to the C verses must be deemed to demonstrate that he knew Matthew? This is the nub of the problem; but is so, obviously, because we do not know the answer; though we have expressed above a reasoned preference for the former possibility. And the point is, on Dr. Farrer's argument, Luke did not know the answer either. On Dr. Farrer's argument, we have to suppose that Luke sat down (or stood) with Matthew's and Mark's works before him. He must have then, we have suggested, decided to follow Matthew (he has only three Markan words not in Matthew, and two are in another context). But for some incomprehensible reason, he decides not to follow Matthew throughout, but to follow Matthew *only where the latter has added new material to Mark or has largely altered him*. He notes that one and a half sentences exactly quote Mark, and so omits them. It is not that he is going to use them somewhere else. He just arbitrarily excludes them, in one case actually in favor of writing his own version (verses 21-22): so it is not even that he finds the Markan material repetitive. It is not that he objects either, to Mark as such, for on Dr. Farrer's thesis, Luke does not *know* (as we have noted) that the B material is not basically Mark, but slightly emended; and he includes this, quite happily. All that he excludes is the material in Mark that Matthew obviously saw fit to include pretty well as it stood!

It seems very much more sensible to assume that Luke did not know Matthew's use of Mark, and in fact here reproduced his own version of the B and C (= Q) material, with no reference either to Matthew or Mark. The similarities between Luke and Matthew, and the others between Luke, Mark and Matthew (barring coincidental alterations in the same direction independently by the evangelists) already stood in the material they had before them. After all, we were surely right that Mark and C are describing the same controversy. At least, Matthew thought so. A failure to coincide at some points would be very remarkable indeed.

Of course, two missing strangers do not form a queue—but it is possible to point to this same phenomenon (''the Lukan omissions of pure Mark from his rendering of material similar to that which Matthew has conflated with Mark'') in other contexts in which Matthew is generally admitted to have had (or at least, supposed himself to have) in addition to a

Markan account further traditional material referring to the same event or teaching.

There are the baptism narratives (Mt. 3:1ff.; Mk. 1:1ff.; Lk. 4:1ff.). Here Matthew has a great deal of C material (Matthew not Mark): John's Preaching of Repentance (verses 7-10), his further description of The Coming One (last word of verse 11? and verse 12), a conversation about the propriety of Jesus' request for Baptism (verses 13-14), and the triple Temptation (4:3-10). He has some B material (Matthew ‖ Mark)(verses 1:1-3a, 5b, 11, 16-17, 4:1-2, and 11); but the divergences from Mark are not as great as they were in the Beelzebul controversy, and it seems unlikely that he had extensive parallels. Mostly his material was supplementary. Verse 5b, introduction to the preaching, verse 11, the first part of the announcement of the Coming One, and 4:1-2, alone seem likely to have had parallels in Matthew's additional source, which could hardly otherwise have made sense. Apart from these, the B material diverges probably just through editorial action. Then there is A (Matthew ⌒ Mark) material, the Description of the Baptist (3:4-5a, 6); and of course the quotation from Isa. 40 (omitting that from Mal. 3) (verse 3b),

Again, Luke reproduces almost all the C material (less any equivalent of Mt. 3:14-15), the preaching of John, very faithfully, the Temptation less so. For the B material he has often his own version of Mark (so this time, if he has Matthew and Mark before him, he is surely using both) but reproduces almost all of it. Of the A material, Matthew's faithful quoting of Mark, he omits completely the larger part, 3:4-5a (he uses 5b independently, Lk. 3:3a) and verse 6. He does include the quotation from Isaiah (and omits Malachi from Mark); but the correction is obvious, and the remaining quotation essential to the Markan context that he retains. So again, Luke seems deliberately to ignore just the Markan material that Matthew has seen fit to reproduce exactly. Again, he seems to be reproducing Matthew's material independently of Matthew's use of Mark. Or else, he is just objecting to places where Matthew has nothing new to add, or no adaptation to make, but for no obvious reason.

Of course, it might be argued that Luke omitted these verses because he did not mean the Baptist to look like Elijah,[12] but there are further instances still.

---

[12]Cf. H. Conzelmann, *The Theology of St Luke* (1960) 22ff. He points out that the identification is, however, there in Lk. 1:17.

In Matthew's version of the Sending out of the Twelve (Mt. 9:35-10:16) there is a considerable amount of C (Matthew not Mark) material (9:35b, 37-38; 10:1b, 5-8, 12-13, most of 14 [?], 15-16). There is B material (Matthew ‖ Mark), 9:35a, 10:1a, 2-4, 9-11 (14a?). There is A class material (Matthew ⌐ Mark): Matthew cites Mark precisely in 9:36. And again, Luke reproduces a lot of the C material, almost verbatim. He reproduces most of the B material, but often offers his own version of Mark: if he has Matthew and Mark before him, he is using both. But he omits Mt. 6:36 = Mk. 6:34, the only verse of Mark that Matthew has included as it stood in his own conflation of his two sources. It has every sign of 'Luke-pleasingness' (to quote Dr. Farrer: cf. Lk. 7:13; 10:33; 15:4-6, 20). He does not use it elsewhere. He just omits it, though he preserves parallels to both sides of its Matthean context. He just does not seem to know Matthew's clear uses of Mark.

The last examples come from the Apocalypses in Mt. 24 (and 25), Mk. 13, and from Lk. 12, 17, 19, and 21. Here again, there is C type material (Matthew not Mark), Mt. 24:10-12, 14, 26-28, 30a; 24:37-25:46.[13] There is B material (Matthew ‖ Mark), 24:29-30, 42; 25:13-15b. There is a great deal of A material (Matthew = Mark), 24:4-9, 13, 15-25, 31-36.

Luke treats this section rather differently from the way in which he dealt with the Beelzebul controversy. Here (in the Markan context) he follows Mark, and it is Matthew that he ignores.[14] In fact, he omits a lot of the A class material, or rewrites the Markan original in his own way. Even his omissions from Mark bear no significant relation to Matthean omissions.

However, he does reproduce the new Matthean material elsewhere, in other contexts. On Dr. Farrer's thesis, he must be "credited with measuring the Markan text against St. Matthew's augmented version of it, before he reaches the place."[15] Dr. Farrer somehow knows this would be

---

[13]It is assumed that the parallels in Mt. 25:13, 14, 15b to the end of Mark's Apocalyptic discourse, 13:33-37 (to which Matthew offers no previous parallels), allow it to be taken that right into this block of material Matthew was still consciously conflating his sources with Mark. He omitted Mk. 13:33-37, knowing that his other parabolic material would only repeat these verses of Mark. Certainly at 24:42 he seems still directly to be quoting Mark (13:35a). That is, this is still material of the sort we have been considering up to now.

[14]Unless γάρ in Lk. 21:8 and 9, and ἕως ἄν in Lk. 21:32 be taken as evidence to the contrary.

[15]Farrer, "On Dispensing with Q," 84.

easy for Luke to do, for he would have the Markan apocalypse off "by heart" (*sic*). And Luke has to be credited with again a very strangely punctilious attention to detail. For instance, Matthew has followed a very close quotation of Mark 13:21-23, with a section of his own that contains a similar key phrase: "See here. . . . " Matthew has changed Mark's ἰδέ to a uniform ἰδού. This talks of lightning, and the gathering eagles (Mt. 24:23-28). Luke has parallels to the "new" material in his apocalyptic section in chapter 17. But he does not include anything parallel to Matthew's Markan verses. For Matthew's Ἐὰν οὖν εἴπωσιν ὑμῖν· ἰδοὺ ἐν τῇ ἐρήμῳ ἐστίν, μὴ ἐξέλθητε· ἰδοὺ ἐν τοῖς ταμιείοις, μὴ πιστεύσητε Luke does have Καὶ ἐροῦσιν ὑμῖν· ἰδοὺ ἐκεῖ, ἰδοὺ ὧδε· μὴ ἀπέλθητε μηδὲ διώξητε. But, obviously, if the ἐκεῖ . . . ὧδε . . . echoes any source of Luke we possess, it is Mark (13:21), and not Matthew, who has changed Mark to ὧδε . . . ὧδε. . . . Again we have Luke, if he is using Matthew, refusing any of Matthew's amalgam of his material with Mark. (That Luke sees his verses as roughly equivalent to Mk. 13:21-23 is further suggested by the fact that he omits them when he comes to write his version of most of Mark 13.) Of course an alternative description of the relationship could be written, which might seem to favor Dr. Farrer's case: Luke has condensed Mt. 24:23-25 into 17:23a, and 26-27 into 23b-24, while maintaining the connection Matthew made. But this only restates our problem. If this is really what Luke has done, why did he prefer Mark for his conflation to the Matthean version of Mark that he was supposedly following? It seems much simpler to suppose that he did not know Matthew; and that if his version of these sentences does echo the Markan passage Matthew also connected with them, that was inherently likely in the material itself. Certainly, Luke reproduces the "Eagle" saying (Mt. 24:28; Lk. 17:37) much later in the chapter, quite apart from the (Matthean) context of "See here. . . . "

Luke follows his version of the Lightning saying with a prophecy of the suffering of the Son of Man, and then goes into a comparison with the days of Noah, which Matthew has included in his Apocalypse, at the point where he was coming to the end of his Markan material (Mt. 24:37-41; Lk. 17:26-27). Quite without parallel in Matthew, he then recounts a similar comparison with the days of Lot. He inserts a saying about gaining or losing life (which on Dr. Farrer's thesis he earlier had remembered to omit when he was copying Mt. 10:37-39 in his own (Luke) 14:26-27; or now remembered that he had not yet included). He returns to the theme of the

arbitrary slaughter (17:34) and completes it with a version of the words in Mt. 24:40-41, and 24:28. It is interesting that he has material to supplement what he has that is parallel to Matthew for the construction of 17:20-37, material that (save perhaps for verses 32? and 33) fits well the context—or could it be that Luke is recording in full a section that Matthew has pruned, because part of it has similarities with material from Mark that he had repeated almost immediately before (Lk. 17:31 and 34; cf. Mt. 24:17-18 = Mk. 13:15-16)? Anyway, Luke seems to be ignoring not only Matthew's use of Mark in this section, but Matthew's use of Matthew; or Q. We suggest the ignoring is due to ignorance.

The next ten verses of Matthew, Luke (on the thesis we are examining) uses earlier still (Mt. 24:42-51; Lk. 12:39-46). He precedes them with a passage that has some superficial similarities to the parable of the Ten Virgins (which follows the Matthean passage referred to above, Mt. 25:1-13): λύχνοι, λαμπάδας; τῶν γάμων, τοὺς γάμους (but has otherwise little else: the actors in Luke are male, in Matthew female). Matthew ends this parable with what may be a quotation from Mk. 13:37; at least it is enough of a parallel for Matthew to omit any further use of the verse from his use of Mark: and Luke omits this, though it might have provided a good transition. More significantly, Matthew precedes his Householder and Thief with a similar sentence (Mt. 24:42), again reminiscent of Mark (Mk. 13:35), a verse to which again Matthew offers no further parallel: and Luke omits this too, although for the rest he is reproducing the Matthean material almost verbatim (only 16 words out of 145 are not in Matthew; about as many from Matthew not in Luke, save for verse 42, as mentioned, and the very Matthean verse 51b). Luke is not retaining these verses for use elsewhere. He just shows no sign of knowing Matthew's mixture of Mark with Matthew's own other source or sources.

Lastly, Matthew follows the parable of the Ten Virgins with that of the Talents (Mt. 24:14-30) of which Luke has a rather different version (Lk. 19:12-27), Matthew has either assimilated Mk. 13:34 to his 24:14-15b, or has at least again seen this as a doublet, and refrained from any further use of it. And neither of the incidental parallels appears in Luke.

This then is the major problem of the relation of Luke and Matthew: the Lukan omissions of Mark (particularly ''pure'' Mark) from his rendering of material similar to that which Matthew has conflated with Mark.

It is not the similarities in other contexts, in minor details, between Luke's and Matthew's handling of Mark that raise an insuperable problem. As Dr. Farrer has said, ''One cannot say that Dr. Streeter's plea that

these similarities are in different ways coincidental is incapable of being sustained.''[16] The real difficulty is to be found in attempting to explain why it was that a Luke who (on this theory) often followed Matthew very precisely in minor and unimportant stylistic changes of Mark, yet so objected to any attempt by Matthew to integrate matter taken intact from Mark with similar material from elsewhere, that he went to as great lengths as the various contexts would allow to unravel the mixture; often with such success that not a sign of it remains; and yet this without any aim in view (it seems) for the freed Markan sentences or phrases or words. This is such an inconsistent Luke (not the intelligent writer that Dr. Farrer mind-reads): he follows ''pure'' Mark for himself and ''pure'' Matthew, and even what may be Matthew's editorial restyling of ''pure'' Mark; but if *Matthew* uses pure Mark in the context of what seems to be some teaching from another source, then whatever is at all clearly of Mark must come out, or at least, be further disguised.[17]

We would suggest it is much more reasonable to suppose that Luke's apparent ignoring of every *clear* use by Matthew of Mark is due to Luke's ignorance of Matthew's use of Mark. Luke knew Matthew's source (or sources) ''before'' it had had its parallels with Mark conflated with the latter; and this source (or ''these sources'') is what has come to be known in part as Q.

II

Dr. Farrer admitted that the Q ''hypothesis wholly depends on the incredibility of St. Luke having read St. Matthew's book,'' but suggested

---

[16]Ibid., 62.

[17]Dr. Farrer can suggest only two instances of Luke's ''transcription of . . . Markan sentences embedded in Matthean discourse'': the Beelzebul controversy, and the sermon on the Little Ones; ''On Dispensing with Q,'' 83. We have suggested above that Luke seems to have left only ''Matthean'' sentences, and no obvious Markan ones, in the former discourse; and the latter is a further illustration of Luke's dependence of Matthew at *just this point* of Matthew's marriage of similar material in Mark and his other source(s). In Mt. 18:6-9, to a Markan saying about causes of stumbling is *appended* a complete saying on the same subject, the necessity of *skandala,* and ''woe to the man through whom the *skandalon* comes.'' This is the only context in Mark where *skandala* are discussed in these terms, and here it is at length. Luke has a similar saying to that in Matthew, and of course, if he is to add it at all, he will add it here. In fact, he uses it to *introduce* the Markan saying, and omits all of the words of Mark that Matthew reproduces, save περὶ τὸν τράχηλον αὐτοῦ and εἰς τὴν θάλασσαν, which are anyway the irreducible minimum of the saying. He makes his conflation with no sign at all of any dependence on Matthew for it.

that there was no such incredibility. We have suggested that, on the contrary, there is a greater degree of incredibility than has perhaps hitherto been realized. Dr. Farrer then offered some supporting contentions, with which we must now briefly deal.

According to Dr. Farrer, Q as it is normally analyzed has no shape or cohesion or character; it starts with vivid narrative, and peters out into unconnected oracles. It is hard to tell who would want such a work, for which there is no contemporary analogy. Q is "unevidenced and unique."

However, it needs only a slightly more sympathetic and a little more accurate description of Q to change the picture considerably. Unless a critic wishes to prove a "Proto-Luke" theory, there is no need to insist on the *narrative* exordium to Q. All that seems to be there are a few references to to actions that are the setting for discourses, a couple of geographical references, one healing, and for the rest a number of unelicited sayings of Jesus, and a number of dialogues between him and disciples. And this is formally very like the gnostic Gospel of Thomas.[18] It is composed of sayings and discourses, and once a conversation between disciples, with occasionally the setting described in one sentence (for example, Logion 23). Thomas certainly sees the Wicked Husbandmen and the Corner Stone as referring to Jesus (Logia 66-67), but like Q has no Passion Narrative. This is not to suggest any direct dependence of Thomas on Q.[19] It is just to point out what has surely now been noticed, that someone else, not far removed in time at all from the period when Q was still, it is supposed, in circulation, thought it worth while to write a "gospel" in this form. Of course, Thomas was perhaps a gnostic—but there is little in Thomas that is as "gnostic" as the Revelation saying in Mt. 11:25-26 = Lk. 10:21-22. And Q disappeared just as Mark almost did when the Matthean conflation was published; and as the four gospels almost did when Tatian's conflation was published.[20]

---

[18]R. M. Grant and D. N. Freedman, *The Secret Sayings of Jesus* (1960).

[19]Though he may have received his material independently of our gospels (and so, quite early?), he includes material in all the synoptists, with perhaps some echoes of the Fourth Evangelist added later. See K. Grobel, "How Gnostic is the Gospel of Thomas?" *NTS* 8 (1962): 367-73; R. E. Brown, "The Gospel of Thomas and St. John's Gospel," *NTS* 9 (1963): 157-77; also J. P. Brown, "The Form of 'Q' known to Matthew," *NTS* 8 (1961) esp. 38ff.

[20]See J. P. Brown, "The Form of 'Q'." The present writer would not, even to meet Dr. Farrer's challenge, be willing to attempt to work out the precise extent of Q (Dr. Brown

We have already dealt with Dr. Farrer's claim that Q is mere hypothesis; and have mentioned his admission that if it can be shown to be incredible that Luke knew Matthew's book, then Dr. Streeter's piecemeal dismissal of the minor similarities between Luke and Matthew in their use of Mark is acceptable.

He wrote that the hypothesis of Luke using Matthew must be exploded before the hypothesis of a common source, Q, be considered. It would be interesting to see whether the argument of this essay produces such an explosion: a bang or a whimper.

---

does attempt this speculation), and would only treat the passages where Matthew and Luke are very largely in agreement, say 70 per cent and over, as Q, where this was to serve as the basis for a further argument. However, from their treatment of Markan parables (for example, the Sower) Matthew and Luke might well be expected to differ largely in their use of Q parables (for example, the Pounds-Talents) and these might need to be judged separately. It is perhaps worth noting, even at this late point, that in this discussion of Dr. Farrer's hypothesis, I have joined him in assuming for the moment without argument that both Luke and Matthew had before them a copy of Mark much as we have it.

IN DEFENSE OF Q

E. L. Bradby*

Bradby's purpose is to suggest a rough-and-ready method of judging Austin Farrer's hypothesis in "On Dispensing with Q" that Luke had available and used as the basis of his gospel both Mark and Matthew. Bradby maintains that Farrer's thesis can fairly be judged by reference to a small number of key-passages from the Triple Tradition in which Matthew's text is *fuller* than Mark's. In these instances, if Farrer is right, we should surely find some instances in which Luke has reproduced material from Matthew which neither Matthew nor Luke could have gotten from Mark, because it is not paralleled in Mark.

Bradby considers four sets of passages from the Triple Tradition:

1. the walk through the cornfields and its sequel
2. the parable of the sower
3. the charge to the apostles
4. Peter's confession at Caesarea Philippi.

Bradby concludes that Farrer's thesis cannot be "proved" or "disproved." But in the four instances examined, if Farrer's thesis is correct, then Luke has consistently spurned the latter and fuller version in Matthew in favor of the earlier and shorter version in Mark. Bradby prefers to fall

*E. L. Bradby, "In Defence of Q," *The Expository Times* 68 (1956-1957): 315-18.

back on the theory of the priority of Mark and the use of Mark and Q by both Matthew and Luke.

Dr. Austin Farrer's stimulating essay, "On Dispensing with Q" in *Studies in the Gospels: Essays in Memory of R. H. Lightfoot*, edited by Professor D. E. Nineham (1955), must have sent many of us back to the Gospels eager to test his hypothesis against that which we have grown to regard as traditional. Dr. Farrer, it will be remembered, challenges the view that the writers of the First and Third Gospels both used a common source in addition to using the Gospel according to St. Mark, and seeks to establish instead that St. Luke has available and used as the basis of his Gospel both the Gospel according to St. Mark and that according to St. Matthew.

To deal fully with this contention would require the reexamination of a whole mass of books and articles based on the "two-document" theory—or later elaborations of it—and written over a period of more than half a century past. It is to be hoped that scholars who are qualified to do so will be provoked into making such a reexamination on a proper scale; but it will take time.

The purpose of the present article is to suggest a rough-and-ready method of judging Dr. Farrer's hypothesis without waiting for such a complete survey. It will be argued that the new theory can fairly be judged by reference to quite a small number of key-passages, in which all three of the Synoptic Gospels treat the same material, passages to which, remarkably enough, Dr. Farrer makes no reference at all in his essay.

For Dr. Farrer argues mainly from certain passages which are common to Matthew and Luke. He suggests, with great dialectical skill, that Luke has rearranged the material that he found in Matthew in the interests of clearer and more forceful presentation, grouping, for example, two passages about prayer which in Matthew were separate. But these facts may equally well be explained by suggesting that Luke found the passages linked in Q and preserved Q's order, whereas Matthew split them up, in accordance with his characteristic thematic treatment (abundantly shown already by his treatment of Markan material). Such passages can therefore be used to support either side of the argument, and cannot be conclusive.

Surely the hope of conclusive evidence must lie in the passages where all three of the Synoptic Gospels treat the same material. Now there are certain of such passages where the treatment is so nearly identical in all

three Gospels that nothing can be deduced regarding priority. Such a passage is the call of Matthew (Mk. 2:13-17; Mt. 9:9-13; Lk. 5:27-32). Granted that Luke had Mark in front of him when he wrote there is no means of telling whether he also had Matthew, for Matthew is virtually identical with Mark.[1]

Another type of passage from which no conclusion can be drawn is represented by the account of the Transfiguration (Mk. 9:2-13; Mt. 17:1-13; Lk. 9:28-36). Here Luke is shorter than Matthew and Mark, and they are almost identical with each other. It is therefore arguable that Luke abbreviated either Mark or Matthew, or both.

What we want is obviously a passage where all three writers are in parallel but Matthew is *fuller* than Mark. Then we shall surely find, if Dr. Farrer is right, some instances where Luke has reproduced material from Matthew which neither of them can have got from Mark, because it is not in Mark.

Luckily we have several suitable sets of passages, and four of of them will now be considered.

1. The walk through the cornfields and its sequel (Mk. 2:23-3:6, Mt. 12:1-21; Lk. 6:1-11). Here Matthew has clearly followed Mark very closely, but has characteristically inserted some additional material in three places: verses 5-7 (an elaboration of the argument about the priests in the Temple, capped by another saying of Jesus and a quotation from the Old Testament); verses 11-13 (parabolic allusion to a sheep fallen into a pit, with another saying of Jesus); and verses 15-21 (which completes the narrative by informing us that Jesus withdrew and charged the crowds not to make him known, this being capped by another Old Testament quotation).

Now if we read Luke's account we find that he has followed Mark almost verbatim; but of Matthew's insertions there is not so much as a trace. It is, of course, understandable that Luke should omit the Old Testament references; but if he had Matthew in front of him as well as Mark, and might therefore have copied the passage equally well from either, it is surely surprising that he did not think fit to reproduce here *any* of Matthew's additions, which were closely bound into the narrative, and which

---

[1] It is, however, noteworthy that Luke follows Mark in using the name "Levi" and not the first Gospel's "Matthew."

preserved two of the actual sayings of Jesus, sayings not reproduced else-where in Luke.[2]

2. *The Parable of the Sower* (Mk. 4:1-20; Mt. 13:1-23; Lk. 8:4-15). Here again, all three Gospels give most of the material in almost identical form. But in verse 12 and from verse 14 to verse 17 Matthew is alone; that is, he has inserted two passages into Mark's account. Of these passages there is again no trace whatever in the parallel passage from Luke.

Let us look at the Matthaean insertions in detail: the first (Mt. 13:12) is the familiar saying of Jesus; "whosoever hath, to him shall be given," etc. Now this occurs in *two* other contexts in Luke: (1) Lk. 8:18. This is only a few verses later than the Parable of the Sower, but interestingly enough it is in a Markan passage *not* reproduced by Matthew but repro-duced in full by Luke, namely, the short Parable of the Candle under a bushel. (2) Lk. 19:26, where it forms the conclusion of the Parable of the Pounds, being paralleled by a second occurrence in Matthew (Mt. 25:29) at the end of the corresponding Parable of the Talents.

A second saying comes at Mt. 13:16-17: "But blessed are your eyes, for they see," etc. This Luke introduces at 10:23, in his account of the re-turn of the seventy disciples.

Between these two sayings of Jesus, Matthew gives an expanded ver-sion of the reference to Isaiah (given shortly in Mk. 4:12 and Lk. 8:10), with a longer quotation. Luke's omission of this passage is less remark-able, for he might well have considered it as of less interest to his Gentile readers.

What is the upshot of all this? Simply that Luke is clearly following Mark and not Matthew in his account of the Parable of the Sower, although this involves him (according to Dr. Farrer's hypothesis) in leaving aside two important sayings which Matthew incorporates into this parable and bringing them in *later*. Surely here if anywhere he might have followed Matthew, since he intended to introduce the two sayings: to suggest that he changed their context for literary reasons seems far-fetched; is it not much more likely that—not having Matthew before him—he did not know of them as part of this parable?

---

[2] "In this place is one greater than the temple" (Mt. 12:6); and "It is lawful to do well on the sabbath days" (Mt. 12:12). The omission of the parable of the sheep in the pit in this context is in itself striking, but it might be argued that Luke has changed it into the closely similar parable of the ox or ass at Lk. 14:5.

3. The Charge to the Apostles (Mk. 6:7-11; Mt. 10:1-42; Lk. 9:1-5). Here Matthew's account is much fuller than Mark's or Luke's. All three accounts start off with almost identical wording.[3] Luke is a little shorter than Mark, not because he has omitted anything essential, but because he has summarized Mark's account. By the end of verse 5 Luke has reached the same point in the narrative as Mark at verse 11a; "shake off the very dust from your feet for a testimony against them."

Now Matthew's much fuller version is also following Mark, with additional material interspersed. Thus he has reached the injunction about shaking the dust off at verse 14. He follows this up—again transcribing Mark—by the saying "It shall be more tolerable for Sodom and Gomorrah in the day of judgment, than for that city." There Mark's account has ended. But Matthew adds a further long passage, starting with "Behold, I sent you forth as sheep in the midst of wolves" (verse 16), and ending at verse 42. This passage consists of a considerable number of sayings, very various in kind, but obviously brought together here because of their reference to the rigors of discipleship.

Luke includes none of these sayings in his account of the charge to the Twelve, but at 10:1-16 he gives an account of *another* charge, to seventy disciples (an incident not mentioned in Mark or Matthew), and in this charge he incorporates much of the material contained in Mt. 10:1-42. Some of it repeats in fuller form material that he has already used in relation to the sending of the Twelve, for example, "carry neither purse, nor scrip, nor shoes" (Lk. 10:4; cf. 9:3); "even the very dust of your city, which cleaveth on us, we do wipe off against you" (Lk. 10:11; cf. 9:5). But it also contains fresh material closely resembling items in Matthew's account of the sending of the Twelve. Thus Luke's "If the son of peace be there, your peace shall rest upon it" (10:6) recalls Matthew's "If the house is worthy, let your peace come upon it" (10:13) and Matthew's "sheep in the midst of wolves" (10:16) appears as "I send you forth as lambs among wolves" (Lk. 10:3).

The passages would repay more detailed study than can be given here; but enough has been said to show the problem which confronts us. On the old hypothesis of Q there was no difficulty: Luke 9:1-5 was following Mk. 6:7-11, which was the only source he had about the sending out of the

---

[3]Leaving aside the list of apostles, which Matthew gives between verses 1-5, but which Mark and Luke have introduced earlier in the narrative (Mk. 3:16-19; Lk. 6:14-16).

Twelve. But Q had another passage, giving a similar, but longer, charge, referred to a different occasion, namely, the sending out of the Seventy. Luke has reproduced this fairly fully as a separate incident at 10:1-16, but Matthew has conflated the Q passage with the Markan one, giving one long charge to the Twelve instead of a short one to the Twelve and a longer one to the Seventy. But on Dr. Farrer's hypothesis what has happened? Presumably this, that Luke, coming to the incident of Christ's charge to the twelve apostles, finding Mt. 10:1-42 too long for the movement of his narrative, and preferring Mark's shorter version (6:7-11), has given a short version at 9:1-5; but, not wanting to lose the valuable sayings given in Mt. 10:16-42, he has transferred them to *another* incident, although this was not referred to either in Mark or in Matthew (did he invent the incident or did he know of it from some other source?). On this new incident Luke has lavished, we must suppose, many (but not all) of the sayings which his source Matthew had attributed to the earlier incident, together with a few others (for example, "the harvest truly is great, but the laborers are few," 10:2) which he has lifted from other Matthean contexts (cf. Mt. 9:37).

Can this be justified as an economical explanation of the facts?

4. Peter's Confession at Caesarea Philippi (Mk. 8:27-9:1; Mt. 16:13-28; Lk. 9:18-27). The first four verses in Mark (verses 27-30) are reproduced in closely similar words and almost identical length in Matthew (verses 13-16, 20) and Luke (verses 18-21). But between the last two verses Matthew has inserted a passage of great importance, in which Jesus gives St. Peter his special charge as the "rock" on which he will build his church. This is not in either Mark or Luke, either here or elsewhere. During the rest of this narrative Matthew is following Mark very closely: Luke also follows Mark (or Matthew?) closely where he treads at all, but he has entirely omitted the incident of Peter's rebuke. His omission of this incident is surprising in itself (though not, of course, inexplicable); the degree of surprise must be considerably heightened if we suppose that he rejected it in spite of its inclusion in almost identical form by *two* sources, both of which were before him (Mk. 8:32-33; Mt. 16:22-23). Once again there is nothing to suggest that Luke is following Matthew, and a certain amount which suggests that he is following Mark without knowing of Matthew's additions.

Other instances could be given, though the ones quoted appear to be the most striking. In the last resort Dr. Farrer's thesis cannot be "proved" or "disproved," at least in the present state of our documentation. (Sup-

porters of the historicity of Q may, however, legitimately hope that excavations will yet present the world with at least some fragments of it.) Our view of the matter must therefore depend on the results of careful reading of the Gospels, helped by whatever imagination and literary insight we can bring to bear. We may be encouraged in this task by reflecting that these are the very qualities which Dr. Farrer has often commended, and by which much of his own work is guided.[4]

If St. Luke had Matthew as well as Mark before him when he wrote, we can picture him following Mark verbatim whenever he had him, and Matthew verbatim when he had not Mark. But what, then, would happen when he had rival versions of an incident from Mark and from Matthew? What we should normally expect any conscientious historian to do is to take the later and fuller version, in this case Matthew (since *ex hypothesei* Luke knew as well as we do that Matthew had incorporated Mark's shorter Gospel in his longer one). We might, however, concede that for certain literary reasons he might follow sometimes one and sometimes the other. But if we find, as we have found in four important passages, that the later and fuller version is consistently spurned in favor of the earlier and shorter, and that there is not one clear instance in these sections of any non-Markan passage which Luke has derived from Matthew, we can hardly be blamed if we fall back, with relief, on the alternative hypothesis, that in many passages Luke has used Mark and in many others Luke and Matthew have each used a common source other than Mark, that is, Q.

---

[4]See, for example, A. M. Farrer, *A Study of St. Mark* (1951) 9.

THE ORIGINAL ORDER OF Q

V. Taylor*

In light of challenges to the Q hypothesis by such scholars as Lummis, Jameson, Butler, and Farrer, Vincent Taylor believes it is timely to reexamine the order of Q in its bearing on the Q hypothesis. Taylor proposes to discuss only the argument from order reflected by the sayings, which is, in his view, the most objective and decisive argument in support of Q. All Taylor hopes to attempt is to consider whether the order of the sayings commonly assigned to Q is such as to render probable the view that this source lay before Matthew and Luke in the form of a document at the time they wrote.

Taylor discusses the order of the Q sayings in Luke as compared with that presented in the five great discourses in Matthew (The Sermon on the Mount, Mt. 5-7; The Mission Charge, Mt. 10; The Discourse on Teaching in Parables, Mt. 13; The Discourse on Discipleship, Mt. 18; and The Eschatological Discourse, Mt. 23-25) and in the rest of the Gospel of Matthew outside these discourses. In all five Matthean discourses we meet with the same features—respect in the main for the order of Q as it appears in Luke, and editorial activity on the part of Matthew where the order is different. The same is true of the use of Q in the rest of Matthew outside

---

*V. Taylor, "The Original Order of Q," *New Testament Essays: Studies in Memory of T. W. Manson, 1893-1958*, ed. A. J. B. Higgins (Manchester University Press, 1959) 246ff.; reprinted in V. Taylor, *New Testament Essays* (Epworth Press, 1970) 95-118.

the five great discourses; changes of order are editorial or due to conflation with Mark.

Taylor concludes that his investigation has confirmed the view that Luke has preserved the order of Q and has followed it with great fidelity. It has further shown that Matthew knew the same order and was aware of it when he made editorial adjustments and conflated Q with Mark and M. Q is not "an unnecessary and vicious hypothesis" (B. C. Butler), but a written collection of sayings and parables that actually existed when Matthew and Luke wrote. What we are able to recover from a comparison of the parallel material in Matthew and Luke is the form in which Q was current at least as early as the decade A.D. 50-60 and perhaps even earlier.

In view of the great contribution which Professor T. W. Manson has made to the study of Q, a contribution for which all students of Gospel origins are deeply grateful, it seems not inappropriate to offer in this essay a few comments on the order of this source. There are several reasons why such an investigation is desirable. First, it will be agreed that, while many important contributions have been made to this question, the results cannot be regarded as completely satisfactory. Again, and not unconnected with this situation, there has been a shift of interest which has caused a temporary halt to these discussions. For something like a generation the earlier interest in literary criticism, so virile during the latter part of the nineteenth century and the opening decades of the twentieth, has abated owing to the competing claims of Form Criticism, New Testament Theology, Typology, and existentialist assessments of the Gospel tradition. These newer and fruitful interests are not to be regretted and it was perhaps necessary that the well-tilled fields of literary criticism should lie fallow for a time. Nevertheless, it seems necessary, without neglecting the later disciplines, to return to the study of the older problems and to consider how far they are capable of a solution. Further, in the interval, the existence of Q has been vigorously assailed, notably by such scholars as E. Lummis,[1] H. G. Jameson,[2] B. C. Butler,[3] and A. Farrer.[4] These scholars have revived the hypothesis that Luke used the Gospel of Matthew as a source, and Abbott Butler has gone so far as to describe Q as "an unnecessary and vicious hy-

[1]E. Lummis, *How Luke Was Written* (1915).
[2]H. G. Jameson, *The Origin of the Synoptic Gospels* (1922).
[3]B. C. Butler, *The Originality of St. Matthew* (1951).
[4]A. Farrer, *A Study in St. Mark* (1951).

pothesis.''[5] The Two Document Hypothesis has been strongly attacked. These attacks have not changed the views of its advocates, but in some quarters a certain uneasiness is manifest. There is a tendency to speak of Q as ''a hypothetical document'' and its alleged unity has been questioned.[6] On the other hand, there has been what must be described as a closer approach to the Q Hypothesis on the part of some Roman Catholic scholars. In the New *Catholic Commentary on Holy Scripture* (1953) Père Benoit has maintained that an original Aramaic Gospel of Matthew was used as a source by the three Synoptists. Similarly Dr. Alfred Wikenhauser,[7] who maintains that the Greek Matthew and Luke are both dependent on Mark, suggests that Matthew composed the *logia* in Aramaic, the Greek translation being the common source used in the Greek Matthew and Luke.

In these circumstances it may be timely to reexamine the order of Q in its bearings on the Q Hypothesis. At any rate this is the theme of the present essay.

I

In this inquiry I shall use the symbol Q to represent those sayings and parables in Matthew and Luke which are commonly assigned to this source, accepting the view that Q was a document as ''a working hypothesis.'' I shall leave aside the possibility that Q was preceded by earlier groups of sayings and examine the common source which, by hypothesis, lay before them as a unity. Several arguments have been held to support this hypothesis—the linguistic agreements between Matthew and Luke, the order reflected by the sayings, and the presence of doublets in the two Gospels which point to the use of Mark and at least one other source. I do not propose to discuss all these arguments, but only the question of order, which in many respects is the most objective and decisive argument of all. I shall use the sign M as a convenient symbol for the sayings and parables which are found only in Matthew. With Streeter and Bussmann I believe that M was also a document, but it will not be possible within the limits of this essay to discuss this hypothesis, although the investigation will have

---

[5]Butler, *Originality*, 170.

[6]See the important essay of C. K. Barrett, ''Q: A Re-examination,'' *ET* 54 (1942-1943): 320-23 [reprinted in this volume].

[7]A. Wikenhauser, *Einleitung in das Neue Testament* (1953) 162-182.

something to contribute to it. It will not be necessary to examine the L hypothesis, and I must content myself with stating the belief that it was a body of oral tradition which Luke was the first to give a written form. All I wish to attempt is to consider whether the order of the sayings commonly assigned to Q is such as to render probable the view that this source lay before the two Evangelists in the form of a document at the time when they wrote.

In this endeavor I am compelled to refer to an article on "The Order of Q" which I contributed to the *Journal of Theological Studies*[8] in April 1953, since the present essay carries further conclusions there suggested. In that article I made a new approach to the question of order by suggesting that we must not be content to study parallel passages in Matthew and Luke in two columns, with Luke on the left, as presumably representing better the original order of Q, and Matthew on the right. Such lists point to a common order, as many scholars have argued, but the breaches of order in the lists are so many that the case has been felt to be much less strong and convincing than, in fact, it is. In the article referred to I set down the Lukan passages on the left, but instead of one column for Matthew I used *six*, including the Q sayings in the five great discourses in Matthew, in 5-7, 10, 13, 18, and 23-25 and a sixth column containing the Q sayings in the rest of Matthew. The result was to show an astonishing range of agreement, not continuous throughout but visible in groups or series of passages in the same order in both Gospels. In all, only ten sayings stood apart from these series breaking their continuity, and it was suggested that, unless Luke used Matthew as a source, a strong argument existed in favor of the hypothesis that both evangelists drew upon the document Q as one of their principal sources.

Obviously the tabulated series cannot be the result of happy chance, but, in default of any criticisms of the article known to me, I may perhaps be permitted to say that the table is open to two objections. First, I excluded a group of sayings and parables on the ground that in them by wide consent Matthew's preference, while possibly using Q, is dependent upon another source, with the result that the order of Q, as reflected in Matthew and Luke, may be obscured.[9] Secondly, I did not discuss in detail the ten

---

[8]Taylor, "The Order of Q," *JTS* New Series 4 (1953): 27-31.

[9]The passages omitted were the Great Commandment (Lk. 10:25-28; Mt. 22:34-39), the Signs of the Times (Lk. 12:54-56; Mt. 16:2-3), the Narrow Gate (Lk. 13:23-24; Mt.7:13-14), the Shut Door (Lk. 13:25-27; Mt. 25:10-12), the Great Supper (Lk. 14:15-24; Mt. 22:1-10), the Lost Sheep (Lk. 15:4-7, 10; Mt. 18:12-14), and the Pounds (Lk. 19:12-27; Mt. 25:14-30).

short sayings which stand in a different order in the two Gospels. The table was left to speak for itself.

In the present essay I shall include all the passages mentioned, with the exception of Matthew 16:2 which is textually suspect. The effect is to break to some extent the regularity of the agreements, although not in one or two cases, but in any case it makes the investigation more complete. I now propose to discuss the order of the Q sayings in Luke as compared with that present in the five great discourses in Matthew and in the rest of this Gospel outside these discourses.

II
THE SERMON ON THE MOUNT

Luke	Matthew 5-7
6:20-23	5:3-6, 11-12
6:27-30	5:39b-42
6:31	(7:12)
6:32-36	5:44-48
6:37-38	7:1-2
6:41-42	7:3-5
6:43-45	7:16-20
6:46	7:21
6:47-49	7:24-27
11:2-4	6:9-13
11:9-13	(7:7-11)
11:33	(5:15)
11:34	6:22-23
12:22-31	6:25-33
12:33b, 34	(6:20-21)
12:57-59	(5:25-26)
13:23-24	7:13-14
13:25-27	7:22-23
	[25:10-12]
14:34-35	(5:13)
16:13	(6:24)
16:17	5:18
16:18	5:32

Notes:

1. The greater part of Matthew's Version consists of sayings from M. In particular, 5:21-48 includes six "Antitheses," together with an introduction in 5:17-20. Into these sections Q sayings have been inserted. It is not surprising, therefore, that in these cases, Matthew and Luke do not agree in order.

2. Further, there is an original group of M sayings in 6:1-8, 16-18 (and perhaps also in 19-21). This also affects the order in which Q is used.

3. In these circumstances the agreement in the order of Q in the two gospels is remarkable. The order is not continuous, but consists of sequences in common, of which the first (broken by 7:12) is considerable, and the second (broken by 7:7-11 and 5:15) is hardly less notable. Two briefer sequences, consisting of two sayings each, follow. The bracketed passages are those which differ in order.

4. It will be seen that Matthew has used practically the whole of Luke's Sermon on the Plain in Matthew 5 and 7, and in 6 various sayings from Luke 11-14 and 16. This distribution has the appearance of a consciously adopted plan.

5. The passages in brackets obviously call for special discussion, and it will be useful to consider first those in Matthew 5:17-48, and then those in the rest of the Matthean Sermon.

The Q sayings in Matthew 5:17-48. The six Antitheses are (1) 21ff. on Murder, (2) 27ff. on Adultery, (3) 31-32 on Divorce, (4) 33ff. on Vows and Oaths, (5) 38ff. on Retribution, and (6) 43ff. on Love of one's neighbour. The theme of the Introduction, 5:17-20, is the Attitude to be taken to the Law. Of the Q sayings in 5:17-48 that on reconciliation in 25-26 is loosely appended to 24 in No. 1 and it is not surprising that the Lukan order is broken. What is surprising is that 18 (in the Introduction) and 32 in No. 3 stand in their Lukan order, and that the same is true of 39b-42 and 44-48 in Nos. 5 and 6. Nos. 2 and 4 contain no Q sayings.

These facts are naturally explained if Matthew has edited the Introduction and has himself added Nos. 3, 5, and 6 to an original group of three Antitheses in Nos. 1, 2, and 4. This hypothesis has independently been suggested by M. Albertz[10] and W. L. Knox[11] on literary grounds[12] and receives further support from the order of the Q sayings. With the exception of the editorial use of Matthew 5:25-26, dependence on Q in Matthew 5:17-48 in an order common to Matthew and Luke is a reasonable assumption. Matthew 5:18 and 32 are used earlier than the parallel sayings in Luke because they are inserted by Matthew into this complex.

The Q Sayings in the Rest of the Sermon on the Mount. In their Lukan order these sayings are Matthew 7:12, 7:7-11, 5:15, 6:20-21, 5:13, 6:24; and with these 7:13-14 and 22-23 may with advantage be considered.

---

[10]M. Albertz, *Die synoptischen Streitgespräche* (1921) 146-49. The hypothesis is discussed in my *Formation of the Gospel Tradition* (1933) 97-99.

[11]W. L. Knox, *The Sources of the Synoptic Gospels* (1957) 2:19-25.

[12]T. W. Manson, *The Sayings of Jesus* (1949) [first published as Part II of *The Mission and Message of Jesus,* 1937] 162, suggests that the original arrangement was: introduction, 17 and 20; No. 1, 21-22; No. 2, 27-28; No. 3, 31-32; No. 4, 33-34; No. 5, 38-39; No. 6, 43-44; Conclusion, 48.

(1) Mt. 7:12 (Lk. 6:31): "All things therefore whatsoever ye would that men should do unto you, even do so ye also unto them; for this is the law and the prophets."

Apart from the Matthean addition in the final clause, Matthew and Luke agree closely.[13] Dependence on Q is highly probable, and the only question to consider is why Matthew incorporates the saying at a later point. In reply, it is to be noted that both Evangelists use it as a summary passage. The position in Luke is much to be preferred since it is the conclusion to a group, Lk. 6:27-30, arranged in Semitic parallelism and revealing both rhyme and rhythm when translated back into Aramaic.[14] Apparently, Matthew has delayed his use of the saying to sum up the considerable number of Q sayings in 6:22-7:11. In short, he alters Luke's order for editorial reasons.

(2) Mt. 7:7-11 (Lk. 11:9-13): On Answer to Prayer.

The agreement is close, but the clue to the difference of position in the two Gospels is obscure. McNeile says that in Matthew the saying stands in no apparent relation to the context.[15] In Luke it appears in a section on Prayer (11:1-13) following the Lord's Prayer (2-4) and the parable of the Friend at Midnight (5-8). Knox[16] suggests that the section is a (pre-Lukan) tract on Prayer, but, if so, this suggestion does not exclude the probability that in Q Luke 11:9-13 originally followed immediately Luke 11:2-4. Why, then, in Mt. 7:7-11 is it separated from the Prayer (Mt. 6:9-13) by several passages from Q and M, placed immediately after the M saying, "Give not that which is holy to the dogs," and before the summary saying, 7:12, on doing to others as we wish them to do to us? No completely satisfactory answer has been given to this question, and it may be insoluble. Only a conjecture can be offered. The natural place for the passage in Matthew would be after the Lord's Prayer (Mt. 6:9-13) as in Luke. But at this point Matthew uses a saying from Mark or M on forgiveness (Mt. 6:14-15). This change of theme leaves the passage on Answer to Prayer on his hands; and he finds no place for it, save in an unsuitable context, after

---

[13]Ibid., 18-19, suggests that "whatsoever" (Matthew) and "as" (Luke) may be alternative renderings of an Aramaic original, and that "all things" and "therefore" are probably editorial.

[14]Ibid., 50; C. F. Burney, *The Poetry of our Lord* (1925) 113, 169; M. Black, *An Aramaic Approach to the Gospels and Acts* (1967) 137-38.

[15]A. H. McNeile, *The Gospel according to St. Matthew* (1961) 91.

[16]Knox, *Sources*, 60-61.

the extracts from Q and M immediately before 7:12 as indicated above. In any case and whatever may be the explanation, Matthew's use of 7:7-11 is probably editorial.

(3) Mt. 5:15 (Lk. 11:33): "Neither do men light a lamp, and put it under the bushel, but on the stand, and it shineth unto all that are in the house."

Mt. 5:15 stands in an M context (Mt. 5:13-16) and may even belong to M. In this case no problem arises: Matthew follows the order of M. More probably, however, the saying has been taken from Q. The parallel passage in Luke 11:33 has a doublet in Luke 8:16 (= Mk. 4:21) and shares with it the words οὐδείς, ἅψας, and εἰσπορευόμενοι and the idea that those who see the light enter from without. This explains the linguistic differences between Lk. 11:33 and Mt. 5:15.[17] That a common source is used is suggested by the fact that Mt. 5:15, 6:22-23, and 6:25-33 follow in the same relative order as Lk. 11:33, 34-35, and 12:22-31.[18] The earlier position of Mt. 5:15 is caused by its insertion in its present M context (see above).

(4) Mt. 6:20-21 (Lk. 12:33b-34): Treasure on Earth and in Heaven.

Apart from the closing words (Mt. 6:21 and Lk. 12:34) the linguistic differences are considerable. These differences and the variation of rhythm[19] in the two forms suggest that Matthew is drawing upon M and Luke on Q. In this case the difference in position is not surprising.

(5) Mt. 5:13 (Lk. 14:34-35): On salt.

Here again Matthew's source may be M.[20] If he is using Q the difference of order in Matthew and Luke is due to the M context in which Mt. 5:13 appears.

(6) Mt. 6:24: On serving Two Masters.

The two versions are in almost verbatim agreement; the only difference is that Luke has οἰκέτης with οὐδείς. With the last saying this is one of those "scattered fragments" which Streeter[21] says there is good reason to assign to Q, although they are not found embedded in the mass of

---

[17]Matthew is probably nearer to the original in his use of the impersonal plural καίουσιν.

[18]It is noteworthy that if the differences of position of 7:7-11; 5:15; 6:20-21; 5:25-26 are editorial, the agreement in order extends from 6:9-13 to 7:22-23.

[19]Cf. Burney, *Poetry*, 115.

[20]Cf. Manson, *Sayings*, 132.

[21]Streeter, *Four Gospels*, 285-89.

other material from that source. Easton[22] soundly observes that its place in Q is quite uncertain.

It is possible to state a case in favor of the order of either of the Evangelists. Luke attaches it to a group of L sayings (Lk. 16:10-12) which follow the parables of the Unjust Steward (16:1-9) and the connection seems determined *ad vocem* by the word "Mammon." This arrangement appears to be artificial as compared with that of Matthew who uses the saying to introduce the passage on Anxiety (6:25-34). The two are connected by the phrase διὰ τοῦτο and the idea suggested is that, as we cannot serve two masters, we are not to be anxious for our life. This connection is good, but somewhat artificial. Luke has the passage on Anxiety earlier (12:22-31) after the parable of the Rich Fool (12:13-21), and in this arrangement διὰ τοῦτο seems to point back to the preceding Q saying on the guidance of the Holy Spirit in a time of anxiety (12:11-12). As in Matthew this connection is good, but perhaps superficial. Anxiety about food and clothing and about one's defense before a legal tribunal are connected by little save the idea of anxiety itself. No compelling argument enables us to decide between Matthew and Luke and we must agree with the opinion of Easton, cited above, that the place of the saying on Serving Two Masters in Q is uncertain. Editorial activity has been at work in either Matthew or Luke, and perhaps in both.

(7) Mt. 7:13-14 (Lk. 13:23-24): The Two Ways, and Matthew 7:22-23 (Lk. 13:26-27): The Shut Door.

Linguistically the two sayings have so little in common that it is possible that both have been taken from M.[23] Moreover, Mt. 7:13-14 speaks of the narrow *gate* which leads to the ways of destruction and life, whereas Luke speaks of the narrow *door* which many are not able to enter. The sayings on the Shut Door also agree only in the common use of Psalm 6:9. Phrases in Lk. 13:25 recall the parable of the ten Virgins in M (Mt. 25:1-13).

The two sayings are considered here in order to have as many facts before us as possible because (a) they stand in the same order in Matthew and Luke, and (b) the intervening passages, Mt. 7:16-20 (Lk. 6:43-44) and Mt.

[22]B. S. Easton, *The Gospel According to St. Luke* (1926) 246.

[23]For this reason they were omitted with five other sayings in the *Journal of Theological Studies* article mentioned at the outset (Group A); see note 8 above.

7:21 (Lk. 6:46), *also* stand in the same order.[24] Moreover, Mt. 7:16-20 and 21 also, like 7:13-14 and 22-23, may come from M. If the source is Q, Matthew has followed its order; if M, he (or the compiler of M) is aware of Q's order or of a tradition common to Q and M. Probably the editorial work is that of Matthew himself. He connects 7:16-20 and 21 because they stand in that order in the Lukan Sermon on the Plain (Q) and 7:13-14 and 22-23 because they follow in the same order in those passages outside the Lukan Sermon which he uses in compiling the Sermon on the Mount.

Conclusions regarding the Sermon on the Mount. From the above investigation it would appear that, apart from cases of conflation with M, and insertions and additions to it, Matthew has followed the order of Q as it stood in Luke. The necessity of discussing cases where the order is broken must not obscure the fact that for the most part the agreement or order is patent and therefore does not need discusson. In the cases examined conflation and editorial changes are departures from the order present in Luke, except on rare occasions when Luke is responsible for the differences. A point of interest is that M supplies about two-thirds of the whole, which suggests that M itself contained a version of the Sermon beginning with Beatitudes. If so, Matthew has followed M in 5:3-11 with additions and modifications suggested by Q.

THE MISSION CHARGE

Luke	Matthew 9:37–10:42
6:40	(10:24-25)
10:2	9:37-38
10:3-12	10:9-16
10:16	(10:40)
12:2-3	10:26-27
12:4-7	10:28-31
12:8-9	10:32-33
12:11-12	(10:19-20)
12:51-53	10:34-36

---

[24]See the table of texts relating to the Sermon on the Mount. The correspondences (with the Matthean passages on the left) may be represented as follows:

Matthew	Luke	Luke
7:13-14		13:23-24
7:16-20	6:43-44	
7:21	6:46	
7:22-23		13:26-27

14:26-27	10:37-38
17:33	10:39

Notes:

1. The Matthean discourse contains material from M and Mark, but mainly from Q. (For 10:9-16 see footnote 26.)

2. It will be seen that, apart from 10:24-25, 40, and 19-20, the Q passages listed (24 verses) agree exactly in order in Matthew and Luke.

3. Obviously the three exceptions (5 verses) call for examination in order to see why they appear in a different order.

(1) Mt. 10:24-25 (Lk. 6:40): "A disciple is not above his master, nor a servant above his lord" (Matthew); "The disciple is not above his master; but every one when he is perfected shall be as his master" (Luke).

It should be noted that Lk. 6:39 has a parallel in Mt. 14:14 which is also not in Luke's order. Lk. 6:39-40 is a unit, not connected closely with its context in the Lukan Sermon, which Matthew has not included in the Sermon on the Mount. In 15:14 he applies 39 to the Pharisees[25] and, as we see, sets 40 in the Mission Charge. Both Matthean sayings stand in an M context and both may belong to M,[26] but the artificiality of the construction in 15:12-14 and 10:23-25 raises the question whether after all both have been derived from Q.

A common dependence on Q is suggested by the agreements and by the fact that Matthew's modifications appear to be secondary. Instead of the general application which the sayings have in Lk. 6:39-40 he applies 39 to the Pharisees and adapts 40 for use in the Mission Charge in 10:24-25, where the context and the double use of the term "his lord" suggest that he is thinking of Jesus himself.

All this is true even if Lk. 6:39-40 is not in its original order. Creed[27] says that its position is editorial and Easton[28] thinks the connection is artificial. But there is not a little to be said for the view that Luke retains the order of Q. Lk. 6:39-40 follows the saying on Not Judging (6:37-38) and precedes that on the Mote and the Beam (6:41-42). The idea appears to be that the man who condemns others is a blind guide who can benefit no one.

---

[25]This passage is considered later in the section headed "The Rest of Matthew."

[26]Cf. Manson, *Sayings*, 57. Manson also suggests that Mt. 10:9-16 is a conflation of material from Mark, Q, and M (180).

[27]J. M. Creed, *The Gospel according to St. Luke* (1960) 97.

[28]Easton, *Luke*, 92.

Teacher and disciple alike will fall into a pit, for the disciple's insight will rise no higher than that of his teacher even if the lesson is learned perfectly. Moreover, the man who judges is blind in another sense. He sees the mote in his brother's eye, but not the beam in his own eye, and thus deceives himself. This connection of thought seems too subtle to be editorial. It is easier to suppose that Luke is reproducing the order of Q.[29] If so, on his understanding of the sayings, Matthew has regarded them as unsuitable for the Sermon on the Mount and has transferred them to the contexts in which they now stand.

(2) Mt. 10:40 (Lk. 10:16): "He that receiveth you receiveth me, and he that receiveth me receiveth him that sent me" (Matthew); "He that heareth you heareth me; and he that rejecteth you rejecteth me; and he that rejecteth me rejecteth him that sent me" (Luke). Cf. Mk. 9:37, "Whosoever shall receive one of such little children in my name, receiveth me; and whosoever receiveth me, receiveth not me, but him that sent me."

It is important to note that, while these versions of the saying are not in the same order in Matthew and Luke, each belongs to the conclusion of the Mission Charge in the two Gospels. Apparently, Matthew has postponed the use of it deliberately until he has used additional sayings from Q, M, and Mark. It is not certain, however, that Q is his source. Mt. 10:40-41 may be from M and 10:42 is probably taken from Mk. 9:41. Dr. Manson[30] says that Lk. 10:16 is to be assigned to Q, but that one may have doubts whether Mt. 10:40 should be labelled Q or M. He further suggests that Mt. 10:40, Mk. 9:37, and Lk. 10:16 may go back to a fuller common original. The possibility arises that, if Matthew 10:40 is drawn from M, its position at the close of the Charge is suggested by the place of Lk. 10:16. In any case, whether it be from Q or M, its use by Matthew is determined by editorial considerations.

(3) Mt. 10:19-20 (Lk. 12:11-12): "But when they deliver you up, be not anxious *how* or *what* ye shall speak. For it is not ye that speak, but the Spirit of your Father that speaketh in you" (Matthew); "And when they bring you before the synagogues, and the rulers, and the authorities, be not

---

[29]The opinion that "He spake also a parable to them" (Lk. 6:39) is editorial, is supported by Lk. 5:36; 8:4; 12:16; 13:6; 14:7; 15:3; and 18:1; but W. Bussmann, *Synoptische Studien* (1929) 2:48, n1, suggests that perhaps it is original and lost through Matthew's change of position. It may be a necessary connecting link in the sense of "Take an illustration."

[30]Manson, *Sayings,* 78, 182.

anxious *how* or *what* ye shall answer, or what ye shall say: for the Holy Spirit shall teach you in that very hour what ye ought to say'' (Luke). Cf. Mk. 13:11 and Lk. 21:14-15.

The difference of order in Matthew and Luke is explained by the fact that the closer parallel to Mt. 10:19-20 is Mk. 13:11. Matthew's source in 10:17-22 is Mk. 13:9-13. It is often maintained that Lk. 12:11-12 is from Q because of its small linguistic agreements with Mt. 10:19-20 which are not present in Mark, especially the phrase "how or what." This view is weakened if, as Streeter thinks, the phrase is due to textual assimilation,[31] but it is not altogether destroyed. Streeter points out that in both Gospels the saying stands in the same discourse as Lk. 12:2ff. = Mt. 10:26ff., though separated by a few verses, and argues that the presence of Lk. 12:11-12 explains the use of the saying in both Gospels.[32] Q may have suggested to Matthew the use of Mk. 13:9-13 in the Mission Charge rather than in the eschatological discourse in Mt. 24 where it is merely summarized (Mt. 24:9, 13).

Conclusions regarding the Mission Charge. In considering the above passages one must not forget that, even more impressively than in the Sermon on the Mount, much the greater number of Q sayings (approximately four-fifths) are in the same order in Matthew and Luke. Where there is a difference of order, the arrangement in Matthew (and possibly occasionally in Luke) is due to editorial reasons or the use of other sources and that in some cases (10:19-20 and 40) Matthew appears to be aware of the order he deserts. Thus, the differences do not weaken the hypothesis of a common order, but tend to confirm it.

THE DISCOURSE ON TEACHING IN PARABLES

In this, the third of Matthew's five discourses, most of the material is taken from the two sources, Mark (4:1-9, 10-12, 13-20, 30-32) and M (Mt. 13:24-30, 36-43, 44, 45-46, 47-50, 51-52). The Q material is limited to one saying and two parables (The Mustard Seed and the Leaven), of which the Mustard Seed (Mt. 13:31-32) is a conflation of the Q version with Mk. 14:30-32.[33] This material, arranged in the Lukan order, is as follows:

---

[31]Streeter, *Four Gospels*, 280.
[32]Ibid.
[33]Ibid., 246-48.

Luke	Matthew	
10:23-24	13:16-17	"Blessed are the eyes which see."
13:18-19	13:31-32	The Mustard Seed.
13:20-21	13:33	The Leaven.

Notes:

1. There are no Q passages in an order other than that of Luke.

2. It is reasonable to suppose that in constructing the discourse Matthew takes his point of departure from Mk. 4:1, adding a considerable amount of parabolic matter from M, and inserting extracts from Q.

3. He conflates the Q version of the Mustard Seed (Lk. 13:18-19) with Mk. 4:30-32, and appends the parables of the Leaven because the two stood together in Q.

4. Already Matthew has on his hands the saying, "Blessed are your eyes" (Lk. 10:23-24 = Mt. 13:16-17), having replaced this passage by the M saying, "Come unto me, all ye that labor" (Mt. 11:28-30), after the saying, "I thank thee, O Father, Lord of heaven and earth" (Lk. 10:21-22 = Mt. 11:25-27). He places the saying after the Markan passage on the Purpose of Parables (Mk. 4:10-12 = Mt. 13:10-15), adding the phrase "and your ears, for they hear" and substituting "righteous men" for "kings." As Easton[34] says, the arrangement is obviously artificial. Matthew chooses the best place he can find for the saying previous to the second and third extracts from Q fixed by the use of Mk. 4:30-32, the parable of the Mustard Seed.

5. It is to be noted that Matthew had already used all the Q material in Luke which stands before 11:23-24, as well as all the sayings between this passage and the parable of the Mustard Seed (Lk. 13:18-19), with the exception of the saying on the Great Commandment (Lk. 10:25-28). Thus, the three extracts from Q stood together ready for use in Mt. 13.

Conclusions on the Discourse on Teaching in Parables. The amount of Q sayings in the discourse is small, but, so far as it goes, it confirms the hypothesis that Matthew follows the order of Q as it is reflected in Luke.

THE DISCOURSE ON DISCIPLESHIP

The fourth Matthean discourse is constructed like the third. It consists of material taken almost wholly from Mark (9:33-37, 42-48) in 18:1-9 and from M in 18:10-35. A few Q sayings appear to be used in the order in which they are found in Luke.

---

[34]Easton, *Luke*, 168.

Luke	Matthew	
14:11	18:4	On humbling oneself.
(15:4-7, 10)	(18:12-14)	The Lost Sheep.
17:1-2	18:6-7	On stumbling-blocks.
17:3-4	18:15, 21	On forgiveness.

The extent to which Matthew uses Q in these passages is debatable. It is open to question if the second belongs to Q. Mt. 18:4 differs considerably from Lk. 14:11, and Mt. 18:6-7 and 15, 21 are conflations of material from Q and M.

All the more remarkable is the agreement in order shown above. Moreover, Matthew had not to search for the Q sayings: they probably lay immediately before the eye He had already drawn upon all the sayings in Q which precede Lk. 14:11 and those also which lie between this saying and Lk. 17:1, which, with the exception of the sayings listed above, stood in succession ready for use in 18.

In view of the difficult questions which arise in these sayings it is necessary to examine them in detail.

(1) Mt. 18:4 (Lk. 14:11): "Whosoever therefore shall humble himself *as this* little child, the same is the greatest in the kingdom of heaven" (Matthew); "For every one that exalteth himself shall be humbled; and he that humbleth himself shall be exalted" (Luke). Cf. Lk. 18:14b and Mt. 23:12, which are in almost verbatim agreement with Lk. 14:11.

Lk. 14:11 is attached loosely to the section on Table Manners (14:7-10) and similarly the doublet in Lk. 18:14b is a pendant to the parable of the Pharisee and the Taxgatherer (18:9-14a). Mt. 23:12 stands at the end of an M section which condemns the habit of seeking respect from others, and Mt. 18:4, which is the passage under review, is an insertion in the story derived from Mk. 9:33-37 on True Greatness.

Many scholars describe the passage as "a floating saying"[35] or as "a short proverbial saying" for which there is no need to postulate a written source at all.[36]

On the whole it seems best to assign Lk. 14:11 = Mt. 18:4 to Q and to explain Lk. 18:14b and Mt. 23:12 as repetitions of the saying. Hesitation to take this view is natural, for at first sight Mt. 18:4 seems widely different from Lk. 14:11. But the differences, underlined above, are mod-

---

[35]Cf. Manson, *Sayings*, 312.
[36]Cf. Streeter, *Four Gospels*, 285.

ifications due to the Markan context in which it appears (cf. Mk. 9:34, 36). Thus, Mt. 18:4 is more than "a reminiscence of Q;"[37] it is a conscious modification of Q for editorial reasons.

(2) Mt. 18:12-14 (Lk. 15:4-7, 10): The Lost Sheep. This parable is widely assigned to Q,[38] but the opinion of Streeter,[39] endorsed by T. W. Manson,[40] that Matthew's version belongs to M and Luke's to L, is highly probable. The words common to both are those without which the story could not be told, and where the versions can differ, they do. Some of the differences are apparently translation variants.[41] The setting and the moral of the two versions are also different. In Matthew the parable is set in an M context and is related to the despising of "little ones;" in Luke it precedes two other similar parables from L (the Lost Coin and the Lost Son) and its theme is the mercy of God in forgiving sinners. An inordinate amount of editorial modification has to be assigned to Luke if both versions are drawn from a common source, whereas the differences are intelligible if they come from different cycles of tradition.

If this view is taken, the variation in order is irrelevant. Just because this fact is consistent with the main contentions of this essay it is necessary to consider what follows if the common source is Q. In this case the different order is the result of editorial adjustments with the other sources mentioned above on the part of one or both of the Evangelists.

(3) Mt. 18:6-7 (Lk. 17:1-2): On Offenses.

Matthew's version is widely held to be a conflation of Mark and Q, a view which accounts for the reverse form in which the saying appears in Matthew and Luke.[42]

(4) Mt. 18:15, 21-22 (Lk. 17:3-4): On Forgiveness.

The verbal agreements are slight, and from these it is impossible to maintain that the two versions are derived from one common source. Moreover, the number of the acts of forgiveness differs (Matthew seventy

---

[37]Easton, *Luke*, 227.

[38]Cf. Bussmann, *Synoptische Studien*, 2:86-87; Easton, *Luke*, xix, 235-36; Creed, *Luke*, lxv; G. D. Kilpatrick, *The Origins of the Gospel according to St. Matthew* (1946) 28-29; S. E. Johnson, *The Interpreter's Bible* (1951) 7:471.

[39]Streeter, *Four Gospels*, 244-45.

[40]Manson, *Sayings*, 283.

[41]Cf. ibid., 208; J. Jeremias, *The Parables of Jesus* (1963) 29, 106.

[42]Cf. Streeter, *Four Gospels*, 265, 281n; Easton, *Luke*, 256; Creed, *Luke*, 214; E. Klostermann, *Das Lukasevangelium* (1929) 170.

times seven, or seventy-seven; Luke, seven times), and "I repent" is peculiar to Luke. But there is agreement in the succession of themes (Offenses and Forgiveness).[43] The presumption is that Matthew is giving the fuller M version in 18:15-22 in preference to that of Q for liturgical reasons.

Conclusions regarding the Discourse on Discipleship. Although the Q sayings used or reflected in the discourse are few, they follow without exception the Lukan order. It is possible that order of thought in Q, humility, offenses, and forgiveness, is the clue to Matthew's disposal of Markan and M material in 18:1-9 (Mark) and 10-35 (M).

THE ESCHATOLOGICAL DISCOURSE

Whether Matthew 23 (the Condemnation of the Scribes and Pharisees) should be separated from the Eschatological Discourse proper in Mt. 24-25 is a disputed question. Certainly 23 is self-contained, but it is not concluded by the formula, "And it came to pass, when Jesus had finished all these words," which appears at the end of the five great discourses (cf. 26:1). It appears to be Matthew's intention to connect 23 with 24-25 (cf. 23:38). Since, however, it forms a whole, it will be useful to examine it separately.

Luke	*Matthew*
11:39-48	23:4-31
11:49-51	23:34-36
11:52	(23:13)
13:34-35	23:37-39

Notes:

1. It will be seen that there is a relative agreement of order broken, apparently, at Mt. 23:13.

2. The table, however, is delusive unless we consider Mt. 23:4-31 (to which verse 13 belongs) in detail, since M forms the backbone of this section, Mk. 12:38b-40 is inserted in 23:6-7a and 13(-14) almost verbatim. Several of the parallels in Lk. 11, which presumably are from Q, are slight and not in the Lukan order. In these circumstances it will be helpful to set out the whole of Mt. 23 in a table indicating the parallel sayings in Luke and the extent to which they agree linguistically.

---

[43]Cf. Streeter, *Four Gospels*, 281: "Seeing there is no very obvious connection between the two topics, the connection (Offenses-Forgiveness) must have been made in the common source Q."

In their Matthean order the parallel sayings are as follows:

Matthew 23	Luke	Agreement
1		
2-3		
4	11:46	Small
5		
6-7a	11:43	Small
7b-10		
11		
12	(cf. 14:11)	Almost verbatim
13-14	11:32	Small
15-22		
23:23	11:42	Considerable
24		
25-26	11:39-41	Considerable
27-28	11:44	Negligible
29-31	11:47-48	Small
32-33		
34-36	11:49-51	Considerable
37-39	13:34-35	Almost verbatim

Note:
    The horizontal lines separate the seven "Woes" in Matthew from the rest of the chapter.

From this table it can be seen that the first five parallels stand in a different order in Matthew and Luke. They appear to be cases in which a definite preference has been given to the order and text of M. Only Matthew 23:12 is a probable insertion from Q and 23:23 may be a conflation of Q and M. In these circumstances the difference of order in the five parallels is not in the least surprising.

All the more remarkable is the complete agreement of order in the last five parallels. Moreover, apart from Matthew 23:27-28 and 29-31 the linguistic agreement is much greater. Apparently in these two sayings Matthew is still dependent on M. The agreement in order might be accidental or due to the original tradition lying behind M and Q, but the considerable degree of linguistic agreement of 23:25-26, 34-36, and 37-39[44] with their

---

[44]Dr. Manson, *Sayings*, 102, points out that, taking Luke's shorter version as the standard, the amount of agreement in Mt. 23:34-35 is nearly 90 percent.

Lukan counterparts suggests rather a knowledge of the order of the five sayings in Q, and 23:23 may well have drawn Matthew's attention to this series.

We must conclude that, although Matthew follows M in the main in 23, he is well aware of the order of Q and observes it in the latter part of the discourse.

Mt. 24-25. In the Eschatological Discourse proper the parallel passages in their Lukan order are:

Luke	Matthew
12:39-40	24:43-44
12:42-46	24:45-51
17:23-24	24:26-27
17:26-27	24:37-39
17:34-35	24:40-41
17:37	(24:28)
19:12-27	25:14-30

Notes:

1. There are two parallel series, the second of which is broken by Mt. 24:28 (the Gathering Vultures).

2. The questions to be discussed are why 24:43-51 (the Parables of the Thief and the Faithful and Unfaithful Servants) appears later in Matthew, and why 24:28 is used earlier than in Luke.

(1) Mt. 24:43-51. The first question is easily answered. The two parables are attached to the Markan saying (13:35) in Mt. 24:42 to form the first and second of a group of five parables (the last three of which, the Ten Virgins, the Talents,[45] and the Sheep and the Goats, are from M) in Mt. 24:43-25:46 (that is, at the end of the Discourse).

(2) Mt. 24:28: "Wheresoever the carcass is, there will be the vultures gathered together" (Matthew), "And they answering said unto him, Where Lord? And he said unto them, Where the body is, thither will the vultures also be gathered together" (Luke).

In Matthew, without an opening question, it stands in a good connection after the saying on the suddenness of the Coming of the Son of Man; in Luke it closes the Eschatological Discourse. In Matthew it affirms the inevitability of the Parousia, in Luke it amounts to a refusal to answer the

---

[45]The parable of the Talents (in Luke, the Pounds) appears to be a conflation of M and Q (cf. Mt. 25:24-29 and Lk. 19:20-26).

question, "Where, Lord?" Commentators are very divided on the question of its original position, and this is not strange since the saying is a proverbial utterance. The roughness of Luke's enigmatic form may be more original than Matthew's smoother version, but a certain decision is perhaps not possible. In any case the editorial activity of one or other of the Evangelists is responsible for the difference of position.

Conclusions regarding the Eschatological Discourse. As in 23, Matthew used material from M and Mark with which he has connected extracts from Q. In the latter Matthew and Luke agree in order apart from editorial rearrangements in Matthew 24:43-51 due to use of M, and perhaps also in 24:28 where Q alone is in question.

In all the five discourses we met with the same features—respect in the main for the order of Q as it appears in Luke and editorial activity usually on the part of Matthew where the order is different. It remains now to ask if the same is true of the use of Q in the rest of Matthew outside the five great discourses.

THE REST OF MATTHEW

The Q passages in the Lukan order are as follows:

Luke	Matthew
3:7-9, 12, 16-17	3:7-12
3:21-22	3:16-17
4:1-13	4:1-11
6:39	(15:14)
6:43-45	(12:33-35)
7:1-10	8:5-10, 13
7:18-23	11:2-6
7:24-28	11:7-11
7:31-35	11:16-19
9:57-60	(8:19-22)
10:13-15	11:21-23
10:21-22	11:25-27
10:25-27	(22:34-39)
11:14-23	12:22-30
11:24-26	12:43-45
11:29-32	12:38-42
12:10	(12:32)
13:28-29	(8:11-12)
13:30	(20:16)
14:15-24	[22:1-10]
16:16	(11:12-13)
17:5-6	17:20
22:28, 30b	19:28

Notes:

1. It is a remarkable fact that, with the exception of the passages in brackets and the inversion of Matthew 12:43-45 and 38-42, all the sayings stand in the same order in Matthew and Luke.

2. The passage in square brackets is the parable of the Marriage Feast (Mt. 22:1-10, Lk. 14:15-24, the Great Supper). It is included for the sake of completeness. Linguistically Matthew and Luke have very little in common and conflation in Matthew of Q with another parable is a probable explanation.[46]

3. Of the remaining passages in brackets Matthew 12:32 (cf. Mk. 3:28-29) and 22:34-39 (cf. Mk. 12:28-34) are conflations of Q and Mark which, as many examples have shown, result in a difference of order.

4. The passages left for discussion are Mt. 15:14, 12:33-35, 8:19-22, 8:11-12, 20:16, and 11:12-13.

The inversion of Matthew 12:43-47, 38-42 and Luke 11:24-26, 29-32. Editorial rearrangement is the cause of the inversion. In Matthew the sections on the Sign of Jonah and the Ninevites are brought together because they relate to Jonah, and the addition, "Even so shall it be also unto this generation," brings the saying on Demon Possession (12:43-45) into harmony with the whole. In Luke the saying on Demon Possession stands first after the section on Collusion with Beelzebub, presumably because both deal with exorcism. Opinions will differ regarding the original order of Q. Matthew, I think, is responsible for the inversion, but in either case a common order is presupposed.

(1) Mt. 15:14 (Lk. 6:39): "Let them alone: they are blind guides. And if the blind guide the blind, both shall fall into a pit"(Matthew); "And he spoke also a parable unto them, Can the blind guide the blind? shall they not both fall into a pit?" (Luke).

It will be recalled that the saying which follows (Lk. 6:40 = Mt. 10:24-25) was discussed earlier, and that the view taken was that Luke 6:39-40 preserves the order of Q, Mt. 10:24-25 owing its position to the M context in which it stands. A similar explanation accounts for the position of Mt. 15:14 which reflects editorial rearrangement.[47]

(2) Mt. 12:33-35 (Good and Corrupt Trees); cf. Mt. 7:16-20 and Lk. 6:43-45 discussed earlier.

The relationships between Mt. 7:16-20 and 12:33-35 are difficult to determine. Easton[48] suggests different forms in which the saying was spo-

---

[46]Cf. Manson, *Sayings*, 129, 225.

[47]Cf. Ibid., 57.

[48]Easton, *Luke*, 92.

ken. With greater probability Hawkins[49] suggests that Matthew uses the saying twice, adapting it to the context in which he places it, in 7:16-18 to bring out the criterion of true and false teachers, in 12:33-35 to bring out the importance of words as proofs of the state of men's hearts.[50] If this is so, editorial activity accounts for the fact that 12:33-35 is not in the Lukan order.

(3) Mt. 8:19-22 (Candidates for Discipleship); cf. Lk. 9:57-60.

Why does Matthew place these sayings at an earlier point than that of Luke? Easton[51] gives the answer when he says that in both Matthew and Luke this is the last discourse section before the Mission Charge. *After* the Charge Matthew places those relating to the Baptist (11:2-6, 7-11, 16-19), while Luke has the parallel sayings *before* it (7:18-23, 24-28, 31-35). Further, Matthew has used 8:19-22 as a preface to a considerable group from Mark and M containing many miracle stories. The purpose of this arrangement is to prepare the way for 11:5-6 (Lk. 7:22-23), which is the message to John about the mighty works being wrought by Jesus. Luke meets the same need by the editorial passage, 7:21, "In that hour he cured many of diseases and plagues and evil spirits; and on many that were blind he bestowed sight." Both evangelists exercise editorial freedom, but in Matthew the order of Q is affected.

(4) Mt. 8:11-12 (Lk. 13:28-29): "Many shall come from the east and the west. . . . "

Matthew has used the saying earlier by inserting it into the story of the Centurion's Servant (8:5-10, 13) and has inverted the sentences in order to get a better connection.

(5) Mt. 20:16 (Lk. 13:30) (the Last First and the First Last).

The transposition of No. 4 (above) left the saying[52] isolated and Matthew has attached it to the parable of the Laborers in the Vineyard (20:1-15).

(6) Mt. 11:12-13 (Lk. 16:16): "From the days of John the Baptist."

---

[49]J. C. Hawkins, *Horae Synopticae* (1909) 85.

[50]Cf. Manson, *Sayings*, 59: "It is difficult to resist the conclusion that the Q material given here (Lk. 6:43-45) in Luke has been freely adapted in Matthew to other purposes."

[51]Easton, *Luke*, 155.

[52]The source of the doublet in Mt. 19:30 is Mk. 10:31 where, as in Matthew, the clauses are inverted (the First Last and the Last First).

In the interests of a better order Matthew has transferred the saying to an earlier point after the testimony of Jesus to John (11:7-11). Luke would hardly have moved it from this position if Q had so placed it.[53]

Conclusions regarding the Rest of Matthew. The use of Q in its Lukan order is as pronounced as in any of the five great discourses. It may be conjectured that, if the discourses were constructed first, the Q sayings were left standing as they appear in Luke. The changes of order are editorial or due to conflation with Mark. They arise from the necessity of inserting the sayings in the Markan framework and the desire to bring together and to adjust those relating to the Baptist.

III
CONCLUSIONS REGARDING Q AS A WHOLE

The investigation has confirmed the view that Luke has preserved the order of Q and has followed it with great fidelity. It has shown further that Matthew knew the same order and was aware of it when he made editorial adjustments and conflated Q with Mark and M. If we reject, as we must, the hypothesis of Luke's dependence on Matthew, the result of a comparison of the order of the sayings in Matthew and Luke is to demonstrate the existence of Q, so far as this is possible in the case of a source known to us only from its use in the two Gospels. Q is not "an unnecessary and vicious hypothesis," but a collection of sayings and parables which actually existed when Matthew and Luke wrote. Its earlier history is a matter for conjecture; it is not excluded that earlier groups of sayings and parables have been combined in it. But this stage was past when the Gospels were compiled, and what we are able to recover is the form in which Q was current at least as early as the decade A.D. 50-60 and perhaps even earlier. It is probable that some of the sayings peculiar to Luke belong to it, including 6:24-26, 9:61-62, 12:35-38, 47-48, and 54-56, but not sayings found only in Matthew.

It is desirable that M should be investigated more closely. This task has been waiting for a generation,[54] and it will always prove difficult, since the sayings are found in Matthew only.

---

[53]Cf. B. H. Streeter, *Oxford Studies in the Synoptic Problem*, ed. W. Sanday (1911) 156-57.

[54]An important contribution has been made by Professor Pierson Parker in *The Gospel Before Mark* (1953), who has shown that "since Q has not been assimilated to Matthaean types of expression," and "the style of Q does not pervade M, therefore Q and M have different origins" and "Q is really from an autonomous source" (30-31).

THE CASE
AGAINST
THE Q
HYPOTHESIS

ON DISPENSING WITH Q

A. M. Farrer*

Farrer argues that the Q hypothesis depends wholly on the incredibility of Luke's use of Matthew. The hypothesis of Luke's use of Matthew must be conclusively exploded before we can consider that Matthew and Luke have both drawn independently from a common source, Q.

The possibility of a common source would be strengthened: (1) if the passages common to Matthew and Luke had a strong distinctive flavor; or (2) if the passages common to Matthew and Luke cried out to be strung together in one order rather than in any other, and being so strung together made up a satisfyingly complete little book; or (3) if the lost source proposed were of a sort of book known to be plentiful at the time.

In the case of the synoptic gospels, Farrer believes that none of these points is operative. Furthermore, Farrer finds it incredible that Q should open with the strongly narrative character of the Baptist's preaching and Jesus' appearance, proceed to the elaborate symbolism of Jesus' temptations and the Sermon, and then peter out into miscellaneous oracles, and conclude without any account of Jesus' death, the event which, to the Christian faith, is supremely significant. Farrer labels as "a plea against apparent evidence" Streeter's management of the agreements of Matthew

---

*A. M. Farrer, "On Dispensing with Q," *Studies in the Gospels: Essays in Memory of R. H. Lightfoot*, ed. D. E. Nineham (Oxford: Blackwell, 1955) 55-88.

and Luke against Mark by his dividing of the evidence into several groups and finding a distinct hypothesis for each.

Farrer then offers critical comments on five reasons why Luke cannot have used Matthew: (1) there are texts in Matthew which Luke would not have omitted; (2) Luke's wording is sometimes more primitive than Matthew's in the Double Tradition; (3) Luke's use of Matthew would be quite different from his use of Mark; (4) the order of material from the Double Tradition in Luke is mostly less appropriate and less coherent than its order in Matthew; and (5) Luke does not place his material from the Double Tradition in the Markan contexts in which it is usually found in Matthew.

Rather, according to Farrer, Luke's plan is to begin his gospel with lively narrative (1:1-10:24), give the teaching (10:25-18:30), and return to unencumbered narrative for the events at Jerusalem (18:31-24:53). Dispensing with Q, Farrer attempts to analyze a specimen of Luke's reworking in chapters 10-18 of material taken from Matthew and then proceeds to analyze Luke's reworking of the basic structure of Matthew's gospel (or, as he calls it, Matthew's hexateuch).

Farrer concludes by looking at the "mystery" of Luke's wrenching Matthew's non-Markan material away from its Markan contexts and concludes that it is no mystery at all but rather happens much as we might expect. In conclusion, Farrer speculates that the literary history of the gospels will turn out to be simpler than is generally supposed: Matthew will be seen to be an amplified version of Mark; Luke will be found to presuppose Matthew and Mark; and John to presuppose the other three.

I

Why dig up solid foundations, why open questions long taken for settled? Much critical and expository work rests squarely on the Q hypothesis, and if the hypothesis loses credit, the nuisance will be great. The books we rely upon to guide our thought about the history of Christ will need to be read with painful and unrelaxing reinterpretation. Nor is it only the effect on past studies that disquiets us. We want an accepted foundation for our present studies, and it seems a grievous thing that we cannot proceed with them until we have reinvestigated what was unanimously settled by a previous generation. Is there to be no progress in learning? Now that criticism is a science, are we not to hold any established positions as permanent conquests, from which a fresh generation can make a further advance? Minds of high ability and scrupulous integrity were brought to bear on the Q question in the great days of source criticism. They sifted to the bottom, they counted every syllable, and they agreed in the substance

of their findings. Is it likely that we, whose attention is distracted by the questions of our day, can profitably do their work again? And what reason have we to trust our judgments against theirs, if we find ourselves dissenting from their conclusions?

It would certainly be impertinence to suggest that the scholars who established the Q hypothesis reasoned falsely or misunderstood their own business; no less an impertinence than to talk of the great Scholastics so. St. Thomas understood the business of being an Aristotelizing Augustinian, and if I am not his disciple, it is not because I find him to have reasoned falsely. It is because I do not concede the premises from which he reasoned. And if we are not to be Streeterians, it will not be because Dr. Streeter reasoned falsely, but because the premises from which he reasoned are no longer ours.

I take the situation to be this. Since Dr. Streeter wrote, our conception of the way in which the Gospels were composed has gradually altered; so gradually, that we have not observed the extent of the alteration. Nevertheless the change that has taken place removes the ground on which the Q hypothesis stood. For the hypothesis wholly depends on the incredibility of St. Luke's having read St. Matthew's book. That incredibility depends in turn on the supposition that St. Luke was essentially an adapter and compiler. We do not now, or ought not now, so to regard him. And being once rid of such a supposition, we can conceive well enough how St. Luke could have read St. Matthew's book as it stands, and written the gospel he has left us. Then at one stroke the question is erased to which the Q hypothesis supplied an answer. For the hypothesis answered the question, "From what does the common non-Markan material of Matthew and Luke derive, since neither had read the other?"

If there is no difficulty in supposing St. Luke to have read St. Matthew, then the question never arises at all. For if we find two documents containing much common material, some of it verbally identical, and if those two documents derive from the same literary region, our first supposition is not that both draw upon a lost document for which there is no independent evidence, but that one draws upon the other. It is only when the latter supposition has proved untenable that we have recourse to the postulation of a hypothetical source. Now St. Matthew and St. Luke both emanate from the same literary region—both are orthodox Gentile-Christian writings composed (let us say) between A.D. 75 and A.D. 90, in an area in which St. Mark's Gospel was known. Moreover, St. Luke's own pref-

ace informs us that he writes ''in view of the fact that several authors have tried their hands at composing an account of the things fulfilled among us.'' He claims to know, and, one would naturally suppose, to profit by, more than one gospel-narrative other than his own. By all agreement he knew St. Mark's, but what other did he know? It would be natural for him to know St. Matthew's, supposing always that it had been in existence long enough.

The point we are making is that the hypothesis of St. Luke's using St. Matthew, and the hypothesis of their both drawing independently from a common source, do not compete on equal terms. The first hypothesis must be conclusively exploded before we obtain the right to consider the second at all. Such is the actual case. There are, of course, possible cases in which the hypothesis of a lost and unevidenced source might compete on equal terms with the hypothesis of simple borrowing. Suppose, for example, that the passages common to A and B have a strong distinctive flavor, unlike the remaining parts of either A or B. Suppose further that the common passages, once we have extracted them, cry aloud to be strung together in one order rather than in any other; and that being so strung together they make up a satisfyingly complete little book, with beginning, middle and end. Then indeed we might postulate the existence of a common source, without waiting to prove that B cannot derive directly from A, nor A from B.

But in the case before us neither supposition holds good. To begin with the second—it is notorious that Q cannot be convincingly reconstructed. No one reconstruction, to say the least of it, is overwhelmingly evident, and no proposed reconstruction is very firmly patterned. It is fair enough to object that Q may in fact have been a somewhat shapeless writing. It may indeed, but if it was, then no positive argument can be drawn from its shapeliness or cohesion to its existence as a single distinct work. Then to take the other supposition. Can we say that the Q sections of St. Matthew's Gospel have a strong distinctive flavor, marking them off from the rest of his writing? We cannot. They have a special character of a sort, but a character which can be plausibly enough described as Luke-pleasingness. It seems a sufficient account of them to say that they are those parts of St. Matthew's non-Markan material which were likely to attract St. Luke, in view of what we know about the general character of his Gospel, or can conjecture about his aims in writing it. For example, St. Luke was not interested in the detail of the anti-Pharisaic controversy and neglects much

teaching of Christ which attacks the Pharisees on their own ground. Must we therefore distinguish in Matthew two elements, M and Q, M rabbinic in tone, Q popular and nonrabbinic, of which St. Luke knew Q, but not M? Will it not do as well to say that St. Luke let alone what he did not care for, namely, the rabbinic parts of Matthew?

There is another supposition which, if we could make it, might raise the hypothesis of a lost and unevidenced common source to something like a priori equality with the hypothesis of direct borrowing by one of our documents from the other. And that would be, if the lost source we proposed to postulate were a sort of book known to have been plentiful at the time. For example, suppose we were struck by certain resemblances between two Victorian novels, suggestive of actual literary affinity. Then there would be scarcely any a priori disparity between the two hypotheses (*a*) that one borrowed direct from the other (*b*) that both were indebted to some third novel unknown to us. For there were a great number of novels published at the time, and many of them have since sunk into oblivion.

But unhappily the postulation of Q is quite the opposite of such a case. We have no reason to suppose documents of the Q type to have been plentiful. It is vain to cite Streeter's M and L, for the M and L hypotheses are corollaries to the Q hypothesis and have no independent standing. No, in postulating Q we are postulating the unique, and that is to commit a *prima facie* offense against the principle of economy in explanation. St. Luke's preface is evidence that several authors earlier than himself had undertaken the composition of an account of the things fulfilled in the Christian dispensation. But Q does not answer to the description. The "things fulfilled" are, in St. Luke's view, the death and resurrection of Jesus above all. Q is not supposed to have contained an account of them, and therefore Q is not covered by St. Luke's words. He was talking about gospels, about the sort of book he himself proposed to write. And Q was not a gospel.

There was a time when appeal was made from the silence of St. Luke to the supposed informativeness of the elder whom Papias cited. "Matthew arranged the revelations (λόγια) in Jewish speech." Had we not here, perhaps, a reference to the Aramaic original of Q? Our Gospel of St. Matthew was certainly not written by the apostle whose name it bears, nor was it written in Aramaic. Perhaps, then, what St. Matthew really did compose was the Aramaic Q, and it was to this that the elder referred. Such was the suggestion. I do not propose to deal with it in this essay, partly because it has now been generally abandoned, and partly because I have

written what I have to say about Papias's elder in the first chapter of my book called *A Study in St. Mark.*

So there is no independent evidence for anything like Q. To postulate Q is to postulate the unevidenced and the unique. But there is worse yet to come. For it may seem tolerable to postulate even the unique and the unevidenced if the circumstances of the time were such as (in our judgment) to call for its production. "We have no evidence that the primitive Christians ever put together a Q or anything like it. Never mind; we can see that a Q is just what they would have wanted to produce towards the year 60." Can we indeed? I am afraid we cannot. But let us look once more at the familiar story. "In the middle of the first century, men recited the saving Passion as a set piece. Its dramatic quality made it easily memorable and the need to commit it to writing was not early felt. But the teaching of Jesus Christ was another matter. It was miscellaneous and not easy to hold in one's head as a whole body of doctrine. Nor was there any occasion for the continuous recitation of the whole teaching, in the way in which we presume the whole Passion to have been recited. And so it was natural that the Christian teacher should be equipped with a written manual of the teaching, and no less natural that the narrative of the Passion should be omitted from it. And such a manual we take Q to have been."

It is a well-sounding story, but unfortunately it does not square with the Q which the gospel facts require. For Q has to be allowed to possess a strongly narrative exordium, not to mention narrative incidents elsewhere interspersed. It is no simple manual of Christ's teaching. It tells us with considerable fullness how John Baptist preached before the public manifestations of Jesus, and how Jesus, appearing in fulfillment of John's prophecies—and, it would seem, undergoing baptism at his hands—endured a threefold temptation in the wilderness, after which he ascended a mountain, and was joined by disciples there. Having delivered beatitudes and precepts of life, he "concluded his words" and presently made his way into Capernaum, where his aid was invoked by a centurion on behalf of his servant.

Not only is the narrative character of such an opening strongly marked; it further betrays a vigorous symbolical interest in the order of the events. It treats the Lord's temptations in the wilderness as the manifest antitypes to the temptations of Israel in the wilderness, three times citing the appropriate verses of Deuteronomy. Then it proceeds to bring Christ, as Israel was brought, to a mountain where divine teaching of special weight is de-

livered. If Q would have to be credited with a narrative of Christ's baptism immediately preceding his temptations (and it seems that it would), then another piece is added to the symbolical pattern. For, says St. Paul, it was after Israel had been "baptized unto Moses in the cloud and in the sea" that the people underwent their several temptations, in trial of their steadfastness in the race they had received (1 Cor. 10:1-11). So Christ's baptism in Jordan and the descent upon him of the Spirit will answer to the passage of the Red Sea and the descent of the Shekinah.

This pattern of symbolism and narrative finds a natural place in St. Matthew's text, where, in our opinion, it indubitably originated. But what sort of place would it find in the imaginary Q? After an exordium so full of dogmatic weight and historical destiny, is it credible that the book should peter out in miscellaneous oracles, and conclude without any account of those events which, to a Christian faith, are supremely significant? A primitive Christian writer might well string together the teaching of Christ and leave it at that. Or again, he might despair of the attempt to describe the ministry historically, and treat it as simply the field of a teaching activity, but provide it nevertheless with a historical exordium and a historical conclusion. What is hard to believe is that he should supply the exordium, while omitting the conclusion, that he should set in train the only story of unique importance, and break it off.

It can fairly be said that it took time for the whole body of Christian teaching to be brought into relation with Christ's redemptive acts. Men who knew themselves to be saved through Christ alone might make homilies on duties and virtues, citing the Old Testament, citing examples from common life, and making no mention of redemption through Christ. St. James's Epistle is not, perhaps, one of the earlier pieces in the New Testament, but it is arguable that it represents the survival of an early attitude. Such an attitude might find expression in the composition of a collection of Christ's sayings, without any narrative of his passion. But for an author to set about the narrative of Christ's life, and never conclude it with his death, is another thing.

Appeal has been made to the example of Old Testament prophecies. The call of an Isaiah, Jeremiah or Ezekiel is carefully narrated, and so are the acts in which the prophet begins to fulfill his calling. But the conclusion of the book is not the conclusion of his life, but (it may be) certain of his weightiest oracles. Isaiah was supposed to have suffered under Manasseh as Christ suffered under Pilate, but the book of Isaiah does not record

his death. Why should not the author of Q follow the scriptural example, and write a "prophetical biography" of Christ beginning with history, proceeding to discourse, and ending with eschatological oracles? Why should he not? Because Christ was no mere prophet. Isaiah was no more than a prophet, an instrument of the Lord's word. It concerns us to know the history of his call, and how it was obeyed, for therein his authentication lies. The story of his end might be edifying, but it would be irrelevant to his message. The divine act in Isaiah is his call, not his death. It is otherwise with Christ.

It has sometimes been supposed that there was a primitive Christianity—perhaps, indeed, the most primitive of all—which attached no positive value to Christ's death and resurrection, nor believed Christ to have attached any such value to these events beforehand. Christians of this school had only one concern about the Passion—to palliate with scriptural excuses a disconcerting interlude between the coming of Messiah and the Kingdom of God. I have yet to be convinced that there were such Christians or that their existence in the first days was a psychological possibility. They were presumably Jews, and no Jew could hold a negative attitude to Messiah's suffering an accursed death. No Jew could apologize for the cross unless he could glory in it. Yet Jews of a kind (I take it) are credited with having composed Q, and passed it current upon the Gentile churches.

It is sometimes thought that a decent agnosticism about the shape and nature of Q is a safe and honorable position. Why not be content to say that our two evangelists drew from a common written source, or sources, may be, but that we are in no position to decide what sort of writing, or writings, they drew from? Very well; but if so, the Q hypothesis must be allowed to lose heavily in a priori probability. The postulation of unevidenced writing of an indeterminable sort is a hazardous proceeding. If we were dealing with a rich and various literature it might be tolerable. If, for example, we return to our imaginary case of the two Victorian novels. Then we might say, "The common source may be another novel, or a magazine story, or a newspaper report of a law-court drama, or one or more of several other things." But what did the primitive Christians write, besides letters and homilies and gospels? Q was neither a letter nor a homily, nor was it a gospel. "Some writing or other, never mind what" will scarcely pass.

So far we have said nothing new. The difficulties of the Q hypothesis have been fully canvassed by its candid admirers, and subsidiary hy-

potheses have been introduced to meet them. A good deal of such hypothesis may be found in Dr. Streeter's *Four Gospels*, all of it developed with undeniable care and skill. But the palm should surely be awarded to his management of "the agreements of Matthew and Luke against Mark."

The difficulty Dr. Streeter has to face is that St. Luke, in a fairly large number of places, makes small alterations in the wording of his Markan original which St. Matthew also makes. Now this is just what one would expect, on the supposition that St. Luke had read St. Matthew, but decided to work direct upon the more ancient narrative of St. Mark for himself. He does his own work of adaptation, but small Matthean echoes keep appearing, because St. Luke is after all acquainted with St. Matthew. Such is the apparent evidence against Dr. Streeter; such is the single hypothesis which springs immediately to our minds and covers all the facts.

What does Dr. Streeter do? He divides the evidence into several groups and finds a distinct hypothesis for each. In some cases he supposes that scribal error has assimilated St. Luke's text to St. Matthew's where no such similarity originally stood. In other cases it will be St. Matthew's text that has been assimilated to St. Luke's. In a third set of cases St. Matthew and St. Luke may really have coincided, but the original of their coincidence stood in St. Mark's text, from which scribal error has subsequently effaced it. In a fourth group of instances stylistic, and in a fifth doctrinal interests may have suggested the same emendation of St. Mark to St. Matthew and St. Luke independently. There remains a sixth group, where the coincidences are coincidences of substance, not amenable to any of the five methods hitherto advanced. In these cases it will be fair to suppose in Q itself a parallel to that Markan paragraph upon which St. Matthew and St. Luke are both principally working. They both happen to incorporate the same Q features in their Markan transcripts—that is all.

Thus the forces of evidence are divided by the advocate, and defeated in detail. His argument finds its strength in the fewness of the instances for which any one hypothesis needs to be invoked; but the opposing counsel will unkindly point out that the dimunition of the instances for each hypothesis is in exact proportion to the multiplication of the hypotheses themselves. One cannot say that Dr. Streeter's plea is incapable of being sustained, but one must concede that it is a plea against apparent evidence, and that, other things being equal, we should accept the evidence and drop the plea. Of course, on Dr. Streeter's view, other things are by no means equal. There are solid grounds for denying that St. Luke can have known

St. Matthew. Here is the heart of the matter. It is these grounds that we have to examine. But before we proceed to do so, let us sum up our preliminary survey.

The Q hypothesis is not, of itself, a probable hypothesis. It is simply the sole alternative to the supposition that St. Luke had read St. Matthew (or vice versa). It needs no refutation except the demonstration that its alternative is possible. It hangs on a single thread; cut that, and it falls by its own weight.

II

Why is it said that St. Luke cannot have read St. Matthew? Five reasons may be considered.

1. There are texts in St. Matthew which St. Luke would not have omitted, had he been acquainted with them.

2. Where St. Matthew and St. Luke give the same saying of Christ, St. Luke's wording sometimes has the more primitive appearance.

3. Our indubitable evidence for St. Luke's manner of using a written source is his use of St. Mark, whom he follows in continuous order over considerable stretches. Whereas if he used St. Matthew we should have to suppose that he treated him in a quite different way, dividing his text into small pieces and making a fresh mosaic of them.

4. The order in which St. Luke places the material common to himself and to St. Matthew is mostly less appropriate and less coherent than the order it has in St. Matthew.

5. In St. Matthew much of the material common to him and to St. Luke alone is placed in the context of Markan paragraphs. St. Luke, even when he reproduces the same Markan paragraphs, does not place the material we are speaking of in them, but somewhere else.

I shall make immediate comments on these five considerations, and afterwards proceed to a more systematic argument.

1. No one has ever attached decisive importance to St. Luke's unexplained neglect of certain Matthean texts, and whatever importance it ever had derived from an antiquated view of St. Luke's attitude to his work. If we regard him as essentially a collector of Christ's sayings, then the omission of some particularly striking blossom from his anthology may seem incompatible with his having known it. But if he was not making a collection but building an edifice, then he may have omitted what he omitted be-

cause it did not seem serviceable to his architecture nor come ready to his hand in the building of it.

2. The suggestion appears to be that we should take separate units of discourse in isolation and pronounce on their degree of nearness to the spoken words of Christ. And where we find greater primitivity of form in this sense we are to impute literary priority. If the more primitive form were always St. Matthew's, then we might suppose that St. Luke had used, and in using modified, him. But since (it is alleged) the more primitive form is sometimes St. Matthew's and sometimes St. Luke's, it is more reasonable to suppose that they used a common source, which now the one modified, and now the other.

There is a deceptive simplicity about the proposed method of argument which evaporates as soon as we try to apply it. There is scarcely an instance in which we can determine priority of form without invoking questionable assumptions. "If I by the Spirit of God cast out devils," writes St. Matthew, and St. Luke, "If I by the finger of God." St. Luke's version contains a forcible allusion which St. Matthew lacks (Ex. 8:19; Mt. 12:28; Lk. 11:20). Is such an allusion more likely to be original, and later effaced by a more commonplace substitute, or adventitious, and due to our evangelist's Bible learning? "Until heaven and earth pass away, not one jot nor one tittle shall pass away from the law, until all be fulfilled." So writes St. Matthew, and St. Luke, "It is easier for heaven and earth to pass away, than for one tittle of the law to fall." Who can say whether the rhetorical fullness of St. Matthew or the pointed brevity of St. Luke is more likely to be original? Is the copiousness of St. Matthew that of the Galilean gospel, or that of (say) the Antiochene pulpit? If we look at the context, we observe that St. Matthew is developing a flowing discourse (5:17-48), whereas St. Luke is giving us one of those short paragraphs packed with gnomic sentences which are an occasional feature of his style (16:15-18, cf. 12:49-53; 16:8-13; 17:1-6). We are left in complete indecision. Either could be adapting the other's text to his own purpose.

Even the apparently plain cases turn out to be not plain at all. We all agree at first sight that Christ is more likely to have blessed the poor, than the poor in spirit. "In spirit" looks like an editorial safeguard against misunderstanding: to be in lack of money is not enough. St. Luke's phrase, then, is the more primitive. But on the other hand St. Luke's eight beatitudes-and-woes with their carefully paired antitheses are not a more primitive affair than St. Matthew's eight beatitudes, but very much the reverse.

And the phrase "in spirit" cannot stand in St. Luke's beatitudes-and-woes without overthrowing the logic of the paragraph. The poor are opposed; to the rich. The poor in spirit would challenge comparison with the rich in flesh, but that does not mean anything. Thus St. Luke may well have read "in spirit" in St. Matthew, and dropped it in obedience to the logic of his own thought.

The case of the Lord's Prayer is equally inconclusive. Here we may hesitate to attribute the greater bareness of the Lukan version either to editorial economy or to the logical requirements of the context. For surely the words of the Lord's Prayer must be sacred to a Christian. But if they are sacred to him, it is because they are hallowed in usage, not because they happen to turn up in a book from over the sea. The presence of the Lord's Prayer in St. Matthew's Gospel may suggest to St. Luke the appropriateness of placing that prayer in his own, but he may nevertheless write it in the form familiar to those for whom he writes. Now it may be true that the prayer current in (let us say) Achaea towards the end of the first century was more primitive than the prayer current in Antioch at the same time and even a decade earlier. But that casts no light whatever on the literary relation between St. Luke and St. Matthew.

We must content ourselves with these few examples of an inquiry which yields no decisive results. To express my own opinion, I agree with the findings of Harnack and of Loisy, rather than with those of Dr. Streeter. For much the most part the Matthean forms *look* the more original. But I would not base any argument on such grounds.

3. The suggestion that St. Luke might be expected to use St. Matthew as he uses St. Mark sounds reasonable on a first hearing, but it will not bear examination. To follow two sources with equal regularity is difficult. Anyone who holds that St. Luke knew St. Matthew is bound to say that he threw over St. Matthew's order (where it diverged) in favor of St. Mark's. He made a Markan, not a Matthean, skeleton for his book. But as to the clothing of the skeleton, was not St. Luke going to do that according to his own wisdom, or where was the peculiar inspiration God had given him to operate? Is it surprising that he should lay his plan on Markan foundations, and quarry St. Matthew for materials to build up his house?

4. It may well be that we shall have to accuse St. Luke of pulling well-arranged Matthean discourses to pieces and rearranging them in an order less coherent or at last less perspicuous. St. Luke would not be either the first planner or the last to prefer a plan of his own to a plan of a predeces-

sor's, and to make a less skillful thing of it. We are not bound to show that what St. Luke did to St. Matthew turned out to be a literary improvement on St. Matthew. All we have to show is that St. Luke's plan was capable of attracting St. Luke. You do not like what I have done to the garden my predecessor left me. You are welcome to your opinion, but I did what I did because I thought I should prefer the new arrangement. And if you want to enjoy whatever special merit my gardening has, you must forget my predecessor's ideas and try to appreciate mine.

5. It is largely true that St. Luke does not give non-Markan material the same Markan setting as St. Matthew gives it. But that is not to say that he transfers it to other Markan settings. He does not incorporate it in Markan episodes at all. What we have to explain is the single fact that St. Luke disencumbers the Markan narrative of St. Matthew's additions to it, and puts them by themselves. The fact is striking enough, and certainly requires explanation. But it is capable of being explained, as we will proceed to show.

III

The Q hypothesis is a hypothesis, that is its weakness. To be rid of it we have no need of a contrary hypothesis, we merely have to make St. Luke's use of St. Matthew intelligible; and to understand what St. Luke made of St. Matthew we need no more than to consider what St. Luke made of his own book. Now St. Luke's book is not a hypothetical entity. Here is a copy of it on my desk. Let me consider what kind of a book it is.

Dr. Streeter says that St. Luke wrote his book in alternate Markan and non-Markan strips. That is, roughly speaking, true, but it casts at the best an indirect light on what St. Luke was trying to do. "Strip-formation" was not his formula for writing a gospel, especially as he was at pains to make the strips invisible. It is only by a tedious comparison of his text with St. Mark's that we establish the division into strips at all. The strip-formation is the by-product of something St. Luke really was trying to do, and it is this that we have to find out. Dr. Streeter's observation is exterior and diagrammatic, like the observation that my journeys to Paddington bunch together in certain months of the year, with wide gaps between the bunches. It is not my purpose to spend a good part of the months of March, May, July and October on the Oxford-Paddington line, while keeping off it in

the intervening months. My doing so is incidental to the execution of more intelligible projects.

St. Luke's non-Markan strips are very far from equal. One of them, in fact, is out of all proportion to the others (9:51-18:14) and it alone corresponds (very nearly) to a single striking and visible feature of this gospel. No one, reading St. Luke for his own sake, would notice the discrepancy between Markan and non-Markan strips in 4-9, but every attentive reader observes that 10:25-18:30 constitutes a prolonged lull in the progress of the action, and that St. Luke uses it to set before us the greater part of the teaching of Christ.

Surely this part of St. Luke's plan is immediately intelligible. If you or I attempted an account of Christ's life, we might do worse than finish the history of the Galilean ministry, and then break off to give an account of our Lord's teaching, illustrated, perhaps, by anecdotes. Then we might resume the narrative style to describe the visitation of Jerusalem, the passion and the resurrection. And that is what St. Luke does, except that he does not formally abandon narrative style in his middle section. It would, of course, be quite alien from the ways of a primitive Christian evangelist to do that. What St. Luke does is to have a sort of narrative standstill. A period in which nothing of decisive historical importance happens provides a setting for the exposition of the teaching.

Such an arrangement is natural in itself, but more particularly it commends itself to a writer who has St. Mark's and St. Matthew's gospels both before him. He is struck by the special excellence of each and would be happy, if he could, to combine them. St. Mark has narrative vigor and rapidity of movement. St. Matthew has fullness of doctrine and exhortation. St. Mark is deficient in discourse, St. Matthew, by constantly exploiting the occasions for discourse which St. Mark supplies, somewhat muffles the action: the discourses run so long that we lose sight of the narrative situation altogether. An obvious way of keeping abundance of doctrine without allowing action to be muffled is to put doctrine in a place by itself. In nine and a half chapters of lively narrative St. Luke gives us the nativity and the childhood, the relations with John Baptist, and the great events of the Galilean ministry: the works of power, the appointment and mission of the Twelve and the Seventy, the feeding of multitudes, the confession of Peter, the Transfiguration. In eight chapters more he gives us the teaching and in the remaining six and a half returns to unencumbered narrative for the events at Jerusalem.

The plan is a happy one, and in its narrative parts it is an undisputed success. It is only in respect of the teaching part that we can find a shadow of justification for Dr. Streeter's *boutade*, that if St. Luke did what he did after reading St. Matthew, he behaved like a madman. St. Luke's teaching section is not so complete a literary success as St. Matthew's great discourses. But then what St. Luke attempted was, on any showing, an awkward task. One great Sermon on the Mount covering eight chapters instead of three was not to be thought of, and three Sermons on the Mount, one after another, would be scarcely more thinkable. It is a paradoxical truth, but a truth nevertheless, that an evangelist who proposed to himself a long continuous teaching was bound to carve it up. The discourses of Christ in St. Luke's middle part are conceived in episodes of moderate length, one following another. And it must be difficult to employ such a method without seeming somewhat monotonous and somewhat miscellaneous. Fresh episodes arise, but nothing much happens; the teaching is the thing, but the teaching is unsystematic because episodic.

But even if St. Luke was going to give the teachings in episodes, not in great discourses, might he not have profited more from the preparatory work St. Matthew had done for him? Could not he have broken the Matthaean discourses as they stood into two or three parts each at the points of logical division, provided each part with a distinct narrative setting, and left it at that? Has he not given himself unnecessary trouble in his handling of Matthean material, and trouble worse than vain, if the Matthean paragraphs are better than St. Luke's mosaics?

To ask such a question is to misunderstand St. Luke's task in 10-18. He is not dividing and rearranging existing material, he is presenting his vision of the gospel according to his inspiration. And inspiration works in such a field as this by novelty of combination. Every episode in these chapters puts together two texts at the least which have not been combined before, and the new combination reveals the point that St. Luke is specially inspired to make. To say that St. Luke's points are less natural or less well made than St. Matthew's is irrelevant. St. Luke was not rewriting, still less abolishing, St. Matthew: St. Matthew remained to teach the Church St. Matthew's lesson. St. Luke was bound to write what was committed to him, and he was not free to cross it out afterwards even if the excellent and candid Theophilus found it inferior to St. Matthew in literary skill.

Every one of the short episodes in Lk. 10:25-18:11 is composite. This fact, so far from being a scandal, so far from making St. Luke's handling of St. Matthew incomprehensible, is our best clue to what St. Luke was doing. It was the standing method of the Jewish preacher to seek his inspiration in the drawing together of old texts into fresh combinations: the striking of the flints brought forth the spiritual fire. The preacher would not merely juxtapose his texts, he would put in his own words what issued from their juxtaposition. St. Luke perhaps adds little of his own except by way of setting and suggestion. He puts the texts down side by side, and leaves them to speak for themselves, like the texts combined in the liturgy for a feast day.

But surely, it will be said, St. Luke was no Jew; it is not permissible to invoke the methods of the Jewish pulpit to explain him. We must answer that the "Jew or Greek?" issue is not so simple as that. No New Testament writer was all that Jewish, and none of them was all that Greek. Let St. Luke have been a Greek; that is to say, an uncircumcised man. That will not have prevented him from standing, year after year, among God-fearing gentiles in the local synagogue, storing his mind with the Septuagint (what primitive Christian knew it better?) and accustoming himself to the methods of the rabbinic expositor. And when he adhered to the Church he would find nothing different. There were the same Greek scriptures, as soon as the congregation had contrived to get a set; and there was the Christian preacher, using the same weapons to vindicate a fuller truth.

What strikes us about St. Luke is not his hellenism but his versatility. His history unfolds in the bosom of Jewish piety and works its way out into the hellenistic agora. The infancy of Christ is written in the spirit of Tobit, the tumult at Ephesus almost in that of Lucian. The appropriate manner comes ready to the matter. The preaching of Jesus Christ is Jewish preaching, and St. Luke becomes the Jewish preacher in delivering it. We must not first assign St. Luke the Grecian label and then argue to the contents of the parcel. We must study to unfold just how Greek and just how Jewish he was.

A few examples of St. Luke's method in 10-18 will have to suffice here.

In the Sermon on the Mount, St. Matthew attaches the Lord's Prayer somewhat loosely to the second paragraph on the unostentatious performance of the three good works, almsgiving, prayer and fasting (6:7-15). A couple of pages later, in what appears the most miscellaneous part of the

Sermon, he has the paragraph "Ask, and it shall be given you, seek and ye shall find" (7:7-12). The Lord's Prayer and the "Ask" paragraph surely demand to be put together. At 11:1-13 St. Luke in fact joins them in a single episode. There is no doubt about its singleness. It is marked off from what precedes by its own narrative introduction, "And it came to pass that, as he was praying in a certain place." It is similarly marked off from what follows by the introduction of the next paragraph "And he was casting out a dumb demon, and it came to pass that. . . ." Let us see how, in the area thus delimited, the new Lukan combination handles the old Matthean material.

St. Matthew's paragraph on the Lord's Prayer ends with a comment: "For if ye forgive men their trespasses, your heavenly Father will forgive you, but if ye forgive not men their trespasses, neither will your Father forgive you your trespasses." The comment fixes our attention on one clause of the prayer particularly, "Forgive us our debts, as we have forgiven our debtors." But if we want to pass on from the prayer to the "Ask and it shall be given you" paragraph, this is not the clause of the prayer to be kept specially in mind, but "Give us this day tomorrow's bread." For that paragraph continues "What man is there of you, of whom his son shall ask bread, and he will give him a stone?" St. Luke smooths the transition by omitting the comment on "Forgive us our debts."

That omission once made, the transition from the one Matthean paragraph to the other could perfectly well be immediate. But St. Luke prefers to embellish the transition with a parable from his own store, preached (as it might seem) on three phrases of the second Matthaean paragraph, "Ask, and it shall be given you"—"Knock, and it shall be opened to you"—"If ye, being evil, know how to give good things. . . . " A man knocks on a friend's door at night to ask for the loan of three loaves. He is not a good friend: he yields to the other's importunity, not to his own good nature; but he yields. After the perfect introduction which such a parable affords, the second Matthean parable follows with redoubled force. And who will hesitate to say that in the episode taken as a whole St. Luke has put an aspect of Christ's true teaching in a fresh and clear light, by means of the combination he has made?

St. Luke gives a twist to the last phrase of the discourse, when he particularizes the "good thing" which above all we should ask of our Heavenly Father. It is "Holy Spirit." By means of this particularization the evangelist eases the transition to his next episode, in which Christ will cast

out an unclean spirit "by the finger of God," and give a warning against leaving the room vacated by the demon empty. It need not be empty, if the Heavenly Father only awaits our prayer to garrison it with Holy Spirit. But the special twist St. Luke gives to the termination of his episode not only opens the way to the next episode, it also echoes the termination of the episode preceding. It is not bread after all (the evangelist is telling us) that we should make most work about, but a diviner gift. And so, to go back a paragraph, Martha had been mistaken in being so preoccupied with the preparation of a meal. There was one thing needful and Mary had chosen the good part in seeking it at Jesus' feet.

To proceed with the next Lukan episode, the Beelzebub sayings (11:14-28). The divination on which St. Luke built that episode was a perception of the relation between two Matthean parables, "Who can enter into the strong man's house and spoil his goods, unless he first bind the strong, and then he will spoil his house"—"When the unclean spirit goes out of a man he wanders through waterless places seeking rest, and finds none. Then he says, I will return to my house whence I came forth," and so on (Mt. 12:29, and 12:43-45). St. Luke perceives that it is actually the same house in the two parables here despoiled of the gear of devilry, there found swept and garnished and reoccupied by the demon. Not content with juxtaposing the two parables, St. Luke equalizes them, writing the first in the style and almost to the scale of the second. "*When the strong man in armor guards his house*, his goods are in peace; but when the stronger than he comes upon him, he prevails over him, and takes his armor wherein he trusted, and divides his spoils. He that is not with me is against me, he that gathereth not with me scattereth. *When the unclean spirit goes out of a man*, he passes through waterless places, seeking rest; and finding none, he saith, I will return to my house whence I came forth. And coming, he finds it swept and garnished. Then he goes and takes seven other spirits more wicked than himself, and entering they dwell there, and the last state of that man is worse than the first."

In Matthew the long discourse which ends in the parable of the house swept and garnished has for its pendant the visit of Christ's mother and brethren. That is a Markan episode, and St. Luke has already reproduced it in a Markan setting (Lk. 8:19-21). He now writes an evident equivalent for it as a pendant to the episode of the disputed exorcism. Not the womb or the paps of Mary are so blessed as they who hear God's word and do it. Would St. Luke have taken the hint from St. Matthew and repeated his

Markan theme here unless it had served him to bring the conclusion of the exorcism episode into line with the conclusions of the two previous episodes? Not Martha, who prepares nourishment for Christ, is so blest as Mary, who listens to his word. It is good to ask daily nourishment from God, but above all it is good to ask for Holy Spirit. Not the womb that bore Christ or the paps that nourished him are so blest as they who hear the word of God and keep it.

In joining the house swept and garnished to the house defended in arms, St. Luke has omitted two intervening paragraphs, the blasphemy of the Holy Ghost and the sign of Jonah. He takes the sign of Jonah for the beginning of his next episode. But he links the new episode to the old in a peculiar way, which clearly betrays dependence on St. Matthew, or (if you will have it so) on a Q which was virtually identical with St. Matthew for a couple of pages.

St. Matthew has two connected episodes, each with its own narrative occasion. (*a*) The accusation ''By Beelzebul'' led Christ to give the Beelzebul parables and to add a warning against blaspheming the Holy Ghost. (*b*) The demand for a sign occasioned Christ to speak about the sign of Jonah and to give the parable of the house swept and garnished. As we have seen, St. Luke forms a single episode from the head of (*a*) and the tail of (*b*), the Beelzebul parables and the parable of the swept and garnished house. Then he begins a fresh episode with the head of (*b*), the sign of Jonah. But instead of giving each episode its own narrative occasion, he puts together both occasions into a joint occasion for the beginning of the first episode. ''*Some of them* said, he casts out devils by Beelzebul the prince of devils, *and others* tempting him, asked of him a sign from heaven.'' By the time we reach the end of the episode the malice of the *some* has been fully answered, but the temptation from the *others* has not been further alluded to. Christ addresses himself to it in the next episode (11:29ff.). ''And as the crowds gathered about him, he proceeded to say: This generation is an evil generation; it seeketh a sign, but there shall no sign be given it save the sign of Jonah.'' The sign of Jonah is only the beginning of the new episode. What makes the episode is the inspired juxtaposition of the sign of Jonah (Mt. 12:38-42) and the lamp of the body (Mt. 6:22-23). The lamp of the body is the eye; the body is enlightened if the eye is good. The ''good eye'' signifies generosity, and St. Matthew is attacking miserliness in the Sermon on the Mount when he records how Jesus had declared that the good eye lets the light into our own person; it

does not merely direct the beam of favor upon our neighbor. It is St. Luke's inspiration to see the connection between the evil eye's exclusion of light, and the evil generation's blindness to a more than Solomon, a more than Jonah in their midst. In divining this connection, St. Luke sees what is particularly characteristic of his own vision of the gospel. What shuts out the light of supernatural revelation is the refusal of a moral demand, and primarily the demand of generosity. Hearing Christ's teaching the Pharisees mocked him, because they were lovers of money (16:14).

The parable of the good and evil eye, if it is to have its full effect, must stand between matter explicitly concerned with failure to see divine signs on the one side and matter explicitly concerned with the denunciation of covetousness on the other. St. Luke makes a further divination no less brilliant than the last, when he passes on from the evil eye to the woes on the Pharisees. The evil eye darkens the whole man within, and Jesus had called the Pharisees blind, because they cleansed the outside of the platter, when they should have taken thought lest what was inside it might be impoverishing the needy. He had proceeded to transfer the outside-inside antithesis from the platter to its owner, a sepulchre whitewashed without, but full of dead men's bones within. So in the episode of the Pharisaic lunch-party (11:37-52) St. Luke goes on to give a carefully arranged anthology of texts from the woes on the Pharisees (Mt. 23). He begins from the topic of miserliness and works round again to the rejection and suppression of divine truth. The Pharisaic brotherhoods are covetous and hypothetical (11:39-44), their scribal teachers are the enemies of God's word (11:46-52). They reject more than Jonah; their fathers killed the prophets, they complete their fathers' work and bring all the blood of God's messengers on their own generation.

We will turn back and pick up a couple of small points. (a) St. Luke simplifies the sign of Jonah by omitting the distracting allegory on the whale's belly and the Easter sepulchre (Mt. 12:40). Our attention is left free to concentrate on the perversity, more than that of Nineveh, which rejects a more than Jonah, and we are ready to be taught the cause of it in the parable of the evil eye. (b) The parable of the eye itself receives a convenient introduction in the form of a sentence culled from the beginning of the Sermon on the Mount: ''No man lighteth a lamp and putteth it in the closet or under the bushel, but on the lampstand, that those who come in may see the light.''

Nothing but a complete exposition of St. Luke's gospel could prove a complete refutation of the Q hypothesis, and, conversely, when such an exposition had been made, no further arguments in refutation of Q would be required. We have merely attempted a specimen of St. Luke's working from St. Matthew in 10-18. So far from his possession of St. Matthew making what he does a mystery, his possession of St. Matthew is the indispensable explanation of what he does. Let us follow St. Luke's eye and memory as they run up and down St. Matthew's pages under the direction of his own inspiration. To enter into the mind of St. Luke at work would be to dissolve the mystery, and, in the nature of the case, nothing else can possibly dissolve it.

IV

We have been discussing the teaching section (Lk. 10:25-18:30). This section, we have said, is roughly equivalent to the widest by far of St. Luke's non-Markan strips. But what are we to say about the contents of the other strips? About those of them that consist of incident we need say nothing at all. That St. Luke should intersperse his Markan narrative with non-Markan incidents or versions of incidents is the most natural thing in the world. So we find him giving the Matthean account of John Baptist's preaching and of the Lord's temptations; having his own views about the migration from Nazareth to Capernaum, which St. Matthew has mentioned in the same place (Lk. 4:16-29; Mt. 4:13) and about the call of Simon Peter (5:1-10); paraphrasing the Matthean story of the centurion (7:2-10); and adding from his own store the widow of Nain (7:11-17) and the sinful woman (7:36-50); adding Zacchaeus to the story of Jericho and adding a parable to Zacchaeus (19:1-27). There is nothing surprising about such embellishments of the Markan story, nor is it at all surprising that they tend to come in groups. St. Luke is following St. Mark as his main narrative guide, and feels the spell. When he has once turned eyes away from the Markan text he is open to think about his other stores of knowledge. When at length he returns to St. Mark the spell reasserts itself and he follows his written guide for some distance before digressing again.

But since we have said that St. Luke's plan assembles the Lord's sustained teaching in a single place (10-18), we may be expected to show why the evangelist gives a Sermon on the Mount (or under it, rather) in 6:20-49, and why Christ's sayings about John Baptist are recorded in 7:18-34.

The placing of the sayings about John presents no difficulty on any showing. They are inseparable from their Matthean introduction, the message from John in prison. By the time St. Luke's long teaching section begins, John has been already reported dead (9:9). An incident from his life in prison could scarcely come later than 7. But constant to his purpose of reserving the bulk of Christ's teaching for the central section, St. Luke detaches all he can from the Lord's discourse upon this occasion according to St. Matthew (Mt. 11:12-15; 11:20-30; cf. Lk. 16:16; 10:12-25).

St. Luke's sermon at the mountain is also vastly shortened from the Matthean form. It has the same beginning and the same end as its original. But in the body of the sermon St. Luke, with a skill from which no one can withhold the praise, extracts a single essence from the wide range of the Matthean sermon, renunciation seen as humility and generosity. Everything which does not belong to the chosen theme is left for a more convenient occasion. But why (it has still to be asked) should St. Luke give us even a short sermon at the mountain, if he has resolved to keep Christ's teaching for the middle part of his book? If the sermon at the mountain is not a formal declaration of the teaching, then what is it?

Why St. Luke did what he did, rather than anything else, cannot be the question. He did what he was moved to do. It is enough if we can see what he did, and what he meant by it. At an earlier point in this essay we imagined St. Luke coolly resolving to put the mass of Christ's teaching where it would least impede the action. And that is what St. Luke did in effect resolve to do, and we may believe that he was not insensitive to the purely literary advantages of the choice he made. But it is not very likely that the choice would present itself to him as a mere point of literary craft. Let us endeavor to give a more plausible story of how a first-century evangelist arrived at such a decision.

We will suppose that St. Luke has St. Matthew before him. Now St. Matthew is a forerunner in the course which St. Luke is about to take: he first has written a new Mark with the Lord's teaching more fully embodied in it. What path has St. Matthew taken? How closely will St. Luke wish to follow it? St. Matthew has not been content simply to exploit such opportunities for the development of discourse as St. Mark happens to afford. He has so arranged his matter as five times to bring the teaching to a head in a set discourse, and in case we should fail to distinguish the five discourses from other passages of dialogue, he has concluded each dis-

course with an identical phrase: "And it came to pass when Jesus had finished these sayings. . . ."

It has been suggested that St. Matthew's five set pieces[1] have something to do with the five books of Moses, as though the evangelist were presenting his gospel as a new Pentateuch. The suggestion, in that form, remains sterile. We are disappointed to discover that the first set piece has nothing to do with Genesis nor the second with Exodus. We have made a mistake somewhere. Our mistake was to miss the first set piece of all, the genealogy, with which the Gospel opens. If that is not a set piece, what is? It cannot, of course, have the set conclusion "When Jesus had finished these sayings," for it does not consist of his sayings but of his ancestors. In any case the set conclusion has not yet been set, and the only reader who looked for it at 1:17 would be the reader who read the book backwards. He who takes it as it comes is put on the right track from the very first moment by a different and far more explicit indication. "Book of Genesis of Jesus Christ" is the title to the genealogy and the first line of the Gospel. The new "Book of Genesis" derives the legal ancestry of Jesus from the hero of the old Genesis, Abraham. Having done with genealogy, St. Matthew resumes: "Now the genesis of Jesus Christ was thus. . . ." So much, then, for Genesis.

The Exodus set-piece is identified neither by heading nor by termination, but by context and character. That the Sermon on the Mount stands out as a formal unity scarcely needs to be said. It is a new law from the mountain, like the law of Sinai, and the setting is strikingly reminiscent. Jesus passes the waters and undergoes forty days' temptation in the wilderness after the pattern of Israel at the Red Sea and in the desert. Then he comes to the mountain of revelation. By using the formula "When Jesus had finished these sayings" by way of conclusion to what is obviously an Exodus discourse in its own right, St. Matthew first gives it significance as the termination to a "set scriptural piece." When it recurs we shall know what to make of it.

---

[1]It is sometimes assumed that the set pieces are each the conclusions of whole "books" into which St. Matthew is divided. There is no obvious reason for that assumption. St. Matthew wrote his book in one continuous script, divided not by chapter headings, but by "stripes" in the subject matter, the "stripes" being these set pieces which carry the set terminations. The additional matter attaching to the "stripe" may be on either side of it, or on both sides.

St. Matthew's Leviticus is the mission-charge which is also, in his Gospel, the institution of the Twelve (10). The example "Book of Genesis" in 1:1 (cf. 1:18) has already shown us that our author is sensitive to the prima facie meaning of a book-title. Now "Leviticus" means "The Book about Levites" and the Apostles are the corresponding ministry of the New Covenant. Similarly, if we are to go by titles, "Numbers" is the muster of the host. St. Matthew's Leviticus (10) sends forth "laborers into the harvest," the Parables which compose his Numbers (13) show how plenteous the human harvest is, how numerous the catch to which fishers of men were previously called (4:19); they deal with the criterion according to which some pass the muster and are admitted to the promised land, while others are rejected.

It remains that the next set piece (Mt. 18) should be a Deuteronomy. The Markan original is already so Deuteronomic at this point that there is little left for St. Matthew to do. The Transfiguration has already brought Moses to witness the divine repetition of his Deuteronomic testimony about his great Successor, "Hear ye him" (Deut. 18:13; Mk. 9:9; Mt. 17:5). In the discourse at Capernaum St. Mark, and St. Matthew following him, proceed to take up the next preceding paragraph of Deuteronomy, the Law of the Kingdom (Deut. 17:14-20; Mk. 9:32-37; Mt. 17:25-18:35). The princes in God's kingdom are not to exert privileges or make exactions like Gentile kings, but to humble themselves among their brethren. St. Matthew goes further than St. Mark by going one paragraph further back in Deuteronomy (Deut. 17:2-13; Mt. 18:15-20). The Israelite who has a grievance against his neighbor must be prepared first to call two or three witnesses, then to have recourse to a higher court: the decree of ultimate authority must be enforced. The sequel to the Matthean set discourse rejoins St. Mark, and remains in step with Deuteronomy. It is the question of divorce (Deut. 24:1-4; Mk. 10:1-12; Mt. 19:1-12). The next paragraph, the embracing and blessing of the children, simply repeats the Deuteronomic theme of princely humility, while the paragraph after that carries us to the very heart of Deuteronomy (Deut. 5-6; Mk. 10:17-31; Mt. 19:16-30). For the episode of the rich man's question associates the keeping of the decalogue with the Oneness of God, the attainment of "life," and "inheritance." The exhortation to make distribution and to shun the snare of riches is no less Deuteronomic.

We have had five Matthean "Books of Moses." There remains one "book" (24-25), the "Book of Jesus" (Joshua) without a doubt. The new

Jesus comes through Jericho, indeed, but it is Jerusalem he condemns to utter overthrow, so that not one stone shall remain upon another. The fall of the city is the sign and the condition of the gathering of Israel into the true land of promise under the leadership of Jesus (23:27-24:2; 24:15-31).

Such in outline is the structure of St. Matthew's hexateuch, and if we are allowed to reason a priori at all, we must suppose it to have been as evident to St. Luke as it is to us, for he was a next-door neighbor and we are visitors from a far country. Supposing then that St. Luke understood it, what did he do with it? Did he adopt it, or reject it? He did neither. He allowed the general pattern to stand, but he redistributed the weight of the teaching, placing as much of it as he could in the Deuteronomic position. Shall we allow the question "Why?" to be asked once more? We have allowed it already in terms of literary propriety and of respect for Markan narrative. Must we answer it over again in terms of scriptural typology? Among all the books of Moses why should Deuteronomy appeal to St. Luke as specially typical of Christ's doctrine? We are not bound to find certain answers to such a question, probable answers will do. If there are still more probable answers than those we find, why, so much the better.

First, then, the primitive Christian saw the Law reasserted and yet transformed in the Gospel, and it would easily strike him that a model for such a relationship was to be found within the Law itself. In his Deuteronomy Moses reasserted his Protonomy, that is, the Law from Exodus to Numbers, and in reasserting it illuminated it. Had not St. John this example in mind when he meditated on the commandment which in being new is also old (1 Jn. 2:7-8)? The very occasion upon which Moses gave his Deuteronomy enforces the same point to the Christian mind. For it was in his last hours and in connection with his giving place to the *Jesus* who could alone fulfill his words, and who was the first to be designated by that promise on which we have already dwelt: "The Lord will raise up unto you a prophet from among your brethren like unto me: to him hearken."

Such considerations, being formal and typological, make less appeal to us, perhaps, than they did to the first-century mind. But there are more material considerations with which our sympathy will be as great as St. Luke's own. Deuteronomy is the book which adds the spirit to the observance, it is the law of love towards God and man, and especially of humility, generosity, and compassion. It is well indeed if these virtues are as dear to us as they were to St. Luke.

St. Luke might desire, therefore, on some grounds as these to place the weight of Christ's teaching in what his predecessors had already marked out as the Deuteronomic position. But logic forbade him to gather the whole of it there. The Deuteronomy will not stand out as Deuteronomy unless there is some resemblance of a Protonomy; without a first law the second law will be second to nothing. The recapitulation on the plains of Moab presupposes a first statement at the foot of Sinai. And so St. Luke gives us a short sermon beneath the Mountain in 6 as well as the long discourses of 10-18.

The Deuteronomic passage in which Moses most clearly draws a new command out of the old is to be found in Deut. 5-6. Here the Lawgiver first recapitulates the decalogue from Exodus and then adds the *Shema* as the heart of the matter. The Lord is One Lord, and is to be loved with entire devotion. Now we have already seen that the passage is commented upon by the paragraph of the Rich Man, in which St. Matthew's Deuteronomic section culminates. St.Luke allows his own Deuteronomy to run out into the same conclusion (18:18-30). But he is not content to conclude with the *Shema*, he must begin from it too (10:25-28). His Deuteronomic exordium anticipates the explicit discussion of the *Shema* between Jesus and the Pharisaic scribe in the temple court, according to Mt. 22:35-40. (That the Matthean version rather than the Markan is St. Luke's model is the natural conclusion to draw from a comparison of the texts. Streeter has to admit a non-Markan source in parallel with the Markan text here.)

The Scribe's Question and the Rich Man's Question are the twin pillars which mark out the extent of St. Luke's Deuteronomy, and the fact is made more evident by the evangelist's assimilation of the one to the other. A doctor of law is the questioner in 10, a ruler of synagogue in 18. Both ask the same question, the Deuteronomic question, "What must I do to inherit eternal life?" Both are credited with a knowledge of the formal answer which the old law supplies. It is the new Deuteronomy, the life-giving exposition of the old precept, that is reserved for Christ.

It seems, then, that St. Luke consciously regarded what he wrote in 10:25-18:30 as a Christian Deuteronomy. How far can we say that the contents of this Deuteronomy are Deuteronomic in order or in detail? They range over the field of human duty as Deuteronomy does, and in a Deuteronomic spirit. But do they follow the topics of the fifth Mosaic book with any particularity? Here is a complicated inquiry, and it is fortunate

for us that Mr. Evans has undertaken it.[2] We need only refer the reader to
what he has written.

So much for St. Luke's Deuteronomy. but what, if anything, has he
made of St. Matthew's Genesis, Exodus, Leviticus, Numbers and Joshua?
He has denuded them of prolonged discourse: but has he entirely effaced
them? Not entirely, but he has rubbed them faint.

As to the Genesis, St. Luke has his own infancy narratives, and their
patriarchal, especially their Abrahamic, flavor is unmistakable. He has his
own genealogy too, though he places it differently: after the end of his
Genesis, not at the beginning. At first sight we are struck by the differences between the two evangelists in their opening chapters; their genealogies are not the same genealogy nor their narratives in any particular the
same narrative. On second thoughts we observe the points of identity. The
Matthean genealogy has an artificial structure and an openly symbolical
value: the Lukan genealogy develops the symbolical architecture of the
Matthean to a further pitch of elaboration, as the reader may see by referring to the note appended to this essay. The Matthean narratives are made
to revolve round two principal points: Jesus, by domicile a Nazarene, was
a Bethlehemite by birth; Jesus, by family, a descendant of David, was Son
of God by supernatural generation. St. Luke's narratives present a story
which a man who had it to tell might surely prefer to the Matthean form,
even if he knew it. But it is to be remarked that he so tells it as to cover the
two principal Matthean points. What shall we say? We used to say: "His
genealogy is a different genealogy, his infancy narratives are different narratives; he had not read St. Matthew." But now we shall say: "St. Matthew's early chapters define a task, which St. Luke takes up and deals with
from his own resources and with his own improvements. It is most unlikely that he had not read St. Matthew's." So much, then, for St. Luke's
Genesis.

St. Luke's Exodus chapters preserve the most striking Matthean feature, the temptations which Christ, after the example of ancient Israel, endured in the wilderness. They add two distinctively Lukan
developments—the rejection at Nazareth, embodying the principal discourse of St. Luke's Exodus; and St. Peter's confrontation with the supernatural in the miraculous fishing. The Scriptural typology of these two

---

[2]The reference is to C. F. Evans's essay "The Central Section of St. Luke's Gospel,"
Studies in the Gospels: Essays in Memory of R. H. Lightfoot (1955) 37-53.

episodes can be studied in St. Stephen's Speech (Acts 7:23-35). They are antitypical to Moses' rejection by his brethren on his first appearance, and to the vision at the Bush (Ex. 2:11-4:17).

After Exodus, Leviticus. St. Matthew's Leviticus is the institution, mission and mission-charge of the Twelve (10) with which the embassy from John Baptist is associated (11). St. Luke holds over the mission and mission-charge for the enrichment of his own "Numbers," but he still is able to present the institution of the Twelve and the embassy from John in close succession (6:12ff.; 7:18ff.). St. Matthew's Sermon on the Mount, that is, Exodus, becomes St. Luke's Sermon after the Mount, that is, his Leviticus: it loses its character of being a comment on the Ten Commandments and becomes the ordination sermon of the new Levites ("Lifting up his eyes upon his disciples he began to say, Blessed are ye poor," and so on).

As the Leviticus begins with the institution of the Twelve, so the Numbers begins with their mission (9:1-10). The "Numbers" typology of the section stands out clearly. When our evangelist is simply following a source (say, St. Mark) it is unsafe to attribute to him a conscious interest in every symbolical feature already embedded in the text he reproduces. But where he introduces his own additions and modifications, as he does here, it is reasonable to make him responsible for their more evident symbolical bearing. We observe the following facts. St. Luke so abbreviates St. Mark as to bring a certain sequence of events into close proximity: the commission of the Twelve (9:1-9), Jesus' reception of them on their return from mission (9:10ff.), the disclosure of the Divine Son to the Twelve and the leaders of the Twelve (9:18-45). After a few short incidents, Markan and non-Markan (9:46-62), St. Luke supplies a parallel cycle: the commission of the Seventy (10:1-16), Jesus' reception of them on their return from mission (10:17-20), and the disclosure of the Divine Son to his disciples (10:21-24). Now that the Divine Son has been twice testified to as the sole revealer (9:35; 10:21-24) his law, his new Deuteronomy, most fitly follows (10:25ff.).

St. Luke is himself responsible for placing the commission of the Seventy in striking and elaborate parallel with the commission of the Twelve. But to do so is undisguisedly to invoke the example of Moses, and of Moses in Numbers. For in Numbers the commission of the Twelve (1-2, cf. 7) is succeeded by that of the Seventy (11), not immediately, but only after the solemn setting forth of Moses and Israel for the promised land

(10). St. Luke, too, places Christ's solemn setting forth between the cycles of the Twelve and of the Seventy (9:51-62). "It came to pass, as the days of his Assumption began to be fulfilled, he set his face to go to Jerusalem." "Assumption" is a word commonly used of the ends of Moses and Elijah. When we hear it, we still have those two saints' voices ringing in our ears. We have just heard them conversing with Christ on the mount of Transfiguration about the exodus he was to complete at Jerusalem (9:31).

In thus developing the theme of Numbers St. Luke lays the appropriate foundation upon which to raise his great Deuteronomic superstructure. For Deuteronomy itself opens with a recapitulation of precisely those incidents in Numbers to which St. Luke has supplied the antitypes (Deut. 1:6-8, the setting forth from Sinai; 1:9-18, appointment of ministers; 1:19ff., the sending of men to prepare the way whither Israel was to come). The Deuteronomic setting of Lk. 10:25ff., could, in fact, scarcely be more strongly marked than it is. To ask for more would be blank ingratitude. It is hardly necessary to say anything about St. Luke's Joshua. For in any case the triumphant passion and resurrection compose the "Book of Jesus" par excellence. If the birth is a Genesis and the ministry a Lawgiving, then the death and resurrection are a Conquest. But we may anyhow observe that St. Luke shows himself fully alive to the Jerusalem-Jericho paradox. It is Jerusalem, not Jericho, that the new Jesus is called upon to overthrow by the trumpet of his prophecy. Jericho, once the city of the repentant harlot (Heb. 11:31), is now the city of the repentant publican, and Jerusalem that of the proud Pharisee. That is the impression which we form, if we read the story of Zacchaeus upon its Lukan background (19:1-27 and 19:41-48; cf. 18:9-30 and 10:30).

V

It is alleged by those who deny the credibility of St. Luke's having used St. Matthew, that St. Luke never places Matthean material (in their language, Q material) in the Markan place which St. Matthew assigns it; and that the fact is very surprising, if St. Luke knew St. Matthew's book. The allegation is not wholly true, to begin with; and what truth it has is no cause for surprise. Have we sufficiently considered the bewildering way in which Mk. 1-6 is used in Mt. 3-14? To find the "Markan place" of any one paragraph in these chapters may be a teasing puzzle. If St. Luke began with the best will in the world to use Matthew as a direct comment on

Mark, is it surprising that he gave it up in the maze of Mt. 3-14, simply followed Mark through, and dealt with the Matthean additions afterwards on a system of his own?

What, in fact, had St. Matthew done in these chapters? Four times he skipped selectively over the same Markan ground, each time making a fresh selection until the material was exhausted. In 3-7 he covered Mk. 1:1-3:13, recounting the teaching of John, the baptism and temptations of Jesus, Jesus' coming into Galilee and fixing upon Capernaum, his calling of the four; how a mission throughout Galilee (Mk. 1:39ff.) led to the collection of a vast crowd from all the quarters of Palestine, which are named (Mk. 3:8) and how, in face of the crowds, Jesus ascended the mountain and his chosen disciples came up to him. So far St. Luke follows St. Matthew and refers all St. Matthew's special material to the corresponding Markan places, *including the Sermon at the Mountain*. But when, in 8, St. Matthew jumps back to the scene in St. Peter's house, according to Mk. 1, St. Luke deserts him, and is he to be blamed? St. Matthew, unaccompanied by St. Luke flies over Mk. 1:29-5:21 in 8, leaps back to Mk. 2:1 and flies forward as far as Mk. 6:15 in 9-11, returns to Mk. 2:23 and reaches as far as 6 again in 12-14, after which he goes on steadily forward. But we are not concerned to unravel St. Matthew's doings ourselves; we are merely excusing St. Luke for not making the attempt.

We will clear up an allied difficulty, and so make an end. It is common form to say: If St. Luke drew the so-called Q material from St. Matthew, and yet did not produce it in the Markan settings St. Matthew had given it, we must suppose that he went carefully through his text of Matthew blocking out the Markan parts, before he could see what was available for his own Q passages. And it is unlikely that St. Luke did this.

It is more than unlikely, but then there is no need to suppose it. Up to the point at which St. Luke makes his great desertion of St. Mark (9:50 = Mk. 9:40) the issue does not arise at all. The Matthean material in Lk. 3-6 has its Markan place; in 7:1-9:50 there are two Matthean episodes, the centurion's message (7:2-10) and the Baptist's message (7:18-34). Each is already a distinct and self-contained episode in St. Matthew, wholly unconfused with its Markan context, and St. Luke could be in no hesitation at all where to draw the boundaries round either. He shortens both, and makes internal rearrangement in the second, but that has no bearing on the point.

When, on the other hand, St. Luke laid St. Mark aside at 9:40 and took up St. Matthew for the composition of his long teaching section, he had already made such use as he wished to make of the Markan elements in Mt. 3-18. And so, when he set about quarrying these chapters, all he needed to do was to bear in mind what elements in them he had used already. St. Matthew's Markan material was marked off for him by the mere fact that he had just been using it in its pristine Markan form. Equally, of course, he had already used some of the Matthean material, for example in the Sermon and in the reply to John's disciples. He had no difficulty in letting alone what he had used, and picking up what he had neglected. He has no strict rule against Markan material in his teaching section, but only against used material. He is perfectly ready to transcribe unused Markan sentences embedded in Matthean discourses, for example, in the Beelzebul controversy (Lk. 11:15-22 and 12:10) or in the sermon on the little ones (17:2).

There is no difficulty, then, about the selection of non-Markan material from Mt. 3-18 for incorporation in Lk. 10-18. If there is a difficulty, it will concern the incorporation in these Lukan chapters of material from the Matthean chapters which St. Luke has not yet skimmed of their Markan elements, that is to say, from Mt. 19-25. For here we can no longer invoke the explanation we have given for the ready discrimination of Markan from non-Markan in St. Luke's use of Mt. 3-18.

The difficulty melts away on examination, because the anticipations of Mt. 19-25 which St. Luke does make in 10-18 are, with one exception, massively simple and not such as to lay up trouble for the future. There are six in all, and five of them are so whole and single, that they come away clean from their settings. Here is the list.

(a) The lawyer's question (Mt. 22:35-40; Lk. 10:25-28).
(b) Woes on scribes and Pharisees (Mt. 23:1-36; Lk. 11:39-52).
(c) Servants watching (Mt. 24:42-25:12; Lk. 12:35-46).
(d) Jerusalem that slays the prophets (Mt. 23:37-39; Lk. 13:34-35).
(e) Invited guests (Mt. 22:1-4; Lk. 14:16-24).

The sixth, and exceptional, case is the apocalyptic cento in Lk. 17:22-37, put together from non-Markan details of the augmented Markan apocalypse in Mt. 24:23-41. Here, and here only, St. Luke must be credited with measuring the Markan text against St. Matthew's augmented verson of it, before he reaches the place. But there is no great difficulty in believ-

ing that St. Luke already knew that he meant to give the substance of the Markan apocalypse in its Markan place. Its Markan place is also, of course, its Matthean place: and if we are right in supposing that St. Luke was ranging forward through St. Matthew's text when he composed Lk. 17, we may reasonably suppose also that he saw the Markan apocalypse through its Matthean wrappings and realized that he would need it later in its own position. To suppose this is further to suppose that St. Luke had the Markan apocalypse virtually by heart. But there is no text he is more likely to have had by heart than that.

So much for the six anticipations in Lk. 10-18. They are neatly made, but they do not in fact altogether avoid trenching on Markan material. When in due course St. Luke arrives at Mk. 12, he discovers that he has already used up the good scribe's question in the lawyer's question (Lk. 10:25-28), so he allows the merest vestige of it to appear in its own place (20:39-40). Mk. 13:21-23 is found to have been anticipated in the apocalyptic cento (Lk. 17:22-23) and so St. Luke omits it at 21:24-25. Mk. 13:33-37 has been anticipated in the parables of the watching servants (Lk. 12:35-46). St. Luke substitutes a generalizing paraphrase for it in 21:34-36).

Besides these anticipations in the Lukan Deuteronomy, there is one which falls outside it. In the story of Christ at Jericho, St. Luke anticipates a piece of the Matthean apocalyptic discourse, the parable of money on trust (Mt. 25:14-30; Lk. 19:11-27). This anticipation creates no kind of difficulty. The parable is a single unit and manifestly non-Markan; it has not the least tendency to bring Markan masonry away with it when it is pulled out of its Matthean setting.

Thus, when we come to look at the alleged mystery about St. Luke's wrenching of St. Matthew's non-Markan material away from its Markan contexts, it turns out to be no mystery at all. Everything that happens happens much as we might expect.

It is time that we concluded the whole discussion. Let us hope we have sufficiently stated the principles required for dispensing with the Q hypothesis, and done something besides to illustrate the application of those principles to the task. We have certainly not given a complete demonstration, for to do that would be nothing less than to write a complete exposition of St. Luke, beginning from the beginning and unfolding the movement of his thought as it comes. But, on the rash assumption that the fulfillment of such a labor would confirm our guesses, let us indulge ourselves a little here, and prophesy.

The literary history of the Gospels will turn out to be a simpler matter than we had supposed. St. Matthew will be seen to be an amplified version of St. Mark, based on a decade of habitual preaching, and incorporating oral material, but presupposing no other literary source beside St. Mark himself. St. Luke, in turn, will be found to presuppose St. Matthew and St. Mark, and St. John to presuppose the three others. The whole literary history of the canonical Gospel tradition will be found to be contained in the fourfold canon itself, except in so far as it lies in the Old Testament, the Pseudepigrapha, and the other New Testament writings.

The surrender of the Q hypothesis will not only clarify the exposition of St. Luke, it will free the interpretation of St. Matthew from the contradiction into which it has fallen. For on the one hand the exposition of St. Matthew sees that Gospel as a living growth, and on the other as an artificial mosaic, and the two pictures cannot be reconciled. If we compare St. Matthew with St. Mark alone, everything can be seen to happen as though St. Matthew, standing in the stream of a living oral tradition, were freely reshaping and enlarging his predecessor under those influences, practical, doctrinal and liturgical, which Dr. Kilpatrick has so admirably set before us in his book.[3] But then the supposed necessity of the Q hypothesis comes in to confuse us—these apparently free remodelings of St. Mark cannot after all be what they seem, nor are they the work of St. Matthew in his reflection on St. Mark, for they stood in Q before St. Matthew wrote. And that is not the end of the trouble, for if the so-called Q passages were in a written source, so, we must suppose, were other Matthean paragraphs which have the same firmness of outline as the Q passages and are handled by the evangelist in the same way. They were not in Q, or St. Luke would have shown a knowledge of them, which he does not do. Never mind, we can pick another letter from the alphabet: if these are not Q passages let them be M passages, or what you will. Once rid of Q, we are rid of a progeny of nameless chimaeras, and free to let St. Matthew write as he is moved.

NOTE:
THE GENEALOGIES OF CHRIST

A

The Matthean genealogy is commented on by its author. Three fourteens of generations correspond to three periods, before the kingdom, the

---

[3] G. D. Kilpatrick, *The Origins of the Gospel According to St. Matthew* (1946).

kingdom, since the kingdom. The suggestion is, "And now the kingdom again" (2:2; 3:2; 4:17). That *three* spans should bring us to the kingdom of Christ, seems inevitable to any one acquainted with the Gospel tradition, "On the third day" or "After three days" (12:40; 16:21; 17:23; 27:63). The three spans are of *fourteen* each, and a fourteen strikes the Jewish mind as a fortnight, a double seven. Three fortnights—otherwise put, six weeks, a working-week of weeks—and then, of course, the Sabbatical week, the Messianic kingdom, must follow. The total number of generations contained in the six weeks has the same significance—*forty*: "After forty years of wandering and temptation, the Promised Land" (4:2).

The number forty is not obtained without art—7 × 6 = 42, but St. Matthew makes it forty by making David and Jeconias each do double duty: they end one fortnight and begin another. Such a reckoning may suggest a similar function for the name of Jesus—he fulfills the working days and initiates the sabbath.

By noting the irregular marriages in the genealogy (Thamar, Rahab, Ruth, Bathsheba) St. Matthew shows that God can "of the stones raise up children to Abraham" (3:9) and in particular graft his Son into Abraham's stock by a virginal conception.

This genealogy has two formal faults:

(1) The artificial doubling of two names, as indicated.
(2) The omission of several generations from the biblical list between David and Jeconias.

Both faults are eliminated in St. Luke's rewriting.

B

The Lukan genealogy was conceivably written out by its author in groups of seven names each, a division disregarded by his copyists. However that may be, the clue for counting in sevens remains embedded in the the beginning of the list. Jesus is both the son of a Joseph, and the seventh descendant of another Joseph; and this remoter Joseph is himself both the son of a Mattathias and the seventh descendant of another Mattathias. For our present purpose it suffices to write down the beginnings and the ends of St. Luke's sets of sevens, leaving the middles blank.

1. Jesus, Joseph . . . . Jannai

2. Joseph, Mattathias .... Meath
3. Mattathias .... Zerubbabel
4. *Shealtiel* .... *Er*
5. Jesus .... Judah
6. Joseph .... Nathan
7. David .... Admin
8. *Arni* .... *Abraham*
9. Terah .... Shelah
10. Cainan .... Enoch
11. Jared .... God.

The genealogy is written backwards. The name of Joseph in (2) suggests the family background of Jesus, Mattathias in (3), being the name of the father of the Maccabees, suggests the second Jewish kingdom, Shealtiel father of Zerubbabel in (4) brings us to the exile. The rhythm is then repeated: it runs through an earlier Jesus and an earlier Joseph to David, the father of the former kingdom, as Mattathias was of the later. And so we arrive with (8) at the previous exile—Arni lived under Egyptian bondage, as did Shealtiel under Babylonish captivity.

By italicizing the exilic lines (4) and (8) as we have done, we reveal at a glance the meaning of the list. St. Matthew had a threefold division in his genealogy, of which Babylonish captivity marked the second period. St. Luke's system is likewise divided threefold, but now exile marks both the points of division. After a first captivity the Davidic kingdom arises, and in declining towards a second brings forth the name of Jesus, though not yet of *the* Jesus. After the second captivity the Maccabean state, declining towards a third captivity (the fall of Jerusalem, 21:24) brings forth Jesus Christ. But this coming of Jesus Christ closes no more than the *eleventh* "week" of generations, and the eleven "weeks" of St. Luke, like the six "weeks" of St. Matthew, are an incomplete number (Acts 1:13-26). As the Matthaean six point forward to a seventh, so the Lukan eleven point forward to a twelfth, the week of the fall of Jerusalem in which St. Luke lives, a week destined to last until the times of the Gentiles are fulfilled (Lk. 21:24). And that is the end (21:9, 27). The first advent occupies the seventy-seventh (11 × 7th) place, the eighty-fourth (12 × 7th) "year" is that perfect period at which the Son of Man, returning, finds faith in the "poor widow" who awaits him with constant prayer (2:36-38; cf. 18:1-8).

How does St. Luke obtain the liberty to construct so balanced a scheme as his genealogy? By deserting scriptural tradition from David to Jesus, he

has the greater part of the list under his absolute control. He derives Jesus not from Solomon, but from his brother Nathan, whose descendants are nowhere listed in scripture.

A diagram of historical providence composed by the grouping of generations in ''weeks'' or sevens could be found by our Evangelists already standing in 1 Enoch 93.

THE WORDS OF JESUS
AND THE FUTURE
OF THE "Q" HYPOTHESIS

T. R. Rosché*

Rosché sets forth certain steps of procedure under which a reexamination of the evidence for Q might be carried forth most profitably:

1. Deliberations about the order of Synoptic composition must be separated from the question of "Q," since the "Q" controversy is meaningful only for those who have accepted the priority of Mark.

2. Matthew and Luke usually followed the context and order of sayings taken from the known source Mark; conversely they made extensive changes both of meaning and order in narrative material taken from the same source.

3. A study of the Triple Tradition indicates that Matthew and Luke treated the Markan sayings more carefully and faithfully than narrative material taken from Mark.

4. Because the "Q" material is primarily sayings material, it is necessary to relate conclusions concerning the use of Markan sayings in the Triple Tradition to the sayings found in the Double Tradition (that is, "Q" material).

5. When the method used to correlate the non-Markan common results in the Triple Tradition (Step 3) is applied to the 217 verses of "Q," one finds that an average of 54 percent of the words in the shorter non-Markan

*T. R. Rosché, "The Words of Jesus and the Future of the 'Q' Hypothesis," *Journal of Biblical Literature* 79 (1960): 210-20.

versions have parallels in the other version. But 68 percent of the most widely agreed upon verses of "Q" show less than the average (that is, 54 percent) of verbal correspondence.

6. Rosché believes that the evidence gathered leads most naturally to the conclusion that there was no common document "Q." It is, in his view, improbable a priori that Matthew and Luke would have followed one standard of evaluation for the sayings of Jesus found in the Triple Tradition and yet another for the sayings of the same Jesus found in the Double Tradition.

In Rosché's view, the future demands adherents of the "Q" document to appraise realistically the ways by which Matthew and Luke used Markan sayings and those who reject the document "Q" to define more carefully what is common in Matthew and Luke and how this common element is to be explained.

Adolf von Harnack once described source analysis of the Synoptic gospels as "scavenger's labors in which one is choked with dust." Although such a remark suggests little reward, one can take courage in the fact that the dust has never been allowed to settle. I certainly do not expect to settle it, but I hope that the future course of source analysis of the Synoptics will be more clearly seen after this particular scavenger's labors.

Various lines of argument have been advanced recently which imply that the "Q" hypothesis has outlived its usefulness. The most insistent voices come from two camps, those of the "Oxford school" under Austin Farrer, and those of the "Matthean school" under Dom B. C. Butler of Downside.[1] The view of the former school is that both Matthew and Luke used Mark; in the latter case both Mark and Luke used Matthew. In both views a written document "Q" is no longer needed, for Luke used Matthew in addition to Mark.

There is a real danger that current reexaminations of the "Q" hypothesis (or any hypothesis of source criticism) may be the result of attempts to organize the gospel evidence around a priori beliefs and assumptions as to what necessarily that evidence will show. What is required, therefore,

---

[1]Examples of the "Oxford school" include A. M. Farrer, "On Dispensing with Q," in D. E. Nineham, ed., *Studies in the Gospels* (1955); see also Farrer, *A Study in Saint Mark* (1952). For a secondary account, see H. W. Huston, "The 'Q Parties' at Oxford," in *JBR*, 25 (1957): 123-28. From the "Matthean school" see B. C. Butler, *The Originality of St. Matthew* (1951); L. Cerfaux, "Le problème synoptique," in *NRT* 76 (1954); J. Levie, "L'Évangile araméen de S. Matthieu est-il source d l'évangile de S. Marc?" in *NRT* 74 (1952); and J. Schmid and A. Vögtle, eds. *Synoptische Studien.*

is a minute examination of all the evidence in the gospels themselves to see whether in fact "Q" can stand. This paper sets forth certain steps of procedure under which a reexamination of the evidence might be carried forth most profitably.

Step One

"Q" by definition accepts the priority of Mark for Matthew and Luke. The first step, therefore, separates deliberations about a different order of synoptic composition from the question of "Q." The disposition of the approximately 200 verses usually assigned to "Q" cannot be allowed to govern considerations of gospel priority which involve 1,100 verses in Matthew and 1,200 verses in Luke (to say nothing of the 660 verses in Mark which contain little, if any, of "Q"). The case for Markan priority has been made often enough and is based upon the whole of each gospel.[2] If a new priority is to be advanced, it must be decided first in a way which will include *all* the Synoptic material, not just the non-Markan common pericopes, although these passages must be accounted for in any such analysis.

Further, the least committal of all definitions of "Q" is the description of the location of its material, namely, that it is non-Markan common material found in Matthew and Luke. Such a definition distinguishes between the pericopes which make up "Q" and/or the document which may or may not be the source of these pericopes (called "S" by B. W. Bacon). For those who do not hold to the priority of Mark, the removal of Markan material from Matthew and Luke (uncovering the non-Markan common pericopes, or the "Q" of this definition) reveals absolutely nothing which suggests a common non-Markan document.

Therefore, by itself the "Q" controversy is meaningful only for those who have first accepted the priority of Mark. The definition of the problem requires that Matthew be regarded as a fresh edition of Mark and that Luke be recognized as using about one-half of Mark. These requirements are ac-

---

[2]Classic treatments of Markan priority include H. J. Holtzmann, *Die synoptischen Evangelien* (1863) and *Die Synoptiker* (1899); P. Wernle, *Die synoptische Frage* (1899); W. G. Sanday, ed., *Studies in the Synoptic Problem* (1911); E. DeW. Burton, *Some Principles of Literary Criticism and their Application to the Synoptic Problem* (1904); B. H. Streeter, The Four Gospels (1924).

cepted by the Farrer group, but the Butlerites are lost for the rest of this article.

Step Two

The most effective way by which one can determine the literary methods by which Matthew and Luke appropriated the lost source "Q" (granting its existence for the moment) is to examine how each used material he took from Mark. One ought to move from the known source Mark to the supposed source "Q." It is reasonable to assume that the concerns which are evident in the ways by which Matthew and Luke used Mark (whatever these ways may be) were also in operation when they used other deduced and nonextant sources, provided of course that these other sources contain the same form or type of material. When Markan priority is granted, it is necessary to demonstrate the nature and extent of the changes made by Matthew and Luke in this triple tradition. The results of an investigation of Matthew's and Luke's use of Mark are summarized under the following *Results A, B, C*, and *D*.

RESULT A:

Luke reproduced Mark's *sayings* of Jesus more faithfully than that source's *narrative* material. He distinguished between his license as a narrator and his responsibility as a transmitter of Christian *halakhah* found in the sayings of Jesus. This is seen clearly in Markan pericopes used by Luke within which are found both narratives and sayings of Jesus.[3] These passages reveal: (1) Mark's introductory narrative sentences were handled with the greatest amount of freedom; an average of only 25 percent of Luke's words have a parallel in Mark; (2) In the body of the narrative about 45 percent of Luke's words correspond with the Markan account; (3) The proportion drops to 35 percent in Luke's concluding words of narrative; (4) However, 78 percent of the Lukan words of Jesus are paralleled in Markan sayings. Clearly, Luke followed Mark's words of Jesus more closely than narrative words taken from the same source.

The dichotomy in Luke's treatment between Markan sayings and narratives is substantiated by the distribution of "characteristically Lukan words and phrases" in Luke. Since the works of H. J. Holtzmann,

---

[3]Lk. 4:31-37; 5:12-16, 17-26, 27-32; 6:1-5, 6-11; 8:19-21, 22-25, 26-39, 40-56; 9:1-6, 10-17, 18-22, 37-43a, 43b-44; 46-48, 49-50; 18:15-17, 18-30, 31-34, 35-43.

Wernle, Cadbury, Hawkins, and others,[4] it has been reasonable to assume that these words are a valid indication of Luke's editorial presence (or absence). However, the assumption that these words are scattered uniformly among Luke's narratives and sayings alike has never been tested. He used about 413 verses taken from Mark of which 184 contain words of Jesus and 229 do not. Using the list of John Hawkins,[5] 82 percent of Luke's characteristic words and phrases are found in narrative verses while only 18 percent are found in Markan sayings of Jesus. Luke's editorial hand is less evident in sayings of Jesus taken from Mark than is the case in narrative sections taken from the same source.

RESULT B:

The changes Luke did make in the sayings from Mark involve word choice rather than meaning and are overwhelmingly grammatical rather than theological in their concern. They were necessitated by Mark's rather scanty Greek vocabulary, his fondness for overemphasis, pleonasm, anacoluthon, asyndetic construction, and so on. Indeed, there are many instances in which Luke retained the meaning of Mark's saying at the cost of internal consistency, for example, Lk. 9:27 which understands the eschaton in a future literal sense (as does Mk. 9:1), contrary to Lk. 11:20 and 17:20-21.[6] There may be as few as thirteen instances in which Luke changed the Markan meaning of the same saying.[7] Although it is questionable whether some of these changes alter the essential meaning of Mark or whether they merely make explicit what is implied, nevertheless these changes are few in number when compared to the many lesser grammatical and stylistic changes. But changes of all kinds over Markan sayings occur much less frequently than the myriad alterations Luke made over narrative material taken from the same source.

---

[4]H. J. Holtzmann, *Die Synoptiker* and *Die synoptischen Evangelien*; P. Wernle, *Synoptische Frage*; H. J. Cadbury, *The Style and Literary Method of Luke* (1920); J. Hawkins, *Horae Synopticae*, 2d ed. (1909). See also B. S. Easton, *The Gospel according to Saint Luke* (1926).

[5]J. Hawkins, *Horae Synopticae*, 16-30.

[6]Other examples of Luke's faithfulness to Mark include Lk. 8:10 (use of Mark's ἵνα); 8:45 (implies something less than omniscience for Jesus); 18:18 (contains Rabbinic inaccuracy of Mark); 18:30 (contradicts rewards system in Lk. 16:18). See also the Lukan parallels to Mk. 1:44; 2:20; 3:3; 10:17-18, 33.

[7]Lk. 4:43; 5:35, 37-39; 6:3-5; 8:21, 13, 18; 11:18-22, 23, 26, 30, 31-33.

RESULT C:

Matthew, too, treated sayings of Jesus taken from Mark with more care and restraint than Markan narratives (although probably for reasons different from Luke). In the thirty Matthean pericopes which afford any basis for comparison,[8] the results are similar to those found in the case of Luke: (1) Matthew was most free with Mark's introductory narrative sentences, for an average of 36 percent of his words have a parallel in Mark; (2) the average rises to 52 percent in the narrative body; (3) the same percentage is maintained in Matthew's concluding sentences; (4) however, closest correspondence with Mark is found among the words of Jesus where an average of 79 percent of Matthew's words have a parallel in Mark.

Matthew's special use of Markan sayings is substantiated by the distribution of "peculiarly Matthean words and phrases." One-half of the 516 Matthean verses taken from Mark contain sayings of Jesus. However, there are four times as many characteristically Matthean words in the narrative verses than can be found in sayings taken from the same source.[9]

RESULT D:

As far as *content* is concerned, possibly only in eleven pericopes is there any evidence that Matthew gave to his Markan saying a meaning which is not found (either implicitly or explicitly) in his source.[10] All other changes of Mark's sayings involve poor grammar, precision of statement, better word choice, elimination of unnecessary conversational words of Jesus, etc. If it is correct to picture Matthew as writing to a Jewish audi-

---

[8]Mt. 4:12-17, 18-22; 8:1-4, 23-27, 28-34; 9:1-8, 9-13, 18-27; 10:1-4, 9-12, 14; 12:1-8, 9-14, 46-50; 13:53-58; 14:13-21, 22-23; 15:21-28, 32-39; 16:1, 4, 13-16; 17:9-13, 14-21, 22-23; 18:1-5; 19:1-9, 13-15, 16-30; 20:17-19, 20-28, 29-34.

[9]The distinction between words of Jesus and deeds by Jesus is an integral part of the organization of Matthew's gospel. Each of the five "books" can be subdivided into a narrative and a discourse section. Note the transitional verses which separate these subdivisions, for example, Mt. 4:23; 9:35. This same distinction is found in Luke-Acts, for example, Lk. 4:14-15, 31-32, and Acts 1:1. In fact Luke's treatment of the sayings taken from Mark is in direct contrast to the speeches he "composed" for Peter and Paul in Acts. In the gospel, he exercised a *prophetischer Stil*; in Acts, he followed the contemporary Greek historiographer's method.

[10]Mt. 5:32; 10:18; 12:39; 13:11-15; 15:3-11, 16-20; 15:24; 19:3, 9; 19:17, 21.

ence through the adaptation of the gentile Gospel of Mark, one would expect more evidence of his "judaizing tendency" in Markan material. However, such Jewishness is found in the *non*-Markan teachings.[11] When using Markan sayings he retained even a rejection of Jewish scribal traditions and the Corban rule (for example, Mt. 15:1-20 and Mk.7:1-23). It seems that Matthew was compelled to parallel such Markan sayings in spite of his better Jewish judgment which he exercised in the non-Markan parts of his gospel.

Concerning *order*, it has been stated often that Mark's order was changed extensively in the first half of Matthew. This is true of narrative pericopes but is not an accurate generalization where Markan words of Jesus are involved, for they are found in the same order and/or sequence in Matthew. For example, Mk. 1:14-3:30 contains sayings in 1:14-15, 16-20, 40-45; 2:1-12, 13-17, 18-22, 23-28; 3:1-6, 23-30 which have parallels in exactly that order in Mt. 4; 8; 9; and 12. However, the narratives interspersed with the same Markan series (namely, Mk. 1:21-22, 29-31, 32-34, 39; 3:7-12, 13-19a, 19b-22) are *not* found in their proper Markan order but in Mt. 7:28-29; 8:14-17; 4:23-24; 9:35; 4:25 and 10:1-4. There are about sixty verses containing Markan sayings which seem to be out of Markan order in Matthew, but the significance of this number should be reduced for the following reasons: (1) several of these verses have a doublet form in Matthew which occurs in the proper Markan order;[12] (2) other verses involve local transpositions;[13] (3) with the exception of four separate verses (namely, Mt. 10:26; 13:12; 12:30; and 5:13), the remaining sayings verses in Matthew are found in the same Markan sequence even though they are out of order.[14] Matthew maintained Mark's sequence out of order!

---

[11]Examples of Matthew's Jewishness are found in Mt. 5:17-19; 7:6; 15:24; 18:17; and 19:28—all of which are found in peculiarly Matthean pericopes.

[12]For example, Mt. 12:39 is related to Mt. 16:1 and 4 (paralleling the order of Mk. 8:11-12); Mt. 10:38 may be a doublet of Mt. 16:24-25 (found in proper Markan order with Mk. 8:34-35); Mt. 10:40 has a doublet in Mt. 18:1-2, 5, which is parallel with Mk. 9:33ff.; Mt. 5:29-30 has a doublet in Mt. 18:6-9, which is parallel with Mk. 9:42-43, 47-48; Mt. 5:32 has a doublet in Mk. 19:1ff., which is parallel with Mk. 10:1-2.

[13]For example, Mt. 13:12 comes before the interpretation of the Parable of the Sower whereas in Mk. 4:25 it comes after the interpretation; Mt. 13:43 comes after Matthew's special material (13:36-43) following the interpretation and not after Mt. 13:23.

[14]Cf. the following parallels: Mt. 5:15 and Mk. 4:21; Mt. 7:3 and Mk. 4:24; Mt. 8:23-27 and Mk. 4:35-41; Mt. 8:28-34 and Mk. 5:1-20; Mt. 9:18-26 and Mk. 5:21-43; Mt. 10:1 and 9-11 and Mk. 6:7-12. The Matthean pericopes are in Markan sequence.

In contrast to the transposed narrative sections taken from Mark, Matthew kept (successfully) Mark's sayings in the same order and/or sequence.

Results A, B, C, and D in Step Two combine to make this conclusion: Matthew and Luke usually followed the content and order of sayings taken from the known source Mark; conversely, they made extensive changes both of meaning and order in narrative material taken from the same source.

Step Three

The results of *Step Two* may be checked by comparing Matthew and Luke where Mark has been their common source. The correct method for correlating these non-Markan versions of triple tradition is *not* achieved by placing the total number of words in the Markan version beneath the number of Markan words which Matthew and Luke hold in common; this would assume either that at least one of the two non-Markan forms made no change over Mark or that both gospels made exactly the same omissions and changes. Rather, one must note the number of Markan words which the shorter non-Markan form has in common with the other version (whether Matthew or Luke) to determine the *maximum* basis for common Markan words. As an example, Matthew's version of Mk. 2:3-12 is the shorter non-Markan form. It contains 38 of Mark's *narrative* words of which 26 are found also in Luke (or 68 percent of maximum possibility). But there are 27 Markan words in Matthew's *sayings* of Jesus of which 24 have a parallel in Luke (or 89 percent of maximum possibility). Again, Luke's version of Mk. 2:13-17 is the shorter, containing 46 Markan words in its narrative of which 36 (or 78 percent) are paralleled in Matthew. But Matthew parallels all 17 of Luke's words of Jesus taken from Mark.[15]

Such a comparison of non-Markan versions in triple tradition substantiates the results of *Step Two*. Insofar as Matthew and Luke both used Markan *narrative* material, an average of 52 percent of these Markan words are found in both non-Markan parallels. Insofar as they both used Markan words for the *sayings* of Jesus, the percentage increases to 88 percent. Both exercised a similar kind of judgment when they included most

---

[15]The following pericopes were used as a basis for comparing the non-Markan versions of triple tradition: Mk. 1:40-45; 2:3-12, 13-17, 18-22, 23-28; 3:1-6, 31-35; 4:1-9, 10-12, 13-20, 30-32, 35-41; 5:1-20, 21-43; 6:30-44; 8:27-33, 34-39; 9:1, 14-29, 30-32, 33-37; 10:13-16, 17-31, 32-34, 41-45, 46-52.

of the same Markan words in their sayings of Jesus; Matthew did not use one set of Markan words and Luke another. One used more Markan words than the other, and neither used all of Mark; but their common parallels to the triple tradition prove that they treated the Markan sayings more carefully and faithfully than narratives taken from the same common source.

Step Four

Turning from triple to double tradition, one must note the nature of the pericopes which are usually assigned to the non-Markan common source "Q." Overlooking the fact that in recent years a total of 487 *different* verses in Luke (or 42 percent of that gospel) have been identified with "Q,"[16] this paper will follow the "Q" source as defined by Dr. F. C. Grant, which contains 217 verses in Luke.[17]

Two facts come to light concerning the nature of these "Q" verses: (1) 88 percent of them contain sayings of Jesus with little or no narrative material; (2) The so-called "narrative" pericopes in "Q"[18] exhibit the same dichotomy of treatment between the sayings of Jesus and narratives about Jesus found in triple tradition. One suspects that these "narratives" ought more properly to be considered as loosely paralleled settings for closely paralleled sayings (or "pronouncements") of Jesus.

Because of the preponderance of sayings in double tradition and the closer correspondence found in sayings among the "narrative" material in "Q," it becomes necessary to relate conclusions concerning the use of Markan sayings in triple tradition to sayings in double tradition. This can be done by testing the following trial sequence of logic which contains the usual solution to this problem.

> *Proposition A*: Matthew and Luke treated the sayings of Jesus taken from Mark with great care. For this reason, one finds a common element of triple tradition in Matthew and in Luke which shows close verbal correspondence and common order with Mark and with each other. (This proposition has been proved by *Steps Two* and *Three*.)

---

[16]The reconstructions of "Q" used for this figure were those of Grant, Harnack, Streeter, Hawkins, Crum, Stanton, T. W. Manson, Moffatt, Wernle, H. J. Holtzmann, and J. Weiss.

[17]F. C. Grant, *The Gospels: Their Origin and Their Growth* (1957) 58ff.

[18]Lk. 4:1-3, 5-7, 9-11, 13; 7:1-8, 10, 18-21, 29-30; 9:49; 11:14-16, 45. Total: 29 verses.

Proposition B: There is another source which contains sayings of Jesus, usually called "Q." Matthew and Luke drew upon it in addition to Mark.

Proposition C: Since Matthew and Luke treated the sayings of Mark with great care, it is reasonable to expect them to treat this other common source of sayings with the same care.

Proposition D: One should expect, therefore, to find non-Markan common elements in Matthew and Luke which exhibit close verbal correspondence and similarity in order beyond the common Markan elements in these gospels.

Proposition E: Such correspondence and similarity is found in the non-Markan common material, thereby recommending the probable existence of a non-Markan common document "Q."

Step Five

In order to test the accuracy of this sequence it is necessary to examine *Proposition E* to see if in fact the non-Markan material does show common correspondence in wording and in order. This can be done by applying the method used to correlate the non-Markan common results in triple tradition (*Step Three*) to the 217 verses of "Q." The shorter version of double tradition is taken as the *maximum* basis for possible correspondence with the other non-Markan version. For example, Luke's version of the Beatitudes (Lk. 6:20-23) is shorter than Mt. 5:3-4, 6, 11ff. Of the 73 words in Luke's sayings, Matthew parallels 31 (or 43 percent of maximum possibility). Again, Matthew's narrative of the Temptation of Jesus (Mt. 4:3-12), being the shorter, contains 124 words, for which 88 have parallels in Lk. 4:3-13 (or 66 percent). However, Luke has fewer words of Jesus, using 25, of which 24 are found in Matthew (or 96 percent).

When this procedure is followed for all 217 verses assigned to "Q," one finds that an average of 54 percent of the words in the shorter non-Markan versions have parallels in the other version; actually 2,124 of the 3,924 words used in "Q" sayings have common parallels. If *Proposition E* is correct, approximately the same number of verses of "Q" ought to fall on either side of this average mean of 54 percent. Such an assumption is warranted because Matthew and Luke must have been uniform in their respective treatments of the common document "Q." They would have employed their individual literary methods (whatever these methods were) to "Q" with a detectable amount of regularity—unless, of course, one pictures "Matthew" and "Luke" as fitful (not intentional) editors (not authors).

However, when verses which have a parallel form in Mark are discounted because of the distinct possibility that they may not be double tradition at all but triple tradition,[19] only 78 verses (or one-third) have a verbal correspondence of 54 percent and higher. Conversely, 68 percent of these most widely agreed upon "Q" verses show less than the average degree of verbal correspondence.

Regarding common order among these verses, it is absolutely impossible to find any common order and/or sequence following Lk. 11:24-26 and Mt. 12:43-45. Over half the verses prior to this point are out of common order.

One must reject, therefore, the accuracy of *Proposition E* as previously stated and revise it to read:

> *Proposition E*: But no such verbal similarities exist for over two-thirds of this material, nor is there any discernible common order in the double tradition.

This revision, however, has invalidated the whole logical sequence.

Step Six

It is necessary now to repair *Propositions B, C*, and *D* so they can be brought into correct logical relationship with the facts as stated in *Propositions A* and *E*. Any one of the following three alternatives is possible:

> *Alternative 1* states that *Proposition B* is true and *Proposition C* is false, i.e., that the document "Q" is affirmed because it does not necessarily follow that Matthew and Luke would have treated the sayings source in the same way in which they treated sayings taken from Mark.
>
> *Alternative 2* asserts that *Proposition B* is false and *Proposition C* is true, i.e., that the hypothesis of a common written document "Q" must be rejected because Matthew and Luke would have treated these common sayings to some extent as they treated sayings taken from their other common source.
>
> *Alternative 3* suggests that *Proposition B* and *C* are both true and false at the same time. This alternative is suggested by the fact that about one-third of the double tradition shows an average or better degree of verbal correspondence, thereby

---

[19]For example, Lk. 3:16 (parallel in Mt. 3:11) has another parallel form in Mk. 1:7-8 in which 18 of the 21 non-Markan common words appear! Again, 12 of the 14 non-Markan common words in Mt. 4:1-2 (parallel Lk. 4:1-2) have a parallel in Mk. 1:11-12. Other "Q" sayings with possible triple tradition include Lk. 6:37-38; 7:27; 9:47, 48a, 48b, 49, 50; 10:4-5, 40; 11:15, 17, 18, 21-22, 23, 29, 42; 12:2, 8-9, 10, 12, 39-40; 13:18-19, 30; 14:26-27, 34-35; 16:18; 17:1-2, 6, 31, 33.

recommending the possibility that the ''Q'' document could have contained at least these 78 verses.[20]

This last alternative can be dismissed from serious consideration for the following reasons: (1) there is no common order among these 78 verses; (2) about one-third of these verses presuppose at least an awareness of (if not use of) other versions of the same saying now found in Mark;[21] (3) it is highly improbable that Matthew and Luke would have used a common non-Markan document which makes up less than 5 percent of each gospel when the other common source used (namely, Mark) makes up 50 percent of Matthew and at least one-third of Luke; (4) the nature of these sayings with closest verbal correspondence is such that the hypothesis of a common written document is not required to explain the phenomenon. These are short, disconnected sayings which are not integrally connected to their present contexts, as is indicated by the different uses to which Matthew and Luke put them.[22] Such sayings probably remained relatively unaltered through their long history of oral transmission because of their simple mnemonic quality and because it was possible to apply them independently to different contexts.

One must decide, then, between *Alternative 1* and *Alternative 2*. Whatever the choice, in the future greater concern must be paid to the distinction between Markan sayings and narratives used by Matthew and Luke. For if the ''Q'' document is to be affirmed in the future (as it undoubtedly will be), it must be upheld with the full realization that there is some disparateness involved in the estimates of the literary methods used by Matthew and Luke in triple and double tradition. It may be possible to justify satisfactorily the different treatments given the two common sayings sources used by Matthew and Luke. However, I know of no statement which is addressed to the problem. Why do the literary methods by which

---

[20] This shorter ''Q'' would include Lk. 3:7-9, 16-17; 4:3-13; 6:31, 39-42, 45; 7:1-9, 22-28, 31-35; 9:48a; 10:2-3, 12-16, 21-24; 11:2-4, 9-13, 19-20, 23-26, 29-32, 34-35, 42; 12:2-7, 22-31, 39-40, 42-46, 58-59; 13:20-21, 27-30, 34-35; 16:13, 17-18; 17:23-24, 33, 37.

[21] For example, Lk. 4:4, 7, 10; 6:39, 7:27; 9:48; 10:2, 3, 12, 16; 11:19-20, 23, 24-26, 29-30, 43; 12:2, 39-40; 13:30; and 16:18.

[22] For example, Lk. 6:31 is within a lesson On Loving One's Enemies (Lk. 6:27-36), whereas Matthew appended it to God's Answering of Prayer (Mt. 7:7-11). Luke places 6:39 in his section On Judging (Lk. 6:37-42), but the same saying is found in What Defiles a Man in Mt. 15:1-20.

Matthew and Luke appropriated Markan sayings seem different from the ones they used in their common sayings source "Q"?

Until the adherents of "Q" shoulder this burden of proof, it seems far more logical that the other of the two alternatives best fits the evidence, namely, that there was no common document "Q." It is improbable a priori that Matthew and Luke would have followed one standard of evaluation for the sayings of Jesus found in triple tradition and yet another for sayings of the same Jesus in double tradition. At least the Markan words of Jesus seem to have been regarded by two different Christian communities as containing a special authority for Christian living.

However, *Alternative 2* also has its burden of proof, for it must explain why some of the non-Markan material in Matthew and Luke has close verbal correspondence. This is not too heavy a burden for the following reasons: (1) The large majority of "Q" verses have such a low verbal correspondence and no common order that in most cases the agreements are found only among the most minimal skeletal words necessary in order to call these verses "common" sayings. These can be explained best as the result of independent courses of oral, pregospel transmission. (2) The minority of "Q" verses which have closer verbal correspondence are more difficult to explain. However, as noted above, most of these verses are made up of separate and detached units which fit no common context. They need not presuppose a common written document but require only the versatility of being easily memorized and freely applied. Such a nature made these sayings less susceptible to change during the preliterary stage of gospel tradition.

What, then, are the demands made by the future? On the one hand, the adherents of the "Q" document must summon Herculean strength to appraise realistically the ways by which Matthew and Luke used Markan sayings. On the other hand, those who reject the document "Q" must define more carefully what is common in Matthew and Luke and how this common element is to be explained. Whatever position one affirms, the "scavenger's labors" offer more of a reward than to be "choked with dust."

EVIDENCE FOR THE VIEW
THAT ST. LUKE USED
ST. MATTHEW'S GOSPEL

*A. W. Argyle**

Argyle notes that there are a number of editorial agreements between Matthew and Luke that are best explained not by their use of a common source (Mark), but by the fact that one of them was acquainted with the work of the other. The evidence at the beginning of Matthew 5 suggests unmistakably that Luke followed Matthew.

Argyle examines a number of passages to show how Luke has dealt with material from Matthew and argues that the differences between Matthew and Luke are no obstacle to the belief that Luke uses Matthew's gospel, a belief for which the very many agreements of Matthew and Luke against Mark afford sufficient warrant.

After examining in detail several passages in the Triple Tradition, Argyle concludes on the basis of the evidence that the view that Luke knew and used Matthew's gospel is not only a possible one, but is very probable.

There are a number of editorial agreements between Matthew and Luke which are not naturally explained by their use of a common source, but seem to point to the fact that one of the evangelists was acquainted with the work of the other. For instance, both Matthew and Luke date the

---

*A. W. Argyle, "Evidence for the View that St. Luke Used St. Matthew's Gospel," *Journal of Biblical Literature* 83 (1964): 390-96.

cleansing of the temple on the day of the triumphal entry into Jerusalem, whereas Mark dates it on the day after. Again, Mk. 3:20-21 reads: "And he cometh into a house. And the multitude cometh together again, so that they could not so much as eat bread. And when his friends heard it, they went out to lay hold on him: for they said, He is beside himself." According to Mk. 3:31, the "friends" of Jesus include his mother and brothers. Both Matthew and Luke omit Mk. 3:20-21, and both substitute the casting out of a demon as the introduction to the Beelzebub controversy; and both use the phrase, not in Mark, "[Jesus], knowing their thoughts, said to them" (Mt. 12:25; Lk. 11:17). In Matthew the word for "thoughts" is ἐνθυμήσεις. In Luke it is διανοήματα.

So far we might infer either that Matthew used Luke or that Luke used Matthew. But there is another piece of evidence which suggests unmistakably that Luke followed Matthew. Matthew at the beginning of ch. 5 says that Jesus took his disciples apart up on to a mountain and taught them. (Only four disciples had so far been called.) Then follows the Sermon on the Mount. At the end of the sermon Matthew says: "the multitudes were astonished at his teaching, for he taught them as one having authority and not as their scribes." So the sermon, which began by being addressed to the disciples alone, ended by being addressed to the crowds. The explanation is that Matthew is here using the words of Mk. 1:22, where we learn that the congregation in the synagogue at Capernaum "were astonished at his teaching; for he taught them as having authority, and not as the scribes." But in Luke too the Sermon (on the Plain), which began by being addressed to the disciples alone (all twelve), ends by being spoken "in the ears of the people" (7:1). But Luke is not, like Matthew, using Mk. 1:22; for he has already used that at Lk. 4:22. The natural inference is that Luke is following Matthew.

Let us now in imagination put ourselves in Luke's place, and try to see how his mind works as he deals with Matthew's gospel from the beginning. First, he is confronted by the genealogy of Jesus as presented by Matthew. In both Mt. 1 and Lk. 3:23-38, the descent is traced through Joseph, not Mary. Matthew traces the descent through the direct royal line (David and Solomon), and Luke by a side line through David's son Nathan, 2 Sam. 5:14. The two lists coincide again at the names of Zerubbabel, the founder of the second temple, and his father Shealtiel, and again part company until they reach Mary's husband, Joseph. Matthew traces

the genealogy downwards from Abraham; Luke traces the genealogy upwards to Adam, the son of God.

Several problems arise. (1) Why does Luke place the genealogy after the baptism of Jesus, whereas Matthew places it at the beginning of the gospel? Luke has a special reason. According to the most likely reading at Lk. 3:22 the heavenly voice at the baptism said to Jesus: "Thou art my Son: this day I have begotten Thee" (= Ps. 2:7). This is the reading of D (the Western text) and is confirmed by Justin, Clement, Origen, Methodius, Hilary, Augustine, and a host of other early authorities. It is the reading adopted by Streeter, who convincingly argues that the change to "Thou art my beloved Son, in thee I am well pleased" is due to assimilation to the other synoptic gospels and to a desire to avoid the suggestion of Adoptionist heresy. Luke is here concerned to verify that Jesus was the Son of God in as many ways as possible. He was the eternal Son of God, being conceived by the Holy Ghost, born of the virgin Mary. God said to Him at his baptism "Thou art my Son." And finally Luke traces his genealogy up to Adam, "the son of God."

(2) Why are the persons mentioned in the genealogy so different in Luke from those in Matthew? Almost all the women mentioned in Matthew's genealogy were women of dubious reputation. It was unusual to mention women at all in a Jewish genealogy. Matthew seems to have gone out of his way to choose the most disreputable women. Tamar was first the wife of Er, then of Onan, then of Judah, by whom she bore Perez and Zarah. The way in which this happened was a disgrace to Judah (Gen. 38). Rahab was a harlot. Bathsheba, wife of Uriah, was the illegitimate wife of David in the sense that David had her husband killed so that he could marry her himself. No wonder that Luke shrank from this genealogy, and preferred his own. Similarly Luke naturally preferred his own incomparably beautiful nativity narrative to that which he found in Matthew. He was far too good an artist to attempt to conflate them, which would have spoiled both.

When Luke begins to use Mark as well as Matthew, he follows Matthew in omitting the quotation from Mal. 3:1 which Mark wrongly ascribed to Isaiah, just as later he follows Matthew in omitting the erroneous words "when Abiathar was high priest" at Mk. 2:26.

In the account of the ministry of John the Baptist, both Matthew and Luke have "all the region round about the Jordan" (Mt. 3:5; Lk.3:3). These words are not in Mark. John's preaching of repentance (Mt. 3:7-10;

Lk. 3:7-9) occurs in almost identical Greek words in exactly the same order in Luke as in Matthew, and there is nothing corresponding to it in Mark, except the bare statement that John preached a baptism of repentance unto the remission of sins (Mk. 1:4). Matthew omits "unto the remission of sins" because he wants to insert it into the saying of Jesus at the Last Supper. But the extended preaching of John is non-Markan matter common to Matthew and Luke in virtually identical Greek.

In the account of the baptism of Jesus which is based on Mark, Luke follows Matthew in altering Mark's σχίζομαι to ἀνοίγω. In the account of the temptation of Jesus Matthew alters Mark's ἐκβάλλω to ἀνάγω. Luke alters it, very similarly, to ἄγω (Mt. 4:1; Lk. 4:1).

In the detailed account of the three temptations, to which there is nothing corresponding in Mark, Luke reverses the order of the second and third temptations which he finds in Matthew, because our Lord's last reply ("Thou shalt not tempt the Lord thy God") forms a better conclusion to the series. The words are a quotation from Deut. 6:16, where the reference to putting God to the test is explained by Israel's putting God to the test in Ex. 17:1-7. The moral is that to test God's good faith is to show one's own lack of faith. It is wrong to presume upon God's providence. But by placing the quotation at the end of the series Luke is able to suggest a second meaning also: "thou shalt not tempt me, Jesus, the Lord thy God"; and so the devil ceases to do so "for a season" (Lk. 4:13), that is, until Peter tempts him not to seek a Messiahship of suffering (Mk. 8:33), when Jesus says to Peter: "Get thee behind me, Satan," though Luke omits the saying there.

In the rejection at Nazareth Luke in essence agrees with Matthew against Mark. For where Mk. 6:3 has "Is this not the carpenter, the son of Mary?" both Matthew and Luke made the question relate to Joseph, not Mary: "Is this not the carpenter's son?" (Mt. 13:55); "Is this not the son of Joseph?" (Lk. 4:22).

In the healing of the paralytic both Matthew and Luke add to Mark's narrative the statement: "He departed into his house" (Mt. 9:7; Lk. 5:25—exactly the same Greek words in exactly the same order). Further, both Matthew and Luke omit Mark's "take up thy bed" (Mk. 2:9) and have simply "Arise and walk."

In the saying about new wine in old wine skins Matthew and Luke agree in using ἐκχέω instead of Mark's ἀπόλλυται (Mk. 2:22; Mt. 9:17; Lk. 5:37).

The common omissions of Matthew and Luke when they are both following Mark are significant, and there are many of them, for example, Mk. 3:5; Mk. 3:9. Mk. 3:17 tells us that Jesus gave to James and John the surname "sons of thunder." Both Matthew and Luke omit this and both add the fact that Andrew was the brother of Peter.

In the stilling of the tempest (Mk. 4:35-41) both Matthew and Luke omit Mark's statement that it was evening, and that other boats accompanied Jesus. Both omit reference to the cushion on which Jesus rested his head to sleep. Both omit "Carest thou not?" Both omit the Lord's command to the wind and the sea "Hush, be silent." Both omit his words to the disciples, "Why are you such cowards?" But, most striking of all, both Matthew and Luke add the note of astonishment to Mk. 4:41.

We turn now to the Great Sermon. Matthew has nine beatitudes, Luke four, which are balanced by four so-called woes, beginning with οὐαί ("alas"). The beatitudes are more briefly expressed in Luke than in Matthew, and all in the second person plural, whereas Matthew has the third person plural. Matthew has "Blessed are the poor in spirit" (5:3); Luke has "Blessed are you poor" (6:20). Why this change in Luke? (1) Luke's interests are what would now be called "socialistic." He is interested in vindicating the poor. Hence in Luke alone we find the parable of Dives and Lazarus, and the incident of Zacchaeus who wins salvation simply by distributing ill-gotten gains among the poor. (2) Luke wants to balance his first beatitude with the first woe: "Alas for you rich" (6:24).

Compare now Matthew's third beatitude (5:6) with Luke's second (6:21). Matthew has "Blessed are they who hunger and thirst after righteousness"; Luke, "Blessed are you hungry." Once again Luke's "socialism" appears, and he has to balance the beatitude with "Alas for you who are filled now."

It is impossible in the space of this article to go right through the synoptic gospels. But enough has been said to show that the differences between Matthew and Luke are no obstacle to the belief that Luke used Matthew's gospel, a belief for which the very many agreements of Matthew and Luke against Mark afford sufficient warrant.

Mt. 5:48 reads: "Ye shall therefore be perfect as your Father in heaven is perfect." "Perfect" (τέλειος) is never applied to God in the OT, for the very good reason that τέλειος means "fully grown," "mature," a conception which neither the Jew nor the Christian would naturally apply to God. Hence Luke has "Be ye merciful, even as your Father is merci-

ful'' (6:36). "Merciful" is an epithet frequently applied to God in the OT. Note too that Luke has "Father" where Matthew has "Heavenly Father." Luke knew from his Markan source that Jesus addressed God simply as "Abba" (Father). Hence in the Lord's Prayer, too, Luke substitutes "Father" for Matthew's more liturgical address.

Further differences in the Lord's Prayer call for comment. Luke tries to explain Matthew's mysterious word ἐπιούσιος as meaning "day by day" and so substitutes the present imperative of "give" for Matthew's aorist "Give us today." Matthew has "Forgive us our debts"—a Hebrew way of describing sins. But Luke is writing for gentile readers and so writes "Forgive us our sins," though he betrays knowledge of Matthew's text by afterwards describing the sinner as a debtor.

In the passage concerning hearers and doers of the word, with the parable of the two builders (Mt. 7:24-27, Lk. 6:47-49) we find in Luke an interesting reinterpretation of Matthew. In Matthew the two builders choose different sites, the wise man rock, the foolish man sand. In Luke the two come to the same place, but the wise man "dug deep and laid the foundation on rock," while the foolish man built on the soil without foundations. Matthew speaks of rains, floods, and wind. Luke mentions only the river. Matthew ascribes the security of the wise man to his having built on rock; Luke to the fact that the house was "soundly built." Matthew is already looking forward to our Lord's saying to Simon: "Thou art Peter, and upon this rock I will build my church" (Mt. 16:18), a passage which is suited to Matthew's ecclesiastical interest, but which Luke, with other interests, intends to omit.

Other parts of Matthew's Sermon on the Mount have a Judaistic and antigentile bias: for example, Christ's attitude to the Jewish law (5:17-20); on fasting (6:16-18); on casting pearls before swine, a term of reproach applied to the gentiles in (7:6). Such passages and others Luke omits, partly because he is writing for gentiles, partly because he wants to leave room for much of the material peculiar to his own gospel, especially the expansion from oral tradition with which he wants to fill out Mark's passion narrative.

The Gadarene demoniac (Mk. 5:1-20; Mt. 8:28-34; Lk. 8:26-39). Matthew and Luke considerably abbreviate Mark. Especially to be noticed is the passage which they both agree to omit, namely, Mk. 5:3b, 4, 5: "and no man could any more bind him, no, not with a chain: because he had been often bound with fetters and chains, and the chains had been rent

asunder by him, and the fetters broken in pieces, and no man had the strength to tame him. And always, night and day, in the tombs and in the mountains, he was crying out and cutting himself with stones.'' Matthew omits these graphic details, and Luke does likewise. Agreement on which passages to omit is just as significant as agreement in alterations and additions.

Jairus's daughter and the woman with the issue of blood (Mk. 5:21-43; Mt. 9:18-26; Lk. 8:40-56). Note first that Mk. 5:22 speaks of ''one of the rulers of the synagogue'' (εἷς τῶν ἀρχισυναγώγων), named Jairus. Both Matthew and Luke avoid this expression, and both use simply ''ruler'' (ἄρχων), though Luke, trying to do justice to Mark as well as to Matthew, adds ''of the synagogue.'' Matthew omits the name Jairus. Surely all this is very significant. Both Matthew and Luke abridge Mark's account, Matthew so much that he represents the daughter of Jairus as dead from the start (ἄρτι ἐτελεύτησεν). Luke is not prepared to go so far. He honors his Markan source by agreeing with Mark (ἐσχάτως ἔχει) that at the time of the first report the girl was dying (ἀπέθνησκεν).

With regard to the woman with the issue of blood Matthew omits entirely the statement ''she had suffered many things of many physicians, and had spent all she had, and was nothing bettered, but rather grew worse'' (Mk. 5:26). Luke tones it down: ''she had spent all her livelihood on physicians, but could not be healed by any of them.''[1] Both Matthew and Luke omit ''having heard the things concerning Jesus'' and add to the account that the woman touched the tassel, that is, the sacred part, of Jesus' garment.

To return to Jairus's daughter: both Matthew and Luke omit Mark's statement in 5:40: ''But he, having put them all outside, takes the father of the child and her mother and those that were with him, and goes in where the child was.'' Both Matthew and Luke omit Mark's Aramaic ''Talitha cumi,'' the fact that the girl was twelve years old, and the words ''They were straightway amazed with a great amazement.''

The sending out of the Twelve. Here we have a very significant piece of evidence indeed—not only an agreement of Matthew and Luke against Mark, but a point on which Matthew and Luke agree in contradicting Mark. Mk. 6:8 informs us that Jesus instructed the Twelve to take nothing with them for the journey except a staff. That is, he permitted them to take

---

[1] BD syˢ omits ἰατροῖς προσαναλώσασα ὅλον τὸν βίον.

a staff. Matthew contradicts this (10:10), saying they are to take no staff—no collecting bag, neither two shirts, nor shoes, nor staff. Luke agrees with Matthew that Jesus forbade them to take a staff (Lk. 9:3). Not only this: Luke read the following words, which are in Matthew, but not in Mark: "for a laborer is worthy of his food." But Luke decides to reserve this for his second mission, that of the Seventy or Seventy-two (Lk. 10:7), but there he gives it his own form: "for the laborer is worthy of his reward" (cf. 1 Tim. 5:18; 1 Cor. 9:7ff.). In Mk. 6:9 Jesus permits the wearing of sandals. Both Matthew and Luke omit this. And both Matthew and Luke omit Mark's statement in Mk. 6:13, "And they cast out many devils, and anointed many sick ones with oil," though Luke shows that he has read the Markan, as well as the Matthean text, by saying that they preached (εὐαγγελιζόμενοι, 9:6, corresponding to ἐκήρυξαν, Mk. 6:12) and healed everywhere.

Much of the material which Matthew adds to Mark's account of the mission charge Luke includes in his charge to the Seventy or Seventy-two: e.g., "The harvest is plenteous, but the reapers are few. Pray ye therefore the Lord of the harvest that he send forth labourers into his harvest" (Mt. 9:37-38 = Lk. 10:2—exactly the same Greek words in exactly the same order). Similarly: "Behold, I send you out as lambs in the midst of wolves" (Lk. 10:3); "Behold, I send you out as sheep in the midst of wolves" (Mt. 10:18).

Let us proceed now to the Return of the Twelve and the Feeding of the Five Thousand. Both Matthew and Luke omit Mark's statement (Mk. 6:31): "And he says to them: Come ye yourselves apart into a deserted place and rest for a little while. For there were many coming and going and they had no opportunity even to eat." Similarly both omit Mark's statement, "many ran together on foot from all the cities to that place and went before them." Both Matthew and Luke omit Mark's quotation of Num. 27:17, "they were as sheep who had no shepherd" (Mk. 6:34; cf. 1 Kings 22:17). Now Luke is very fond of OT allusions: we would have expected him to retain these which he found in Mark. But he notes that Matthew has omitted them here,[2] and reflects that his need is the same as Matthew's, namely, to leave room in his scroll for the material peculiar to himself.

Both Matthew and Luke omit Mark's statement that the loaves which the disciples ironically suggested that they should go and buy would cost

---

[2] Cf. Mt. 9:36.

two hundred denarii, though the fourth evangelist took due note of it (Jn. 6:7). All three synoptists agree that twelve baskets full of the fragments were taken up, but Matthew and Luke both add the phrase "that which was left over" (τὸ περισσεῦον), a quite unnecessary addition. This agreement of Luke with Matthew against Mark is significant.

In the discourse on leaven (Mk. 8:14ff.; Mt. 16:5ff.; Lk. 12:1) note that whereas Mark has ὁρᾶτε, βλέπετε (8:15), Matthew has προσέχετε and Luke follows Matthew against Mark, despite the fact that Matthew's alteration of Mark is quite unnecessary.

We proceed to the Lord's first prediction of his passion after Peter's confession at Caesarea Philippi (Mk. 8:31; Mt. 16:21; Lk. 9:22). Mark has the grammatically correct ὑπό. Matthew and Luke substitute the less satisfactory ἀπό. Mark has "rise after three days." Matthew alters this to "be raised on the third day." Luke copies Matthew.

In the healing of the epileptic (Mk. 9:14-29; Mt. 17:14-21; Lk. 9:37-43) both Matthew and Luke alter Mark's οὐκ ἴσχυσαν (verse 18) to οὐκ ἠδυνήθησαν. Mark has simply "O faithless generation"; Matthew and Luke have "O faithless and perverse (καὶ διεστραμμένη) generation." Both Matthew and Luke omit a good deal of conversation, and both add the information that the epileptic was a child.

Mk. 9:31 has "is betrayed." Both Matthew and Luke have "is about to be betrayed." Passing over much relevant material to reach the end of Mark's gospel we observe that there Matthew and Luke agree against Mark in affirming that the woman announced to the disciples the angel's message of the Lord's Resurrection.

On the basis of the evidence we venture to suggest that the view that Luke knew Matthew's gospel is not only a possible one, but is very probably true.

THE MAJOR AGREEMENTS
OF MATTHEW AND LUKE
AGAINST MARK

R. T. Simpson*

Simpson maintains that the more strongly we plead the case for Q as a means of explaining all those resemblances between Matthew and Luke that are not attributable to their common use of Mark, the more we undermine the theory of the priority of Mark: and the more we stress in importance the Matthean and Lukan "improvements" of Mark, the more the significance of those 'minor agreements' (which are such a difficulty for the defenders of Q) will be enhanced.

Simpson observes that there are difficulties in reconciling the priority of Mark with the Q hypothesis, and it is in those passages where Matthew and Luke make use of both Markan and Q material that the difficulties are most acute. Simpson belives that the evidence for the priority and independence of Mark is as good in these passages as it is anywhere in the gospels, and further once this is conceded then the case for believing that the major agreements could have been produced only as a result of Luke's use of an edited version of Mark (that is, Matthew) is entirely convincing.

Simpson examines closely three such passages: The Baptism and Temptation of Jesus (Mk. 1:1-13), The Beelzebul Controversy (Mk. 3:22-27), and The Great Commandment (Mk. 12:28-34). In all three passages he is concerned to show two things: first, that the changes made by Mat-

---

*R. T. Simpson, "The Major Agreements of Matthew and Luke Against Mark," *New Testament Studies* 12 (1965-1966): 273-84.

thew and Luke in the text of Mark are editorial *improvements* of that gospel; secondly, that Luke must have known a version of Mark which incorporated the *same* editorial improvements as those which are found in Matthew.

Although Simpson allows that the Synoptic Problem may well turn out to be insoluble, he does believe that a study of the major agreements of Matthew and Luke against Mark greatly strengthens the probability that Matthew was one of the sources employed by Luke in the composition of his gospel.

The problem of the relationship between the first three gospels still awaits a final solution. Even the priority of Mark, the keystone of Synoptic criticism as it was developed by such scholars as B. H. Streeter, has been challenged in recent years.[1] However, the majority of critical scholars are agreed that the careful study of the discrepancies between Mark itself, and those sections of Matthew and Luke which are closest to Mark, leads to the conclusion that St. Matthew and St. Luke worked directly from the written text of that gospel. Even Abbot Butler, the most thoroughgoing of the protagonists of the priority of Matthew, does not in fact deny that Matthew and Luke frequently offer what appears to be an "improved" version of Mark. No doubt it is *possible* to explain the more primitive character of Mark as Butler does, by supposing that St. Peter may have made Matthew the basis of his preaching, and that Mark therefore represents a Petrine version of Matthew. Nevertheless, the majority of scholars are (rightly) agreed in adopting the more economical explanation that the Matthean and Lukan "improvements" upon the text of Mark indicate that both St. Matthew and St. Luke had a copy of that gospel before them as they wrote.

If this explanation of the relationship between Mark and the other two synoptists is accepted, it would seem to be only reasonable to suppose that wherever we find "improvements" of this kind in Matthew and Luke, they ought to be explained on the same hypothesis, namely that these evan-

---

[1]Cf. B. H. Streeter, *The Four Gospels* (1930). Streeter's case has been strongly criticized by Christopher Butler, *The Originality of St. Matthew* (1951) 62ff. [reprinted in this volume]. G. M. Styler discusses Butler's conclusions in an appendix to C. F. D. Moule, *The Birth of the New Testament* (1962) Excursus IV [reprinted in this volume]. Styler points out that even if Butler's case against the logic of Streeter's arguments is admitted, nevertheless a comparison of the style of Mark with that of Matthew and Luke still provides evidence for the priority of Mark. In effect this means that the whole case for the priority of Mark can now be seen to rest upon the kind of evidence produced by Sir John Hawkins, *Horae Synopticae* 2d ed. (1909) 114ff.

gelists are deliberately modifying the text of Mark. Nevertheless, this conclusion has not so far been generally accepted. The difficulty is that a number of these changes are common to both Matthew and Luke—that is, that they sometimes agree in modifying Mark in precisely the same way. It is obvious that the simplest explanation of this phenomenon is that either Matthew or Luke made use of *both* the other synoptists. There are however a number of general considerations which militate against this theory, and some of these will be discussed briefly later on. It was the consideration of these difficulties which led Streeter and others to adopt the ''Q hypothesis'' as a means of explaining all the genuine resemblances between Matthew and Luke other than those attributable to their common use of Mark. But it is clear that the one thing that this theory cannot explain is the agreement between Matthew and Luke in their treatment of *Mark*. To the extent that these ''minor agreements'' are in fact nearly all ''improvements'' of Mark, we may say therefore that the general lines of Streeter's argument in favor of the Q hypothesis run counter to the whole tendency of the argument in favor of the priority of Mark. There can be no doubt therefore that Dr. Farrer has done us a service in drawing attention to the weaknesses of the Q hypothesis.[2] For, the more strongly we plead the case for Q as a means of explaining all those resemblances between Matthew and Luke which are attributable to their common use of Mark, the more we undermine the theory of the priority of Mark: and the more we stress the importance of the Matthean and Lukan ''improvements'' of Mark, the more the significance of those ''minor agreements'' which are such a difficulty for the defenders of Q will be enhanced.

The actual history of the debate on Q will serve to reinforce this point. The problem posed by the minor agreements becomes most acute in those passages of Matthew and Luke where we find incorporated alongside material taken from Mark a certain amount of additional common material not found in Mark—that is ''Q material.''[3] Streeter himself offered two different explanations of the presence of this Q material.[4] In *The Four Gos-*

---

[2]A. M. Farrer, ''On Dispensing with Q,'' in *Studies in the Gospels*, ed. D. E. Nineham (1955) [reprinted in this volume].

[3]This phrase is used simply to describe material common to both Matthew and Luke, but not present in Mark. Its use is not, of course, meant to imply that there ever was a document of the kind that is sometimes labelled ''Q.''

[4]It was Abbot Butler, *Originality*, 109, who pointed out that between the publication of *Oxford Studies in the Synoptic Problem* (1911) and *The Four Gospels* (1924) Streeter completely reversed his opinion on his matter.

pels Streeter argued that this could be explained on a theory of "parallel conflation:"[5] that is, he held that the evangelists were independently conflating the same two narratives. But this by no means does justice to the fact (which we hope to demonstrate later) that Matthew and Luke do not merely add to Mark, but also *improve* it, often in precisely the same way. What is more, there is in a few cases a very close connection between the Q material and that taken from Mark, so that the Q material is quite unable to stand alone. It is rather strange that in fact this latter point was very convincingly made by Streeter himself in his *earlier* essay in *Oxford Studies*. It is tempting to guess that the reason that Streeter allowed his earlier arguments quietly to drop out of sight was that he began to see that they were very difficult to reconcile with the arguments he later put forward in favor of the priority of Mark. For since he had already decided on other grounds that Luke could not have read Matthew (or *vice versa*), in *Oxford Studies* he suggested that where Mark and Q appear to be parallel, we must regard Mark as a secondary verson of Q. This he supposed, was the explanation of the close connection between the Q material and that taken from Mark. Once again, this does much less than justice to the fact that the changes made by Matthew and Luke in Mark often appear to be *improvements* of that gospel. What is more, as Abbot Butler has since pointed out, and as no doubt Streeter saw before him, if we regard Mark as a secondary version of Q, there is very little reason why we should not go one stage further, and treat Mark as a secondary version of *Matthew*.

It is clear then that there are difficulties in reconciling the priority of Mark with the Q hypothesis, and it is in those passages where Matthew and Luke make use of both Markan and Q material that the difficulties are most acute. We believe that the evidence for the priority and independence of Mark is as good in these passages as it is anywhere in the gospels, and further, that once this is conceded then the case for believing that the major agreements[6] could have been produced only as a result of St. Luke's use of an edited version of Mark is entirely convincing.[7] We propose therefore

---

[5]"Parallel conflation": this phrase is used to describe the theory that St. Matthew and St. Luke made use of a tradition parallel to that reproduced in Mark, and independently conflated the two accounts.

[6]"Major agreements": the inclusion of Q material alongside certain of the minor agreements gives them an importance which distinguishes them from the other agreements against Mark.

[7]For the moment we wish to leave open the question of whether that editor was identical with St. Matthew or not. For the purpose of discussion it is convenient to assume that this was the case, but the question will be considered at greater length later on.

to examine three of these passages in order to see what evidence they will provide for the priority of Mark over against Matthew, Luke and any possible reconstruction of "Q." Two of these passages (Mk. 1:1-13: The Baptism and Temptation of Jesus; and Mk. 3:22-27: The Beelzebub Controversy) in their present form are, we suggest, to a large extent Markan constructions. If this is the case, it is obvious that it is extremely unlikely that there ever was any close parallel to them in the tradition, as the reigning theory of parallel conflation requires us to suppose. What is more, some of the most significant agreements against Mark are to be found in verses which make use of Mark's *editorial* material. The other passage we shall consider is "The Great Commandment" (Mk. 12:28-34). The first section of this (Mk. 12:28-31) seems to consist of a single block of traditional material. It is by no means impossible therefore that other versions of this passage may have been in existence at the time when the gospels were written. Nevertheless, we hope to show that the particular changes made by St. Luke in the text of Mark presuppose a knowledge of Matthew's editing of Mark. In all three passages therefore we shall be concerned to show two things: first, that the changes made by St. Matthew and St. Luke in the text of Mark are editorial *improvements* of that gospel; secondly, that St. Luke must have known a version of Mark which incorporated the *same* editorial improvements as those which are found in Matthew.

I

The first passage which we shall consider is Mk. 1:1-13.

(*a*) It seems very likely that the construction of this narrative in its present form is the work of St. Mark, on the basis of a number of small independent pieces of tradition. The connection between the Baptist and his preaching and the Baptism of Jesus, for example, is not so much logical as theological: while the baptism of Jesus *may* have been a traditional feature of descriptions of the beginning of his ministry, and of course this does presuppose the introduction of John, nevertheless the way in which John, the messenger, is contrasted with Jesus, the Son (Mk. 1:2; 1:11), so that the whole narrative is constructed between two of Mark's curiously mixed Old Testament quotations, suggests that it is St. Mark himself who is responsible for devising this introduction to the ministry of Jesus. This impression is confirmed by a closer look at the text:

(i) Mk. 1:1 is obviously Mark's own introduction to his gospel. But Mk. 1:2-3 are dependent on verse 1, for the possessive pronouns of Mk. 1:2 ("Thy" face, "Thy" way) refer back to the mention of Jesus Christ in verse 1. What is more, the adaptation of Is. 40:3 by the substitution of αὐτοῦ for the original (LXX) τοῦ θεοῦ ἡμῶν gives a messianic significance to Mk. 1:3 also, so that it too looks back to Mk. 1:1. We must suppose therefore that Mk. 1:2-3 owe their present position to St. Mark himself. But the only resemblances between Mk. 1:1-6 and Lk. 3:1-6[8] are in Lk. 3:3 (where St. Luke is obviously using a Markan phrase) and Lk. 3:4—the latter consisting of the quotation given in Mk. 1:3, pruned of non-Isaianic material, expanded for another two verses, and still in the amended form adopted by Mark. Apart from Lk. 3:3, therefore, the only part of Lk. 3:1-6 which is at all close to Mark is Lk. 3:4, and here Luke reproduces material which cannot have been part of the pre-Markan tradition in its present form and present context. St. Luke therefore betrays no knowledge of any tradition *parallel* to Mk. 1:1-6.

(ii) Familiarity with the versions of Matthew and Luke is apt to obscure the fact that in Mark, John's Messianic Preaching (1:7-8) and the Baptism of Jesus (1:9-11) go together. The prediction that Jesus would baptize with holy spirit (πνεύματι ἁγίῳ) finds confirmation in the descent of *the* Spirit (τὸ πνεῦμα) upon Jesus at his baptism. In its present form, this is a single narrative. It is sometimes suggested that Luke's version of this incident is really more original, and reflects the standpoint of Q (Lk. 3:16, 17 = Mt. 3:11, 12). However, the more sharply we distinguish between the preaching of John in Matthew and Luke, and the account of it which is given by Mark, the plainer it becomes that there is really nothing in common between Mark's distinctively "Christian" view that Jesus is the recipient and donor of the Spirit, and the tradition incorporated into Lk. 3:17, which makes Jesus an eschatological judge. This Q material is in fact totally irrelevant to any account of Jesus' *baptism*, and cannot have formed part of any kind of parallel account to that given in Mark. Mk. 1:8 finds its proper conclusion in Mk. 1:10, and the curious juxtaposition of "Holy Spirit" and the fire of judgment in Lk. 3:16 (= Mt. 3:11) strongly sug-

---

[8]Since Luke here, as almost always, is further away from Mark than Matthew is, it follows that if we have to choose between Matthew and Luke in order to reconstruct the text of Q, Luke will most probably be nearer to Q and further from Mark. For the purpose of comparison therefore it is convenient to start from Luke rather than from Matthew.

gests that St. Luke is not here relying on any kind of duplicate *baptism* narrative, but on an edited version of Mark into which some extraneous eschatological material has been intruded—that is, on Matthew.

(iii) Streeter himself also pointed out in *The Four Gospels* that while it is easy to believe that St. Matthew and St. Luke may have known and used Mk. 1:12-13 in the composition of their Temptation narratives, it is very hard to believe that the borrowing could have been in the other direction, or, we might add, that the narratives could be regarded as parallel traditions. For Mark knows nothing of Jesus' *fasting*: on the contrary, he is fed by angels in the desert. But the first temptation, to turn stones to bread, necessarily presupposes an account of his fasting, and while it is possible that Matthew and Luke have amended and expanded Mark to allow for this, it is hardly credible that St. Mark should have passed over such a matter had he known of it.

There are good reasons therefore for supposing that the whole of Mk. 1:1-13 is a Markan compilation, and that there never was any parallel to it in the tradition. It seems likely that such traditional material as was employed by St. Mark was of a fragmentary nature only.

(*b*) A number of the changes made by both Matthew and Luke in the text of Mk. 1:1-13 are not so much additions to Mark as editorial amendments and improvements of the Markan material.

(i) The awkwardness of Mk. 1:1-4 is smoothed out in Matthew and Luke by the introduction of John and his preaching *before* the quotation from Isaiah which invests it with its proper eschatological significance. The *Markan* phrase ἐν τῇ ἐρήμῳ is actually used in this new position by both the other evangelists.

(ii) Both Matthew and Luke omit the first part of Mark's quotation, so that the reference to Isaiah ('Hσαίου τοῦ προφήτου, in each case) is now followed by the citation of Is. 40:3. Both use the first part of Mark's quotation later, in the same context (Mt. 11:10 = Lk. 7:27). The significance of this striking agreement against Mark should not be underestimated. Even if both St. Matthew and St. Luke had known this quotation in another context, their agreement in editing Mark in the same way at this point would still be something of a coincidence. But in fact there are two points which suggest that the original context of this quotation is in Mk. 1:2. In the first place, it can be omitted from Lk. 7:27 (or Mt. 11:10) without difficulty: in fact the messianic overtones of the saying make it rather out of place in a passage which finds its climax not in a description of the

messianic role of Jesus but in an exposition of the privileges of the kingdom. Secondly, the very fact that this curious combination of Ex. 23:20 and Mal. 3:1, which, as we have seen, is very probably a Markan construction, should appear in the *same form*[9] in a totally different context in both Matthew and Luke, suggests that a *single* editor of Mark is responsible for these changes.

(iii) If it is conceded that St. Mark was very probably the first to construct a connected account of John's baptizing, his messianic preaching, and his baptism of Jesus, it must be regarded as a surprising coincidence that both St. Matthew and St. Luke should introduce an account of John's preaching of repentance (Lk. 3:7-9) at the same point in the Markan narrative. This is of course an addition to rather than an amendment of Mark, and for that reason it is less conclusive than the other evidence we have cited. Nevertheless it is worth noting that equally suitable opportunities to introduce this teaching are provided by the original mention of John's preaching (Lk. 3:3; Mt. 3:2), and by the examples of John's preaching given at Lk. 3:17 (= Mt. 3:12).

(iv) Lk. 3:16-17 contain two very striking adaptations of Mark which are virtually identical with the changes made in the parallel narrative in Matthew. The clumsy Markan phrase, ἐγὼ ἐβάπτισα ὑμᾶς ὕδατι is reproduced by Matthew and Luke in the more polished form, ἐγὼ μὲν (ἐν) ὕδατι βαπτίζω ὑμᾶς, and both writers move the saying to a new and more emphatic position. Once the independence of Mark is conceded, this is in itself sufficient to demonstrate the dependence of Luke upon Matthew. But Lk. 3:16-17 contains another important agreement against Mark. We have already seen that the Q material in Lk. 3:17 (= Mt. 3:12) must be viewed as a deliberate expansion and modification of a narrative constructed by St. Mark. That both the other evangelists should have independently thought to modify Mark in this way would be something more than a coincidence, the more so as the eschatological teaching introduced so skillfully at this point is really quite out of context. What is even more remarkable is that both St. Matthew and St. Luke modify the last clause of Mk. 1:8 in the *same way,* to form a new and more sophisticated introduction to John's teaching, changing Mark's αὐτὸς δὲ βαπτίσει ὑμᾶς πνεύματι ἁγίῳ into αὐτὸς ὑμᾶς βαπτίσει ἐν πνεύματι ἁγίῳ (καὶ πυρί˙ οὗ τὸ πτύον . . .). What makes it quite certain that these

---

[9]Both Matthew and Luke also give the quotation a new conclusion, ἔμπροσθέν σου.

alterations are of an editorial nature, however, is that the new teaching appended to Mk. 1:8 is not in fact self-contained: it actually begins with a pronoun (οὗ) which refers back to the subject (αὐτός) of the clause taken from *Mark* which immediately precedes it.[10]

(v) There are two small but significant agreements against Mark in the Lukan Baptism narrative, Lk. 3:21, 22. First, it is not said that Jesus *saw* the heavens rent open (σχιζομένους), but rather that the heavens were opened (ἀνεῳχθῆναι). Secondly, the Spirit is no longer said to descend εἰς αὐτόν but ἐπ' αὐτόν (Jesus).[11] Once again, these are *improvements* of Mark.

(vi) Two further small agreements are to be found against Mark's temptation narrative, Mk. 1:12-13; the use of διάβολος (Lk. 4:2; Mt. 4:1) in place of Mark's σατανᾶς; and, of course, the fact that both the later evangelists modify Mk. 1:13 by referring to Jesus' fasting and hunger so as to fashion it into a suitable introduction for their Temptation narratives. We would suggest that once the priority and independence of Mark is conceded, these six groups of agreements against Mark provide conclusive evidence of St. Luke's knowledge of Matthew.

II

The second passage which we shall consider is Mk. 12:28-31 (Lk. 10:25-28), the "The Great Commandment." This passage is in a different category from the one we have just considered, for it cannot be shown that Mark was responsible for composing this narrative—indeed it is more than

---

[10]Abbot Butler points this out (*Originality*, 111); it was first noticed by Streeter himself (in *Oxford Studies*).

[11]The Lukan baptism narrative is at first sight so different from that of Mark that it may be doubted whether St. Luke could possibly have been using Mark as a main source at this point. However, the difficulty disappears when we see that St. Luke has his own particular view of the baptism which leads him to modify the text of Mark. He saves the reference to John's baptism of the people (Mk. 1:5) to this point in order to solve the difficulty presented by John's baptism of Jesus, which is thus included with that of "all the people," cf. J. M. Creed, *St. Luke*, 57. This enables him to place the account of Jesus' baptism, together with the conventional reference to Jesus' praying, within a genitive absolute—virtually within brackets. The fact that the Western text of Lk. 3:22 assimilates the voice at the baptism to the text of Ps. 2:7 demonstrates the tendency of St. Luke (or even of later Christian scribes) to correct Mark's quotations. It is significant that while St. Luke uses none of the additional material introduced here by Matthew, he does make use of two of Matthew's modifications of Mark.

likely that he was not. Nor does St. Luke follow Matthew's changes in Mark altogether exactly. We would suggest however that the changes which St. Luke does make in Mark are unintelligible unless we suppose that he knew Matthew's version of Mark.

The fact that the independence of Mark cannot be demonstrated makes the two outstanding agreements against Mark, the conversion of the questioner into a lawyer[12] who tempts Jesus ([ἐκ] πειράζων), and the omission of the opening words of the *Shema^c* (Mk. 12:29) less impressive than they would otherwise be. Nevertheless, the last point has some weight, for an agreement in omission involves a certain amount of coincidence even on a theory of parallel conflation. The most interesting feature of the passage, however, is the treatment of the quotation in Mk. 12:30. The number of the textual variants serves to demonstrate the difficulty which this last verse has caused to later scribes. We would suggest that the clue which offers the most likely solution to the problem is the fact that καρδία and διάνοια are virtually synonyms, and may be regarded as translation variants.[13] Mark's rendering of the *Shema^c* is in fact unique, and cannot be paralleled from any of the numerous versions of this formula which are at present known to us. Although Matthew gives the quotation in a more Semitic form therefore, replacing Mark's ἐκ by ἐν and restoring the traditional "three tones" of the *Shema^c*, his retention of διάνοια as well as καρδία makes it clear that he is not reproducing an independent tradition, but simply editing Mark. Nevertheless, he removes the implication that Jesus has quoted the *Shema^c* incorrectly by simply omitting the traditional introductory verse (Deut. 6:4; Mk. 12:29b). But once it is seen that Matthew is simply editing Mark at this point, then Luke's dependence on Matthew is quite clear. For Luke too can have known of no tradition other than

---

[12]Streeter, *Four Gospels*, 320, claimed that νομικός was interpolated into Matthew from Luke. Luke, however, normally uses the word in the plural in a rather formal manner (cf. Lk. 7:30; 11:45, 46; 14:3).

[13]Krister Stendahl, *The School of St. Matthew* (1954) 73ff., gives all the relevant textual evidence for this passage. He believes that Matthew is dependent on Mark, but does not draw any further conclusion in regard to Luke. Stendahl also draws attention to the fact that καρδία and διάνοια are translation variants (p. 75, n5). He denies that Mk. 12:30 has been influenced by 2 Kings, as suggested by A. H. McNeile, *The Gospel According to St. Matthew* (1961), on the grounds that it is very unlikely that a liturgical text would be subject to assimilation in this way. It may be, however, that Mark's form of the text indicates that its liturgical origins have been forgotten.

Mark which mistakenly included both καρδία and διάνοια, and yet he also reproduces both nouns. What is more, although he expands his text to include all four of the nouns given by Mark, he follows *Matthew* in putting διάνοια in the final place, and in replacing Mark's ἐκ by Matthew's ἐν before the last three nouns (according to the version of B—whose mixed prepositions are unlikely to have been produced by any kind of scribal correction). In the light of this, Luke's omission of the opening words of the *Shema^c* must also be attributed to his dependence on Matthew. The conclusion that he must have known Matthew's version of Mk. 12:28-31 is inescapable.

III

The Beelzebub Controversy (Mk. 3:22-27; Lk. 11:14-23). The key to this passage is to be found in Mk. 3:26. This seems to be an attempt to reconcile two distinct themes: the impossibility of Satan's expelling Satan (Mk. 3:23), and "United we stand, divided we fall" (Mk. 3:24, 25). Thus in Mk. 3:26 the expulsion of Satan (which is the main point of the story) is linked with the idea of the *division* of Satan (which is the point of Mk. 3:24, 25) by the suggestion that if Satan were, in the person of Jesus, to expel his own demons, this would be equivalent to attributing to Satan a kind of split personality. But while this successfully links the idea of expulsion with that of division, it does so at the expense of obscuring the real point of 3:23, namely that to drive out the servants of Satan is not the proper work of Satan himself, but of his enemies. The impression that this linking of sayings is editorial is confirmed by the fact that in 3:27 we have another similar, but slightly different saying, which Luke seems to know in a different version (Lk. 11:21,22). But if the association of Mk. 3:24-26 with Mk. 3:22-23 is the work of St. Mark then it is extremely unlikely that any hypothetical parallel version of this passage would have included parallels to Mk. 3:24-26, and especially to Mk. 3:26 (which we have seen to be editorial). But, in fact, Lk. 11:17-18 and Mt. 12:25-26 do have a number of agreements against Mk. 3:24-27. The following marked verses should make this sufficiently clear[14] (Lk. 11:17, 18):

---

[14]Direct borrowings from Mark are underlined with a single line, those from Matthew with a double one. Phrases borrowed from either of these sources which are reproduced in a modified form, are indicated by broken lines, single (Mark), or double (Matthew). It is also worth noting that ἐρημοῦν occurs in the New Testament on three other occasions only, all in the Apocalypse.

αὐτὸς δὲ εἰδὼς αὐτῶν τὰ διανοήματα εἶπεν αὐτοῖς·
πᾶσα βασιλεία ἐφ' ἑαυτὴν διαμερισθεῖσα
ἐρηνοῦται καὶ οἶκος ἐπὶ οἶκον πίπτει.
εἰ δὲ καὶ ὁ σατανᾶς ἐφ' ἑαυτὸν διεμερίσθη
πῶς σταθήσεται ἡ βασιλεία αὐτοῦ;
ὅτι λέγετε ἐν βεελζεβοὺλ ἐκβάλλειν με
τὰ δαιμόνια. . . .

Corroborative evidence of St. Luke's dependence on Matthew is provided by Lk. 11:14. This appears to be a free version of Mt. 12:22; but
St. Luke's reference to the 'throwing out' of the demon, and his substitution of a deaf demon for one that is both deaf and dumb (Mt. 12:22) suggests that St. Luke has made use of Mt. 9:32-34 as well as 12:22, 23 in
writing this section. This is confirmed by St. Luke's use of Mt. 9:34 in
rewriting Mk. 3:22 (Lk. 11:15).[15] Finally, the fact that St. Luke follows
Matthew in adding another independent saying (Lk. 11:23 = Mt. 12:30)
to the Markan narrative also shows St. Luke's knowledge of Matthew.
(The saying occurs in a different form at Mk. 9:40.) It has a significant part
to play in Matthew's version of the Beelzebub Controversy. Mk. 3:28-29
seem to imply that *any* blasphemy is forgivable except blasphemy against
the Spirit. But the insertion of Mt. 12:30 before Mt. 12:31 (= Mk. 3:28)
prepares the way for St. Matthew to change a pronouncement about the
forgiveness of blasphemy in general into a concession to those who are
"against" Jesus that their words will be forgiven (Mt. 12:32) *unless* they
blaspheme the Spirit. In this way Mark's prophetic warning is turned into
a kind of law prohibiting blasphemy against the Spirit. But Mt. 12:30 (=
Lk. 11:23) fulfills no useful function at all in *Luke*, and its presence can

---

[15]Streeter regarded Mt. 9:34 as a "Western interpolation" (*Four Gospels*, 170), and
supposed that Mt. 9:34 had been interpolated from Lk. 14:15. The purpose of this interpolation remains obscure however, and we may well think that the scribe who was responsible for it employed a great deal of skill to very little purpose. For, once Mt. 9:34 is
deleted, there is little to connect this incident with the Beelzebub Controversy, and it is hard
to believe that a scribe could have had any reason for making an interpolation of this kind.
Mt. 12:22, 23 is really a duplicate of the exorcism in Mt. 9:32-34, and it is introduced in
order to allow St. Matthew to drop the unedifying story given in Mk. 3:20, 21. Meanwhile
Mt. 9:34 provides a kind of remote preparation for the Beelzebub Controversy when it
comes. This view of the matter is confirmed by the fact that St. Matthew also introduces a
reference to Beelzebub at 10:25.

be explained only on the theory that St. Luke knew Matthew's version of Mk. 9:27, 28.

The study of the major agreements of Matthew and Luke against Mark in these three passages appears to leave us with only two alternatives. Either we must suppose that St. Mark knew and modified "Q" (or even Matthew), or we must suppose that St. Luke knew Matthew as well as Mark. In every case we have considered, it is Mark who appears to give the more primitive version, and it is obvious that the simplest solution to the problem is that St. Luke made use of Matthew. Nevertheless, there is one other possibility.

Hawkins suggested[16] that some of the agreements against Mark which we have been considering may be explained on the theory that both St. Matthew and St. Luke made use of a deutero-Mark, a kind of second edition which has since been lost. This would explain all the evidence which we have so far considered. There is however one strong objection to this hypothesis. In a number of places, St. Luke appears to conflate St. Matthew's "improved" version of Mark with the original; examples in the passages which we have been considering may be found at Lk. 3:4a and 3:16. There are a sufficient number of such cases to suggest that if St. Luke knew deutero-Mark, he must have known our Mark as well. The same can be said of St. Matthew. In Matthew those passages where the major agreements occur are found in their Markan position: Luke on the other hand places them in the middle of the Q sections of his gospel (with the exception of the Baptism–Temptation narrative, of course, which could hardly be moved from its Markan position). This suggests that the major agreements and the Q material are in some way related to each other, and, further, that if they are both to be explained by reference to a deutero-Mark, then the order of deutero-Mark must be represented by Luke rather than Matthew. But in that case we must suppose that St. Matthew also knew *both* versions of Mark, and corrected the order of deutero-Mark against that of the original. It seems unlikely that both the later synoptists would have known two versions of Mark, and it is simpler to suppose that Matthew itself is the second edition of Mark on which St. Luke relied.[17]

---

[16] Hawkins, *Horae Synopticae*, 152.

[17] C. S. C. Williams, *Peake's Commentary*, rev. ed. (1962) 749, sec. 654a, also denied the possibility of two editions of Mark, on the grounds that it is improbable that both re-

There are of course a number of well-known objections to the theory that St. Luke knew Matthew, most of which are conveniently set out by Mr. Blyth Martin in an article in *Theology*.[18] There is no space to do justice to his argument here, but we would suggest that his objections are valid only against the form of this theory which supposes that St. Luke must have used Matthew as a *main source*. The discrepancies between the *order* of the Q material in Matthew and its order in Luke, for example, are easily explained if we suppose that St. Luke regarded the Matthean material as of secondary importance, and simply fitted it into his own scheme at what seemed to him to be suitable points. On the face of it, a greater difficulty

---

dactions would have lacked the original ending. This is not altogether convincing however: apart from the question as to whether there ever was an "original ending" of Mark other than the one we have, it is difficult to see why deutero-Mark should not have been constructed from the same mutilated edition of Mark used by St. Matthew, St. Luke and ourselves. The connection between the Q material and the major agreements is a more significant point. If we assume that St. Luke read Matthew, however, this connection is easily explained on the theory that St. Luke earmarked certain passages of Matthew for his own use, and then simply inserted this material (some of which would have been originally Markan—hence the major agreements), into the non-Markan section of his own gospel. This theory also explains those coincidences in order between the Q material in Matthew and that in Luke noted by Vincent Taylor, *JTS* 4 (1953): 27-31, while it allows for those dissimilarities which have led Dr. C. K. Barrett, "Q, A Re-examination," *ET* (1942-1943): 320 [reprinted in this volume] and others to doubt whether Q could be regarded as a single document.

[18]R. H. Blyth Martin, "The Indispensibility of Q," *Theology* 59 (1956): 182-88. An interesting attempt to justify the Q hypothesis is to be found in a recent article by F. G. Downing, "Towards the Rehabilitation of Q," *NTS* 11 (1964-1965): 169-81 [reprinted in this volume]. Mr. Downing emphasizes the importance of the passages we have considered (along with others), but assumes throughout his study that there is a real possibility that Q may have contained large sections closely parallel to Mark. He therefore sees in St. Luke's divergences from Mark a sign that he is following Q, and gives a number of instances where Matthew follows Mark, and Luke does not. He regards these divergences not as evidence that St. Luke was rewriting his sources, but as an indication that he was following an alternative source: " . . . Luke seems to ignore just the Markan material that Matthew has seen fit to reproduce exactly. . . . He seems to be reproducing Matthew's material independently of Matthew's use of Mark" (176). But these two statements seem to be at variance with each other. Mr. Downing does not deny that Matthew makes *some* use of Mark even where he does not quote him exactly. The fact that Luke sometimes seems to avoid those passages of Mark which Matthew quotes exactly does not suggest that he is following Q but that he "deliberately . . . [ignores] just the Markan material that Matthew has seen fit to reproduce exactly!"

is provided by the fact that the Lukan version of the Q material often appears to be the more original. Two things must be said about this. In the first place, the fact that St. Luke may have read Matthew does not exclude the possibility of his having access to other traditions. An obvious example is provided by the parable of the 'Great Supper' (Lk. 14:15-24), which is clearly a parallel tradition to Mt. 22:1-10. It is very probable that a number of St. Luke's divergences from Matthew should be explained on the same hypothesis. Secondly, however, it is clear that St. Luke often prefers to rewrite his sources to produce a version which is clearly his own. This tendency can be illustrated from his account of the Transfiguration (Lk. 9:28-36), where St. Luke uses only 51 of the 121 words of Mark (Mt. has 83), and adds 129 words of his own (as compared with Matthew's 69). It is in fact often the dialogue which St. Luke reports fairly faithfully (cf. Lk. 9:33, 35), while the narrative portions of Mark are sometimes heavily rewritten.

Our conclusion is therefore a modest one. It seems very likely that there will always be some doubt about the sources of St. Luke, as of the other synoptic gospels, just because the evangelists saw themselves not as compilers but as *authors*. Our contention is that editorial improvements, and these alone, provide a real indication of the true relationship among the first three gospels. It is this kind of evidence which shows that Matthew and Luke depend on Mark. It is the same kind of evidence which alone can show where Luke is dependent on Matthew. In one sense therefore the Synoptic Problem may well turn out to be insoluble. There will always be room for argument about the sources of the synoptic gospels. Nevertheless, we believe that the study of the major agreements of Matthew and Luke against Mark greatly strengthens the probability that Matthew was *one* of the sources employed by St. Luke in the composition of his gospel.

A FRESH APPROACH TO Q

W. R. Farmer*

Farmer observes with respect to the content or even the existence of "Q" that there is great uncertainty amounting to a theoretical impasse for contemporary scholarship. In this essay he seeks to contribute toward the resolution of this impasse by exploring the question: "How is material common to Matthew and Luke (that is, material of the so-called Double *and* Triple Tradition) viewed on the Griesbach hypothesis?"

Farmer views Matthew as having composed his gospel first out of a great variety of preexisting Greek texts, including several important collections of *logia* material. In addition to having a copy of Matthew before him, the author of Luke also had access to other source material—not another "source"—but a plurality of other written Greek texts. Most of what on the two-document hypothesis is called "Q" material is best explained on the Griesbach hypothesis as material Luke copied from Matthew, although this must not obscure the fact that the Griesbach hypothesis affords support for the view that there were collections of the sayings of Jesus circulating in the churches at a very early date.

Farmer notes that on the Griesbach hypothesis Luke combined his sources, in general utilizing in a very free manner the basic outline of Mat-

*W. R. Farmer, "A Fresh Approach to Q," *Christianity, Judaism, and Other Greco-Roman Cults: Studies for Morton Smith at Sixty*, ed. Jacob Neusner, Part One: New Testament (Leiden: E. J. Brill, 1975) 39-50.

thew, except in that section of his gospel constituted by chapters 12-18. In doing so he freely alters Matthew's outline and frequently substitutes tradition from his other sources for corresponding material in Matthew, for example, birth stories, genealogy, parables, gnomic material, stories, and so on, and often compiles material from different sources according to an intelligible principle of association.

The idea of ''Q'' is currently exercising a significant influence on scholarship. That there was such an early collection of the sayings of Jesus, and that scholars have reliable access to this collection through the Gospels of Matthew and Luke is presupposed in most contemporary speculation about the origins of Christianity, and in attempted reconstructions of early Christian history and theology. Ironically, never in the last century has uncertainty concerning the content or even the existence of ''Q'' been greater than it is at present.[1] This points to a serious difficulty amounting to a theoretical impasse for contemporary scholarship.

---

[1]Richard A. Edwards in ''An Approach to a Theology of Q,'' *JR* (1971): 247-69, represents the current tendency to build on ''Q.'' He reviews earlier work in this tradition and cites the writing of Norman Perrin, M. Jack Suggs, James M. Robinson, William A. Beardslee, and Paul D. Meyer among others. R. Schnackenburg in his review of D. Lührmann's *Die Redaktion der Logienquelle* (1969), published in *Biblische Zeitschrift* (1971): 279-81, recognizes a new theological interest in ''Q'' and surveys Roman Catholic work on the Christology and theology of ''Q'' recently completed and in progress. Support for the ''Q'' hypothesis among scholars in recent years has come from E. L. Bradby, ''In Defence of Q,'' *ET* 68 (1956-1957): 315-18 [reprinted in this volume]; F. G. Downing, ''Towards the Rehabilitation of Q,'' *NTS* 11 (1964-1965): 169-81 [reprinted in this volume]; W. H. B. Martin, ''The Indispensibility of Q,'' *Theology* 59 (1956): 182-88. Critics dubious of Q include A. W. Argyle, ''Agreements Between Matthew and Luke,'' *ET* 73 (1961-1962): 19-22; A. M. Farrer, ''On Dispensing with Q,'' *Studies in the Gospels*, ed. D. E. Nineham (1955), 55-88 [reprinted in this volume]; J. Jeremias, *New Testament Theology* (1971) 1:38-39; S. Petrie, '' 'Q' Is Only What You Make It,'' *NT* 3 (1959): 28-33; R. T. Simpson, ''The Major Agreements of Matthew and Luke Against Mark,'' *NTS* 12 (1966): 273-84 [reprinted in this volume]. In their ''Once More—Statistics and Q,'' *HTR* 64 (1971): 59-78, Charles E. Carlston and Dennis Norlin are almost certainly correct in rejecting Jeremias's views that ''Q'' material in Matthew and Luke can be explained by appeal simply to the hypothesis of their dependence on oral tradition. But their dependence on the work of A. M. Honoré for their confidence in the two-document hypothesis has been criticized by David Wenham whose analysis of the statistical work of Honoré raises serious questions about its reliability. See A. M. Honoré, ''A Statistical Study of the Synoptic Problem,'' *NT* 10 (1968): 95-147, and Wenham's analysis in ''The Synoptic Problem Revisited,'' *Tyndal Bulletin* (1973): 13-17.

What follows is intended as a contribution toward the resolution of this impasse, and presupposes the viability of the Griesbach hypothesis. Few adherents of the two-document hypothesis are unaware of the serious difficulties that face the critic who attempts to explain all the synoptic data on that hypothesis, and a growing number of experts are becoming aware of the real advantages of the Griesbach hypothesis.[2] For this reason it may be a timely exercise for some critics (certainly including those who while continuing to adhere loosely to the two-document hypothesis are open-minded on the question) to reflect on the problem of "Q" from a fresh perspective. One way in which this can be done, and the way taken in this essay, is by attempting to explore the question: "How is material common to Matthew and Luke viewed on the Griesbach hypothesis?"[3]

On the Griesbach hypothesis the Gospel of Matthew was composed before Mark, Luke and John. In writing the first volume of his two-volume work, the author of Luke-Acts followed the general outline of Matthew but often substituted different tradition for that found in Matthew. Mark and John were written after Matthew and Luke, which accords with our earliest external evidence bearing on the question of the sequence in which the gospels were written, namely the testimony of Clement of Alexandria who reports that he "received it from the elders that the gospels with genealogies were written before those without genealogies."

The problem of understanding the relationship between Matthew and Luke is both constituted and complicated by the circumstance that, as Augustine noted, "no one of the evangelists did his work in ignorance of that of his predecessors." For those like Augustine, who believe that the Gospels were written in the traditional order Matthew, Mark, Luke, and John, the point at which to begin a study of their literary interdependence would be to consider the relationship between Matthew and Mark. On the Griesbach hypothesis, however, the point at which to begin is with the relationship between Matthew and Luke. There is some advantage, therefore, in concentrating attention upon the material common to Matthew and Luke.

---

[2]For the view that the Griesbach hypothesis has emerged as the chief rival of the two-document hypothesis, see Robert Morgenthaler, *Statistiche Synopse* (1971) 27; W. R. Farmer, "A Response to Robert Morgenthaler's *Statistiche Synopse*," *Biblica* 54 (1973): 417-33.

[3] This essay was first prepared at the request of M. Jack Suggs, Chairman of the Gospel Seminar of the Society of Biblical Literature, for the first meeting of the Task Group on the Sequence of the Gospels held in New York, 1970, and chaired by William Beardslee.

For on the Griesbach hypothesis, this material can be considered without reference to the complicated problem of what Mark and John may have done. However, before considering this material on the Griesbach hypothesis, we first need to consider how it has traditionally been treated on the two-document hypothesis.

On the two-document hypothesis, which presupposes that Matthew and Luke have independently copied Mark, the material common to Matthew and Luke is frequently divided into two categories: double tradition and triple tradition. On the Griesbach hypothesis, however, these categories are otiose. The double tradition is simply material taken by Luke from Matthew which Mark did not use. Whereas, the so-called triple tradition is material Luke took from Matthew which the author of Mark conflated into his gospel. In other words, on the Griesbach hypothesis, the "double" and "triple" tradition categories are artificial literary creations of the two-document proponents and have no meaning at all so long as one is restricting his attention to Matthew and Luke. For all those who conventionally think in "two-document" terms, it is important to grasp the point that on the Griesbach hypothesis the material common to Matthew and Luke is inclusive of what is regarded as the double *and* triple tradition on the two-document hypothesis. Once this point is firmly grasped, several matters which on the two-document view are perplexing, find a ready explanation.

For example, on the two-document hypothesis, it has often been noted that, although the double tradition has come to Matthew and Luke from some early written collection of the sayings of Jesus, this document seems also to have included material that would have been more appropriate in another gospel, for example, John the Baptist tradition, temptation story, healing of the centurion's son, and so on.

Speaking broadly, on the Griesbach hypothesis material common to Matthew and Luke includes whatever Luke took from Matthew, *plus* whatever Luke may have copied from other sources closely paralleling material copied by Matthew. Sometimes it appears that the author of Luke has conflated or combined texts he found in his special source material with the Matthean form of the same tradition. The Parable of the Talents may be a case in point (Lk. 19:12-27 ‖ Mt. 25:14-30). In other cases, as for example with the Parable of the Great Feast (Lk. 14:16-24 ‖ Mt. 22:1-10) and the Parable of the Lost Sheep (Lk. 15:4-7 ‖ Mt. 18:12-14), the author of Luke has simply chosen one form of the tradition to the exclusion

of the other. That is, these parables in Luke have been taken from his special source material, and the form of the same parables in Matthew has exercised no visible influence upon the Lukan text. In all such cases where the author of Luke had access to sayings of Jesus in his special source material which have parallels in Matthew, he was in a position to preserve these sayings in a form which plausibly would be closer to the original than the same sayings as found in Matthew.

As early as the first half of the nineteenth century it was noted that sometimes Luke and sometimes Matthew has a saying of Jesus that seems to be more original than the parallel form of the saying in the other Gospel. This led some of the nineteenth-century advocates of the Griesbach hypothesis to postulate that behind Matthew and Luke was an extensive proto-gospel, known to both evangelists, and that sometimes one evangelist preserved the text of this proto-gospel more faithfully than did the other. Some advocates of the Griesbach hypothesis went so far as to hold that Matthew and Luke probably were entirely independent of one another, in which case all the material common to these two Gospels would have been derived from this imagined proto-gospel.

Our present two-gospel hypothesis developed out of this latter form of the proto-gospel hypothesis: namely Matthew and Luke have copied an extensive proto-gospel (much longer than Mark since it included such material as the sermon on the mount) *and* they were otherwise quite independent of one another. The essential new element which paved the way for the two-document hypothesis was the idea of an extensive collection of sayings copied by Matthew and Luke. This removed the necessity that the proto-gospel account for the great bulk of the sayings of Jesus common to Matthew and Luke, and paved the way for Holtzmann and his followers to think of the proto-gospel as an "Ur-Marcus." Sometimes the collection of sayings ("Q") was conceived as a second proto-gospel, that is, a proto-Matthew, so that the two proto documents behind our canonical Gospels were Ur-Markus and Ur-Matthaeus, as with Bernhard Weiss. As between Holtzmann and Bernhard Weiss, it was the former's views that prevailed in the form the two-document hypothesis had assumed by the time of Streeter; that is, Matthew and Luke have independently copied Mark and "Q."

The never ending problem of defining the content of "Q," or the problem of the overlap between Mark and "Q," or the problem of whether "Q" is a single written source or a plurality of written and/or oral sources,

all disappear on the Griesbach hypothesis, at least as that hypothesis can be understood and defended *today*. We must emphasize the word "today" because an important development in Gospel studies has taken place since the heyday of this hypothesis in the nineteenth century. This development concerns Form Criticism.

Before the advent of Form Criticism there was a tendency to think in terms of dating all material in a document at the time of the composition of that document. Thus when it was discovered that what was believed to be the earliest Gospel (Matthew) was written after the eyewitness period, a discovery effectively verified by 1832 in the work of Sieffert, the reliability of the Gospels as historical sources for a knowledge of Jesus was seriously challenged. The radical solution was to deny the possibility of reliable knowledge of Jesus, and out of this developed the Christ myth theory according to which Jesus never existed as an historical figure and the Christ of the Gospels was a social creation of a messianic community.

A reactionary solution to this development was to deny the validity of the historical-critical method and to retreat into Orthodoxy. However, most theologians chose what came to be called a mediating solution. They accepted a late date for Matthew and the other canonical Gospels but moved around these late Gospels in various ways to get to the earlier eyewitness period. In moving around these late canonical Gospels, theologians still thought in terms of datable documents rather than in form-critical terms. The proto-gospel and sayings collection in which they believed were datable to the eyewitness period by the external evidence of Papias. According to Schleiermacher, to whom we are indebted for the origin of the Logia idea, when Papias referred to Mark it was not to our canonical Mark, obviously late, but to an Ur-Markus. And when he referred to τὰ λόγια he referred to a collection of the sayings of Jesus made by the Apostle Matthew. By adhering to texts where two or three of the Synoptic Gospels agreed, scholars in the mediating school were confident that the texts of these "datable" (to the apostolic period) documents could be reconstructed in such a fashion as to constitute a reliable foundation for their theological systems.

The collapse of such nineteenth-century liberal theologies is well known. Nineteenth-century liberal theologies, however, did not die easily. They were replaced by dialectical theology only after considerable polemicizing during which the attempt to ground theology upon the historical Jesus was effectively discredited. This theological polemicizing has not

only distorted our understanding of the importance of source criticism, it has also obscured the full importance of the discipline of form criticism, which came to the fore at the very time when nineteenth-century liberal theology was being discredited.

Only in recent times has it become clear that form criticism can put the quest for the historical Jesus upon a secure basis. Form criticism enables the critic to recognize that in a particular Gospel not all the material is to be dated at the time of that Gospel's composition. The Gospels preserve older traditions. Some of the sayings attributed to Jesus in the Gospels go back to Jesus himself. The task of delineating the origin and development of the Jesus tradition in the Gospels is not complete. But no one today who is engaged in this task labors under the assumption that he must discover some Gospel datable to the eyewitness period—nor even some particular apostolic collection ("Q") of the sayings of Jesus. Form criticism enables the critic to treat each literary unit separately, and frees the student to think in terms of a multiplicity of pregospel sources. Actually Herder in the eighteenth century, and later Schleiermacher in his classic work on Luke, anticipated this development. But not until Dibelius and Bultmann did this understanding of the development of the Gospel tradition begin to become normative among students of the Gospels.

All this has been said preliminary to our approaching the Gospels of Matthew and Luke on the Griesbach hypothesis. The historical note helps explain why today an adherent of the view that Luke copied Matthew, and that Mark worked with both Matthew and Luke, will generally work with the hypothesis somewhat differently than those nineteenth-century scholars who held this same basic solution to the Synoptic Problem but oft-times combined it with the notion of a proto-gospel and its corollary, the independence of Matthew and Luke.

In any case, the twentieth-century adherent of the Griesbach hypothesis will not do as did F. C. Baur, and think of Matthew as a reliable recension of an earlier apostolic Gospel of the Hebrews. Rather will he think of the author of Matthew composing his gospel out of a great variety of preexisting materials, including several important collections of logia material. As examples of such preexisting collections we may consider those found in the following sections of Matthew: 5:1-7:29; 10:5-42; 13:3-50; 18:1-35; 23:1-39; 24:4-25:46. Some of these collections of sayings materials may have been known to the evangelist Matthew combined in one or more large composite sources from which he has made selections. How-

ever, it is equally likely that they all come to him first independently and probably from different communities. Or the evangelist may in some cases have combined even these sections of his gospel out of materials which came to him separately. Such questions must be decided upon the basis of redaction and tradition criticism. On the Griesbach hypothesis, there is no redactional evidence to suggest that the author of Matthew has composed any of the tradition in these collections. On the contrary they all seem to have been edited into his work largely unaltered from preexisting texts written in Greek. These preexisting Greek texts seem themselves to have been relatively late and represented the Jesus tradition at a rather advanced stage of its development (post-Pauline). Form criticism, redaction, and tradition criticism, however, enable the student to work with these developed collections of the Jesus tradition and assist him in separating the earlier material from its later modifications.

To a considerable degree, on the Griesbach hypothesis, the study of Matthew can be carried forward with little regard to the Lukan text. However, this is certainly not the case in studying Luke. Here there must be frequent reference to the question of what the author of Luke may have done with the text of Matthew.

Luke's Treatment of Matthew
on the Griesbach Hypothesis

The beginning of wisdom in dealing with the question of the relationship between Luke and Matthew on the Griesbach hypothesis is to recognize that in addition to having a copy of Matthew before him, the author of Luke also had access to other source material—not *another* "source" be it noted—but a plurality of other written Greek texts. Much of Luke's special material has no parallel in Matthew. Some of it, however, as noted above, corresponds to the materials utilized by the author of Matthew, and in some cases this correspondence is so close as to suggest common written sources. In no case, however, are these latter indications of common written sources extensive enough to support the *conventional* "Q" hypothesis. Most of what on the two-document hypothesis is called "Q" material is best explained on the Griesbach hypothesis as material Luke copied from Matthew. This must not obscure the fact, however, that the Griesbach hypothesis affords support for the view that there were collections of the sayings of Jesus circulating in the churches at a very early date.

For on the Griesbach hypothesis it is necessary to postulate such collections not only to explain a great part of the text of Matthew, but also to explain much of the text of Luke.[4]

If one makes a careful redactional and form-critical analysis of Luke on the view that its author had access to a copy of Matthew, it is not dif-

---

[4]On the surface it may appear that to concede the necessity of positing the existence of collections of "sayings material" behind Matthew and Luke is to surrender the advantage of the economy of hypotheses. I do not accept this as a valid criticism of the Griesbach hypothesis. In chapter 6 of my book, *The Synoptic Problem* [reprinted in this volume], I point out that while it is possible to multiply the number of hypotheses by imagining that the evangelists used hypothetical sources, and it might even be legitimate to do this, that procedurally one ought to try to explain the verbatim agreement between the synoptics without appealing to hypothetical sources. The reason for this procedure is not that the simplest explanation is necessarily the correct one, but it is wrong to multiply hypothetical possibilities unnecessarily. I do not say that it is wrong to hypothecate a hypothetical source if it is necessary. As indicated above, on the Griesbach hypothesis (and indeed on *all* historical-critical solutions to the Synoptic Problem), it is necessary to postulate collections of Jesus tradition. This is done because of the indications that the evangelists have copied such sources. This is clearly the case with Lukan parables. Many of these parables are not in Matthew. Where did the author of Luke get them? He must have gotten them from some source other than Matthew. So one is not in that case hypothecating source material unnecessarily. The evidence requires it. There is nothing wrong in hypothecating the existence of an otherwise unknown source or sources if there exists evidence that is best explained thereby. But for the sake of economy this is not to be done without good reason. This is not an infallible rule, but it is accepted procedure in literary criticism as well as in other disciplines, and one which commends itself by the results achieved when it is followed compared to whose which are achieved when it is ignored. This relates to step one. In step three I take this matter up again. While it is possible to conceive of an infinite number of variations of the 18 basic relationships between these documents, by positing additional hypothetical documents, these 18 should be given first consideration. This does not mean that the investigator should assume that there were no additional hypothetical documents: on the contrary, he should be open to the possibility that such actually existed. There are instances in literary historical studies where circumstantial evidence requires the investigator to posit the existence of a document for which he has no direct evidence. But a critic should not posit the existence of hypothetical sources until he has made an attempt to solve the problem without appeal to such sources. In other words, on the Griesbach hypothesis, in dealing with the parables in Luke, the proper procedure requires that one look at all parables in Luke that are parallel to Matthew, and consider the possibility that Luke has copied them from Matthew before concluding that they have not been copied from Matthew but in fact come from some source or sources quite independent of Matthew. One does not need to assume the existence of a source otherwise unknown until he has checked out the possibilities of accounting for these materials in terms of existing documents. In order to explain most of the vast amount of material common to Matthew and Luke on the Griesbach hypothesis one need not hypothecate an extensive collection of sayings copied by Matthew and Luke ("Q"), but it *is* necessary to hypothecate the existence of a large amount of parabolic material copied by Luke which material is quite independent of the source material copied by Matthew.

Only after the investigator has been unable to understand the relationship between Matthew, Mark and Luke without appealing to unknown sources, is he justified in hypothecating the existence of such unknown sources as may be required to explain phenomena which otherwise would be inexplicable. This is a very serious hang-up for those who hold

ficult to understand the problem of the relationship between these two Gospels. In general it may be said that the author of Luke is at no point required to behave in a manner unnatural to an author engaged in the production of a work like Luke-Acts. For example in working with Matthew, the author of Luke tends to move forward through this source. This is a natural literary practice for an author or editor to follow—especially when dealing with narrative material.

The fact that the author of Luke has utilized material in Matthew is obscured by the circumstance that he worked forward in Matthew not once,

---

to the Markan hypothesis. They feel that this way of proceeding rules out in advance the two-document hypothesis. It does not, however, rule out in advance the Griesbach hypothesis. It simply says that before you consider the two-document hypothesis, if you are going to proceed in a sound way, consider explaining the phenomena without appealing to "Q." If you need "Q," according to an arrangement where Matthew and Luke are dependent upon Mark, well, then see whether you can put Matthew first and Luke second and Mark third, or in some other arrangement and explain the phenomena, and if you find that as a matter of fact you can explain the phenomena in one or more of these ways, then there's no necessity for thinking that the true paradigm is provided by the one necessitating "Q." When I say explain all the phenomena, I mean all of the phenomena that are relevant to the synoptic problem, and the synoptic problem classically is the problem of explaining the literary relationship between Matthew, Mark, and Luke.

There is in Chapter 17 of Luke some apocalyptical material that is parallel to apocalyptical material in Matthew 24, and it seems to me that the Lukan form of that material is more original than the form of the material in Matthew 24. Therefore, I cannot derive that apocalyptical material in Luke 17 from Matthew 24. At that point it is necessary for me to hypothecate, just as I do in the case of the special Lukan parabolic material, another source, an apocalyptical source, that Luke has copied. In my book I make the point that that source, copied by Luke on the one hand in Chapter 17, might have been copied by Matthew at an earlier period in Chapter 24. Professor Hare of Pittsburgh Theological Seminary has made the point that here I have a "Q." What I actually have is the acknowledgment of the possibility that in this one instance I may have a source common to Luke and to Matthew. That's not an impossibility. "But then why not broaden it," asks Professor Hare, "and use it to explain all of the other agreements between Matthew and Luke" (quoted from "A Review of *The Synoptic Problem*," a transcription (mimeo) from tapes of a colloquy held at Pittsburgh Theological Seminary, April 3, 1967). I simply answer that I do not do that because that is not the simplest way to explain the evidence. In most instances you can explain the text of Luke by simply recognizing that he has modfied the text of Matthew. Now, if one can explain most of the text of Luke without hypothecating an extended "Q"-like source, with miracle stories, John the Baptist tradition, etc., in my view that is still a definite advantage of the Griesbach hypothesis over the Markan hypothesis, where the whole of the agreement between Matthew and Luke not covered in Mark must be explained in terms of "Q." In other words, it is not simply a question, "How many hypothetical sources do you need?" but "How extensive is the dependence upon these hypothetical sources which is required in order to account for the evidence?" It would be possible to extend considerably the list of such passages in Luke and Matthew which call for a common source or sources, and one would still not be required to hypothecate anything like the "Q" that has traditionally and conveniently been required by the two-document theory. If, however, one thinks of "Q" not as a document written in Greek which, if it were available, would account for the verbatim agreement between Matthew and Luke where this agree-

but repeatedly. A further obscuring factor is the circumstance that between chapters twelve and eighteen he abandons Matthean order rather completely and utilizes material from Matthew following the basic order of some other source or sources. In fact on the Griesbach hypothesis it becomes clear that essentially what the author of Luke did was to combine his sources, in general utilizing in a very free manner the basic outline of Matthew, except in that section of his gospel constituted by chapters 12-18. In so doing he freely alters Matthew's outline and frequently substitutes traditions from his other sources for corresponding material in Matthew, such as birth stories, genealogy, parables, gnomic material, stories, and so on, and often compiles material from different sources according to an intelligible principle of association. In the successive redactional movements of going back over and then moving forward through Matthew made while composing chapters 9-12, the author of Luke incorporates into his text material from his other sources while following the general sequence of this material in Matthew. For chapters 12-18, however, as has been pointed out, he appears to follow the order of another source or sources while continuing to compile material according to the same principle of association, thus further utilizing material remaining in his text of Matthew *but not at all in Matthean order*.

At 18:15 the author of Luke returns to Matthew and follows that narrative freely to the end of his Gospel. This is all perfectly in accord with intelligible literary practice. However, on the two-document hypothesis, where one attempts to view Lukan and Matthean order through dependence upon Mark, and treats their editorial dependence on Mark separately from their dependence on "Q," the whole procedure is obscured, and we consequently find the ironical and confusing situation where *differences* in the order between Matthew and Luke in so-called "Q" material are appealed to as evidence that Luke did not know Matthew, thus lending credence to the existence of "Q" (Streeter), while *similarity* in the order of "Q" material is appealed to as evidence that Matthew and Luke did know "Q" (Taylor), which again supports belief in the existence of "Q."[5] Such

---

ment cannot be accounted for through the dependence of Matthew and Luke upon Mark, but rather thinks in terms of "Q" as a loose term to refer generally to sayings materials commonly available to Matthew and Luke, the grounds for discussion are open on a new basis.

[5]B. H. Streeter, *The Four Gospels* (1953) 183; Vincent Taylor, "The Order of Q," *JTS* (1953): 27-31, and "The Original Order of Q," *New Testament Essays*, ed. A. J. B. Hig-

similarity as exists in order between Matthew and Luke is most naturally explained by direct dependence of Luke on Matthew, and such differences as exist seem to me to pose no serious problem for an author-editor responsible for a freely created work like Luke-Acts. In fact, the most unusual differences that do exist, when once properly understood in terms of Lukan dependence on Matthew, are actually supportive of the view that the author of Luke either had access to Matthew or to the text of a gospel very similar to the text of Matthew. The demonstration of this particular contention, however, requires a full exhibition of the redactional procedures of the author of Luke, and goes beyond the scope of this paper. This paper has been designed to orient the reader (especially the reader who, while he is open to the Griesbach hypothesis, still tends to think in "two-document" terms), to the manner in which one approaches the general problem of explaining the material common to Matthew and Luke on the Griesbach hypothesis.

The import of this discussion for the resolution of the present impasse over 'Q' is that it opens up and initiates an exploration of a way in which theological and historical projects can continue to presuppose a considerable corpus of early Jesus *logia* tradition without necessitating any dependence on a dubious hypothetical document written in Greek, which, if we could find it, would help explain the differences between Matthew and Luke in passages common to those Gospels, but not paralleled in Mark. This description has for over one hundred years given scholars the technical meaning of "Q." In this sense "Q" is not only problematic as most critics understand, but as this study has shown, it is unnecessary for the pursuit of responsible historical and theological study of early Christianity, providing one accepts the validity of form criticism and/or the viability of the Griesbach hypothesis, or for that matter any solution of the synoptic problem which allows for and envisions the author of Luke having access to and making extensive use of the Gospel of Matthew.

---

gins (1959) 246-269 [reprinted in this volume]. Such partial, selective, and preferential treatment of the evidence by critics is clearly explained in Thomas Kuhn's discussion of the role of basic paradigms in scientific communities in his book *The Structure of Scientific Revolutions* (1962).

THE ARGUMENT FROM ORDER AND THE RELATIONSHIP BETWEEN MATTHEW AND LUKE

E. P. Sanders*

Sanders's purpose is to reexamine some of the facts on which the argument from order rests and to see whether they do support Matthew's and Luke's independent use of Mark and Q, or whether it appears that there are agreements between Matthew and Luke that cannot be accounted for by their independent use of the same sources.

Sanders cites the six reasons F. H. Woods used to prove that the original basis of the Synoptic Gospels coincided in its *range* and *order* with our Mark and then proceeds in his essay to consider more closely two of Woods's points: (1) the order of the whole of Mark, excepting of course what is peculiar to that Gospel, is confirmed either by Matthew or Luke, and the greater part of it by both; and (2) a passage parallel in all three Synoptists is never *immediately* followed in both Matthew and Luke by a *separate incident or discourse* common to these two evangelists alone.

In the body of his essay Sanders notes the exceptions to the usual claims about synoptic order. The statement that both Matthew and Luke generally support Mark's order is a great oversimplification, and Sanders notes the following exceptions to the traditional claims: (1) to the claim that Matthew and Luke never agree against Mark in a point of arrangement, there are four clear exceptions; (2) there are five passages that are

*E. P. Sanders, "The Argument from Order and the Relationship Between Matthew and Luke," *New Testament Studies* 15 (1968-1969): 249-61.

differently placed by each of the three evangelists; (3) there are four instances in which either Matthew or Luke has a different order from that of Mark, while the other omits; and (4) there are several instances where Matthew and Luke agree in placing the same common (Q) material at the same place or at basically the same place relative to the Markan outline. Sanders then asks how many of these exceptions to the usual statements about order could be explained by the theory that Mark and Q overlapped.

Sanders concludes that we must become more open to the possibility that there was more contact between Matthew and Luke than their independent employment of the same two sources, Mark and Q. The simple explanation is that one knew the other, most likely that Luke used Matthew.

Recent discussions have shown that the absence of agreement between Matthew and Luke against Mark with regard to the relative sequence of events does not prove our Mark to be directly prior to Matthew and Luke. The "argument from order" was originally developed to show that Mark's sequence of events is closest to that of the Ur-Gospel, and it cannot logically prove Mark to be directly prior to Matthew and Luke, although many scholars used it as if it could.[1] But the argument from order was also used to show that Matthew and Luke *independently* copied two sources. They both chose to follow the order of one (Mark), while inserting material from the other (Q) at different places in the Markan outline. The purpose of this essay is to reexamine some of the facts on which the argument from order rests and to see if they do support Matthew and Luke's independent use of Mark and Q, or if it appears that there are agreements between Matthew and Luke which cannot be accounted for by their independent use of the same sources.[2]

---

[1]See B. C. Butler, *The Originality of St. Matthew* (1951) 62-71 [reprinted in this volume]; W. R. Farmer, *The Synoptic Problem* (1964) 63-67, 211-215; N. H. Palmer, "Lachmann's Argument," *NTS* 13 (1967): 368-378, esp. 369, 377-78 [reprinted in this volume].

[2]The argument from order which I am discussing is the one which depends upon the absence of agreement between Matthew and Luke against Mark. As Palmer has shown, there is another argument from order, one which attempts to show that Mark's order can be demonstrated to be the source of Matthew and Luke at individual points by adducing reasons why Matthew and Luke would have altered Mark's order if they had it before them. This was Lachmann's argument; but as Palmer ("Lachmann's Argument," 377) points out, "it may also be that we could find 'reasons' telling the opposite way in each single case." For a recent attempt to show that Mark has the earlier order at individual points, see H. G. Wood, "The Priority of Mark," 65 (1953-54): 17-19 [reprinted in this volume]. He argues, for example, that the connection of the conflict stories in Mk. 2:1-3:6 is *better* than it is in Matthew.

I

Of all the synoptic phenomena, the phenomenon of order is perhaps the most difficult to state in general terms which can claim accuracy. That Matthew, Mark and Luke have approximately the same arrangement of material is obvious, but the attempt to state just what the interrelations of the orders of the gospels are is agonizing. F. H. Woods confessed in his influential essay that it "seemed at times a hopeless task."[3] He is nevertheless able to lay down six statements which are generally true. The passage is worth quoting at length.

> I will now give the reasons which seem to me to prove conclusively that the original basis of the Synoptic Gospels coincided in its *range* and *order* with our St. Mark. (1) The earliest and the latest parallels in all three Gospels coincide with the beginning and end of St. Mark. . . . (2) With but few exceptions we find parallels to the whole of St. Mark in either St. Matthew or St. Luke, and to by far the larger part in both. (3) The *order* of the whole of St. Mark, excepting of course what is peculiar to that Gospel, is confirmed either by St. Matthew or St. Luke, and the greater part of it by both. (4) A passage parallel in all three Synoptists is never *immediately* followed in both St. Matthew and St. Luke by a *separate incident or discourse* common to these two evangelists alone. (5) Similarly in the parts common to St. Matthew and St. Luke alone, no considerable fragments, with some doubtful exceptions,[4] occur in the same relative order, so that it is *unlikely* that they formed part of the original source. (6) To this we may add the fact that in the same parts the differences between St. Matthew and St. Luke are generally greater than those which are common to all three.[5]

Similar arguments had already been advanced in Germany,[6] but we may take Woods as presenting the argument from order in its typical and most complete form. All of the points he makes are not of equal significance, however. Woods points out that

> the third argument is by far the most important, and requires some fuller explanation. When we say that the order of St. Mark is maintained either by St. Matthew

---

[3]F. H. Woods, "The Origin and Mutual Relations of the Synoptic Gospels" (1886, 1890), *Studia Biblica et Ecclesiastica* II:60.

[4]Here Woods, ibid., has a footnote listing the "doubtful exceptions": Mt. 12:22-30 = Lk. 11:14-23; Mt. 13:38-42 = Lk. 11:29-32; Mt. 12:43-45 = Lk. 11:24-26. Perhaps also Matthew 12:33-35 = Lk. 6:43-45.

[5]Ibid., 61-62 (italics in original).

[6]See, for example, C. H. Weisse, *Die evangelische Geschichte* (1838), cited by W. G. Kümmel, *Das neue Testament* (1958) 184.

or St. Luke, we mean the relative order, without taking into account the insertion by either of what is not in St. Mark at all, or the omissions from St. Mark by both.[7]

That Woods's point number three is indeed the most important is indicated by Streeter's utilizing it as his third ''proof'' for the priority of Mark. He states it this way:

> The order of incidents in Mark is clearly the more original; for wherever Matthew departs from Mark's order Luke supports Mark, and whenever Luke departs from Mark, Matthew agrees with Mark. The section Mk. 3:31-34 alone occurs in a different context in each gospel; and there is no case where Matthew and Luke agree together against Mark in a point of arrangement.[8]

Scarcely less important for the solution of the synoptic problem, however, are Woods's points four and five. As a matter of fact, points three, four, and five taken together have been the most persuasive argument for the two-document hypothesis. There is a classic passage in Streeter which shows the force of point four.

> Sir John Hawkins once showed me a Greek Testament in which he had indicated on the left-hand margin of Mark the exact point in the Markan outline at which Matthew has inserted each of the sayings in question [that is, the so-called Q material] with, of course, the reference to chapter and verse, to identify it; on the right-hand margin he had similarly indicated the point where Luke inserts matter also found in Matthew. It then appeared that, subsequent to the Temptation story, there is not a single case in which Matthew and Luke agree in inserting the same saying at the same point in the Markan outline. If then Luke derived this material from Matthew, he must have gone through both Matthew and Mark so as to discriminate with meticulous precision between Markan and non-Markan material; he must then have proceeded with the utmost care to tear every little piece of non-Markan material he desired to use from the context of Mark in which it appeared in Matthew—in spite of the fact that contexts in Matthew are always exceedingly appropriate—in order to re-insert it into a different context of Mark having no special appropriateness. A theory which would make an author capable of such a proceeding would only be tenable if, on other grounds, we had reason to believe he was a crank.[9]

---

[7]Woods, ''Origin,'' 63.

[8]B. H. Streeter, *The Four Gospels*, 2d ed. (1930) 161. Streeter applies Woods's point three to proving Mark's direct priority to Matthew and Luke. Woods uses the argument to show that Mark's range and order were identical with the range and order of the Ur-Gospel.

[9]*Ibid.*, 183. Streeter's statement is curious, because actually Hawkins knew very well that there are several places at which Matthew and Luke agree in placing the same Q material at the same point in the Markan outline. Hawkins gives a list of ten such places in *Oxford Studies in the Synoptic Problem* (1911) 102, and *Horae Synopticae*, 2d ed. (1909)

Thus we see how the phenomenon of order was used not only to show that Mark was the best representative of the Ur-Gospel (which was eventually done away with, leaving Mark first), but also how it was used to show that Luke and Matthew used Mark and Q independently, neither one knowing the other. It is the second conclusion which we wish to test.

For the purposes of this paper, we are going to consider only Woods's points three and four. These two points actually make more than two assertions. We may briefly list the different assertions involved:

1. Both Matthew and Luke support Mark's order the greater part of the time.

2. If Matthew or Luke disagrees with Mark's relative order the other supports it. This point has corollaries:

(*a*) Matthew and Luke never place a Markan[10] passage in the same context which is different from its context in Mark.

(*b*) With one exception (Mk. 3:31-35) no Markan passage occurs in different contexts in all three gospels.

(*c*) No Markan passage is ever rearranged by either Matthew or Luke while being omitted by the other. (It is not usually recognized that this last is a corollary to Wood's point three, but it is. If Matthew departs from Mark's order and Luke omits, neither has supported Mark's order; while the claim is that *one always supports Mark's order* except where both omit.

3. Matthew and Luke never agree in the placement of Q material relative to Markan material, subsequent to the Temptation story.

If all of this were true, it would be a striking occurrence of phenomena. That it is true is never questioned today. The facts of order, thus stated, have had a stronger influence on the formation of the two-document hypothesis than any of the other phenomena.[11] There is no doubt that the ar-

---

208. The text which Hawkins showed Streeter must have been based on full pericopes in Tischendorf's synopsis. The ten places which Hawkins discusses are all instances in which Matthew and Luke have the same Q material within a Markan passage, and in which the entire passage (both Markan and Q material) is considered by Tischendorf to be one pericope. The pericope division, of course, is artificial. A different division would permit at least ten clear exceptions to Streeter's statement and to Woods's point four. See Section VI below.

[10]I use "Markan" to refer to a passage in Mark which is also in Matthew and/or Luke, without prejudice as to whether Matthew and Luke copied it directly from our Mark or not. Similarly, I use "Q" only to indicate the tradition common to Matthew and Luke alone.

[11]See, for example, Sir John Hawkins, *Horae Synopticae*, 2d ed., 114, n3. Bultmann,

gument from order is a powerful one once the Q material is considered. If Matthew and Luke generally agree with Mark (but not with each other against Mark) in the arrangement of the Markan material, but disagree in the arrangement of the Q material, there is really only one explanation. Matthew and Luke have used two sources independently. Both generally followed the order of one source, but one or the other or both used the material from the second source without regard to its order. But any agreements, even minor ones, between Matthew and Luke on a point of order which cannot be attributed to their independent use of Mark and Q will argue strongly that there must have been some other contact between the first and third gospels. Minor *verbal* agreements between Matthew and Luke against Mark have been noted and accounted for (whether rightly or wrongly) on a number of grounds.[12] But agreements in order will be very hard to explain away. They could hardly have been introduced in the course of textual transmission, and very few could be attributed to a common desire on the part of Matthew and Luke to "improve" Mark in the same way.

Now we must ask what constitutes an agreement in order. This issue is of crucial importance. The argument from order, as outlined above, deals only with full pericopes, and further, with full pericopes as they are presented in Tischendorf's synopsis. The restriction of the question to full pericopes was quite reasonable when the goal of research was to find a biographical outline of Jesus' life to substitute for the Johannine outline, confidence in which had been destroyed by Strauss. Naturally only the main events were significant. Whenever two gospels agreed on the placement of a pericope, their agreement was attributed to faithful copying of the Ur-Gospel, which could be presumed to have presented a largely ac-

---

in assessing the evidence for the two-document hypothesis, writes, "Das Hauptgewicht aber fällt auf die Reihenfolge. . . ," *Die Erforschung der synoptischen Evangelien*, 3d ed. (1960) 8. See also Farmer, *Synoptic Problem*, 63ff. The belief that Mark's style is that of dictation from an eyewitness also was very influential when the two-document hypothesis was first being formulated. The difference between the style of Mark and that of Matthew and Luke was regarded as "the difference which always exists between the spoken and the written language. Mark reads like a shorthand account of a story told by an impromptu speaker. . . . " (Streeter, *Four Gospels*, 163). Few people today would hold to this view, although they still may regard Mark as earlier. The view that some of it, at least, represents dictation is still held in some quarters, however. See, for example, Vincent Taylor, *The Formation of the Gospel Tradition*, 2d ed. (1935) ix.

[12]See Streeter, *Four Gospels*, 293-331.

curate scheme of Jesus' life.[13] But once the question becomes the strictly literary one of whether there was some contact between Matthew and Luke other than their independent use of the same sources, it is clear that the limitation to full pericopes is unwarranted. The small points at which Matthew and Luke agree against Mark in a point of order are just as difficult to explain as large ones would be. But the small points have never been investigated.

The use of Tischendorf's synopsis by Woods, Hawkins and others is also significant. On the whole, Tischendorf's pericopes are longer than those in the synopsis of Huck, his successor.[14] As we shall see below, some instances in which neither Matthew nor Luke supports Mark's order were overlooked because they were not full pericopes in Tischendorf's synopsis. I have already pointed out that Woods's point four is dependent upon using Tischendorf's long pericopes, which include both Markan and Q material under one heading, and so prevent one from finding a *separate* incident of discourse in which Matthew and Luke agree in the placement of Q material. The true exceptions to Woods's point four are given in section VI below. Once the question becomes the literary relation between Matthew and Luke rather than the sequence of events in Jesus' life, the insistence on a *separate* incident becomes irrelevant.

We may now note the exceptions to the usual claims about synoptic order. The purpose of doing so is not to attempt to explain the synoptic order, but simply to see to what extent the usual picture is accurate.

II

In the first place, the statement that both Matthew and Luke generally support Mark's order is a great oversimplification. This statement, to be

---

[13]On the significance of the sequence of events for research on the life of Jesus, see Schweitzer's chapters on Strauss and on the Markan hypothesis in *The Quest of the Historical Jesus* (1961). Lachmann's original discussion of the synoptic order was apparently motivated by interest in the "precise chronology of the history of Jesus." He argued that since the three synoptics show a common order, except where one or the other alters the order for his own purpose, "no greater weight can be placed on the witness of three evangelists than if a single and indeed unknown author had testified." The gospels reveal the order of the Ur-Gospel, which order then must be investigated for information about the chronology of Jesus' ministry. See Palmer, "Lachmann's Argument," 375-76.

[14]Tischendorf's synopsis was first published in 1851 and was revised in 1864. I have used the fifth edition of 1884. Huck's synopsis was first published in 1892. Sanday, writing in 1911, noted that the Oxford Seminar used Tischendorf, but referred to other synopses, including Huck's (*Oxford Studies*, viii). See also Hawkins's remark (ibid., 102, n1).

sure, claims nothing more than that the three synoptics have basically the same order, but this is true only in the most general sense. Sir John Hawkins recognized the degree of oversimplification, although his qualification of the general statement has been pretty well forgotten. Concerning the statement that Matthew and Luke do not desert the relative order of Mark, Hawkins writes,

> that general statement, however, does not apply to what forms nearly a quarter of the First Gospel, viz. Matthew 8-13, containing 252 verses, nor to what forms nearly one-third of the Third Gospel, viz. Luke 9:51-18:14, containing 350 verses (omitting 17:36 as spurious). Of neither of these two large departments of the Gospels bearing the names of Matthew and Luke can it be said that much account is taken of the Markan arrangement and order.[15]

We might also note that Luke's Passion narrative is notorious for differing in order from Mark's. That Hawkins has stated the matter more accurately than is usually done will be quite obvious to anyone who tries to trace the "Markan" order in the first half of Matthew. I frankly doubt that it is justifiable to speak of a Markan order in the section of Matthew mentioned by Hawkins at all.

To speak more specifically, we may divide Mark (following Huck's arrangement) into 101 pericopes. These fall basically into two groups—the narrative and sayings material before the entry into Jerusalem (1:1-10:52) and that after (11:1-16:8). We might antecedently expect there to be more agreement in order among the various recorders after the entry into Jerusalem than before. This is precisely the case. Dividing Mk. 1:1-10:52 into 61 pericopes, and giving the benefit of every doubt to support for Mark, we find that in only 28 of them do Matthew and Luke both support Mark's order. This is somewhat under half. In the 40 pericopes following the entry into Jersualem, Matthew and Luke both support Mark's order 30 times. That is so, however, only if we overlook the constant rearrangement by Luke of large portions of the material within the Passion narrative pericopes. Of the total 101 pericopes, 58 are supported in order by both Matthew and Luke. This is, of course, only slightly over half. As Woods said, the greater part of Mark is confirmed in order by both Matthew and Luke, but it is barely the greater part. It is usually not recognized that so small a majority of Mark's pericopes is confirmed in order by both Matthew and Luke, not that, apart from the section where considerable

---

[15]*Oxford Studies*, 29-30.

uniformity could be expected even from independent sources, a minority of Mark's pericopes is so supported. It might lead to better comprehension of the phenomenon if we said that both Matthew and Luke support Mark's order three-fourths of the time after the entry into Jerusalem, but less than half the time before the entry, rather than that the greater part of Mark's order is confirmed by both Matthew and Luke.

Let us now turn to the task of noting exceptions to the more particular claims of the argument of order. We shall begin by noting the places in which Matthew and Luke agree against Mark in a point of order.

III

To the claim that Matthew and Luke never agree against Mark in a point of arrangement, there are four clear exceptions.

1. Matthew (7:2) and Luke (6:38) place the saying about Measuring in the context of the Sermon on the Mount (Plain). In both, it is after the saying about Judging and before the saying about the Splinter and the Beam. Mark (4:24b) places it in the context of the sayings on the Right Use of Parables.

2. Matthew (11:10) and Luke (7:27) place the ἰδοὺ ἀποστέλλω quotation concerning John the Baptist in the context of the Baptist's question and Christ's testimony to him. Mark (1:2) places it in the context of the Baptist's preaching.

3. Matthew (3:2) and Luke (3:3) place John's call to repentance and baptism before the quotation from Isaiah. Mark (1:4) places it after.

4. Matthew (3:11) and Luke (3:16) place the sentence ''I baptize you with water'' before John's statement about the one who is stronger than he. Mark (1:7-8) has the reverse order.

There are also two passages which are not so obvious.

5. Matthew (21:10-17) and Luke (19:45-46) have Jesus cleanse the temple when he first enters. Mark places the cleansing on the next day, after the Return to Bethany (11:11, 15-19). The issue is clouded because Luke omits the Return to Bethany altogether, and perhaps this passage should be placed in the third category, to be considered below. It is nevertheless a striking instance in which neither Matthew nor Luke supports Mark's order.

6. Matthew (25:14) and Luke (19:12-13) are, despite differences, parallel to Mk. 13:34. Both Matthew and Luke use this statement as an intro-

duction to the Parable of the Pounds. Mark uses it to close the apocalyptic discourse. Mt. 24:42 is parallel to Mk. 13:35, but is differently placed. Luke's 12:40 can hardly be considered a parallel. Any parallel between Mk. 13:36-37, Mt. 25:13, and Lk. 12:38 is doubtful. If there is one, Mark's order is not supported by either Matthew or Luke. In short, none of Mk. 13:33-37 is supported in order by Matthew or Luke, while in one verse (Mk. 13:34), they both agree against Mark.

There is one important instance in which Matthew and Luke agree against Mark in the placing of a phrase.

7. Matthew (6:33) and Luke (12:31) place καὶ προστεθήσεται ὑμῖν in the saying on Cares (which, while evidencing a high degree of verbatim agreement, is itself differently placed by Matthew and Luke). Mark (4:24c) places the phrase with the saying on Measuring.

IV

We may now note the passages which are differently placed by each of the three evangelists. Streeter, as we have seen, said that Mk. 3:31-35 was such a passage. This is curious, because it has the same relative order in Matthew as in Mark: after the Beelzebub controversy and before the Parable of the Sower. There are some genuine instances of different placing by each evangelist, however.

1. Mark places the saying about Salt (9:50) after the saying about Offenses. Matthew places it (5:13) in the Sermon on the Mount. Luke has it (14:34) in his greater interpolation, at the end of his paragraph on the cost of discipleship. The saying about Salt is a separate pericope in Huck's synopsis, but not in Tischendorf's.

2. Matthew (10:2-4) and Luke (6:13-16) place the Call of the Twelve Apostles before the Healing of Multitudes (Mt. 12:15; Lk. 6:17-19), although in different places. Mark (3:13-19) has the Call after the Healing (3:7ff.).

3. Mark places Rejection at Nazareth (6:1-6a) directly after Jairus's Daughter and the Woman with the Issue of Blood. Luke (4:16-30) has it before that pericope, however, Matthew (13:53-58) places it considerably later, with several Markan pericopes intervening between it and Jairus's Daughter. In Matthew, the displacement is only partial, since it is followed by material in the Markan order, but not preceded by such material. It is really virtually impossible to say whether Matthew supports the order

of Mk. 6:1a or not. Woods thought that Matthew does support Mark, but granted that this was "the only point in [the] examination to which . . . any exception can possibly be taken."[16] The problem is that this is part of that section where Matthew's and Mark's orders are hard to reconcile. Immediately before Mt. 13:53-58 is a large body of material peculiar to Matthew (13:36-52). Immediately before Mk. 6:1-6a is a large body of material which is paralleled by Matthew in his chapters eight and nine (Mk. 4:35-5:43 = Mt. 8:18-34; 9:18-26). Moreover, in the pericope immediately after Mk. 6:1-6a Matthew's parallel is once again in chapter nine. So it is hard to say whether Mt. 13:53-58 is the only pericope in this section in Markan order or the only one *not* in Markan order.

There are also two phrases which are differently placed by the three evangelists.

4. Mark places the saying "he who has ears . . . " in the Right Use of Parables (4:23). Matthew has it in Christ's Testimony to the Baptist (11:15) and the Interpretation of the Parable of the Tares (13:43). Luke has it in the Cost of Discipleship (14:35). (In addition, it appears in the Parable of the Sower, Mt. 13:9 = Mk. 4:9 = Lk. 8:8).

5. Mark (12:34c) is differently placed by Matthew (22:46) and by Luke (20:40).

V

Thirdly, there are instances in which either Matthew or Luke has a different order from that of Mark, while the other omits. These are not full passages, but all are significant.

1. Matthew places the saying on Forgiveness after the Lord's Prayer (6:14b), while Mark has it in the Meaning of the Withered Fig Tree (11:25). Luke omits.

2. Matthew has "locusts and wild honey" before the description of those who came to hear John (3:4-6). Mark has the reverse (1:4-6). Luke omits both.

3. Mark has the saying on the giving of a drink and the subsequent reward at the end of the Strange Exorcist (9:41). Matthew lacks the Strange Exorcist and has the saying in a different context (10:42). Luke has the Strange Exorcist (9:49-50), but omits the saying.

---

[16]Woods, "Origin," 66.

4. The quotation of the phrase "as sheep not having a shepherd" from Num. 27:17 is in another context in Matthew (9:36b) than in Mark (6:34b). Luke omits. It is true that Mt. 9:36a is a doublet of Mt. 14:14a, which is parallel to Mk. 6:34a, but the quotation (which does not agree precisely with any passage in the LXX) is differently placed by Matthew and by Mark, and is omitted by Luke.[17]

Thus we see that, while it is generally true that either Matthew or Luke supports Mark's order, there are important exceptions when neither does.

VI

The final group of exceptions to the traditional claims concerns those places where Matthew and Luke agree in placing the same common (Q) material at the same place relative to the Markan outline.

1. After John the Baptist (Mt. 3:1-6; Mk. 1:1-6; Lk. 3:1-6), Matthew and Luke place John's Preaching of Repentance (Mt. 3:7-10; Lk. 3:7-9). Streeter notes this by saying the rule applies only subsequently to the temptation. Woods, however, considered it to be "almost certain" that Matthew 3:7-10, 12 was in the Ur-Gospel and was omitted by Mark.[18]

2. After the Parable of the Mustard Seed (Mt. 13:31-32; Mk. 4:30-32; Lk. 13:18-19), Matthew and Luke place the Parable of the Leaven (Mt. 13:33; Lk. 13:20-21).[19]

There are two important instances in which Matthew and Luke basically place the same material in the same place relative to the Markan outline, but in a slightly different order or with one having a passage the other lacks.

3. After the Beelzebub Controversy (Mt. 12:25-37; Mk. 3:23-30; Lk. 11:17-23), Matthew places Against Seeking for Signs (12:38-42) and the Return of the Evil Spirit (12:43-45). Luke places the Return of the Evil Spirit (11:24-26), the Blessedness of Christ's Mother (11:27-28), and Against Seeking for Signs (11:29-32).

4. After About Offenses (Mt. 18:6-9; Mk. 9:42-48; Lk. 17:1-2), Matthew places The Lost Sheep (18:10-14), On Reproving One's Brother

---

[17]It would be easy to increase the number of items in this category by considering less significant phrases. See, for example, "why are you afraid" (Mt. 8:26; Mk. 4:40) and "and leaving him, they departed" (Mt. 22:22; Mk. 12:12).

[18]Woods, "Origin," 94.

[19]Cf. Hawkins, *Oxford Studies*, 50.

(18:15-20), and On Reconciliation (18:21-22). Luke places On Reproving One's Brother (17:3) and On Reconciliation (17:4).

We may note here two important instances in which Matthew and Luke place in the same place in the Markan outline different passages which make the same point. Although the material is approximately the same, there is no verbatim agreement between Matthew and Luke.

5. Matthew (26:25) and Luke (22:23) agree in having the disciples (or one of them) question Jesus after his "woe to that man" speech (Mk. 14:21).

6. Matthew (26:50) and Luke (22:48) agree against Mark (14:45) in having Jesus address a question to Judas after the kiss of betrayal.

We may also list here some instances in which Matthew and Luke break the Markan order at the same point, but with different material.

7. After A Preaching Journey in Galilee (Mt. 4:23; Mk. 1:39; Lk. 4:44) Matthew places The Sermon on the Mount (5-7), Luke The Miraculous Draught of Fishes (5:1-11).

8. Where the Parable of the Seed Growing Secretly stands in Mark (4:26-29), Matthew and Luke not only both lack it, but have other material. Matthew has the Parable of the Tares (13:24-30), and Luke Christ's Real Brethren (8:19-21).

To the same point, although not contradicting one of the usual claims, are five pericopes in which Matthew and Luke have considerable material in common with each other in addition to material common to them and Mark.[20] This list differs from the one above in that the additions common to Matthew and Luke are not separate incidents or discourses, but expansions of a Markan passage. Woods, in his point four, explicitly avoided discussing such instances. These agreements of Matthew and Luke are no less important for that.

9.   Mt. 3:11-12 = Mk. 1:7-8 = Lk. 3:15-18.
10.   Mt. 4:1-11 = Mk. 1:12-13 = Lk. 4:1-13
11.   Mt. 12:22-37 = Mk. 3:20-30 = Lk. 11:14-23.
12.   Mt. 10:1-16 = Mk. 4:7-13 = Lk. 10:1-12.
13.   Mt. 24:23-28 = Mk. 13:21-23 = Lk. 17:21-37.[21]

---

[20]Cf. the list given by Hawkins, *Oxford Studies*, 102, and *Horae Synopticae*, 208.

[21]If Huck's arrangement is followed, this passage is an instance in which Matthew and Luke add the same *separate* discourse after a Markan pericope. Huck divides the pericopes thus: (1) Mt. 24:23-25 = Mk. 13:21-23 = Lk. 17:21; (2) Mt. 24:26-28 = Lk. 17:23-24, 37. He does not, however, count Lk. 17:21 as a full parallel to Mt. 24:23-25 and Mk. 13:21-23.

VII

It is noteworthy that a number of exceptions are concentrated in a single section of Mk. 4:21-42. In this section, a common order is simply nonexistent, as the following chart will make clear. The sign * indicates a passage in Matthew or Luke which is not in Mark's order. The sign ** indicates that Matthew and Luke have the same order against Mark. Mark's passages which are supported in order by neither Matthew nor Luke are shown by bold figures.

MATTHEW	MARK	LUKE
	The Saying on Light	
5:15*	4:21	8:16
	Hidden and Revealed	
10:26*	4:22	8:17
	He Who Has Ears	
11:15*; 13:43*	**4:23**	14:35*
	Take Heed What You Hear	
————	4:24a	8:18a
	Measuring	
7:2**	**4:24b**	6:38**
	It Will be Added to You	
6:33**	**4:24c**	12:31**
	He Who Has . . .	
13:12*	4:25	8:18b
	The Seed Growing Secretly	
————	**4:26-29**	————
	The Mustard Seed	
13:31-32	4:30-32	13:18-19*
	The Leaven	
13:33**	————	13:20-21**
	The Use of Parables	
13:34-35	4:33-34	————
	The Stilling of the Tempest	
8:23-27*	4:35-41	8:22-25

VIII

Now let us ask how many of these exceptions to the usual statements about order could be explained by the theory that Mark and Q overlapped. For the purpose of deciding this, we shall invoke Streeter's criterion that "we have no right to call in the hypothesis of the influence of Q . . . except in places where the existence of different versions, or of doublets very dis-

tinctly defined, provides us with objective evidence of the presence of Q.''[22] The hypothesis of an overlap between Mark and Q has been used to explain the verbatim agreements of Matthew and Luke against Mark in such passages as the Beelzebub Controversy. Now we shall see if it will explain the agreements in order of Matthew and Luke.

Some of the agreements in order that we have noted occur in passages where it is usually said that Mark and Q overlap. These, of course, are explicable on that ground. Those who, like myself, have little or no faith in the existence of a single document Q, as it is usually defined, will be able to see even in the passages we are now about to list further evidence of Matthew's or Luke's knowledge of the other. It must be granted, however, that if the Q hypothesis could explain all of the agreements of Matthew and Luke against Mark, it would gain somewhat in probability.

The agreements in order of Matthew and Luke against Mark which concern a passage usually attributed to Q are as follows:

> Mt. 7:2; Mk. 4:24b; Lk. 6:38 (see III. 1 above).[23]
> Mt. 11:10; Mk. 1:2; Lk. 7:27 (see III. 2 above).
> Mt. 3:11; Mk. 1:8; Lk. 3:16 (see III. 4 above).[24]
> Mt. 6:33; Mk. 4:24c; Lk. 12:31 (see III. 7 above).[23]
> Mt. 5:13; Mk. 9:50; Lk. 14:34 (see IV. 1 above).

I do not include V. 4 above, because the phrase in question does not itself appear in a doublet.

Some of the instances of Matthew and Luke's placing the same common (Q) material in the same place in the Markan outline can be explained if the preceding Markan pericope was also in Q. Matthew and Luke's agreement would be caused by their following the order of Q.

> Mt. 3:7-10; Lk. 3:7-9 (VI. 1 above).
> Mt. 12:38-45; Lk. 11:24-32 (VI. 3 above).
> The five pericopes from VI. 9-13.[24]

---

[22]Streeter, *Four Gospels*, 306.

[23]While these three sayings are usually assigned to Q, their Matthean and Lukan forms are not really different from their Markan forms. Thus we might protest that they are improperly assigned to Q, apparently on the basis of context alone. This is not an adequate reason for attributing a passage which occurs in all three of our synoptics to that hypothetical document, as is well recognized. The sayings in question, however, are too short to admit much variation in any case, so I have left the passages in the list.

[24]Even so, these pericopes are instances in which Matthew and Luke agree in the placement of Q material.

Many would wish to place the Parable of the Leaven (see VI. 2 above) in this category, primarily on the ground that the preceding parable, that of the Mustard Seed, is an overlap of Mark and Q. Without going into detail we may simply note that there is really no clear internal evidence in the Parable of the Mustard Seed sufficient to prove that it has been preserved in two different traditions. The only real reason for attributing the Mustard Seed to Q is that Matthew and Luke both follow it with the same pericope. But we can hardly argue that the reason we know the Mustard Seed was in Q is that it stood together with the Leaven in Q. This is to presuppose the point at issue. We must emphasize that Q material cannot be decided on the basis of context alone.[25]

To summarize, there are points in Mark which are supported in order by neither Matthew nor Luke, at which Matthew's and Luke's failure to support cannot be attributed to the influence of Q, objectively ascertained. The Markan passages which are thus inexplicably unsupported, in the order of their occurrence in this paper are as follows:[26] Mk. 1:4 (III. 3 above); 11:11, 15-19 (III. 4); 13:33-37 (III. 5); 3:13-19 (IV. 2); 6:1-6a (IV. 3);[27] 4:23 (IV. 4); 12:34c (IV. 5); 11:25 (V. 1); 1:4-6 (V. 2); 9:41 (V. 3); 6:34b (V. 4).

Points where Matthew and Luke agree, to some extent at least, in placing the same material at the same place in the Markan outline, where such agreement cannot be attributed to the influence of Q, are as follows: Mt. 13:33 = Lk. 13:20-21; Mt. 18:10-22 = Lk. 17:3-4. The passages dis-

---

[25]For arguments in favor of assigning the Parable of the Mustard Seed to Q, see Hawkins, *Oxford Studies*, 50-53, and Harnack, *The Sayings of Jesus* (1908) 26-27. Both mention first the connection of the parable with the Parable of the Leaven and then the fact that Matthew agrees partially with Mark and partially with Luke. These points are taken as establishing the existence of different versions, one Markan and one Q. The argument from context is irrelevant. The fact that Matthew and Mark have "shrubs" and Matthew and Luke have "tree" (to mention the most striking agreement in the second point) does not seem sufficient evidence for the existence of different versions which are conflated in Matthew. Or if it is taken as such, what will one make of the fact that Mk. 3:8 agrees with Lk. 6:17 in reading "Tyre and Sidon" and with Mt. 4:25 in having "beyond the Jordan"?

[26]The parallels to Mk. 1:4; Mt. 3:2; and Lk. 3:3 are not placed in Q by either Harnack or Hawkins, but Streeter *Four Gospels*, 291, does assign them to Q. I do not see that there is any objective basis for assigning these verses to Q, following Streeter's own criterion, and so have followed Harnack and Hawkins.

[27]Assuming that Matthew does not support Mk. 6:1-6a. See IV. 3 above.

cussed in VI. 5 and VI. 6 above perhaps should be placed here, but I have omitted them because of the lack of verbatim agreement.

In sum, the assurance with which it is usually said that Matthew and Luke were independent of each other rests on the assertion that they *never* agree together in such a way that it cannot be explained by reference to their independent use of Mark and Q. When we note the number of instances where they do, the assurance we have felt in the traditional hypothesis must be correspondingly weakened. We must then become more open to the possibility that there was more contact between Matthew and Luke than their independent employment of the same two sources. The simplest explanation is that one knew the other; evidence not discussed here makes it likely that Luke used Matthew.[28]

---

[28]Of course the suggestion that Luke used Matthew has often been made; but it has been countered by the argument from order: why do Luke and Matthew never agree in the placing of Q material if Luke knew Matthew? See W. G. Kümmel, *Introduction to the New Testament* (1965) 50. I have just shown that they do so agree, and so perhaps one impediment to accepting Luke's use of Matthew is removed. The number of agreements in order between Luke and Matthew is too large to attribute to chance. For recent articles which accept Luke's use of Matthew, see A. W. Argyle, "Evidence for the View that St Luke used St Matthew's Gospel," *JBL* 83 (1964): 390-96 [reprinted in this volume]; R. T. Simpson, "The Major Agreements of Matthew and Luke Against Mark," *NTS* 12 (1965-1966): 273-84 [reprinted in this volume]. For a recent article which takes another view, see H. Philip West, Jr., "A Primitive Version of Luke in the Composition of Matthew," *NTS* 14 (1967): 75-95.

CRITIQUE OF THE Q HYPOTHESIS

*D. L. Dungan**

Dungan's critique of the Q hypothesis consists of two parts: (1) a literary-critical discussion that puts some questions that require explanation if the Q hypothesis is to stand; and (2) an inquiry into the historical and philological arguments commonly advanced in support of the Q hypothesis.

(1) For example:

   (a) How big was Q?

   (b) What was the relation between Q and Mark?

   (c) Why did Mark ignore so much of Q?

(2) For example:

   (a) Some studies have found traces of Q in the Apostolic Fathers, Justin Martyr, and the Oxyrhynchus Papyri.

   (b) What is the relationship of Q to the newly discovered Gospel of Thomas?

Dungan maintains that no matter how many sources, *logia*-collections, and baptism catechisms the early church may have had, all we can deduce is that such groupings of tradition were no doubt available to Matthew and Luke (and Mark) when they wrote their Gospels. But nothing is

---

*D. L. Dungan, "Critique of the Q Hypothesis," from "Mark—The Abridgement of Matthew and Luke," *Jesus and Man's Hope* (Pittsburgh Theological Seminary, 1970) I:74-80.

thereby demonstrated either about the actual existence of Q, its specific size, or its concrete contents.

This critique will consist of two parts, the first being a literary-critical discussion which shall, for the sake of argument, concede the priority of Mark as well as the existence of Q in order to put some questions that require explanation if the Q hypothesis is to stand. The second part will contain an inquiry into the historical arguments commonly advanced in support of the Q hypothesis.

1. What was Q?

Hamlet: *Do you see yonder cloud, that's almost in shape of a camel?*
Petronius: *By the mass, and 'tis like a camel indeed!*
Hamlet: *Methinks it is like a weasel.*
Petronius: *It is backed like a weasel.*
Hamlet: *Or, like a whale?*
Petronius: *Very like a whale.*[1]

Only naive graduate students think that Q is (by definition) the non-Markan sections in Matthew and Luke which more or less closely resemble each other. To be sure, this may be what Q is in part, but it overlooks the far more useful and important part of Q. As Styler's remark . . . plainly shows,[2] the real value of the Q hypothesis is that it provides a way for those doing research in the Synoptic Gospels to handle all of the passages which clearly belie the theory of Mark's originality. In other words, the true essence of the contents of the Q source consists not in the *non*-Markan matter in Matthew and Luke, but precisely in those passages of Triple Tradition in which Matthew and Luke jointly (or singly) attest *more primitive Mark-like matter*; where Q, to coin a phrase, "overlaps" Mark. Streeter couldn't have said it more perfectly: "to put it paradoxically, the overlapping of Mark and Q *is more certain than is the existence of Q*" (italics added).[3]

---

[1]*Hamlet, Act. 3, Sc. 2*; superscription to S. Petrie, " 'Q' Is Only What You Make It," *NT* 3 (1959): 28.

[2]Dungan refers to the following statement from G. Styler, "The Priority of Mark," in C. F. D. Moule, *The Birth of the New Testament* (1962) 223-24 [reprinted in this volume]: "It was not necessary to maintain that Mk.'s version must at every point be older than Mt.'s parallel version, since it was possible to say that anything in Mt. which in fact seemed more original than Mk. could have been derived from Q."

[3]B. H. Streeter, *The Four Gospels: A Study of Origins* (1924) 186. Italics added.

The truth is, these Q-Mark overlaps raise all sorts of problems. For example, how big was Q? In view of the fact, mentioned above (B)[4] that negative and positive agreements against Mark sometimes link up with Q sections before and after Triple Tradition sections, it begins to appear that Q was quite large: larger than Mark at any rate. Not only that, it does not seem to have been primarily a collection of sayings at all, but began with and continued to have strictly narrative sections all through, including an account of the Passion. What was the reaction between this gospel-Q and Mark? Why did Mark ignore it so much? And so on; the questions could be multiplied.

Interestingly enough, I have always found that adherents of the Two-Document hypothesis fell back quite painlessly upon the idea that there may have been an Urgospel, shaped like Mark in some way. But this seems to be because most of them have never given the idea up anyway (that is, the vestiges of the older original hypothesis still hang around).[5] But now it finally comes clear what promiscuous invoking of Q all over the place really signifies: the Markan priorists all have an Ur-gospel tucked in their back pockets, called Q, which surfaces now here, now there, in any of the three Gospels at any point. Here also we finally understand why so many consider it to be the special genius of form criticism that it can tap this underground reservoir of more primitive tradition working indiscriminately through any of the Gospels, and therefore independently of any particular solution of the Synoptic Problem. Indeed, some are even rash enough to claim that with the techniques of form criticism in our possession, no particular solution of the Synoptic Problem is even necessary,[6] which, of course, is utter nonsense. Indeed, it does not even seem to be true to say that form-critical research can locate primitive traditions with much certainty.[7]

However that may be, as we shall see,[8] the willingness to entertain hypotheses involving the existence of large, now lost, Gospels of various

---

[4]See D. L. Dungan, "Mark—The Abridgment of Matthew and Luke," *Jesus and Man's Hope* (1970) 1:55-60 [reprinted in this volume].

[5]See, for example, E. P. Sanders, *The Tendencies of the Synoptic Tradition* (1969) 6, nn2-3 for references on Bultmann, Hawkins, and others.

[6]See, for example, the reviews of Farmer's *The Synoptic Problem: A Critical Appraisal* by Rhys and of Vaganay's *Le problème synoptique* by P. Vielhauer, *TLZ* 80 (1955): 647ff.

[7]See Sanders, *Tendencies*, 21ff.

[8]See Dungan in *Jesus and Man's Hope*, 1:81ff. [reprinted in this volume].

types is not at all unpopular these days: But here we must raise a final question. If one is willing to dispense with what seems to be the only logical starting-point: namely, "to earn the right" (Farrer) to postulate these lost sources by proving conclusively that one cannot make any sense out of the documents we do have without them, then one is thrown back entirely upon the stylistic and grammatical arguments mentioned elsewhere.[9] But in that case, at least as Sanders's study shows by way of a preliminary examination, the matter is hopeless; that type of criteria will permit mutually contradictory conclusions. Thus the situation would be at a stalemate until some new way of discovering these hypothetical sources with greater certainty were found.[10]

---

[9]See ibid., 65-71.

[10]See, for the best discussion of the peculiar problem posed for the Two-Document hypothesis precisely by the Q-Mark overlaps, the article by R. T. Simpson, "The Major Agreements of Matthew and Luke Against Mark," *NTS* 12 (1966): 273-84 [reprinted in this volume]; A. W. Argyle, "Agreements between Matthew and Luke," *ET* 73 (1961): 19-22; N. Turner, "Minor Verbal Agreements," *SE,* TU (1957): 223-34. But the essential point was stated long ago by E. W. Lummis: "Tentative reconstructions of Q by various scholars have exhibited such various results, and have been exposed to such destructive criticism from men who confidently accept the Q hypothesis in general, that Professor Burkitt (with whom Canon Hawkins agrees) has pronounced all such attempts 'futile.' Q cannot be determined, *because in order to work at all Q must remain indeterminate.* Each critic in turn in view of the particular part of the Synoptic Problem on which he is working, must be able to apply a specially adapted conception of this purely hypothetical document" (*How Luke Was Written* [1915] 31, italics added).

This *argumentum ad hominem* is not as out of place as one might think. The evidence actually seems to require it. If someone as enamoured of and skillful at finding "characteristic" words and phrases as Hawkins was, had to admit that he could not find "any expressions which I could definitely label as characteristic of Q" (*Horae Synopticae,* 2d ed. [1909] 113), if J. Jeremias asserts that "the *logia* as a written source is in my opinion a figment of the imagination" (quoted in A. Robert, et al., *Introduction to the New Testament,* 281), if C. K. Barrett concludes that, after examining the relationship of the Q sections in Matthew and Luke no common order is apparent and consequently no single document should be postulated ("Q, A Re-examination," *ET* 54 [reprinted in this volume]): what are we to make of all these reconstructions of Q which others have so obligingly furnished us? To be sure, some of them such as W. Haupt, *Worte Jesus und Gemeinde-überlieferung* (1913), or J. P. Brown, "Mark as a Witness to an Edited Form of Q," *JBL* 80 (1961): 29-44 (he finds evidence of *five distinct recensions of Q*), are such virtuoso performances that the very richness of their hypotheses, like some of the early airplanes which had five wings, renders them impractical. But even simple questions such as, how did the

2. Historical discussion of Q

There is a considerable literature on the Q source from the historical and philological perspectives. For example, many studies have sought to find traces of the influence of Q in later writings, such as the Apostolic Fathers, Justin Martyr, and the Oxyrhynchus papryri. Or, working back in the other direction, Q sections of Matthew and Luke have been analyzed for Semitisms, poetic structure, and the like, in order to locate its contents more securely in Jesus' contemporary linguistic usage. But most significant in recent times for the general discussion of the basic character and contents of Q has been the discovery of just such a collection of sayings as Q is generally supposed to have been, namely the Gospel of Thomas.[11]

---

two Gospel editors use Q?, seem to provoke these hyperthyroid reactions. See, for example, V. Taylor's hopelessly convoluted answer to this question after several attempts, "The Original Order of Q," in *New Testament Essays: Studies in Memory of T. W. Manson* (1959) 246-69 [reprinted in this volume]. His claim that his argument from order is "the most objective and decisive argument of all" for the existence of Q (247) may be forgiven as a bit of special pleading. The fact is, as T. R. Rosché has demonstrated, no matter which generally accepted reconstruction one uses (he chose F. C. Grant's), "no . . . verbal similarities exist . . . , nor is there any discernible common order in the double tradition," ("The Words of Jesus and the Future of the Q Hypothesis," *JBL* 79 [1960]: 218 [reprinted in this volume]). Rosché's conclusion was anticipated by C. S. Petrie, who examined the *seventeen* reconstructions of Q printed in J. Moffatt's *Introduction to the New Testament,* 3d ed. (1918) 197-202, namely, those of Reville, Barnes, Burton, Wernle, von Soden, Stanton, Barth, Allen, Holtzmann, Harnack, Wellhausen, Roehrich, Wendt, Hawkins, J. Weiss, B. Weiss, and Moffatt, and came to the astounding discovery that *not a single verse of Matthew was common to all seventeen reconstructions,* and only eighteen verses from Luke. Petrie understandably enough considered this "absence of even a mild display of unanimity" to be something of a disgrace in the household of advanced biblical science, something the neighbors in "the hard sciences" probably ought not to find out about. Indeed, he was moved to make the following caustic observation: "the malleability of this nebulous hypothesis makes 'Q' a letter to conjure with. Its protean nature allows the magician to endow his production with whatever characteristics he may choose, and he is encouraged to adopt for 'Q' the principle that Humpty-Dumpty paraded when Alice sought for a definition of 'glory': 'it means just what I choose it to mean—neither more nor less' " (" 'Q' Is Only What You Make It," 31); see also Petrie, "The Proto-Luke Hypothesis," *ET* 54 (1942-1943): 172-77, with an answer by V. Taylor, 219-22, and rejoinder by Petrie, *ET* 55 (1943-1944): 52-53.

[11]Out of the literature on these subjects the following may be cited, which should be consulted for further bibliography. For Q and the Apostolic Fathers, see especially H.

Although studies such as these are frequently very informative, they do not provide more than a general probability for the Q source's own actual existence and character. For there is no way to tell from specific quotations of Synoptic(-like) traditions in later literature whether one has a reference to Q, or some anonymous "free tradition," or dependence upon a baptismal catechism, or catena of canonical Gospel sayings, or whatever. Even if the saying in question is one corresponding roughly to something half in Luke and half in Matthew (which is frequently the case), one cannot prove that this is a quote from Q, and not just a harmonistic usage of the two written Gospels such as is frequently seen in Old Testament quotations. As far as that goes, how justifiable is it to posit imaginary sources rather than seek for direct influences of written documents which we know existed and actually possess?[12]

Koester, *Synoptische Überlieferung bei den apostolischen Vätern* TU (1957); further J. P. Brown, "The Form of 'Q' Known to Matthew, " *NTS* 8 (1961): 27-42. For Q and Justin Martyr, see esp. A. J. Bellinzoni, *The Sayings of Jesus in the Writings of Justin Martyr* (1967). For Semitisms and poetic structure in Q, see M. Black, *An Aramaic Approach to the Gospels and Acts,* 3d ed. (1967). On the implications of the Gospel of Thomas for the Q hypothesis, see especially J. M. Robinson, "Logoi Sophon Zur Gattung der Spruchquelle Q," in *Zeit und Geschichte. Dankesgabe an R. Bultmann zum 80 Geburtstag* (1964) 77-96, trans. in *Trajectories Through Early Christianity* (1971) 71-113; see also, H. Montefiore and H. E. W. Turner, *Thomas and the Evangelists* (1962); R. North, "Chenoboskion and Q," *CBQ* 24 (1962): 154-70. Finally, in case anyone wanted to know what became of Q, see G. D. Kilpatrick, "The Disappearance of Q," *JTS* 42 (1941): 182-84 (it disappeared).

[12]Studies which attempt to approach the second century Gospel question in this way are, for example, the massive investigation of the influnce of the Gospel of Matthew by E. Massaux, *Influence de l'Évangile de saint Matthieu sur la littérature chrétienne avant saint Irenée* (1950) and "Le text du sermon sur la montagne de Matthieu utilisé par saint Justin," *ETL* 28 (1952): 411-48; further B. C. Butler, "The Literary Relations of Didache 16," *JTS* 11 (1960): 265-83. J. P. Brown, "The Form of 'Q' Known to Matthew," can be read so as to support the contention that it was not Matthew's *form of Q* which was so popular in the early church but Matthew itself. J. Jeremias's book, *Unknown Sayings of Jesus* (1957), is a consistent effort at understanding the Oxyrhynchus sayings without the aid of the Q hypothesis. W. Schrage, in *Das Verhältnis des Thomas-Evangeliums zur synoptischen Tradition und zu den koptischen Evangelienübersetzungen* (1964), argues that the Synoptic sayings in Thomas are simply free harmonizations of the sayings of Jesus as contained in various Coptic translations of the Gospels. The study on Thomas by R. M. Grant and D. N. Freedman, *The Secret Sayings of Jesus According to the Gospel of Thomas* (1960) also avoids using Q to explain the Synoptic material in Thomas. In other words, nothing in the

No matter how many sources and *logia*-collections and baptismal cat-echisms the early church may have had, and we see signs at numerous points that it did have these types of collections in its possession, all we can deduce from this is that such groupings of tradition were no doubt available to Matthew and Luke (and Mark) when they wrote their Gospels. To be sure, this is all the more likely, now that a collection of such sayings has actually turned up. But nothing is thereby demonstrated either about the actual existence of Q, or its specific size or its concrete contents. As a means of directly verifying and conclusively demonstrating the existence, structure, and contents of the alleged source underlying the non-Markan sections of Matthew and Luke, such studies are finally quite inconclusive.

text of the Gospel of Thomas requires us to assume anything one way or the other about the contents of Q, or, since Q seems to have been Gospel-like in general scope, its form either (*pace* Robinson).

CONCLUSION

THE TWO-SOURCE HYPOTHESIS: A CRITICAL APPRAISAL

Joseph B. Tyson

The essays printed here appeared originally over a period of almost sixty years, from 1924-1981. They represent only a small part of the volume of books and articles that have, during this time, dealt with the Synoptic problem. The editor of this book did not intend to feature the various theories about the solution to the Synoptic problem but rather to bring together the major arguments for and against the two-source hypothesis. A serious reading of these essays should provide some understanding of the course of debate on the hypothesis as well as an assessment of where we now stand in reference to it.

It was decided to focus attention on the two-source hypothesis, first, because during the period covered by these essays, it has been the reigning solution to the Synoptic problem. G. M. Styler correctly described the situation with regard to the priority of Mark when he wrote in 1962,

> After a century or more of discussion, it has come to be accepted by scholars almost as axiomatic that Mark is the oldest of the three synoptic gospels, and that

it was used by Matthew and Luke as a source. This has come to be regarded as 'the one absolutely assured result' of the study of the synoptic problem.[1]

But Styler was quite aware that the theory of Markan priority was being challenged. This fact constitutes a second reason for concentrating on the two-source hypothesis: it has been the reigning theory, but it has been challenged at fundamental points.

The arrangement of the essays is intended to show how the leading scholars attacked and defended the hypothesis in regard to its two fundamental assertions—the priority of Mark and the existence of Q. Unfortunately, this arrangement obscures some chronological relationships among the various writers. Styler's reply to Butler, for example, comes here before Butler's argument. In addition, it should be stressed that not all the writers who are included under a particular category embrace the same source hypothesis. For example, Austin Farrer and W. R. Farmer agree that Q is not necessary since Luke used Matthew. But Farrer accepts the priority of Mark, while Farmer rejects it. Thus, their approaches to the composition of Luke are very different from one another. One might also observe the range of viewpoints among those who support the Q hypothesis, from Vincent Taylor, who believes it was "a collection of sayings and parables which actually existed when Matthew and Luke wrote,"[2] to C. K. Barrett, who does not think of Q as a single written document. Since, however, the essays had to be arranged in some fashion, the present one seemed to the editor to be the best way to exhibit the various arguments about the two-source hypothesis.

After reading these essays, it is difficult to avoid the conclusion that nothing convincing has emerged from this long and tortuous discussion. With so many voices raised in protest, it surely is no longer accurate to refer to the two-source hypothesis as the "assured result" of Synoptic criticism. But neither has this hypothesis been driven from the field. Serious and expert scholars have come to its defense, and most NT scholars continue to support it and utilize it in their studies of the gospels and the history of early Christianity. The two-source hypothesis has been damaged, but its adherents have not surrendered.

---

[1]G. M. Styler, "The Priority of Mark," in C. F. D. Moule, *The Birth of the New Testament* (1962) 223.

[2]Vincent Taylor, *New Testament Essays* (1970) 117.

Inevitably, readers of these essays will appraise them quite differently and assess the current situation in various ways. In a concluding chapter, it seems appropriate to attempt a restatement of the major problems that have been dealt with in the essays, an assessment of the failure to agree, and a prognosis for future research on the Synoptic problem. No attempt will be made to summarize all the essays or to cover all the issues that have been raised in them.

It is enlightening to recognize that B. H. Streeter's statements about the facts that are relevant for a solution to the Synoptic problem have received remarkably wide acceptance. There is significant agreement, sometimes implicit, among our authors that Streeter called attention to those areas that required explanation. This is not to say that there is basic agreement with Streeter's statements about these facts, much less with his utilization of the facts to support his thesis. The statements have been challenged as biased—a fact that even some supporters recognized—and, in some cases, inaccurate. But the areas that Streeter cited seem to have been generally accepted as constituting those matters that require explanation, namely agreements among the Synoptic gospels in content, wording, and order, the data that come from comparisons of language, and the distribution of materials. Supporters of the two-source hypothesis tend to repeat Streeter's statements. Opponents either correct them or evaluate them differently, but they do not ignore them. This fact may itself be an indication that Streeter knew where to look for the relevant facts that had to be explained by any solution to the Synoptic problem.

Among the areas that Streeter cited, two seem to be more problematic than the others. At least, that judgment emerges from a review of the essays printed here. One is the problem of order; the other is a complex of problems that relate to the composition of the Synoptic gospels.

THE PROBLEM OF ORDER

There is little disagreement that similarities among the Synoptic gospels in respect to the order of pericopes require some explanation. Most scholars are convinced that these similarities can be explained only by some theory of literary relationships. Although the use of oral sources might explain some of the relevant phenomena, extended agreement between two documents in respect to the sequence of apparently unrelated narratives or sayings seems to be explicable only by a theory of literary

relationships. But in order to move from this point of consensus, it is necessary to say something precise about the character of sequential agreement. Streeter's statement involves an acceptance of Markan priority and is, as David Dungan says, "inexcusably prejudicial."[3] It goes as follows: "The relative order of incidents and sections in Mark is in general supported by both Matthew and Luke; where either of them deserts Mark, the other is usually found supporting him."[4]

The bias in Streeter's statement may be shown by rephrasing it along the lines of a different hypothesis; say, the Farrer theory. Here one may say that Matthew usually supports Mark's order and that Luke supports both when they agree and Mark when they do not. The same phenomenon may be described by an adherent of the Griesbach hypothesis: Luke frequently follows Matthew's order when he uses Matthew's material; Mark, when he uses material in both Matthew and Luke, follows the order of both when they agree and one when they do not. None of these statements is free from bias, and none adequately describes the situation with the precision that is needed.

Despite the bias that he recognized in Streeter's statement about order, Dungan agreed that Streeter had most of his facts right. E. P. Sanders, however, has challenged the facts themselves. He called attention to the fact that Streeter and others overlooked narratives and sayings that Matthew or Luke may have omitted from their texts, and he contended that if one author has relocated a pericope from his source and the other has omitted it, it is fair to say that both have deserted the order of their common source. Sanders pointed to a number of such desertions by Matthew and Luke. Moreover, he challenged the tool that most previous scholars used in making judgments about sequence, namely the synopsis of Tischendorf.[5] If one should define the units differently, one would probably come up with a different perception of the phenomenon of order, and Sanders made some suggestions along these lines. Whether we accept Sanders's conclusions or not, we should agree with him that, "of all the synoptic phenomena, the phenomenon of order is perhaps the most difficult to state in general terms which can claim accuracy."[6]

---

[3]David L. Dungan, "Mark—The Abridgement of Matthew and Luke," in *Jesus and Man's Hope* (1970) 1:60.

[4]B. H. Streeter, *The Four Gospels* (1924) 151.

[5]See Constantin von Tischendorf, *Synopsis Evangelica* (1851).

[6]E. P. Sanders, "The Argument from Order and the Relationship between Matthew and Luke," *NTS* 15 (1969): 249.

The discussion of the so-called "Lachmann fallacy" represents some of the difficulties involved in describing the phenomenon of order. A number of writers have shown that Lachmann's argument about order applied only in the situation that Lachmann himself presupposed—namely the mutual use by Matthew, Mark, and Luke of a hypothetical Ur-Gospel. To say that, on this assumption, the order of Mark agrees best with the order of the hypothetical primitive gospel is not the same as saying that Mark is the oldest of the Synoptic gospels. That fallacy has been sufficiently exposed, and it is good to know, thanks to N. H. Palmer, that Lachmann himself did not commit the Lachmann fallacy.

But there is another aspect of Lachmann's argument that has not received much attention. In Palmer's translation, Lachmann says:

> The ordering of the gospel stories does not vary as much as most people think. The variation appears greatest if all three writers are compared together, or if Luke is compared with Matthew: it is less if Mark is compared with the others one by one. That shows what I should do: first compare Mark with Matthew, and afterwards consider the order of Luke and Mark.[7]

To be sure, if there are any sequential agreements among three writers, there will likely be more between some pairs and less among all three. But is it a fair statement of the phenomenon of order to isolate the pairs that show the highest agreements and to ignore the others? Agreements in order among all three Synoptic writers form part of the total picture and should not be overlooked. But Lachmann's procedure has been influential. Neirynck, for example, believes that "the basic phenomenon to be reckoned with is the common order between Mark and Matthew and between Mark and Luke."[8]

Discussion of the order of Q poses a very different topic from the discussion of order in respect to materials shared by Mark and one or both of the other Synoptic gospels. This is so because of the hypothetical nature of Q. Referring to the work of Sir John Hawkins, Streeter observed that Matthew and Luke almost never agreed either on the order or the context of Q material.

> It then appeared that, subsequent to the Temptation story, there is not a single case in which Matthew and Luke agree in inserting the same saying at the same point in the Markan outline. If then Luke derived this material from Matthew, he

---

[7]N. H. Palmer, "Lachmann's Argument," *NTS* 13 (1967): 370.

[8]F. Neirynck, "Synoptic Problem," *The Interpreter's Dictionary of the Bible* (1976) Supp.:846.

> must have gone through both Matthew and Mark so as to discriminate with metic-
> ulous precision between Markan and non-Markan material; he must then have pro-
> ceeded with the utmost care to tear every little piece of non-Markan material he
> desired to use from the context of Mark in which it appeared in Matthew—in spite
> of the fact that contexts in Matthew are always exceedingly appropriate—in order
> to re-insert it into a different context of Mark having no special appropriateness.[9]

In this quotation Streeter is pointing to two distinct, though related, phenomena. He emphasizes the disagreement between Matthew and Luke in
respect to the Markan contexts of the Q material. But he also notes the disagreement in respect to the order of that material. For him, the disagreement between Matthew and Luke in their contextual and sequential
placement of the two hundred or so non-Markan verses common to them
was an argument for the existence of Q. Presumably, if Luke had used
Matthew, there would be a higher rate of agreement, both in respect to
context and in respect to sequence, in this material.

Some later scholars have, however, been able to find evidence in Matthew and Luke of an underlying agreement on the order of Q material.
While not denying the disagreement in respect to context, Vincent Taylor
claimed that Luke faithfully preserved the order of Q and that Matthew
"knew the same order and was aware of it when he made the editorial adjustments and conflated Q with Mark and M."[10] He concluded:

> If we reject, as we must, the hypothesis of Luke's dependence on Matthew, the
> result of a comparison of the order of the sayings in Matthew and Luke is to dem-
> onstrate the existence of Q, so far as this is possible in the case of a source known
> to us only from its use in the two Gospels.[11]

It is remarkable that contrary observations about the phenomenon of
order can lead to the same conclusion. For Streeter, lack of sequential
agreement between Matthew and Luke suggests the existence of Q; for
Taylor, indications of an underlying agreement in order demonstrate the
existence of Q. Admittedly, the two were not pointing to exactly the same
phenomenon. Streeter was looking at the different contexts and locations
of Q material. Taylor was looking for subtle indications that Matthew was
aware of the Lukan order of the Q material. Streeter talks about disagreement at the surface, and Taylor talks about underlying agreement. Never-

---

[9] Streeter, *Four Gospels* 183.
[10] Taylor, *Essays*, 117.
[11] Ibid.

theless, these essays show that the phenomenon of order may be perceived in quite different ways and may be used to support quite different arguments.[12]

Taylor's argument rests on a number of assumptions, and it is not clear what, if anything, it actually demonstrates. If we had a document such as the one he describes, that is, Q in the Lukan order, and if we had reason to suppose that Matthew and Luke used it, Taylor's analysis would show how we might understand Matthew's editorial procedures. It would show that Matthew distributed the Q material in his five great discourses but, within each discourse, largely respected the order of Q. But since Q is hypothetical and its original order unknown, it is not clear that the analyses show anything more than the remarkable ingenuity of a modern scholar. They do not demonstrate that Luke's order is more original, for that was presupposed, and they do not show that Matthew respected the original order of Q.

Austin Farrer has questioned the force of Streeter's observations at this point. He agreed that, for the most part, Luke's placement of the Q material is less coherent than Matthew's, but he did not think that in itself was an argument against Luke's use of Matthew. An author who uses an earlier document as a source will not necessarily improve on the source. As Farrer says, "St. Luke would not be either the first planner or the last to prefer a plan of his own to a plan of a predecessor's, and to make a less skillful thing of it."[13] Surely, logic is on Farrer's side at this point, although he did not answer Streeter's implied objection about the different ways Luke would, under Farrer's hypothesis, have treated the Markan and the non-Markan material in Matthew.

These observations show that there is a need for a more accurate and unbiased description of the phenomenon of order. Such a description would need to make clear what an agreement in order is. It would also need to develop some principles for setting the limits of the units to be dealt with. Sanders's point about Tischendorf's synopsis is well taken, although most of us may not wish to deal with units as small as the ones Sanders

---

[12]Note that W. G. Kümmel accepts Taylor's judgment as does Joseph Fitzmyer. By contrast, Theodore A. Rosché cites the lack of common order in Q as a problem for adherents of the Q hypothesis.

[13]A. M. Farrer, "On Dispensing with Q," in *Studies in the Gospels: Essays in Memory of R. H. Lightfoot* (1955) 65.

uses. Above all, an accurate description of sequential agreement among the Synoptic gospels would include analyses of agreements between Mark and Matthew, Mark and Luke, Matthew and Luke, and all three.[14] In addition, there is a need for great care in constructing arguments on the basis of such a description of the phenomenon of order.

Moreover, the discussions represented in the essays have led to some conclusions and have helped to clarify some problems. One conclusion that might be drawn is a negative one, but it is valuable nevertheless. The patterns of sequential agreement in the Synoptic gospels do not require any one explanation. B. C. Butler was right in his remarks about the so-called triple tradition. The patterns that Streeter, et al., observed in the order of these materials are explicable by any hypothesis in which Mark is the linking term. Among the possibilities are the following: Matthew and Luke used Mark; Mark used Matthew and was then used by Luke; Mark used Luke and was then used by Matthew; Mark used both Matthew and Luke. Perhaps more precise statements of the phenomenon of order or about other aspects of the situation may make one of these theories more likely than the others, but as things stand now, no one theory has the edge.

In regard to the existence of Q, observations on order lack probative value. It seems necessary to have Q only if one finds it impossible to believe that Luke used Matthew, or vice versa. Farrer is right at this point, and he is correct in saying that the disagreements in the order of common non-Markan materials do not make it impossible to believe that Luke used Matthew. In this case, Luke might be described as a crank, to use Streeter's term, but one would be hard put to say that such editorial processes are impossible. Moreover, Farmer has been able to show that Luke's procedure in using Matthew is explicable on the assumption that he worked through it several times and did not have Mark.

THE PROBLEM OF COMPOSITION

The term *composition* is used here to cover a complex of phenomena, including language and redaction. It involves comparisons among the Synoptic gospels on linguistic style, the identification of redactional passages and procedures, and differences between primary and secondary documents.

---

[14]One way this may be done is shown in my article, "Sequential Parallelism in the Synoptic Gospels," *NTS* 22 (1976): 276-308.

Streeter used observations about the language of Mark and about Matthean and Lukan redaction of Mark's language in one of his arguments for the priority of Mark.

> The primitive character of Mark is further shown by (a) the use of phrases likely to cause offense, which are omitted or toned down in the other Gospels, (b) roughness of style and grammar, and the preservation of Aramaic words.[15]

He called attention to such things in Matthew and Luke as more reverential terms for Jesus. He also characterized Mark's linguistic style as "a shorthand account of a story by an impromptu speaker—with all the repetitions, redundancies, and digressions which are characteristic of living speech."[16] Matthew and Luke, by comparison, used a more careful written style. They omitted most of Mark's Aramaic phrases, and they corrected his grammatical errors. Streeter assumes that, in primitive Christian history, a source is likely to be closer to oral communication, more apt to use Aramaic, and grammatically inferior to the books that made use of it.

Whether Streeter is correct in his observations and whether or not his assumptions are valid, he has pointed to the need for close comparison of compositional aspects of the gospels. The problem of order may be thought of as requiring macrostudies, in which one takes a broad overview of the gospels and examines the arrangement of large blocks of material. The problem of composition requires microstudy, in which one looks within the pericopes and observes the verbal and stylistic differences among the gospels.[17]

Several of our essayists have engaged in such microstudies. B. C. Butler closely examined a number of pericopes that he thought were explicable on the assumption that Mark used proto-Matthew. Styler replied by citing several passages which he thought showed that Matthew had used Mark. In some of these, Styler attempted to show that Matthew had misunderstood Mark and, hence, had gone astray. He was also impressed with the "freshness and circumstantial character" of Mark's style. Styler rec-

---

[15]Streeter, *Four Gospels*, 151ff.

[16]Ibid., 163.

[17]William O. Walker, Jr. has used the terms "atomistic" and "holistic" to make essentially the same distinction. He refers to the current debates between W. R. Farmer, et al. (favoring a holistic approach) and Reginald H. Fuller, et al. (favoring an atomistic approach). He analyzes the issues in "The Son of Man Question and the Synoptic Problem," *NTS* 28 (1981-1982): 374-88.

ognized that scholars may choose the pericopes that are favorable to their own view and difficult for others. He wrote, "Our explanation of *his* [Butler's] favorable cases may be cumbersome; but his explanation of *our* favorable cases is incredible."[18]

The problem of composition has not only played a role in the question of the priority of Mark but also in that of the existence of Q. In this connection, our collection of essays includes two treatments of the Beelzebul controversy (Mt. 12:22-30; Mk. 3:22-27; Lk. 11:14-23), one by F. G. Downing, who supports the existence of Q, and the other by R. T. Simpson, who does not. A comparison of these two treatments may help to highlight some aspects of the problem of composition.

The Beelzebul passage appears in all three Synoptic gospels, with verbal agreements between Matthew and Mark and between Luke and Mark, but also significant agreements between Matthew and Luke. In fact, the agreements that Matthew and Luke share in this passage are greater than those that either shares with Mark. At best, Matthew and Mark agree on 52 words, Luke and Mark on 18, and Matthew and Luke on 95. To one who accepts the priority of Mark and the existence of Q (Downing), this passage would be a case of a Q-Mark overlap. On the Farrer hypothesis (Simpson), the passage shows how Luke used both Matthew and Mark.

Downing sets the limits of the Beelzebul controversy to include Mt. 12:22-45; Mk. 3:20-29; Lk. 11:14-26 (with Lk. 12:10; 6:43-45). This arrangement includes sayings of Jesus about the sin against the Holy Spirit, the sign of Jonah, and the return of the evil spirit. He begins by comparing Matthew and Mark and classifying the material as (A) material on which there is nearly *verbatim* agreement between Matthew and Mark; (B) material that is parallel in Matthew and Mark but in which verbal agreements are not high; and (C) material that is in Matthew but not in Mark. Then Downing examines Luke and attempts to show that Luke used none of the A material, most of the B material, and almost all of the C material "here or elsewhere." The Lukan avoidance of the A material is, for him, the most damaging evidence against the Farrer hypothesis. If Luke used Matthew, he followed him *"only where the latter has added new material to Mark or has largely altered him."*[19] The only thing that Luke left out was "the material in Mark that Matthew obviously saw fit to include pretty

---

[18]Styler, "Priority," 231.

[19]F. G. Downing, "Towards the Rehabilitation of Q," *NTS* 11 (1964-1965): 175.

well as it stood."[20] Downing concludes that Luke depended for his narrative only on Q. Evidently Matthew combined Mark and Q.

Downing may have exaggerated the differences between the A and B material in his analysis. Some of the B verses have about as much verbal agreement between Matthew and Mark as the A verses. Mt. 12:24b (B material) has as many words in common with Mark as Mt. 12:31a (A material). Mt. 12:25b-26a has proportionally more.[21] Distinctions between verses that are nearly verbatim and verses that are similar sometimes rest on shaky judgments rather than on objective observations. Moreover, it is not quite correct to say that Luke has no parallels with the A material. In Lk. 11:21, "the strong one" may have come from Mt. 12:29. Finally, Downing's A material constitutes a sampling, that is, only two unrelated sayings, that is too small to be of much significance.

Although Simpson deals with the Beelzebul controversy, he makes no reference to Downing's article, which had appeared in the previous volume of *NTS*. His approach is to claim that Mk. 3:26 is an editorial attempt to reconcile 3:24-25 with 3:23. If that is so, says Simpson, it is unlikely that Q would have had parallels that included this editorial material. But if you look at the parallel verses in Matthew and Luke, you find not only agreements between them and Mark but also agreements between them against Mark. If these agreements did not come from Q, which is unlikely, they must have come from Luke's use of Matthew as well as Mark. In addition, both Matthew and Luke have added a saying that is not found in Mark at this point. It appears in a different form in Mk. 9:40 and Lk. 9:50, but it is identical in Mt. 12:30 and Lk. 11:23—"He who is not with me is against me, and he who does not gather with me scatters." Although the connection with the Beelzebul story is not obvious, both include it at about the same point.[22]

Simpson rightly looks upon Mk. 3:26 as the key to his argument. If one is not convinced that the verse is editorial, the way is open to an analysis of the entire passage on the Q hypothesis. The contrast that Simpson draws

---

[20]Ibid.

[21]Mt. 12:31a (A material in Downing's classification) has 9 out of 14 words, or 64 percent, in agreement with Mark. Mt. 12:24b (B material) has 9 out of 13 words, or 69 percent, in agreement with Mark. Mt. 12:24b-26a (B material) has 19 out of 26 words, or 73 percent, in agreement with Mark.

[22]Cf. R. T. Simpson, "The Major Agreements of Matthew and Luke Against Mark," *NTS* 12 (1965-1966): 282. The reference in line 4 to Mt. 18:30 should be to Mt. 12:30.

is that Mk. 3:23 talks about expulsion, while 24-25 talk about division. Mk. 3:26 links the two concepts. Many readers will think this is an overly subtle point, too small to build a convincing case against Q. Without it, there is nothing against the view that Matthew and Luke are independently conflating Mark and Q at this point.[23]

A comparison of the articles by Downing and Simpson raises a number of methodological questions. One question relates to the identification of editorial sections. This is manifestly an important consideration in solving the source problem, since it is clear that one of the things the evangelists did was to edit traditional material, whether that material came in oral or written form. They had to make basic decisions about the compositional structure of their gospels and about the treatment of the individual pericopes. They wrote introductions, conclusions, transitions, summaries, and explanatory notes, and they provided geographical and chronological settings. If it can be shown that traces of editorial sections from one gospel, say Mark, show up in another, say Luke, that would constitute evidence that Luke used Mark. Simpson's article shows that arguments relating to the influence of editorial sections from one gospel to another are potentially useful. His essay also shows that great care is needed in the determination of editorial sections. One must be certain that a particular theory of Synoptic relationships has not affected one's judgment about redaction.

Another aspect of the study of composition in the gospels is the redactional procedure itself. Each theory of Synoptic relationships requires a certain understanding of the redactional procedures of the individual evangelists. The power that a particular theory has to convince lies partly in the credibility of its understanding of the editorial procedures of the individual gospel writers. In the two-source hypothesis, one needs to show how Matthew and Luke, respectively, used Mark (and Q). In the Griesbach hypothesis, it is necessary to show how Luke used Matthew and how Mark used Matthew and Luke. Contrariwise, it is often felt that one can destroy a hypothesis by showing that the redactional procedure it would require is incredible. This was what Downing attempted to do against the Farrer hypothesis. To him it was incredible that Luke would avoid those verses in which Matthew closely followed Mark. Here it is necessary to sound a cautionary note. It is inevitable that the standard of judgment we make of

---

[23]Unfortunately, there is not, to my knowledge, an analysis of the Beelzebul story from the perspective of the Griesbach hypothesis.

this matter is our own, but what appears credible or incredible to any one of us may be idiosyncratic or ethnocentric. What Luke did with his sources may have made perfect sense to him but not to us. Or, what is more likely, we may not be able to discern the sense that things made to an ancient author. Thus, it is difficult to attribute probative value to those arguments that attempt to show the credibility or incredibility of a certain redactional procedure, even if we are able to describe that procedure.

A final problem relating to the matter of composition is that of distinguishing between primary and secondary versions of parallel accounts. In those cases where we are almost certain that there is a literary relationship between two versions of a narrative, what things do we look for as signs of dependence? Streeter was certain that an oral style is prior to a written style, that poor grammar comes before correct grammar, and that higher titles for Jesus come later. Form criticism has played a significant role here, in showing us how primitive forms frequently take on secondary characteristics. In this respect the appendix from E. P. Sanders's *The Tendencies of the Synoptic Tradition* is significant.[24] He has gathered a number of verses from Mark that ''representative scholars'' regard as secondary to the parallels in Matthew or Luke. Some of the ''representative scholars,'' such as Bultmann, are noted for their form-critical studies, and all of them hold to the two-source hypothesis. The impressive aspect of this list is its size. Sanders's intention in compiling the list evidently is to raise doubts about the priority of Mark. He asks if Mark can come first if it has so many verses, that, on form-critical grounds, appear to be secondary to the gospels which allegedly made use of it.

Sanders's book, from which our excerpt is taken, is a test of the validity of some commonly applied criteria for distinguishing between primary and secondary documents. In it, he examines the characteristics of length, detail, Semitism, the use of direct discourse, and conflation. His conclusion is that no criteria are hard: ''On all counts the tradition developed in opposite directions.''[25] He adds, ''For this reason, *dogmatic statements that a certain characteristic proves a certain passage to be earlier than another are never justified.*[26] Perhaps Sanders has not had the last word, but unless new evidence requires an alteration of his judgment, ar-

---

[24]E. P. Sanders, *The Tendencies of the Synoptic Tradition* (1969).
[25]Ibid., 272.
[26]Ibid.

guments based on the criteria that he cited should be regarded as inconclusive.[27]

In this light, we must look again at the criteria offered by W. R. Farmer in his "New Introduction to the Problem."[28] He has three "canons of criticism," to which he adds six principles originally suggested by E. D. Burton. Farmer's first canon claims that, in the Synoptic tradition, a Palestinian provenance is primary to a non-Palestinian provenance. As a criterion, it appears to make use of the Semitisms that Sanders examined and discarded. It should be noted, however, that Sanders dealt only with formal Semitisms, that is, "the way in which something is said."[29] He did not deal with Semitisms of content, that is, "what is said." Sanders also observed that "Semitisms of content are seldom dealt with as such, and the word Semitisms usually refers to formal Semitisms."[30] By calling attention to the "Palestinian provenance," Farmer seems to have in mind the second category of Semitisms, the ones with which Sanders did not deal. Even so, it would seem difficult to eliminate the possibility that a certain saying or narrative with Palestinian characteristics has entered the tradition at a relatively late date or has undergone "re-Palestinianization." The second canon, that a version of a saying or narrative with an explanatory gloss is secondary to one without it, commends itself as probably useful. The third deals with the appearance of one gospel's redactional material in another gospel.[31] Burton's six principles, as principles, seem un-

---

[27]In the essay by Pierson Parker, taken from a longer article, we may see the application of a number of criteria to show that Mark is secondary. Parker believes that Mark is secondary to a document, K, on which Matthew also depended. The criteria that he uses seem, however, to suggest that Mark is secondary to the situation that prevailed in the life of Jesus. Thus, Parker calls attention to such things as Markan errors about Judaism, the scriptures, Palestinian geography, and doubtful statements about Jesus. It is evident that Parker means to use the word "secondary" in a sense other than the way it is being used here, that is, to distinguish literary characteristics in the Synoptic gospels. Elsewhere Parker has outlined his views on this matter; see "A Second Look at *The Gospel Before Mark*," *JBL* 100 (1981): 406-408. Some of the criteria he uses there have been questioned by Sanders.

[28]W. R. Farmer, *The Synoptic Problem* 2d ed. (1976) 227-29.

[29]Sanders, *Tendencies*, 193.

[30]Ibid.

[31]In the first edition published in 1964, Farmer had an additional canon on specificity. It stated that the more specific form of the tradition is secondary to the less specific form. Farmer was convinced by the work of Sanders to omit this as a valid criticism; cf. Farmer, *Synoptic Problem* (1964) 228.

arguable. If, for example, we can properly identify material in one gospel that is a manifest misunderstanding of material in another, or if we can spot an interrupting insertion or omission, then we will have discovered an important clue to the source problem. The canons and principles that Farmer sets forth (except for the first) seem valid. The rub comes in applying them. An examination of the essays in this book should show that the identification of glosses, redactional material, and interrupting insertions is a hazardous occupation. Yet it is in applying such principles as these that progress will probably be made.

The application of the above canons and principles will require literary studies that do not make use of a source hypothesis. The tricky part of this work lies in the identification of the relevant literary characteristics which are thought to have a bearing on the source problem, and if this process of identification is theory dependent, it is flawed. Ironically, hope for a solution to the Synoptic problem now seems to rest on studies in the area of a kind of literary criticism that brackets the source question.

In any event, the examination of the essays here, in respect to their contribution to the study of composition in the Synoptic gospels, shows that greater precision is needed in the identification of relevant compositional characteristics. In addition, greater attention needs to be given to the development of an appropriate method of comparing compositional characteristics. Scholars have not yet agreed on what constitutes relevant evidence, what valid criteria may be applied, or what kinds of arguments carry conviction.

It has not been my purpose in this essay to survey all the contributions and summarize their arguments. As a result, it is likely that some important points have not been mentioned here. I am aware, for example, of the importance in the history of discussion of the minor agreements of Matthew and Luke against Mark. The essays show that there is a good deal of dissatisfaction with the way Streeter dealt with these agreements, which some interpret as evidences that Luke used Matthew. The matter of doublets has also received appropriate attention in several essays. My purpose has been to call attention to two major areas of discussion—order and composition—and to the problems in these areas, in the hope that an examination of these problems will indicate something significant about the state of Synoptic studies.

It appears now necessary to embrace the conclusion that was tentatively stated at the beginning of this essay. The discussion of the two-

source theory during the past sixty years has seriously damaged the reigning hypothesis, but it has not completely dislodged it. One who continues to regard it as an "assured result of critical study" has apparently chosen to ignore the discussions here and elsewhere. So has anyone who regards the two-source hypothesis as dead.

There is a sense in which the essays printed here are not totally representative of the current state of the problem. Since it was decided to focus on the pros and cons of the two-source hypothesis, it was necessary to include challenges from proponents of various alternative hypotheses. It seems fair to say, however, that the Griesbach hypothesis, especially as represented in the work of W. R. Farmer, has now emerged as the leading alternative solution to the Synoptic problem. This fact suggests that future research on the source problem will be carried on largely by persons in the Griesbach and the two-source camps.

This collection has shown that the challenges to the two-source hypothesis are serious and should be taken seriously. On an even more basic level, it has uncovered a number of methodological weaknesses, which are evident on both sides of the discussion. It is imperative that future research on the source problem concern itself with the development of sounder procedures of analysis, particularly for the study of order and composition of the gospels. Much has been done, but more remains.

BIBLIOGRAPHY
AND INDEXES

BIBLIOGRAPHY

Abbott, E. A. *The Corrections of Mark Adopted by Matthew and Luke*, Diatesserica II. London: A. & C. Black, 1901.

_____. *The Fourfold Gospel*, 5 volumes. Cambridge: The University Press, 1913-1917.

_____. "Gospels." In *Encyclopedia Biblica*, ed. T. K. Cheyne and J. S. Black, II:1761-1840. New York: The Macmillan Company, 1901.

_____ and W. G. Rushbrooke. *The Common Tradition of the Synoptic Gospels*. London: Macmillan and Co., 1884.

Aland, Kurt. *Synopsis of the Four Gospels*. Greek-English Edition of the *Synopsis Quattuor Evangeliorum*, 3d ed. Stuttgart: United Bible Societies, 1979.

Albertz, Martin. *Die Botschaft des Neuen Testaments*. Zollikon-Zürich: Evangelischer Verlag. I, 1 (1947); I, 2 (1952).

_____. *Die synoptischen Streitgespräche. Ein Beitrag zur Formgeschichte des Urchristentums*. Berlin: Trowitzsch und Sohn, 1921.

Allen, W. C. *The Gospel According to St. Matthew*. The International Critical Commentary. Edinburgh: T. & T. Clark, 1907.

Appel, Heinrich. *Einleitung in das Neue Testament*. Leipzig: Erlangen, 1922.

Argyle, A. W. "Agreements between Matthew and Luke," *The Expository Times* 73 (1961-1962): 19-22.

_____. "Evidence for the View that St. Luke Used St. Matthew's Gospel," *Journal of Biblical Literature* 83 (1964): 390-96.

————. "The Methods of the Evangelists and the Q Hypothesis," *Theology* 67 (1964): 156-57.

Audet, Jean Paul. *La Didaché, instructions des apôtres*. Paris: Librarie Lecoffre, J. Gabalda, 1958.

Bacon, Benjamin W. *Is Mark A Roman Gospel?* Harvard Theological Studies 7. Cambridge: Harvard University Press, 1919.

————. *Studies in Matthew*. New York: Henry Holt and Co., 1930.

Badham, F. P. *St. Mark's Indebtedness to St. Matthew*. London: T. Fisher Unwin, 1897; New York: E. R. Herrick and Co., 1897.

Balz, Horst R. *Methodische Probleme der neutestamentliche Christologie*. Wissenschaftliche Monographien zum Alten und Neuen Testament 25. Neukirchen-Vluyn: Neukirchener Verlag des Erziehungsvereins, 1967.

Bammel, E. "Das Ende von Q," *Verborum Veritas, Festschrift for Gustav Stählin*. Wuppertal: Theologischer Verlag Brockhaus, 1970.

Barnikol, Ernst. *Das Leben Jesu der Heilsgeschichte*. Halle: M. Niemyer, 1958.

Barr, Allen. *A Diagram of Synoptic Relationships*. Edinburgh: T. & T. Clark, 1938.

Barrett, C. K. "Q: A Re-examination," *The Expository Times* 54 (1942-1943): 320-23.

Bauer, J. B. "The Synoptic Tradition in the Gospel of Thomas," *Studia Evangelica* III, Texte und Untersuchungen zur Geschichte der altkirchlichen Literatur 88 (1964).

Beare, Francis W. *The Earliest Records of Jesus*. London: Blackwell, 1962; New York and Nashville: Abingdon Press, 1962.

Bellinzoni, Arthur J. *The Sayings of Jesus in the Writings of Justin Martyr*. Novum Testamentum Supplements 17. Leiden: E. J. Brill, 1967.

Benoit, Pierre. *L'Évangile selon S. Matthieu*, 3d ed., rev. Paris: Éditions du Cerf, 1961.

Betz, Otto. *What Do We Know About Jesus?*, trans. Margaret Kohl. London: S. C. M. Press, 1968.

Black, Matthew. *An Aramaic Approach to the Gospels and Acts*, 3d ed. Oxford: The Clarendon Press, 1967.

Bleek, Friedrich. *Einleitung in das Neue Testament*, 2d ed. English translation by William Urwic, *An Introduction to the New Testament* in Clark's *Foreign Theological Library*. Edinburgh: T. & T. Clark, 1869; 3d ed., 1875; 4th ed. rev. by W. Mangold, 1886.

Boismard, M.-E. *Synopse des quatre évangiles en français*, II: Commentaire. Paris: Éditions du Cerf, 1972.

Boman, Thorleif. *Die Jesusüberlieferung im Lichte der neueren Volkskunde*. Göttingen: Vandenhoeck und Ruprecht, 1967.

Bornkamm, Günther. "Evangelien, synoptische." In *Die Religion in Geschichte und Gegenwart*, 3d ed., I:753-66. Tübingen: Mohr, 1958.

————. *Handbuch zum Neuen Testament*, begründet von Hans Leitzmann in Verbindung mit Fachgenossen. Tübingen: J. C. B. Mohr, 1949.

————. *Jesus of Nazareth*, trans. Irene and Fraser McLuskey with James M. Robinson. London: Hodder and Stoughton, 1960; New York: Harper and Brothers, 1960.

Bradby, E. L. "In Defence of Q," *The Expository Times* 68 (1956-1957): 315-18.

Brown, John P. "An Early Revision of the Gospel of Mark," *Journal of Biblical Literature* 78 (1959): 215-27.

————. "The Form of 'Q' Known to Matthew," *New Testament Studies* 8 (1961-1962): 27-42.

————. "Mark as Witness to an Edited Form of Q," *Journal of Biblical Literature* 80 (1961): 29-44.

Brown, Milton P. *The Authentic Writings of Ignatius. A Study of Linguistic Criteria*. Duke Studies in Religion 2. Durham: Duke University Press, 1963.

Brown, Raymond E. "The Gospel of Thomas and St. John's Gospel," *New Testament Studies* 9 (1963): 155-77.

Bultmann, Rudolf. *Die Erforschung der synoptischen Evangelien*, 3d ed., 1960; trans., "The Study of the Synoptic Gospels." In *Form Criticism*, ed. F. C. Grant. New York: Harper Torchbooks, 1962.

_____. *Form Criticism: A New Method of New Testament Research*, trans. and ed. F. C. Grant. Chicago: Willett, Clark, 1934; rev. 1962.

_____. *Die Geschichte der synoptischen Tradition* (und *Ergänzungsheft*), 4. Auflage. Göttingen: Vandenhoeck und Reprecht, 1958.

_____. *The History of the Synoptic Tradition*, trans. John Marsh. London: Blackwell, 1963; 2d ed. 1968 (translation of 2d German edition of 1931).

Burkitt, F. C. *The Earliest Sources for the Life of Jesus*. Boston: Pilgrim Press, 1910.

_____. *The Gospel History and Its Transmission*. Edinburgh: T. & T. Clark, 1906.

Burney, Charles F. *The Poetry of Our Lord. An Examination of the Formal Elements of Hebrew Poetry in the Discourses of Jesus Christ*. Oxford: The Clarendon Press, 1925.

Burton, Ernest De W. *Some Principles of Literary Criticism and Their Applications to the Synoptic Problem*. Chicago: University of Chicago Press, 1904.

_____ and Edgar J. Goodspeed. *A Harmony of the Synoptic Gospels*. New York: Charles Scribner's Sons, 1917.

Bussby, F. "Is Q An Aramaic Document?" *The Expository Times* 65 (1953-1954): 272-75.

Bussmann, W. *Synoptische Studien*, 3 volumes. Halle/S.: Buchhandlung des Waisenhauses, 1925, 1929, 1931.

Butler, B. C. "The Literary Relations of the Didache, ch. 16," *Journal of Theological Studies* 11 (1960): 265-83.

_____. "M. Vaganay and the 'Community Discourse,' " *New Testament Studies* 1 (1955): 283-90.

_____. *The Originality of St. Matthew: A Critique of the Two-Document Hypothesis*. Cambridge: University Press, 1951.

_____. "St. Luke's Debt to St. Matthew," *Harvard Theological Review* 32 (1939): 237-308.

_____. "St. Paul's Knowledge and Use of St. Matthew," *Downside Review* 64 (1948): 367ff.

_____. "The Synoptic Problem," *A New Catholic Commentary on Holy Scripture*, ed. R. C. Fuller, L. Johnston, and C. Kearns, 815-21. New York: Nelson, 1969.

_____. "The Synoptic Problem Again," *Downside Review* 73 (1954-1955): 26ff.

_____. "The 'Two Ways' in the Didache," *Journal of Theological Studies* (1961): 27-38.

Cadbury, Henry J. *The Making of Luke-Acts*, 2d ed. New York: The Macmillan Co., 1958.

_____. *The Style and Literary Method of Luke*. Harvard Theological Studies 6. Cambridge: Harvard University Press, 1920.

Carlston, Charles E. and Norlin, Dennis. "Once More—Statistics and Q," *Harvard Theological Review* 64 (1971): 59-78.

Cassian. "The Interrelation of the Gospels: Matthew—Luke—John," *Studia Evangelica* 1, Texte und Untersuchungen zur Geschichte der altkirchlichen Literatur 73 (1958): 129ff.

A Catholic Commentary on Holy Scripture, ed. Bernard Orchard, et al. New York: Nelson, 1953.

Cerfaux, L. "Le problème synoptique," *Nouvelle Revue théologique* 76 (1954).

Chaine, J. *L'Épître de S. Jacques. Études bibliques.* 2d ed. Paris: J. Gabalda et Cie., 1927.

Chapman, John. *Matthew, Mark and Luke. A Study in the Order and Interrelation of the Synoptic Gospels*, ed. John M. T. Barton. London: Longmans, Green and Co., 1937.

Cherry, R. S. "Agreements between Matthew and Luke," *The Expository Times* 74 (1962-1963): 63ff.

Cole, R. A. *The Gospel According to Mark: An Introduction and Commentary.* Tyndale New Testament Commentaries. Grand Rapids: Wm. B. Eerdmans, 1961.

Conzelmann, Hans. *The Theology of St. Luke*, trans. Geoffrey Buswell. New York: Harper and Brothers, 1960.

Couchoud, Paul-Louis. "L'Évangile de Marc a-t-il été écrit en Latin," *Revue de l'Histoire des Religions* (1926): 161-92; trans., "Was the Gospel of Mark Written in Latin?" *Crozer Quarterly* 5 (1928): 35-79.

Creed, John M. *The Gospel According to St. Luke.* The International Critical Commentary. London: Macmillan and Co., 1960.

Cullmann, Oscar. "Das Thomasevangelium und die Frage nach dem Alter der in ihm enthaltenen Tradition," *Theologische Literaturzeitung* 85 (1960): 322-34.

Dahl, Nils A. "Die Passiongeschichte bei Matthäus," *New Testament Studies* 2 (1956): 17-32.

Dalmau, W. M. *A Study on the Synoptic Gospels. A New Solution to an Old Problem. The Dependence of the Greek Gospels of St. Matthew and St. Luke Upon the Gospel of St. Mark.* New York: Robert Speller, 1964.

Davidson, Samuel. "The Gospel of Mark—'Analysis of Contents,' and 'Relation of Mark to Matthew and Luke.' " In *An Introduction to the Study of the New Testament, Critical, Exegetical, and Theological*, 2d ed., 1:542-63. 1882.

Dibelius, Martin. *From Tradition to Gospel*, trans. B. L. Woolf. New York: Charles Scribner's Sons, 1935.

Dodd, C. H. *The Parables of the Kingdom.* New York: Charles Scribner's Sons, 1961.

_____. "Matthew and Paul," *The Expository Times* 58 (1947): 293ff.

Downing, F. G. "Towards the Rehabilitation of Q," *New Testament Studies* 11 (1964-1965): 169-81.

Dungan, D. L. "Mark—The Abridgement of Matthew and Luke." In *Jesus and Man's Hope.* 1:51-97. Pittsburgh: Pittsburgh Theological Seminary, 1970.

Dupont, Jacques. *Les Béatitudes*, new ed. Bruges: St. André, 1958.

Easton, Burton S. *The Gospel according to St. Luke: A Critical and Exegetical Commentary.* New York: Charles Scribner's Sons, 1926.

Edwards, Richard A. "An Approach to a Theology of Q," *Journal of Religion* (October 1971): 247-69.

Eichhorn, Johann Gottfried. "Über die drei ersten Evangelien." In *Allgemeine Bibliothek der biblischen Literatur.* 5:759-996. 1794.

Ellis, Edward E. *The Gospel of Luke.* The Century Bible, New Ed. London: Nelson, 1966.

Evans, C. F. "The Central Section of St. Luke's Gospel." In *Studies in the Gospels: Essays in Memory of R. H. Lightfoot*, ed. D. E. Nineham, 37-53. Oxford: Basil Blackwell, 1955.

Evans, Owen E. "Synoptic Criticism Since Streeter," *The Expository Times* 72 (1960-1961): 295-99.

Farmer, William R. "A Fresh Approach to Q." In *Christianity, Judaism, and Other Greco-Roman Cults: Studies for Morton Smith at Sixty*, ed. Jacob Neusner. Part One: New Testament, 39-50. Leiden: E. J. Brill, 1975.

_____. "The Lachmann Fallacy," *New Testament Studies* 14 (1967-1968): 441-43.

_____. "A Response to Robert Morgenthaler's *Statistische Synopse*," *Biblica* 54 (1973): 417-33.

_____. "A 'Skeleton in the Closet' of Gospel Research," *Biblical Research* 6 (1961): 18-42.

_____. *The Synoptic Problem: A Critical Analysis*. New York: Macmillan, 1964; 2d ed., Mercer University Press, 1976.

_____. *Synopticon: The Verbal Agreement between the Greek Texts of Matthew, Mark and Luke Contextually Exhibited*. Cambridge: University Press, 1969.

_____. "The Two-Document Hypothesis as a Methodological Criterion in Synoptic Research," *Anglican Theological Review* 48 (1966): 380-396.

Farrer, Austin M. "On Dispensing with Q." In *Studies in the Gospels: Essays in Memory of R. H. Lightfoot*, ed. D. E. Nineham, 55-88. Oxford: Basil Blackwell, 1955.

_____. *St. Matthew and St. Mark*. Westminster, England: Dacre Press, 1954.

_____. *A Study of St. Mark*. London: Dacre Press, 1951; New York: Oxford University Press, 1952.

Fascher, Erich. *Die formegeschichtliche Methode*. Beiheft, Zeitschrift für die neutestamentliche Wissenschaft und die Kunde der älteren Kirche 2. Giessen: A Töpelmann, 1924.

_____. *Textgeschichte als hermeneutisches Problem*. Halle: M. Niemeyer, 1953.

Feine, Paul and Johannes Behm. *Einleitung in das Neue Testament*. Heidelberg: Quelle und Meyer, 1963.

_____, Johannes Behm, and Werner G. Kümmel. *Introduction to the New Testament*. Nashville: Abingdon, 1966.

Filson, Floyd V. "New Testament Greek and Coptic Gospel Manuscripts," *Biblical Archaeologist* 24 (1961).

Fitzmyer, Joseph A. "The Priority of Mark and the 'Q' Source in Luke." In *Jesus and Man's Hope*. 1:131-70. Pittsburgh: Pittsburgh Theological Seminary, 1970.

_____. "The Use of *Agein* and *Pherein* in the Synoptics." In *Verborum Veritas, Festschrift for Gustav Stählin*. Wuppertal: Theologischer Verlag Brockhaus, 1970.

Fortna, Robert T. "Redaction Criticism, NT." In *The Interpreter's Dictionary of the Bible*. Supp.:733-35. Nashville: Abingdon, 1976.

Fuchs, A. "Sprachliche Untersuchungen zu Mt und Lk. Ein Beitrag zur Quellenkritik," *Analytica Biblica* 49 (1971).

Fuller, Reginald H. *A Critical Introduction to the New Testament*. London: Gerald Duckworth and Co., Ltd. 1966.

_____, Ed P. Sanders, and Thomas R. W. Longstaff. "The Synoptic Problem: After Ten Years," *Perkins School of Theology Journal* 28 (1975): 63-74.

Gaboury, Antonio. *La structure des évangiles synoptiques. La structure-type à l'origine des Synoptiques*, Novum Testamentum Supplements 22. Leiden: E. J. Brill, 1970.

Gärtner, Bertil. *The Theology of the Gospel of Thomas*, translated by Eric J. Sharpe. New York: Harper, 1961.

Gardner, Helen L. *The Business of Criticism*. Oxford: Clarendon Press, 1959.

Gerhardsson, Birger. *Memory and Manuscript: Oral Tradition and Written Transmission in Rabbinic Judaism and Early Christianity.* Lund: C. W. K. Gleerup, 1961.

Gigot, Francis E. "Synoptics." In *The Catholic Encyclopedia,* ed. Charles G. Herbermann and others, XIV. New York: Robert Appleton Company, 1912.

Gilmour, S. MacLean. "Exegesis of the Gospel According to Saint Luke." In *The Interpreter's Bible.* 8:3-434. Nashville: Abingdon Press, 1952.

Glasson, Thomas F. and C. S. C. Williams. "Did Matthew and Luke Use a 'Western' Text of Mark?" *The Expository Times* 56 (1944-1945): 41-45; 57 (1945-1946): 53-54; 58 (1946-1947): 251.

Glasson, Thomas F. "Did Matthew and Luke Use a 'Western' Text of Mark?" *The Expository Times* 55 (1943-1944): 180-84.

_____. "An Early Revision of the Gospel of Mark," *Journal of Biblical Literature* 85 (1966): 231-33.

Goguel, Maurice. *Introduction au Nouveau Testament.* I-IV, 1/2. Paris, 1922-1926 (incomplete).

Goodspeed, Edgar J. *An Introduction to the New Testament.* Chicago: The University of Chicago Press, 1937.

_____. *New Chapters in New Testament Study.* New York: The Macmillan Co., 1937.

Goulder, M. D. "The Composition of the Lord's Prayer," *Journal of Theological Studies.* New Series 14, i:32-45.

Grant, F. C. *The Gospels: Their Origin and Their Growth.* New York: Harper and Brothers, 1957.

Grant, Robert M. *The Earliest Lives of Jesus.* London: S.P.C.K., 1961; New York: Harper and Brothers, 1961.

_____. *A Historical Introduction to the New Testament.* New York: Harper and Row, 1964.

_____. and David Noel Freedman. *The Secret Sayings of Jesus According to the Gospel of Thomas.* Collins: Fontana, 1960.

Griesbach, Johann J. *Synopsis Evangeliorum Matthaei Marci et Lucae una cum iis Joannis pericopis quae omnino cum caeterorum Evangelistarum narrationibus confederendae sunt.* Halle: 2d ed., 1797; 3d ed., 1809; 4th ed., 1822; trans. B. Orchard, "A Demonstration that Mark was Written after Matthew and Luke." In *J. J. Griesbach: Synoptic Text-Critical Studies,* ed. B. Orchard and T. R. W. Longstaff. Cambridge: University Press, 1977.

Grobel, Kendrick. *Formgeschichtliche und synoptische Quellenanalyse.* Forschungen zur Religion und Literatur des Alten und Neuen Testaments, Neue Folge 35. Göttingen: Vandenhoeck und Ruprecht, 1937.

_____. "How Gnostic is the Gospel of Thomas?" *New Testament Studies* 8 (1962): 367-73.

Grundmann, Walter. *Das Evangelium nach Lukas.* Theologischer Hand-Kommentar zum Neuen Testament, 2d ed. Berlin: Evangelischer Verlagsanstalt, 1961.

_____. *Das Evangelium nach Markus,* Theologischer Hand-Kommentar zum Neuen Testament, 5th ed. Berlin: Evangelischer Verlagsanstalt, 1971.

Güttgemanns, E. *Offene Fragen zur Formgeschichte des Evangeliums. Eine methodische Skizze der Grundlagenproblematik der Form- und Redaktionsgeschichte.* Beiträge zur evangelischen Theologie 54. Munich: C. Kaiser, 1970.

Guillaumont, Antonio. *Gospel According to Thomas,* with Coptic text. Leiden: E. J. Brill, 1959; New York: Harper, 1959.

Guthrie, Donald. *New Testament Introduction: The Gospels and Acts.* London: Tyndale, 1965.

Haardt, R. "Das koptische Thomasevangelium und die ausserbiblischen Herrenworte." In *Der historische Jesus und der Christus unseres Glaubens,* ed. Kurt Schubert. Vienna: Herder, 1962.

Haenchen Ernst. "Literatur zum Thomasevangelium," *Theologische Rundschau* Neue Folge 27 (1961-1962): 147-78, 306-38.

Harnack, Adolf von. *The Sayings of Jesus: The Second Source of St. Matthew and St. Luke*, trans. J. R. Wilkinson (New York: Putnam, 1908).

_____. *Sprüche und Reden Jesus; Beiträge zur Einleitung in das Neue Testament* II. Leipzig: J. C. Hinrichs, 1907.

Hauck, Friedrich. *Das Evangelium des Lukas.* Theologischer Hand-Kommentar zum Neuen Testament. Leipzig: Deichert, 1931.

Haupt, W. *Worte Jesu und Gemeinde-überlieferung.* 1913.

Hawkins, John C. *Horae synopticae: Contributions to the Study of the Synoptic Problem.* 2d ed. Oxford: Clarendon, 1909.

_____. "Three Limitations to St. Luke's Use of St. Mark's Gospel: The Disuse of the Markan Source in St. Luke ix. 51-xviii. 13." In *Oxford Studies in the Synoptic Gospels*, ed. W. Sanday, 29-59. Oxford: The Clarendon Press, 1911.

Held, Heinz Joachim. "Matthew as Interpreter of the Miracle Stories." In *Tradition and Interpretation in Matthew*, ed. Günther Bornkamm and others. Philadelphia: The Westminster Press, 1963.

Helmbold, Heinrich. *Vorsynoptische Evangelien.* Stuttgart: E. Klotz, 1953.

Hennecke, Edgar. *New Testament Apocrypha* I, ed. Wilhelm Schneemelcher; trans. and ed. R. McL. Wilson. Philadelphia: The Westminster Press, 1963.

Heuschen, J. "La Formation des Évangiles," *Recherches Bibliques* 2 (1957): 11-23.

Higgins, Angus J. B. "The Gospel of Thomas." In *The Tradition About Jesus.* Scottish Journal of Theology Occasional Papers 15. 30ff. Edinburgh: Oliver & Boyd, 1969.

Hirsch, Emmanuel. *Frühgeschichte des Evangeliums.* I: *Das Werden des Markus.* Tübingen: J. C. B. Mohr, 1940, 1951; II: *Die Vorlagen des Lukas und das Sondergut des Matthäus.* 1941.

Höpfl, Hildebrand and B. Gut. *Introductionis in sacros utriusque Testamenti libros compendium.* Volume III: *Introductio specialis in Novum Testamentum*, 4th ed. Naples: M. D'Auria, 1838; 6th ed., 1962, curavit A. Metzinger.

Hoffmann, P. "Die Anfänge der Theologie in der Logienquelle." In *Gestalt und Anspruch des Neuen Testaments*, ed. Joseph Schreiner with the collaboration of G. Dautzenburg. Würzburg: Echter-Verlag, 1969.

Holtzmann, Heinrich J. *Die synoptiker.* Hand Kommentar zum Neuen Testament. Freiburg, 1889.

_____. *Die Synoptische Evangelien. Ihr Ursprung und Geschichtlicher Charakter.* Leipzig: Wilhelm Engelmann, 1843.

Honey, T. E. Floyd, "Did Mark Use Q?" *Journal of Biblical Literature* 62 (1943): 319-31. ✓

Honoré, A. M. "A Statistical Study of the Synoptic Problem," *Novum Testamentum* 10 (1968): 95-147.

Howard, W. F. "The Origin of the Symbol 'Q,' " *The Expository Times* 50 (1938-1939): 379-80. ✓

Huck, Albert. *Deutsche Evangelien-Synopse mit Zugrundelegung der Übersetzung Karl Weizsäckers.* Tübingen: J. C. B. Mohr, 1961.

_____ and Hans Lietzmann. *Synopsis of the First Three Gospels*, ed. F. L. Cross. London: Blackwell, 1951.

Hummel, Reinhart. *Die Auseinandersetzung zwischen Kirche und Judentum im Matthäusevangelium.* Munich: Christian Kaiser, 1966.

Hunzinger, Claus-Hunno. "Aussersynoptisches Traditionsgut im Thomas-Evangelium," *Theologische Literaturzeitung* 85 (1960): 843-46.

Huston, Hollis W. "The 'Q Parties' at Oxford," *Journal of Bible and Religion* 25 (1957): 123-28.

Isaksson, Abel. *Marriage and Ministry in the New Temple*. Acta Seminarii Neotestamentici Upsaliensis 34. Lund: Gleerup, 1965.

Jameson, Hampden G. *The Origin of the Synoptic Gospels: A Revision of the Synoptic Problem*. Oxford: Blackwell, 1922.

Jeremias, Joachim. *New Testament Theology*, Part One. London: S. C. M. Press, 1971.

_____. *The Parables of Jesus*. 2d English ed., trans. S. H. Hooke. New York: Charles Scribner's Sons, 1963.

_____. *The Sermon on the Mount*. London: University of London: Althone Press, 1961.

_____. *Unknown Sayings of Jesus*. London: S. P. C. K., 1957.

_____. "Zur Hypothese einer schriftlichen Logienquelle Q," *Zeitschrift für die neutestamentliche Wissenschaft und die Kunde der älteren Kirche* 29 (1930): 147ff.

Johnson, Sherman E. "The Gospel According to St. Matthew: Introduction and Exegesis," *The Interpreter's Bible*. 7:231-625. Nashville: Abingdon-Cokesbury Press, 1951.

_____. *A Commentary on the Gospel according to St. Mark*. Harper New Testament Commentary. New York: Harper, 1960.

Jouvyon, M. "Papias." In *Dictionnaire de la Bible*. Supplement VI:1104-1109. 1960.

Jülicher, Adolf. *Einleitung in das Neue Testament*. 1894; 7th ed., 1931, rev. in collaboration with E. Fascher; trans., *Introduction to the New Testament*, by Janet Penrose Ward. London: Smith, Elder and Co., 1904.

Käsemann, Ernst. "On the Subject of Primitive Christian Apocalyptic." In *New Testament Questions for Today*. Philadelphia: Fortress Press, 1969.

Kee, H. C. *Jesus in History: An Approach to the Study of the Gospels*. New York: Harcourt, Brace and World, Inc., 1970.

Kilpatrick, G. D. "The Disappearance of Q," *Journal of Theological Studies* 42 (1942): 182-84.

_____. *The Origins of the Gospel according to St. Matthew*. Oxford: Clarendon Press, 1946.

Kittel, Gerhard. *Theologisches Wörterbuch zum Neuen Testament*; trans., *Theological Dictionary of the New Testament*, 10 volumes. Grand Rapids: W. B. Eerdmans, 1964-1976.

Klijn, Albertus F. J. *An Introduction to the New Testament*. Leiden: E. J. Brill, 1967.

_____. "A Survey of the Researches into the Western Text of the Gospels and Acts," *Novum Testamentum* 3 (1959): 1-27, 161-173.

Klostermann, Erich. *Das Lukasevangelium*. Handbuch zum Neuen Testament, 2d ed. 1929.

Knox, W. L. *The Sources of the Synoptic Gospels*. I: *St. Mark*; II: *St. Luke and St. Matthew*, ed. H. Chadwick. Cambridge: The University Press, 1953, 1957.

Koester, Helmut. "Gnomai Diaphoroi: The Origin and Nature of Diversification in the History of Early Christianity." In *Trajectories Through Early Christianity*, by James M. Robinson and Helmut Koester, 114-57. Philadelphia: Fortress Press, 1971; also in *Harvard Theological Review* 58 (1965): 270-318.

_____. "One Jesus and Four Primitive Gospels," In *Trajectories Through Early Christianity*, by James M. Robinson and Helmut Koester, 158-204. Philadelphia: Fortress Press, 1971; also in *Harvard Theological Review* 61 (1968): 203-47.

_____. *Synoptische Überlieferung bei den apostolischen Vätern*. Texte und Untersuchungen zur Geschichte der altkirchlichen Literatur. Berlin: Akademie-Verlag, 1957.

Kühn, Heinz-Wolfgang. "Der irdische Jesus bei Paulus als traditionsgeschichtliches und theologisches Problem," *Zeitschrift für Theologie und Kirche* 67 (1970): 295-320.

Kümmel, Werner G. *Introduction to the New Testament*. Nashville: Abingdon Press, 1973, 1975.

_____. *The New Testament: The History of the Investigation of its Problems*, trans. S. M. Gilmour and H. C. Kee. Nashville: Abingdon Press, 1972.

_____. Review of *Rediscovering the Teaching of Jesus*, by Norman Perrin. *Journal of Religion* 49 (1969): 59-66.

_____. *The Theology of the New Testament According to Its Major Witnesses: Jesus-Paul-John*, trans. John E. Steely. Nashville: Abingdon Press, 1973.

_____. *Verheissung und Erfüllung*, Abhandlung zur Theologie des Alten und Neuen Testaments 6, 3d ed. Zurich: Zwingli-Verlag, 1956; trans., *Promise and Fulfillment*. London: S. C. M. Press Ltd., 1957.

Kuhn, Thomas S. *The Structure of Scientific Revolutions*. Chicago: University of Chicago Press, 1962.

Kundsin, Karl. "Primitive Christianity in the Light of Gospel Research." In *Form Criticism: The Study of the Synoptic Gospels*, by Rudolf Bultmann and Karl Kundsin. New York: Harper Torchbooks, 1962.

Lachmann, Karl. "De ordine narrationum in evangeliis synopticis," *Theologische Studien und Kritiken* 8 (1835): 570-90.

Lagrange, Marie-Joseph. *The Gospel of Jesus Christ* 1. London: Burns, Oates & Washbourne, Ltd., 1938.

_____. *L'Évangile selon Matthieu, Études Bibliques*, 4th ed. 1927.

Lambrecht, J. "Die Logien-Quelle von Markus 13," *Biblica* 47 (1966): 321-60.

Leany, Alfred R. C. *A Commentary on the Gospel According to St. Luke*. Harper New Testament Commentary. New York: Harper, 1958.

Lehmann, Karl. *Aufweckt am dritten Tag nach der Schrift*. Questiones disputatae 38. Freiburg: Herder, 1968.

Léon-Dufour, X. "Les évangiles synoptiques." *Introduction à la Bible* II. 1959.

_____. "Interpretation des Évangiles et problème synoptique." *De Jésus aux Évangiles: Tradition et rédaction dans les Évangiles synoptiques*. Bibliotheca Ephemeridum Theologicarum Lovaniensium 25: Donum natalicum Josepho Coppens, 2:5-16. Gembloux: Duculot, 1967.

_____. "The Synoptic Problem," *Introduction to the New Testament*, ed. A. Robert and A. Feuillet, trans. P. W. Skehan and others. New York: Desclee, 1965.

Levie, J. "L'Évangile araméean de S. Matthieu est-il source de l'évangile de S. Marc?" *Nouvelle Revue théologique* 74 (1952).

Lightfoot, Robert H. *History and Interpretation in the Gospels*. London: Hodder and Stoughton, Ltd., 1935.

Lindsey, Robert L. *A Hebrew Translation of the Gospel of Mark*. Jerusalem: Dugith Publishers Baptist House, n.d.

_____. "A Modified Two-Document Theory of Synoptic Dependence and Interdependence," *Novum Testamentum* 6 (1953): 239-63.

Linton, O. "Evidences of a Second-Century Revised Edition of St. Mark's Gospel," *New Testament Studies* 14 (1967-1968): 321-55.

Lührmann, Dieter. *Die Redaktion der Logienquelle*. Wissenschaftliche Monographien zum Alten und Neuen Testament 33. Neukirchen-Vluyn: Neukirchener Verlag, 1969.

Lummis, E. W. *How Was Luke Written: Considerations Affecting the Two-Document Theory with Special Reference to the Phenomenon of Order in the Non-Markan Matter Common to Matthew and Luke*. Cambridge: University Press, 1915.

McArthur, Harvey K. "The Gospel according to Thomas." In *New Testament Sidelights: Essays in Honor of A. C. Purdy*. 1960.

McCown, C. C. "The Scene of John's Ministry and Its Relation to the Purpose and Outcome of His Mission," *Journal of Biblical Literature* 59 (1940): 113-31.

McLoughlin, S. "Les accords mineurs Mt-Lc contre Mc et le problème synoptique; Vers la théorie des Deux Sources." In *De Jésus aux Évangiles: Tradition et rédaction dans les évangiles synoptiques*. Bibliotheca Ephemeridum Theologicarum Lovaniensium 25: Donum Natalicum Josepho Coppens, 2:17-40. Gembloux: Duculot, 1967.

_____. "Le problème synoptique." In *De Jésus aux Évangiles: Tradition et rédaction dans les évangiles synoptiques*. Bibliotheca Ephemeridum Theologicarum Lovaniensium 25: Donum Natalicum Josepho Coppens, 2. Gembloux: Duculot, 1967.

_____. *The Synoptic Theory of Xavier Léon-Dufour. An Analysis and Evaluation*. Louvain, unpublished, 1965.

McNeile, A. H. *The Gospel according to St. Matthew*. London: Macmillan and Co., 1961.

_____. *An Introduction to the Study of the New Testament*. 1927; 2d ed., ed. C. S. C. Williams. Oxford: The Clarendon Press, 1953.

Manson, Thomas W. *The Sayings of Jesus as Recorded in the Gospels According to St. Matthew and St. Luke*. London: S. C. M. Press, 1949; first published as *The Mission and Message of Jesus*, Part 2. 1937.

Martin, W. H. Blyth. "The Indispensibility of Q," *Theology* 59 (1956): 182-88.

Marxsen, Willi. *Introduction to the New Testament: An Approach to its Problems*. Philadelphia: Fortress Press, 1968.

Massaux, E. *Influence de l'Évangile de saint Matthieu sur la littératur avant saint Irenée*. Louvain, 1950.

_____. "Le texte du sermon sur la montagne de Matthieu utilisé par saint Justin," *Ephemerides Theologicae Lovanienses* 28 (1952): 411-48.

Masson, C. *L'Évangile de Marc et l'Église de Rome*. 1968.

Meynell, H. "The Synoptic Problem: Some Unorthodox Solutions," *Theology* 70 (1967): 386-97.

Michaelis, Wilhelm. *Einleitung in das Neue Testament. Eine Einführung in ihre Probleme*. 1963.

Moffatt, James. *An Introduction to the Literature of the New Testament*, 3d edition. Edinburgh: T. & T. Clark, 1918.

Montefiore, Hugh and Henry E. W. Turner. *Thomas and the Evangelists*. Studies in Biblical Theology 35. Naperville: Alec R. Allenson, 1962.

Morgenthaler, Robert. *Statistische Synopse*. Zurich and Stuttgart: Gotthelf-Verlag, 1971.

Moule Charles F. D. *The Birth of the New Testament*. London: Adam and Charles Black, 1962.

Moulton, J. H. *A Grammar of New Testament Greek*. Volume II: *Accidence and Word Formation*, ed. W. F. Howard. Edinburgh: T. & T. Clark, 1956.

Narborough, Frederick D. V. "The Synoptic Problem." In *A New Commentary on Holy Scripture*. 1928.

Neirynck, F. "The Argument from Order and St. Luke's Transpositions." In *The Minor Agreements of Matthew and Luke Against Mark with a Cumulative List*, ed. in collaboration with T. Hansen and F. Van Segbroeck, 291-322. Leuven: University Press, 1974.

_____. *Duality in Mark. Contributions to the Study of the Markan Redaction*. Leuven: The University Press, 1972.

_____. "The Gospel of Matthew and Literary Criticism: A Critical Analysis of A. Gaboury's Hypothesis." In *L'Évangile selon Matthieu*, ed. M. Didier, 37-69. Bibliotheca Ephemeridum Theologicarum Lovaniensium 29. 1972.

_____. "Q." In *The Interpreter's Dictionary of the Bible*, 4:715-716. Nashville: Abingdon, 1976.

_____. "Rédaction et structure de Matthieu." *De Jésus aux Évangiles: Tradition et rédaction dans les Évangiles synoptiques*. Bibliotheca Ephemeridum Theologicarum Lovaniensium 25: Donum Natalicum Josepho Coppens, 2:65ff. Gembloux: Duculot, 1967.

_____. "Synoptic Problem." In *The Interpreter's Dictionary of the Bible*, Supp.:845-58. Nashville: Abingdon Press, 1976.

_____. "Urmarcus redivivus? Examen critique d l'hypothèse des insertions matthéennes dans Marc." In *L'Évangile selon Marc*, ed. M. Sabbe, 103-145. Bibliotheca Ephemeridum Theologicarum 34. 1974.

_____, in collaboration with T. Hansen and F. Van Segbroeck. *The Minor Agreements of Matthew and Luke Against Mark with a Cumulative List*. Leuven: University Press, 1974.

North, Robert. "Chenoboskion and Q," *Catholic Biblical Quarterly* 24 (1962): 154-170.

Orchard, Bernard. "Thessalonians and the Synoptic Gospels," *Biblica* 19 (1938): 19-42.

Palmer, N. H. "Lachmann's Argument," *New Testament Studies* 13 (1966-1967): 368-78.

Parker, Pierson. "The Authorship of the Second Gospel," *Perspectives in Religious Studies* 5 (1978): 4-9.

_____. *The Gospel Before Mark*. Chicago: University of Chicago Press, 1953.

_____. "A Second Look at *The Gospel Before Mark*," *Journal of Biblical Literature* 100 (1981): 395-405; also in *Society of Biblical Literature 1979 Seminar Papers* 1, 151-61. Missoula: Scholars Press, 1979.

Pelletier, André. *Flavius Josèph, Adapteur de la Lettre d'Aristée. Une réaction atticisante contre la Koiné*. 1962.

Perrin, Norman. *Rediscovering the Teaching of Jesus*. New York: Harper and Row, 1967.

Petrie, Stewart. "The Proto-Luke Hypothesis," *The Expository Times* 54 (1942-1943): 172-77.

_____. " 'Q' is Only What You Make It," *Novum Testamentum* 3 (1959): 28-33.

Price, James L. *Interpreting the New Testament*. New York: Holt, Rinehart and Winston, 1961.

Quecke, H. *La Venue du Messie*. Recherches Bibliques 6. 1962.

Quentin, Henri. *Essais de critique textuelle*. Paris and Bruges, 1926.

Quispel, G. "Some Remarks on the Gospel of Thomas," *New Testament Studies* 5 (1958-1959): 276-90.

Rawlinson, Alfred E. J. *The Gospel According to St. Mark*. London: Methuen & Co., Ltd., 1947.

Redlich, Edwin B. *The Student's Introduction to the Synoptic Gospels*. London: Longmans, Green and Co., 1926.

Rehkopf, F. "Synoptiker." In *Biblisch-historisches Handwörterbuch*, 3:1910ff. 1966.

Rengstorf, K. H. *Das Evangelium nach Lukas*. Das Neue Testament Deutsch. Neues Göttinger Bibelwerk 3, 9th ed. Göttingen: Vandenhoeck & Ruprecht, 1962.

Riddle, Donald W. and Harold H. Hutson. *New Testament Life and Literature*. Chicago: University of Chicago Press, 1946.

Robert, A. and others. *Introduction to the New Testament*. New York: Desclee, 1965.

Robinowitz, I. " 'Be opened' = 'Εφφαθά (Mk. 7:34): Did Jesus Speak Hebrew?" *Zeitschrift für die neutestamentliche Wissenschaft* 53 (1962): 229-38.

Robinson, Armitage. *The Study of the Gospels.* 1902.

Robinson, James M. *Kerygma und historischer Jesus.* 2d ed. Zurich and Stuttgart: Zwingli-Verlag, 1967.

—————. "Logoi Sophon: On the Gattung of Q." In *Trajectories Through Early Christianity*, by James M. Robinson and Helmut Koester, 71-113. Philadelphia: Fortress Press, 1971.

—————. *The Problem of History in Mark.* Studies in Biblical Theology 21. London. SCM Press, 1957.

—————and Helmut Koester. *Trajectories Through Early Christianity.* Philadelphia: Fortress Press, 1971.

Robinson, John A. T. *Jesus and his Coming: The Emergence of a Doctrine.* London: SCM Press, 1957.

Robinson, William C., Jr. "The Theological Context for Interpreting Luke's Travel Narrative (9:51ff.)," *Journal of Biblical Literature* 79 (1960): 20-31.

Ropes, James H. *The Synoptic Gospels.* Cambridge: Harvard University Press, 1934; 2d ed., London, 1960.

Rosché, T. R. "The Words of Jesus and the Future of the 'Q' Hypothesis," *Journal of Biblical Literature* 79 (1960): 210-20.

Rudolph, K. "Gnosis and Gnostizismus, ein Forschungsbericht," *Theologische Rundschau* Neue Folge 34 (1969): 181-231.

Rushbrooke, W. G. *Synopticon: An Exposition of the Common Matter of the Synoptic Gospels.* London: Macmillan, 1880.

Sanday, William, ed. *Oxford Studies in the Synoptic Problem.* Oxford: Clarendon Press, 1911.

Sanders, Ed Parish. "The Argument from Order and the Relationship Between Matthew and Luke," *New Testament Studies* 15 (1968-1969): 249-261.

—————. *The Tendencies of the Synoptic Tradition.* Monograph Series of Studiorum Novi Testamenti Societas 9. Cambridge: University Press, 1969.

Schaefer, Aloys. *Einleitung in das Neue Testament.* 4th ed., rev. M. Meinertz, 1933; 5th ed., 1950.

Schlatter, Adolf von. *Das Evangelium des Lukas aus seinen Quellen erklärt,* 2d ed. Stuttgart: Calwer, 1960.

—————. *Der Evangelist Matthäus.* 1929.

Schmid, Josef. *Einleitung in das Neue Testament.* Freiburg: Herder, 1973.

—————. *Matthäus und Lukas: Eine Untersuchung des Verhältnisses ihrer Evangelien.* Freiburg im Breisgau: Herder and Co., 1930.

Schmid, Josef and A. Vögtle, eds. *Synoptische Studien.*

Schmithals, W. "Kein Streit um des Kaisers Bart." *Evangelische Kommentare* 3. 1970.

Schnackenburg, Rudolf. Review of *Die Redaktion der Logienquelle*, by Dieter Lührmann. *Biblische Zeitschrift* (1971): 279-81.

—————. *Synoptische Studien für A. Wikenhauser.* 1953.

Schrage, Wolfgang. *Das Verhältnis des Thomas-Evangeliums zur synoptischen Tradition und zu den koptischen Evangelienübersetzungen.* Beiheft, *Zeitschrift für die neutestamentliche Wissenshaft* 29. 1964.

Schramm, Tim. *Der Markus-Stoff bei Lukas.* Monograph Series of Studiorum Novi Testamenti Societas 14. 1971.

Schürmann, H. "Die Dublettenvermeidungen im Lk" (The Avoidance of Doublets in Luke), *Zeitschrift für Kirchengeschichte* 76 (1954): 83ff.

_____. "Das Thomasevangelium und das luk. Sondergut," *Biblische Zeitschrift* Neue Folge 7 (1963): 237ff.

_____. "Sprachliche Reminiszenzen an abgeänderte oder ausgelassene Bestandteile der Spruchsammlung im Lukas- und Matthäusevangelium," *New Testament Studies* 6 (1959-1960): 193-210.

_____. *Traditionsgeschichtliche Untersuchungen zu den synoptischen Evangelien Beiträge. Kommentare und Beiträge zum Alten und Neuen Testament.* Düsseldorf: Patmos Verlag, 1968.

Schultz, S. *Die Stunde der Botschaft. Einführung in die Theologie der vier Evangelisten.* 1967.

Schweitzer, Albert. *The Quest of the Historical Jesus,* trans. W. Montgomery. New York: Macmillan Co., 1961.

Schweizer, Eduard. *Jesus Christus im vielfältigen Zeugnis des Neuen Testaments.* Munich: Siebenstern-Tauschbuch 126, 1968; trans., *Jesus* by David E. Green. London: SCM Press, 1971.

Simpson, R. T. "The Major Agreements of Matthew and Luke Against Mark," *New Testament Studies* 12 (1966): 273-84.

Solages, Bruno de. *La Composition des évangiles. De Luc et de Matthieu et leurs sources.* Leiden: E. J. Brill, 1973.

_____. *A Greek Synopsis of the Gospels: A New Way of Solving the Synoptic Problem.* Leiden: E. J. Brill, 1959.

Sparks, Hendley F. D. *The Formation of the New Testament.* London: SCM Press, 1952.

Stanton, V. H. "Gospels." In *Hastings Dictionary of the Bible,* 234-49. New York: Charles Scribner's Sons, 1899.

_____. *The Gospels as Historical Documents.* Part II: *The Synoptic Gospels.* Cambridge: The University Press, 1909.

Steck, Odil H. *Israel und das gewaltsame Geschick der Propheten.* Wissenschaftliche Monographien zum Alten und Neuen Testament 23. Neukirchen-Vluyn: Neukirchener Verlag, 1967.

Stein, Robert H. "The 'Redaktionsgeschichtliche' Investigation of a Markan Seam (Mk. 1:21f.)," *Zeitschrift für die neutestamentliche Wissenschaft* 61 (1970): 70-94.

_____. "What is Redaktionsgeschichte?" *Journal of Biblical Literature* 88 (1969): 45-56.

Stendahl, Krister. *The School of St Matthew and Its Use of the Old Testament.* Philadelphia: Fortress Press, 1968.

Stoldt, Hans-Herbert. *History and Criticism of the Marcan Hypothesis,* trans. and ed. Donald J. Niewyk. Macon GA: Mercer University Press, 1980.

Strecker, G. "Zur Geheimnistheorie im Mk." In *Studia Evangelica* III. Texte und Untersuchungen zur Geschichte der altkirchlichen Literatur 88, 87ff. Berlin, 1964.

Streeter, B. H. *The Four Gospels: A Study of Origins.* London: Macmillan and Co., 1924, 1930.

_____. "St. Mark's Knowledge and Use of Q." In *Studies in the Synoptic Problem,* ed. William Sanday. Oxford: Clarendon Press, 1911.

Styler, G. M. "The Priority of Mark." In *The Birth of the New Testament,* ed. C. F. D. Moule, 223-32. New York: Harper and Row, 1962.

Suggs, M. Jack. *Wisdom, Christology, and Law in Matthew's Gospel.* Cambridge: Harvard University Press, 1970.

Taylor, Vincent. *Behind the Third Gospel: A Study of the Proto-Luke Hypothesis.* Oxford: The University Press, 1926.

_____. *The Formation of the Gospel Tradition.* London: Macmillan and Co., Ltd., 1933; 2d ed., 1935.

_____. *The Gospel according to St. Mark.* London: Macmillan, 1952, 1953.

_____. "The Order of Q," *Journal of Theological Studies* New Series 4 (1953): 27-31.

_____. "The Original Order of Q." In *New Testament Essays: Studies in Memory of T. W. Manson, 1893-1958,* ed. A. J. B. Higgins, 246ff. Manchester University Press, 1959; reprinted in Vincent Taylor. *New Testament Essays,* 95-118. London: Epworth Press, 1970.

_____. "Some Outstanding New Testament Problems: I. The Elusive Q," *The Expository Times* 46 (1934-1935): 68-74.

Thompson, J. M. *The Synoptic Gospels.* Oxford: Clarendon Press.

Throckmorton, Burton H., Jr. "Did Mark Know Q?" *Journal of Biblical Literature* 67 (1948): 319-29.

Thüsing, W. "Erhöhungsvorstellung und Parusieerwartung in der ältesten nachösterlichen Christologie," *Biblische Zeitschrift* Neue Folge 12 (1968): 54-80.

Tischendorf, Constantin von. *Synopsis Evangelica.* Leipzig: H. Mendelssohn, 1851.

Tödt, Heinz E. *Der Menschensohn in der synoptischen Überlieferung.* 1959; trans., *The Son of Man in the Synoptic Tradition,* by Dorothea M. Barton. Philadelphia: The Westminster Press, 1965.

Torrey, Charles C. *The Four Gospels.* New York and London: Harper & Brothers, 1933.

_____. *Our Translated Gospels.* New York: Harper and Brothers, 1936.

Toynbee, Arnold J. *Greek Historical Thought from Homer to the Age of Heraclitus.* New York: E. P. Dutton & Co., 1924.

Turner, N. "The Minor Verbal Agreements of Mt. and Lk. against Mk." In *Studia Evangelica* 1. Texte und Untersuchungen zur Geschichte der altkirchlichen Literatur 73, 223-34. Berlin: Akademie-Verlag, 1957.

_____. "Q in Recent Thought," *The Expository Times* 80 (1968-1969): 324-28.

Tyson, Joseph B. "Sequential Parallelism in the Synoptic Gospels," *New Testament Studies* 22 (1976): 276-308.

Vaganay, Léon. *Le problème synoptique: Une hypothèse de travail.* Bibliotheque de théologie, 3/1. Paris: Desclée, 1954.

_____. *L'Évangile de Pierre.* Études Bibliques. Paris, 1930.

Vielhauer, P. *Aufzätze zum Neuen Testament.* 1955.

_____. Review of *Le problème synoptique,* by L. Vaganay. *Theologische Literaturzeitung* 80 (1955): 647ff.

Vögtle, A. *Das NT und die neuere katholische Exegese. I. Grundlegende Fragen zur Entstehung und eigenart des NT.* 1966.

Walker, William O., Jr., ed. *The Relationships among the Gospels: An Interdisciplinary Dialogue.* San Antonio: Trinity University Press, 1978.

_____. "The Son of Man Question and the Synoptic Problem," *New Testament Studies* 28 (1981-1982): 374-88.

Weinreich, O. *Tübinger Beiträge zur Altertumswissenschaft.* Stuttgart: Kohlhammer, 1929.

Weiss, Johannes. *Das älteste Evangelium.* Göttingen: Vandenhoeck und Ruprecht, 1903.

_____. *Die Predigt Jesu vom Reiche Gottes*. Göttingen: 1892.

_____. *Synoptische Tafeln zu den drei älteren Evangelien mit Unterscheidung der Quellen in Vierfachem Farbendruck*, 3d ed. rev. R. Schutz. Göttingen: Vandenhoeck und Ruprecht, 1929.

Weisse, Christian H. *Die evangelische Geschichte kritisch und philosophisch bearbeitet*, 2 vols. Leipzig: Breitkopf und Hartel, 1838.

Wellhausen, Julius. *Einleitung in die drei ersten Evangelien*. Berlin: G. Reimer, 1905; 2d ed., 1911.

Wenham, David. "The Synoptic Problem Revisited," *Tyndale Bulletin* (1973): 13-17.

Wernle, Paul. *Die synoptische Frage*. Tübingen: J. C. B. Mohr (Paul Siebeck), 1899.

West, H. Philip, Jr. "A Primitive Version of Luke in the Composition of Matthew," *New Testament Studies* 14 (1967): 75-95.

Wette, Wilhelm de. "Evangelium des Marcus," *Kurze Erklärung der Evangelien des Lukas und Markus in Kurzgefasstes exegetisches Handbuch zum Neuen Testament*, Ersten Band, Zweiter Theil: 127-200.

_____ and F. Bleek. "Erklärung des Verhältnisses zwischen Marcus und den beiden andern Evangelisten durch die Annahme, dass er sie benützt hat." In *Lehrbuch der historisch-kritischen Einleitung in die kanonischen Bücher des Neuen Testaments*, 5th ed. Berlin; trans. O. B. Frothingham. Boston, 1858.

Wikenhauser, Alfred. *Einleitung in das Neue Testament*. Freiburg: Herder, 1953; 4th ed., 1961, slightly rev. A. Vögtle; trans. from the 2d ed. by J. Cunningham, *New Testament Introduction*. New York: Herder and Herder, 1958.

Wilkens, W. "Zur Frage der literarischen Beziehung zwischen Matthäus und Lukas," *Novum Testamentum* 8 (1966): 48-57.

Williams, Charles S. C. "The Synoptic Problem." In *Peake's Commentary on the Bible*, rev. ed., 748-55. New York: Thomas Nelson and Sons, 1962.

_____. See also under Glasson, Thomas F.

Wilson, R. McL. "Farrer and Streeter on the Minor Agreements of Mt and Lk against Mk." In *Studia Evangelica* 1. Texte und Untersuchungen zur Geschichte der altkirchlichen Literatur 73, 254-57. Berlin: Akademie-Verlag, 1959.

_____. *Studies in the Gospel of Thomas*. London: Mowbray, 1960.

_____. " 'Thomas' and the Growth of the Gospels," *Harvard Theological Review* 53 (1960): 231-50.

Wood, H. G. "The Priority of Mark," *The Expository Times* 65 (1953-1954)): 17-19.

Woods, F. H. "The Origin and Mutual Relation of the Synoptic Gospels." In *Studia biblica et ecclesiastica: Essays Chiefly in Biblical and Patristic Criticism*, 59-104. Oxford: Clarendon, 1886, 1890.

Wrede, Wilhelm. *Das Messiasgeheimnis in den Evangelien*. Göttingen: Vandenhoeck & Ruprecht, 1901; 2d ed., 1913; 3d ed., 1963; trans. M. C. G. Grieg, *The Messianic Secret*. Cambridge: J. Clarke, 1971.

Wrege, H.-T. *Die Überlieferungsgeschichte der Bergpredigt*. Wissenschaftliche Untersuchungen zum Neuen Testament 9. Tübingen: J. C. B. Mohr (Paul Siebeck), 1968.

INDEX OF BIBLICAL CITATIONS

Genesis
38 373

Exodus
2:11-4:17 348
8:19 331
17:1-7 374
23:20 388

Leviticus
19:18 208

Numbers
1-2 348
7 348
10 349
11 348
27:17 .... 378, 420

Deuteronomy
1:6-8 349
1:9-18 349
1:19ff. 349
5-6 .... 344, 346
6:4 390
6:16 374
17:2-13 344
17:14-20 344
18:13 344
24:1-4 344

2 Samuel
5:14 372

1 Kings
22:17 378

2 Chronicles
24:20-21 238

Psalms
2:7 .... 373, 389 n11
6:9 303
22:1 .... 29, 208

Isaiah
40 279

40:3 .... 386, 387
42:1 208

Zechariah
9:9 .... 71 n19

Malachi
3 279
3:1 .... 208, 373, 388

1 Enoch
93 356

Matthew
1 372
1:1 344
1-2 .... 222 n1
1:17 343
1:18 344
1:38-39 268
2:2 354
3-7 350
3-14 .... 349, 350
3-18 351
3:1ff. 279
3:1-3a 279
3:1-6 420
3:1-4:11 271
3:1-4:22 57
3:2 ... 354, 388, 417, 424 n26
3:3 213
3:3b 279
3:4-5a 279
3:4-6 419
3:5 373
3:5b 279
3:6 279
3:7-10 .....34, 172, 222, 231,
            279, 373, 420, 423
3:7b-10 251
3:7-12 .... 232, 268, 314
3:7-17 267
3:9 .... 68 n8, 354
3:11 .... 279, 367 n19, 386,

            417, 423
3:11-12 .... 34, 386, 421
3:12 .... 279, 386, 388, 420
3:13 210
3:13-14 279
3:14-15 279
3:16 59
3:16-17 ....279, 314
3:17 ....208, 249
4 .... 80, 363
4:1 ....374, 389
4:1-2 .... 279, 367 n19
4:1-11 .....34, 172, 267, 314,
                            421
4:2 354
4:2-11 232
4:2-10 279
4:3-12 366
4:11 279
4:12-17 .... 362 n8
4:13 .... 213, 341
4:15-16 213
4:17 354
4:18 249
4:18-22 .... 362 n8
4:19 344
4:20 128
4:22 128
4:22ff. 235
4:23 .... 57, 362 n9, 421
4:23a 90
4:23b 91
4:23c 91
4:23-24 363
4:23-25 57
4:23-11:1 .... 89, 90, 92
4:24 126
4:24-25 127
4:24-13:58 123
4:24a 91
4:24b 91

4:25 .... 91, 363, 424 n25
5 .... 115, 300, 371, 372
5-7 ..... 57, 90, 91, 231, 295,
            298, 299, 421
5:1a 91
5:1-7:27 267
5:1-7:29 403
5:2 92
5:3 .... 68 n8, 248 n7, 375
5:3ff. 234
5:3-4 .... 34, 366
5:3-6 .... 232, 299
5:3-11 304
5:3-7:27 90
5:6 ...... 34, 248 n7, 366, 375
5:11 .... 264 n7
5:11-12 .... 34, 232, 299
5:11ff. 366
5:12 .... 264 n7
5:13 . 35, 265, 299, 300, 302,
            418, 423
5:13a 363
5:13-16 302
5:15 ... 34n, 35, 48, 232, 253,
   265, 266, 299, 300, 302, 302
            n18, 363 n14, 422
5:17 .... 300 n12
5:17-19 .... 363 n11
5:17-20 .... 299, 300, 376
5:17-48 .... 300, 331
5:18 .... 35, 266, 299, 300
5:20 .... 300 n12
5:21-22 .... 300 n12
5:21ff. 300
5:21-48 299
5:22 189
5:23-24 201
5:24 300
5:25-26 .... 35, 265, 299, 300,
            302 n18
5:27-28 .... 300 n12
5:27ff. 300
5:29 201
5:29-30 .... 233, 363 n12
5:31-32 .... 300, 300 n12
5:32 . 35, 115, 201, 233,
   247 n5, 265, 299, 300,
            362 n10, 363 n12
5:33-34 .... 300 n12
5:33ff. 300
5:38-39 .... 300 n12
5:38ff. 300
5:39-40 34
5:39-42 232
5:39b-42 .... 299, 300
5:42 34
5:43-44 .... 300 n12
5:43ff. 300
5:44 34
5:44-48 .... 299, 300
5:45 34

5:45-48 .... 299, 300
5:46-47 34
5:48 .... 34, 300 n12, 375
6 300
6:1-8 299
6:5 206
6:6-13 .... 248 n7
6:7-15 336
6:9-13 ..... 35, 232, 299, 301,
            302 n18
6:9-15 266
6:14b 419
6:14-15 .... 206, 301
6:16-18 .... 299, 376
6:19-21 .... 35, 232, 299
6:19-33 267
6:20-21 . 299, 300, 302,
   302 n18
6:21 302
6:22-23 .... 35, 232, 265, 266,
            299, 302, 339
6:22-7:11 301
6:24 .. 35, 251, 299, 300, 302
6:25-33 ... 35, 232, 299, 302
6:25-34 303
6:33 .... 418, 422, 423
6:36 280
7 .... 266, 300
7:1-2 .... 34, 299
7:1-5 232
7:2 .. 34n, 237, 417, 422, 423
7:3 .... 363 n14
7:3-5 .... 34, 172, 251, 299
7:6 .... 363 n11, 376
7:7-11 ..... 35, 231, 232, 251,
   266, 299, 300, 301, 302,
   302 n18, 368 n22
7:7-12 337
7:12 .. 34, 299, 300, 301, 302
7:13-14 ...... 35, 263, 298 n9,
   299, 300, 303, 304, 304 n24
7:16-18 .... 34, 316
7:16-20 . 299, 303, 304,
   304 n24, 315
7:16-21 232
7:20 34
7:21 . 35, 299, 303-304,
   304 n24
7:22-23 ... 35, 254, 263, 299,
   300, 302 n18, 303, 304,
   304 n24
7:24-27 .... 35, 189, 232, 299,
            376
7:28 107
7:28-29 363
7:28b-29 92
7:29 32
8 .... 57, 80, 350, 363
8-13 416
8:1-4 .... 50, 57, 362 n8
8:1-17 91

8:1-9:34 91
8:2 .... 61 n17, 172
8:2-4 .... 91, 92
8:5-10 .... 35, 314, 316
8:5-13 .... 90, 232, 267
8:6 126
8:7-10 171
8:11-12 ....35, 108, 263, 314,
            315, 316
8:13 .... 35, 314, 316
8:14 200
8:14-16 92
8:14-17 .... 57, 363
8:16 .... 59, 81, 81 n3, 126
8:17 213
8:18 92
8:18-34 419
8:18-9:34 91
8:19-22 ...... 35, 90, 91, 108,
   232, 267, 314, 315, 316
8:23 48
8:23-27 ...... 362 n8, 363 n14,
            422
8:23-34 .... 57, 92
8:25 .... 69 n13
8:26 .... 420 n17
8:27 200
8:28-34 .. 146 n8, 362 n8, 363
            n14, 376
8:30 215
9 .... 57, 81, 363
9-11 350
9:1 210
9:1-8 .... 40, 173, 362 n8
9:1-17 .... 55, 57, 92
9:2 .... 59, 200
9:3-4 50
9:7 .... 48, 51, 374
9:9 249
9:9-13 ...... 40, 289, 362 n8
9:9-17 57
9:14 70
9:14-17 40
9:17 374
9:18 55
9:18-25 92
9:18-26 .. 57, 73 n26, 146 n8,
            363 n14, 377, 419
9:18-27 .... 362 n8
9:20 .... 51, 61 n17
9:27-31 213
9:27-34 .... 91, 222 n1
9:30 213
9:30b-31 91
9:32-34 .... 213, 392, 392 n15
9:34 .... 392, 392 n15
9:35 .... 95, 362 n9, 363
9:35a 280
9:35b 280
9:35-10:16 .... 271, 280
9:35-10:42 55

9:36 .... 280, 378 n2
9:36a 420
9:36b 420
9:37 292
9:37-38 .... 35, 126, 280, 304, 378
9:37ff. 90
9:37-10:14 267
9:37-10:15 232
9:37-10:16 90
9:37-10:42 304
10 ...... 31, 83, 91, 113, 114, 231, 232, 295, 298, 344, 248
10:1 ....91, 254, 363 n14
10:1a 280
10:1b 280
10:1-4 ... 42 n11, 57, 362 n8, 363
10:1-5 .... 291 n3
10:1-14 ....55, 92
10:1-16 ....233, 421
10:1-42 ....291, 292
10:2-4 .... 127, 280, 418
10:3-15 ....78 n2
10:5 ....189, 214
10:5ff. 57
10:5-8 280
10:5-42 ....126, 403
10:7 249
10:7-8 ....35, 91
10:9 35
10:9-10 200
10:9-11 .... 280, 363 n14
10:9-12 .... 362 n8
10:9-14 106
10:9-16 .... 304, 305, 305 n26
10:10 378
10:10a 35
10:10b 35
10:10-12 254
10:11-13 35
10:12 .... 264 n7
10:12-13 280
10:13 291
10:14 . 254, 280, 291, 362 n8
10:14a 280
10:14-15 35
10:15-16 280
10:16 .... 35, 291
10:16-42 ....291, 292
10:17-22 ..90, 112, 113, 114, 307
10:18 .... 362 n10, 378
10:19-20 ...... 233, 304, 305, 306, 307
10:20 202
10:22 ....213, 233
10:23-25 305
10:24-25 ...34, 304, 305, 315
10:25 .... 392 n15
10:26 ......34n, 48, 253, 263, 422

10:26-27 304
10:26ff. 307
10:26-33 ...35, 231, 232, 267
10:28-31 304
10:32 233
10:32-33 304
10:33 254
10:34-36 .... 35, 304
10:37-38 .... 35, 305
10:37-39 281
10:38 ....363 n12
10:38-39 ....233, 254
10:39 305
10:40 .... 201, 304, 305, 306, 307, 363 n12
10:40-41 306
10:42 .... 291, 306, 419
11 ....231, 348
11:1 107
11:2-6 ....314, 316
11:2-11 35
11:2-19 ....90, 172, 232, 267
11:2-30 55
11:4-6 ....231, 251
11:5 126
11:5-6 316
11:7-11 .... 314, 316, 317
11:7b-11 251
11:7-19 126
11:7-30 126
11:10 ..... 213, 387, 417, 423
11:12-13 .... 35, 262, 265-66, 314, 315, 316
11:12-15 342
11:15 ....419, 422
11:16-19 .... 35, 314, 316
11:20-24 90
11:20-30 342
11:21-23 . 108, 232, 252, 314
11:21-24 35
11:25-26 ....232, 284
11:25-27 ... 35, 90, 108, 252, 308, 314
11:27 .... 236 n26, 241 n44
11:28-30 ....234, 308
11:30 126
12 .... 82, 363
12-14 350
12:1 91
12:1-8 .... 40, 362 n8
12:1-14 ....55, 92
12:1-21 .... 57, 289
12:5-7 .... 214, 249, 289
12:6 .... 290 n2
12:9-10 48
12:9-14 .... 40, 362 n8
12:10 331
12:11-13 289
12:12 .... 290 n2
12:15 418

12:15-16 92
12:15-21 40
12:15-50 55
12:15-21 289
12:18-21 213
12:22 ...... 273, 392, 392 n15
12:22ff. 274-77
12:22-23 . 213, 273, 392, 392 n15
12:22-27 35
12:22-30 ...232, 314, 411 n4, 446
12:22-32 92
12:22-37 421
12:22-45 . 267, 269, 271, 446
12:22-13:35 57
12:23 ...... 273, 392, 392 n15
12:24a 273
12:24b 272, 447, 447 n21
12:24b-26a 447 n21
12:25 372
12:25a 273
12:25-26 391
12:25b-26a 447
12:25c 273
12:25-31 233
12:25-32 .... 78 n2, 106
12:25-37 420
12:25-45 ....126, 266
12:26a 272
12:26b 273
12:27 273
12:28 ....273, 331
12:28-42 274
12:29 .... 272, 338, 447
12:30 .... 273, 363, 392, 447, 447 n22
12:31 ....267, 392
12:31a 272, 447, 447 n21
12:31b 273
12:31b-32a 273
12:31-33 ....78 n2
12:32 ......35, 240, 267, 314, 315, 392
12:32a 273
12:32b 273
12:33 267
12:33-35 ..34, 273, 314, 315, 316, 411 n4
12:33-42 277
12:33-43 273
12:33-45 .... 55, 273
12:34 267
12:35 267
12:36 ....213, 273
12:36-37 267
12:38 48
12:38-40 ....34n
12:38-42 ..35, 172, 232, 314, 315, 339, 411 n4, 420
12:38-45 423

12:39 .... 362 n10, 363 n12
12:40 ....340, 354
12:43-45 ..35, 231, 232, 252,
274, 314, 315, 338, 367,
411 n4, 420
12:43-47 315
12:46-50 .... 92, 362 n8
12:48 50
12:50 214
12:53-58 92
13 .....31, 91, 272, 295, 298,
308, 344
13:1-9 40
13:1-23 290
13:1-35 92
13:1-52 72
13:3-50 403
13:3-52 126
13:9 ....34n, 419
13:10 .... 48, 213
13:10-15 .... 70 n14, 308
13:10-17 40
13:11 61
13:11-15 ....362 n10
13:12 .... 34n, 233, 253, 290,
363, 363 n13, 422
13:12a 249
13:14 ....249, 290
13:14-15 213
13:16-17 ...35, 108, 234 n18,
240, 241 n44, 266, 290, 308
13:17 290
13:18-23 40
13:23 ....363 n13
13:24ff. 54
13:24-30 ....307, 421
13:31-32 ..35, 106, 200, 307,
308, 420, 422
13:31-33 .... 58, 232
13:33 ......35, 308, 420, 422,
424
13:34-35 .... 58, 422
13:35 213
13:36-43 .... 307, 363 n13
13:36-52 .... 57, 419
13:38-42 .... 411 n4
13:43 ...... 363 n13, 419, 422
13:44 307
13:45-46 307
13:47-50 307
13:51 58
13:51-52 307
13:53 107
13:53-58 .... 57, 362 n8, 418,
419
13:55 374
13:58 .... 28, 69 n13
14 83
14-28 27
14:1 ...... 59, 71 n18, 89, 209
14:3 209

14:3-12 .... 71, 146 n8
14:4 ....215 n11
14:5 209
14:9 ...... 59, 71, 71 n18, 209
14:12-13 71
14:13 209
14:13-21 .... 362 n3
14:14 305
14:14a 420
14:21 .... 71 n19
14:22-33 .... 362 n8
14:23 421
14:28ff. 222 n1
14:28-31 ....216, 248
14:34 209
15:1-20 .... 363, 368 n22
15:3-6 90
15:3-11 ....362 n10
15:4 206
15:12-14 305
15:14 ....34, 305, 314, 315
15:15 216
15:16-20 ....362 n10
15:21-28 ....200, 212, 362 n8
15:24 . 200, 362 n10, 363 n11
15:29 212
15:30 .... 222 n1
15:31 213
15:32-39 .... 169, 362 n8
15:39 ....209, 212
16 116
16:1 ....362 n8, 363 n12
16:2 .... 81, 299
16:2-3 ..35, 254, 264, 298 n9
16:4 ...... 48, 362 n8, 363 n12
16:5ff. 379
16:5-12 70
16:9 212
16:13-16 .... 292, 362 n8
16:13-23 ..... 40, 74 n29, 201
16:13-28 292
16:16 216
16:16b 249
16:16ff. 248 n6
16:16b-19 247-48
16:17-19 201
16:17-20 216
16:18 376
16:20 292
16:21 ....354, 379
16:22 201
16:22-23 292
16:24 213
16:24-25 .. 233, 254, 363 n12
16:24-28 .... 40, 173
16:27 ....233, 254
17:1-9 40
17:1-13 289
17:3 .... 51, 214
17:5 ....213, 344
17:9-13 .... 362 n8

17:13-14 254
17:14 201
17:14-21 ..... 146 n8, 362 n8,
379
17:17 .... 51, 61 n17
17:20 ..31, 35, 216, 267, 314
17:22-23 ....254, 362 n8
17:23 354
17:24ff. 222 n1
17:24-27 214
17:25-18:35 344
17:30 213
18 .....31, 91, 295, 298, 309,
344
18:1-2 ....363 n12
18:1-5 .... 362 n8
18:1-9 ....308, 311
18:1-35 403
18:4 ....309, 310
18:5 ....363 n12
18:6-7 .. 35, 78 n2, 106, 267,
309, 310
18:6-9 ..... 283 n17, 363 n12,
420
18:8-9 ....201, 233
18:10ff. 231
18:10-14 420
18:10-22 424
18:10-35 ....308, 311
18:12-14 .... 35, 254, 298 n9,
309, 310, 400
18:13 267
18:15 .... 35, 309, 310
18:15-20 ....344, 421
18:15-22 311
18:17 ....363 n11
18:21 309
18:21-22 ...35, 267, 310, 421
18:30 ....447 n22
19 115
19-25 351
19:1 107
19:1ff. 363 n12
19:1-9 .... 362 n8
19:1-12 344
19:3 ....362 n10
19:4-6 90
19:8 115
19:9 .. 115, 233, 247, 247 n5,
362 n10
19:10-12 31
19:12 ....34n
19:13-15 .... 173, 362 n8
19:16 .... 206 n3
19:16-17 .... 69 n13
19:16-30 .... 344, 362 n10
19:17 .... 28, 59, 362 n10
19:18-19 208
19:20 69
19:21 ....362 n10
19:23 212

19:26 69
19:28 ....31, 314, 363 n11
19:28b.........................36
19:30 ....31, 316 n52
20:1-15 316
20:1-16 .... 74 n29
20:16 ..... 263, 314, 315, 316
20:17-19 .... 362 n8
20:20 ....216 n12
20:20-28 .... 216, 362 n8
20:21 201
20:27 213
20:29 ....216 n12
20:29-34 .... 213, 362 n8
21:2ff. 71 n19
21:4 213
21:5 213
21:10-17 417
21:11 210
21:12-13 90
21:12-17 210
21:13 212
21:14 .... 222 n1
21:15 213
21:16 213
21:21 213
21:23-27 173
21:33ff. 31
21:33-46 173
21:39 211
21:42 214
22:1-4 351
22:1-10 ...... 36, 254, 298 n9,
          314, 315, 395, 400
22:15-16 210
22:15-22 41
22:22 ....420 n17
22:23-33 .... 41, 173
22:31 214
22:34-39 ...254, 298 n9, 314,
                             315
22:34-40 .... 41, 106
22:35-40 ..... 78 n2, 346, 351
22:36 201
22:40 214
22:41-46 41
22:43 202
22:44 214
22:46 419
23 ..231, 263, 267, 311, 313,
                        314, 340
23-25 ....295, 298
23:1 312
23:1-36 351
23:1-39 403
23:2-3 312
23:4 ....35, 232, 312
23:4-31 311
23:5 ....189, 312
23:6-7a 35, 311, 312
23:7b-10 312

23:11 ....213, 312
23:12 .... 35, 309, 312
23:13 .... 35, 311
23:13-14 ....311, 312
23:15-22 312
23:23 ...35, 264 n7, 312, 313
23:23-25 232
23:24 312
23:25-26 .... 35, 312
23:26 .... 264 n7
23:27 .... 35, 262
23:27-28 312
23:29-31 .... 35, 312
23:29-36 232
23:31 .... 264 n7
23:32-33 312
23:34-35 ....312 n44
23:34-36 ....35, 311, 312
23:35 237
23:37 210
23:37-38 252
23:37-39 ..35, 172, 232, 267,
                 311, 312, 351
23:27-24:2 345
23:38 311
24 ...114, 267, 280, 307, 406
                               n4
24-25 ....91, 311, 313, 344
24:4-8 173
24:4-9 280
24:4-26 271
24:4-25:46 403
24:9 ....90, 213, 233, 307
24:9-13 213
24:9-14 .... 112, 113, 114
24:10 213
24:10-12 280
24:11 213
24:12 213
24:13 .... 233, 280, 307
24:13-14 90
24:14 ....113, 280
24:14-15b 282
24:14-30 282
24:15 214
24:15-25 280
24:15-31 345
24:17-18 282
24:20 ....189, 213
24:23-25 .... 281, 421 n21
24:23-28 ....281, 421
24:23-41 351
24:26-27 ....35, 281, 313
24:26-28 .. 232, 280, 421 n21
24:28 ......36, 281, 282, 313,
                               314
24:29-30 280
24:30a 280
24:31-36 280
24:37ff. 231
24:37-39 .... 35, 313

24:37-41 ....232, 281
24:37-25:46............112, 280
24:40-41 ....36, 282, 313
24:42 ... 34n, 112, 280,
      280 n13, 282, 313, 418
24:42-51 282
24:42-25:12..................351
24:43-44 .... 112, 267, 313
24:43-51 ...35, 232, 313, 314
24:43-25:46..................313
24:45 112
24:45-51 .... 231, 252, 313
24:51b........................282
25 .... 32, 231, 280
25:1-13................282, 303
25:10-12 ...254, 263, 298 n9,
                               299
25:13 .... 280 n13, 418
25:13-15 ....34n
25:13-15b 280
25:14 .... 280 n13, 417
25:14ff. 236
25:14-30 ..36, 112, 231, 232,
      254, 298 n9, 313, 352, 400
25:15b.................280 n13
25:24-29 ....313 n45
25:29 .... 233, 253, 290
26:1 ....107, 311
26:13 212
26:17 207
26:20 211
26:20-29 170
26:21 212
26:25 421
26:36-46 170
26:50 421
26:52-54 .... 222 n1
26:58 207
26:61 202
26:64 202
26:67 .... 207 n3
26:67-68 48
26:68 ....51, 61, 61 n19
26:70-74 217
26:71 .... 207 n3
26:75 51
27:3-10................... 222 n1
27:14 202
27:19 .... 222 n1
27:24-25 .... 222 n1
27:33 .... 29, 58 n10
27:40 .... 58 n10
27:45 215
27:46 .... 29, 208
27:51b-53 .... 222 n1
27:62-66 .... 222 n1
27:63 354
28:8 48

Mark
1.................... 80, 91, 350
1-6 349

1-13 .... 110, 114
1:1 .... 34, 47, 203, 386
1:1ff. 279
1:1-4 387
1:1-6 .... 386, 420
1:1-13 .... 271, 381, 385, 387
1:1-15 ....40, 56
1:1-20 57
1:1-3:13 350
1:1-6:6 56
1:1-10:52 416
1:2 . 110, 114, 208, 213, 385,
        386, 387, 417, 423
1:2-3 386
1:3 ....213, 386
1:4 ...374, 417, 424, 424 n26
1:4-6 ....419, 424
1:5 ....389 n11
1:5-6 34
1:7-8 ... 34, 87, 367 n19, 386,
        417, 421
1:8 ..206, 386, 388, 389, 423
1:9 210
1:9-11 386
1:10 .... 59, 386
1:11 .... 200, 208, 249, 385
1:11-12 ....367 n19
1:12-13 ..... 34, 87, 110, 387,
        389, 421
1:13 ....208, 389
1:14 203
1:14-15 .... 91, 213, 363
1:14-3:30.................... 363
1:15 203
1:16 249
1:16ff. 57
1:16-20 .. 34, 42, 56, 93, 128,
        363
1:18 128
1:20 128
1:21 ....91, 92
1:21-22 .... 237 n28, 363
1:21ff. 57
1:21-28 170-71
1:21-39 .... 40, 56, 90
1:21-6:13.................... 123
1:22 ....32, 91, 92, 372
1:23-28 .... 34, 249 n10
1:28 91
1:29 ....62 n21, 200, 209
1:29ff. 57
1:29-31 363
1:29-34 ....57, 92
1:29-5:21 350
1:29-6:11 ....58 n7
1:32 .... 29, 81, 91
1:32-34 363
1:33 200
1:34 ....59, 91
1:35 200
1:35-38 34

1:39 .... 57, 363, 421
1:39a..........................90
1:39b..........................91
1:39ff. 350
1:40 .... 61 n17
1:40-45 . 57, 92, 172-73, 363,
        364 n15
1:40-3:6 56
1:40-3:19........................40
1:43-45 91
1:44 .... 361 n6
2-3 55
2:1 ....210, 350
2:1-12 ......40, 173, 210, 363
2:1-22 .... 55, 57, 91, 92
2:1-3:6............... 81, 410 n2
2:3 .... 39, 200
2:3-12 .... 364, 364 n15
2:4 .... 58, 59, 208
2:7 58
2:9 374
2:12 48
2:13-17 ..... 26, 40, 289, 363,
        364, 364 n15
2:14 ....209, 249
2:15 59
2:18 70
2:18-22 ......40, 363, 364 n15
2:19 214
2:20 .... 361 n6
2:22 374
2:23 .... 91, 350
2:23-28 ......40, 363, 364 n15
2:23-3:6 .... 55, 92, 289
2:23-3:12......................57
2:25 214
2:26 .... 203, 208, 373
2:26-27 249
2:27 .... 34, 47, 203, 214
3 233
3:1 48
3:1-6 ....40, 363, 364 n15
3:3 .... 361 n6
3:5 375
3:6 210
3:7-8 91
3:7ff. 418
3:7-12 .... 40, 42, 56, 92, 93,
        363
3:7-19 .... 126, 127
3:7-35 55
3:8 .... 212, 350, 424 n25
3:9 375
3:13 .... 91, 210
3:13ff. 57
3:13-19a.................... 363
3:13-19 ... 42, 55, 56, 57, 91,
        92, 93, 418, 424
3:14-15 211
3:16-19 .... 291 n3
3:17 ....215, 375

3:18 209
3:19 210
3:19b-22 363
3:20 .... 54, 392 n15
3:20ff. 274-76
3:20-21 .. 34, 47, 82, 372,
        392 n15
3:20-29 .... 269, 271, 446
3:20-30 ....127, 421
3:21 .... 70 n17, 216, 392 n15
3:22 ....210, 392
3:22-23 391
3:22-27 ..... 34, 35, 381, 385,
        391, 446
3:22-30............. 87, 92, 110
3:22-4:34..........................57
3:23 .... 210, 391, 447, 448
3:23-30 ... 106, 233, 363, 420
3:24 391
3:24-25 .... 391, 447, 448
3:24-26 391
3:24-27 391
3:25 391
3:26 .... 391, 447, 448
3:27 ....272, 391
3:28 ....272, 392
3:28-29 .....35, 237, 315, 392
3:28-30 34
3:29 273
3:31 372
3:31-34 412
3:31-35 ... 27, 42, 56, 92, 93,
        127, 364 n15, 413, 418
3:32 .... 70 n17
3:34 213
3:35 214
4 ....31, 110, 272
4:1 308
4:1-9 ....40, 307, 364 n15
4:1-20 290
4:1-25 .... 56, 127
4:1-34 .... 57, 92, 93
4:1-9:41 40
4:7-13 421
4:9 ....34n, 419
4:10 .... 48, 213
4:10-12 ...... 40, 70 n14, 307,
        308, 364 n15
4:11 61
4:12 ....249, 290
4:13 215
4:13-20 ......40, 307, 364 n15
4:21 ...34n, 35, 48, 253, 302,
        363 n14, 422
4:21-24 34
4:21-25 110
4:21-42 422
4:22 ....34n, 35, 48, 253, 422
4:23 ..... 34n, 419, 422, 424
4:24 .... 34n, 363 n14
4:24a........................ 422

4:24b 417, 422, 423
4:24c 418, 422, 423
4:25 ...... 34n, 233, 249, 253,
                363 n13, 422
4:26-29 ....34, 47, 54, 178,
                421, 422
4:28 215
4:30-32 .. 34, 35, 42, 87, 106,
127, 237, 307, 308, 364 n15,
                420, 422
4:31-32 200
4:31-34 91
4:33-34 .... 34, 422
4:35 ....81, 81 n3, 203
4:35ff. 57
4:35-41 .... 363 n14, 364 n15,
                375, 422
4:35-5:20 57
4:35-5:43 .....56, 91, 92, 419
4:36 .... 48, 203
4:38 ..29, 39, 69 n13, 72 n20,
                215
4:40 .... 420 n17
4:41 ....200, 375
5:1-20 ... 171, 363 n14,
364 n15, 376
5:1-8:17 91
5:3b 376
5:4 376
5:5 376
5:11 215
5:18-20 212
5:21ff. 57
5:21-43 ...... 57, 73 n26,
363 n14, 364 n15, 377
5:22 ..... 206, 206 n3, 207 n3,
                377
5:26 377
5:27 .... 61 n17
5:31 215
5:35 .... 70 n17
5:40 377
5:41 215
5:43 ....211, 213
5:43-44 213
6 .... 82, 350
6:1ff. 57
6:1-6 ..... 34, 42, 56, 57, 128,
                243 n47
6:1-6a 92, 93, 418, 419,
                424, 424 n27
6:3 .... 203, 206, 211, 374
6:4 216
6:5 28
6:5-6 .... 69 n13
6:6 271
6:6b 90,92
6:6-11 35
6:6b-11 91
6:7 .... 56, 271
6:7ff. 31, 237

6:7-11 . 87, 91, 92, 249, 290,
                291, 292
6:7-12 ....363 n14
6:7-13 .... 110, 214, 232, 233
6:8 377
6:8-9 200
6:8-11 .... 106, 254, 271
6:9 378
6:11a 291
6:12 378
6:13 ....203, 378
6:13-19 271
6:14 .... 59, 209
6:14-27 209
6:14-16:8 ....27, 89
6:15 .... 207 n3, 350
6:16-20 56
6:17 209
6:17-18 42
6:17-29 ....34, 71
6:18 ....215 n11
6:19 212
6:21 208
6:26 59
6:27 208
6:30 34
6:30-44 ....364 n15
6:31 ....210, 378
6:31-44 ....254 n23
6:34 .... 271, 280, 378
6:34a 420
6:34b 420, 424
6:37 215
6:45 209
6:45-8:26 .... 26, 34, 40, 60
6:50 248
6:52 215
6:55 209
7:1ff. 61
7:1-23 363
7:2-4 47
7:2-13 214
7:3-4 .... 34, 207
7:10 206
7:13 207
7:17 ....210, 216
7:19b 214
7:24 ....210, 211
7:24ff. 61
7:24-30 212
7:24-31 200
7:27 200
7:31 ....209, 212
7:31-37 54
7:32-35 178
7:32-37 ....34, 47
7:34 .... 156 n34, 215
7:36 211
7:37 213
8:1 212
8:1-10 .... 170, 254 n23

8:3 212
8:10 209
8:11-12 ....363 n12
8:12 ....35, 48
8:14 29
8:14ff. 379
8:14-21 70
8:15 .... 34, 110, 379
8:17-18 215
8:19-21 212
8:22-26 ... 34, 47, 54, 89, 178
8:27 209
8:27-30 292
8:27-33 ...... 40, 74 n29, 201,
                364 n15
8:27-9:1 292
8:28 .... 207 n3
8:29 248
8:29b 249
8:31 379
8:32-33 ....201, 292
8:33 374
8:34 .... 35, 213
8:34-35 ... 233, 254, 363 n12
8:34-39 ....364 n15
8:34-9:1 .... 40, 110, 173
8:35 203
8:38 .... 35, 233, 254
9:1 .... 361, 364 n15
9:2-10 40
9:2-13 289
9:4 214
9:9 344
9:10 215
9:10-13 34
9:14 ....201, 203
9:14-29 .... 216, 364 n15, 379
9:17 .... 207 n3
9:18 379
9:19 .... 61 n17, 215
9:27 393
9:28 .... 34, 210, 393
9:29 ....34, 47
9:30-31 203
9:30-32 ....364 n15
9:31 379
9:32 215
9:32-37 344
9:33 210
9:33ff. 363 n12
9:33-37 ....31, 110, 214, 308,
                309, 364 n15
9:33-50 91
9:34 ....215, 310
9:35 ....213, 233
9:35-37 .... 203, 254 n23
9:36 310
9:37 ....201, 306
9:37-40 171
9:38-40 34
9:39b 34

9:40.........35, 350, 392, 447
9:41.........34, 306, 419, 424
9:42..................... 34, 106
9:42-43.....................363 n12
9:42-48............31, 308, 420
9:43-47................ 34, 201
9:47-48....................363 n12
9:48-49....................34, 47
9:49.........................54
9:50.........34, 265, 418, 423
10:1-2 ....363 n12
10:1ff............................61
10:1-10.......................34
10:1-12...................... 344
10:10 210
10:11 ....201, 247
10:11-12 34
10:12 215
10:13-16 .... 173, 364 n15
10:13-13:32..................40
10:17 .... 206 n3
10:17-18 ...... 69 n13, 361 n6
10:17-31 .. 171, 344, 364 n15
10:18 ....28, 59
10:19 208
10:20 69
10:23 212
10:24 215
10:27 69
10:29 203
10:30 110
10:31 .... 34, 316 n52
10:32 215
10:32-34 ....364 n15
10:33 .... 361 n6
10:35-40 110
10:35-41 34
10:35-45 215
10:37 201
10:38 110
10:38-39 215
10:40-45 91
10:41-45 ....364 n15
10:42-45 ....34, 93
10:43-44 .... 233, 254 n23
10:43ff. 201
10:44 213
10:45 201
10:46 ....210, 215
10:46-52 .... 213, 364 n15
11:1-16:8 416
11:11 .... 210, 417, 424
11:11a 34
11:12-14 34
11:15 210
11:15-19 .... 210, 417, 424
11:16 211
11:17 ....203, 212
11:20-22 34
11:20-26 211
11:21 44

11:22-23 35
11:23 .... 34, 213
11:24 34
11:25 ......34, 201, 206, 419, 424
11:27-33 .... 26, 173
12 352
12:1-12 173
12:8 211
12:10 214
12:12 ....420 n17
12:13 210
12:13-17 41
12:18-27 .... 41, 173
12:25 201
12:28 .... 201, 207 n3
12:28-31 .... 385, 389, 391
12:28-34 ...... 34, 41, 87, 93, 106, 201, 315, 381, 385
12:29 390
12:29b 390
12:30 .... 390, 390 n13
12:31 214
12:32 214
12:33-34 214
12:34c 419, 424
12:35-37 41
12:36 ....202, 214
12:37 212
12:38-40 .... 35, 110
12:38b-40 311
12:38b-44 171
12:40-44 34
12:41-44 .... 90, 249 n10
12:42 214
13 .....31, 91, 202, 237, 280, 281
13:1 .... 207 n3
13:1-2 202
13:1-32 112
13:5-8 173
13:5-37 271
13:9 ....202, 233
13:9-10 90
13:9-13 ....90, 110, 112, 113, 307
13:10 .... 34, 113
13:11 ....202, 307
13:12c-13 90
13:13 ....213, 233
13:13b 202
13:14 214
13:15-16 .... 34, 282
13:18 34
13:21 .... 35, 281
13:21-23 ..34, 281, 352, 421, 421 n21
13:27 .... 34, 212
13:32 .... 34, 112
13:33-37 .... 34, 47, 112, 280 n13, 352, 418, 424

13:34 ....36, 282, 417, 418
13:34b....................... 112
13:35 .... 282, 313, 418
13:35a....................280 n13
13:36-37 418
13:37 282
14:1-16:8 40
14:3-9 .... 34, 93, 128
14:9 212
14:10 .... 207 n3
14:12 207
14:13 207
14:17 211
14:17ff. 34
14:17-21 202
14:17-25 170
14:17-16:8 34
14:18 .... 207 n3
14:19-21 93
14:20 .... 207 n3, 216
14:20-21 42
14:21 421
14:22-25 202
14:26-28 34
14:29-30 93
14:30 ....34n, 203
14:30-32 307
14:31 216
14:32-42 170
14:40 216
14:43 .... 207 n3
14:45 421
14:51 54
14:51-52 .... 34, 47, 90
14:54 216
14:55 207
14:57-58 212
14:58 202
14:62 202
14:65 ....48, 61, 61 n19
14:66 .... 207 n3, 210
14:68-70 210
14:72 203
15:1 207
15:3-5 34
15:5 202
15:6 59
15:11-12 209
15:16-20 34
15:25 ....203, 215
15:34 .... 29, 208, 215
15:42 207
15:44-45 202
15:46 207
16:1-8 39
16:8 48

Luke
1:1 187
1:1-4:30 32
1:1-10:24.................... 322
1:17....................279 n12

2:36-38 355
3-6 350
3:1ff. 108
3:1-6 386,420
3:1-18 257
3:1-22 271
3:1-4:15 ....40, 56
3:1-4:30 ....268 n10
3:2-22 267
3:3 . 373, 386, 388, 417,
424 n26
3:3a 279
3:4 ....213, 386
3:4a 393
3:7-9 ......34, 172, 222, 229,
232, 250, 314, 368 n20, 374,
388, 420, 423
3:7b-9 251
3:7-14 40
3:8 ....68 n8
3:12 314
3:15-18 421
3:16 .... 237, 367 n19, 386,
393, 417, 423
3:16-17 .. 34, 232, 314,
367 n20, 386, 388
3:17 .... 229, 250, 386, 388
3:19 209
3:19-20 42
3:21 389
3:21-22 ...... 257, 314, 389
3:22 ...... 200, 208, 249, 373,
389, 389 n11
3:23-38 ....40, 372
4-9 334
4:1 374
4:1ff. 279
4:1-2 ....367 n19
4:1-3 ....365 n18
4:1-13 ....34, 172, 257, 267,
271, 314, 421
4:2 ....374, 389
4:2-13 .... 232, 235, 250
4:2b-13 40
4:3-13 .... 366, 368 n20
4:4 ....368 n21
4:5-7 ....365 n18
4:7 ....368 n21
4:9-11 ....365 n18
4:10 ....368 n21
4:13 .... 365 n18, 374
4:14-15 .... 362 n9
4:16-29 341
4:16-30 .. 34, 42, 56, 93, 128,
418
4:22 ....372, 374
4:22ff. 243 n47
4:23 57
4:31 213
4:31-32 .... 362 n9
4:31ff. 57

4:31-37 .... 171, 360 n3
4:31-38 128
4:31-44 ....40, 56
4:31-6:19....................32
4:33-37 ....249 n10
4:38 .... 57, 128, 200
4:40 59
4:42 200
4:43 .... 361 n7
4:44 421
5:1 210
5:1ff. 57
5:1-10 341
5:1-11 ... 34, 42, 56, 93, 128,
421
5:3 249
5:8 216
5:11 128
5:12 .... 61 n17, 210
5:12-16 ......172, 173, 360 n3
5:12-6:11....................56
5:12-6:19....................40
5:16 210
5:17 210
5:17-26 .... 40, 173, 360 n3
5:17-39 55
5:18 200
5:19 208
5:25 .... 48, 374
5:27 249
5:27-32 .... 40, 289, 360 n3
5:28-29 128
5:29 59
5:33-39 40
5:35 .... 361 n7
5:36 ....306 n29
5:37 374
5:37-39 .... 361 n7
6 346
6:1-5 .... 40, 360 n3
6:1-11 .... 55, 289
6:3-5 .... 361 n7
6:4-5 249
6:6 48
6:6-11 .... 40, 360 n3
6:12ff. 348
6:12-16 .... 42, 56, 93
6:12-19 127
6:13-16 ....271, 418
6:14-16 .... 291 n3
6:14-19 127
6:17 ....424 n25
6:17-19 .. 40, 42, 56, 93, 418
6:20 .... 68 n8, 248 n7, 375
6:20ff. 56, 234, 235
6:20-23 .....34, 232, 299, 366
6:20-26 263
6:20-49 . 43 n11, 55, 90, 267,
341
6:20-7:35.................... 235
6:20-8:3 .... 32, 40, 267

6:21 .... 248 n7, 375
6:22 .... 264 n7
6:23 .... 264 n7
6:24 375
6:24-26 317
6:27-30 .... 232, 299, 301
6:27-33 34
6:27-36 ....368 n22
6:29 262
6:31 . 299, 301, 368 n20,
368 n22
6:32-36 ....232, 299
6:35-36 34
6:36 376
6:37-38 ....34, 232, 299, 305,
367 n19
6:37-42 ....368 n22
6:38 .... 417, 422, 423
6:39 .... 305, 306 n29, 314,
315, 368 n21, 368 n22
6:39-40 .... 34, 305, 315
6:39-42 ....368 n20
6:40 .... 304, 305, 315
6:41-42 ....34, 172, 251, 299,
305
6:41-49 232
6:43-44 .... 303, 304 n24
6:43-45 ....34, 267, 271, 277,
299, 314, 315, 316 n50,
411 n4, 446
6:45 ....368 n20
6:46... 35, 299, 304, 304 n24
6:47-49 .....35, 189, 299, 376
7 342
7:1 ....107, 372
7:1-8 ....365 n18
7:1-9 ....368 n20
7:1-10 . 34, 90, 91, 232, 235,
267, 314
7:1-8:3 55
7:1-9:50 350
7:2-10 ....341, 350
7:6-9 172
7:10 ....365 n18
7:11-17 341
7:13 280
7:18ff. 348
7:18-20 35
7:18-21 ....365 n18
7:18-23 .... 235, 314, 316
7:18-34 ....341, 350
7:18-35 .....90, 172, 232, 267
7:21 316
7:22-23 ....251, 316
7:22-28 .... 35, 368 n20
7:24-28 .... 314, 316
7:24b-28 251
7:27 .. 213, 367 n19, 368 n21,
387, 417, 423
7:29-30 ....365 n18
7:30 ....390 n12

7:31-35 .. 35, 314, 316, 368 n20
7:36-50 .... 34, 93, 341
7:38-50 128
7:44-47 212
7:49 128
8:1-3 128
8:4 .... 55, 306 n29
8:4-8 40
8:4-15 290
8:4-18 .... 56, 93, 127
8:4-9:50 .... 32, 40
8:8 419
8:9 48
8:9-10 40
8:10 .... 61, 290, 361 n6
8:10-11 249
8:11-15 40
8:13 .... 361 n7
8:16 .... 48, 253, 302, 422
8:17 .... 48, 253, 422
8:18 ... 233, 253, 290, 361 n7
8:18a 422
8:18b 249, 422
8:19-20 .... 42, 43 n11
8:19-21 ..... 56, 93, 127, 338, 360 n3, 421
8:20 214
8:21 .... 361 n7
8:22 48
8:22-25 .... 360 n3, 422
8:22-56 56
8:26-39 ...... 171, 360 n3, 376
8:32 215
8:37b-39 212
8:40-56 .... 360 n3, 377
8:43 .... 377 n1
8:44 .... 61 n17
8:45 .... 361 n6
9 232
9-12 407
9:1-5 .... 249, 271, 291, 292
9:1-6 .... 360 n3
9:1-9 348
9:1-10 348
9:3 .... 291, 378
9:3-4 200
9:3-5 254
9:5 291
9:6 378
9:7 209
9:9 342
9:10ff. 349
9:10-17 .... 360 n3
9:11 209
9:17 40
9:18-21 292
9:18-22 .... 40, 200, 360 n3
9:18-27 292
9:18-45 348
9:20b 249

9:22 379
9:23-24 .... 233, 254
9:23-27 .... 40, 173
9:26 254
9:27 361
9:28-36 .... 40, 289, 395
9:30 214
9:31 349
9:33 395
9:35 .... 348, 395
9:37 200
9:37-43 379
9:37-43a 360 n3
9:40 351
9:41 61
9:43b-44 .... 360 n3
9:45 215
9:46-48 .... 360 n3
9:46-62 348
9:47 .... 367 n19
9:48 .... 368 n21
9:48a 367 n19, 368 n20
9:48b 367 n19
9:48-50 171
9:49 .... 365 n18, 367 n19
9:49-50 ...... 249 n10, 360 n3, 419
9:50 .... 350, 367 n19, 447
9:51ff. 250
9:51ff. 250 n11
9:51-62 349
9:51-18:14 . 32, 40, 103, 104, 182, 182 n7, 231, 334, 416
9:53 250
9:57-60 ..... 35, 232, 314, 316
9:57-62 90
9:57-10:12 91
9:57-10:24 .... 108, 267
9:57-13:34 235
9:61-62 .... 234, 317
10 .... 232, 346
10-18 .... 322, 335, 336, 341, 346, 351, 352
10:1 233
10:1-6 291
10:1-12 .... 233, 271, 421
10:1-16 .... 292, 348
10:2 ... 35, 304, 368 n21, 378
10:2-3 .... 368 n20
10:2-12 90
10:3 .... 291, 368 n21, 378
10:3-12 .... 35, 304
10:4 .... 233, 254, 291
10:4-5 .... 367 n19
10:4-11 106
10:5 .... 264 n7
10:5-7 254
10:6 291
10:7 378
10:10-11 254
10:11 291

10:12 .... 368 n21
10:12-16 .... 368 n20
10:12-25 342
10:13-15 ... 35, 90, 232, 252, 314
10:13-11:32 266
10:16 ...... 304, 306, 368 n21
10:17-20 348
10:21-22 ... 35, 90, 232, 239, 252, 284, 308, 314
10:21-24 .... 348, 368 n20
10:23 290
10:23-24 ...35, 234 n18, 266, 308
10:25-26 201
10:25ff. 348, 349
10:25-27 314
10:25-28 ... 34, 93, 106, 254, 298 n9, 308, 346, 351, 352, 389
10:25-18:11 336
10:25-18:30... 322, 334, 341, 346
10:30 349
10:33 280
10:40 .... 367 n19
11 .... 233, 263, 266, 311
11-14 300
11:1-4 .... 232, 266
11:1-13 .... 301, 337
11:2-4 . 35, 248 n7, 266, 299, 301, 368 n20
11:4 34
11:5-8 301
11:9-13 ....35, 232, 251, 266, 299, 301, 368 n20
11:14 .... 213, 273, 392
11:14ff. 274-77
11:14-16 .... 365 n18
11:14-23 ... 34, 35, 232, 235, 314, 391, 411 n4, 421, 446
11:14-26 . 127, 269, 271, 446
11:14-28 338
11:14-32 267
11:15 .... 367 n19, 392
11:15-22 351
11:17 ...... 367 n19, 372, 391
11:17a 273
11:17b 273
11:17-18 391
11:17-23 .... 106, 233, 420
11:18 .... 367 n19, 391
11:18a 273
11:18b-20 273
11:18-22 .... 361 n7
11:19-20 ... 368 n20, 368 n21
11:20 .... 331, 361
11:21 .... 391, 447
11:21-22 .. 278, 367 n19, 391
11:22 391
11:23 . 273, 361 n7, 367 n19,

368 n21, 392, 447
11:23-24 308
11:23-26 ....368 n20
11:24-25 252
11:24-26 ..35, 232, 274, 314, 315, 367, 368 n21, 411 n4, 420
11:24-32 423
11:26 .... 361 n7
11:27-28 ....266 n9, 274, 420
11:29 .... 48, 367 n19
11:29-30 ....368, 433
11:29ff. 339
11:29-32 ..35, 172, 232, 235, 274, 277, 314, 315, 368 n20, 411 n4, 420
11:30 .... 361 n7
11:31-33 .... 361 n7
11:32 312
11:33 .35, 48, 253, 265, 266, 299, 302
11:33-34 266
11:33-35 232
11:34 299
11:34-35 ....35, 302, 368 n20
11:34-36 ....265, 266
11:37-52 340
11:39 .... 264 n7
11:39-41 312
11:39-44 .... 35, 340
11:39-48 311
11:39-52 .... 232, 267, 351
11:41 .... 264 n7
11:42 .312, 367 n19, 368 n20
11:43 .... 312, 368 n21
11:44 ....262, 312
11:45 .... 365 n18, 390 n12
11:46 .... 312, 390 n12
11:46-48 35
11:46-52 340
11:47-48 312
11:48 .... 264 n7
11:49-51 ....311, 312
11:49-52 35
11:50-51 237
11:52 311
12 280
12-18 ....398, 407
12:1 .... 34, 379
12:2 ... 48, 253, 367 n19, 368 n21
12:2-3 304
12:2ff. 307
12:2-7 ....368 n20
12:2-9 35
12:2-10 232
12:2-12 267
12:4-7 304
12:6 262
12:8-9 .... 233, 241 n44, 304, 367 n19

12:9 254
12:10 .34, 35, 106, 267, 271, 276, 314, 351, 367 n19, 446
12:10a 273
12:10b 273
12:11-12 ...... 233, 303, 304, 306, 307
12:12 ....367 n19
12:13-21 303
12:16 ....306 n29
12:20 241
12:22-31 ...... 266, 299, 302, 303, 368 n20
12:22-32 35
12:22-34 ....232, 267
12:31 .... 418, 422, 423
12:33-34 .... 35, 266
12:33b......................... 299
12:33b-34 302
12:34 ....299, 302
12:35-38 317
12:35-46 ....351, 352
12:35-59 267
12:38 418
12:39-40 . 313, 367 n19, 368 n20, 368 n21
12:39-46 .... 35, 232, 282
12:40 418
12:42-46 .. 252, 313, 368 n20
12:47-48 317
12:49-53 331
12:50 215
12:51-53 .... 35, 304
12:54ff. 264
12:54-56 . 35, 254, 264, 298 n9, 317
12:57-59 .... 265, 266, 299
12:58-59 .... 35, 368 n20
13:6 ....306 n29
13:18-19 .....34, 35, 42, 106, 127, 237, 257, 308, 367 n19, 420, 422
13:18-21 232
13:20-21 ...35, 257, 308, 368 n20, 420, 422, 424
13:22 250
13:22-30 ....263, 267
13:23-24 ...35, 254, 266, 298 n9, 299, 303, 304 n24
13:25 303
13:25-27 ....254, 298 n9, 299
13:25-30 263
13:26-27 . 35, 266, 303, 304 n24
13:27-30 ....368 n20
13:28-29 ...35, 108, 314, 316
13:30 ......34, 264, 314, 316, 367 n19, 368 n21
13:31 210
13:34-35 ..35, 172, 232, 241, 252, 267, 311, 312, 351,

368 n20
14:3 ....390 n12
14:5 .... 290 n2
14:7 ....306 n29
14:7-10 309
14:11 .... 35, 309, 312
14:15 ....392 n15
14:15-24 ... 36, 254, 298 n9, 314, 315, 395
14:16-24 ....351, 400
14:26-27 . 35, 281, 305, 367 n19
14:27 .... 233, 241, 254
14:31-32 265
14:34 .... 34, 418, 423
14:34-35 ..35, 266, 299, 302, 367 n19
14:35 419
15:3 ....306 n29
15:4-6 280
15:4-7 .35, 254, 298 n9, 309, 310, 400
15:10 ....298 n9, 309, 310
15:20 280
16 300
16:1-9 303
16:8-13 331
16:10-12 303
16:13 ......35, 251, 266, 299, 368 n20
16:14 340
16:15-18 331
16:16 ......35, 262, 314, 316, 342
16:17 .... 35, 299
16:17-18 ....368 n20
16:18 ... 34, 35, 201, 247 n5, 265, 299, 361 n6, 367 n19, 368 n21
17 ..... 280, 281, 352, 406 n4
17:1 309
17:1b 106
17:1-2 .... 35, 309, 310, 367 n19, 420
17:1-6 ....267, 331
17:2 ....34, 106, 351
17:3 421
17:3-4 ......35, 309, 310, 424
17:4 421
17:5-6 314
17:6 .... 34, 35, 367 n19
17:11 250
17:20-21 361
17:20-37 282
17:21 ....421 n21
17:21-37 421
17:22-23 352
17:22-37 .... 232, 267, 351
17:23 34
17:23a......................... 281
17:23-24 ...35, 313, 368 n20,

421 n21
17:23b-24 281
17:26-27 .... 35, 281, 313
17:31 ....34, 282, 367 n19
17:32 282
17:33 ... 233, 282, 305,
 367 n19, 368 n20
17:34 282
17:34-35 .... 36, 313
17:36 416
17:37 .... 36, 281, 313,
 368 n20, 421 n21
18 ....309, 346
18:1 ....306 n29
18:1-8 355
18:9-14a.................... 309
18:9-30 349
18:14b 35, 309
18:15 407
18:15-17 .... 173, 360 n3
18:15-43 32
18:15-21:33...................40
18:18 .... 361 n6
18:18-30 ....171, 346, 360 n3
18:20 208
18:30 .... 361 n6
18:31-34 .... 360 n3
18:31-24:53................ 322
18:35-43 .... 360 n3
19 280
19:1-27 ...... 32, 40, 341, 349
19:11ff. 236
19:11-27 .... 36, 352
19:11-28 232
19:12-13 417
19:12-27 ...254, 282, 298 n9,
 313, 400
19:20-26 .... 313 n45
19:26 .... 233, 253, 290
19:28 250
19:28-22:13.................32
19:41-44 40
19:41-48 349
19:45-46 ....210, 417
10:46 212
20:1-8 173
20:2 128
20:9-19 173
20:15 211
20:17 214
20:20-26 41
20:27-40 .... 41, 173
20:34-36 201
20:37 214
20:39-40 .... 93, 352
20:40 419
20:41-44 41
20:42-43 214
20:46-21:4 171
21 280
21:6 202

21:8 .... 280 n14
21:8-11 173
21:8-36 271
21:9 .... 280 n14, 355
21:12 233
21:12-13 202
21:14-15 307
21:17 233
21:19 202
21:20-36 202
21:24 355
21:24-25 352
21:27 355
21:32 .... 280 n14
21:34-36 ....116, 352
22:1-23:11 40
22:7 207
22:10 207
22:14 .... 32, 211
22:14ff. 32, 34
22:14-18 202
22:19-20 202
22:21-23 .... 56, 93, 202
22:23 421
22:24ff. 201
22:24-27 93
22:25-27 34
22:27 201
22:27-32 40
22:28 314
22:28-32 216
22:29 .... 235 n20
22:30b 36, 235 n20, 314
22:31-34 93
22:34 .... 34n
22:35 233
22:35-38 40
22:48 421
22:56-66 56
22:64 ....48, 61, 61 n19
22:66 207
22:70 202
23:11 34
23:18 59
23:21-23 42
23:27-32 40
23:39b-43 40
23:44 215
23:47b-49 40
24:9 48

John
1:45 210
2:13-22 210
2:19 212
6:1 209
6:5 209
6:7 379
6:16 209
12:7-8 212
13:1-2 211
18:18 216

18:25 216
19:14 215
21:15-17 216

Acts
1:1 .... 362 n9
1:13-26 355
4:27 210
6:14 212
7:23-25 348
10:11-14 214
10:38 210
11:5-8 214
12:10 215
12:12-13 .... 28 n12
13:1 209
13:15 206
20:35 224

1 Corinthians
7:10 .... 235, 247 n5
7:12 235
7:25 235
9:7ff. 378
9:14 235
10:1-11 327
11:23ff. 235
11:25 240
15:3ff. 240

Galatians
2:7-8 116

1 Thessalonians
4:15 235
5:3 116

1 Timothy
5:18 378

Hebrews
11:31 349

1 John
2:7-8 345

INDEX OF NAMES

Abbott, 16, 47 n27, 130, 130 n8, 131, 134, 135, 135 n5, 138 n16, 145 n4, 147, 147 n12
Achtemeier, 217 n14
Aland, 242 n45
Albertz, 236 n24, 237 n28, 300, 300 n10
Allen, 27 n10, 431 n10
Appel, 231 n12
Argyle, 18, 49 n32, 146 n8, 147 n13, 148, 148 n14, 157, 229 nn3-4, 247 n4, 371, 371n, 398 n1, 425 n28, 430 n10
Audet, 117, 117 n26
Augustine, 4, 4 n3, 5, 7, 10, 24, 38, 45, 101, 150, 150 n16, 151, 157, 159, 180, 181, 182, 183, 183 n9, 184, 323, 373, 399

Bacon, 156 n34, 260, 260 n1, 359
Badham, 115, 115 n21
Balz, 241 n43
Bammel, 235 n20
Bannwart, 102 n6
Barnes, 431 n10
Barnikol, 59 n12
Barr, 56 n6, 232 n13
Barrett, 18, 253 n22, 255, 255 n27, 259, 259n 260, 297 n6, 394 n17, 430 n10, 438
Barth, 431 n10
Bauer, 243 n47, 243 n49
Bauerfeind, 238 n31
Baur, 403
Beardsley, 398 n1, 399 n3
Beare, 270, 271 n6, 272 n11
Behm, 52 n44, 59 n12, 144 n1, 237 n28, 252, 252 n20
Bellinzoni, 3, 432 n11

Benoit, 102, 103, 103 n11, 104, 297
Betz, 230 n9
Black, 200, 201, 202, 236 n21, 301 n14, 432 n11
Bleek, 184 n10, 185, 185 n12
Boismard, 11, 11 n19, 86 n3, 87 n10, 93
Boman, 241 n43
Bornkamm, 38 n1, 52 n44, 59 n12, 146 n8, 236 n22, 239, 240, 270, 270 n5
Bradby, 18, 229 n7, 248 n9, 287n, 398 n1
Brown, J. P., 52 n43, 61, 86 n5, 230 n10, 237 n28, 255 n26, 257 n30, 284 nn19-20, 430 n10, 431 n11, 432 n12
Brown, M. P., 158 n37
Brown, R. E., 284 n19
Buchanan, 207 n4
Bultmann, 52 n44, 144 n1, 200, 201, 202, 243 n47, 256 n29, 270, 270 n4, 403, 413 n11, 429 n5, 432 n11, 449
Burkitt, 16, 24, 25, 25 n2, 41 n8, 131, 134, 135, 135 n7, 136, 136 n13, 137, 137 n14, 139, 139 n18, 141 n24, 149 n14, 150 n16, 224 n3, 430 n10
Burney, 108, 108 n14, 111, 113, 136 n13, 140, 141, 189 n15, 301 n14, 302 n19
Burton, 27 n7, 156, 182, 194, 359 n2, 431 n10, 450
Bussby, 231 n10, 234 n16, 251 n17
Bussmann, 156, 234 n17, 237 n28, 255 n27, 260, 260 n3, 261 n4, 297, 306 n29, 310 n38
Butler, 7, 7 n10, 8, 9, 15, 16,

38 n4, 41, 41 n8, 41 n9, 42, 44, 44 n15, 44 n17, 45, 45 n18, 45 n19, 55 n5, 63, 64, 65, 65 n2, 66, 66 n4, 67, 67 nn6-7, 68, 69, 70, 70 n15, 71, 71 n18, 72, 73, 73 n24, 74, 77, 78, 78 n1, 79, 80, 81, 83, 88, 88 n17, 89 n20, 97, 97n, 98, 104 n13, 111 n19, 116 n24, 117 n25, 117 n28, 119, 120, 120 n1, 121, 130, 131, 131 n10, 133, 133n, 134, 136 n13, 140 n20, 148 n14, 149 n16, 150 n16, 152 n26, 156 n34, 157, 159, 159 n41, 229 n3, 249 n3, 247 n4, 248 n6, 251, 251 n16, 295, 296, 296 n3, 297 n5, 358, 358 n1, 360, 382, 382 n1, 383 n4, 384, 389 n10, 410 n1, 432 n12, 438, 444, 445, 446

Cadbury, 158 n37, 361, 361 n4
Carlston, 231 n11, 398 n1
Cassian, 229 n3
Cerfaux, 358 n1
Chaine, 116 n24
Chapman, 98, 102, 102 n8, 103, 111 n19, 148 n14, 151 n20, 157, 157 n35
Cherry, 255 n27
Cole, 230 n10, 236 n24
Conzelmann, 43 n11, 279 n12
Coppens, 58 n7, 61 n17
Couchoud, 156 n34
Creed, 305, 305 n27, 310 n38, 310 n42, 389 n11
Cross, 271 n10
Crum, 365 n16
Cullmann, 242 no46, 242 n47
Cunningham, 230 n10

Dahl, 87 n12

Dalmau, 58 n7
Davidson, 185 n12, 196,
    196 n20
Denzinger, 102 n6
De Wette, 186, 186 n12
Dibelius, 236 n22, 239 n35,
    256 n28, 403
Dodd, 116, 116 n23, 260 n1
Downing, 18, 229 n7, 242 n46,
    248 n9, 251, 251 n15, 269,
    269n, 270, 394 n18, 398 n1,
    446, 446 n19, 447, 447 n20,
    447 n21, 448
Dungan, 16, 54 n2, 55 n5, 143,
    143n, 144, 151 n18, 151 n21,
    152 n24, 153 n26, 159 n38,
    427, 427n, 428 n2, 429 n4,
    429 n8, 430 n9, 440, 440 n3
Dupont, 118, 118 n29, 248 n7

Easton, 217, 217 n13, 303,
    303 n22, 305, 305 n28, 308,
    308 n34, 310 nn37-38, 310
    n42, 315, 315 n48, 316, 316
    n51, 361 n4
Edwards, 398 n1
Eichhorn, 3 n1, 228
Ellis, 230 n9
Enslin, 10, 156 n34
Evans, O. E., 6 n7, 41 n9, 42
    n10, 230 n10, 253 n22, 347,
    347 n2

Farmer, 6 n7, 9, 9 n13, 10, 12,
    12 n23, 16, 19, 26 n6, 38, 38
    n3, 39 n5, 41, 41 nn8-9, 43, 43
    n12, 45, 45 n20, 48 n31, 49
    n36, 50, 50 n37, 50 n38, 50
    n39, 55-56 n5, 75 n30, 88 n16,
    93 n22, 98, 100, 100 n2, 104,
    109, 114, 117, 122, 122 n3,
    130 n8, 144 n1, 145 n4, 145
    n5, 146, 146 n8, 147, 147
    nn10-11, 147 n13, 148-149
    n14, 149 n16, 150 n16, 151
    n22, 152, 152 nn25-26, 153
    n26, 155, 156 n34, 160, 160
    n45, 163, 163n, 166 n2, 166
    n3, 179 n5, 182 n8, 184 n11,
    185, 187 n13, 188 n14, 192,
    192 n16, 193, 193 n17, 195
    n18, 229 n3, 247 nn4-5, 248
    n6, 397, 397n, 399, 405 n4,
    410 n1, 414 n11, 429 n6, 438,
    444, 445 n17, 450, 450 n28,
    450 n31, 451, 452
Farrer, 4, 5, 5 n5, 9, 10, 18, 49,
    49 n33, 49 n34, 49 n35, 67 n7,
    68 n10, 87 n8, 147 n13, 160
    n42, 229 n3, 247, 247 n3, 248
    nn8-9, 249 n10, 250, 251 n14,
    257, 269, 270, 270 n1, 271,
    271 n7, 271 n9, 273, 278, 280,

280 n15, 281, 282, 283, 283
    nn16-17, 284, 284 n20, 285,
    285 n20, 287, 288, 289, 290,
    292, 293, 293 n4, 295, 296,
    296 n4, 321, 321n, 322, 326,
    358, 358 n1, 360, 383, 383 n2,
    398 n1, 429 n6, 430, 438, 440,
    443, 443 n13, 444, 446, 448
Fascher, 6 n7, 236 n22, 237 n28
Feine, 52 n44, 59 n12, 144 n1,
    237 n28, 252, 252 n20
Feuillet, 38 n2
Filson, 242 n46
Fitzmyer, 10 n15, 15, 17, 18,
    37, 37n, 38, 48 n30, 229 n4,
    245, 245n, 246, 443 n12
Fortna, 86 n1
Freedman, 243 n49, 284 n18,
    432 n12
Fuchs, 59 n12, 86, 86 n7
Fuller, 60 n14, 88 n18, 97n, 236
    n22, 239 n36, 445 n17

Gaboury, 11, 11n20, 87 n13, 90
Gärtner, 243 n49
Gardner, 249 n10
Gerhardsson, 10 n16, 12
Gigot, 7 n8
Gilmour, 230 n10
Gingrich, 48 n30
Glasson, 52 n43, 61 n20, 86 n4
Goguel, 237 n28, 239 n34
Goodspeed, 27 n7, 237 n28
Goulder, 270 n2
Grant, F. C., 60 n14, 144 n1,
    237 n27, 365, 365 n16, 365
    n17, 431 n10
Grant, R. M., 152 n23, 230 n9,
    243 n49, 284 n18, 432 n12
Grieg, 11 n21, 211 n8
Griesbach, 4, 4 n4, 5, 9, 9 n13,
    9 n14, 10, 16, 38, 38 n2, 58,
    88, 89, 93, 105, 114, 125, 145
    n4, 149 n14, 150, 150 n16,
    155, 159, 177, 184, 184 n11,
    185, 247 n5, 397, 399, 399 n2,
    400, 401, 402, 403, 404, 405,
    405-406 n4, 407, 408, 440,
    448, 448 n23, 452
Grobel, 6 n7, 284 n19
Grundmann, 230 n10
Güttgemanns, 237 n28
Guillaumont, 242 n45
Gut, 230 n9
Guthrie, 44 n13, 58 n8, 230 n9

Haardt, 242 n47
Haenchen, 242 n45, 243 nn48-
    49
Hampe, 55 n3
Hansen, 87 n13
Hare, 406 n4

Harnack, 140, 224 n3, 234 n17,
    254 n24, 332, 358, 365 n16,
    424 nn25-26, 431 n10
Hauck, 59 n12
Haupt, 430 n10
Hawkins, 16, 24 n1, 29, 29
    nn13-14, 30, 44, 44 n16, 47
    n27, 58 n10, 61 nn18-19, 116,
    131, 134, 135, 135 n8, 146,
    147, 147 n11, 150, 155 n33,
    182 n7, 206 n3, 223, 233 n14,
    254 n23, 316, 316 n49, 361,
    361 nn4-5, 365 n16, 382 n1,
    393, 393 n16, 412 n9, 413, 413
    nn9-11, 415, 415 n14, 416, 416
    n15, 420 n19, 421 n20, 424
    nn25-26, 429 n5, 430-31 n10,
    441
Held, 146 n8
Helmbold, 231 n10, 235 n19
Hennecke, 242 n45
Herder, 403
Heuschen, 60 n14
Higgins, 243 n47, 295n, 407-
    408 n5
Hirsch, 231 n10, 234 n17, 235
    n19
Höpfl, 230 n9
Hoffmann, P., 231 n10, 240,
    240 n41
Holtzmann, 6 n7, 59, 97, 101,
    101 n4, 144 n1, 150 n16, 359
    n2, 360, 361 n4, 365 n16, 401,
    431 n10
Honey, 257 n30
Honoré, 55 n3, 398 n1
Howard, 246 n2, 264 n7
Huck, 27 n7, 271 n10, 415, 415
    n14, 416, 418, 421 n21
Hummel, 62 n21
Hunzinger, 242 nn46-47
Huston, 230 n10, 358 n1

Isaksson, 247 n5

Jameson, 41, 41 n9, 109 n15,
    145, 145 nn3-4, 150, 151, 152
    n26, 157, 159, 160 n42, 247
    n4, 295, 296 n2
Jeremias, 70 n16, 230 n9, 256
    n28, 261 n4, 270, 270 n3, 310
    n41, 398 n1, 430 n10, 432 n12
Johnson, 60 n14, 310 n38
Johnston, 97n
Jones, 103, 103 n12
Jouvyon, 117 n27
Jülicher, 179 n5, 237 n28, 239
    n34

Käsemann, 240, 240 n42
Kearns, 97n
Kee, 239 n36

Kilpatrick, 310 n38, 353, 353 n3, 432 n11
Kittel, 202
Klijn, 52 n43, 60 n14, 236 n22
Klostermann, 310 n42
Knox, 230 n9, 300, 300 n11, 301, 301 n16
Koester, 239, 239 n38, 240, 240 n39, 243 n47, 256 n29, 431-32 n11
Kühn, 234 n16, 239 n37, 241 n44, 408 n5
Kümmel, 6 n7, 15, 17, 18, 52 n44, 53, 53n, 55 nn4-5, 58 n9, 60 n13, 87 n14, 144 n1, 227, 227n, 228 228 n1, 230 n10, 234 n18, 236 n25, 237 n29, 240 n40, 252, 252 n20, 425 n28, 441 n6, 443 n12
Kundsin, 200

Lachmann, 41, 41 n8, 55, 55 n5, 59, 78, 80, 89, 100, 109, 116, 119, 119n, 120, 120 n1, 121, 122, 122 n4, 123, 126 n6, 129, 130, 133, 133n, 134, 135, 135 n3, 136, 136 n13, 138, 139, 150 n16, 179, 410 nn1-2, 415 n13, 441, 441 n7
Lagrange, 97, 98, 101, 102, 102 n7, 103, 236 n24
Lambrecht, 237 n28
Leaney, 230 n10
Lehmann, 241 n43
Léon-Dufour, 11, 11 n18, 38 n2, 39 n5, 49 n32, 51 n41, 87 n11, 101 n5, 236 n22, 255 n26
Lessing, 160, 187, 188
Levie, 358 n1
Lietzmann, 271 n10
Lightfoot, 5 n5, 49 n33, 141, 141 n22, 147 n13, 247 n3, 288, 321n, 347 n2, 443 n13
Lindsey, 4, 5, 5 n6, 6, 9, 10
Linton, 52 n43
Loisy, 332
Longstaff, 88 n18
Lührmann, 228 n2, 231 n10, 234 n16, 234 n17, 236 nn23-26, 239 n34, 241 n44, 243 n49, 298 n1
Lummis, 41, 41 n9, 148 n14, 157, 295, 296, 296 n1, 430 n10

McArthur, 242 n46, 243 n48
McCown, 208 n5
McLoughlin, 51 n40, 61 n17, 61 n19, 87 n15, 97, 101, 101 n5
McNeile, 144 n1, 236 n24, 301, 301 n15, 390 n13
Manson, 239 n34, 252 n21, 295n, 296, 300 n12, 301 nn13-14 302 n20, 305 n26, 306, 306

n30, 309 n35, 310, 310 nn40-41, 312 n44, 315 nn46-47, 316 n50, 365 n16, 431 n10
Martin, 251 n15, 394, 394 n18, 398 n1
Marxsen, 7, 7 n9
Massaux, 432 n12
Masson, 59 n12
Mattill, 252 n20
Meinertz, 236 n22
Metzger, 242 n45
Metzinger, 230 n9
Meyer, 398 n1
Meynell, 152 n26
Michaelis, 60 n14, 236 n24, 237 n28
Michel, 238 n31
Moffatt, 254 n24, 365 n16, 431 n10
Montefiore, 243 n47, 432 n11
Morgenthaler, 54 n1, 55 n3, 56 nn5-6, 60 n16, 61 n18, 87 n9, 267 n11, 231 n12, 233 nn14-15, 399 n2
Moule, 58 n8, 63n, 88 n18, 121 n2, 152 n26, 288 n1, 382 n1, 428 n2, 438 n1
Moulton, 264 n7

Narborough, 16, 131, 134, 135, 135 n10
Neirynck, 15, 17, 58 n7, 85, 85n, 86, 86 n2, 87 n13, 231 n10, 441, 441 n8
Neusner, 397n
Nineham, 147 n13, 270 n1, 288, 321n, 358 n1, 383 n2, 398 n1
Norlin, 231 n11, 398 n1
North, 230 n9, 432 n11

Orchard, 38 n2, 116 n22

Palmer, 16, 41 n8, 55 n5, 119, 119n, 120, 150 n16, 410 nn1-2, 415 n13, 441, 441 n7
Parker, 8, 8 n11, 8 n12, 9, 16, 98, 102, 103 n9, 117 n28, 152 n26, 156, 205, 205 n1, 206 n2, 214 n9, 253 n22, 317 n54, 450 n27
Pelletier, 158 n37
Perrin, 240 n39, 240 n40, 398 n1
Petrie, 230 n9, 251, 251 n16, 398 n1, 428 n1, 431 n10
Price, 144 n1
Procksch, 202
Purdy, 242 n46

Quecke, 242 n45, 243 n47
Quentin, 131, 131 n9
Quispel, 242 n47

Rawlinson, 16, 110, 110 n16, 111, 131, 134, 135, 135 n9,

140, 140 n21, 141
Redlich, 16, 131, 134, 135, 135 n11
Rehkopf, 230 n9
Rengstorf, 229 n3, 247 n4
Reville, 431 n10
Rhys, 429 n6
Riddle, 230 n10
Robert, 38 n2, 430 n10
Robinowitz, 156 n34
Robinson, A., 139 n17
Robinson, J. A. T., 202
Robinson, J. M., 11 n22, 18 n24, 239, 239 n37, 240, 243 n47, 256 n29, 398 n1, 432 n11, 433 n12
Robinson, W. C., 250 n11
Roehrich, 431 n10
Ropes, 229 n3, 247 n4
Rosché, 19, 158 n37, 230 n9, 250 n12, 357, 357n, 358, 431 n10, 443 n12
Rudolph, 242 n45, 243 n48, 243 n49
Rushbrooke, 27 n7, 43, 43 n12, 130 n8

Sanday, 25 n4, 27 n11, 33 n17, 111 n18, 144 n1, 148 n14, 182 n7, 224 n3, 272 n11, 317 n53, 359 n2, 415 n14
Sanders, 16, 19, 45, 45 n21, 46, 46 nn22-24, 46 nn25-26, 55 n3, 55 n5, 58 n10, 88 n18, 89, 89 n19, 144 n1, 146 n8, 157, 158, 158 n37, 193, 199, 199n, 199 n1, 229 n3, 229 n5, 243 n48, 409, 409n, 410, 429 n5, 429 n7, 430, 440, 440 n6, 443, 449, 449 nn24-26, 450, 450 n27, 450 n29, 450 nn30-31
Schaefer, 236 n22
Schlatter, 229 n3, 247 n4
Schleiermacher, 123, 126, 129, 160, 188, 228, 236, 402, 403
Schmid, 49 n32, 60 n14, 61 n18, 62, 62 n21, 87 n15, 229, 229 n7, 230 n8, 248 n9, 358 n1
Schmithals, 237 n28
Schnackenburg, 60 n14, 398 n1
Schneemelcher, 242 n45
Schrage, 243 n48, 432 n12
Schramm, 60 n14, 61 n17, 87 n12, 243 n47
Schubert, 243 n47
Schürmann, 60, 60 nn14-15, 231 n10, 234, 243 nn47-48
Schutz, 229 n6
Schultz, 237 n28
Schweitzer, 144 n1, 415 n13
Schweizer, 231 n10
Segbroeck, 87 n13

Sieffert, 402
Simpson, 19, 148 n14, 229 n3, 247 n4, 381, 381n, 382, 398 n1, 425 n28, 430 n10, 446, 447, 447 n22, 448
Skehan, 38 n2
Smith, 397n
von Soden, 431 n10
de Solages, 47 n27, 54 n1, 61, 87 n15, 181 n6, 229 n6, 231 n11, 233 n14, 233 n15
Sparks, 230 n10
Stählin, 235 n20
Stanton, 16, 131, 134, 135, 135 n4, 136 n13, 146 n8, 199, 202, 261, 261 n5, 365 n16, 431 n10
Steck, 238 n30, 238 n32, 238 n33
Stein, 237 n28
Stendahl, 390 n13
Stoldt, 3 n1, 4, 4 n2, 6 n7
Strauss, 414, 415 n13
Strecker, 237 n28
Streeter, 15, 16, 17, 18, 23, 24n, 25 n3, 25 n5, 27 n8, 27 n9, 32 n15, 32 n16, 34n, 37, 38, 38 n1, 41 n9, 43, 44, 44 n15, 45, 47, 47 n28, 47 n29, 48, 48 n31, 49, 49 n35, 50, 60 n14, 61 n17, 64, 64 n1, 66 n4, 86, 97, 99, 99 n1, 101, 106, 107, 111, 111 n18, 114 n20, 122, 131, 133, 134, 134 n1, 135, 136 n13, 137, 138, 139, 140, 140 n19, 141, 143, 144, 144 nn1-2, 145, 145 nn5-6, 146, 146 n7, 147, 147 n9, 147 n13, 148 n14, 149, 149 nn14-15, 150, 150 nn16-17, 151, 151 n19, 152, 152 n26, 153, 153 n27, 153 nn29-30, 154, 154 n31, 155, 155 n32, 156, 156 n34, 157 n35, 158, 159, 159 nn39-40, 160, 160 nn43-44, 161, 178, 178 n4, 179, 200, 221, 221n, 222, 222 nn1-2, 224 nn3-4, 225 n5, 230 n10, 234 n17, 250 n13, 252 n19, 253 n22, 254 n24, 257, 260, 260 n2, 263, 266, 266 n8, 267, 271, 271 n8, 282, 285, 297, 302, 302 n21, 307, 307 nn31-33, 309 n36, 310, 310 n39, 310 n42, 311 n43, 317 n53, 321, 323, 325, 329, 332, 333, 335, 346, 359 n2, 365 n16, 373, 382, 382 n1, 383, 383 n4, 384, 387, 389 n10, 390 n12, 392 n15, 401, 407, 407 n5, 412, 412 nn8-9, 413 n9, 413 n11, 413 n12, 418, 420, 422, 423 n22, 424 n26, 428,

428 n3, 439, 440, 440 n4, 441, 442, 442 n9, 443, 444, 445, 445 n15, 445 n16, 449, 451
Styler, 15, 58 n8, 59 n11, 63, 63n, 64, 88 n18, 121, 121 n2, 152 n26, 153, 153 n28, 161, 161 n46, 382 n1, 428, 428 n2, 437, 438, 438 n1, 445, 446 n18
Suggs, 239 n37, 241 n44, 398 n1, 399 n3

Taylor, 17, 18, 44 n14, 51, 52 n42, 59 n12, 60 n14, 110, 110 n17, 200, 201, 202, 206 n3, 230 n10, 231 n12, 232, 234 n17, 235, 252 n21, 253, 253 n22, 254, 254 n25, 255, 255 n26, 295, 295n, 296, 298, 298 n8, 300 n10, 303 n23, 394 n17, 407, 407 n5, 414 n11, 431 n10, 438, 438 n2, 442, 442 nn10-11, 443, 443 n12
Thompson, 27 n7
Throckmorton, 231 n10, 237 n28, 257 n30, 271 n10
Thüsing, 241 n43
Tischendorf, 413 n9, 414, 415, 415 n14, 418, 440, 440 n5, 443
Tödt, 231 n10, 239 n34, 240, 241
Torrey, 264 n7
Toynbee, 152 n23
Turner, 49 n32, 148, 148 n14, 229 n3, 234 n16, 243 nn47-48, 248 n9, 430 n10, 432 n11
Tyson, 437, 444 n14

Vaganay, 6 n7, 11, 11 n17, 49 n32, 58, 87 n10, 98, 102, 103, 103 n10, 104, 104 n13, 115, 146 n8, 156, 156 n34, 230, 230 n8, 246 n1, 250 n11, 250 n13, 429 n6
Vielhauer, 240 n39, 429 n6
Vögtle, 60 n14, 230 n10, 358 n1

Walker, 9 n14, 445 n17
Weinreich, 215 n10
Weiss, B., 401, 431 n10
Weiss, J., 200, 228 n2, 229 n6, 365 n16, 431 n10
Weisse, 89, 89 n21, 97, 101, 101 n3, 136 n13, 144 n1, 228, 441 n6
Wellhausen, 16, 131, 134, 135, 135 n6, 140, 237, 237 n28, 264 n7, 431 n10
Wendt, 431 n10
Wenham, 398 n1
Wernle, 58 n10, 228 n2, 239 n34, 359 n2, 361, 361 n4, 365 n16, 431 n10

West, 86, 86 n6, 246 n1, 425 n28
Wikenhauser, 60 n14, 87 n15, 230 n10, 297, 297 n7
Wilkens, 229 n3, 229 n4, 247 n4
Wilkinson, 254 n24
Williams, 52 n43, 236 n24, 393 n17
Wilson, 49, 49 n35, 242 n45, 242 n47, 243 n49
Wink, 43 n11
Wood, 15, 42, 42 n10, 58, 77, 77n, 410 n2
Woods, 41 n8, 145 n4, 409, 411, 411 nn3-5, 412, 412 nn7-8, 413 n9, 415, 416, 419 n16, 420, 420 n18, 421
Wrede, 11, 11 n21, 211 n8
Wrege, 230 n9